BANNED BOOKS

LITERATURE SUPPRESSED ON

Religious Grounds

Third Edition

MARGARET BALD

Preface by
KEN WACHSBERGER

Facts On File
An Infobase Learning Company

Facts On File, Inc.
An imprint of Infobase Learning
132 West 31st Street
New York NY 10001

Library of Congress Cataloging-in-Publication Data
Bald, Margaret.
Literature suppressed on religious grounds / Margaret Bald. — 3rd ed.
     p. cm. — (Banned books)
Includes bibliographical references and index.
ISBN 978-0-8160-8230-8 (acid-free paper)
1. Censorship—Religious aspects. 2. Censorship—Religious aspects—Christianity.
3. Prohibited books—Bibliography. 4. Religious literature—Censorship.
5. Censorship—History. I. Title.
BL65.C45B35 2011
098'.11—dc22   2010030408

Facts On File books are available at special discounts when purchased in bulk quantities for businesses, associations, institutions, or sales promotions. Please call our Special Sales Department in New York at (212) 967-8800 or (800) 322-8755.

You can find Facts On File on the World Wide Web at
http://www.InfobaseLearning.com

Text design by Cathy Rincon
Composition by Publication Services, Inc.
Cover printed by Yurchak Printing, Landisville, Pa.
Book printed and bound by Yurchak Printing, Landisville, Pa.
Date printed: June 2011
Printed in the United States of America

10 9 8 7 6 5 4 3 2 1

To prohibit the reading of certain books
is to declare the inhabitants to be
either fools or slaves.
—Claude-Adrien Helvétius

One idea can only be opposed by another idea.
—Naguib Mahfouz

Contents

ACKNOWLEDGMENTS

I am grateful to Jonathan Pollack, Philip Milito, Alice Tufel, Daniel Calvert, Elizabeth Calvert-Kilbane, and Marie Calvert-Kilbane for writing entries, as bylined, for this volume. Thanks go to Ken Wachsberger for his keen editorial eye and unflagging encouragement and enthusiasm during the publication of the first edition of this book, to my literary agent Gene Brissie, and to Jeff Soloway at Facts On File. The staff of the American Library Association's Office for Intellectual Freedom deserves special mention for their research and advocacy on the issue of censorship in the United States and for their assistance. A special thanks to Jonathan Calvert for the constancy of his loving support and to my children, André and Daniel, longtime proponents of free speech, for technological and editorial assistance. This book is dedicated to the memory of Siobhan Dowd (1960–2007), who wrote the foreword to the first edition of this volume. Siobhan was the former program director of PEN American Center's Freedom-to-Write Committee, a tireless defender of human rights and free expression, and an acclaimed author of novels for young adults. Her work is carried on by the Siobhan Dowd Trust, which brings books and reading to disadvantaged young people in the United Kingdom.

PREFACE

We Americans are proud of our Constitution, especially its Bill of Rights. The First Amendment right to freedom of speech and religion has inspired dissenters and nonconformists everywhere. Censored writers such as Salman Rushdie, Pramoedya Ananta Toer, and Aleksandr Solzhenitsyn have looked to our country's example for strength as they battled for their rights to express their own thoughts, and that of others to read them, even at the risk of their lives.

Yet censorship has been a major part of American history from the time of Roger Williams and other early colonial freethinkers. Many of our richest literary works—*Adventures of Huckleberry Finn, The Color Purple, The Grapes of Wrath, The Jungle, Uncle Tom's Cabin, Tropic of Cancer*—have been censored at one time or another. Even today, school boards, local governments, religious organizations, and moral crusaders attempt to restrict our freedom to read or to learn alternative viewpoints. Witness the Texas State Board of Education's attempts to revise American history and tear down the wall separating church and state through its revisionist textbooks. Advancing technology has provided more diverse targets—the record, film, and television industries and the Internet—for the censors and would-be censors to aim at, as they work their strategies to restrict free expression and the freedom to read, watch, and listen, dumbing down material in order to shield their children, and you, from original or disturbing thoughts.

As Margaret Bald shows in this expanded volume, religious censorship over the years and around the world has never been a characteristic solely of the secular Left or the fundamentalist Right, but clearly today the Right is now the dominant censor in the United States, particularly in the battle over textbooks that discuss evolution. Internationally, the current hard-line Islamic regime in Iran deserves a spotlight for its increase in repression, censorship, and persecution of its own writers, both contemporary (*Touba and the Meaning of Night*) and dead for more than half a century (*The Blind Owl*). Furthermore, fear of reprisals by Islamic terrorists has motivated publishers in the United States to preemptively censor books (*The Cartoons That Shook the World* and *The Jewel of Medina*).

I called the last edition the Harry Potter volume because J. K. Rowling's first five books—which came out too late to be included in the first edition—were published in quick succession between 1999 and 2003. All were so heavily censored, and for largely the same reasons—glorification of witch-craft, magic, wizardry, the occult—that Bald summarized each one indi-vidually and then wrote one collective censorship history. In this third edition, they are joined by Rowling's next two volumes: *Harry Potter and the Half-Blood Prince* and *Harry Potter and the Deathly Hallows.* The censorship history of other new books in this third edition show the international reach of censorship. They include *The Battle for God, The Da Vinci Code,* and Philip Pullman's His Dark Materials trilogy *(The Golden Compass, The Subtle Knife,* and *The Amber Spyglass).*

Fortunately, our country has a strong tradition of fighting censorship as well. Groups such as the National Coalition Against Censorship, the American Library Association's Office for Intellectual Freedom, People for the American Way, the American Civil Liberties Union, the PEN American Center, and the National Writers Union exist to defend the First Amend-ment and support independent writers, through legal action and by raising public awareness.

The first edition of the Facts On File Banned Books Series came out as a four-volume hardcover set in 1998. The second edition, which was pub-lished in 2006, added 50 additional titles to the list. The four volumes in this dynamic revised and expanded third edition add to our rich First Amendment tradition by spotlighting approximately 500 works that have been censored for their political, social, religious, or erotic content, in the United States and around the world, from biblical times to the present day. While many of these have been legally "banned"—or prohibited "as by official order"—all indeed have been banned or censored in a broader sense: targeted for removal from school curricula or library shelves, condemned in churches and forbid-den to the faithful, rejected or expurgated by publishers, challenged in court, even voluntarily rewritten by their authors. Censored authors have been ver-bally abused, physically attacked, shunned by their families and communities, excommunicated from their religious congregations, and shot, hanged, or burned at the stake by their enemies, who thus made them heroes and often enough secured their memory for posterity. Their works include novels, histories, biographies, children's books, religious and philosophical treatises, dictionaries, poems, polemics, and every other form of written expression.

It is illuminating to discover in these histories that such cultural land-marks as the Bible, the Qur'an, the Talmud, and the greatest classics of world literature have often been suppressed or censored from the same motives, and by similar forces, as those we see today seeking to censor such books as *Daddy's Roommate* and *Heather Has Two Mommies.* Every American reading these volumes will find in their pages books they love and will be thankful that their authors' freedom of expression and their own freedom to read are constitutionally protected. But at the same time, how many will be gratified by the cruel fate of books we detest? Reader-citizens capable of acknowledging their own contradictions will be grateful for the existence of the First Amendment and will thank its guardians, including the authors of this series, for protecting us against our own worst impulses.

It is to Facts On File's credit that it has published this new version of the original Banned Books series. May the day come when an expanded series is no longer necessary.

***

To prevent redundancy, works banned for multiple reasons appear in only one volume apiece, based on the judgment of the editor and the volume authors. The alphabetical arrangement provides easy access to titles. Works whose titles appear in SMALL CAPITAL LETTERS within an entry have entries of their own elsewhere in the same volume. Those whose titles appear in *ITALICIZED SMALL CAPITAL LETTERS* have entries in one of the other volumes. In addition, each volume carries complete lists of the works discussed in the other volumes.

—Ken Wachsberger

Ken Wachsberger is a longtime author, editor, educator, and member of the National Writers Union. He is the editor of the four-volume Voices from the Underground series, a landmark collection of insider histories about the Vietnam era underground press (www.voicesfromtheundergroundpress.com).

INTRODUCTION

In 1989, an edict from Tehran brought a shocking reminder of religious censorship, regarded by many as a specter from the distant past of the Inquisition and the burning of heretics. The Ayatollah Khomeini's death decree against author Salman Rushdie and the widespread banning of Rushdie's novel *The Satanic Verses* for blasphemy against Islam was a startling example of a phenomenon that is as old as history and, with the current wave of religious fundamentalism, as recent as today's headlines.

Censorship has existed in every society to protect the prevailing moral and social order. Book censorship in Western culture can be traced to the earliest years of Christianity, when the church began to suppress competing views as heretical. In the second century, the Council of Ephesus burned superstitious works and prohibited the *Acta Pauli*, a history of St. Paul, and in the fifth century, the pope issued the first list of forbidden books.

The flood of unauthorized Bible translations and religious tracts that followed the invention of the printing press in 1450 and the rise of religious dissent during the Protestant Reformation motivated the church to expand its censorial functions. In 1559, Pope Paul IV published the first Index librorum prohibitorum (Index of Forbidden Books). The Index, referred to as the Roman Index, was administered by the Roman Inquisition. It was binding on all Roman Catholics, who represented most of the population of continental Europe, and was enforced by government authorities. At the same time, similar indexes were also prepared by theological faculties in Paris and Louvain and by the Spanish Inquisition.

As church and state in Europe began to separate in the 16th century, national monarchies instituted their own mechanisms of religious and political censorship to supplement or substitute for that of the church. In the areas where they had political control, the new Protestant faiths began to ban the writings of Catholics or dissenters.

From the earliest times, religious orthodoxy and politics have been intimately connected. To be a heretic was often to be considered a traitor, subject to punishment by secular authorities. And manipulation of religious sensibilities for political purposes has a long and sordid history, with recorded examples dating to the trial of Socrates in 399 B.C.

As Europe became more politically fragmented and means of communication more sophisticated, state censorship was rarely thorough enough to prevent forbidden books from circulating. By the 18th century, the proliferation of underground publishing, as France's book censor Chrétien-Guillaume de Lamoignon de Malesherbes said, meant that "a man who had read only books that originally appeared with the formal approval of the government would be behind his contemporaries by nearly a century."

It is impossible to discuss religious censorship of books without referring to the Roman Index, one of the most successful and enduring censorial devices in history. Sixty-one of the books discussed in this volume, many subject to multiple forms of censorship, were listed on the Index. When it was finally abolished by the Vatican in 1966 after four centuries, it had outlived its effectiveness. The church had long before lost the authority to enforce it, and this list was widely viewed as anachronistic.

In the 42nd and final Index issued in 1948 and in print until 1966, a total of 4,126 books were still prohibited to Catholics: 1,331 from the 17th century or earlier, 1,186 from the 18th century, 1,354 from the 19th century, and 255 from the 20th century. Though many were obscure theological titles or works that were controversial in their day but had been forgotten for centuries, literary and philosophical classics by dozens of authors representing a Who's Who of Western thought also were included: among them, Bentham, Bergson, Comte, Defoe, Descartes, Diderot, Flaubert, Gibbon, Hobbes, Hume, Kant, Locke, Mill, Montaigne, Montesquieu, Pascal, Rousseau, Sand, Spinoza, Stendhal, Voltaire, and Zola. Rather than banning books, the church's post-Index book censorship has focused primarily on sanctioning dissident Catholic theologians for their writing or pressuring the occasional Catholic author to hew to orthodoxy.

Though the First Amendment bars government authorities from practicing religious censorship in the United States, individuals and organized religious fundamentalists have successfully pressed to remove books viewed as anti-Christian from public and school libraries and curricula. The majority of these instances have focused on perceived immorality, profane language, or treatment of sexuality rather than religious content per se, and have been discussed in another volume in this series. Their targets, however, have included textbooks that teach evolution without presenting the alternative theories of "creationism," or "intelligent design," books said to promote the religion of "secular humanism," and material with references to Eastern religions, "New Age" thought, and witchcraft or the occult, such as J. K. Rowling's Harry Potter books.

Although Rushdie's *Satanic Verses* is the most notorious international case of book censorship in the 20th century, it is not unique. The freedom of expression and safety of authors, editors, and publishers continues to be threatened by governments that censor or prosecute those whose writing offends Islamic religious authorities and by militant Islamic groups and terrorists.

Since the Islamic revolution of 1979 in Iran, thousands of writers, journalists, and other intellectuals have been jailed, and unknown numbers executed or assassinated. Iranian novelist Shahrnush Parsipur was repeatedly imprisoned because of her writing and had to leave the country. During the 1990s, fundamentalist terrorists murdered Egyptian writer Farag Fouda and Algerian novelist and journalist Tahar Djaout, among many others. In 1994, the Egyptian Nobel laureate Naguib Mahfouz was stabbed and seriously wounded. Other writers, such as Taslima Nasrin of Bangladesh, have been driven into exile by death threats or, like Egyptian novelist Alaa Hamed, sentenced to prison for blasphemy. The writing of feminists such as Nasrin, Nawal El Saadawi of Egypt, and Fatima Mernissi of Morocco, who challenge interpretations of Islamic dogma that restrict women, has particularly angered both governments and Islamists.

The books discussed in this volume represent a sampling of the thousands that have been targets of religious censorship over the centuries. They include texts of the world's major religions, novels, and classic works of philosophy, science, and history representing the intellectual heritage of Western civilization. They also include contemporary works that offended church authorities, governments, or Christian, Muslim, or Hindu fundamentalists. A few entries, such as Charles Dickens's *Oliver Twist*, chronicle censorship attempts in the United States that were ultimately unsuccessful but that merit attention because they involved legal challenges.

Many of these books were branded with the charge of heresy. Heresy is defined as opinion or doctrine that is at variance with orthodox religious teaching, or, as religious historian David Christie-Murray observed, "the opinion held by a minority of men which the majority declares is unacceptable and is strong enough to punish." Others were charged with blasphemy, speaking in a profane or irreverent manner of the sacred. All were censored because they were seen as dangerous—to orthodoxy, to faith and morals, or to the social and political order.

Some authors—Henry Cornelius Agrippa, Erasmus, Cyrano de Bergerac, Blaise Pascal, Bernard Mandeville, Jonathan Swift, Daniel Defoe, Montesquieu, Voltaire, Anatole France, and Rushdie—ran afoul of censors for what Swift called "the sin of wit": irreverence in the form of satire, parody, irony, or mockery in combination with dissenting ideas on religion or philosophy.

Philosophers, scientists, and historians—from Peter Abelard in the 12th century to Galileo Galilei, René Descartes, John Locke, and Charles Darwin—who advocated the use of reason or the experimental or scientific method, were condemned for what might be called the sin of thinking.

The works of Sebastian Castellio, Thomas Helwys, Hugo Grotius, Pierre Bayle, Roger Williams, and Baruch Spinoza were censored for advocating religious freedom, the sin of tolerance. And the sin of disputation was committed by dissidents and reformers such as John Wycliffe, Jan Hus, Martin Luther, John Calvin, William Tyndale, William Penn, John Toland,

Matthew Tindal, Emanuel Swedenborg, and contemporary theologians Leonardo Boff, Hans Küng, and Tissa Balasuriya.

Some writers paid for their sins against orthodoxy with silencing, prison, or banishment. Others, notably Hus, Michael Servetus, Tyndale, and Giordano Bruno, were victims of what George Bernard Shaw called the ultimate form of censorship—assassination.

The history of censorship is one of inhumanity, of lives and livelihoods lost, talent or genius snuffed out, and work unfinished, withheld, deleted, or destroyed. Literary history and the present are dark with silences, Tillie Olsen has written. It is also a history of rebellion, of defiance in the face of mortal danger, and perseverance against harassment, discouragement, and disdain.

Yet to review the censorship of the books discussed in this volume is to be struck by its futility. As historian Leonard W. Levy observed, the verdicts of time mock judgments and alter sensibilities. Insurgent faiths become established and revolutionary ideas lose their power to shock. For centuries censorship has created best sellers because, as Michel de Montaigne said, "To forbid us anything is to make us have a mind for it." Like water leaking slowly through a dike to become a steady trickle or a flood, words and ideas inexorably elude the censor's grasp.

"A book cannot be killed," commented Moroccan writer Nadia Tazi on Rushdie's censorship. "It lives and dies on its own. Once the 'vases' are 'broken,' the fragments of life spread throughout the world; voices escape, going their adventurous ways; and there are always encounters, mutations, and festivals of the spirit."

NOTES ON THE THIRD EDITION

Since the first edition of this book was published in 1998 and the second in 2006, would-be censors have found new targets, but their motives and methods remain the same. In the United States, public schools and public libraries are still the primary arenas for battles over book banning. During the period 1990 to 2008, the American Library Association (ALA) logged more than 9,600 attempts to limit access to books or remove them entirely from schools or libraries. Many of the people who would restrict the freedom to read are parents and organized Christian conservatives who wish to shield young people from sexual content, offensive language, portrayals of violence, or political, social, or religious viewpoints with which they disagree. During the years 2000 to 2009, J. K. Rowling's Harry Potter novels were at the top of the ALA's list of "challenged" books because their depiction of wizards and witches offended Christian fundamentalists. In 2007 and 2008, Philip Pullman's award-winning trilogy of fantasy novels, *The Glass Compass*, *The Subtle Knife*, and *The Amber Spyglass*, were among the most frequently targeted books because they were seen as anti-Catholic and antireligious. And more than 85 years after the Scopes "monkey trial," the teaching of evolution and its discussion in textbooks is still hotly contested around the country on religious grounds.

Writers around the world continue to face bans, persecution, and violence for offending religious authorities or religious sensibilities or for diverging from political ideology masquerading as religion. This volume tracks the wholesale banning of books in Malaysia that discuss Islam, including Karen Armstrong's *The Battle for God*. It also discusses the stepped-up suppression of writers in Iran and the increase in book banning since 2005 by the hard-line Islamic regime of Mahmoud Ahmadinejad—including international best sellers such as *The Da Vinci Code* (also banned in Lebanon, Pakistan, Egypt, and some Indian states) and classic works of Persian literature by Iran's greatest writer, Sadegh Hedayat, and the contemporary novelist Shahrnush Parsipur.

This edition also sheds light on an ominous development, an example of the stranglehold that extremism can have on freedom of expression—preemptive censorship by publishers motivated by fear of violence. In 2008, Random House, the world's largest trade book publisher, canceled the publication of *The Jewel of Medina*, a novel by Sherry Jones about Muhammad's wife A'isha, because the company feared terrorist attacks by radical Muslims. After Random House's decision, the London home of the book's British publisher was firebombed.

In 2009, also fearing violence, Yale University Press decided to remove all the images of the prophet Muhammad from *The Cartoons That Shook the World*, a scholarly study by Jytte Klausen of the international furor that erupted after a Danish newspaper published 12 cartoons of Muhammad in 2005. Subsequently, the British anticensorship publication *Index on Censorship* declined to publish the cartoons, which were to accompany an interview with Klausen on the very subject of Yale's censorship. The publisher cited fear of reprisals similar to the firebombing in London.

When research began for the first edition of this volume, the fatwa against the writer Salman Rushdie seemed like a "terrible anachronism," as French writer Christian Salmon put it. In 2001, we realized that it was a harbinger of a greater tragedy: wholesale murder by terrorists in the name of religion. Perhaps writers are like canaries in a mine. "When people first started to make a connection between me and 9/11, I resisted because of the disparity of the scale," Rushdie told the *Times* of London in 2005. "But I have come to feel that what happened with *The Satanic Verses* was a kind of prologue and that now we are in the main event."

—Margaret Bald

WORKS DISCUSSED IN THIS VOLUME

LEVIATHAN
Thomas Hobbes

THE LIFE OF JESUS
Ernest Renan

MARY AND HUMAN LIBERATION
Tissa Balasuriya

MEDITATIONS ON FIRST PHILOSOPHY
René Descartes

THE MERITORIOUS PRICE OF OUR REDEMPTION
William Pynchon

THE METAPHYSICS
Aristotle

MEYEBELA: MY BENGALI GIRLHOOD
Taslima Nasrin

THE NEW ASTRONOMY
Johannes Kepler

THE NEW TESTAMENT
William Tyndale, trans.

NINETY-FIVE THESES
Martin Luther

OF THE VANITIE AND UNCERTAINTIE OF ARTES AND SCIENCES
Henricus Cornelius Agrippa

OLIVER TWIST
Charles Dickens

ON CIVIL LORDSHIP
John Wycliffe

ON JUSTICE IN THE REVOLUTION AND IN THE CHURCH
Pierre-Joseph Proudhon

ON MONARCHY
Dante Alighieri

LITERATURE
SUPPRESSED ON
RELIGIOUS GROUNDS

ADDRESS TO THE CHRISTIAN NOBILITY OF THE GERMAN NATION

Author: Martin Luther
Original date and place of publication: 1520, Switzerland
Literary form: Theological tract

SUMMARY

The German monk and theologian Martin Luther was the founder of the Protestant Reformation. His NINETY-FIVE THESES, posted on the door of Wittenberg Castle church in 1517, marked the beginning of a movement that would shatter the structure of the medieval church.

On August 18, 1520, he published *Address to the Christian Nobility of the German Nation*, an open letter to the ruling class of the German-speaking principalities advocating control by the nobility of German ecclesiastical matters and calling for the help of the princes in reforming the church. The *Address*, called "a cry from the heart of the people" and a "blast on the war-trumpet," was Luther's first writing after he was convinced that his breach with the Roman Catholic Church was irreparable.

He expressed his anger at corruption of the Renaissance papacy and exploitation of Germans by the church and proposed reforms to severely limit the pope's power and authority over secular rulers. Each local community, he believed, should take charge of its own affairs and elect its own ministers and bishops. He denied that the pope was the final interpreter of Scripture and enunciated his doctrine of the priesthood of all believers.

"To call popes, bishops, priests, monks and nuns the religious class, but princes, lords, artisans and farm-workers the secular class," Luther wrote, "is a specious device. . . . The fact is that our baptism consecrates us all without exception and makes us all priests." Moreover, the claim that the pope alone can interpret Scripture or confirm any particular interpretation is a "wicked, base invention, for which they cannot adduce a tittle of evidence in support."

Luther detailed a sweeping program of church reorganization and purification to strip away its temporal power so that it could better perform its spiritual functions. Recalling the example of Christ on foot and comparing it to the image of the pope in a palanquin, he recommended that the papacy return to apostolic simplicity. The number of cardinals should be reduced, the temporal possessions and claims of the church abandoned, and its income from fees and indulgences curtailed. Monks should be relieved of hearing confession and preaching. The number of monastic orders should be cut and the practice of irrevocable monastic vows eliminated. The clergy should be permitted to marry. Litigation by church courts involving Germans should be tried under a German primate. Luther urged the German states to refuse to pay papal taxes and exactions and to expel papal legates from their territories.

"Heretics should be vanquished with books, not with burnings," Luther recommended. The church's response to the *Address* and his next major tract of 1520, THE BABYLONIAN CAPTIVITY OF THE CHURCH, was hostile. Shortly after the publication of the two tracts, Luther received word that the pope had pronounced him a heretic and ordered the burning of his books.

CENSORSHIP HISTORY

See NINETY-FIVE THESES.

FURTHER READING

Bainton, Roland H. *Here I Stand: The Life of Martin Luther.* New York: Penguin Group, 1995.

Bokenkotter, Thomas S. *A Concise History of the Catholic Church.* Garden City, N.Y.: Doubleday, 1977.

Christie-Murray, David. *A History of Heresy.* Oxford: Oxford University Press, 1989.

Haight, Anne Lyon. *Banned Books: 387 BC to 1978 AD.* Updated and enlarged by Chandler B. Grannis. New York: R. R. Bowker, 1978.

Putnam, George Haven. *The Censorship of the Church of Rome.* Vol. 1. New York: G. P. Putnam's Sons, 1906–07.

Spitz, Lewis W., ed. *The Protestant Reformation.* Englewood Cliffs, N.J.: Prentice Hall, 1966.

Wilcox, Donald J. *In Search of God and Self Renaissance and Reformation Thought.* Boston: Houghton Mifflin, 1975.

THE ADVANCEMENT OF LEARNING

Author: Francis Bacon
Original date and place of publication: 1605, 1623, England
Literary form: Scientific treatise

SUMMARY

English philosopher and statesman Francis Bacon was a pioneer in the use of the modern inductive method and the logical systemization of scientific procedures. He is credited with the slogan, "Knowledge is power." He planned the writing of a large scientific work, the *Instauratio Magna* (Great restoration of science), but completed only two parts. The first part, *The Advancement of Learning*, a sketch in English of his key ideas, was published in 1605 and expanded in Latin in 1623 as *De Augmentis Scientiarum*. The second part, the *Novum Organum*, was published in 1620.

In *The Advancement of Learning*, Bacon explained his intention to survey the sciences and methods of attaining truth in order to develop a system of classifying the various branches of knowledge. But first he had to deliver scientific learning from "the discredits and disgraces which it hath received, all from ignorance, but ignorance severally disguised, appearing sometimes in the zeal and jealousy of divines, sometimes in the severity and arrogancy of politiques, and sometimes in the errors and imperfections of learned men themselves."

Bacon believed that knowledge was best attained through what he called the "initiative method," as opposed to the "magistral method." "The magistral method teaches," he wrote, "the initiative intimates. The magistral method requires that what is told should be believed; the initiative that it should be examined." As opposed to the prevailing deductive Aristotelian Scholastic approach to knowledge, Bacon advocated an empirical and inductive method, which began with observations of particular things and events and moved toward wider and wider generalizations. He recommended investigation as the key to knowledge, rejecting theories based on insufficient data and, as he described further in the *Novum organum*, ideas drawn from individual propensities and prejudices, "the idols and false notions which are now in possession of human understanding."

He proposed a strict separation of the study of nature from the study of the divine, opposing St. Thomas Aquinas's doctrine that knowledge of the supernatural was sought through the natural. "We do not presume, by the contemplation of nature to attain to the mysteries of God," he declared. Rather, the value and justification of knowledge, he believed, consisted in its practical application and utility. The function of knowledge was to achieve material progress by extending the dominion of human beings over nature.

CENSORSHIP HISTORY

Bacon is often described as the father of modern empiricism. The clear functional style of his writing and his advocacy of sober and dispassionate inquiry free of preconceived notions had a powerful impact on the generation that followed him. Seventeenth-century clerics, who believed that it was sinful to inquire into nature, strongly opposed his rejection of prevailing Aristotelian orthodoxy and the a priori method of medieval Scholasticism.

While medieval Scholastics argued from premises established by past authority and religious revelation, Bacon bypassed the tenets of received knowledge to recommend the discovery of general principles through observation. In 1640, the Spanish Inquisition banned all of Bacon's works, and in 1707 the Spanish Index of Forbidden Books condemned Bacon's *opera omnia* (all his works). In 1668, *De augmentis scientiarum* was placed on the Index of Forbidden Books in Rome, listed with the notation *donec corrigantur* (until corrected). Bacon's work remained on every edition of the Roman Index until it was abolished in 1966.

FURTHER READING

Bacon, Francis. *Francis Bacon: A Selection of His Works*. Edited by Sidney Warhaft. Indianapolis: Odyssey Press, 1981.

Collinson, Diané. *Fifty Major Philosophers: A Reference Guide*. London: Routledge, 1988.

Copleston, Frederick. *A History of Philosophy*. Vol. 3: *Late Medieval and Renaissance Philosophy*. New York: Doubleday, 1993.

Haight, Anne Lyon. *Banned Books: 387 BC to 1978 AD*. Updated and enlarged by Chandler B. Grannis. New York: R. R. Bowker, 1978.

THE AGE OF REASON

Author: Thomas Paine
Original dates and place of publication: 1794–95, France
Literary form: Philosophical treatise

SUMMARY

The Anglo-American political theorist, writer, and revolutionary Thomas Paine was one of the greatest pamphleteers in the English language. *The Age of Reason*, an uncompromising attack on Christianity based on the principles of rationalism, became the most popular deist work ever written.

The son of an English Quaker, Paine immigrated to America in 1774 and became active in the independence movement. His pamphlet, *Common Sense*, published in January 1776, called for the founding of an American republic and galvanized the public toward independence.

In 1787, Paine returned to England, where he published in 1791–92 THE RIGHTS OF MAN, a work defending the French Revolution and attacking social and political inequities in Britain. It was to sell an estimated half-million copies in the next decade and become one of the most widely read books in England. Indicted for seditious libel by the British government for *The Rights of Man*, Paine fled to Paris, where he participated in the French Revolution as a member of the National Convention. For 10 months in 1794, during the Reign of Terror, he was imprisoned by Maximilien Robespierre and the Jacobins before being rescued by the American ambassador to France, James Monroe.

On his way to prison Paine delivered to a friend the manuscript of part one of *The Age of Reason*, which was published in Paris in 1794. After his release from prison, he completed part two, which appeared in 1795. During his stay in France, Paine became convinced that popular revulsion against the reactionary activities of the French clergy, who plotted against the Revolution in alliance with the forces of aristocracy and monarchy, was leading the French people to turn to atheism. In *The Age of Reason*, Paine resolved to rescue true religion from the Christian system of faith, which he regarded as a "pious fraud" and "repugnant to reason."

Paine, in common with many prominent American and European intellectuals, such as Benjamin Franklin, Thomas Jefferson, Voltaire, and Jean-Jacques Rousseau, was a deist. Deism, a religious expression of scientific rationalism, proposed that the existence of God could be inferred from the order and harmony of creation. Deists saw formal religion as superfluous and scorned claims of supernatural revelation as a basis for belief. God's creation, deists believed, was the only bible.

In *The Age of Reason*, Paine popularized deism, removed it from the sphere of the intellectual elite, and made the philosophy accessible to a mass audience. Though critics described the book as "the atheist's bible," Paine repudiated atheism. He opened the book with a profession of faith: "I believe in one God, and no more; and I hope for happiness beyond this life."

Paine's declared objective in all his political writings, beginning with *Common Sense*, was to rescue people from tyranny and false principles of government. *The Age of Reason* was written in the same vein. "Of all the tyrannies that affect mankind," Paine wrote, "tyranny in religion is the worst; every other species of tyranny is limited to the world we live in; but this attempts to stride beyond the grave, and seeks to pursue us into eternity." Organized religion was set up to "terrify and enslave mankind, and monopolize power and profit." The only true theology was "natural philosophy, embracing the whole circle of science."

Paine criticized insincere claims of belief as "mental lying." Every national church or religion claims some special mission from God, communicated to certain individuals, and every church proclaims certain books to be revelation or the word of God. "It is a contradiction to call anything a revelation that comes to us second-hand, either verbally or in writing," Paine wrote.

Paine believed that mystery, miracle, and prophesy were three frauds and that the Old and the New Testaments could not be attributed to revelation. "I totally disbelieve that the Almighty ever did communicate anything to man . . . other than by the universal display of Himself in the works of the creation, and by that repugnance we feel in ourselves to bad actions, and the disposition to do good ones." It was the "Bible of Creation," not the "stupid Bible of the Church," to which men should turn for knowledge. "My own mind is my own church," he proclaimed.

While in part one of *The Age of Reason* Paine disputed in general terms the tenets of Christianity, in part two he attacked both the Old and the New Testaments in tones of ridicule and sarcasm. Challenging the authenticity of the five books of Moses, Paine asserted that they had not been written in the time of Moses; rather, they represented an "anonymous book of stories, fables and traditionary or invented absurdities, or of downright lies." He described the Old Testament as being full of "obscene stories, the voluptuous debaucheries, the cruel and tortuous executions . . . a history of wickedness that has served to corrupt and brutalize mankind; and for my part, I sincerely detest it as I detest everything that is cruel."

Criticizing the New Testament, Paine wrote that the Gospels, having appeared centuries after the death of Christ, were not written by the apostles. He admitted that Jesus was a virtuous and honorable man but denied that he was God. He took offense at the Christianity of the church, "a religion of pomp and revenue" contradictory to the character of Jesus, whose life was characterized by humility and poverty. He described the story of the Immaculate Conception as "blasphemously obscene." He deplored the depiction of miracles for "degrading the Almighty into the character of a showman."

Of all the systems of religion, none is "more derogatory to the Almighty, more unedifying to man, more repugnant to reason, and more contradictory in itself, than this thing called Christianity," Paine wrote. "As an engine of power, it serves the purpose of despotism; and as a means of wealth, the avarice of priests; but so far as respects the good of man in general, it leads to nothing here or hereafter."

As Christianity worships a man rather than God, it is itself a species of atheism, a religious denial of God, Paine contended. "The creation is the Bible of the Deist. He there reads, in the handwriting of the Creator himself, the certainty of his existence and the immutability of His power, and all other Bibles and Testaments are to him forgeries."

CENSORSHIP HISTORY

Paine wrote *The Age of Reason* in an accessible, easy-to-read style. Deistic organizations distributed it free of charge or at low cost in America and Europe. In America, in the mid-1790s, Paine's book went through 17 editions, selling tens of thousands of copies. *The Age of Reason* became the bible of American deists, Paine their hero, and deism a mass movement allied with republicanism.

However, the book also aroused the hostility of clergy and believers on both sides of the Atlantic—a hostility that endured even long after Paine's death. A century later, for example, Theodore Roosevelt referred to Paine as "a filthy little atheist." *The Age of Reason* outraged the leaders of the religious establishment. But it also angered religious reformers who shared Paine's critique of religious conservatism but who parted company with him when he rejected the Bible and all forms of Christianity.

Like its seditious predecessor, *The Rights of Man*, *The Age of Reason* was regarded by the British government as genuinely dangerous because it appeared in the context of mass unrest stirred by the French Revolution. Though Paine was out of reach of British law in France and America, his publishers and booksellers in Britain were not. They were relentlessly prosecuted and imprisoned by the British government over a period of more than 25 years.

In 1797, Thomas Williams of London was tried by a special jury before the Court of King's Bench and found guilty of the crime of blasphemy for having published *The Age of Reason*. The prosecution contended that Paine's book, by subverting the truths of Christianity, undermined the government and the constitution, both of which rested on Christianity. Further, *The Age of Reason* robbed the poor by depriving them of a belief in a happier afterlife. Williams was sentenced to a year at hard labor and a £1,000 fine.

In 1812, the British Crown prosecuted publisher Daniel Isaac Eaton for blasphemy for publishing and selling a new edition of *The Age of Reason*. Eaton had earlier been imprisoned for publishing *The Rights of Man*. "Our civil and religious institutions are so closely interwoven together," the prosecutor told the jury, "that they cannot be separated—the attempt to destroy either is fraught with ruin to the state." Eaton was sentenced to stand in the pillory and to serve 18 months in Newgate Prison. Upon his release from prison, he again defied authorities by publishing *The Age of Reason*; once again, he was prosecuted and convicted of blasphemy. However, because of his age and poor health, he was not sentenced.

The highest price for the defense of Paine's right to publish his ideas was paid by publisher Richard Carlile, a radical exponent of freedom of the press, who between 1817 and 1835 served more than nine years in prison for publishing *The Age of Reason* and other deist tracts. In 1818, he read *The Age of Reason* for the first time and became a deist. He decided to republish the book knowing that its previous publishers had been imprisoned for blasphemy. Indicted for blasphemy, Carlile defiantly kept selling the book. He was brought to trial in October 1819 and in his own defense read the entire book to the jury, taking 12 hours the first day of the trial. By reading it into the court proceedings, he ensured that the work would be republished as part of the public record. It sold 10,000 copies in this form thanks to publicity surrounding the trial.

Carlile was found guilty of blasphemy and sentenced to two years in prison and a £1,000 fine for publishing *The Age of Reason*, as well as another year in prison and a £500 fine for publishing Elihu Palmer's deist book, *The Principles of Nature*. Within an hour of his conviction, government officers seized the contents of his shop and closed it down. Carlile was bankrupted and spent six years in prison, as he could not pay his fines. His wife, his sister, and more than 20 of his workers were also prosecuted and jailed in the years that followed for continuing to publish *The Age of Reason* and other material judged blasphemous.

Rather than succeeding in suppressing Paine's work, Carlile's prosecution aroused interest in it. Four years later more than 20,000 copies were in circulation in England. According to the philosopher John Stuart Mill, writing in 1824, "as among the poorer classes it is notorious that there are several readers to one purchaser, it may be estimated that at least one hundred thousand persons have been led to the perusal of that work under circumstances highly favourable to its making an impression on their minds."

FURTHER READING

Foner, Eric. *Tom Paine and Revolutionary America*. London: Oxford University Press, 1976.

Levy, Leonard W. *Blasphemy: Verbal Offense against the Sacred, from Moses to Salman Rushdie*. New York: Alfred A. Knopf, 1993.

Paine, Thomas. *The Age of Reason*. Introduction by Philip S. Foner. Secaucus, N.J.: Citadel Press, 1974.

ALCIPHRON, OR THE MINUTE PHILOSOPHER

Author: George Berkeley
Original dates and places of publication: 1732, Ireland and England; 1803, United States
Literary form: Philosophical dialogue

SUMMARY

The Anglo-Irish philosopher and Anglican bishop George Berkeley is regarded as among the outstanding and influential classical British empiricists. Among his most important works, written in his younger years, were *An Essay Towards a New Theory of Vision* (1709), *A Treatise Concerning the Principles of Human Knowledge* (1710), and *Three Dialogues Between Hylas and Philonous* (1713).

Berkeley's philosophy of subjective idealism held that matter does not exist independent of perception, and that the observing mind of God makes possible the continued apparent existence of material objects. Qualities, rather than things, are perceived and the perception of qualities is relative to the perceiver. Berkeley characterized his immaterialism with the phrase, *esse est percipi*, "to be is to be perceived."

The most popular and accessible of his works was *Alciphron, or the Minute Philosopher*, published in Dublin and London in 1732 and in The Hague in French in 1734. A third edition was published in London in 1752, the year before Berkeley's death. *Alciphron* was directed against freethinkers—English deists and atheists—and attempted to vindicate Christianity. Berkeley believed that the growth of atheistic freedom from religious restraints was the primary cause of England's social maladies, because atheism withdraws the strongest motive for promoting the common good. He charged the "minute" (meaning "small") philosophers with anticlericalism, intellectual arrogance, and contempt for religion, attributing their atheism to their limited intellectual vision.

"The Author's design being to consider the Free-thinker in the various lights of atheist, libertine, enthusiast, scorner, critic, metaphysician, fatalist, and sceptic," Berkeley wrote in the introduction to *Alciphron*, "it must not therefore be imagined that every one of these characters agrees with every individual Freethinker; no more being implied that each part agrees with some or other of the sect. . . . Whatever they pretend, it is the author's opinion that all those who write, either explicitly or by insinuation, against the dignity, freedom, and immortality of the Human Soul, may so far be justly said to unhinge the principles of morality, and destroy the means of making men reasonably virtuous."

The seven dialogues that make up *Alciphron* occur over the seven days of one week, during which Euphranor, a prosperous farmer, and Crito, a neighboring distinguished gentleman, debate the tenets of "minute philosophy" with Alciphron and Lysicles, both confirmed freethinkers. Their conversations are reported in a letter to a friend by Dion, who observes but does not participate in the discussions. Alciphron and Lysicles are depicted as comic figures. The pedantic Alciphron is influenced by the deistic philosophy of the third earl of Shaftesbury, who posited that true morality was found in a balance of egoism and altruism. Lysicles is a follower of the philosophy of Bernard Mandeville, who, in his THE FABLE OF THE BEES, argued the social utility of vice.

In Berkeley's view, neither Shaftesbury nor Mandeville understood the function of reason in moral life, nor did they provide a motive for altruistic conduct. In the dialogues, Berkeley defends the individual and social utility of Christianity and declares the universal providence of God as indispensable to the vitality of virtue and the practice of morality.

CENSORSHIP HISTORY

Unlike many other British thinkers of the period, Berkeley was a devout Christian. Predictably, freethinkers attacked *Alciphron* soon after its appearance. Mandeville, in his *Letter to Dion*, complained of misrepresentation by Berkeley. A number of other books and tracts critical of *Alciphron* were published. But Berkeley's censors were not the freethinkers.

In *Alciphron* Berkeley, who used the terms "popery and papists" when referring to Catholicism and Catholics, suggested that the "minute philosophers" might be dupes of the Jesuits. At the end of the second dialogue, Euphranor argues that if the opinions of freethinkers were to prevail and destroy the Protestant Church and clergy, they would leave way for "a harvest by popery."

"I am credibly informed there is a great number of emissaries of the church of Rome disguised in England," Euphranor says. "[W]ho can tell what harvest a church so numerous, so subtle, and so well furnished with arguments to work on vulgar and uneducated minds, may be able to make in a country so despoiled of all religion, and feeling the want of it?" In effect, one of Berkeley's arguments against freethinking was that it would lead to a resurgence of Catholicism, which he, as an Anglican, abhorred.

In 1742, despite Berkeley's defense of Christianity against deism and atheism, his anti-Catholic views led the Catholic Church to place *Alciphron* on the Roman

Index of Forbidden Books. It was retained on the Index of Pope Leo XIII in 1897 and remained listed through the last edition, compiled in 1948 and in print until 1966. Mandeville's *The Fable of the Bees*, which Berkeley attacked in *Alciphron*, was also placed on the Index and was still listed in the last 20th-century edition.

FURTHER READING

Berkeley, George. *The Works of George Berkeley*. Vol. 2: *Philosophical Works, 1732–33*. Preface by Alexander Campbell Fraser. Oxford, U.K.: Clarendon Press, 1931.
Collinson, Diané. *Fifty Major Philosophers: A Reference Guide*. London: Routledge, 1988.
Cook, Richard I. *Bernard Mandeville*. New York: Twayne Publishers, 1974.
Copleston, Frederick. *A History of Philosophy*. Vol. 5: *Modern Philosophy: The British Philosophers from Hobbes to Hume*. New York: Doubleday, 1994.

THE ANALECTS

Author: Confucius (Kong Fuzi)
Original date and place of publication: Third–fourth century B.C., China
Literary form: Religious and philosophical text

SUMMARY

The Analects is a collection of sayings and short dialogues attributed to Confucius (551–479 B.C.) and first compiled by his disciples during the third and fourth centuries B.C. Confucius was China's greatest philosopher and the founder of the ethical and religious system of Confucianism, which dominated China's social and political thinking for millennia. All educated men in China memorized *The Analects* as a guide to ethics and morality in personal and political life.

Though it is chiefly through *The Analects* that Confucianism has been known to the West, many of the pithy maxims and remarks in *The Analects* are extracts from longer discourses found in other works of the Confucian canon. In the centuries after Confucius's death, five works attributed to Confucius were collected into the *Five Classics:* one on ritual, two on history, one on poetry, and one on cosmology and divination (*I Ching* [*Yi Jing*]). In the 12th century A.D., selections from the *Five Classics*, including *The Analects*, the sayings of Confucius's follower Mencius, and two selections from the book on ritual dealing with human nature and moral development were formed into the *Four Books*. The *Four Books* were thought to embody the essence of Confucius's teachings. The *Five Classics* and the *Four Books* became the basis for state examinations required for government service in China. Until the second half of the 19th century, China's educational system was based entirely on Confucian thought.

The Analects emphasizes rational thinking rather than dogma and stresses the virtue of altruism. In Confucius's dialogues with statesmen and students, he is portrayed as a shrewd and modest teacher who tested himself and others for character flaws while promulgating faith in the power of moral example and virtuous action. Confucius believed that intellect and learning rather than inherited privilege should determine man's place in society.

Social relations function smoothly by a strict adherence to *li*, a term denoting a combination of etiquette and ritual. Filial piety—the hierarchical code governing behavior among family members (respect of son for father, wife for husband, and younger brother for older brother)—extended to homage to the emperor, who is regarded as the embodiment of wisdom and moral superiority.

Confucius taught four subjects, or precepts: literature, personal conduct, being one's true self, and honesty in personal relationships. He denounced arbitrary opinions, dogmatism, narrow-mindedness, and egotism and was described as gentle but dignified, austere but not harsh, and polite and completely at ease. "Whenever walking in a company of three," Confucius said, "I can always find my teacher among them (or one who has something to teach me). I select a good person and follow his example, or I see a bad person and correct it in myself." He advised his followers to criticize their own faults rather than those of others. When asked if there was one single word that would serve as a principle of conduct for life, Confucius replied, "Perhaps the word *reciprocity (shu)*: Do not do unto others what you do not want others to do unto you."

The golden rule and the golden mean—moderation in all things—are essential principles expressed in The Analects. "To go a little too far is as bad as not going far enough." Many of the maxims of The Analects describe the qualities of the superior man. "To know what you know and know what you don't know is the characteristic of one who knows," Confucius said. "A man who has committed a mistake and doesn't correct it is committing another mistake. . . . The superior man understands what is right; the inferior man understands what will sell. . . . The superior man blames himself; the inferior man blames others."

Confucius's views of political ethics were extensions of his view of personal ethics. "When wealth is equally distributed, there is no poverty; when the people are united, you cannot call it a small nation, and when there is no dissatisfaction (or when the people have a sense of security), the country is secure," he said. When a ruler does what is right, he will have influence without giving commands, and when the ruler does not do what is right, his commands will be of no avail.

CENSORSHIP HISTORY

Though Confucius himself was an agnostic, a popular religion developed around his teachings. Temples dedicated to Confucius sprang up across

China, especially near his birthplace in Qufu, in what is now Shandong Province. In 221 B.C., the first ruler of the Qin dynasty, Shi Huangdi, unified China. He abolished the system of warring feudal states and established a centralized feudal system known as Legalism, with an appointed bureaucracy, laws, and standardized currencies, weights, and measures. In 213 B.C., the emperor, who saw the traditional culture of China as a challenge to Legalism and the centralized state, ordered Confucian books burned and threatened to execute anyone who dared to quote them. Only practical works on agriculture, medicine, and divination were exempted from the burning and preserved in the imperial library. In the following year, 460 Confucian scholars were buried alive. The imperial library was destroyed during a civil war in 206 B.C.

In 191 B.C., the rulers of the Han dynasty rescinded the book-burning edict. Because the teachings of Confucius were handed down orally from master to disciple, scholars were able to reconstruct the texts from memory and from hidden manuscripts that escaped destruction.

In the 20th century, *The Analects* and the Confucian canon were again attacked. During the Great Proletarian Cultural Revolution of 1966–74, Mao Zedong and the leaders of the Chinese Communist Party called for a comprehensive attack on the "four old" elements within Chinese society—culture, thinking, habits, and customs. Though Mao had quoted aphorisms of Confucius in his essays and poems, possession of Confucian writings became dangerous. Youths organized as Red Guards charged intellectuals with feudal or reactionary modes of thinking and destroyed libraries and art collections. Confucian temples in Qufu were vandalized.

During 1973–74, the Communist Party launched a major propaganda campaign against the teachings of Confucius as well as against former defense minister Lin Biao, who was regarded as a reactionary parallel to Confucius. The party criticized Confucian thinking as promoting an ideology of exploitation, elitism, social hierarchy, and preservation of a status quo in which people knew and kept their place in a static society and obeyed the prescribed rites for their station in life. Party leaders asserted that Lin Biao promoted Confucian ideology and had opposed Mao Zedong, just as conservative Confucian thinking opposed the politically centralizing policies of the first emperor in the third century B.C. The anti–Lin Biao, anti-Confucius campaign was the focus of mass rallies and discussions in party cells, the army, agricultural communes, and factories. The burning of Confucian books and the execution of scholars in the third century B.C. were defended in the campaign as historically necessary to overthrow the feudal landlords of the slave-owning aristocracy.

The end of the Cultural Revolution brought about a change in government attitudes toward Confucian thought. In 1989, a few months after the repression of prodemocracy demonstrations in Beijing's Tiananmen Square, China's newly appointed Communist Party chairman, Jiang Zemin, attended an official ceremony commemorating the anniversary of Confucius's birth, marking the complete rehabilitation of Confucianism. It is now one of China's officially approved religions.

Confucianism is enjoying a resurgence in China. Study of Confucian thought is widespread at all levels of the Chinese educational system, and a book based on a popular television program explaining *The Analects* has sold more than 4 million copies. By 2007, the Chinese Communist Party had opened 145 Confucius Institutes in more than 52 countries to promote Chinese language and culture. The emphasis in Confucianism on order, harmony, and respect for authority is appealing to the Communist Party. For ordinary Chinese, it is providing an alternative ideology both to communism and rampant materialism and a source of philosophical and spiritual values during a time of rapid economic and social changes.

FURTHER READING

Fan, Maureen. "Confucius Making a Comeback in Money-Driven Modern China." *The Washington Post* (July 24, 2007). Available online. URL: http://www.washingtonpost. com/wp-dyn/content/article/2007/07/23/AR2007072301859.html. Accessed June 6, 2010.

Lin, Yutang, ed. *The Wisdom of Confucius*. New York: Random House, 1966.

Mooney, Paul. "Confucius Comes Back." *The Chronicle of Higher Education* (April 20, 2007). Available online. URL: http://chronicle.com/article/Confucius-Comes-Back/34363. Accessed June 6, 2010.

Spence, Jonathan D. *The Search for Modern China*. New York: W. W. Norton, 1990.

ARCANA COELESTIA

Author: Emanuel Swedenborg
Original dates and place of publication: 1747–58, England
Literary form: Theological treatise

SUMMARY

The writings of Emanuel Swedenborg, the Swedish scientist, philosopher, and theologian, form the doctrinal basis of the church of the New Jerusalem, or New Church, founded after his death. Swedenborg was an engineer and assessor of the Swedish Royal Bureau of Mines. He wrote many notable scientific volumes between 1720 and 1745, including *Principia*, a groundbreaking mathematical, rational explanation of the universe, the first part of the three-volume *Philosophical and Mineralogical Works*.

Swedenborg adopted his religious philosophy, generally called Swedenborgianism, during 1744 and 1745, when he had a number of dreams and mystical visions in which he believed God directly called him to bring a new revelation to the world. In 1747, he resigned his post of assessor to dedicate himself to spiritual matters and for the next quarter century, wrote voluminous theological works expounding "the true Christian religion," a body of spiritual law meant to revivify all churches.

In his theosophic teachings he declared that two worlds exist, both emanating from God. The "New Jerusalem" is the spiritual world to which man will ultimately be restored by a process of purification through divine love. The second is the world of nature in which human beings live. A symbolic counterpart to everything in our world exists in the spiritual world. All creative forces, both in the spiritual and in the natural kingdom of consciousness, flow from the divine center of the universe. Man's spirit or soul was created to be a receptacle of divine life, whose essence is love and wisdom.

Between 1747 and 1758, Swedenborg wrote and published the eight-volume *Arcana coelestia*, or *Heavenly Secrets*, his first major theological work, a 7,000-page, 3 million–word commentary on the Books of Genesis and Exodus. *Arcana*, as well as his other theological works, Swedenborg believed, were dictated to him by God. Between his chapters of biblical exegesis, Swedenborg inserted his personal accounts of experiences "from the other world," copied or transposed from his own spiritual diaries.

In *Arcana*, Swedenborg interpreted the Bible according to the doctrine of correspondences, by which everything that is outward or visible has an inward or spiritual cause. "The universal heaven is so formed as to correspond to the Lord, to His Divine Human; and man is so formed that all things in him, in general and in particular, correspond to heaven, and through heaven, to the Lord," he wrote. He believed that God inscribed within the historical narratives of the Bible an interior spiritual sense. The early chapters of Genesis, for example, were allegorical and did not literally describe the creation of the universe and the origins of the first human beings. He interpreted Genesis as descriptive of man's spiritual regeneration. Adam and Eve represented the human race or human nature in the abstract, Adam standing for its intellectual qualities and Eve for its emotional side. Through the language of correspondences, the familiar Bible stories revealed basic divine teachings on life after death, relationships between the spiritual and natural worlds, human nature and religion. In the preface to *Arcana*, Swedenborg maintained that without an understanding of the internal meaning of the Scriptures, they were like "a body without a soul."

Central elements of Swedenborg's theology diverged from both Catholic and Protestant doctrines. He taught that rewards and punishments have no place as incentives to virtue. He denied that there were three persons in the Holy Trinity, believing instead in the exclusive divinity of Jesus Christ. He also took issue with the doctrine of Atonement and called the Catholic Church "Babylon" for its desire for dominion over men's souls. He attacked the Lutheran belief that faith without works is sufficient for salvation, holding that true faith could not be disassociated from a life of charity and active usefulness. He saw good in all churches and criticized Protestants for their self-righteousness.

In 1758, Swedenborg published the three-volume *Heaven and Hell*, extracts from *Arcana* describing the nature of heaven and hell, as well as the world of the spirits, the transitory state between natural life and heaven or hell, where human beings prepare for their ultimate fate. Whether human beings go to heaven or hell depends on the quality of their lives in the natural world. Swedenborg believed that spirits go to hell when their selfish lives on earth cause them to find the unselfish love of heaven oppressive.

CENSORSHIP HISTORY

The eight volumes of *Arcana coelestia*, written in Latin, were published anonymously during the years 1749 to 1756 in London, where Swedenborg had settled. Despite its size, Swedenborg insisted that the book be sold cheaply. He advanced the money for its publication, dedicating all profits to "the propagation of the gospel."

As only the second volume was issued with an English translation, the book appealed primarily to the learned, and few copies were sold. Swedenborg gave away many copies anonymously to clergymen, including the bishops of Sweden, England, Holland, and Germany, as well as to universities and libraries. Though his expectation was that some would accept his teachings and spread them, most of the clergy either ignored his doctrines or regarded them with contempt.

Swedenborg's efforts to remain anonymous in his theological writings lasted until 1759. That year in Stockholm, in a well-publicized incident, Swedenborg apparently demonstrated clairvoyance by correctly predicting a fire. As a result of the general curiosity about this and other examples of his unusual abilities, he became a public figure. He became known in Sweden as the author of *Arcana coelestia* and *Heaven and Hell*, and copies published in London began to trickle into Sweden.

His theological writings caused great controversy in Göteborg's Lutheran consistory. In September 1768, a country parson introduced a resolution objecting to Swedenborg's writings and calling for measures to stop the circulation of works such as Swedenborg's that contradicted Lutheran dogma. However, some members insisted that Swedenborg's works should not be judged until the entire membership had studied them. But Dean Ekebom, the ranking prelate, announced that, even though he was unacquainted with Swedenborg's religious system and had not read much of it, he found his doctrines to be "corrupting, heretical, injurious, and to the highest degree objectionable." He concluded that Swedenborg's views on the nature of the divine, the Bible, the Holy Supper, faith, and other basic teachings should be suppressed as dangerous to established religious concepts. He also charged Swedenborg with the anti-Trinitarian heresy of Socinianism.

Swedenborg, who had gone to Amsterdam in 1769 to publish a new book, replied by letter in his own defense, stating, "I look upon the word Socinian as a downright insult and diabolical mockery." The clergy, however, regarded Swedenborg's letter as "sinister," because he also argued that his doctrine of the New Church had come directly from God, who had asked his servant Swedenborg to introduce it to the world.

The case of Swedenborg's heresy was brought before the Swedish Diet. The chief prosecutor urged that "the most energetic measures be taken to stifle, punish and utterly eradicate Swedenborgian innovation and downright heresies by which we are encompassed . . . so that the boar which devastates and the wild beast which desolates our country may be driven out with a mighty hand."

The royal council, appointed through the Diet, issued its final report in April 1770. It "totally condemned, rejected and forbade the theological doctrines contained in Swedenborg's writings." Swedenborg's supporters among the clergy were forbidden to read or propagate his teaching, and customs officials were directed to impound his books and stop their circulation unless the nearest Lutheran consistory granted permission.

Swedenborg continued to protest the council's decision. The royal council referred the matter to the Götha court of appeals, which asked several universities to thoroughly study his ideas. The universities found nothing objectionable in his writing but asked to be excused, as they were not inclined to put bishops and consistories on trial for false accusations. Eventually the controversy abated. Some Lutheran clergymen preached Swedenborgian ideas without interference, and Swedenborg continued to write and speak, dividing his time among Sweden, London, and Amsterdam. But because of censorship in Sweden, his religious ideas found the most fertile ground elsewhere. Toward the end of his life, Swedenborg's works were widely translated and circulated. In a letter written in 1771 he stated that the *Arcana* "can no longer be obtained either here in Holland or in England, as all the copies are sold." He was most influential in England, where societies formed for the study of his works.

Swedenborg had not intended to establish a religious sect, for he saw his ideas as relevant to all Christians. However, after his death in 1772, his English followers began to organize the New Church. The first public services of its congregation were held in 1788 in London. Swedenborg's teachings were introduced into the United States in 1784, and a congregation of the New Church was formed in Baltimore in 1792.

Swedenborg's reputation increased in the 19th century, when he was admired by many European and American intellectuals. His book on marriage and sex, *Conjugal Love*, condemned by Swedish authorities shortly after its publication in 1768, became popular in Germany and France. It attracted public attention in the United States in 1909 when it was seized by Philadelphia post office authorities on grounds of obscenity.

Despite Swedenborg's divergence from Catholic dogma as expressed in such works as *Arcana*, the Catholic Church condemned only Swedenborg's early scientific work *Principia; or the First Principles of Natural Things*, published in 1721. It placed the book on the Index of Forbidden Books in 1738. *Principia* remained there through the final edition of the Index compiled in 1948 and in effect until 1966. In the Soviet Union, all of Swedenborg's works were banned in 1930 in an effort to suppress mystical and religious works generally.

FURTHER READING

Haight, Anne Lyon. *Banned Books: 387 BC to 1978 AD*. Updated and enlarged by Chandler B. Grannis. New York: R. R. Bowker, 1978.

Synnestvedt, Sig. *The Essential Swedenborg*. New York: Twayne Publishers, 1970.

Toksvig, Signe. *Emanuel Swedenborg: Scientist and Mystic*. Freeport, N.Y.: Books for Libraries Press, 1972.

Trowbridge, George. *Swedenborg, Life and Teaching*. New York: Swedenborg Foundation, 1938.

THE BABYLONIAN CAPTIVITY OF THE CHURCH

Author: Martin Luther
Original date and place of publication: 1520, Switzerland
Literary form: Theological tract

SUMMARY

In 1520, Martin Luther, the German founder of the Protestant Reformation, published a radical tract whose uncompromising assault on Roman Catholic doctrine led to an irreparable breech with the church hierarchy. In *The Babylonian Captivity of the Church*, Luther definitively abandoned traditional Catholicism and presented a new theory about the nature of the church and its sacramental system. He denied the authority of the priesthood to mediate between the individual and God and rejected the sacraments except as aids to faith.

On the grounds that a sacrament must have been directly instituted by Christ and based on the authority of Scripture, Luther reduced the number of the sacraments from seven to two. Confirmation, marriage, ordination, penance, and extreme unction were eliminated. Only baptism and the Eucharist, radically transformed, remained. Luther's repudiation of ordination, the sacrament granting priests the power to celebrate the Eucharist and marking them with an indelible character, provided the basis for Luther's priesthood of all believers, ending the "detestable tyranny of the clergy over the laity."

Ordination as a sacrament, Luther wrote, "was designed to engender implacable discord whereby the clergy and the laity should be separated farther than heaven and earth. . . . All of us who have been baptized are priests without distinction, but those whom we call priests are ministers, chosen from among us so that they should do all things in our name and their priesthood is nothing but a ministry."

In eliminating the sacrament of penance, Luther recognized the usefulness of confession but believed that it could be made to any Christian rather than only to a priest. He regarded confirmation, the rite that confirms the initiation into the church by baptism, and marriage, which he felt should be allowed for priests, as useful ceremonies rather than as sacraments.

He proposed that the efficacy of extreme unction, or anointing of the sick, depended on the faith of the recipient. The church taught that a sacrament's benefits could not be impaired by any human weakness, as it operates by virtue of itself. Luther viewed this interpretation of the sacraments as mechanical and magical. "I may be wrong on indulgences," Luther declared, "but as to the need for faith in the sacraments I will die before I will recant."

Luther accepted the scriptural origins of baptism but believed that no vow beyond the baptismal vow should ever be taken, thereby repudiating the vows taken by monks. Although he retained the sacrament of the Eucharist, he held that the Mass is not a repetition of Christ's sacrifice. Thus he rejected the doctrine of transubstantiation, by which the bread and wine are held to be transformed into the Body and Blood of Christ. He proposed instead his doctrine of consubstantiation, meaning that after their consecration the substances of bread and wine remain along with the Body and Blood of Christ. The priest does not "sacrifice Christ" and effects no miracle because Christ is present everywhere and at all times.

CENSORSHIP HISTORY

See NINETY-FIVE THESES.

FURTHER READING

Bainton, Roland H. *Here I Stand: The Life of Martin Luther.* New York: Penguin Group, 1995.

Bokenkotter, Thomas S. *A Concise History of the Catholic Church.* Garden City, N.Y.: Doubleday and Co., 1977.

Christie-Murray, David. *A History of Heresy.* Oxford: Oxford University Press, 1989.

Haight, Anne Lyon. *Banned Books: 387 BC to 1978 AD.* Updated and enlarged by Chandler B. Grannis. New York: R. R. Bowker, 1978.

Putnam, George Haven. *The Censorship of the Church of Rome.* Vol. 1. New York: G. P. Putnam's Sons, 1906–07.

Spitz, Lewis W., ed. *The Protestant Reformation.* Englewood Cliffs, N.J.: Prentice Hall, 1966.

Wilcox, Donald J. *In Search of God and Self: Renaissance and Reformation Thought.* Boston: Houghton Mifflin, 1975.

THE BATTLE FOR GOD

Author: Karen Armstrong
Original date and place of publication: 2000, United States
Original publisher: Alfred A. Knopf
Literary form: Nonfiction

SUMMARY

In *The Battle for God*, Karen Armstrong, one of the most prolific and respected commentators on the ethical, cultural, and psychological aspects of religions and their believers, turns her formidable intellect to an examination of the foundations of fundamentalism and its rise to its current position of influence.

Armstrong considers the development of fundamentalism in terms of two contrasting modes of experience. One life view is based on *mythos*, which is intuitive and rooted in the unconscious levels of the human mind; it provides a meaning and a context for a society's beliefs and code of conduct. The other mode is *logos*, which is rational; it resides in the conscious mind and is concerned with discursive knowledge and the practical applications in this material world we all inhabit. Operating on the accumulation and manipulation of data, *logos* would be inadequate to ponder the ultimate questions of life; that is the ground *mythos* covers.

Premodern peoples were capable of keeping separate and balancing these two ways of knowledge in their daily living. But efforts to make either mode fill the other's purpose inevitably leads to disaster. Armstrong gives the example of the Crusades. As a military maneuver to extend the power of the church, the plan was within the realm of reason and succeeded, creating colonies and establishing trade in the Middle East. However, when the crusaders based their policies on mystical visions, they ended up committing murderous atrocities in the name of Christ.

Using this conceptual template, Armstrong proceeds to focus on the three great monotheisms, examining the development of Jewish fundamentalism in Israel, Islamic fundamentalism in Egypt and Iran, and Protestant fundamentalism in the United States. Armstrong points out in her introduction, however, that fundamentalism is not monolithic; it has its own character as determined by the tenets of the religion from which it develops. Any religion can be a breeding ground for fundamentalism. But regardless of their origin, all forms of fundamentalism share basic characteristics: an absolute rejection of secular values and an attempt to reintroduce the "sacred" into society.

Positing 1492 as the beginning of our modern era, Armstrong explains how Judaism and Islam developed from agrarian societies, where a reliance on the conservation and replenishment of resources led to a generally conservative worldview that also emphasized preservation of ideas, an identification with the past, and the importance of tradition. In these societies, *mythos* gave people social cohesion, made manifest in prayer and ritual.

When Catholic monarchs Ferdinand and Isabella expelled the Jews and the Muslims from Spain in 1492, the Muslims had only lost an opportunity to expand Islamic interests in Spain; they had maintained *mythos* in thriving empires established in the Middle and Far East. For the Jews, however, the banishment launched them into a new exile. The sense of dislocation destroyed all aspects of shared community and religious belief. In many of the lands where any sanctuary could be found, many Jews turned to atheism.

Throughout Europe at this time, rationalism was gaining ascendancy, as scientific advances brought greater industrial and commercial success. Instead of the conservation of resources, society was now capable of reproducing and multiplying materials. As the triumphs of science and technology yielded greater wealth and established the primacy of secular values, *logos* came to be seen as the sole way of perceiving truth; *mythos* was now seen as superstition. It was in this climate of wholesale change that Martin Luther rose to prominence. Luther suffered from "agonizing depressions" in his formative years, personal conditions that the practices of established faith could do nothing to alleviate. Luther came to dismiss prayer and ritual as meaningless and stressed an adherence to doctrine. The authority of Scripture provided the basis for individual interpretation, and thus one would be justified by one's faith alone, contingent upon the mercy of a benevolent God. Positing God as separate and utterly absent from his creation, Luther, like many others, exhibited an existential dread that was not unlike the atheism of the exiled Jews of the Diaspora. Confused and bewildered by the loss of a context they had known, they could not endure life outside the norms of their traditional religions and had lost all sense of the divine in this world.

This feeling of helplessness and the fear of annihilation bred an intense desire to reaffirm religious identity, which in turn formed the beginnings of fundamentalism as we know it today. As industrialization continued to obliterate the past, fundamentalism turned to *logos*—rational thought—to project God back into the human world. The prevailing ethos was formed by eschatology, a doctrine of "last things," in which life on earth was seen as the battlefield for a cosmic war between good and evil, in which the truly faithful would ultimately be vindicated in their religious beliefs and be delivered from their worldly oppressors.

In Judaism, Armstrong sees this element as present, for example, in the 17th-century messianic movement of Shabbateanism, which turned to the mystical tradition of the Kabbalah for illumination and guidance. However, eschatology is, perhaps, most actively prominent in American Protestant fundamentalism, as exemplified by the likes of John Nelson Darby, whose biblical literalism led him to espouse the notion of the Rapture, during which true believers would be physically lifted into the air by God to be spared the agonies of the Time of the Tribulation, as Christ returns to establish the Heavenly Kingdom on an earth purged of "evildoers."

As Armstrong astutely notes in the book's afterword, "Fundamentalists have turned the *mythos* of their religions into *logos*, either by insisting that their dogmas are scientifically true or by transforming their complexity into a streamlined ideology. . . . As a result, all have neglected the more tolerant, inclusive and compassionate teachings and have cultivated theologies of rage, resentment and revenge." Armstrong further points out that while fundamentalists' violent attempts to bring God back into the world undermine the very sanctity of their religions, secularism's own "cult of rationality" has had its episodes of irrationality. In Armstrong's words, "The liberal myth that humanity is progressing to an ever more enlightened and tolerant state looks as fantastic as any of the other millennial myths we have considered in this book. Without the constraints of a 'higher,' mythical truth, reason can on occasion become demonic and commit crimes as great as, if not greater than, any of the atrocities perpetrated by fundamentalists."

The Battle for God lucidly shows that the divide between *mythos* and *logos* is a permanent condition of the world but one that is not necessarily unbridgeable. Armstrong urges a return to compassion, so that, at the least, dialogue may open between adherents of these antagonistic tendencies. In an atmosphere of mutual respect, the ravening fears of the fundamentalists may be assuaged, and the smug incomprehension of the secularists may be humbled to bring about a greater understanding between them.

CENSORSHIP HISTORY

On January 8, 2010, the Associated Press reported that violence had erupted in Malaysia over a December 31, 2009, High Court decision to overturn a government ban on Roman Catholics using the word *Allah* when writing or speaking of God. Angry Muslims firebombed three churches in protest, in a country whose constitution guarantees freedom of religion. It is not surprising, then, that a book of such lucidity, even-handedness, and depth of intellectual penetration as *The Battle for God* should run afoul of the tendencies of fundamentalism that Karen Armstrong examines in the book.

This particular controversy began in 2006, when the book was banned by Malaysia's Ministry of Internal Security, under the Printing Presses and Publications Act of 1984, which prohibits the reproduction and distribution of materials deemed capable of "disrupting peace and harmony." Article 19, the Global Campaign for Free Expression, based in London, has pointed out that section 9 (1) of the act allows the ministry to ban any expression in any form or medium it considers to be harmful to public order, morality, and security; to excite public opinion or be illegal; or is otherwise prejudicial to the public or national interest.

It was under this act in 2006 that the ministry had revoked the publishing licenses of local newspapers for running articles about the Danish cartoons that mocked the prophet Muhammad, or for reprinting those cartoons. Other books banned in that year under the act include *Sharing Your Faith with a Muslim*, by Akbidayah Akbar Abdul-Haqq; *Islam Revealed: A Christian Arab's View of Islam*, by Dr. Anis A. Shorrosh; and *What Everyone Needs to Know about Islam*, by John Esposito, professor of religion and international affairs, professor of Islamic studies, and founding director of the Prince Alwaleed bin Talal Center for Muslim-Christian Understanding at Georgetown University.

What is strange about the banning of *The Battle for God* is that the book, along with two previous Armstrong works that were banned in 2005 (*The History of God* and *Muhammad: A Biography*), was fully available, widely read, and highly praised previously in Malaysia. James Wong Wing-on, former member of the Eighth Parliament (1990–95) under then–prime minister Dr. Mahathir bin Mohamad and now a political commentator, wrote in his *Clare Street* blog that the censors are "becoming irrational paranoiac and arbitrary . . . [even if] it is a subversive book, the ban imposed in 2006 is really too late and it shows how inefficient the censors are." He expressed dismay that while, for instance, Armstrong's and Esposito's books had been banned, other works critical of Islam, such as *Crisis in Islam* by Professor Bernard Lewis, remained available.

Odder still was the fact that despite the banning of her books, Armstrong was still welcomed as a lecturer. On June 16, 2007, at the invitation of the Institute of Diplomacy and Foreign Relations, she delivered a talk in Kuala Lumpur on "The Role of Religion in the 21st Century" at a conference on Islam and the West. Two days later in Kajang, she gave another talk on "Building a Universal Civilization of Peace" at a conference organized by the International Movement for a Just World and the World Assembly of Muslim Youth.

The International Freedom of Expression Exchange suggested a more patently political reason for the bans. Prime Minister Abdullah Ahmad Badawi, who came into office in 2004 on pledges of democratic reforms, had the practical concern of balancing his endeavors to ensure open dialogue on Islamic plurality while maintaining a strong base of support among Muslim conservatives.

In the United States, conservative commentator Daniel Pipes, noting the proscription on Esposito's and Armstrong's books, described them as "two of the West's leading apologists for radical Islam." This statement would make anyone familiar with *The Battle for God* wonder whether Pipes had read the book at all. As deep and solid a work of scholarship as *The Battle for God* is, Armstrong writes with insight and compassion. It is this sense of tolerance that has caused many Muslims to embrace the book, feeling grateful that a Western writer has shown respect for, instead of hatred of, their faith.

In 2006, the Kuala Lumpur–based women's rights group Sisters-in-Islam protested the ministry's censorship policy by trying to gather support to have recent and past bans lifted. The group stated, "Malaysians are being deprived of ideas and debate. . . . There should be opportunity for readers and writers to question decisions being made and the reasons behind the bans."

A year later, the Muslim Youth Movement of Malaysia (Abim) joined the protest by asking the government to lift the ban on Armstrong's books. Azril Mohdamin Amin, vice president of the group, was quoted as saying, "Armstrong has made some very fair judgments on certain issues in Islam. We can learn from that. And we can see that she is also sincere in her opinion."

The Malaysian government instituted the Media Council Bill (2006) in an attempt to mitigate some of the abuses of the 1984 act with regard to the local media. It does not seem to have made any difference. Since then, the ministry has banned more books, including *The Two Faces of Islam: Saudi Fundamentalism and Its Role in Terror* by Stephen Schwartz, and has chosen to keep all existing bans in place.

—Philip Milito

FURTHER READING

Bunting, Madeleine. "A Question of Faith." *Guardian* (October 6, 2007). Available online. URL: http://www.guardian.co.uk/books/2007/oct/06/society1.html. Accessed October 7, 2009.

Joshi, Vijay. "Three Malaysian Churches Attacked in 'Allah' Dispute." *Yahoo News.* Available online. URL: http://news.yahoo.com/s/ap/20100108/ap_on_re_as/as_malaysia_allah_ban/print.html. Accessed January 8, 2010.

"Karen Armstrong: It's OK to Listen to Her but Don't Read Her Works" (June 11, 2007). Centre for Independent Journalism, Malaysia. Available online. URL: http://www.cijmalaysia.org/content/view/214/6/.html. Accessed October 7, 2009.

"Malaysia: 18 Books Banned for Disrupting Peace and Harmony." Article 19 (July 10, 2006). Available online. URL: http://www.article19.org.html. Accessed October 7, 2009.

"Malaysian Government Bans Eighteen Books on Islam and Religion." International Freedom of Expression Exchange (July 4, 2006). Available online. URL: http://www.ifex.org/en/content/view/full/75464/.html. Accessed June 15, 2009.

Nee, Ooi Ying. "The Bane of Book Banning." The Nut Graph (August 8, 2008). Available online. URL: http://www.thenutgraph.com/the-bane-of-book-banning. html/ Accessed October 7, 2009.

Pipes, Daniel. "John Esposito and Karen Armstrong Banned in Malaysia." Daniel Pipes Blog (June 15, 2006, updated January 31, 2008). Available online. URL: http://www.danielpipes.org/blog/2006/06/john-esposito-and-karen-armstrong-banned-in.html. Accessed June 3, 2009.

Wing-on, James Wong. "M'sia Bans Oxford University Book on Islam." Clare Street: James Wong Wing-on Online (June 20, 2006). Available online. URL: http://jameswongwingon-online.blogspot.com.html. Accessed October 7, 2009.

Yusop, Husna, and Jacqueline Ann Surin. "Abim: Lift Ban on Armstrong Books." *Sun,* June 18, 2007, p. 2.

THE BIBLE

Literary form: Religious text

SUMMARY

The Bible is a collection of books containing the sacred writings of the Jewish and Christian religions. Both religions regard the Bible as inspired by God. The Christian Bible has two parts: the Old Testament, which includes the Hebrew Bible that is sacred to Jews, and the NEW TESTAMENT, which includes specifically Christian writings. The Hebrew Bible is divided into three sections: the Law, or Torah (also known as the Pentateuch), consisting of the first five books—Genesis, Exodus, Leviticus, Numbers, and Deuteronomy—the Prophets, books of history and prophecy; and the Writings, containing prayers, poems, and maxims.

The books of the Bible were written over centuries by many different authors. The authorship of the Old Testament was traditionally attributed to great Jewish leaders, among them Moses, Samuel, David, Solomon, and various prophets. Modern scholars, however, have concluded that many of the books are later compilations of early traditions and writings. Scholars believe that the earliest books of the Bible began as oral literature and were first written down following the reign of King David, after 1000 B.C. The Book of Genesis, for example, contains passages that may date to the 10th century B.C., but the entire book was probably not written down in its present form until the fifth century B.C. The whole Torah, or first five books of the Bible, was in use by about 400 B.C.

The Old Testament—written in Hebrew, with some sections in Aramaic— tells the story of Creation and provides information on pre-Israelite times and the history and religious life of ancient Israel from about 1300 B.C. to the second century B.C. Christians and Jews regard the Old Testament as the record of a covenant or testament made by God with man and revealed to Moses on Mount Sinai.

The canonical books of the Old Testament and their order vary within the Jewish, Catholic, and Protestant religions. The Hebrew Bible revered by Jews consists of 24 books. The Christian Old Testament divides some of the books, increasing their number to 39. The Catholic Bible also includes as authentic seven books of the Old Testament that Protestants consider to be of doubtful authority and refer to as the Apocrypha.

The 27 books of the New Testament, sacred only to Christians, chronicle the years from the birth of Jesus Christ to about A.D. 100 and consist of the earliest documents extant on the life and teaching of Jesus and the establishment of the Christian church. Christians believe that Jesus Christ proclaimed a new covenant, or new testament, that both fulfilled and superseded the covenant revealed to Moses.

The New Testament is divided into four sections: the Gospels, or biographies of Jesus; the Acts of the Apostles; the Letters, or Epistles, of the apostles; and

Revelation, a book of prophecy. Written in Greek between A.D. 70 and 100, the New Testament was compiled in the second century. Although the New Testament is traditionally considered to have been written by the apostles and disciples of Jesus, modern scholars have questioned the apostolic authorship of some of the books.

Both the Old and New Testaments were translated into Latin by Saint Jerome in about A.D. 400 and compiled as the standard and definitive text in the sixth century. The Roman Catholic Church designated his translation, known as the Vulgate, as the authorized Bible. It remained so for 1,000 years, up to the time of the 16th-century Reformation. The first book printed in Europe, the famous Gutenberg Bible of 1456, was an edition of the Vulgate.

CENSORSHIP HISTORY

"Both read the Bible day and night, But thou read'st black where I read white." These words of the poet William Blake aptly describe the origins of censorship of the Bible. Battles over the correct version of the Bible began in the early years of Christianity, when many of the church's first decrees established certain books as acceptable parts of the Bible and disclaimed others. Throughout the later Middle Ages, the Catholic Church discouraged translation of its official Latin Vulgate edition for fear that the text might be corrupted or misinterpreted. In the late 14th century, in defiance of the church's restrictions, the first complete translation of the Vulgate into English appeared, the work of the scholar and reformer John Wycliffe and his followers.

Wycliffe, whose treatise ON CIVIL LORDSHIP was condemned for heresy, maintained that all people had the right to read the Gospel "in that tongue in which they know best Christ's teaching." Reading the Wycliffe Bible was forbidden in England except by ecclesiastical permission. In 1409, the Synod of Canterbury at Saint Paul's in London issued a decree forbidding translation of the Scriptures or the reading of any new translations without a special license, under penalty of excommunication. Although Bible translations were undertaken in other European countries, no others appeared in England until the Protestant Reformation. Despite the ban, the Wycliffe Bible was frequently copied, and some portions of it were later adopted by William Tyndale, the first of the Reformation translators.

The 16th-century Protestant reformers held that because God speaks directly to human beings through the medium of the Bible, it is the right and duty of every Christian to study it. They either sponsored or undertook themselves translations of the Bible into their own languages. By 1522, when Martin Luther's German translation was published, or shortly thereafter, there were already 14 printed German Bibles, and vernacular versions had appeared in France, Italy, Spain, Portugal, Bohemia, the Netherlands, and Scandinavia.

Protestant reformers believed that the Bible should be understood literally and historically by readers without interpretation by church authorities.

This doctrine, *sola scriptura* (Scripture alone), was seen as threatening by the Catholic Church, faced with a widespread loss of its authority as the Protestant revolt spread throughout Europe. Catholic censorship focused on the burgeoning number of Protestant vernacular versions of the Bible, notably Luther's in Germany, Tyndale's in England and Robert Estienne's in France. Protestants also censored biblical material, banning titles by dissenting Protestants as well as by Catholics. But Protestants could censor only within their own political boundaries. Because of the fragmentation of Protestant Europe, Protestant censorship was not as comprehensive as that of the Catholic Church.

The most violently suppressed Bible translation was Tyndale's. He was the first person to translate the Bible into English from its original Hebrew and Greek and the first to print it in English. His translation of the New Testament, printed in Cologne and Worms, Germany, in 1524–26, was smuggled into England, where the church banned and publicly burned it. His translations of the Pentateuch in 1530, the Book of Jonah in 1531, and a revised New Testament in 1534 were also prohibited and burned. Despite the bans, many reprints of Tyndale's translations were smuggled into the country and circulated.

In a plot masterminded by English authorities, Tyndale was arrested by authorities in Antwerp, Belgium, tried for heresy, and strangled and burned at the stake near Brussels in 1536 with copies of his Bible translation. Despite its repression, Tyndale's translation survived to form a considerable portion of later Bibles, including the Authorized or King James Version published in 1611.

Miles Coverdale, Tyndale's colleague, produced a complete English Bible in 1535. Because it could not be licensed to be printed in England, it was published in Germany. The popular demand for the Bible in English and the growing difficulty of suppressing its publication led King Henry VIII to name an authorized version, Matthew's Bible, based on Tyndale's and Coverdale's work. It appeared in 1537 with prefaces and annotations by John Rogers, who used the pseudonym John Matthew. Rogers was a Catholic priest who converted to Protestantism and a friend of Tyndale's. Matthew's Bible was the first in English to be licensed by the government. But on the accession of the loyal Catholic queen Mary I, Rogers was among the first of 300 martyrs to be imprisoned and burned as heretics in 1554.

Bans on new Bible versions were not confined to England. In 1539, Henry VIII issued his own Great Bible, a revision by Coverdale of his earlier work, which was to be the official version in the newly reformed Church of England. When he decided to print it in Paris, authorities moved to stop it. François Regnault, the famous Parisian printer of English books, was seized by the Inquisition and imprisoned. Sheets of the Great Bible were smuggled out of France in hats and taken to every church in England with the king's directive that each man should interpret Scripture for himself.

In 1546, the doctors of theology at the Sorbonne secured the condemnation in the Louvain Index of Forbidden Books of a Bible edition printed by the renowned humanist Robert Estienne, the official printer of King Francis I. The king responded by prohibiting the printing or circulation in France of the Louvain Index and ordering the withdrawal of strictures on the Estienne Bible. With the death of the king in 1547, however, the prohibition was renewed and Estienne had to move his press to Geneva. But Protestant Geneva, under the authority of the Protestant reformer John Calvin, was not a bastion of religious toleration. The Calvinists also condemned the Estienne Bible.

Spain under the Inquisition moved to suppress Bible editions influenced by Protestantism. In 1551, the Index of Valladolid listed 103 editions condemned because of errors and heresies to suppression, correction, or cancellation.

The restoration of papal authority, ecclesiastical courts, and the laws against heresy in England under the Catholic regime of Mary I reconfirmed the ban on Protestant Bibles. In 1555, a royal proclamation commanded "that no manner of persons presume to bring into this realm any manuscripts, books, papers . . . in the name of Martin Luther, John Calvin, Miles Cover-dale, Erasmus, Tyndale . . . or any like books containing false doctrines against the Catholic faith." Protestants from England who took refuge in Frankfurt and Geneva published the Calvinist "Breeches Bible" in 1560. Although its use was forbidden in churches in England, it went into 140 editions between 1560 and 1644.

In 1546, the Catholic Church's Council of Trent declared the Latin Vulgate of Saint Jerome to be the sole canonical text of the Bible. In opposition to the Protestant reformers, the council decreed that dogma is transmitted through the church's teaching, whose authority is equal to that of the Bible, and forbade the reading of any unapproved translation. The first English version approved for Catholics was a translation of the New Testament from the Vulgate by church scholars published in Rheims in 1582 and printed in 1610 with an approved Old Testament as the Rheims-Douay version.

In 1631, the word *not* was inadvertently omitted from the seventh commandment (Thou shalt not commit adultery) in an edition of 1,000 copies of the Bible printed in England by R. Barker. The printers were heavily fined, and the edition, known as the "wicked Bible," was so vigorously suppressed that few copies have survived.

Because the copyright of the Authorized (King James) Version was held by the British Crown, the right to print in England in the 17th century was held by the royal printers. Only the universities of Oxford and Cambridge were exempt from the restriction. This meant that no authorized Bible could be printed in the American colonies until after their independence. The first Bible printed in America was not the King James Version, but the *Up-Biblum God*, John Eliot's Bible translation for the Algonquian Indians, published in 1661–63. The Bible in English was probably not published in the United States until 1782 in Philadelphia, though historians have found evidence that a Bible may have been secretly printed in Boston about 1752.

The prudish sensibilities of the 19th century in England and the United States led to a new kind of censorship of the Bible—the publication of expurgated editions. *The Holy Bible, Newly Translated*, by John Bellamy, a Swedenborgian, was published in 1818. Declaring that no major biblical figure could have committed actions he found unacceptable, Bellamy decided that the translation from Hebrew must be at fault, and he revised passages he considered indecent. *The New Family Bible and Improved Version*, by Dr. Benjamin Boothroyd, a Congregationalist who wanted to circumvent "many offensive and indelicate expressions" in the Bible, was published in several editions beginning in 1824. That year, in *The Holy Bible Arranged and Adapted for Family Reading*, John Watson, a Church of England layman, replaced offensive sections with his own writing and dropped the numbering of traditional chapters and verses so that it was difficult for readers to notice what had been cut. In 1828, William Alexander, a Quaker printer, published *The Holy Bible, Principally Designed to Facilitate the Audible or Social Reading of the Sacred Scriptures*. He changed words and passages "not congenial to the views and genius of the present age of refinement."

The first expurgated Bible in America was published in 1833 by the lexicographer Noah Webster, who made thousands of alterations in material he considered indecent. Although his Bible was adopted by the state of Connecticut in 1835, endorsed by Yale, and widely used in Congregational pulpits for about 20 years, Webster's desire to make changes even in "decent" parts of the Bible met with criticism. The third edition, published in 1841, was the last.

Twentieth-century government censorship of the Bible has been most widespread in socialist countries. In 1926, the Soviet government instructed libraries throughout the USSR to remove all religious books such as the Bible. It was allowed to remain only in the country's largest libraries. Its importation was forbidden, and it was not printed again in the Soviet Union until 1956. In China, during the Cultural Revolution of the 1960s and 1970s—a campaign to destroy "the four olds" of culture, thinking, habits, and customs—Bibles were burned, and all places of Christian worship were closed.

A 1986 government-authorized printing of a Bible used by the Baptist Church in Romania marked the first time since 1951 that the Bible had been published there. The socialist military government of Ethiopia in 1986 banned several books of the Bible as "contrary to the ongoing revolution." A shipment of more than 45,000 Bibles destined for a church in Ethiopia was held indefinitely in customs.

Many attempts to censor the Bible have been recorded in the United States. Parents or religious groups who denounced the teaching of the Bible as comparative literature or believed it should be taught only as the sacred word of God from their own perspective and interpretation have tried to remove it from school libraries or curricula. Challenges to the Bible have also often been based in misunderstanding of Supreme Court decisions prohibiting prayer in the public schools. In 1963, in *District of Abington Township v. Schempp*, the U.S. Supreme Court prohibited devotional exercises in public schools. The Court, however, did not forbid the study of the Bible as literature, or of religion in historical or social studies. In its decision the Court declared, "In addition, it might well be said that one's education is not complete without a study of comparative religion or the history of religion and its relationship to the advancement of civilization. Nothing we have said here indicates that such study of the Bible or of religion, when presented objectively as part of a secular program of education, may not be effected consistently. . . ."

In an early challenge to the Supreme Court decision, a conservative religious organization sued the University of Washington for having offered an elective course on the Bible as literature. It argued that such a course could not be offered in a public institution and that the approach taken conflicted with its religious views. The Washington state courts upheld the inclusion of the course in a broad curriculum.

A 1982 study of 17 surveys conducted of school libraries during the previous two decades found that the presence or use of the Bible in schools had been challenged by students, parents, or teachers who thought it was illegal or who objected to the interpretation used. Similar challenges were reported during the 1980s and 1990s. For example, in 1989 an elementary school in Omaha, Nebraska, banned the reading or possession of the Bible on school premises. In a settlement of a suit in federal district court that never came to trial, it was agreed that students could read the religious literature of their choice at school during their free time. In 1991, a library patron who believed that public funds could not be spent on religious books challenged the presence of the *Evangelical Commentary on the Bible* and the *Official Catholic Directory* in the Multnomah, Oregon, public library. The books were retained by the library. In May 1981, Christian fundamentalists burned copies of *The Living Bible* in Gastonia, North Carolina.

A spate of attempts during the 1990s to restrict access to the Bible, reminiscent of Victorian-era attempts to bowdlerize it, were motivated by the view that it contains indecent material. In 1992 in the Brooklyn Center, Minnesota, independent school district, an atheist "seeking to turn the tables on the religious right" challenged use of the Bible, declaring that "the lewd, indecent, and violent contents of that book are hardly suitable for young children." In 1993, the Bible was challenged as "obscene and pornographic," but was retained at the Noel Wien Library in Fairbanks, Alaska. Near Harrisburg, Pennsylvania, protesters attempting to remove it from the West Shore schools cited "more than 300 examples of obscenities in the book" and objected that it "contains language and stories that are inappropriate for children of any age, including tales of incest and murder."

Though the Bible is among the most censored books in history, it has been translated more times and into more languages than any other and has outsold every book in the history of publishing. In the English language alone, some 450 different editions are in print. The long history of Bible censorship has had little impact on its availability and influence today.

FURTHER READING

Burress, Lee. *Battle of The Books: Library Censorship in the Public Schools, 1950–1985.* Metuchen, N.J.: Scarecrow Press, 1989.

Daniell, David. *Let There Be Light: William Tyndale and the Making of the English Bible.* London: British Library, 1994.

———. *William Tyndale: A Biography.* New Haven, Conn.: Yale University Press, 1994.

Doyle, Robert P. *Banned Books: 2004 Resource Guide.* Chicago: American Library Association, 2004.

Haight, Anne Lyon. *Banned Books: 387 B.C. to 1978 A.D.* Updated and enlarged by Chandler B. Grannis. New York: R. R. Bowker, 1978.

Hentoff, Nat. *Free Speech for Me, but Not for Thee.* New York: HarperCollins, 1992.

Jenkinson, Edward B. "The Bible: A Source of Great Literature and Controversy." In *Censored Books: Critical Viewpoints*, edited by Nicholas J. Karolides, Lee Burress, and John M. Kean, 98–102. Metuchen, N.J.: Scarecrow Press, 1993.

Lofmark, Carl. *What Is the Bible?* Buffalo, N.Y.: Prometheus Books, 1992.

Manguel, Alberto. *A History of Reading.* New York: Viking Press, 1996.

New York Public Library. *Censorship: 500 Years of Conflict.* New York: Oxford University Press, 1984.

O'Neil, Robert M. "The Bible and the Constitution." In *Censored Books: Critical Viewpoints*, edited by Nicholas J. Karolides, Lee Burress, and John M. Kean, 103–108. Metuchen, N.J.: Scarecrow Press, 1993.

Perrin, Noel. *Dr. Bowdler's Legacy: A History of Expurgated Books in England and America.* Garden City, N.Y.: Anchor Books, 1971.

Putnam, George Haven. *The Censorship of the Church of Rome.* Vol. 1. New York: G. P. Putnam's Sons, 1906–07.

Tinguet, Margaret. "Ethiopia: Destroy the Muslims." *Index on Censorship* 16, no. 4 (April 1987): 33–35.

THE BLIND OWL

Author: Sadegh Hedayat
Original date and place of publication: 1937, India; 1957, United Kingdom
Original publisher: Self-published; John Calder
Literary form: Novel

SUMMARY

Sadegh Hedayat, Iran's foremost 20th-century fiction writer, was as well read in modern Western literature as he was in Persian history and folklore.

Poe, Kafka, Rilke, and Omar Khayyam stood together easily in Hedayat's creative imagination. These strong influences fused in Hedayat's masterpiece, *The Blind Owl* (*Buf-e Kur*), considered to be one of the most important works of modern Iranian literature.

Constructed more as a long prose poem than a conventional novella and written in the first person, *The Blind Owl* concerns the interior life of a man struggling with madness. Alone in his room, the narrator considers his isolation from the rest of humanity, as his shadow clings to a wall in the lamplight. He is determined to make himself known to his shadow by recording his experiences. His tale is fully informed by a central image: an old man in a cloak, a scarf, and a turban, squatting under a cypress tree, holding a finger to his lips. Standing before him is a young girl in a long black dress, offering him a morning glory flower across a small stream separating them. The narrator, a decorator of pen cases by trade, repeats this scene continuously.

These two figures are the templates for the characters, as in intensely surreal episodes, phrases repeat like refrains, and characters, images, actions, and scenes recur, mirroring one another in shifting variations. The women are united by references to eyes and hands; the men are denoted by scarves, turbans, knives, and "a hollow, grating laugh, of a quality to make the hairs on one's body stand on end."

In one episode, the narrator confronts the figures from his pen-case decoration when they appear in his front yard, then mysteriously depart. Nights later, the girl reappears at his house, where she promptly dies. The narrator dismembers her body and puts the parts in a suitcase. The turbaned man, who appears as a hearse-driving grave digger, assists him in burying the body.

In another section, we learn of the breach in the marriage of the narrator's parents. The father's identical twin brother has sexual relations with the narrator's mother, who realizes she has been lured into infidelity and rebukes both brothers. She demands that the men undergo a "trial by cobra," in which they are locked in a closed cell with a cobra; the one who survives the ordeal is the one to whom she will belong. One man emerges alive, but he has become white-haired and crazed and shakes with "hollow, grating" laughter. Because the men are twins, "like two halves of the one apple," no one is sure which brother survived. Accompanied by the diminished man, the narrator's mother abandons the narrator to his aunt. The narrator eventually marries his cousin, who cuckolds him repeatedly while refusing to have sexual relations with him. Driven by his derangement, he rapes and stabs her. As she lies dead, he glances at the mirror and finds himself transformed into the turbaned man.

As Massoume Price contends in an essay on the symbolism of women in *The Blind Owl*, much of the narrator's distress can be understood as an expression of sexual fear instilled by an association of women with death, an ironic reminder that the narrator is not all that different from the men of his society from whom he feels so estranged, as his individual pathology is reinforced by a masculine Iranian culture's disdain for the feminine. For the narrator, the sexual act is a fall from grace. In raping and stabbing his unfaithful wife, he feels contaminated by the contact; he has forgotten his higher self and copulated like a beast, while she remains as she always was—a bringer of death. In dismembering the ethereal woman from his pen-case illustration, he is subconsciously aware that she embodies his mother, who was not and never had been a pure spiritual force but was, rather, an ordinary woman, fallen as a result of the very act of sex that generated him.

Price maintains that in order to reestablish and affirm his identity, the narrator would need to conjure some ideal woman, untouchable in mind, neither sexual nor mortal, who could synthesize the feminine aspects of his own nature. The mother, the wife, and the ethereal woman are all, finally, one woman, slain by the narrator in a manic denial of objective, external reality. All the manifestations of the woman and of the turbaned man are merely reflections of himself, and the depth and intensity of his disorder are revealed in withdrawal from contact with the world at large and in regression, fueling a resentment toward the mother who had abandoned him.

A comprehensive narcissism, expressed in loss of affect and a sense of superiority, predicates his displacement from ordinary reality. The narrator disdains the common man, whom he calls the "rabble-men," and who "for thousands of years . . . have been saying the same words, performing the same sexual act, vexing themselves with the same childish problems." He feels no connection to them: "As for mosques, the muezzin's call to prayer, the ceremonial washing of the body and the rinsing of the mouth, not to mention the pious practice of bobbing up and down in honor of a high and mighty Being . . . these things left me completely cold." In his antipathy to the "nonsense and lies" of religion that condition the conduct of the "rabble-men," the narrator feels as if he "had become a miniature god," alone in his own mind and above such concerns. But as weary of life as he is afraid of death, the narrator rejects suicide and the idea of an afterlife, which, after all, would mean that he would have to deal with yet another world of other souls. The narrator hopes fervently for oblivion, absolute nothingness, after death.

The narrator, at last, returns to his own shadow, whose presence compelled him to write his account. His shadow is now in the shape of an owl, "leaning forward, read[ing] intently every word I wrote. When I looked out the corner of my eye . . . I felt afraid."

CENSORSHIP HISTORY

The Blind Owl was written in the early 1930s, during the latter years of Reza Shah's ruthless regime. Hedayat attempted to publish it in Tehran in 1936 but was forbidden to do so unless he removed passages that Iranian clerics found atheistic. (Though the clerics had no actual political power, they were a strong and influential moral voice.) Hedayat refused and went to Bombay, where he published the book in 1937 in a limited edition stamped, "Not for sale or publication in Iran."

In 1941, after the Anglo-Soviet invasion of Iran forced Reza Shah's abdication, his son, Mohammad Reza Pahlavi, became the new shah and suspended all censorship restrictions. *The Blind Owl* came home to Iran, where it ran serially in the daily paper *Iran*. The work remained an important and powerful best seller in subsequent editions.

In 1979, however, the book was again banned when the radical Islamic Republic deposed the shah. Religious authorities found Hedayat's bleak, godless existential vision to be antireligious and regarded the narrator's likening himself to a miniature god to be blasphemous.

In 1993, *The Blind Owl* was allowed publication in Iran only in a heavily censored version. Iranian authorities removed all passages viewed as antireligious, as well as many sexual passages. This version remained available through the brief cultural revival experienced under the presidency of reformist Mohammad Khatami from 1997 to 2005.

Since 2005, with the ascension to power of Mahmoud Ahmadinejad's hard-line government, *The Blind Owl* has once again been banned in Iran, along with most of Hedayat's other major writings, in the sweeping purge conducted by the Ministry of Culture. Yet Hedayat's great modern classic of despair and self-alienation endures. While major publishing outlets are routinely inspected for violations of bans, it has been suggested that in small, out-of-the-way secondhand bookstores, original editions of *The Blind Owl* may still be located and purchased.

—Philip Milito

FURTHER READING

Dehghan, Saeed Kamali. "The Gag Is Tightened." *Guardian* (January 6, 2008). Available online. URL: http://www.guardian.co.uk/books/2008/Jan/06/fiction. iran/print. Accessed July 8, 2009.

———. "Iranian Writers in a Literary Depression." PowellsBooks.Blog. Posted October 3, 2007. Available online. URL: http://www.powells.com/blog/?p=2492. Accessed June 16, 2009.

Hedayat, Sadegh. *The Blind Owl*. Translated by D. P. Costello. New York: Grove Weidenfeld, 1989.

Jones, Derek, ed. *Censorship: A World Encyclopedia*. Chicago and London: Fitzroy, Dearborn, 2001. Available online. URL: http://www.thefileroom.org/documents/dyn/DisplayCase.cfm/id/1212. Accessed June 16, 2009.

Price, Massoume. "Symbolism of Women in Hedayat's 'Blind Owl.'" *Persian Language and Literature*. Iran Chamber Society, 2001. Available online. URL: http://www.iranchamber.com/literature/articles/women_hedayat_blind_owl.php. Accessed July 9, 2009.

Sarkouhi, Faraj. "Iran: Book Censorship the Rule, Not the Exception." Radio Free Europe/Radio Liberty (November 26, 2007). Available online. URL: http://www.rferl.org/articleprintview/1079193. Accessed July 8, 2009.

Tait, Robert. "Bestsellers Banned in New Iranian Censorship Purge." *Guardian* (November 17, 2006). Available online. URL: http://www.guardian.co.uk/world/2006/nov/17/books.iran.print. Accessed July 8, 2009.

THE BLOUDY TENENT OF PERSECUTION

Author: Roger Williams
Original date and place of publication: 1644, England
Literary form: Religious text

SUMMARY

Roger Williams, a founder of the Rhode Island colony, brought a radical liberty of conscience to the shores of New England. In *The Bloudy Tenent of Persecution for Cause of Conscience*, he espoused the ideas of religious toleration and intellectual freedom under both secular and ecclesiastical governments. The trajectory of Williams's life represented the dissenting currents in British Protestant thought. Born into a family that belonged to the Church of England, he became a Puritan while at Cambridge in the 1620s and was a Separatist Puritan by the time he joined the Massachusetts Bay Colony in 1631.

In 1635, his disenchantment with the Separatists in Massachusetts led to his banishment, and he and a group of followers moved to Rhode Island, at that time a wilderness between the British colonies of Massachusetts and Connecticut. Williams was dissatisfied with the way churches began as fundamentalist, back-to-basics movements and gradually developed their own orthodoxies. His desire for a pure church led him to question the idea of an official church decreed by a political entity, such as a local or colonial government.

In the summer of 1643, Williams returned to England to persuade Parliament to grant him a charter for Rhode Island, which would establish it as an official colony, free to govern its own affairs. England in this period was racked with religious controversy, particularly over the boundaries between church and state authority and individual liberty. By the spring of 1644, Williams had made a name for himself arguing for a balance of church, state, and individual interests that would favor individual conscience. Observing the proliferation of new Protestant sects, he believed that no church or state power could control this impulse toward fragmentation. Liberty of conscience, which Williams defined as the freedom to worship as one saw fit, should not be restricted.

Williams published his ideas in *The Bloudy Tenent of Persecution*, officially a rebuttal to John Cotton, the most powerful Puritan minister in Massachusetts and a skillful politician who wanted to curry favor with Parliament. Cotton had endorsed new legislation that increased the church's power in civil affairs. Williams's book argued against the right of Parliament to demand and enforce conformity in interpretation and practice of scriptural principles. He claimed that the Massachusetts Puritans were trying to build a modern state based on the Ten Commandments. He criticized the idea that the abstract and absolute principles of Moses could be used to govern society thousands of years later.

Williams had his own religious and philosophical reasons for opposing Cotton's ideas. Williams believed that the British government's enforcement of the First Commandment, that there is one God to be obeyed, was offensive to Christian tradition, because the New Testament superseded Mosaic law. Williams also objected because, as he put it, prayer offered insincerely "stinks in God's nostrils."

The Bloudy Tenent of Persecution continued in this vein, offering copious evidence from religious and secular history that the state and the church had separate realms. Williams denounced the philosophy and practice of religious repression. The earth has been "made drunk with the bloud of its inhabitants," he wrote, slaughtering each other with indiscriminate zeal as each sect seeks to aggrandize itself at the expense of others. "Those churches cannot be truly Christian . . . which either actually themselves, or by the civil power of kings and princes . . . doe persecute such as dissent from them or be opposite against them." Unless reason and charity prevail, the result will be the ruin of the church and the devastation of civil society.

Williams was all too familiar with the power of an official church. In *The Bloudy Tenent* he stated that his exile to Rhode Island was a result of his campaigning for liberty of conscience and that the Puritans sent him to a remote outpost to silence him. The example of his own life, he hoped, would persuade readers of the harm of religious doctrine enforced through civil punishment.

Williams wrote *The Bloudy Tenent* in the form of a dialogue between Peace and Truth, as a parable about his fight with the established churches of his day. He was particularly troubled by the role of nonbelievers in English and colonial society. He wondered what was to be gained in forcing someone who was not a sincere Protestant to mouth the words of Protestant doctrine. Williams believed that the salvation of nonbelieving individuals would come from their own conversion experiences, rather than through the commands of a religious orthodoxy.

To Williams, religion was primarily an inner belief, as opposed to the outward expression of religion practiced by most Puritans in Massachusetts and Presbyterians in the English Parliament. Official religion, state celebration of religious holidays, and courts empowered to enforce religious doctrine offended his religious sensibilities. Mixing the private religious sphere and the public governmental sphere resulted in a cheapening of religion: Religious doctrine came straight from divine sources, while political leaders were merely appointed or elected by other humans. This latter idea offended King Charles I, who still clung to the idea that his power could be traced to divine origins.

Williams's ideas in *The Bloudy Tenent*, as they attacked the relationship between church and state—which most Britons took for granted—became infamous. But his inflammatory language won few converts to his ideas. However, his book did not hinder his achieving another goal. One month after its publication, he returned to the wilderness of Rhode Island with the charter in hand that established Rhode Island as a British colony.

CENSORSHIP HISTORY

Upon its publication in July 1644, *The Bloudy Tenent of Persecution* failed to persuade Parliament and the British reading public of the importance of separating religious doctrine from civil policy. Given the imperative that Parliament placed on religious conformity, it is hardly surprising that Parliament ordered all copies of Williams's 400-page book to be burned publicly in August 1644.

Williams's style of organization was partly to blame as well. He had composed his book in fits and starts over nearly 25 years. This gradual formation of a religious philosophy showed up in the muddled prose of the original work. It is unlikely that most members of Parliament, or anyone else, read far enough into the book to be persuaded by Williams's defense of his ideas through painstaking analysis of scriptural passages.

Hostility toward this book may also have been generated by its subtitle: "for cause of Conscience." Liberty of conscience was a radical concept in England at this time. When members of such dissenting sects as the Quakers were jailed for their beliefs and Catholics and Jews faced more violent suppression, a plea for complete religious tolerance was unlikely to be persuasive.

By the time Williams's book was burned, he was on a ship bound for New England. He never faced jail or other personal punishment for writing *The Bloudy Tenent of Persecution*. He did, however, have to answer attacks on his ideas. In 1647, his old nemesis John Cotton wrote *The Bloudy Tenent, Washed, and Made White in the Bloud of the Lamb*, in which he denied that Williams had been expelled from Massachusetts for religious reasons. He contended, rather, that Williams had spoken against the Boston government, preaching sedition, and had to be punished. Explicit in Cotton's argument was the idea that there was no separation between religious and civil authorities, that a dispute with the religious practice of civil leaders was tantamount to a civil dispute, and that this constituted advocating rebellion. Cotton attacked Williams as self-serving and dismissed Williams's claims that he was persecuted for his religious beliefs.

Five years after Cotton's rebuttal, Williams published *The Bloudy Tenent yet More Bloudy: by Mr. Cotton's endeavour to wash it white in the Bloud of the Lambe*. Williams stood by his original principles, especially the scriptural justification for religious tolerance. In his opinion, forcing people to worship in churches against their will resulted in the sin of hypocrisy. Thus, the Massachusetts authorities were requiring their citizens to sin. Forcing non-members to attend a church was to Williams a greater sin than was lack of belief in Christianity.

While Parliament's burning of *The Bloudy Tenent of Persecution* did not stop Roger Williams from publishing his ideas or from prospering in his colony of Rhode Island, this censorship signaled the beginning of an era of religious intolerance in both England and New England. Respect for William's belief in freedom of conscience grew, however, over the following 150 years. His philosophy of religious tolerance inspired the rights to "life, liberty, and the pursuit of happiness" in the Declaration of Independence, as well as the Constitution's First Amendment guarantees of freedom of religion and speech. In 1936, 300 years after Williams's exile to Rhode Island, the state of Massachusetts pardoned him for his offense.

—Jonathan Pollack

FURTHER READING

Covey, Cyclone. *The Gentle Radical: A Biography of Roger Williams*. New York: Macmillan, 1966.

Gaustad, Edwin S. *Liberty of Conscience: Roger Williams in America*. Grand Rapids, Mich.: Wm. B. Eerdmans, 1991.

Green, Jonathon. *Encyclopedia of Censorship*. New York: Facts On File, 1990.

Haight, Anne Lyon. *Banned Books: 387 B.C. to 1978 A.D.* Updated and enlarged by Chandler B. Grannis. New York: R. R. Bowker, 1978.

Jordan, W. K. *The Development of Religious Toleration in England*. Vol. 3. Gloucester, Mass.: Peter Smith, 1965.

Morgan, Edmund S. *Roger Williams: The Church and the State*. New York: Harcourt, Brace & World, 1967.

Polishook, Irwin H. *Roger Williams, John Cotton, and Religious Freedom: A Controversy in New and Old England*. Englewood Cliffs, N.J.: Prentice Hall, 1967.

Zagorin, Perez. *How the Idea of Religious Toleration Came to the West*. Princeton, N.J.: Princeton University Press, 2003.

THE BOOK OF COMMON PRAYER

Authors: Thomas Cranmer and others
Original date and place of publication: 1549, England
Literary form: Religious text

SUMMARY

The Book of Common Prayer contains the prescribed forms of public worship for the Church of England and the churches of the Anglican Communion around the world. Known for the beauty of its language and its comprehensiveness as a source of religious thought, it was produced mainly by Thomas Cranmer, archbishop of Canterbury, who served King Henry VIII and his successor, Edward VI. Cranmer shaped the doctrine and liturgical transformation of the Church of England during Edward's reign.

In 1548, Cranmer presided over an assembly of scholars that convened to discuss the draft of the book he had prepared, which was based mainly on translations from the Sarum or Salisbury Missal rendered in Cranmer's sonorous prose. The book approved by the assembly reflected liturgical reforms based on Lutheran influences, such as the abolition of the elevation of the host during the Mass and elimination of the Mass's sacrificial nature. Cranmer's intention was to purge the service of innovations that had crept into it over the centuries and to return to the old practices of the primitive church. It also provided that the whole of the Mass was to be said in English, rather than in Latin, so that it could be better understood. This change was among those that aroused conservative religious revolts against the prayer book when it was put into use throughout England.

The Prayer Book, brought into compulsory use in the Church of England in 1549 by act of Parliament, was the first complete service book in English to be published under one cover. It was revised by Cranmer in 1552, with the aid of Protestant reformers from the Continent, as the Second Prayer Book. This substantial revision altered baptism, confirmation, and funeral services and swept away all traces of the old Mass.

It has been periodically revised over the centuries both in England and in the United States, where it is the prayer book of the Episcopal Church. Controversial modern revisions have changed the language of Cranmer to make the book more relevant to contemporary concerns. It includes prayers, liturgies, and scriptural readings for the sacraments, for all occasions, seasons, and holy days. It also contains a catechism, historical documents of the church, including the Articles of Religion, and tables for finding the date of holy days.

CENSORSHIP HISTORY

Upon her accession to the throne in 1553, the Catholic queen Mary I legally restored the Roman Catholic Church in England and banned use of the Prayer Book. Cranmer was convicted of treason, then tried for heresy in 1555. He was excommunicated, degraded from his office as archbishop, and sentenced to death. Cranmer signed six documents admitting the supremacy of the pope and the truth of all Roman Catholic doctrine except transubstantiation, but when asked to repeat his recantation in public at the stake, he refused. Along with two other leading Protestant reformers, Hugh Latimer and Nicholas Ridley, he was burned at the stake in Oxford on March 21, 1556.

In 1559, under Queen Elizabeth I, the Prayer Book of 1552 was restored in altered form. From 1645 to 1660, under the Puritan Commonwealth

Protectorate and the rule of Oliver Cromwell, it was suppressed again. Despite government prohibition of its use, Anglican services were held freely, and no systematic effort was made to enforce the ordinances against it.

In 1662, a new post-Restoration revision of the book was declared by King Charles II to be the only legal service book for use in England. It remains in use today in revised form. The Book of Common Prayer, adapted to fit the needs of the American community, was adopted in 1789 by the first general convention of the Protestant Episcopal Church of the United States and is today the standard of faith and worship among Episcopalians.

Because it promulgated non-Catholic religious devotions, the Book of Common Prayer was placed on the Catholic Church's Index of Forbidden Books, where it remained through the first 20th-century edition prepared under Pope Leo XIII in 1897.

In 1975, the Prayer Book Society was formed in Britain to uphold the use of the 1662 edition and protest modern changes to Cranmer's language.

FURTHER READING

The Book of Common Prayer. New York: Seabury Press, 1977.
Jordan, W. K. *The Development of Religious Toleration in England.* Vol. 3. Gloucester, Mass.: Peter Smith, 1965.
Ridley, Jasper. *Thomas Cranmer.* Oxford, U.K.: Clarendon Press, 1962.
Welsby, Paul A. *A History of the Church of England 1945–1980.* Oxford: Oxford University Press, 1984.

THE CARTOONS THAT SHOOK THE WORLD

Author: Jytte Klausen
Original date and place of publication: 2009, United States
Original publisher: Yale University Press
Literary form: Scholarly political science analysis

SUMMARY

On September 30, 2005, the Danish newspaper *Jyllands-Posten* published 12 cartoons depicting the prophet Muhammad. The cartoons, drawn by different artists, were accompanied by statements explaining that they were being published as a blow against intimidation and self-censorship because various artists "were afraid—or should be afraid—to treat Muslims as they would members of any other religious group." The publication of the cartoons touched off violent protests during which 200 or more people died and sparked an international debate on free speech, blasphemy laws, and modern Islam.

The Cartoons That Shook the World examines the events following the publication of the cartoons in *Jyllands-Posten*. The book's author, Jytte Klausen, is a native of Denmark who lives in the United States and teaches comparative politics at Brandeis University. She deconstructs the arguments and motives that drove the escalation of the conflict and concludes that the reaction was primarily "an orchestrated," though uncoordinated, "political action" by those who wished to influence elections in Denmark and Egypt. Later, the issue was taken up by Islamic extremists whose aim was to destabilize governments in Pakistan, Lebanon, Libya, and Nigeria, rather than a spontaneous emotional outburst and "a colossal cultural misunderstanding," which is how it was widely perceived.

Klausen describes the 12 drawings at the center of the conflict, as well as the cartoonists' bewildered and angry responses to the developing crisis. Some of the cartoons were, in fact, caricatures, or wordless line drawings that satirize, mock, or ridicule; others could be properly described as political cartoons, which tell a story or comment on current events. One cartoon in particular, by Kurt Westergaard, which depicted Muhammad with a bomb in his turban, inspired the most rage—although Westergaard, says Klausen, intended only "to show that radical Muslims use the Prophet's name to justify violence."

Klausen explains that the early reaction to the cartoons was nonviolent, though Muslims and others saw them as derogatory and evidence of an Islamophobic environment in Denmark. It was to call attention to an ongoing "smear campaign" against Muslims that, following the cartoons' publication, a group of Muslim ambassadors in Copenhagen wrote to the Danish prime minister Anders Fogh Rasmussen and requested a meeting. Among their concerns were demeaning statements made by the Danish culture minister Brian Mikkelsen and representatives of the far-right Danish Peoples' Party (DPP), an ally of the governing party. When Fogh Rasmussen responded, as he did similarly to two other letters from the Organization of the Islamic Conference (OIC) and the Arab League (who would become key players in the controversy), he defended Denmark's tradition of free speech, said that the government had no influence over the press, and ignored the request for a meeting. He maintained this stance in the ensuing weeks and months as the crisis simmered. This response (or lack of it), Klausen asserts, all but guaranteed the subsequent controversy, of which, she says, Fogh Rasmussen and his government should have been well aware.

Klausen examines Fogh Rasmussen's possible motives, which include his political ambitions and his ties to the DPP, a party that wielded considerable political clout. Moreover, says Klausen, the issue was not just free speech; it was the perception that *Jyllands-Posten* had exploited the issue of free speech specifically to deride Muslims. Many decried what they saw as a double standard that favored Christians and Jews—the most common complaint that Muslims expressed during the crisis. (Denmark, like other countries in Europe, has laws against blasphemy and racial hate speech.)

Klausen traces the events as they unfolded, beginning with diplomatic efforts in fall 2005 to quell a growing crisis that included death threats against the cartoonists and the *Jyllands-Posten* editors. Egypt, in particular, became a major player in the events that followed. Toward the end of October, the Egyptian foreign ministry voiced its expectation that the Danish government should condemn "the mockery of the Prophet" and complained to the United Nations, the Organization for Security and Co-operation in Europe, and the European Union that the Danes had violated nondiscrimination resolutions. Klausen discusses the possible reasons for Egypt's involvement, including the government's wish to compare favorably with the opposition party, the Muslim Brotherhood; an attempt to discourage Western pressure to democratize; and an effort to help establish Islamophobia as a human rights offense. At around the same time, the Arab League and the OIC accused Denmark of violating UN resolutions on human rights.

In December 2005, a group of Danish imams assembled a dossier containing, among other documents, copies of the cartoons and more incendiary drawings (which were incorrectly attributed to *Jyllands-Posten*, though they had never appeared in the paper). Copies of these materials, which were distributed at an OIC summit meeting, became "the primary source of information for Middle Eastern religious authorities, and it shaped their view about the treatment of Muslims in Denmark," despite the fact that, as Klausen notes, the "impression conveyed by the dossier was . . . misleading and on some points plainly false." Following the OIC summit and the release of a communiqué condemning the cartoons, the world's Muslims—who by and large knew little about the controversy until that time—were put on alert. The OIC meeting "encouraged the religious establishments to become involved and various governments and parliaments in Islamic countries to publicly condemn the cartoons."

In January 2006, expressing disappointment at the Danish government's continuing refusal to apologize, the Muslim Brotherhood clerics who belonged to the International Union of Muslim Scholars condemned the cartoons, encouraged Arab and Muslim governments to apply political and diplomatic pressure on Denmark, and recommended a trade boycott. In February 2006, Islamic scholar and preacher Yusuf al-Qaradawi, who had ties to the Muslim Brotherhood, urged Muslims to stage a "day of rage" against the cartoons, though not all Muslims—including his supposed allies—agreed with him. At that time, "clerics and political leaders from the radical opposition in Muslim countries . . . joined the campaign," and violence erupted around the world.

The protests, says Klausen, ultimately "had less to do with outrage at the cartoons than with a broader strategy of collective mobilization and agitation," as radical groups across the Muslim world co-opted the cartoons "to mobilize popular anger against local governments for purposes that had nothing to do with the feelings of observant Muslims or the human rights of Danish Muslims." She notes that only a small fraction of Western Europe's small population of Muslims support Islamist extremism, and she highlights the mixed reactions of Muslims to the cartoons, observing that "the protests against the cartoons revealed deep fissures in the Muslim countries between secularists, electoral Islamists, and extremists," with "political arguments . . . as common as religious opinions."

The violent protests that erupted in February and March 2006 were brought on, Klausen writes, by a combination of motives that, while appearing to be part of a "coordinated global protest," were actually part of a fragmented movement with varying goals and players. "The governments of Muslim countries aimed to make symbolic statements and influence international debates about human rights, democracy, and Muslims. . . . The radical extremists aimed to destabilize Islamic governments and turned the cartoons against them. The Danish mosque activists wanted to change things in Denmark and shake up Danish Muslims, and . . . European Muslim associations and the Muslim Brotherhood pursued legal avenues of redress in order to obtain recognition and promote the rights of Muslims in the context of national politics."

Klausen emphasizes that it was not until other European newspapers began to reprint the cartoons, months after their initial publication, that the crisis became full blown. While a number of European newspapers reprinted them as a way to demonstrate their solidarity in refusing to cave in to "political correctness," many Muslims saw the reprinted cartoons "as a coordinated campaign of denigration." (In fact, during two weeks in February, the cartoons were also reprinted in Russian, African, Latin American, Asian, and Australian papers. By the end of February, one or more of the cartoons had been reprinted in at least 143 newspapers in 56 countries. Among the news outlets that reproduced the cartoons were 12 or more papers, magazines, or news stations in Arab and Muslim countries.)

"A domestic chain-reaction of protests and counterprotests" followed each reprint, Klausen explains. Except in the British and American media, which by and large did not reprint the cartoons, this chain reaction occurred worldwide. Finally, says Klausen, "The cartoons were made into a chapter in the undeclared war between the West and Islam only as a result of the political processes that took place before the eruption of violent demonstrations." In the end, the "cartoons and the protests against them confirmed existing prejudices on both sides."

CENSORSHIP HISTORY

In August 2009, Jytte Klausen noted, in an address to members of a Washington think tank, "It is obviously a strange situation for an author to end up becoming another chapter in her own book." In July, a few months before the scheduled fall publication of *The Cartoons That Shook the World*, Klausen learned that Yale University Press, the book's publisher, had decided to remove the illustrations of the 12 cartoons from the book. They also excised all representations of Muhammad, including renderings of the scene of "Muhammad in Hell" in Dante's *Inferno*, drawn by such masters as Doré, Rodin, and Blake, and an image from a children's book.

In a publisher's statement printed at the front of the book, Yale University Press said that it had considered the civil unrest occasioned by the publication of the cartoons and, in consulting with "experts in the intelligence, national security, law enforcement . . . fields, as well as with leading scholars in Islamic studies," was persuaded that reprinting the images risked inciting violence.

In an author's statement, printed on the same page, Klausen "reluctantly" consented to the removal of the illustrations, saying that Muslim scholars and political activists and leaders with whom she had spoken "urged me to include the cartoons . . . with the purpose of encouraging reasoned analysis and debate" on the entire episode.

Debates over Yale's action began to rage, in a more intellectual way, with as much passion as Muslim demonstrators displayed in their condemnation of the cartoons. James Bone, writing in the *Times* of London, and Christopher Hitchens, posting on *Slate*, berated Yale for its cowardice in censoring itself. PEN American Center, the National Coalition Against Censorship, the American Booksellers Foundation for Free Expression, the American Civil Liberties Union, the American Library Association, and the American Association of University Professors (AAUP) were among the groups that protested. "What is to stop publishers from suppressing an author's words if it appears they may offend religious fundamentalists or groups threatening violence," wrote Cary Nelson, president of the AAUP in an open letter. The university's action "compromises the principle and practice of academic freedom, undermines the independence of the press, damages the university's credibility, and diminishes its reputation for scholarship," wrote Joan Bertin, executive director of the National Coalition Against Censorship on behalf of 11 other organizations.

John Donatich, director of Yale University Press, defended the removal of the images. He cited the arrest in 2008 by Danish police of Muslims who attempted to murder Kurt Westergaard, the artist who depicted Muhammad with a bomb in his turban, as a continued reaction to the publishing of the cartoons. Donatich also quoted one of the experts consulted by Yale—Ibrahim Gambari, United Nations special adviser to the secretary-general—as saying, "You can count on violence if any illustration of the prophet is published. It will cause riots, I predict, from Indonesia to Nigeria."

However, Reza Aslan, a scholar of religion and author of *No god but God: The Origins, Evolution and Future of Islam*, disagreed and withdrew the blurb he had written in praise of the book. The book is "a definitive account of the controversy," he said, "but not to include the actual cartoons is to me, frankly, idiotic. . . . This is an academic book for an academic audience by an academic press. . . . There is no chance of this book having a global audience, let alone causing a global outcry."

Klausen, also, found Gambari's assertions "laughable," but was more disturbed by Yale's insistence that as a condition of being able to read the summary of recommendations made by the consultants, she sign a confidentiality agreement forbidding her to discuss their findings. She refused. One of the consultants, Fareed Zakaria, then editor of *Newsweek International*, who serves on Yale's governing board, came forward and said that he told Yale he believed reprinting the images would have provoked violence.

As Brendan O'Neill wrote in London's *Independent* (and as others have observed), publishing the cartoons in an academic work is very different from reprinting them in various newspapers, which was the action that gave rise to the riots. The real problem, he wrote, "is the cultural cowardice in the West itself, over-caution amongst the supposed guardians of ideas and arguments, that leads to the removal of offending material." Citing other cases in which material was suppressed before it reached the public—including Random House's reneging on its contract to publish Sherry Jones's THE JEWEL OF MEDINA (about Muhammad's wife A'isha and which was later released by another publisher)—O'Neill notes that, "In each case, it wasn't threats or actions by agitated Muslims that gave rise to censorship; rather, elite fear of agitated Muslims generated self-censorship."

The *Washington Post*'s editorial of August 23, 2009, said: "Yale's self-censorship establishes a dangerous precedent. If one of the world's most respected scholarly publishers cannot print these images in context in an academic work, who can? . . . In effect, Yale University Press is allowing violent extremists to set the terms of free speech. As an academic press that embraces the university's motto of *Lux et Veritas*, it should be ashamed."

Jytte Klausen herself has observed that, as her book shows, the violence had "little connection to the original protests in Denmark or the international diplomatic protests." She notes that most of the deaths occurred in Nigeria, where a "virtual civil war" is ongoing. And al-Qaeda's bombing of the Danish embassy in Islamabad in 2008 had more to do with "a string of attacks on diplomatic foreign missions" than with the cartoons. "The deaths," she wrote, "resulted from violence in long-running conflicts where the cartoons became a new symbol in an old terrorist campaign or a rallying point in a protracted standoff between extremists and local governments."

So while Klausen reluctantly agreed to go ahead with the book's publication on Yale's terms, she has written subsequently that "nothing could substitute for looking at the cartoons and parsing their multiple and contradictory meanings and interpretations." In addition, she observed, "The removal of the other illustrations poses problems for the text, which was written to the illustrations . . . these illustrations were intended to awake the reader to the history of depiction of Muhammad in Ottoman, Persian, and Western art—and to show also how we live with images and do not examine them. Well, they will not be examined this time."

In December 2009, the self-censorship controversy took a startling new turn when *Index on Censorship*, a respected British organization and publication that documents and campaigns against censorship, declined to publish images of the cartoons alongside an interview with Klausen about Yale's censorship. Jonathan Dimbleby, chair of *Index*, cited the firebombing of the home and offices in London of the publisher of Gibson Square Books, who had proposed publishing the novel *The Jewel of Medina*, and wrote: "Re-publication of the cartoons would put at risk the security of our staff and others, which on balance, could not be justified on 'freedom of expression' grounds alone."

Critics of *Index*'s decision could not resist pointing out the obvious. "They at least know the value of free expression, and would not let purely notional imaginary projected risks cause them to censor themselves," wrote Ophelia Benson in London's *Guardian*. "Surely. But Index on Censorship did just that, thus seeing and raising Yale's bet in the irony stakes."

Dissenting *Index* board member Kenan Malik wrote, "[W]e cannot in good conscience criticize others for taking decisions that we ourselves have taken and for the same reasons. . . . Almost every case of pre-emptive censorship, including that of Yale University, has been rationalised on the grounds that the censored material was not necessary anyway. Once we accept that it is legitimate to censor that which is 'unnecessary' or 'gratuitous', then we have effectively lost the argument for free speech. . . . what I fear is that in refusing to publish the cartoons, *Index* is not only helping strengthen the culture of censorship, it is also weakening its authority to challenge that culture."

—Alice Tufel and Philip Milito

FURTHER READING

Applebaum, Anne. "Chipping Away at Free Speech." *Washington Post* (September 15, 2009). Available online. URL: http://www.washingtonpost.com. Accesssed June 6, 2010.

Benson, Ophelia. "Fear and Censorship." *Guardian* (January 5, 2010). Available online. URL: http://www.guardian.co.uk/commentisfree/belief/2010/jan/04/religion-islam. Accessed June 6, 2010.

Bone, James. "Yale University Press Accused of Cowardice over Muhammad Cartoons." *Times* (London) (August 18, 2009). Available online. URL: http://www.timesonline.co.uk/tol/news/world/us_and_americas/article679968. Accessed June 6, 2010.

Broder, Henryk M. "After Attack on Danish Cartoonist, the West Is Choked by Fear." Spiegel Online International (January 4, 2010). Available online. URL: http://www.spiegel.de/international/Europe/0,1518,669888,00.html. Accessed June 6, 2010.

Christoffersen, John. "Yale Criticized for Nixing Muslim Cartoons in Book." Associated Press (September 8, 2009). Available online. URL: http://abcnews.go.com/US/wireStory?id=8512341. Accessed June 6, 2010.

Cohen, Patricia. "PEN Urges Yale to Publish Images of Muhammad." *New York Times* (September 11, 2009). Available online. URL: http://www.campus-watch.org/article/id/8289. Accessed June 6, 2010.

————. "Yale Press Bans Images of Muhammad in New Book." *New York Times* (August 13, 2009). Available online. URL: http://www.nytimes.com/2009/08/13/books/13book.html. Accessed June 6, 2010.

Devi, Sharmilia. "Book on Danish Cartoons Sparks Ruckus." *National* (September 9, 2009). Available online. URL: http://www.campus-watch.org/article/id/8273. Accessed June 6, 2010.

Dimbleby, Jonathan. *Index on Censorship* (December 18, 2009). Available online. URL: http://www.indexoncensorship.org/2009/12/jonathan-dimbleby/. Accessed June 6, 2010.

Dworkin, Ronald. "The Right to Ridicule." *New York Review of Books* (March 23, 2006). Available online. URL: http://www.nybooks.com/articles/18111. Accessed June 6, 2010.

Eltahawy, Mona. "Yale's Misguided Retreat." *Washington Post* (August 29, 2009). Available online. URL: http://www.washingtonpost.com. Accessed June 6, 2010.

Flood, Alison. "Publisher Bans Images of Muhammad in New Book." *Guardian* (August 14, 2009). Available online. URL: http:/www.guardian.co.uk/books/2009/aug/14/publisher-bans-images-muhammad/print. Accessed June 6, 2010.

Goldstein, Evan R. "The Book That Shook Yale." *Chronicle of Higher Education* (September 29, 2009). Available online. URL: http://chronicle.com/article/The-Book-Shook-Yale/48634. Accessed June 6, 2010.

Hitchens, Christopher. "Yale Surrenders." Slate (August 17, 2009). Available online. URL: http://www.slate.com/toolbar/aspx?action=print&id=2225504. Accessed June 6, 2010.

Howard, Jennifer. "Academic and Free-Speech Groups Join Criticism of Yale U. Press Over Cartoons in Book." *Chronicle of Higher Education* (September 16, 2009). Available online. URL: http://chronicle.com/article/AcademicFree-Speech/48441/. Accessed June 6, 2010.

Klausen, Jytte. "'Not Everything Can Be Explained by Words Alone.'" *Yale Alumni Magazine* (September 9, 2009). Available online. URL: http:/www.yalealumnimagazine.com/extras/yup/klausen149.html. Accessed June 6, 2010.

Malik, Kenan. "Why We Should Not Censor Ourselves." *Index on Censorship* (December 18, 2009). Available online. URL: http://www.kenanmalik.com/debates/index_cartoons.html. Accessed June 6, 2010.

O'Neill, Brendan. "Censorship Is Being Justified by Imaginary Muslim Outrage." *Independent* (October 22, 2009). Available online. URL: http://license.icopyright.net/user/viewFreeUse.act?fuid=NTQ3MTY3NA%3D%3D. Accessed June 6, 2010.

Pasha, Kamran. "Yale and the Danish Cartoons." Huffington Post (September 8, 2009). Available online. URL: http://www.huffingtonpost.com/kamran-pasha/yale-and-the-danish-carto_b_279463.html. Accessed June 6, 2010.

Ritter, Karl. "Muhammad Cartoonist Defiant After Attack." Associated Press (May 13, 2010). Available online. URL: http://www.google.com/hostednews/ap/article/ALeqM5gfyTngzJoXl5VLnRYFKryLwR. Accessed June 6, 2010.

"Self-Muzzled at Yale." *Washington Post*. Editorial (August 23, 2009). Available online. URL: http://www.washingtonpost.com. Accessed June 6, 2010.

"Somali Charged over Attack on Cartoonist." BBC News (January 2, 2010). Available online. URL: http://news.bbc.co.uk/2/hi/Europe/8437652.stm. Accessed June 6, 2010.

Sjolie, Marie Louise. "The Danish Cartoonist Who Survived an Axe Attack." *Guardian* (January 4, 2010). Available online. URL: http://www.guardian.co.uk/world/2010/jan/04/danish-cartoonist-axe-attack. Accessed June 6, 2010.

"Writers Issue Cartoon Row Warning." BBC News. (March 1, 2006). Available online. URL: http://news.bbc.co.uk/2/hi/Europe/4663520.stm. Accessed June 6, 2010.

CHILDREN OF THE ALLEY

Author: Naguib Mahfouz
Original dates and places of publication: 1959, Egypt; 1988, United States
Original publishers: *Al-Ahram* newspaper; Three Continents Press
Literary form: Novel

SUMMARY

The Egyptian author Naguib Mahfouz (1911–2006), awarded the Nobel Prize in literature in 1988, was the most celebrated contemporary Arab writer of his time, with 33 novels, 13 anthologies of stories, and 30 screenplays to his credit over a half-century. Many of Mahfouz's richly detailed novels portray life in Cairo's teeming working-class neighborhoods. Among them are the three novels of his masterpiece *The Cairo Trilogy*, written between 1945 and 1957, chronicling the fortunes of three generations of a Cairo family.

Children of the Alley (also known by the title *Children of Gebelawi*) is the history of an imaginary Cairo alley and a retelling in allegorical form of the lives of Adam and Eve, Cain and Abel, and Moses, Jesus, and Muhammad. The novel can be read on many levels. It is an evocative account of the vanished world of Mahfouz's childhood in the alleys of Gemalia, in Cairo, and an engrossing fictional narrative. It is also a fable that echoes the history of Judaism, Christianity, and Islam, as well as a critique of religious intolerance and political and economic repression.

Narrated by an unnamed resident of the alley who is a professional writer, the story begins in the shadow of the mansion of Gabalawi, master of the estate at the foot of Muqattam Mountain. Gabalawi, whose despotic presence looms over generations of his descendants, represents God, or as Mahfouz has said, a certain idea of God that people have created.

Gabalawi's son, Adham, and Adham's wife, Umaima, tempted and tricked by Adham's dissolute brother, Idris, are permanently expelled by Gabalawi from the mansion and its fragrant gardens for seeking a look at his forbidden book. One of their two sons, Qadri, kills the other, Humam, in a fight. Qadri marries Hind, the daughter of Idris. They have several children, and from these ancestors all the people of the alley descend.

Gabalawi shuts himself away in his mansion and is not seen again. The management of his estate subsequently becomes a source of conflict. Though the estate's overseer at first follows the good example of Gabalawi, sharing its benefits with all the descendants, greed eventually gets the better of him and he exploits the poor. The neighborhood is run by young gangsters in the overseer's employ, who extort protection money from its hard-working inhabitants.

The first to rise up and rebel against injustice in the alley is the snake charmer Gabal, who defeats the gangsters and takes over leadership of the quarter. Gabal, who applies eye-for-an-eye justice, is honest and upright and shares the estate revenues equally, but he is also feared. He is a symbol of justice and order, but after his death, the era of the dishonest overseers and their threatening gangsters returns.

In another generation, a new leader—Rifaa, the carpenter's son—comes forth to preach against violence and materialism. He calls on Gabal's followers to trust him so that he can deliver them from evil spirits. Rifaa is murdered by the overseer and his gangsters, who see him as a threat to their social order.

A third leader, Qassem, eventually emerges from among the Desert Rats, the poorest and most wretched people of the neighborhood. He says that the people of the alley are all Gabalawi's children and the rule of gangsters must end. Following Rifaa's example, he ushers in an era of brotherhood and peace among the followers of Gabal, Rifaa, and his own disciples. He proclaims that no neighborhood is more closely related to Gabalawi than any other and that the estate belongs to everyone.

But those who succeed Qassem as overseer return to the old system of violence and exploitation. The alley is again divided against itself, with separate quarters for the followers of Gabal, Rifaa, and Qassem. "Gabalawi," the old man Shakrun cries out facing the mansion, "how long will you be silent and hidden? Your commandments are ignored and your money is being wasted. . . . Don't you know what has happened to us?"

Arafa, a magician, resolves to liberate the alley from the overseer's tyranny. He wants to find Gabalawi's book, the cause of Adham's exile, believing that it holds the magic secret of Gabalawi's power. When he breaks into the mansion to search for the book, he kills a servant. Having come in a quest for power to use against evil, he has turned into an evildoer.

In murdering a servant, Arafa indirectly kills Gabalawi, who dies from the shock of the murder in his house. The followers of Gabal, Rifaa, and Qassem squabble over where Gabalawi should be buried, each group believing they have a closer relationship with their ancestor. The overseer instructs the storytellers to sing the story of Gabalawi, emphasizing how he died at the hands of Arafa. But the people favor Arafa and his magic, exalting his name above those of Gabal, Rifaa, and Qassem. Gabalawi is dead, the people of the alley say: "We have nothing to do with the past. Our only hope lies in Arafa's magic, and if we had to choose between Gabalawi and magic, we'd choose magic." The final line of the book looks to the future with hope: "Injustice must have an end, as day must follow night. We will see the death of tyranny, and the dawn of light and miracles."

CENSORSHIP HISTORY

Children of the Alley was serialized in 1959 in the semiofficial Cairo newspaper *Al-Ahram*. Devout Muslims took to the streets in protest, demanding a ban because Mahfouz had suggested in allegorical fashion that the God of Adam, Moses, Jesus, and Muhammad might be dead. It was only upon the intervention of Egypt's president, Gamal Abdel Nasser, a friend of *Al-Ahram*'s editor, Mohammed Heikal, that the serialization was published uncut to the end. However, the scholars of Cairo's powerful government-recognized religious authority, Al-Azhar University, banned *Children of the Alley*, condemning it as "blasphemous," and calling its author a heretic for causing offense to the prophets of Islam and for misrepresenting the character of Muhammad.

Since that time, militant Islamic groups have sustained a relentless campaign against the book and its author, which successfully ensured its banning for more than three decades. *Children of the Alley* was passed from hand to hand in its newspaper version until 1967, when a pirated edition of the novel was published in Beirut, Lebanon, in slightly expurgated form. Smuggled into Egypt, it was sold under the counter at some Cairo bookstores.

In 1979, Mahfouz again incurred the wrath of Islamic fundamentalists in Egypt and elsewhere in the Arab world when he was among the first to support the peace treaty between Egypt and Israel. His novels were banned for several years in many Arab countries.

In 1988, Mahfouz won the Nobel Prize. Fundamentalists, who had never forgiven him for writing *Children of the Alley*, renewed their attacks, fearing that the prize would be used as a pretext to remove the book from the proscribed list. "The novel had basically been forgotten for a period of 30 years," Mahfouz said in a 1989 interview, "but following the prize it was subjected to very heavy attack in all the Islamicist-oriented newspapers and magazines. So the idea of publishing it here isn't even a topic for discussion."

In view of Egyptian president Hosni Mubarak's statement that the novel should be published and its availability in much of the rest of the Arab world, renewed attempts were made to lift the ban on the book. But when the Egyptian monthly *Al-Yasar* began to serialize it in 1989, the Islamic press campaigned so virulently against it that Mahfouz himself asked the magazine to stop the serialization.

Mahfouz again ran afoul of militants that same year when he spoke out against Iran's Ayatollah Ruhollah Khomeini's edict calling for the death of British author Salman Rushdie for having written THE SATANIC VERSES. Sheikh Omar Abdel Rahman, the Egyptian fundamentalist leader of the militant Gamaat Islamia sect (who was later convicted in a plot to blow up New York City landmarks and assassinate U.S. political leaders), issued a statement calling on both Mahfouz and Rushdie to repent. "If they do not, they will be killed," he said. "If this sentence had been passed on Naguib Mahfouz when he wrote *Children of the Alley*, Salman Rushdie would have realized that he had to stay within certain bounds."

In June 1992, Islamist terrorists in Cairo shot and killed Farag Fouda, a prominent Egyptian secular writer, who, like Mahfouz, had spoken out against violent censorship. Shortly after Fouda's slaying, the Egyptian government uncovered a death list including Mahfouz and several other leading writers and intellectuals. Mahfouz was offered but declined police protection.

In early 1994, the weekly magazine *Rose el-Youssef* published extracts from several banned works, including *The Satanic Verses* and *Children of the Alley*, accompanied by a statement in defense of freedom of expression. Most Arab countries, with the exception of Egypt and Kuwait, banned the magazine's distribution. In October 1994, Mahfouz was stabbed several times in the neck as he sat in a car outside his Cairo home. (Two Islamic militants were convicted of attempted murder and executed, and others received lesser sentences.) Mahfouz never regained full use of his right arm and hand after the assault and had to dictate his writings.

Shortly thereafter, the government's minister of information, speaking from Mahfouz's hospital bed, said the government did not support a ban on any of his works. His statement was interpreted as ending the official prohibition of *Children of the Alley*. As Egyptian newspapers rushed to serialize the novel, Mahfouz asked that publication come at a later time. "The issue is diverting attention from a crime against my life to whether this novel is, or is not, against religion," he said. But his request was ignored. A few weeks after the attack, the novel was published in the Egyptian press for the first time in 35 years, but its publication in book form in Egypt remained officially prohibited. Despite the ban, the Lebanese edition of the book had continued to be sold on the black market, and an English translation was available from American University in Cairo Press. Mahfouz died in August 2006 at the age of 94. Four months later, the book was officially published in Arabic in Egypt and became a best seller in Egypt.

FURTHER READING

Abou El-Magd, Nadia. "Book That Nearly Cost Naguib Mahfouz His Life Resurfaces in Egypt." Associated Press (January 12, 2007). Available online. URL: http://thedailynewsegypt.com/article.aspx?ArticleID=4933. Accessed June 6, 2010.

Appignanesi, Lisa, and Sara Maitland, eds. *The Rushdie File*. Syracuse, N.Y.: Syracuse University Press, 1990.

El-Hennawy, Noha. "Publish and Perish." *Egypt Today* (February 2006). Available online.URL: http//www.egypttoday.com/article.aspx?ArticleID=6361. Accessed June 6, 2010.

Pipes, Daniel. *The Rushdie Affair*. New York: Carol Publishing Group, 1990.

Weaver, Mary Anne. "The Novelist and the Sheikh." *New Yorker*, January 30, 1995, 52–59.

THE CHRISTIAN COMMONWEALTH

Author: John Eliot
Original date and place of publication: 1659, England
Literary form: Religious text

SUMMARY

John Eliot, who succeeded the banished Roger Williams as the Anglican minister of the First Church of Roxbury, Massachusetts, gained fame for his missionary work among the Algonquian Indians, the original inhabitants of what became the Boston metropolitan area. While he is most widely known for translating the Bible into Algonquian, he also worked with Algonquian leaders to create a society run according to legal principles of the Old Testament. Eliot wrote the blueprint for such a government in a tract titled *The Christian Commonwealth: or, the Civil Policy of the Rising Kingdom of Jesus Christ.*

Eliot wrote *The Christian Commonwealth* before 1650, shortly after he learned Algonquian and began preaching to the Indians of the area in their own language. Perhaps as a way of discounting local chiefs' authority, Eliot's book emphasizes the ultimate power of God over all civil governments. For Eliot there is no separation of church and state. Because civil authorities acknowledge God's power, God's laws are the basis of laws passed by governments.

Yet Eliot did not intend for his work to convert only the Algonquian. In his preface, he exhorts his audience to "set the Crown of England upon the head of Christ, whose only true inheritance it is, by the gift of his father." In the same chapter, Eliot addresses the British tradition of the rights of elected governments when he writes, "It is the holy Scriptures of God only that I do urge, to be your only Magna Charta, by which you should be ruled in all things; which being, Christ is your King and Sovereign Lawgiver, and you are his people ruled by him in all things." Eliot uses specific examples of British laws to prove the importance of the Bible in underpinning earthly governments.

As Eliot wrote *The Christian Commonwealth*, Oliver Cromwell's reign as lord protector had brought radical changes to England. The English Revolution expanded political liberties and overthrew the monarchy, and Eliot took occasion to address those who might look for salvation in democracy. Eliot warns them: "And when a Christian people are to choose their Government, should they take their Patern from the Nations of the World, we know what an offence that would be to Christ, who intends to rule them himself, by his own Divine Patern and Direction."

Eliot stands clearly against democracy and secular government as an ideal. For these reasons, he was much more acceptable to the Puritan leadership of Roxbury than was the more radically democratic Roger Williams, whose BLOUDY TENENT OF PERSECUTION was burned in London by order of the British Parliament in 1644.

In the eight chapters of *The Christian Commonwealth*, Eliot discusses exactly how a political and legal system could be set up under biblical guidelines. He begins by stressing the hierarchy of the household, where the wife and children serve the husband. In Exodus 18:25, Jethro advises Moses on how the Israelites should govern themselves: They should elect men to represent groups of 10, 50, 100, and 1,000, with the rulers of 10 handling the least consequential decisions, and the rulers of 1,000 responsible for the most important decisions. Eliot's belief in the Old Testament as a literal document led him to think that such a government could work for England, Ireland, and Scotland.

Eliot's role as a missionary to the Algonquian gave him an opportunity to create a "Christian commonwealth" of his own. In 1651, he helped the Algonquian Speene family organize the Christian Indian village of Natick, near Boston. Fewer than 150 people lived in Natick, a population small enough to experiment with Eliot's Old Testament system of governance. According to the few surviving mentions of life in Natick, the system worked for the small community. The Indians who settled Natick had lived among the English for several decades and had already begun to adopt English dress and language. The community agreed with Eliot's idea that all true governing power comes from a divine source, and in September 1651 they assembled to take an oath affirming their status as a holy town. Their special form of governance lasted until 1675–76, when white settlements took over the village.

CENSORSHIP HISTORY

In 1651, Eliot sent *The Christian Commonwealth* back to England, hoping to publish it there, but the book did not appear until eight years later. However, King Charles II, who was restored to the throne in 1660, did not appreciate a religious work that stated that even royal authorities owed their power to a higher source.

Livewell Chapman, Eliot's publisher, tried to avert censorship by including a disclaimer on the book's title page. Under Eliot's full title, Chapman included a note that the book was "Written Before the Interruption of the Government. . . . And Now Published by a Server of the Season." By 1661, copies of the book had made their way back to Massachusetts and, in spite of Chapman's efforts to appease royal suspicions, the Massachusetts general court feared that Eliot's ideas could be misconstrued by the king or his ministers. On May 30 of that year they ordered the book suppressed. Within two weeks, any Massachusetts citizen who owned copies of the banned work had to "cancel or deface" them or bring them to local judges, who would then dispose of them.

Eliot admitted that he had made some mistakes in his work but stood by his original principles, claiming in a statement to the Massachusetts general court that "All forms of Government . . . [are] from God . . . and whatsoever in the whole epistle or book is inconsistent therewith, I do at once most cordially disown." While the judges had hoped that he would admit guilt for denying the king's power, Eliot apologized only for any errors he might have made in his interpretation of Scripture.

Evidently, Eliot's nonadmission of guilt satisfied the court. There is no further record of Eliot being punished by Massachusetts authorities for *The Christian Commonwealth*. He continued to live and work in Roxbury for almost 30 years after his trial. The residents of Roxbury and Natick regarded him fondly for his deep religious faith and his service to the members of the two communities. As in the case of Springfield merchant and amateur theologian William Pynchon, whose MERITORIOUS PRICE OF OUR REDEMPTION was the first work to be publicly burned in North America, Eliot's experience shows how even the most upstanding citizen of early Massachusetts could become a victim of censorship.

—Jonathan Pollack

FURTHER READING

Winslow, Ola Elizabeth. *John Eliot, "Apostle to the Indians."* Boston: Houghton Mifflin, 1968.

CHRISTIANITY NOT MYSTERIOUS

Author: John Toland
Original date and place of publication: 1696, England
Literary form: Religious treatise

SUMMARY

The Irish deist John Toland was brought up as a Roman Catholic and became a Protestant at age 16 before later declaring his affinities for deism and pantheism. He studied at the Universities of Glasgow, Edinburgh, and Leiden and earned his living as a writer and publicist for radical Whig causes. Toland wrote nearly 200 works. The most important of these is *Christianity Not Mysterious*, published in 1696, a book that launched the deist controversy. Deists held that the course of nature alone was sufficient to demonstrate the existence of God. Formal religion was superfluous and the claims of supernatural revelation were scorned as spurious.

In *Christianity Not Mysterious*, Toland attempts to reconcile the scriptural claims of Christianity with John Locke's theory of knowledge as revealed in AN ESSAY CONCERNING HUMAN UNDERSTANDING, asserting that neither God nor revelation is above the comprehension of human reason. The book's purpose is indicated in its subtitle: *A Treatise Shewing, That There is Nothing in the Gospel Contrary to Reason, Nor Above it; And That No Christian Doctrine Can Be Properly Call'd A Mystery.*

On the title page, Toland quotes Archbishop John Tillotson, a liberal Anglican admired by deists: "We need not desire a better Evidence that any Man is in the wrong, than to hear him declare against Reason, and thereby acknowledg[e] that Reason is against him." Toland believed that revelation is a "means of information," rather than a "motive of assent." The Bible should be assessed critically by each person who reads it. "Since Religion is not calculated for reasonable Creatures," he wrote, " 'tis Conviction and not Authority that should bear Weight with them. A wise and good Man will judg[e] of the Merits of a Cause consider'd only in itself, without any regard to Times, Places, or Persons."

Toland insists that everything, including religious revelation, must pass the test of reason or be rejected: "I hold nothing as an Article of my Religion, but what the highest Evidence forc'd me to embrace." Only reason enables people to distinguish between fact and fancy, between what is certain and what is only probable. Toland suggests that God, who endowed human beings with the faculty of reason, would not require belief in the irrational as a condition of salvation. Much of the Bible must be interpreted symbolically, otherwise "the highest Follies and Blasphemies" can be drawn from the letter of Scripture.

Toland concludes *Christianity Not Mysterious* with an expression of the deist's credo: "I acknowledge no ORTHODOXY but the TRUTH; and, I'm sure, where-ever the TRUTH is there must also [be] the CHURCH, of God. . . ."

CENSORSHIP HISTORY

Christianity Not Mysterious was published anonymously in 1695, after expiration of the book censorship provisions of the Licensing Act of 1662. Though Toland insisted that he was a sincere Christian who wished only to purge Christianity of its mysteries and restore it to a rational condition, his critics saw *Christianity Not Mysterious* as a blasphemous expression of the Socinian heresy, which denied the doctrine of the Holy Trinity. The book was described as the first act of warfare between deists and those who held more orthodox Christian views.

By late summer 1696, Toland decided to allow his name to be attached to the book, which was rapidly becoming notorious. By publicly claiming authorship, Toland became a visible target for the heretic hunters. The book was presented by the grand jury of Middlesex, England, but Toland fled to Ireland and escaped criminal or civil penalties. Intense hostility against him in Ireland, led by clergy who viewed the book as denying Christ's divinity, resulted in action by an Irish grand jury. The archbishop of Dublin called on the civil arm of government to "suppress his Insolence." In 1697, the Irish Parliament, acting on the report of an investigating committee, condemned *Christianity Not Mysterious* as heretical and ordered it burned by the public hangman. The government also ordered Toland's arrest and prosecution by the attorney general. He returned in haste to England, where he remained in hiding.

Toland's book infuriated orthodox Christians. The profusion of deistic, anti-Trinitarian books such as *Christianity Not Mysterious* led the House of Commons to press for the passage of a new antiblasphemy statute. The act, adopted in 1698 "for the more effectual suppressing of Blasphemy," provided that any person who professed to be a Christian would be convicted of blasphemy if he denied in conversation or in writing that any one of the persons of the Holy Trinity was God, that the Christian religion was true, or that the Bible had divine authority. The punishment for a first offense was denial of civil, military, or ecclesiastical employment. A second offense would cost the loss of all civil rights and three years in prison without bail. In 1699, Toland decided to take a journey to Holland until the furor over his book had abated.

The act of 1698 remained in effect until 1967, when it was revoked by Parliament. The common law of blasphemy, however, based on judicial precedents dating from 1676 to 1921, still existed. It became a subject of debate in Britain in the 1980s during the controversy over the censorship of Salman Rushdie's THE SATANIC VERSES, when an unsuccessful campaign was launched by Muslim organizations in Britain to extend the common law against blasphemy to protect all religions.

FURTHER READING

Levy, Leonard W. *Blasphemy: Verbal Offense Against the Sacred, from Moses to Salman Rushdie.* New York: Alfred A. Knopf, 1993.
Smith, George H. *Atheism, Ayn Rand and Other Heresies.* Buffalo, N.Y.: Prometheus Books, 1991.
Sullivan, Robert E. *John Toland and the Deist Controversy. A Study in Adaptations.* Cambridge, Mass.: Harvard University Press, 1982.

CHRISTIANITY RESTORED

Author: Michael Servetus
Original date and place of publication: 1552, France
Literary form: Theological treatise

SUMMARY

The Spanish theologian and physician Michael Servetus earned his reputation for religious deviationism at the age of 20. During his law studies at Toulouse, France, he had discovered in the Scriptures the historical person of Jesus of Nazareth, leading him to reject traditional formulations of the nature of Christ and the relationship of the three persons of the Trinity.

Servetus believed that Protestant reformers Martin Luther, John Calvin, and Huldrych Zwingli were not revolutionary enough, because they accepted the doctrine of the Trinity, which he viewed as incomprehensible. Failing to convince the reformers in Basel and Strasbourg of his ideas, Servetus decided to write a book that would persuade all Christians of the truth of his discoveries.

In 1531, he published On the Errors of the Trinity, a treatise asserting that traditional Scholastic theology introduced Greek philosophical terms and nonbiblical concepts into the definitions of the Trinity that were abstract, speculative, and unrelated to the living God. "Not one word is found in the whole Bible about the Trinity, nor about its Persons, nor about an Essence, nor about a unity of the Substance, nor about one Nature of the several beings," he wrote. Orthodox Catholics and many Protestants viewed Servetus's theology as having revived the fourth-century heresy of Arianism, which denied the doctrine of the Trinity by teaching that Jesus as the Son of God was neither equal to nor eternal with God the Father.

In 1552, Servetus recast his earlier tracts in a new book, *Christianity Restored*. It contained a revised edition of *On the Errors of the Trinity* and new material, including 30 letters on theology that he had sent to Calvin. In *Christianity Restored*, Servetus challenged the established churches, both Catholic and Protestant, to return Christendom to the purity of its origins: "A calling of the whole apostolic church to make a fresh start, restored completely in the knowledge of God, the faith of Christ, our justification, regeneration, baptism, and the Lord's Supper. Our restoration finally in the kingdom of heaven, with the loosing of the captivity of ungodly Babylon and Antichrist and his own destroyed."

In the new work, he claimed that Christianity had failed because it had become corrupted in the early fourth century by pagan doctrines and by the church's acquisition of temporal power. He attacked the definition of the Trinity established by the church's Council of Nicaea in the fourth century, as well as the practice of infant baptism, which he termed as unchristian. He accepted the heretical Anabaptist tenet that baptism should be deferred until maturity, when a sinner has experienced Christ and repented. Christ himself was not baptized until he was an adult, Servetus wrote, and becoming a Christian meant sharing a spiritual communion that an infant could not understand.

CENSORSHIP HISTORY

The publication in 1531 of *On the Errors of the Trinity* made Servetus notorious and a hunted man, threatened by both the French and Spanish Inquisitions and the Protestants, who banned his book and closed cities to him. In 1532, the Inquisition in Toulouse issued a decree ordering his arrest. He went underground in Paris and assumed a new identity, adopting the name of Michel de Villeneuve, from the family home of Villanueva, Spain. Fear of persecution in Paris drove him to Lyon, where he worked as a printer's editor, eventually settling in 1540 in the suburb of Vienne.

Using his own name, Servetus began to correspond with Protestant reformer John Calvin in Geneva, instructing him on theology. In all he sent 30 epistolary discourses to Calvin. Calvin sent him a copy of his INSTITUTES OF THE CHRISTIAN RELIGION, which Servetus boldly returned annotated with criticisms. Servetus also presented Calvin with a manuscript copy of part of *Christianity Restored*, apparently hoping that Calvin would view it favorably.

A thousand copies of *Christianity Restored* were printed anonymously and in secret in Vienne by the publishers Balthasar Arnoullet and Guillaume Guéroult in 1552 after publishers in Basel refused to have anything to do with the book. Some copies were sent to the Frankfurt book fair and others to a bookseller in Geneva. There a copy came into the hands of Calvin's colleague, Guillaume Trie, who forwarded the first four leaves of the book to a Catholic cousin in Lyon, revealing Villeneuve's identity and location in Vienne. The cousin placed the material in the hands of the Inquisition, which began an investigation.

Servetus and his publisher Arnoullet denied any knowledge of the book. But at the request of the Inquisition, Trie provided the investigators the manuscript copy of the book sent by Servetus to Calvin, implicating Servetus. Servetus was arrested and held for trial but escaped. In June 1553, the civil tribunal of Lyon condemned him in absentia for heresy, sedition, rebellion, and evasion of prison, fining him 2,000 livres and sentencing him to be burned. In his absence, bales of copies of his books were incinerated with his effigy. His publisher was imprisoned.

In August, on his way to seek refuge in Italy, Servetus passed through Geneva, Calvin's stronghold. There he was recognized and, on Calvin's orders, arrested. Charged with 39 counts of heresy and blasphemy, for more than two months he stood trial before the judges of the Geneva city council. The verdict of the council was that the book Servetus had secretly printed in Vienne had spread "heresies and horrible, execrable blasphemies against the Holy Trinity, against the Son of God, against the baptism of infants and foundations of the Christian religion." The Geneva authorities consulted the magistrates of all the Swiss cantons, who unanimously agreed on the verdict.

Servetus was sentenced to be burned to ashes with his book for trying "to infect the world with [his] stinking heretical poison." The verdict stated further, "And so you shall finish your days and give an example to others who would commit the like." Servetus's last request was to see Calvin. "I told him to beg the pardon of the son of God, whom he had disfigured with his dreams . . .," Calvin reported. "But when I saw that all this did no good I did not wish to be wiser than my Master allows. So following the rule of St. Paul, I withdrew from the heretic who was self-condemned."

Servetus asked to die by the sword rather than by burning. Although Calvin supported this request for mercy, it was denied by the magistrates. "He asked forgiveness for his errors, ignorance and sins, but never made a full confession," wrote Calvin's colleague, Guillaume Farel. "But we could never get him openly to admit his errors and confess that Christ is the eternal son of God." On October 27, 1553, Servetus was burned at the stake.

Calvin urged the destruction of *Christianity Restored* in Protestant countries, as it contained "prodigious blasphemies against God." Only three copies survived. In part the tragic result of a power struggle between Calvin and his opponents, Servetus's execution damaged Calvin's reputation. As Church historian Roland H. Bainton wrote, Servetus had "the singular distinction of having been burned by the Catholics in effigy and by the Protestants in actuality." Servetus was the first person to be executed as a heretic on the authority of a reformed church. His martyrdom came to have a significance greater than any other in his century, as it marked the first important controversy over the issue of toleration within Protestantism.

The movement on behalf of toleration, reflected in Sebastian Castellio's 1554 defense of toleration, CONCERNING HERETICS, was galvanized by widespread revulsion at Servetus's punishment. Yet the systematic repression of *Christianity Restored* minimized Servetus's posthumous influence on religious thought. Almost two centuries later, Richard Mead, the physician to the king of England, tried to publish Servetus's work. In 1723, the government seized and burned the whole printing and imprisoned Mead and his printer.

FURTHER READING

Bainton, Roland H. *Hunted Heretic: The Life and Death of Michael Servetus*. Gloucester, Mass.: Peter Smith, 1978.

Christie-Murray, David. *A History of Heresy*. Oxford: Oxford University Press, 1989.

Haight, Anne Lyon. *Banned Books: 387 B.C. to 1978 A.D.* Updated and enlarged by Chandler B. Grannis. New York: R. R. Bowker, 1978.

Levy, Leonard W. *Blasphemy: Verbal Offense Against the Sacred, from Moses to Salman Rushdie*. New York: Alfred A. Knopf, 1993.

Parker, T. H. L. *John Calvin*. Batavia, Ill.: Lion Publishing Corporation, 1975.

Smith, George H. *Atheism, Ayn Rand, and Other Heresies*. Buffalo, N.Y.: Prometheus Books, 1991.

Spitz, Lewis W., ed. *The Protestant Reformation*. Englewood Cliffs, N.J.: Prentice Hall, 1966.

Zagorin, Perez. *How the Idea of Religious Toleration Came to the West*. Princeton, N.J.: Princeton University Press, 2003.

CHURCH: CHARISM AND POWER: LIBERATION THEOLOGY AND THE INSTITUTIONAL CHURCH

Author: Leonardo Boff
Original dates and places of publication: 1981, Brazil; 1985, United States
Publishers: Editora Vôzes; Crossroad
Literary form: Theological essays

SUMMARY

The Brazilian Catholic theologian Leonardo Boff is a leading exponent of liberation theology, an interpretation of Christian faith drawn from the experience of the poor. *Church: Charism and Power*, a collection of essays, speeches, and lecture notes, contains some of the sharpest criticisms of the Roman Catholic Church to come from Latin America. Boff argues from his experience with the poor in Brazilian base communities—grassroots, Catholic communities led by laity. He urges institutional reform of Catholicism and its transformation into a "liberation Church," not simply *for* the poor, but *of* the poor. Criticizing abuse of hierarchical power, he calls for a return to the collegial structure of early church communities, in which both clergy and laity exercised power.

Boff's central thesis is that the struggle for justice and human rights cannot be separated from a similar struggle within the church itself. The preferential option for the poor demands shifts within Catholicism. The institutional church must move away from its reliance on power and coercion and toward a democratic model of openness and tolerance, the original model upon which Christ founded the church. Boff contends that the church hierarchy took its form only after Jesus' death. When Christianity became the official religion of the Roman Empire, the church began to reflect the empire's feudal structure of authority, including its institutions, laws, and bureaucratic centralization.

Boff distinguishes between two kinds of power: *exousia*, the power of love employed by Jesus, and *potestas*, the power to dominate and rule that characterized Roman officialdom. He describes the exercise of *potestas* by the clergy and the division between the clergy and the laity as a cancer within the church. The charismatic essence of the church, in which everyone has a charism, or gift, to offer, has been extinguished. "Christianity is not against power in itself," Boff writes, "but its diabolical forms which show themselves as dominion and control." Using marxist terminology, Boff refers to the "gradual expropriation of the spiritual means of production from the Christian people by the clergy."

The church must contain charisms, such as teaching, serving, preaching, and administering, as well as power. The papacy does have a special position within the church in maintaining doctrinal unity based on the emerging consensus of the community. Power can be a charism, Boff believes, as long as it serves everyone and is an instrument for building justice in the community.

CENSORSHIP HISTORY

Boff's orthodoxy already had been investigated by the Vatican in 1976 and again in 1980 on suspicion of doctrinal deviation. The 1980 investigation centered on his book *Jesus Christ, the Liberator.* But the Vatican had been generally willing to leave the question of orthodoxy of individual Latin American theologians to their own bishops.

When *Church: Charism and Power* was published in Brazil, Spain, and Italy in 1981, it was not expected to spark widespread debate. It was a further development of ideas expressed in Boff's doctoral thesis and in a previous book on ecclesiology, or the study of the structure of the church. Boff was not optimistic that the book, a loosely connected collection of disparate writings and talks rather than a comprehensive analysis, would find an audience.

Almost immediately, however, it provoked an unusual amount of discussion. Boff had applied the insights of liberation theology, previously directed at the reform of secular society, to the church itself. His choice of the words "symbolic violence" to refer to the Vatican's methods for discouraging dissent and his use of quasi-marxist terminology to analyze the church's structure angered critics.

In the book, he quotes at length a Brazilian Catholic who makes a point-by-point parallel between Kremlin and Vatican styles of governance. In another highly controversial passage, he writes: "It is strange to see that the Church institution has developed into exactly that which Christ did not want it to be."

Boff had earlier described the Vatican's Congregation for the Doctrine of the Faith (CDF) as relying on procedures that are unacceptable in civil society, a "Kafkaesque process wherein the accuser, defender, the lawyer and judge are one and the same." In 1982, a similar process was initiated to investigate Boff's views.

In February 1982, Boff, who knew that his critics had already complained to the Vatican, mailed to Rome as a courtesy a copy of some negative reviews of his book and a response by Rev. Urbano Zilles of Brazil. Three months later, he received a letter from Joseph Cardinal Ratzinger, prefect of the CDF (who became Pope Benedict XVI in April 2005), asking him to respond to criticisms. He wrote a response and published it.

In May 1984, Boff received a six-page letter from Ratzinger criticizing Boff's views as expressed in the book and saying they "did not merit acceptance." The letter referred to Boff's theological method, his analysis of church structure, his concepts of dogma and revelation, and his description of the exercise of power in the church. It criticized his "ecclesiastical relativism" and his "sociological" analysis. Ratzinger accused Boff of using language that was "polemic, defamatory and pamphleteering, absolutely inappropriate for a theologian," drawing on "ideological principles of a certain neo-Marxist inspiration," proposing "a certain revolutionary utopia which is foreign to the church," and holding a "relativizing conception" of church structure and doctrine.

Boff replied with a 50-page document, insisting that he wrote "only to right the balance in the direction of the experience of the laity, the poor, and the contributions of the social sciences." He concluded, "Of one thing I am sure: I prefer to walk in the church than go it alone with my theology. The church is a reality of Faith that I assume. Theology is a product of reason that I discuss."

Rather than going through the Brazilian bishops, who would have supported Boff, Ratzinger summoned him to Rome for a "colloquy" in September 1984. Boff took with him to Rome petitions signed by 50,000 Brazilians and was accompanied by two Brazilian cardinals, who came to show their support. Although Boff would not have selected *Church: Charism and Power* to fully represent his ideas, the colloquy turned out to be a full-scale interrogation on his views as expressed in the book.

In March 1985, the CDF published a Notification, making public the letter Ratzinger had sent the previous year and labeling it an official public document approved by the pope. The CDF stated that its reservations about his book "had not been substantially overcome" and that Boff was guilty of three errors: his statement that the church borrowed societal characteristics from contemporary Roman and later feudal society, his relativistic interpretation of dogma as good for specific circumstances and times, and his statements that clergy had expropriated spiritual means of production from the laity. "The options of Leonardo Boff analyzed herein endanger the sound doctrine of the Faith which this congregation has the task of promoting and safeguarding," the Notification concluded.

In May 1985, Boff received an official notice from the CDF ordering him to begin immediately to observe an "obedient silence" for an unspecified period of time. The notice stated that the period of silence "would permit Friar Boff a time for serious reflection." It required him to abstain completely from writing and publishing, from his duties as editor of the *Revista Ecclesiastica Brasileira*, the most influential theological journal in Brazil, from his work as editor of books on theology at the publishing house Editora Vôzes, and from teaching or lecturing. Boff submitted to the silencing, saying, "As a Christian, Franciscan friar and theologian, it is for me to listen and adhere."

Ten Brazilian bishops, who viewed the Vatican's attack on one of liberation theology's most prominent figures as an unwelcome intrusion of Rome into Latin American matters and a threat to the right of Catholics to think and write freely, took the highly unusual step of publicly criticizing the Vatican's treatment of Boff. Senior Brazilian bishops met with Pope John Paul II in Rome during March 1986. That month, after 10 months of the silencing, Boff's punishment was lifted. Boff said he received the news "as an Easter present" and was sure that it was a gesture of goodwill on the part of the Vatican toward the bishops of Brazil.

In 1991, Boff published a series of articles calling for change in the church's prohibition against marriage for priests. When church officials denied approval for publication of his next manuscript, he resigned from the priesthood. In an open letter to his followers he wrote, "I am leaving the priestly ministry, but not the church. . . . I continue to be and will always be a theologian in the Catholic and ecumenical mold, fighting with the poor against their poverty and in favor of their liberation."

FURTHER READING

Boff, Leonardo. Leonardo Boff's official Web site. Available online. URL: http://fly. to/boff.
"Leonardo Boff." Inter Press Service (December 30, 1999).
Cox, Harvey. *The Silencing of Leonardo Boff: The Vatican and the Future of World Christianity.* Oak Park, Ill.: Meyer Stone Books, 1988.
Sigmund, Paul E. *Liberation Theology at the Crossroads: Democracy or Revolution?* New York: Oxford University Press, 1990.

COLLOQUIES

Author: Desiderius Erasmus
Original dates and place of publication: 1518–33, Switzerland
Literary form: Essays

SUMMARY

The Dutch writer and biblical scholar Desiderius Erasmus, an influential proponent of the values of Christian humanism, was a critic of abuses within the Catholic Church. He advocated the practice of a simpler, purer Christianity, purged of superstition, corruption, and meaningless ceremonies. Among his main works were *Adages* (1500), a collection of classical proverbs; *The Handbook of the Christian Soldier* (1503), a manual of piety taken from Christ's teachings; THE PRAISE OF FOLLY (1511), a satire on theologians and church dignitaries; *Education of a Christian Prince* (1516); and a translation into Latin of the Greek New Testament (1516).

Colloquies, a collection of informal conversations or dialogues on contemporary issues, had its origins during the years 1495 to 1499 when Erasmus supported himself in Paris by tutoring Latin. He prepared some simple exercises for his pupils to improve their writing and conversation. Some 20 years later, in 1518, to Erasmus's surprise and annoyance, Johannes Froben published the exercises in Basel without his authorization, then reprinted them in Paris and Antwerp. The book became a popular textbook for the study of Latin.

Erasmus wrote in 1523: "There had also appeared a small book of 'Colloquies' pieced together partly from familiar conversation and partly from my notes, but with a certain amount of nonsense thrown in which was not only foolish but bad Latin and simply packed with blunders; and this worthless piece was given a surprisingly warm welcome. . . . At length, by taking more than ordinary pains, I added a good deal, to bring it up to the right size for a book." In 1519, Erasmus had the thin volume reissued, with some corrections and his own preface.

Beginning with the 1522 edition, the character of the book changed as Erasmus began to make significant additions to the text, with new dialogues containing elements of social criticism directed as much to adults as to students. Between 1522 and 1533, 12 new expanded editions of the book were published.

The final edition contained some 50 colloquies. Many of them were humorous diversions; others represented lively debates on the moral, religious, and political issues of the day, from discussions of methods of study, sleep, and diet and amusing accounts of the passing scene to sober and provocative reflections on ethics, government, marriage, and money. "Socrates brought philosophy down from heaven to earth," Erasmus said of his *Colloquies*. "I have brought it even into games, informal conversations, and drinking parties."

Many pages in the *Colloquies* made pointed reference to the religious controversies of the day and criticized superstition and lack of spirituality in the church. In "Cyclops," a character who refers to the calamities of the times says, "Kings make war, priests are zealous to increase their wealth, theologians invent syllogisms, monks roam throughout the world, the commons riot, Erasmus writes colloquies."

In "The Godly Feast," in a passage that was censored by the Sorbonne, Erasmus wrote, "Hence those who adorn monasteries or churches at excessive cost, while meanwhile so many of Christ's living temples are in danger of starving, shiver in their nakedness, and are tortured by want of necessities, seem to me almost guilty of a capital crime." It was this thread of social criticism running through many of the dialogues of the *Colloquies* that led to its censorship.

CENSORSHIP HISTORY

Colloquies became a best seller in Europe, with at least 100 editions printed before Erasmus's death in 1536. Erasmus wrote of the book, "And to be sure, as long as there was nothing in that book but the merest trifles, it found surprising favour on all sides. When it began to be useful in many ways, it could not escape the poison-fangs of slander."

After the emergence of Lutheranism, whatever he wrote that related to criticism or reform of the church was closely scrutinized. Erasmus was repeatedly compelled to defend the *Colloquies*. Its critics alleged that certain passages were indecent and that his portrayals of the hypocrisy of monks, friars, and prelates and his attacks on superstition and ignorance were irreverent and heretical.

In 1526, the Sorbonne, the theological faculty of the University of Paris and the most influential body of theologians in Europe, took action. In a petition to the Parlement of Paris, it formally censured *Colloquies*, along with passages from other writings by Erasmus viewed as promoting Lutheranism. Condemning 69 pages as "erroneous, scandalous or impious," it described Erasmus as "a pagan who mocks at the Christian religion and its sacred rites and customs." The Sorbonne recommended that the book be forbidden to all, especially to youth, lest it corrupt their morals. In 1528, the university forbade regents to use the *Colloquies* in their teaching.

In 1535, Holy Roman Emperor Charles V of Spain made it a capital offense to use *Colloquies* in schools. Three years later, an ecclesiastical commission appointed by Pope Paul III recommended that the *Colloquies* "and any other book of this sort" be prohibited as "injurious to youthful minds." When the Index librorum prohibitorum (Index of Forbidden Books) was established in 1559 by Pope Paul IV, the *Colloquies* was included, along with all of Erasmus's other work. The Tridentine Index of 1564, issued by the Council of Trent, removed some of Erasmus's writings from the proscribed list, but the *Colloquies* remained condemned.

Subsequent Indexes in Rome and Spain maintained the bans on the *Colloquies*, and Erasmus was listed on the Roman Index until 1930. Nevertheless, the book continued to be widely read and translated for three centuries, as long as Latin was the basis of study in schools and the accepted international language among the educated.

FURTHER READING

Erasmus, Desiderius. *The Colloquies of Erasmus*. Translated and with an introduction by Craig R. Thompson. Chicago: University of Chicago Press, 1965.
———. *Ten Colloquies of Erasmus*. Translated and with an introduction by Craig R. Thompson. New York: Liberal Arts Press, 1957.
Rummel, Erika, ed. *The Erasmus Reader*. Toronto: University of Toronto Press, 1990.

COMMENTARIES

Author: Averroës
Original dates and places of publication: 1168–90, Spain and Morocco
Literary form: Philosophical commentaries

SUMMARY

The 12th-century Spanish-Arab philosopher and physician Ibn Rushd, known as Averroës, is among the outstanding figures of medieval philosophy. Born in

Córdoba, Spain, into a family of distinguished judges, Averroës was trained in the legal tradition and in theology, medicine, and philosophy. He held judicial posts under the Almohad dynasty (Arab Islamic rulers of Spain and Morocco), first in Seville and later in Córdoba, and became physician to the caliph in 1182.

His extensive commentaries on the works of Aristotle, translated into Latin in the early 13th century, had a great influence on the development of medieval Scholasticism. Averroist schools sprang up at many of the leading universities of Europe. His commentaries rendered Aristotle accessible at a time when knowledge of his writing in the Western world was fragmentary. He also played a crucial role in the transmission of classical philosophy to Islam. In less technical works, such as the *Incoherence of the Incoherence* and *The Decisive Treatise*, he defended philosophy against charges that it opposed the teachings of the KORAN (Qur'an).

Convinced that the genius of Aristotle represented the model of human perfection, Averroës devoted many years to writing his greatest work, in the form of commentaries presenting and interpreting the thought of Aristotle. They can be categorized in three classes: the greater commentaries, in which Averroës presents Aristotle's original text along with comments on it; the middle or lesser commentaries, reproducing only the opening words of particular paragraphs of the Aristotelian text, with extensive interpretation by Averroës; and the little commentaries or paraphrases, in which Averroës gives only Aristotle's conclusions, omitting proofs and historical references.

In his interpretation of Aristotle, Averroës contributed his own philosophy. As a Muslim who believed that philosophy was the highest form of inquiry and that Aristotle was the author of a system representing the supreme truth, he attempted to delimit the separate domains of faith and reason. He held that the two need not be reconciled because they did not conflict but rather followed parallel paths, arriving at the same goals. The same truth is expressed allegorically in theology and understood clearly in philosophy.

Religious teaching expresses truth to the unlettered ordinary person, while philosophy attains it through the use of pure reason for those with the mental ability to undertand it. Averroës's theory, later described as a doctrine of "double truth," allowed science to advance and the free mind to inquire without fetters imposed by either Islam or Christianity.

CENSORSHIP HISTORY

While the Almohad monarch Yusuf the Wise ruled in Spain and Morocco, Averroës was protected from orthodox Islamic theologians who opposed the study of philosophy. When rule of the empire passed to Yusuf's son, Yaq'ub al-Mansur, Averroës at first continued to hold positions of honor as either *qadi* (judge) or court physician in Seville and in Morocco. Al-Mansur, however, succumbed to the pressure of theological scholars and the reaction against philosophy. Averroës was stripped of his honors, banished from court, and imprisoned until a few years before his death in Marrakesh in 1198, when he was reinstated and his honors restored.

The Averroistic interpretation of Aristotle remained influential in western Europe long after his death. By the end of the 12th century, most of his works were available to the Christian world in Latin translation and he was widely known as "the Commentator." His admirer, the Franciscan philosopher Roger Bacon, recommended the study of Arabic at 13th-century Oxford so that students could read Averroës in the original. Emperor Frederick II welcomed Michael Scott, the first translator of Averroës into Latin, to his Sicilian court in defiance of the church, which was alarmed by Averroist thinking.

The dissemination of Aristotelian thought, accompanied by Averroës's commentaries emphasizing its nonreligious character, precipitated a grave crisis for the church. Averroism represented a challenge to religious authority, for it allowed philosophy to claim access to truth outside established religious sources. One of the central controversies of 13th-century thought concerned his theory of "double truth." Saint Thomas Aquinas, Italian philosopher and theologian and the greatest figure of Scholasticism, was respectful of Averroës but attacked the Averroist contention that philosophical truth is derived from reason and not from faith. While Aquinas vindicated the rights of reason against those who wished to suppress Aristotle's thought, he opposed the Averroist views that would separate faith and truth absolutely. He held that reason and faith constitute two harmonious realms and that reason gives a rational content to faith.

Thirteenth-century Scholastics concluded, from reading Averroës's commentary on Aristotle's *De Anima*, that Averroës rejected the reality of individual intellect, thus denying personal immortality. Averroës was led by his understanding of Aristotle to postulate that there is one intellect for all people, which is not a soul. The soul does not survive the death of the body and the world has not been created but is eternal.

In *De unitate intellectus contra Averroistas* Aquinas argued that if the Averroistic theory is accepted, "it follows that after death nothing remains of men's souls but one intellect; and in this way the bestowal of rewards and punishments is done away with." Averroistic theory was incompatible with Christian doctrines of immortality and of sanctions in the next life.

In 1210, bishops who were gathered at the Provincial Council of Paris forbade the public or private teaching of the natural philosophy and THE METAPHYSICS of Aristotle, or commentaries on them. The ban applied to instruction at the University of Paris, the most important center of higher education is Christendom, and was imposed under penalty of excommunication. The ban was reiterated by the papal legate, Robert de Curzon, in 1215. Averroës's commentaries were condemned as the "unholy gloss of infidels." In 1231, Pope Gregory IX prohibited the reading of the works of Aristotle until they were purged of heresy and appointed a commission of theologians to correct them. By 1245, the prohibition was extended to Toulouse by Innocent IV.

The interdictions were gradually lifted when they became impossible to enforce. It is recorded that Bacon lectured on Aristotle as a member of the arts faculty at Paris between 1241 and 1247. By 1255, all the known works of Aristotle and the commentaries on them were officially taught there. Though Averroist doctrines on "double truth," personal immortality, and eternity of matter were again condemned by the pope in 1263 and by the bishop of Paris in 1277, his interpretations of Aristotle remained influential throughout the later Middle Ages and the Renaissance.

FURTHER READING

Bokenkotter, Thomas. *A Concise History of the Catholic Church*. New York: Doubleday, 1977.

Copleston, Frederick. *A History of Philosophy*. Vol. 2: *Medieval Philosophy*. New York: Doubleday, 1993.

Hoffman, Eleanor. *Realm of the Evening Star: A History of Morocco and the Lands of the Moors*. Philadelphia: Chilton Books, 1965.

Landau, Rom. *Morocco*. New York: G. P. Putnam's Sons, 1967.

Urvoy, Dominique. *Ibn Rushd (Averroës)*. Translated by Olivia Steward. Cairo: American University of Cairo Press, 1993.

Wippel, John F., and Allan B. Wolter, eds. *Medieval Philosophy: From St. Augustine to Nicholas of Cusa*. New York: Free Press, 1969.

COMPENDIUM REVELATIONUM

Author: Girolamo Savonarola
Original date and place of publication: 1495, Italy
Literary form: Religious treatise

SUMMARY

Dominican monk and religious reformer Girolamo Savonarola, perhaps the best-known heretic of the Renaissance, made his mark as a charismatic preacher in Florence soon after he was sent there by the Dominican order in 1490. Calling for a regeneration of spiritual and moral values, he warned in his fiery sermons that a great scourge was about to descend on the city. He declared that the wickedness he observed in Florence—the corruption of the church, the excesses of the wealthy, and their exploitation of the poor—was proof that the message of the Apocalypse was soon to be fulfilled.

After the expulsion in 1494 of the Medicis, Florence's ruling family, Savonarola became the spiritual leader of the city and wielded great influence in the new government. Savonarola urged the Florentines who had ejected the Medici tyranny to establish a model government to regulate the moral and religious life of the city and help convert its citizens to the life of the spirit. He saw Florence as a new Zion, the center of a reform that would spread throughout Italy, all Christendom, and ultimately to the entire world.

Savonarola had earlier predicted that Charles VIII of France would invade Italy to wield the sword of God's wrath, and he warned Florentines to repent. When Charles VIII marched through Florence in 1494, Savonarola's prophecies were fulfilled, and his reputation in the city was enhanced. Savonarola and the city of Florence supported Charles's invasion, which was opposed by Pope Alexander VI in league with Milan, Venice, Spain, and Holy Roman Emperor Maximillian. Savonarola hoped that the advent of the French king would lead to the establishment of a democratic government in Florence and the reform of the corrupt and morally lax court of Pope Alexander VI, the ambitious Rodrigo Borgia, of whom Savonarola was an outspoken critic.

Savonarola's enemies sent reports of his preaching and prophecies to the pope. Alexander VI summoned Savonarola to Rome, writing that he had heard that Savonarola "dost assert that thy predictions proceed not from thee but from God." Savonarola asked to be excused from appearing at that time because he had been ill, and his absence from Florence would be detrimental to his reforms. He recommended, instead, that as the pope had expressed the desire to be more fully informed of Savonarola's predictions, he could refer to the *Compendium revelationum*, a new book Savonarola was printing, which would summarize his visions and prophecies. As God had confided in him in secrecy, he was not at liberty to reveal more than what he had written in his book.

In the *Compendium* that Savonarola sent to the pope, published in Latin and Italian in 1495, he explained that God had arranged for his superiors in the Dominican order to send him to Florence on a divine mission to begin the work of conversion that would lead to the reform of the church and of the world. "Almighty God, seeing that the sins of Italy continue to multiply, especially those of her princes, both ecclesiastical and secular, and unable to bear them any longer, decided to cleanse His church with a mighty scourge," he wrote. God wanted the impending scourge to be foretold by Savonarola so that Florence might prepare better to withstand it.

At first, Savonarola wrote, he did not reveal to the people that he had learned these things directly from God, "since it seemed to me that your minds were not ready for a revelation of mysteries." His predictions initially referred to information provided by the Scriptures alone. But later, when he concluded that the minds of the people were better prepared to believe, he began to reveal that he knew of these future events through divine inspiration.

Savonarola described a dramatic vision that came to him during Advent in 1492. A hand brandished a great sword of judgment, filling the air with dense clouds, hail, thunder, arrows, and fire, while wars, plagues, and famine arose upon the Earth. Savonarola explained that he was "compelled to write about my public prophecies, especially the more important ones, because many who have heard them from me in the pulpit have tried to describe them, but being inexpert writers in Latin they have butchered the truth or contaminated it with many errors. . . ."

He recounted some of his earlier predictions that had proven to be correct, such as the time of the deaths of Pope Alexander VI's predecessor, Pope Innocent VIII, and Lorenzo de' Medici, as well as Charles VIII's invasion of Italy and many others, "which, if I wished to recount them now would perhaps not be believed, since they were not generally made known at the time."

As Charles VIII approached Florence, Savonarola recalled, he had preached from the pulpit that these adversities had come to Italy because of its sins. Further, he predicted that Florence would be reformed to a better way of life and that the city would be "more glorious, richer, more powerful than ever before." He said that events had proven the divine will of God, as it was through Savonarola, speaking with divine authority, that the peace of the city had been restored and constitutional reforms adopted.

CENSORSHIP HISTORY

When Pope Alexander VI received his copy of the *Compendium revelationum*, he was already angered by Savonarola's role in mounting Florence's support for the French invasion. He was infuriated by Savonarola's claim in the *Compendium* that his illumination came directly from God and, no doubt, also by Savonarola's thinly veiled attack on the papacy in his references to God's punishment for the sins of "ecclesiastical princes."

The pope sent a brief to the Dominican friars of San Marco in Florence. "We are informed," it read, "that a certain Fra Hieronymo of Ferrara . . . has been led by the disturbed condition of affairs in Italy to such a pitch of folly as to declare that he has been sent by God and that he holds converse with him." The pope had hoped by "patient forbearance" to persuade the friar to acknowledge the folly of his prophecies. Instead Savonarola had written a book for "uninformed readers," in which he had written down the ideas that previously he was bold enough to disseminate only by word of mouth. The pope commended Savonarola's case to Fra Sebastiano Maggi, the vicar general of the Dominican order for the province of Lombardy. Pending examination by Maggi, Savonarola was forbidden to preach.

Savonarola sent a letter to the pope describing himself as "deeply grieved that the malice of men had gone to such lengths that certain people had not scruples to suggest to His Holiness a brief so full of false statements and perverse interpretations of his conduct and motives." He said that his enemies made it impossible for him to emerge from his monastery without taking extraordinary precautions, and that he trusted the Holy Father would not consider him disobedient if he prudently refrained for the moment from complying with the pope's wishes that he come to Rome.

If the pope demanded of him that something he had written should be retracted, he would do so, he wrote, as he submitted himself and all his writings to the correction of the Holy Roman Church. The pope agreed to suspend the investigation of Savonarola, on the condition that he cease preaching until it was possible for him to come to Rome.

During Lent of 1496, he was allowed to preach again. Later that year, the pope tried to bring him under more direct control by commanding that he unite the Dominican monastery of San Marco in Florence, of which Savonarola was prior, with the Tuscan Roman congregation that was more directly subject to the Vatican. Savonarola defied the pope's orders and the following Lent preached boldly against the evils of the church. On May 13, 1497, Savonarola was excommunicated by Alexander VI for having ignored the pope's first brief summoning him to Rome and for refusing to bring San Marco under Roman control.

In response to his excommunication, Savonarola published "Epistle against Surreptitious Excommunication" addressed to "all Christians and believers of God," in which he claimed that the pope's excommunication was based on false insinuations devised by his enemies and thus it had no value in the eyes of God or the church. He also published a letter citing church canon law experts to bolster his claim that he was not obliged to honor an unjust excommunication.

Savonarola continued preaching until the pope threatened Florence with an interdict unless the city silenced Savonarola and sent him to Rome to be tried. At the request of the leaders of the Florentine republic, he stopped preaching in March 1498. Savonarola called upon the sovereign powers of Europe to summon an ecumenical council, declaring that Alexander was neither a true Christian nor a true pope as he had committed the sin of simony by paying for his election to the office of the papacy.

In the meantime, Florentines began to grow weary of Savonarola's demands for asceticism. He had pressed for the passage of laws against "all those things which are pernicious to the soul's health," including gambling, drinking, and indecent dress in women. He organized bands of children to confiscate volumes of works by Ovid, Dante, and Boccaccio, as well as paintings, cards, dice, mirrors, makeup, and carnival masks, which were burned in gigantic bonfires of vanities erected in the Piazza della Signoria.

Hostility against him grew, led by members of the Franciscan religious order, who used the enmity of the pope and local officials to their advantage. Savonarola's downfall came in April 1498 when one of his disciples accepted the challenge of an ordeal by fire to prove Savonarola's holiness. When rain cancelled the event, there were riots and Savonarola and two of his followers were arrested and put on trial for heresy and schism.

Alexander VI sent judges from Rome with instructions to find Savonarola guilty. Under torture, Savonarola was said to have confessed that he was a false prophet who committed heresy in demanding church reforms and denouncing papal corruption. In May 1498, he was hanged and burned with all of his writings.

Fourteen years after his death, renewed circulation of Savonarola's writings led the vicar of the Florentine archdiocese to issue proclamations against unlicensed preaching and the persistent cultic veneration of Fra Girolamo. The authorities believed that the continuing influence of Savonarola's prophetic writings was the root cause of the ferment of apocalytic sects, preachers and tracts.

The Tridentine Index of Forbidden Books, issued by the Council of Trent in 1564 and effective in Belgium, Bavaria, Portugal, Italy, and France, listed the complete writings of Savonarola. A revised index in 1612 confirmed the banning of Savonarola's work in the most severe category of *opera omnia*, or all works condemned.

The 19th century saw a revival of interest in Savonarola and the growth of a cult of Savonarola followers who regarded him as a saint, a prophet, and a martyr. Calling themselves the New Piagnoni, after the friar's original followers, they gathered at the Dominican Convent of San Marco in Florence. Though Savonarola's writings were eventually eliminated from modern editions of the Roman Index of Forbidden Books, efforts to rehabilitate Savonarola's reputation within the Catholic Church and elevate him to sainthood were unsuccessful. Savonarola is remembered today more for his censorial bonfires of the vanities than for his martyrdom and the banning of his writings.

FURTHER READING

Burman, Edward. *The Inquisition: Hammer of Heresy.* New York: Dorset Press, 1992.
Christie-Murray, David. *A History of Heresy.* Oxford: Oxford University Press, 1976.
Erlanger, Rachel. *The Unarmed Prophet: Savonarola in Florence.* New York: McGraw-Hill, 1988.
George, Leonard. *Crimes of Perception: An Encyclopedia of Heresies and Heretics.* New York: Paragon House, 1995.
Weinstein, Donald. *Savonarola and Florence: Prophecy and Patriotism in the Renaissance.* Princeton, N.J.: Princeton University Press, 1970.

CONCERNING HERETICS

Author: Sebastian Castellio
Original date and place of publication: 1554, Switzerland
Literary form: Theological treatise

SUMMARY

French Protestant theologian Sebastian Castellio was Europe's first great defender of religious tolerance, and his book *Concerning Heretics, Whether They Are to Be Persecuted and How They Are to Be Treated (De haereticis)* was a landmark in the struggle against religious persecution.

In 1553, at the instigation of the Protestant leader John Calvin, the Spanish theologian Michael Servetus was burned at the stake in Geneva for his unorthodox views on the Trinity and the efficacy of infant baptism as expressed in his treatise CHRISTIANITY RESTORED. The execution of Servetus prompted Castellio to write the most important work of the century in support of religious toleration. Published in Latin and in French and German translations in 1554 under three different pseudonyms and with a false printer's name, *Concerning Heretics* courageously protested cruelty and persecution carried out by Christians in the name of religious doctrine.

The book consisted of two parts: a preface by Martin Bellius (a pseudonym for Castellio), addressed to a German prince, Christoph, duke of Württemburg, and an anthology of selections from the writing of the early church fathers and Protestant writers on the subject of toleration. The selections included writings by Erasmus, Martin Luther, Calvin, and Castellio himself, under his own name and the pseudonyms Basil Montfort and Georg Kleinberg.

In the book's preface, Castellio presented a parable illustrating that tolerance and mutual love are imperative to Christians. He asked the prince to imagine that he had instructed his subjects to prepare to meet him clad in white garments at some time in the future. When he returned, he found that instead of preparing their robes, they were disputing among themselves about his whereabouts and how he would reappear. What if then, Castellio asked the prince, the controversy degenerated into violence and one group killed those who disagreed with them? And what if those who killed others claimed to have done it in his name and in accord with his commands, even though he had previously expressly forbidden it?

"Although opinions are almost as numerous as men, nevertheless there is hardly any sect which does not condemn all others and desire to reign alone," Castellio continued. "I ask you, then, most Illustrious Prince, what do you think Christ will do when He comes? Will He commend such things? Will He approve of them?"

Castellio declared that he wrote to "stanch the blood" shed by those who are called heretics. After investigating the meaning of heresy, he concluded that heretics are those with whom one disagrees. Each sect views the others as heretical, "so that if you are orthodox in one city or region, you must be held for a heretic in the next." If one travels, one must change one's religion like one's money.

The points of religion on which Christians disagree and persecute one another are uncertain. "Were these matters obvious, that there is one God, all would agree." The wisest course is to condemn no one who believes in God, whatever their religion. Because people will never agree on religious matters, conduct alone should be punishable, never religious belief or worship. On such matters as the doctrine of the Trinity, "each may be left to his own opinion and revelation of the Savior." Religion resides "in the heart, which cannot be reached by the sword of kings and princes." Since faith cannot be compelled, coercion is futile.

In the book's concluding statement by Basil Montfort, Castellio stressed that neither Christ nor the apostles did violence to their enemies and that when religion is not left free, spiritual tyranny and error can flourish.

CENSORSHIP HISTORY

By the time Castellio wrote *Concerning Heretics* in 1554, Calvin already regarded him as an enemy. As a colleague of Calvin, in Geneva, Castellio became head teacher of the Collège de Rive and preached at nearby villages. When he split with Calvin over doctrinal differences, the Geneva magistrates censured him for misconduct. In 1545, he moved to the more tolerant city of Basel, where he worked as a corrector for the noted printer and publisher Johannes Oporinus and became a professor of Greek at the university. Castellio wrote epic poems in Greek and Latin and translated the Bible. The preface to his Latin Bible translation published in 1551 contained his first notable defense of religious toleration and an indictment of religious persecution by Christians. It was Castellio's first salvo in a long battle against Calvinist intolerance, which was galvanized by the execution of Servetus in 1553.

The Calvinists stepped up their harassment of Castellio after the publication of *Concerning Heretics*. Despite Castellio's use of pseudonyms, the Calvinists suspected that he was the author. Calvin and his followers condemned the work as an evil influence and Castellio as a blasphemer who deserved Servetus's fate. Calvin urged the Swiss synods to prohibit the book's circulation.

Later that year, Castellio wrote another tract in defense of his views, an anonymous satirical polemic attacking Calvin's ideas, titled *Against Calvin's Book*. Calvin was able to ensure, however, that no publisher would print it. It circulated only in manuscript form until 1612, when it was published for the first time in the Netherlands. "If Servetus had attacked you by arms, you had rightly been defended by the magistrate," Castellio wrote. "But since he opposed you in writings, why did you oppose them with sword and the fire?. . . Does your piety consist only in hurrying to the fire strangers passing peacefully through your city?"

Christ and his disciples died as heretics and seditious blasphemers, Castellio reminded his readers. "This ought to fill us with fear and trembling when it comes to persecuting a man for his faith and his religion." Servetus had fought with "reasons and writings" and should have been answered the same way, Castellio declared. Now that Servetus has been burned, everybody desires to read his books. "To kill a doctrine is not to protect a doctrine, but it is to kill a man. When the Genevans killed Servetus, they did not defend a doctrine, but they killed a man."

Calvin's disciple, Theodore Beza, wrote a refutation of *Concerning Heretics* in which he described toleration as a diabolical doctrine and its defenders as "emissaries of Satan." In 1555, Castellio responded to Beza with his third major treatise on toleration, *Concerning the Nonpunishment of Heretics*, written again under the pseudonym Basil Montfort. It offered a critique of the theoretical underpinnings of religious persecution, asserting that the killing of heretics was antithetical to Christianity and that heresy was a vice rather than a crime. The work circulated in manuscript copies but remained unprinted during the author's lifetime. It was not published in book form until 1971.

For the next decade, the Calvinists hounded Castellio as he continued to defend the principles of religious freedom. In 1557, Calvin and Beza had Castellio brought before the Basel City Council, but he was cleared of any wrongdoing. In 1563, they finally were able to bring Castellio to trial for religious unorthodoxy. However, he died in December of that year at age 48, while the proceedings were pending, At the time of his death, he had been considering immigrating to Poland, which offered a haven to victims of religious persecution.

In spite of Calvin's efforts to suppress *Concerning Heretics*, it was widely influential in Western Europe. It sparked the first great controversy within Protestantism over the issue of religious freedom and inspired other writers during the 16th and 17th centuries to argue in favor of freedom of conscience.

FURTHER READING

Castellio, Sebastian. *Concerning Heretics, Whether They Are to Be Persecuted and How They Are to Be Treated.* Translated and with an introduction by Roland H. Bainton. New York: Columbia University Press, 1935.
Christie-Murray, David. *A History of Heresy.* Oxford: Oxford University Press, 1989.
Levy, Leonard W. *Blasphemy: Verbal Offenses Against the Sacred, from Moses to Salman Rushdie.* New York: Alfred A. Knopf, 1993.
Smith, George H. *Atheism, Ayn Rand, and Other Heresies.* Buffalo, N.Y.: Prometheus Books, 1991.
Spitz, Lewis W., ed. *The Protestant Reformation.* Englewood Cliffs, N.J.: Prentice Hall, 1966.
Zagorin, Perez. *How the Idea of Religious Toleration Came to the West.* Princeton, N.J.: Princeton University Press, 2003.

THE COURSE OF POSITIVE PHILOSOPHY

Author: Auguste Comte
Original dates and places of publication: 1830–42, France; 1855, United States
Literary form: Philosophical text

SUMMARY

The French philosopher Auguste Comte was the founder of the school of philosophy known as positivism. *The Course of Positive Philosophy*, Comte's main contribution to intellectual history, began as a series of public lectures and was published in six volumes between 1830 and 1842.

In *The Course*, Comte systematized all of science based on two general laws: the Law of the Three States and the Classification of the Sciences. The Law of the Three States, scientifically derived from Comte's observations of patterns of human intellectual development, consists of three progressive stages: the theological, metaphysical, and positive states. In the theological state, events are explained by spiritual forces; in the metaphysical state, natural phenomena are considered to be the result of fundamental energies or ideas; and in the positive state, phenomena are explained by observation, hypotheses, and experimentation.

Comte believed that the science of society had already passed through the first two states and was about to enter the third, definitive state based on positive philosophy. The educational system should be structured along the lines of these stages of intellectual development, and *The Course* would provide the text.

In *The Course*, Comte proposed that the natural hierarchy of the sciences provides a useful classification system. He ranked the sciences according to their complexity. Mathematics was the first science and the basis of natural science, followed by astronomy, physics, chemistry, biology, and, finally, social physics, or *sociology*, a term that Comte originated. Because each science depends in part on the science preceding it, all the sciences contribute to sociology. The new science of sociology would be created by extending scientific methodology to social phenomena.

Comte believed that the moral and political anarchy he observed in his society was caused by intellectual confusion resulting from the outmoded remnants of theological and metaphysical thinking. The first step toward the achievement of social unity was the creation of a unified set of beliefs. Comte's systemization of the sciences and the application of the scientific method to society would supply the intellectual basis of such unity. In Comte's view, only positivism could provide a firm foundation for belief and action. As a science-based philosophy, it was accessible to all reasonable people who assess facts positively, or scientifically, and who respect scientific observation and natural law.

The Course of Positive Philosophy represented Comte's first major step in his program for the reorganization of society. In other works—the four-volume *System of Positive Polity* (1851–54), the *Positivist Catechism* (1852), and the *Subjective Synthesis* (1856)—he presented positivism as a religion, the Universal Church of the Religion of Humanity. In Comte's religion, the Great Being of Humanity was the object of worship. This religion without metaphysics had its own catechism, sacraments, priesthood, and rituals, modeled on those of the Catholic Church, but without God. As the writer T. H. Huxley said, it was "Catholicism minus Christianity."

CENSORSHIP HISTORY

In France the publication of the six-volume *Course of Positive Philosophy* during the years 1830 to 1842 elicited little critical attention. However, in the preface to volume six, published in 1842, Comte wrote a vituperative attack on the "establishment" of the École Polytechnique in Paris, where he was admissions examiner. From that time on, Comte's reappointment was uncertain and in 1844 his position was not renewed. In 1851, he lost the position of assistant lecturer that he had held since 1832.

What Comte described as persecutions were partly a result of the resistance of the intellectual establishment to his ideas. His contemporaries reported, however, that he was an exceedingly difficult person (particularly during the times when he struggled with mental illness), that he did not properly fulfill his academic duties, and that he brought many of his troubles on himself.

It was not until the end of 1844, when the eminent academic and journalist Émile Littré published six articles about Comtean philosophy, that his positivist ideas began to be widely disseminated in France. Comte's thought influenced the work of his contemporary, the English philosopher John Stuart Mill, and such writers as Edward Bellamy, George Bernard Shaw, and George Eliot.

In 1869, the Catholic Church placed the third edition of *The Course of Positive Philosophy* (with a preface by Littré) on the Index of Forbidden Books. It was still prohibited when the last Index was compiled in 1948. Because Comte's positivist philosophy viewed Catholicism as retrograde, excluded metaphysics and revealed religion, and substituted a new religion of humanity and sociological ethics, it was not surprising that the church found it offensive.

The Course of Positive Philosophy, however, was the only work of Comte's to be placed on the Index, though in several later works Comte framed in more detail his plans for a new positivist religion that adapted and parodied many Catholic rituals. Ironically, Comte believed that the church's attempts to impose unity by insisting on absolute faith and repressing dissent were not only necessary, but a real advance. The organization of the church impressed him with its effectiveness in providing unifying beliefs, education and worship for its vast community. Mirroring the church's efforts to censor books that challenged its doctrine, Comte himself in *The System of Positive Polity* proposed "the systematic destructions of the accumulations which now compress or misdirect thought." He drew up a list of 150 books he felt deserved to survive as part of the "Positivist Library" and suggested that all others be destroyed.

FURTHER READING

Putnam, George Haven. *The Censorship of the Church of Rome.* Vol. 2. New York: G. P. Putnam's Sons, 1906–07.

Standley, Arline Reilein. *Auguste Comte.* Boston: Twayne Publishers, 1981.

CREATIVE EVOLUTION

Author: Henri Bergson
Original date and place of publication: 1907, France
Literary form: Philosophical treatise

SUMMARY

The publication in 1907 of *Creative Evolution* estblished the worldwide reputation of the French philosopher Henri Bergson as one of the most influential thinkers of his time. In *Creative Evolution* he sought to reconcile Charles
Darwin's theory of evolution with his own beliefs about the nature of the
universe. He held that matter is propelled by an internal élan vital, or life
force, the eternally creative source of being that permeates the universe and
guides the evolutionary process.

The élan vital is present in all species and organisms and works uncon-
sciously with internal purposefulness to produce progressively higher variations of instinct and intelligence. "The more we focus our attention on the
continuity of life," Bergson explained, "the more we see how organic evolution comes closer to the evolution of consciousness where the past presses
the present to give birth to a new form which is incommensurable with its
antecedents." Bergson believed that this process could only be explained as
the work of divine energy. It is through intuition that we are able to discern
the divine impulse in evolution.

Bergson rejected both materialist and mechanistic accounts of reality,
along with theories that propose that an individual goal or purpose controls
the functioning of each organism. Speaking of the élan vital as God, he
wrote: "Thus defined, God has nothing of the ready-made, he is uninterrupted life, action, freedom. And the creation, so conceived, is not a mystery:
we experience it in ourselves when we act freely." For Bergson, God is not
a thing or a substance but creativity itself. God is timeless, living in the
eternal present.

Bergson's dynamic vision of the universe was regarded as a bold attempt
to reconcile the theory of evolution with Christian traditions of creation.
Creative Evolution offered a system of thought that mediated between rigid
scientific determinism and a Christian worldview. Recent scientific discoveries, Bergson believed, did not conflict with the concept of the immateriality
of consciousness and the idea of God's presence in the universe.

CENSORSHIP HISTORY

Bergson was the target of many attacks after the publication of *Creative
Evolution*. Rationalists viewed his philosophy as opposing analytical reason
and attempting to replace the scientific method with quasi-mystical insights.
Catholic theologians, who saw him as allied to the pernicious movement

of modernism, took issue with what they described as his pantheism and anti-intellectualism.

The influential French Catholic philosopher Jacques Maritain led the critical opposition to Bergson. In his 1913 anti-Bergsonian work, *La philosophie bergsonienne*, he asserted that Bergson's thinking was incompatible with Christian belief, as Bergson regarded faith as purely an inner experience, rather than an assent to revealed truth.

"The Bergsonian doctrine leads imperceptibly and infallibly to a view of dogmas as transitory," Maritain wrote. "If there is no eternal truth and if axioms evolve, why should dogmas not evolve as well?" Bergson promoted the destruction of both faith and reason, Maritain believed. Bergson denied that God could be understood through intellectual efforts and also challenged the concepts of divine creation, free will and the substantial unity of the human soul. His ideas could not be reconciled with the Catholic concepts of the Eucharist or revelation.

Bergson's thought was seen as being in sympathy with a modernist movement among Catholic intellectuals that questioned the church's system of authority and emphasized the importance of personal religious experience. Modernists argued that revelation is transmitted through enlightenment of the individual consciousness by God, rather than by sacred texts. They saw the church's dogmas as provisional and changeable, affected by historical circumstances.

The campaign against modernist heresy was a primary preoccupation of the church of the time. In 1907, the Vatican's Holy Office condemned 65 erroneous statements by modernists. This pronouncement was confirmed the same year in Pope Pius X's encyclical, *Pascendi*, in which he called for disciplinary measures to stamp out what he termed "the synthesis of all heresies." Catholic scholars who held modernist views were excommunicated, and all Catholic priests were required to take an antimodernist oath. This practice remained in force until the mid-1960s, when it was ended by the reforms of the Second Vatican Council.

In 1914, the Catholic Church placed *Creative Evolution* on the Index of Forbidden Books, where it remained through the last edition, published until 1966. Bergson was elected in 1914 to the prestigious French Academy, and in 1927, he received the Nobel Prize in literature. Despite church opposition, Bergson was regarded as the chief intellectual spokesman of his era. His philosophy continued to be read and admired, exercising an important influence on European thinkers before World War II.

Ironically, though his work was condemned by the church, he moved closer to the Catholic faith in his personal beliefs. He had not intended to undermine Catholicism, as it was his conviction that philosophical illumination could in the end only purify and enhance any religious doctrine. In 1937, in his last will and testament, Bergson, whose father was Jewish, stated that he had wished to be baptized as a Catholic, but noting the growth of anti-Semitism preferred to remain among the ranks of the persecuted. On

January 3, 1941, he died of pneumonia in occupied Paris after standing in line for many hours to be registered as a Jew.

FURTHER READING

Collison, Diané. *Fifty Major Philosophers: A Reference Guide*. London: Routledge, 1988.
Kolakowski, Leszek. *Bergson*. Oxford: Oxford University Press, 1985.

THE CRITIQUE OF PURE REASON

Author: Immanuel Kant
Original date and place of publication: 1781, Prussia
Literary form: Philosophical treatise

SUMMARY

Kant's most important work, *The Critique of Pure Reason*, marked the birth of the critical philosophy known as transcendental idealism. It is regarded as one of the most difficult and controversial works in philosophy. To make the ideas of the *Critique* more accessible, Kant wrote a shorter work, *Prolegomena to Any Future Metaphysics*, published in 1783, which is often read in place of the longer, more demanding *Critique*.

Kant recognized the validity of the empiricist claim that sense experience is the source of belief but could not accept its skeptical conclusion that those beliefs cannot be justified. "Although all our knowledge begins with experience," he declared, "it does not follow that it arises from experience."

The rationalists, beginning with René Descartes, posited that systematic knowledge can be derived from reason and that sense perception is a secondary, less certain source of knowledge. The opposing movement of British empiricism began with John Locke's refutation of Plato's doctrine of innate ideas and led finally to the skepticism of David Hume, who denied the possibility of any valid knowledge. In the *Critique*, Kant identifies the merits and defects of both approaches to thought and offers an alternative approach mediating between the two. He criticizes rationalistic claims that reason can know what is beyond sense experience, but defends the possibilities of knowledge from the skepticism of Hume.

Kant's concern in the *Critique* is to discover the extent of a priori knowledge, that is, knowledge that is necessary and independent of experience. The first step in this process is to distinguish between ultimate realities, things in themselves, and phenomena, things as they appear to human minds. Kant finds that metaphysical knowledge—knowledge of such matters as the existence of God, free will, and the immortal soul—cannot be attained through speculative thought. Things lying beyond the realm of experience are unknowable. Their existence is, nevertheless, a necessary proposition, which Kant demonstrates through his moral philosophy. Kant's conception of the "categorical imperative" convinces him by practical reasoning of man's moral nature, freedom, and immortality.

Kant calls his basic insight into the nature of knowledge "the Copernican revolution in philosophy." Nicolaus Copernicus reversed the commonly accepted theory of planetary revolution by removing the Earth from the center of creation. By proposing the theory that objects conform to the mind, rather than assuming that ideas must conform to an external independent reality, Kant removes sense experience from the center and makes it peripheral. Objective reality is known only as it conforms to the structure of the mind. "All objects of any experience possible to us," he writes in the *Critique*, "are nothing but appearances, that is, mere representations which . . . have no independent existence outside our thoughts."

CENSORSHIP HISTORY

Kant's work influenced almost every area of philosophy. *The Critique of Pure Reason* was immediately recognized as a work of major importance, but it was not well understood when it first appeared. Because of Kant's cumbersome and technical style, it proved difficult to translate from German, and its influence spread slowly. Because Kant was a prominent author who enjoyed the confidence of the king, and the *Critique* was not intended for and not likely to be read and understood by the general reader, it was spared the censorship that affected Kant's RELIGION WITHIN THE LIMITS OF REASON ALONE, published in 1793, 12 years after the appearance of the *Critique*.

In October 1794, the Prussian king Frederick William II wrote a personal letter to Kant accusing Kant of having "misused" his philosophy over a long period of time and of "the destruction and debasing of many principal and basic teachings of the Holy Scripture of Christianity." He warned Kant not to write or publish any similar works on religion, or "otherwise you can unfailingly expect, on continued recalcitrance, unpleasant consequences." *Religion within the Limits of Reason Alone* was banned by the Lutheran Church in Prussia.

Kant promised "to refrain entirely in the future from all public discourse concerning religion, natural or revealed, in lectures and in writing alike," and published no further philosophical writing until after the king's death.

The Critique of Pure Reason came to the attention of the Catholic Church in 1827, when an Italian translation was published. Kant's contention that the existence of God can be neither confirmed nor denied through the use of reason caused the book to be placed in the Roman Index of Forbidden Books, where it remained through the last edition, compiled in 1948 and in effect until 1966.

In 1928, *The Critique of Pure Reason*, along with all of Kant's writing, was also prohibited in the Soviet Union, presumably because the metaphysical and transcendental themes of Kant's works were thought to conflict with Marxist-Leninist ideology. All of the works of "such disgraceful writers" as

Kant and Johann Wolfgang von Goethe were also purged from the libraries of Spain under the Franco dictatorship in 1939.

FURTHER READING

Appelbaum, David. *The Vision of Kant.* Rockport, Mass.: Element Books, 1995.

Cassirer, Ernst. *Kant's Life and Thought.* Translated by James Hader. Introduction by Stephan Korner. New Haven, Conn.: Yale University Press, 1981.

Collinson, Diané. *Fifty Major Philosophers: A Reference Guide.* London: Routledge, 1988.

Copleston, Frederick. *A History of Philosophy.* Vol. 6: *Modern Philosophy: From the French Enlightenment to Kant.* New York: Doubleday, 1994.

Green, Jonathon. *The Encyclopedia of Censorship.* New York: Facts On File, 1990.

Kant, Immanuel. *The Philosophy of Kant: Immanuel Kant's Moral and Political Writings.* Ed. and introduction by Carl J. Friedrich. New York: Modern Library, 1993.

——. *The Critique of Pure Reason.* Translated by N. Kemp Smith. New York: St. Martin's Press, 1965.

Popkin, Richard, and Avrum Stroll. *Philosophy Made Simple.* New York: Doubleday, 1993.

Wolff, Robert Paul, ed. *Ten Great Works of Philosophy.* New York: New American Library, 1969.

THE DA VINCI CODE

Author: Dan Brown
Original date and place of publication: 2003, United States
Original publisher: Doubleday
Literary form: Novel

SUMMARY

Few works of popular fiction have captured the imagination of the reading public and stirred as much controversy as the historical thriller *The Da Vinci Code* and its revelation of the secret of the Holy Grail—that Jesus Christ was a mortal man who married Mary Magdalene and sired a bloodline that has endured to this day.

The story begins at the Louvre, where an albino monk named Silas has assassinated Louvre curator Jacques Saunière, who is a Grand Master for the Priory of Sion. The Priory of Sion was founded in 1099 to conceal the Holy Grail relics and protect them from those who would destroy them, most notably the Roman Catholic Church, which views the Grail and its story as a threat to its power. Silas is the ward of Bishop Aringarosa, head of Opus Dei, a conservative Catholic Church organization. Before killing Saunière, Silas forces him to reveal the location of the keystone to the Grail. Aringarosa covets those remains, to ensure and augment Opus Dei's own power. Before Saunière's murder, a figure known only as "the Teacher" had approached

Aringarosa about having the Vatican finance his efforts to attain the Grail, and Aringarosa agreed, putting Silas at the service of the Teacher.

The book's hero enters the narrative here. Robert Langdon, Harvard professor of religious symbology, is in Paris to deliver a lecture and to meet with Saunière at a reception afterward, but Saunière does not show up. Langdon is summoned by the Judicial Police (the French equivalent of the FBI) for questioning and for help in deciphering the bizarre clues Saunière left in his remaining minutes alive. Langdon and Captain Bezu Fache, head investigator of the crime, enter the Louvre's Grand Gallery, where the corpse lies. Saunière is naked on the floor, arms and legs spread-eagle, with a pentacle (a five-pointed star) drawn on his abdomen with the blood of his fatal wound. Fache calls Langdon's attention to a marker in Saunière's hand and uses black-light illumination on the area around the corpse to reveal a series of numbers, two odd phrases, and a circle in which Saunière positioned his dying body, which Langdon at once recognizes as a replica of Leonardo da Vinci's "Vitruvian Man," a symbol of male and female harmony.

At this moment, police cryptographer Sophie Neveu, Jacques Saunière's estranged granddaughter, arrives at the murder scene. She quickly gains Langdon's trust and, together, while Fache absents himself for a moment, they solve these three lines of riddles, which lead them to a key with the Priory's fleur-de-lis symbol and the letters "PS" written on it, along with an address on note paper. Sophie then reveals to Langdon that a tracking device was planted in his coat pocket and that Fache had erased a fourth line of the clue before Langdon arrived on the scene: "PS: Find Robert Langdon." Langdon removes the device, tossing it out a window onto a truck waiting below at a traffic light.

Fache, led to believe Langdon has escaped, has his agents give chase to the truck, orders arrest warrants for Langdon and Sophie, and releases their names and pictures to the media. Langdon and Sophie, meanwhile, flee the museum and locate the address given with the key, which turns out to be that of the Paris branch of the Depository Bank of Zurich. A watchman admits Langdon and Sophie to the bank, where they are confronted by bank president André Vernet, a friend of Jacques Saunière. He is suspicious, but allows them to access Saunière's deposit box, gained by a code composed of the numbers found near Saunière's body. The deposit box contains a rosewood box with a rose inlay on the lid; inside the box is a large cryptex, a cylinder invented by Leonardo himself, which works like a combination lock, for transporting messages securely. Inside the cryptex is a message written on papyrus. If the cryptex is opened incorrectly, a vial of vinegar breaks and dissolves the message. Under the lid inlay is a paper bearing a riddle giving clues to the cryptex's combination.

Vernet returns, having heard the news bulletin of Saunière's murder and the fugitive status of Langdon and Sophie, but he is coerced into helping them escape. Langdon and Sophie hide in a bank transfer truck while Vernet drives through the waiting line of police outside the bank's garage. The truck is let past, but a suspicious agent informs Fache, and the chase resumes. Meanwhile, Silas goes to the Church of Saint-Sulpice, where Saunière has told him to look for the keystone to the Grail, and is admitted by a nun. But Saunière had lied in order to defend the Grail's secret, and Silas realizes he has been tricked. The nun reveals herself to be in league with the Priory, and Silas kills her. Confused, he calls the Teacher to relate what has transpired and awaits further instructions.

Langdon and Sophie ditch Vernet, who calls bank security to activate the truck's homing device, as Langdon and Sophie head for the chateau of Sir Leigh Teabing, Langdon's friend and fellow Grail expert. Grudgingly admitted by Rémy, Teabing's surly manservant, Langdon and Sophie meet with Teabing, who enlightens Sophie on the true nature of the Grail. It is the womb of Mary Magdalene herself, who was of royal descent (the House of Benjamin) and married to Jesus (the House of David). At the time of the Crucifixion, Mary Magdalene was pregnant and fled to Gaul, where she gave birth to a daughter, Sarah, thus establishing the sacred bloodline that was to become the Merovingian dynasty of France. The Priory and the Knights Templar were established to protect the secret and to hide the Grail relics, including the bones of Mary Magdalene.

Silas now breaks into the house, looking for the keystone. He is subdued and taken with Langdon, Sophie, Teabing, and Rémy, as they flee from the police, who have tracked the bank transport truck to Teabing's chateau. They go to a nearby airfield, where they are able to flee for England on Teabing's private jet. In the interim, Bishop Aringarosa has learned of Silas's murderous rampage. Aringarosa realizes that his plan to obtain the Grail has collapsed and suspects that the Teacher may be double-crossing him. Filled with remorse for his arrogance, Aringarosa contacts Fache to confess.

Police at Teabing's villa discover an enormous surveillance setup with bugs in Saunière's office and at the homes of other Priory members. When it is determined that Teabing's jet is bound for England, Fache contacts the English authorities to hold the escapees until he can arrive there himself. He also establishes contact with Aringarosa, hears his confession, and has him travel to England, where he is to wait for Fache at the London headquarters of Opus Dei.

Sophie's estrangement from her grandfather is alluded to throughout the narrative, and now she reveals her story to Langdon: Paying a surprise visit to her grandfather at his country home, Sophie had let herself in and followed strange chanting sounds to a lower-level room. There she found a group of men wearing black tunics and shoes and women wearing white gossamer gowns and golden shoes, holding golden orbs, and all wearing androgynous masks. In their midst, engaged in the sex act, was her grandfather and a large woman with long gray hair. Horrified, Sophie fled and broke contact with her grandfather. Langdon explains to her that what she had witnessed was a pagan sex ritual known as Hieros Gamos, or "sacred marriage," which constituted a spiritual act of worship.

As Langdon and the others are en route to England, he solves the riddle that allows the large cryptex to be safely opened. Inside is a smaller cryptex with another riddle, which speaks of ". . . a knight a Pope interred." On landing in England, the group evades the waiting police and, on a hunch, goes to Temple Church, built by the Knights Templar themselves. They do not find the tomb they are looking for. At the church, Rémy pretends to kidnap Teabing, leaving Langdon and Sophie shaken but able to continue searching for the knight's tomb. Once they have gone, Rémy and Teabing remove Silas's binds, telling him to wait at Opus Dei's London office, while Teabing informs the police anonymously that Silas is hiding there. He then kills Rémy. Teabing is himself the Teacher, who, with information gained by his surveillance, had dispatched Silas on his murderous errands. Teabing had played on Opus Dei's desire to obtain the Grail, never intending to let them have it, and Rémy had been his collaborator. Teabing felt that the Priory had broken its own vow to reveal the secret of the Grail at the so-called End of Days and had vaingloriously taken it upon himself to do so.

Once the riddle is solved, revealing Isaac Newton as the "knight" eulogized by Alexander Pope ("a pope"), Langdon, Sophie, and Teabing meet at Westminster Abbey before Newton's tomb, where Teabing fully reveals his plan. Langdon secretly opens the second cryptex and removes the contents, before smashing it in front of Teabing. Teabing is arrested. He begs to know the answer to the final riddle, but Langdon lets him be led away.

Meanwhile, Silas tries to flee the police and, in the confusion, accidentally shoots Aringarosa. Wounded in the confrontation, Silas escapes but is later found dead in Kensington Gardens. With Silas dead, Teabing in custody, and Aringarosa in the hospital, all that remains is the solving of the final riddle:

> The Holy Grail 'neath ancient Roslin waits.
> The blade and the chalice guarding o'er her gates.
> Adorned in masters' loving art, She lies.
> She rests at last beneath starry skies.

Langdon and Sophie go to Rosslyn Chapel and see a Star of David on the chapel floor (the interlocking blade and chalice triangles). However, Sophie discovers that a young docent at the chapel is her long-lost brother, and the guardian of the chapel is none other than Marie Chauvel Saint-Clair, of the Merovingian line, wife of Jacques Saunière, Sophie's grandmother, and the unrecognized participant in the sex rite that Sophie had witnessed. Sophie is a descendant of Jesus Christ and Mary Magdalene, and the Priory hid her identity to protect her life after suspected Opus Dei operatives had killed her parents. Marie assures Langdon that the Grail is no longer at the chapel, and he and Sophie part company.

Back in Paris, Langdon remembers the final riddle and, on a hunch, heads for the Louvre, following the ancient "Rose Line" (the original prime meridian) to the museum's inverted pyramid (the Chalice) and the small upright pyramid (the blade) below it. Looking up at the starlit night, he realizes that the Grail is buried under these pyramids. Langdon sinks to his knees, as much in amazement as in adoration.

CENSORSHIP HISTORY

The Da Vinci Code quickly became an international blockbuster. By 2009, it had sold some 80 million copies and been translated into 44 languages. It soon also became a target of protest. While some authors and critics disparaged the book for its dubious literary value and inaccurate historical information, and Catholic sources denounced it as a dishonest attack on the church, others objected to what they referred to as the blasphemous nature of the book's subject matter. Both evangelical Protestants and Catholics circulated rebuttals, ranging from church-issued pamphlets and study guides to books such as Rev. Erwin W. Lutzer's *The Da Vinci Deception* and Rev. James L. Garlow's and Peter Jones's *Cracking the Da Vinci Code*. These writings sought to refute the book for fostering, in Garlow's words, "an incorrect and historically inaccurate view . . . people are buying into the notion that Jesus is not divine . . . is not the son of God."

Even though Christians were in the forefront of protests against the book, it was banned primarily in predominantly Muslim countries. The first country to ban it was Lebanon, for fear of reviving the sectarian tensions between Christians and Muslims that lay at the heart of Lebanon's 15-year war (1975–90). The government's national security agency issued the ban after protests by the Catholic Information Center. Lebanese who wanted to read the book, however, were able to download it on the Internet or buy black-market copies. In 2006, Iran, after allowing the publication of eight previous editions of the book, banned any further editions at the request of Christian clergy.

Further bans came in the wake of the new international attention brought to the book by the release of a film adaptation in 2006. The predominantly Christian, northeastern Indian state of Nagaland banned both the film and the book in May 2006, declaring them blasphemous, offensive, and a direct assault on the Christian faith. Following Nagaland's lead in June 2006 and after protests by local Christian leaders, the Indian states of Goa, Punjab, Tamil Nadu, and Andhra Pradesh also banned both the film and the book. India's national government did not ban either. (Indian censors cleared the film after its makers agreed to insert a legal disclaimer saying "it was of a fictitious nature.")

Later that month, after protests by members of Pakistan's small Christian community, Pakistan banned the film as blasphemous and also announced intentions to ban the book, which had been available there for some time. The country's cultural affairs minister, Ghazi Gulab Jamal, said that the decision had been made because the *Code* contravenes Islamic teachings. "Islam teaches us to respect all the prophets of Allah Almighty, and degradation of any prophet is tantamount to defamation of the rest," he said.

Also in 2006, Egypt's Ministry of Culture banned both the film and the Arabic- and English-language editions of the novel, which had been sold in the country since 2003. The police also confiscated 2,000 copies of a pirated DVD of the film and arrested the owner of a local production company.

—Philip Milito

FURTHER READING

Bhaumik, Subir. "India State in Total *Da Vinci* Ban." BBC News (May 23, 2006). Available online. URL: http://news.bbc.co.uk/go/pr/fr/2/hi/south___asia/5009778.stm. Accessed July 8, 2009.

"Da Vinci Code Ban in India State." BBC News (June 1, 2006). Available online. URL: http://news.bbc.co.uk/go/pr/fr/-/2/hi/south___asia/5036094.stm. Accessed July 8, 2009.

"Da Vinci Code Book Banned in Iran" BBC News (July 26, 2006). Available online. URL: http://news.bbc.co.uk/go/pr/fr/-/2/hi/entertainment/5216490.stm. Accessed July 27, 2009.

Faroaq, Umer. "Pakistan Bans *Da Vinci Code*, Christians Happy." Islam Online (June 5, 2006). Available online. URL: http://www.islamonline.net/servlet/Satellite?c=Article__C&cid=1162385911282&pagename. Accessed July 8, 2009.

Garlow, James L., and Peter Jones. *Cracking Da Vinci's Code*. Wheaton, Ill.: Victor Books, 2004.

Goodstein, Laurie. "Defenders of Christianity Rebut *The Da Vinci Code*." *New York Times*, April 27, 2004, A22.

Hiel, Betsy. " 'Da Vinci' Unlikely to Pass Egypt Censors." *Pittsburgh Tribune-Review* (May 14, 2006). Available online. URL: http://www.pittsburghlive.com/x/pittsburghtrib/mostread/s_453828.html. Accessed August 25, 2009.

"Iran Bans *Da Vinci Code* Book after 8 Editions." Christians of Iraq (July 26, 2006). Available online. URL: http://www.christiansofiraq.com/irandavinci.html. Accessed July 8, 2009.

Lutzer, Erwin W. *The Da Vinci Conspiracy*. Carol Stream, Ill.: Tyndale House, 2004.

"Pakistan Bans *Da Vinci Code* Film." BBC News (June 4, 2006). Available online. URL: http://news.bbc.co.uk/go/pr/fr/-/2/hi/south___asia/5045672.stm. Accessed July 8, 2009.

"Punjab Ban for *Da Vinci Code* Film." BBC News (May 25, 2006). Available online. URL: http://news.bbc.co.uk/go/pr/fr/-/2/hi/south___asia/5017498.stm. Accessed July 8, 2009.

Wilson, Scott. "Fearing Repeat of the Past, Lebanon Bans a Book." *Washington Post* (October 17, 2004). Available online. URL: http://www.washingtonpost.com/wp-dyn/articles/A38753-2004Oct16.html. Accessed June 4, 2009.

DE ECCLESIA

Author: Jan Hus
Original date and place of publication: 1413, Bohemia
Literary form: Theological treatise

SUMMARY

The Czech religious reformer Jan Hus, a Catholic priest and theologian, was a forerunner of the Protestant Reformation. He was influenced by the views of English heretic John Wycliffe and became the leading exponent of Wycliffe's teaching in Bohemia. In his sermons in Prague's Bethlehem Chapel, Hus attacked the worldliness and corruption of the Catholic clergy and advocated the purification of the church and a return to the simplicity of its origins. He opposed the condemnation in 1403 of Wycliffe's doctrines by the University of Prague and translated Wycliffe's writing into Czech.

A formal complaint against Hus was brought to the archbishop of Prague and, with the support of the pope, he was deprived of his position as preacher in Bethlehem Chapel. In 1410, the archbishop ordered the burning of Wycliffe's ON CIVIL LORDSHIP and the following year excommunicated Hus and his followers. Hus left Prague in 1412 but continued preaching his opposition to the sale of indulgences and asserting the primacy of Scripture as the chief authority on doctrinal questions.

During two years of exile from Prague, he wrote his chief works, including his treatise De ecclesia, in which he denied the infallibility of the pope and proposed that the state had the right and duty to supervise the church. He allowed for private interpretation of the Bible and declared that it was correct to resist church authority on matters of conscience. In contradiction to Catholic theology, he advocated more frequent communion, claimed that the efficacy of the sacraments depended on the worthiness of the minister, and declared that only the predestined elect, not sinners, belonged to the true church. De ecclesia was publicly read in Bethlehem Chapel upon Hus's return to Prague on July 8, 1413.

CENSORSHIP HISTORY

In 1414, the church convened the Council of Constance in Germany at the request of the Holy Roman Emperor Sigismund. The aim of the four-year-long council was to reform Christian life, extirpate heresy, and resolve a schism in the church in which three men—Gregory XII (since recognized as canonical pope), John XXIII, and Benedict XIII—all claimed to be the true pope. The council was organized as a convention of the nations of Germany, Italy, France, England, and, later, Spain, with each nation having one vote.

Emperor Sigismund, anxious to bring the unrest caused by Hus's preaching to a swift end, invited Hus to justify his views before the council, promising him a safe conduct and suspension of his excommunication if he would appear to present his case. Upon Hus's arrival in Constance, however, on the principle that faith cannot be kept with heretics, his safe conduct was ignored, and he and his follower Jerome of Prague were arrested and put on trial.

The council had already condemned Wycliffe as a heresiarch, or arch-heretic, and ordered his bones exhumed and burned and his ashes thrown into a running stream. Hus was charged with 42 errors extracted from his own writing, among them the charge that *De ecclesia* reflected Wycliffe's views. Hus denied that he accepted all of Wycliffe's teachings but refused to disavow the extracts from his own works that the council claimed were heretical. He maintained that the Scriptures were the only test of doctrine and that he would submit to the judgment of the council only if it did not offend God or his conscience.

The council condemned Hus for both his written errors and those recounted by witnesses and declared him an incorrigible heretic who did not desire to return to the church. It ordered his books burned and his removal from the priesthood. With Jerome of Prague, Hus was sentenced to be executed for heresy. Seven bishops warned him to recant, but Hus declared that he was unable to confess to errors he had not committed, lest he should lie to God. On July 6, 1415, he was burned at the stake, and his ashes were thrown into the Rhine.

Hus became a Czech national hero. He was declared a martyr by the University of Prague and the day of his execution was inserted into the calendar of saints. In 1418, a papal bull condemned the followers of the "arch-heretics" Wycliffe, Hus, and Jerome of Prague, declaring that they "cease not to blaspheme the Lord God" and that their "heretical pravity" must be extirpated. Hus's writings and those of other pre-Reformation heretics were included in the Index librorum prohibitorum of 1559, the first Index of Forbidden Books compiled by the church. Over the centuries, Hus became a central symbol of the Czech nation and his proclamation "Truth prevails" has been adopted as a slogan by every popular Czech revolutionary movement since that time.

FURTHER READING

Burman, Edward. *The Inquisition: Hammer of Heresy.* New York: Dorset Press, 1992.

Christie-Murray, David. *A History of Heresy.* Oxford: Oxford University Press, 1989.

George, Leonard. *Crimes of Perception: An Encyclopedia of Heresies and Heretics.* New York: Paragon House, 1995.

Haight, Anne Lyon. *Banned Books: 387 BC to 1978 AD.* Updated and enlarged by Chandler B. Grannis. New York: R. R. Bowker, 1978.

Lea, Henry Charles. *History of the Inquisition of the Middle Ages.* Vol. 2. New York: Russell and Russell, 1955.

Levy, Leonard W. *Blasphemy: Verbal Offense against the Sacred, from Moses to Salman Rushdie.* New York: Alfred A. Knopf, 1993.

DE INVENTORIBUS RERUM

Author: Polydore Vergil (Virgil)
Original date and place of publication: 1499, Italy
Literary form: Reference Book

SUMMARY

Polydore Vergil was an Italian humanist who for many years lived in England, where he served as the archdeacon of Wells Cathedral. His small book of proverbs, the *Adagia*, was one of the most widely read books of the 16th century. Vergil is also remembered for two influential works: *Anglica Historia*, a history of England, and *De inventoribus rerum*, his account of the beginnings of things, a best-selling book of popular scholarship. First published in three volumes in 1499, *De inventoribus rerum* traced the inventions and discoveries of civilization to their original inventors. Designed to provide scholarly information in a compact and accessible form, it was among the first of many popular reference books published during the 16th and 17th centuries.

Vergil's work was translated into all the major European languages and was familiar to most literate persons in 16th- and 17th-century Europe, as indicated by the comical reference to it in Miguel de Cervantes's DON QUIXOTE. "Another work which I soon design for the press I call a 'Supplement to Polydore Vergil, concerning the Invention of Things,' " the clerk tells Cervantes's knight, "a piece, I will assure you, sir, that shows the great pains and learning of the compiler, and perhaps in a better style than the old author. For example, he has forgot to tell us who was the first that was troubled with a catarrh in the world. Now, sir, this I immediately resolve, and confirm my assertion by the testimony of at least four-and-twenty authentic writers. . . ." The clerk later rejoices at his discovery of the first inventor of playing cards, a fact that will be included in his supplement to Polydore Vergil.

Vergil's method was to state a subject, such as music or geometry and arithmetic, and examine the possible claims of its origins in pagan antiquity, ancient Greece, Rome, Egypt, Syria, or Jewish culture. He cited as sources the Greek and Latin classics, the New and Old Testaments, and early Christian, medieval, and contemporary writers. Vergil's copious use of references, satirized by Cervantes, marked the transition to the scholarly methods that distinguished the later Renaissance. It also provided a valuable guide for later historians to the knowledge of classical texts in the early Renaissance.

His aim was to list all those "who first invented or began all things or arts; who first established particular provinces or towns; by whom the names come of provinces, towns, peoples, islands, rivers, mountains and other matters; in what places, provinces, islands or towns various things were first hit upon; who first held certain offices and dignities; who first did anything splendid or unusual."

Indeed, Vergil's compendium was eclectic and diverse, full of illustrative material drawn from contemporary life, ranging from the marriage customs of Germany and Italy to the gambling games of Flanders and the differences between ale and beer in northern Europe. In Book I, he examined the origins of the word *God* and of creation, language, marriage, divorce, and science; in Book II, law, administration, time, books, and military science; and in Book III, agriculture, architecture, navigation, and prostitution.

In 1521, Vergil revised the book, adding five volumes on Christianity that discussed the sacraments, church services and festivals, monastic vows, relics, indulgences, papal titles, heresy, schisms, church councils, and martyrs. In these new volumes, Vergil, allying himself with the moderate proponents of church reform associated with the humanist scholar Desiderius Erasmus, advocated a return to the simple purity of the early days of Christianity. He criticized corruption in the church and the attention to ceremony and external form, which he felt violated the spirit of Christ's teaching, condemning veneration of relics and statues as "not far removed from impiety." He attacked the immorality of monks and advocated marriage for priests. He also argued that the church's failure to call regular church councils was responsible for a decline in religious belief.

CENSORSHIP HISTORY

For well over a century after its publication, *De inventoribus rerum* was unrivaled as a work of popular scholarship. Before Vergil's death in 1555, it appeared in some 30 editions published in Latin in Venice, Strasbourg, Basel, and Lyon. It was translated into English, French, Italian, German, Spanish, and, in the 18th century, Dutch and Russian. The "battle of the books" of the 17th century—the debate that opposed the knowledge of antiquity and that of modern times—renewed interest in the book. In all, at least 100 editions were issued over the centuries.

The publication of the expanded version of *De inventoribus rerum* in 1521, including Vergil's account of Christian institutions and his criticisms of church practices, aroused the interest of church authorities. The church also viewed with suspicion Vergil's *Commentary on the Lord's Prayer*, which accompanied the 1524 Basel edition of *De inventoribus rerum*. As the Counter-Reformation intensified at mid-century and the Catholic Church moved to suppress reform elements within its ranks, it condemned Vergil's writing for having criticized the morality of the Catholic clergy and the policies of the pope and for passages suggesting that the church's discovery of Purgatory stimulated a market for indulgences. *De inventoribus rerum* was included in a 1551 list of books condemned by the Sorbonne, then in the Spanish Index of Forbidden Books in 1559, the Roman Index of Forbidden Books issued by Pope Paul IV in 1564, and the Liège Index of 1569.

An indication of *De inventoribus rerum*'s continued popularity despite its censorship was the Catholic Church's decision in 1576 to publish its own expurgated edition in Rome, more than two decades after the author's death. Many passages were removed or altered in the censored version: Vergil's views on the meaning of Christ's baptism and mission on earth; his discussion of circumcision; his exposition on the practices of the primitive church as being without ritual confession, monastic rules, or an organized priesthood; his attacks on worldly monks, ignorant priests, and the sale of indulgences; and his criticism of the church for failing to hold general councils every 10 years. The expurgated version was translated into Italian and Spanish, but all other unexpurgated editions remained on the Index.

The 1546 English-language translation, which enjoyed considerable success and was reprinted in several editions, was subjected to another form of censorship. Its translator, Thomas Langley, heavily abridged it, reducing it to less than a tenth of its original size, and added his own commentaries. This gave the work, written from the perspective of a Catholic reformer, a more Protestant flavor. He excised all critical comments on Martin Luther and Lutheranism and references that emphasized pagan, rather than Christian, sources.

FURTHER READING

Haight, Anne Lyon. *Banned Books: 387 BC to 1978 AD.* Updated and enlarged by Chandler B. Grannis. New York: R. R. Bowker, 1978.
Hays, Denys. *Polydore Vergil: Renaissance Historian and Man of Letters.* Oxford, U.K.: Clarendon Press, 1952.

DE L'ESPRIT

Author: Claude-Adrien Helvétius
Original date and place of publication: 1758, France
Literary form: Philosophical treatise

SUMMARY

Claude-Adrien Helvétius was a French philosopher of the Enlightenment and a contributor to the famous ENCYCLOPÉDIE. His utilitarian theories influenced the work of British philosophers Jeremy Bentham, James Mill, and Adam Smith. Helvétius held the lucrative post of farmer-general, or tax collector, a position to which he was appointed through his father's influence with the queen. His first major work was *De l'esprit* (Essays on the mind), published in 1758, which proposed that self-interested pursuit of pleasure and avoidance of pain is the sole motive for human actions.

De l'esprit is divided into four discourses. The first presents the epistemological foundation of his system; the second and most influential deals with ethics;

the third explains his educational ideas, later amplified in a posthumously published work, *De l'homme* (Treatise on man); and the fourth concerns aesthetics.

Helvétius maintains that since consciousness is derived from sensation and is the same in everyone, all forms of intellectual activity originate in sensation. Self-love, directed toward the acquisition of pleasure, is the universal basis of human conduct. Even benevolent virtues can be attributed to self-love. "What is a benevolent man?" Helvétius asks. "One in whom a spectacle of misery produces a painful sensation."

Although self-interest is the fundamental motive of conduct, "the public good is the supreme law." The criterion for the morality of an action is its usefulness to the community. Altruism is psychologically possible if education is directed toward developing benevolent impulses. If children are taught to empathize with those who are unfortunate, for example, the misfortune of others will arouse in them painful sensations and self-love will stimulate a desire on their part to relieve misery.

"To love one's fellow-men, one must not expect much of them," Helvétius believed. Justice and the happiness of the greatest number can be obtained through education and legislation that manipulate and condition people to treat one another well through a system of rewards and punishments. All progress depends on education. "Destroy ignorance, and you will destroy all the seeds of moral evil."

Helvétius felt that the entire educational system of France had to be reconstructed, freed from the control of the church, and assigned to the state. Catholic control of education, he charged, impeded the technical advance of the nation and subjected the minds of children to priestly domination. "There is nothing which the sacerdotal power cannot execute by the aid of superstition. For by that it robs the magistrates of their authority and kings of their legitimate power; thereby it subdues the people, and acquires a power over them which is frequently superior to the laws; and thereby it finally corrupts the very principles of morality."

CENSORSHIP HISTORY

Few books of the 18th century provoked greater opposition from religious and civil authorities than *De l'esprit*. It was condemned as atheistic, materialistic, sacrilegious, immoral, and subversive, the epitome of all the dangerous philosophical trends of the age. The Catholic Church saw Helvétius's theories as antireligious, because earthly happiness, rather than salvation, was the object of his ethical theory. Theologians objected to his reduction of all the powers of the human understanding to sense perception, and to his materialistic ethic of self-interest that posited social utility as the only criterion for morality. The Jesuits objected to his proposals to remove education from their control. The church charged that his deterministic philosophy rejected the doctrine of free will and denied the soul's spirituality and immortality.

De l'esprit was published in 1758 with a royal privilege or permission from the official censor, Jean-Paul Tercier, a principal secretary at the foreign office. "I have found nothing in it which in my judgement ought to prevent its publication," Tercier declared. Soon after its publication, however, the Jesuits at court, the queen and the Parlement of Paris made official complaints about it to Chrétien-Guillaume de Lamoignon de Malesherbes, the director of the book trade. Malesherbes ordered sale of the book suspended until a second censor could examine it.

The second censor detected improper criticism of the church and asked for cuts in the manuscript. Helvétius was ordered to write a retraction. Instead, he provided an introduction defending his writing against charges of heresy. "Of what impiety can they accuse me?" he protested. "I have in no part of this work denied the Trinity, or the divinity of Jesus, or the immortality of the soul, or the resurrection of the dead, or any other article of the papal creed; I have not therefore in any way attacked religion."

Durand, the printer, put the original typesetting aside and printed a second, anonymous version with the changes ordered by the censor and with Helvétius's introduction. This version was approved for publication, but it also met with condemnation. In a futile effort to deter the censors, Helvétius wrote two more submissive retractions disavowing his work and explaining his desire not to offend the church. Jesuits and Jansenists alike attacked it in periodicals and pamphlets, bishops lambasted it from the pulpit, and in November 1758, *De l'esprit* was prohibited by the archbishop of Paris.

Only three weeks before the book's publication, Pope Clement XIII, who was determined to stamp out the new materialistic thought, succeeded the more moderate Benedict XIV. In January 1759, the new pope banned it in a special brief forbidding—under pain of excommunication—the printing, reading, or possession of the work. The pope described Helvétius as doing Satan's work and opening "the broadest possible path to lead souls to perdition." The book was also placed on the Index of Forbidden Books.

In February, the Parlement of Paris, having extended its authority to censor books on its own initiative, without waiting for the verdict of the faculty of theology at the Sorbonne, ordered *De l'esprit* to be burned by the public hangman and prohibited in Paris and in the provinces. In April the Sorbonne finally weighed in with its own condemnation.

Despite its banning, *De l'esprit* became an underground best seller in pirated and clandestine editions. Twenty editions appeared in France within six months, and the work was translated into English and German. Though Helvétius was dismissed from his sinecure as major domo to the queen, he escaped further punishment by virtue of his personal relationships with high-level persons in the court and government, such as King Louis XV's mistress Madame de Pompadour and the duke of Choiseul, the foreign minister, who interceded on his behalf. He was ordered, instead, to retire to his estate for two years. It was said that the penalty might have been more severe if the king had not remembered that his life had been saved by Helvétius's father, who had been physician to the queen.

In 1772, the year following Helvétius's death, *De l'homme* was published. In it he attacked political despotism and called for a more equitable distribution of the national wealth. He also assailed the detrimental influence of revealed or "mysterious" religion, declaring that the power of the church and the Catholic clergy were impediments to reforming education and ensuring the smooth running of society. In 1774, *De l'homme* was also condemned and burned in Paris.

FURTHER READING

Copleston, Frederick. *A History of Philosophy*. Vol. 6: *Modern Philosophy*. New York: Doubleday, 1994.

Curtis, Michael, ed. and intro. *The Great Political Theories*. Vol. 1. New York: Avon Books, 1981.

Durant, Will, and Ariel Durant. *The Age of Voltaire*. New York: Simon and Schuster, 1965.

Smith, D. W. *Helvétius, a Study in Persecution*. Oxford, U.K.: Clarendon Press, 1965.

DIALOGUE CONCERNING THE TWO CHIEF WORLD SYSTEMS

Author: Galileo Galilei
Original date and place of publication: 1632, Italy
Literary form: Scientific monograph

SUMMARY

The work of the great Italian astronomer, mathematician, and physicist Galileo Galilei had a profound effect on the development of science and philosophy, laying the foundations for modern experimental science and enlarging human understanding of the nature of the universe. Although the Polish astronomer Nicolaus Copernicus had argued in ON THE REVOLUTION OF HEAVENLY SPHERES, published in 1543, that the Sun was the center of the universe and the Earth a planet that moved, belief in the geocentric Ptolemaic system (named for the second-century astronomer Ptolemy) remained prevalent in the early 17th century. The Ptolemaic theory placed the Earth motionless at the center of the universe, with the Sun, the Moon, and the five planets moving around it in complex circular motions.

When Galileo, a professor of mathematics at the University of Pisa, first gazed at the sky through the refracting telescope he had designed, it had been a half-century since Copernicus introduced his theory of a heliocentric, or Sun-centered, universe. For the first time, however, actual observations of the heavens through a telescope seemed to confirm Copernicus's hypothesis. In 1610, Galileo published *The Starry Messenger*, a 24-page pamphlet reporting his astronomical observations of the Moon and the planets. Galileo recounted his discovery of four previously unknown heavenly bodies moving around the planet Jupiter, proof that Copernicus's theory was correct. He also noted that the Moon was not a self-luminous body, but was lit by the Sun.

The Venetian senate granted Galileo a salary for his discoveries, and he was appointed mathematician to the duke of Tuscany. In 1613, he published *Letters on the Solar Spots*, in which he declared his belief in the Copernican theory. Galileo was convinced that "the Book of Nature is written in mathematical symbols," and that in observation and quantification lay the science of the future. In 1632, Galileo published the work that was to mark a turning point in the history of science, *Dialogue Concerning the Two Chief World Systems, Ptolemaic and Copernican.*

In this dialogue in the Platonic tradition, Galileo allowed arguments for and against the Copernican system to emerge from a conversation among three friends: a Florentine who believes in the Copernican system, an Aristotelian supporter of the geocentric theory, and a Venetian aristocrat for whose benefit they propose their arguments. Galileo wrote in Italian for the nonspecialist, rather than in Latin, the language of scholars and intellectuals.

In structuring the *Dialogue*, Galileo complied with the church's orders that the heliocentric theory be discussed as a useful mathematical hypothesis, rather than as a representation of physical reality. But the views he expressed in the *Dialogue* were clearly supportive of the Copernican system. Galileo found that the Earth, like the other planets, rotated on its axis and that the planets revolved around the Sun in elliptical paths determined by gravity. He rejected the idea of a finite universe bounded by an outer sphere of unchanging perfection. By showing that the Earth was not the center of creation but, rather, an insignificant part of it, Galileo overturned the medieval system of cosmology based on Aristotelian theories of the motion of bodies.

Galileo expressed two principles in the *Dialogue* that have become the guiding principles of modern science. First, statements and hypotheses about nature must always be based on observation, rather than on received authority; and second, natural processes can best be understood if represented in mathematical terms.

CENSORSHIP HISTORY

In 1616, the system of Copernicus was denounced as dangerous to the faith and Galileo, summoned to Rome, was warned by Pope Paul V not to "hold, teach or defend" Copernican theories. Galileo promised to obey the papal injunction and returned to Florence. In 1619, the pope banned similar theories, published by the German astronomer Johannes Kepler in THE NEW ASTRONOMY. According to the papal bull accompanying these bans, teaching or even reading the works of Copernicus and Kepler was forbidden.

In 1624, Galileo went to Rome again to pay his respects to the newly anointed Pope Urban VIII. Despite the prohibition of 1616, he requested papal permission to publish a book comparing Ptolemaic and Copernican doctrines. The pope refused his request.

Despite warnings by the Vatican, which had cited numerous corrections required before any of Copernicus's theories might be promulgated, in 1632 Galileo published *Dialogue Concerning the Two Chief World Systems.* He attempted to satisfy the authorities by including a preface by a leading Vatican theologian describing Copernican theory as merely an interesting intellectual exercise. But the pope was unconvinced. The book had attracted the attention of all of Europe. The rising threat of Protestantism spurred the pope to respond aggressively to preserve the integrity of the church's dogmas.

Further, Galileo's enemies at the Vatican implied that by publishing the book under the colophon of three fishes—the usual imprint of the Florentine press of Landini—Galileo had made a libelous reference to Pope Urban VIII's three incompetent nephews, whom he had promoted to the church hierarchy. They further suggested that one of the characters in the dialogue, Simplicio, the conservative defender of the geocentric view of the universe, was meant to be a caricature of the pope himself.

In February 1633, the pope summoned Galileo to Rome. Although he was gravely ill in Florence and his doctors warned that a journey in the dead of winter might prove fatal, the pope threatened to forcibly remove him in chains if he did not appear. The grand duke of Florence provided a litter to carry Galileo to Rome, where he was imprisoned. In June he was put on trial for heresy.

The trial focused on technicalities regarding what church authorities had told him during his visit to Rome in 1616 and on how clearly he had understood the papal disapproval of Copernican doctrines. The Inquisition's verdict was that Galileo was "vehemently suspected of heresy, namely of having believed and held the doctrine which is false and contrary to the sacred and divine scriptures that the sun is the center of the world and does not move from East to West and that the earth moves and is not the center of the world and that an opinion may be held and defended as probable after it has been declared and defined to be contrary to Holy Scripture. . . ."

Galileo was sentenced to prison for an indefinite period and required to make a public and formal abjuration. On the morning of June 22, 1633, at the age of 70, Galileo knelt before the court and declared, "With sincere heart and unpretended faith I abjure, curse, and detest the aforesaid errors and heresies and also every other error and sect whatever, contrary to the Holy Church, and I swear that in the future I will never again say or assert verbally or in writing, anything that might cause a similar suspicion toward me. . . ." "And yet it [the Earth] moves," he is said by legend to have muttered after his recantation.

In 1634, the *Dialogue* was formally condemned and banned along with all of Galileo's works. Galileo was confined to a secluded house in Arcetri, outside Florence, where he was allowed no visitors except with the permission of the pope's delegate. During his confinement Galileo was able to complete a new work, *Dialogue Concerning Two New Sciences,* which was smuggled out of Italy and published by the Protestants in Leiden in 1638, four years before his death. During the last four years of his life, Galileo was blind. Eventually the pope allowed him the companionship of a young scholar, Vicenzo Viviani. Still in seclusion, Galileo died on January 8, 1642, a month before his 78th birthday.

The Index of Forbidden Books of 1664 confirmed the condemnation of the works of Copernicus and Galileo and of all other writings affirming the movement of the Earth and the stability of the Sun. In 1753, the Index of Benedict XIV omitted the general prohibition covering books that teach the heliocentric theory.

However, it was not until 1824, when Canon Settele, a Roman astronomy professor, published a work on modern scientific theories, that the church finally announced its acceptance of "the general opinion of modern astronomers." In the next papal Index of 1835, the names of Galileo, Copernicus, and Kepler were removed. On October 31, 1992, Pope John Paul II formally rehabilitated Galileo—359 years, four months, and nine days after Galileo had been forced to recant his heresy that the Earth moved around the Sun.

FURTHER READING

Boorstein, Daniel J. *The Discoverers: A History of Man's Search to Know His World and Himself.* New York: Random House, 1983.

Collinson, Diané. *Fifty Major Philosophers: A Reference Guide.* London: Routledge, 1988.

Garraty, John A., and Peter Gay. *The Columbia History of the World.* New York: Harper & Row, 1972.

Green, Jonathon. *Encyclopedia of Censorship.* New York: Facts On File, 1990.

DIALOGUES CONCERNING NATURAL RELIGION

Author: David Hume
Original date and place of publication: 1779, England
Literary form: Philosophical treatise

SUMMARY

Dialogues Concerning Natural Religion was the last work of the Scottish philosopher and historian David Hume, one of the great empiricists of the 18th-century Enlightenment. Published posthumously in 1779 because Hume felt it was too controversial to be released during his lifetime, it distills his thought on religious skepticism and is regarded as among the most important works on the philosophy of religion.

In earlier works, Hume contributed several influential arguments against both revealed religion and the rationalist arguments for belief. The most famous was his celebrated attack on miracles in AN INQUIRY CONCERNING HUMAN UNDERSTANDING, published in 1748. *Dialogues Concerning Natural Religion* contains a full development of many of the arguments introduced in the notorious sections X and XI of the *Inquiry.*

In the *Dialogues,* Hume examines the rational claims for religious belief. Through the differing views of three characters—Philo, the skeptic; Cleanthes, the empirical or rational theologian; and Demea, the orthodox defender of revealed religion—whose conversations are reported by Pamphilus, the narrator, Hume analyzes the arguments that have been advanced to prove God's existence and benevolence.

His primary target in the *Dialogues* is "the argument from design," advanced by deists and theists alike, which proposes that because the universe works like a machine and shows signs of a designing intelligence, a perfect and immutable designer must have created it. This argument is advanced by Cleanthes in the *Dialogues.* "Look around the world, contemplate the whole and every part of it," he says, "you will find it to be nothing but one great machine, subdivided into an infinite number of lesser machines, which again admit of subdivisions to a degree beyond what human senses and faculties can trace and explain."

The argument is challenged by Philo, the skeptic, who objects to Cleanthes's logic and demonstrates the faultiness of his experimental reasoning. Philo shows that the basic analogy of the argument comparing the universe with a machine is exceedingly weak, that alternative hypotheses not considered by Cleanthes explain the data equally well, and that Cleanthes's conclusion is incompatible with the existence of evil.

Even if we accept the basic premises of the argument from design, Philo points out, it provides no basis for making assumptions about the nature of the designer. It is pure conjecture to state that the designer is necessarily morally perfect or even good. "But were this world ever so perfect a production, it must still remain uncertain whether all the excellence of the work can justly be ascribed to the workman. . . . Many worlds might have been botched and bungled, throughout an eternity, ere this system was struck out; much labor lost, many fruitless trials made, and a slow but continued improvement carried on during infinite ages in the art of world-making."

The argument for design proceeds from the existence of an effect, a designed universe, to the existence of a cause, God the designer. In Philo's view, Cleanthes's data do not support his conclusions. His argument simply rationalizes what he already believes independently of the data. The existence of God is a hypothesis and the argument from design does not provide the evidence necessary to demonstrate its truth.

CENSORSHIP HISTORY

Although Hume did not state which of the views expressed in the *Dialogues* were his own, it is clear that his position was represented primarily by the arguments of the skeptic, Philo. Hume was a resolutely secular thinker who felt that religion was a negative influence on both individuals and society. Though many British intellectuals were hostile to revealed or organized religion, most believed in God. Atheism was unthinkable in the culture of the day and could not be put forward as a serious option, even by deists or freethinkers. In the *Dialogues*, Hume skirted dangerously close to atheism by taking issue with both the tenets of revealed religion and deists' claims on behalf of "natural religion."

Hume believed not only that the arguments put forth for God's existence and benevolent nature did not meet the tests of empirical investigation but also that religion impeded morality. It encouraged people to act for motives other than love of virtue for its own sake and caused anxiety, intolerance, and persecution. In *The Natural History of Religion*, published in 1755, Hume had observed that fanaticism and bigotry increased with the development of monotheism and that in the Christian world philosophy was misused in the service of theological doctrines.

The torrent of criticism Hume faced after publication of *An Inquiry Concerning Human Understanding* in 1748, particularly of the two sections discussing philosophy of religion, "Of Miracles" and "Of a Particular Providence and of a Future State," had led Hume to decide that he could not publish *Dialogues Concerning Natural Religion* during his lifetime.

Hume had been rejected for appointments at the Universities of Edinburgh and Glasgow, and a formal attempt had been made to excommunicate him from the Church of Scotland. The Vatican placed a French version of his first philosophical work, *A Treatise of Human Nature*, on the Index of Forbidden Books in 1761, and a flood of widely circulated attacks on Hume were published during the years after the appearance of the *Inquiry*.

The manuscript of *Dialogues Concerning Natural Religion* had been largely completed by 1751. He circulated it to a few friends, including the philosopher and economist Adam Smith, who advised him not to publish it. More than 20 years later, in a 1776 letter to his publisher, Hume indicated that he planned to print 500 copies of the work. But the decline of his health led him with "abundant prudence" to prepare instead for its posthumous publication.

The book appeared in late 1779, three years after Hume's death. Hume had tried to convince Adam Smith to guarantee its publication, but Smith was reluctant to become involved because of its highly controversial nature. Hume's printer, also a friend, refused to publish it. Finally Hume's nephew, David Hume, had it published anonymously without a publisher's imprint. A French edition appeared the same year and a German one in 1781. The book sold well in Britain, and a second edition was published in 1779.

In 1827, Hume's *History of England* and all his philosophical works, including *Dialogues Concerning Natural Religion* and *An Inquiry Concerning Human Understanding*, were placed by the Catholic Church on the Index of Forbidden Books, where they remained through the last edition of the Index, compiled in 1948 and in effect until 1966.

In 1986, more than 200 years after the publication of *Dialogues Concerning Natural Religion*, the work was censored again—this time by the government of Turkey. A translation by Mere Tuncay of Hume's writing on religion was banned under the Law to Protect Minors. This legislation was enacted in 1985 to allow for restriction of "items of a political nature which may affect minors adversely." Also included in the proscription were the film *Gandhi* and the television program *Dallas*.

FURTHER READING

Boyle, Kevin, ed. *Article 19 World Report 1988.* New York: Times Books, 1988.

Collinson, Diané. *Fifty Major Philosophers: A Reference Guide.* London: Routledge, 1988.

Copleston, Frederick. *A History of Philosophy.* Vol. 5: *Modern Philosophy: The British Philosophers from Hobbes to Hume.* New York: Doubleday, 1994.

Gay, Peter. *The Enlightenment: An Interpretation. The Rise of Modern Paganism.* New York: W. W. Norton, 1995.

Penelhum, Terence. *David Hume: An Introduction to His Philosophical System.* West Lafayette, Ind.: Purdue University Press, 1992.

Popkin, Richard H., and Avrum Stroll. *Philosophy Made Simple.* New York: Doubleday, 1993.

Price, John V. *David Hume.* New York: Twayne Publishers, 1968.

Scott-Kakures, Dion, Susan Castegnetto, Hugh Benson, William Taschek, and Paul Hurley. *History of Philosophy.* New York: HarperCollins Publishers, 1993.

DISCOURSE ON METHOD

Author: René Descartes
Original date and place of publication: 1637, Holland
Literary form: Philosophical text

SUMMARY

Discourse on Method outlined the philosophy of René Descartes, the founder of modern philosophy and mathematics. Published in 1637 along with other important essays on optics, meteorology, and analytical geometry, *Discourse on Method* established Descartes's reputation throughout Europe and introduced philosophy as a field of intellectual inquiry open to all self-critical thinkers. His MEDITATIONS ON FIRST PHILOSOPHY, published four years later, offered a more complete exposition of the ideas introduced in *Discourse on Method*.

Descartes's method of philosophical inquiry was to proceed by rigorous deduction from self-evident premises. He claimed that this method provided a foundation for solving on the basis of available facts any problem that could be resolved by human reason.

Descartes divided *Discourse on Method* into six parts to make it more accessible to the reader. In part one, "Some Thoughts on the Sciences," Descartes stated that the ability to distinguish true from false is the same by nature in all men. Differences of opinion are due not to variations in intelligence, but rather to different approaches to arriving at the truth.

In part two, "The Principal Rules of the Method," Descartes resolved to reject all the opinions he had acquired since birth until he determined how they fit into a rational scheme. He outlined four rules: First, never accept anything as true unless you recognize it to be so. Second, divide difficulties into as many parts as possible. Third, think in an orderly fashion, beginning with the simplest and most easily understood ideas, gradually reaching toward more complex knowledge. Fourth, make complete enumerations and general reviews to be sure that nothing has been omitted.

In part three, "Some Moral Rules Derived from the Method," Descartes recounted the personal code of morality he followed while he was discarding his own opinions in order to reexamine them. He obeyed the laws and customs of his country, retaining the religion of his upbringing. He acted resolutely on all his decisions, even those he was unsure of. He sought to conquer himself and change his desires rather than the established order, believing that nothing except our thoughts is wholly under our control.

In part four, "Proofs of the Existence of God and of the Human Soul," Descartes noticed that while he wished to think everything false, "it was necessarily true that I who thought so was something." Since this truth, "I think, therefore I am" (*Cogito ergo sum*), was so firm and assured, he judged he could accept it as the first principle of the philosophy he was seeking. In ascertaining how he had learned to think of something more perfect than himself, it appeared evident to him that it must have been from some more perfect nature, which was God.

In part five, "Some Questions of Physics," Descartes recounted the discovery of certain laws established by God in nature, the idea of which he had fixed in our minds, leading him to conclude that the soul is immortal. In part six, "Some Prerequisites for Further Advances in the Study of Nature," Descartes outlined his own procedure. He first tried to discover the general principles or first causes of existence. Next he examined the first and most common effects that could be deducted from these causes. But when he wanted to descend to particulars, he found it impossible to distinguish the forms or species of objects found on Earth from an infinity of others that might have been there if God had so willed. It thus appeared impossible to proceed further deductively. To reach understanding, causes would have to be discovered by their effects, through experimentation.

Descartes did not claim that his ideas were original. Rather, he asserted that he did not accept ideas simply because they were maintained by others, but only because reason persuaded him of their truth. "As for my real opinions," Descartes concluded, "I do not apologize for their novelty, especially since I am sure that anyone who attends to the argument will find them so simple and so comfortable to common sense that they will seem less extraordinary and strange than any other opinions that can be held on the same subjects."

CENSORSHIP HISTORY

By attempting to apply the methods, standards, and concepts of mathematical and natural sciences to philosophic inquiry, Descartes launched an intellectual revolution. He changed the emphasis in philosophical inquiry from metaphysics, the study of the ultimate nature of existence, to epistemology, the study of the origins and grounds of knowledge, thereby ushering in a new philosophical era. Descartes's rationalist approach to knowledge, whereby reason alone, unaided by experience, can arrive at basic truths about the world from self-evident premises, challenged Catholic Church doctrine.

As expressed by Saint Thomas Aquinas, church doctrine asserted that not all articles of faith were demonstrable by reason. Descartes, in common with many individuals in his period, discarded the authoritarian system of the Scholastics, the medieval philosophy synthesizing faith and reason that dominated the thinking of the church. He adopted instead the concept of universal doubt and belief in the unique adequacy of each individual's reason to discover truth.

Descartes was a devout Catholic and accepted the existence of God, but he considered moral questions to be separable from the process of scientific observation. The church attacked the scientific method as a form of atheism and branded Descartes's methodology as dangerous to the faith.

Though Descartes's philosophy, as expressed in *Discourse on Method* and *Meditations on First Philosophy*, made rapid advances, it was attacked by church, state, and universities. In France, an officially Catholic country governed by an absolute monarchy, as well as in liberal Holland, his rejection of Scholasticism was regarded as threatening. In 1641, in Holland, the senate of the University of Utrecht voted to condemn his philosophy. At the University of Leiden, any mention of Descartes's philosophy in lectures was forbidden. In 1643, civil authorities in Utrecht took direct action against Descartes, and the open letters he published in his own defense were declared defamatory. Two years later, the city megistrate ordered Descartes to appear in person to answer libel charges. An appeal to the French ambassador, who exercised his influence with the Dutch prince of Orange, led to the charges being dropped.

In France, where all universities were subject to royal and ecclesiastical authorities, repression of Descartes's ideas was particularly severe under the

Catholic absolute monarchy of Louis XIV (1643–1715). Catholic opinion in France was particularly disturbed by the question of whether his philosophy of matter could be reconciled with the dogma of transubstantiation. This dogma holds that the substances of bread and wine of the sacrament of the Eucharist are turned miraculously into the substance of Christ himself. Cartesians attempted to explain the Eucharist using Descartes's philosophy, rather than declaring it a mystery to be accepted on faith.

The debate on the Eucharist after Descartes's death in 1650, led by advocates of Cartesian philosophy who promoted his views on transubstantiation, resulted in further repression of his philosophy. It is thought that Jesuit hostility to Cartesian ideas, particularly the suspicion that Cartesians favored a purely symbolic interpretation of the Eucharist, was responsible in 1663 for the placement on the Index of Forbidden Books of all Descartes's philosophical writings. They were listed on the Index with the notation *d.c.* (*donec corrigantur*), meaning "until corrected," a qualification used to express condemnation in milder form.

In 1671, the debate on the Eucharist again resulted in censure of Cartesian philosophy. A Benedictine monk, Desgabets, published a book offering a Cartesian interpretation of the Eucharist. The king took offense and mounted a major campaign against Cartesianism in French universities. That year the University of Paris complied with a royal ban on teaching of his philosophy, and other French universities followed suit. Religious orders also imposed bans on teaching of Cartesian philosophy.

Despite such bannings, Descartes's philosophy and science won many converts in Holland and France. Cartesian views circulated in informal settings such as the salons of Paris and in universities, where professors were able to find ways to discuss Cartesian ideas while technically complying with official bans. By the mid-18th century, Descartes's ideas had become the philosophy of the establishment.

In 1722, Descartes's 1641 *Meditations on First Philosophy* was prohibited unconditionally in the Index. In 1948, when the last revision of the Index was made by the church, Descartes's philosophical works, including *Discourse on Method*, were still listed. It was not until 1966, when the Vatican abolished the Index, that Catholics were officially allowed to read Descartes.

In 1926 in the Soviet Union, the government suppressed many philosophical works, including those of Descartes.

FURTHER READING

Descartes, René. *Discourse on Method*. Translated and with an introduction by Laurence J. Lafleur. Indianapolis: Bobbs-Merrill, 1956.

Green, Jonathon. *The Encyclopedia of Censorship*. New York: Facts On File, 1990.

Jolley, Nicholas. "The Reception of Descartes' Philosophy." In *The Cambridge Companion to Descartes*. Edited by John Cottingham, 393–423. Cambridge: Cambridge University Press, 1992.

DON QUIXOTE

Author: Miguel de Cervantes Saavedra
Original dates and place of publication: 1605, 1615, Spain
Literary form: Novel

SUMMARY

One of the greatest and most enduring classics of European literature, *Don Quixote de la Mancha* is a burlesque of the popular romances of chivalry. Cervantes's masterpiece tells the story of Don Quixote, a country gentleman of La Mancha, in central Spain, whose mind has become unbalanced by his reading of too many tales of chivalry. He sees himself as a knight-errant whose mission is to travel the world in rusty armor in search of adventure, riding a decrepit horse, Rocinante, and accompanied by his squire, the peasant Sancho Panza. He selects as his knightly belle a country girl, Aldonza Lorenza, and dubs her Dulcinea del Toboso, though she remains unaware of the honor bestowed upon her.

Don Quixote embarks on a series of absurd and extravagant adventures, as in his disordered imagination the land is transformed into a knightly landscape where the most commonplace objects assume fantastic forms. Windmills become giants; an inn, a castle; and a flock of sheep, a great army. Concerned about his safety, his friends trick him into returning to his home, where he recovers his health. Don Quixote's misadventures continue, as he endeavors to free Dulcinea from what he believes is an enchantment by a wicked spell. Finally Don Quixote is induced to abstain from his chivalrous exploits for a year and resolves to live a pastoral life as a shepherd. But falling sick upon his return to his village, he regains his sanity, and renouncing his fantasies of chivalry, he dies.

CENSORSHIP HISTORY

Through Cervantes's vivid portrayal of the panorama of 16th-century society, *Don Quixote* explores two conflicting attitudes toward the world: idealism and realism. Cervantes's brilliant humanistic study of illusion and reality is considered by many critics to be the first modern novel in its pioneering effort to reveal the variety of the individual and translate all human experience into the novel form.

Immediately upon its publication in 1605, *Don Quixote* became a best seller. It was reprinted in six editions in Spain during the first year of its publication and translated into all the major languages of Europe. The popularity of a pirated edition of his idea spurred Cervantes to publish a sequel in 1615. Part two also sold well and was soon bound and marketed together with the first part.

The censorship of *Don Quixote*, though minor in scope and impact, was a notorious example of the fastidious and thorough nature of the Spanish

Inquisition's control over book publishing and distribution. Under penalty of confiscation and death, no bookseller could sell or keep any work condemned by the Inquisition. Agents searched bookstores and private libraries, and a commissioner was appointed to survey ships docked at Spanish ports to prevent the importation of offensive literature. The examiners of the Inquisition read every book published in Spain or imported from abroad for heretical ideas but allowed certain books to circulate if offensive passages were expurgated. Under this system, permission could be given for publication of books that were absolutely prohibited by the Roman Index of Forbidden Books. But the heavy financial loss incurred by printers by suppression of the original edition often discouraged investment in a second, expurgated text and effectively halted publication altogether.

In part one of *Don Quixote*, the knight-errant tears off the tail of his shirt and ties knots in it to serve as a rosary in the wilderness of the Sierra Morena. This passage was pronounced indecent by the church's Holy Office, and in a second edition the shirt-tail was changed to a chapelet of corn-tree nuts. "I would have made the book more amusing," Cervantes commented on the church's restrictions, "had it not been for the Holy Office."

But unaccountably the censors let pass Cervantes's satire on ecclesiastical censorship in chapter six of part one, in which the priest and the barber set themselves up as inquisitors and purge Don Quixote's library of its most deleterious works on chivalry.

In 1640, 25 years after the first publication of part two of *Don Quixote*, the book was placed on the Spanish Index for a single sentence extracted from the half-million words of one of the world's longest novels: "Works of charity performed negligently have neither merit nor value." The church viewed this statement as reflecting Lutheran beliefs. Removal of the sentence in a reprinted edition satisfied the censors and allowed the novel's continued circulation.

In Chile in 1981, the military junta led by General Augusto Pinochet banned *Don Quixote* as subversive because it supports individual freedom and attacks authority.

FURTHER READING

Boorstein, Daniel J. *The Discoverers: A History of Man's Search to Know His World and Himself.* New York: Random House, 1983.

Burman, Edward. *The Inquisition: Hammer of Heresy.* New York: Dorset Press, 1992.

Manguel, Alberto. *A History of Reading.* New York: Viking, 1996.

Putnam, George Haven. *The Censorship of the Church of Rome.* Vol. 1. New York: G. P. Putnam's Sons, 1906–07.

Roth, Cecil. *The Spanish Inquisition.* New York: W. W. Norton, 1964.

DRAGONWINGS

Author: Laurence Yep
Original date and place of publication: 1975, United States
Original publisher: Harper and Row
Literary form: Novel

SUMMARY

Dragonwings is a critically praised, Newberry Honor novel for young adults by Laurence Yep. Yep has written more than 20 books inspired by the Chinese-American immigrant experience and legends of Chinese folk tales. *Dragonwings*, about a boy who emigrates from China to San Francisco in 1905 to join the father he has never met, is a coming-of-age story and a celebration of the courage and industry of the Chinese-American community of the early 20th century.

Eight-year-old Moon Shadow lives with his mother and grandmother in a small village in China. One day he receives a letter from his father, who immigrated years before to the Golden Mountain, or America, asking that Moon Shadow sail to San Francisco to join him. Upon Moon Shadow's arrival in the Land of the Demons, as the people of his village refer to the United States, he meets his father. He is brought to the Company of the Peach Orchard Vow, the laundry that serves as the family headquarters in the neighborhood of the Tang people, San Francisco's Chinatown.

He is soon exposed to the difficult living and working conditions of Chinese immigrants. Moon Shadow's own grandfather had been lynched 30 years before by a mob of white demons. Now a brick shatters the laundry window as a racist mob of drunken white men roams through the neighborhood.

His father, who is called Windrider, was known in China as a master kitemaker. He shows Moon Shadow the electrical devices he has invented and recounts the story of how he received the name Windrider. In a former life the father was the greatest physician of all the dragons. His skill at kitemaking is only a remnant of his former powers.

As Moon Shadow grows to love and respect his father, he studies English and begins to learn the strange customs of the American people. After Windrider fights with a member of the criminal brotherhood in Chinatown and kills the man as he is about to shoot Moon Shadow, he and Moon Shadow must leave the Tang neighborhood. They move to rooms in the house of a landlady, Miss Whitlaw, on Polk Street, where Windrider has found work as a handyman.

Moon Shadow becomes friends with Miss Whitlaw's niece, Robin, the first non-Chinese child he has ever met. With Robin's help, Moon Shadow learns to read and write English. Moon Shadow and his father begin a correspondence with the Wright brothers on the mechanics of flying machines, and Windrider begins to build large glider models.

By 1906, Windrider is saving money, looking forward to opening his own fix-it shop and thinking of the day when he might be able to bring Moon Shadow's mother over from China. One morning in April, a great earthquake shakes the city. Moon Shadow, his father, Miss Whitlaw, and Robin survive; Miss Whitlaw's well-constructed house is the only one still standing on their street. When fires sweep the city, they flee by wagon to Golden Gate Park, then to the Oakland foothills, where they make a home in an abandoned barn.

Windrider dedicates his time and resources for the next three years to building Dragonwings, his flying machine. He makes a successful test flight, but the plane is destroyed and he is injured when it crash-lands. As his broken bones mend, Windrider and Moon Shadow rejoin the company, moving into its sturdy new building in San Francisco. Finally, Moon Shadow's father sails for China to bring Moon Shadow's mother to America.

Moon Shadow knows that many problems and challenges lie before him, but "I knew I could meet them," he says, "with the same courage with which Father had pursued his dream of flight and then given it up, or the same courage with which Mother had faced the long separation from us."

CENSORSHIP HISTORY

Dragonwings was inspired by historical accounts of Fung Joe Guey, a young Chinese man who improved upon the Wright brothers' original airplane design and flew in the hills over Oakland on September 22, 1909, for 20 minutes before a mishap brought his biplane down.

In *Dragonwings*, the author wished to breathe life into the dry historical facts of the experience of Chinese immigrants. "At the same time," Yep wrote, "it has been my aim to counter various stereotypes as presented in the media. . . . I wanted to show that Chinese-Americans are human beings upon whom America has had a unique effect."

Because the novel is written from the point of view of a recently arrived boy, Moon Shadow refers to white Americans as "demons." The Tang word for demon can mean many kinds of supernatural beings, Moon Shadow explains. "A demon can be the ghost of a dead person, but he can also be a supernatural creature, who can use his great powers for good as well as for evil, just like the dragons."

Such allusions to the customs and beliefs of the Chinese immigrants portrayed in *Dragonwings* led to an attempt to ban the book in May 1992. Sylvia Hall, a Pentecostal minister, approached the Apollo-Ridge School Board in Kittanning, Pennsylvania, to ask that *Dragonwings* be removed from the eighth-grade curriculum. She objected to the use of the word *demon* in the book, references to reincarnation and other allusions to Eastern religion and what she described as content relating to the occult and satanism.

When the school board rejected Hall's request to ban the book by a vote of 9-0, she took her case to court, asking for an injunction prohibiting the use of the book. She told the court, "There may be children who will commit suicide because they think they can be reincarnated as something or someone else."

Hall contended the reading of the book in a public school violated the First Amendment prohibition against the establishment of religion. *Dragonwings*, she argued, advanced the religion and beliefs of Taoism and reincarnation. It also promoted the religion of secular humanism by implying that people can achieve their goals without God's intervention.

In a September 15, 1992, ruling, Armstrong Country judge Joseph Nickleach denied the request to ban the book. In his opinion, Nickleach wrote: "The fact that religions and religious concepts are mentioned in school does not automatically constitute a violation of the establishment clause." He stipulated that the book was used for a purely secular purpose and that neither the book nor the teachers who taught it promoted a particular religion as the only correct belief or even the preferred belief. He found that the complainant failed to sustain her burden of proof that Apollo-Ridge School District violated the U.S. Constitution by assigning the book to be read in school.

FURTHER READING

American Library Association. *Newsletter on Intellectual Freedom*, 42, no. 1 (January 1993): 18.
Yep, Laurence. Afterword to *Dragonwings*. New York: Scholastic, 1990.

ÉMILE

Author: Jean-Jacques Rousseau
Original date and place of publication: 1762, France
Literary form: Novel

SUMMARY

An intimate in the circle of French intellectual Denis Diderot and contributor of music articles to the famous ENCYCLOPÉDIE, Jean-Jacques Rousseau launched his own literary career in 1750, when he unexpectedly won the prize of the Dijon Academy for his essay, "Discourse on the Influence of Learning and Art." Rousseau had been encouraged to enter the competition by Diderot, whom Rousseau had visited when Diderot was imprisoned after the publication of LETTER ON THE BLIND. In his essay, Rousseau first expressed the visionary theories that would generate the romantic movement in literature: a belief in human goodness and a call for a return to nature and the primitive virtues corrupted by society.

In 1761, he published an epistolary novel, *Julie, or the New Héloïse*, a love story that popularized the moral beauty of simple living and unaffected virtue. The following year, his two greatest and most influential works appeared: THE SOCIAL CONTRACT, explaining his political philosophy, and *Émile*, a pedagogical novel exemplifying his ideas on education.

In *Émile*, which Rousseau considered to be his best work, he presents a plan for the upbringing of male children based on the principle of the natural goodness of man. The book was first intended to be a "memoir of a few pages." When Rousseau introduced the fictional element of the characters of the Tutor, Émile, and Sophie, the work expanded. In *Émile* Rousseau discourses on a great variety of subjects, including language, history, politics, society, and religion, within a loose fictional framework.

Rousseau structured the book in five parts: the first, on the "age of nature," covering infancy; the second, on boyhood; the third, on the "age of reason"; the fourth, on adolescence; and the fifth, on love and society. In Rousseau's theory of "negative education," giving free rein to nature will result in the best development of human potential. "Nature wants children to be children before being men," Rousseau wrote.

He sees education not simply as imparting or imposing information; rather, it requires a gentle nurturing of what is already within the child. Instruction should proceed by stimulating curiosity and intelligence; the growing child should learn by experience, rather than by rote. The child's mind should develop through conversations and experiments arranged by his tutor that will assist him to use his senses and imagination.

The best preparation for development of healthy, self-reliant children begins in infancy. Babies should be nursed by their own mothers and kept free of swaddling clothes so that the body's natural movements are not impeded. Doctors should be called in as little as possible in order to allow nature's healing powers to operate. As the child grows up, he should participate in athletic activities and commune with nature.

Rousseau was opposed to book learning in childhood. "Reading is the curse of childhood," he believed. The first book he would prescribe for reading at age 12 was Defoe's *Robinson Crusoe*, the story of a man who faced nature with steadfastness and self-reliance. As the child matures, relationships with others begin to be more important and moral and political awareness follows. "The only moral lesson which is suited for a child—the most important lesson for every time of life—is this: 'Never hurt anybody.' "

A child's religious education should begin only when he is familiar with the wonders of the universe. Rousseau would substitute for the dogmas of the church a natural religion based on the principles of deism, in which God's creation is the only Bible and the existence of God is inferred from the order and harmony of the universe, rather than from formal religious teachings.

He recommended against religious books, ritualistic observances, or church attendance. "If I had to depict the most heart-breaking stupidity I would paint a pedant teaching children the catechism," he wrote. As an example of what Émile should learn, Rousseau included a long statement of his own religious belief, "Profession of Faith of a Savoyard Priest," an open attack on Christianity. Book Five begins with a section called "Sophie, or Woman," devoted to the education of women, in which he proposed that a woman's place is in the home and subordinate to that of man.

If his education has spared him unnatural stimulations and energies, eventually the individual is able to exercise his natural powers within a community of rational beings. The child raised according to these methods will become the man who is fit to live in Rousseau's good society, which he analyzed in *The Social Contract*.

CENSORSHIP HISTORY

The deistic religious views expressed by Rousseau in *Émile* offended ecclesiastical authorities. The archbishop of Paris issued a mandate against the book, condemning it for its "abominable doctrines," and prohibited the residents of his diocese from reading or possessing it. In 1762, the Parlement of Paris ordered that the book be publicly torn up and burned. The Parlement condemned *Émile* for its proposals "to re-establish natural religion . . . that criminal system." It also cited its opposition to the idea of an education based on nature, "the kind of knowledge which instinct alone" suggests. It further took issue with the way the author did "misrepresent sovereign authority," destroying "the principles of obedience which is due to kings." The book was also prohibited at the Sorbonne and by the Inquisition.

When the French government ordered his arrest on June 11, 1762, Rousseau fled Paris for Berne but was refused permission to remain there. He took refuge in the Swiss canton of Neuchâtel, then a Prussian possession under the protection of Frederick the Great, king of Prussia. In 1763, *Émile* and *The Social Contract* were attacked by Protestant authorities and condemned by the council of Geneva; copies of the book were burned for having "confused anarchy and liberty, [for having] brought the chaos of the state of nature into the system of civil societies, put an axe to the root of all governments, and in turn exalted and insulted Christianity." An order was given for Rousseau's arrest if he entered the city.

Rousseau was outraged that Geneva, the city of his birth, known as a just and free state, would condemn his work and order his arrest without trial. "I trembled with fear that such an evident and obvious breach of every law, beginning with that of common sense, would throw Geneva upside down," he wrote. When there was little protest in Geneva, Rousseau wrote his *Letter to Christophe de Beaumont*, a long reply to the condemnation of *Émile* by the archbishop of Paris. "Neither the burning nor the decrees will ever make me change my language," he wrote. "The theologians, in ordering me to be humble, will never make me be false and the philosophers, by taxing me with hypocrisy, will never make me profess unbelief." The *Letter* was published in March 1763 in Holland and sold 500 copies in one day in Geneva. When its reprinting was prohibited, Rousseau expected the citizens of Geneva to rally to his defense. When they did not, Rousseau renounced his citizenship.

In 1764, Rousseau published *Letters from the Mountain*, a defense of *Émile* and *The Social Contract* that included an attack on the Geneva council and constitution. When his house was stoned, he moved to St. Pierre, an island in the Lake of Bienne in Berne. In 1765, he was expelled from Berne and went to England at the invitation of the Scottish philosopher David Hume.

In Rome in 1766, the church placed *Émile*, *The Social Contract*, and *Letter to Christophe de Beaumont* on the Index of Forbidden Books. The Spanish Index also prohibited all of Rousseau's writings. Despite its banning, *Émile* was widely read and was extremely influential in its time and in forming modern views of education and childbearing.

One of Rousseau's publishers, François Grasset of Lausanne, recounted to Rousseau in 1765 the response he observed to the suppression of *Émile* in Spain. "I am sure you will be very surprised, my honoured compatriot," he wrote, "when I tell you that I saw your *Émile*, in quarto form, publicly consigned to the flames in Madrid. It took place in the principal Dominican church one Sunday, after High Mass, in the presence of a whole crowd of gaping imbeciles. The immediate consequence was that a number of Spanish grandees and foreign ambassadors began trying to get hold of a copy regardless of cost, arranging for it to be sent them by post." The censorship of *Émile* served only to increase its fame, and it became an underground best seller throughout Europe.

A quarrel with Hume brought Rousseau back to France in 1767. After wandering through the provinces, he settled in 1770 in Paris, where he lived in a garret and copied music, undisturbed by the authorities. There he worked on his famous autobiographical *CONFESSIONS*, which was not published until after his death in 1778.

Both *Émile* and *The Social Contract* remained on the Roman Index through its last edition compiled in 1948 and published until 1966. *Julie, or the New Héloïse* was also placed on the Index in 1806. In 1929, *Confessions* was banned by the United States Customs Department as being injurious to public morals. Rousseau's writing was also banned in the USSR in 1935–36.

FURTHER READING

Collinson, Diané. *Fifty Major Philosophers: A Reference Guide*. London: Routledge, 1988.
Green, Jonathon. *The Encyclopedia of Censorship*. New York: Facts On File, 1990.
Haight, Anne Lyon. *Banned Books: 387 BC to 1978 AD*. Updated and enlarged by Chandler B. Grannis. New York: R. R. Bowker, 1978.
Hornstein, Lillian Herlands, ed. *The Readers' Companion to World Literature*. New York: New American Library, 1956.
Mason, John Hope. *The Indispensable Rousseau*. London: Quartet Books, 1979.
Scott-Kakures, Dion, Susan Castegnetto, Hugh Benson, William Taschek, and Paul Hurley. *History of Philosophy*. New York: HarperCollins, 1993.

ENCYCLOPÉDIE

Editors: Denis Diderot and Jean Le Rond d'Alembert
Original dates and place of publication: 1751–72, France
Literary form: Encyclopedia

SUMMARY

The *Encyclopédie*, a 28-volume encyclopedia of arts and sciences published between 1751 and 1772, epitomized the rational and tolerant spirit of the 18th-century Enlightenment and was instrumental in creating the climate of ideas that culminated in the French Revolution of 1789. The *Encyclopédie* was the monumental life's work of its primary editor, French philosopher, critic, and dramatist Denis Diderot. Diderot's aim in producing the *Encyclopédie* was to "change the general way of thinking" by bringing together the thought of all the outstanding writers and thinkers of the time, collecting in one huge work the summary of all human knowledge as seen from a modern perspective.

Originally planned as a translation from English of Ephraim Chambers's 1728 *Cyclopaedia*, Diderot and mathematician Jean Le Rond d'Alembert decided to launch an entirely new work when disagreements caused the first project to be abandoned. In 1751, Diderot and d'Alembert produced a *Preliminary Discourse* signed by d'Alembert, presenting the philosophical foundations of the project and expressing confidence in human abilities to transform the conditions of material and intellectual life. It traced the sciences and arts to their origins and classified them according to the faculties of memory, reason, or imagination. It also outlined the history of intellectual progress and scientific development since the Renaissance, discussing the contributions of René Descartes, Isaac Newton, and John Locke, as well as those of contemporaries Voltaire (François-Marie Arouet) and Charles-Louis de Secondat, baron de la Brède et de Montesquieu.

Later that year the first folio volume of the *Encyclopédie* appeared, with contributions by the most brilliant writers of the time. Diderot's article "Political Authority" set the rational and democratic tone of the work: "No man has received from nature the right to give orders to others. . . . Power deriving from the consent of the peoples subject to it necessarily presupposes conditions that render the wielding of it legitimate, useful to society, advantageous to the state, and restricted within certain fixed limits."

Diderot's essay "Natural Right," which appeared in the fifth volume published in 1755, exemplified the philosophical thought behind the project. He defended a universal natural law based on human needs and experience, rather than the doctrine of traditional innate or God-given law. "We must in all things, make use of our reason, because man is not merely an animal, but an animal with the power of reason. . . . Everything that you conceive, every course of action you consider, will be good, great, noble, sublime if it is in accordance with the general and common interest."

Despite struggles with government censors, seven folio volumes appeared at the rate of one a year until 1757 and included contributions by such luminaries as Voltaire, Montesquieu, and Jean-Jacques Rousseau. In 1759, the *Encyclopédie* was officially suppressed. After d'Alembert resigned as editor, Diderot carried on the project clandestinely, publishing the last 10 volumes of text in 1765 in the provinces and in 1766 in Paris. Eleven volumes of plates illustrating the industrial arts also appeared under his direction in 1772.

The *Encyclopédie* was immediately successful. Its intellectual and political impact was enormous. It promulgated the work of Francis Bacon, Descartes, Thomas Hobbes, Locke, George Berkeley, Baruch Spinoza, Pierre Bayle, and Gottfried Wilhelm Leibnitz in philosophy and the scientific advances of Nicolaus Copernicus, Johannes Kepler, Galileo Galilei, and Newton. It implicitly advocated social change in its preference for ideas derived from experience and the senses, its glorification of the arts, sciences, and industry, its stress on rationalism and scientific determinism, and its attacks on legal, juridical, and clerical abuses. It championed the principles of religious tolerance, democratic government, and equality, supporting the philosophic doctrine that the dissemination of knowledge would lead to human emancipation.

CENSORSHIP HISTORY

In an entry in the *Encyclopédie* expounding on the meaning of the word *pardonner,* "to pardon," Diderot took the opportunity to defend his work against defamation. "Some men, who produced a silly work which imbecile editors botched further," he wrote, referring to the Jesuit encyclopedia the *Dictionnaire de Trévoux,* "have never been able to pardon us for having planned a better one. These enemies to all good have subjected us to every kind of persecution. We have seen our honor, our fortune, our liberty, our life endangered within a few months' time."

Indeed, the rational secular emphasis of the *Encyclopédie* made government officials uneasy and aroused the hostility of the Jesuits, who attacked the work as irreligious and used their influence to have it suppressed. The opening skirmish of the battle to censor the *Encyclopédie* took place after the publication of the first two volumes in 1752. Among the articles in the second volume was "Certitude," written by Jean-Martin de Prades, a theology student at the Sorbonne. The Parlement of Paris had earlier denounced as heretical the thesis submitted by de Prades for his Sorbonne degree. It was rumored that Diderot had a hand in the thesis, which, in fact, included whole paragraphs taken from the *Preliminary Discourse.* The Sorbonne revoked de Prades's degree and ordered his arrest. He fled to Prussia, but the fallout from the de Prades affair landed squarely on the *Encyclopédie.*

De Prades's contribution was denounced to the king as evidence of the atheistic underpinnings of the project. Jesuit critics also took the editors to task for an article claiming that most men honor literature as they do religion, "as something they can neither know nor practice nor love." On January 31, 1752, the archbishop of Paris condemned the *Encyclopédie* for its subtle attack on religion.

In February, the king's council condemned the first two volumes for their tendency to "destroy the royal authority, set up the spirit of independence and revolt, and under obscure and equivocal language, to raise the foundations of error, of corruptions of morals, of irreligion, and of unbelief." The council forbade further sale or publication and ordered seizure of the volumes.

The publisher, André-François Le Breton, and his associates, Antoine-Claude Briasson, Michel-Antoine David, and Laurent Durand, appealed to the council with the support of Chrétien-Guillaume de Lamoignon de Malesherbes, the liberal director of the book trade and powerful protector of the *Encyclopédie*. Malesherbes arranged the granting of a "tacit permission" for the publication of further volumes and, to placate the clergy, agreed that future volumes would be reviewed by three theologians. In 1754, Louis XV, influenced by anti-Jesuit sentiment within his court, granted a personal *privilège*, or official permit, for continuation of the work.

As publication of the volumes proceeded, the number of subscribers rose far beyond the number anticipated by the publishers to 4,255 by 1757. That year brought the second attempt to ban the *Encyclopédie*. In the wake of an assassination attempt against Louis XV, the Crown issued a declaration in April 1757 reviving an old law that condemned to death authors, publishers, and sellers of books that attacked religion and the state.

The seventh volume of the *Encyclopédie* included an article by d'Alembert on the Calvinist stronghold of Geneva, in which he compared French Catholicism unfavorably with Genevan Protestantism and represented the Calvinist clergy as denying the divinity of Christ. The article offended both Protestants and Catholics. Seizing their opportunity, the opponents of the project pressed again for its suppression. In July 1758, Claude-Adrien Helvétius's book DE L'ESPRIT was condemned by religious and civil authorities as atheistic and subversive. The anti-Encyclopédists charged that Helvétius's book, whose skeptical views were associated with those of the philosophes, was intimately connected with the *Encyclopédie*. The two books were viewed as representing a conspiracy to destroy religion and undermine the state.

The furor over the seventh volume led the king to revoke the license to publish in 1759 and a decree of his council outlawed the *Encyclopédie*. "The advantages to be derived from a work of this sort, in respect to progress in the arts and sciences, can never compensate for the irreparable damage that results from it in regard to morality and religion," the decree stated. The publishers were forbidden to sell the volumes that had already appeared or print any new ones.

On March 5, 1759, the Vatican placed the first seven volumes of the *Encyclopédie* on the Index of Forbidden Books on the grounds that the teaching and propositions contained in it were false and pernicious, tending to the destruction of morality, the promotion of godlessness, and the undermining of religion. Later that year, Pope Clement XII warned all Catholics who owned the volumes to have them burned by a priest or face excommunication.

D'Alembert had resigned as editor in 1758, but Diderot and his printers continued their work in secret. Urged to give up the project and flee the country for his own safety, Diderot wrote to Voltaire that "to abandon the work is to turn one's back on the breach, and do what the rascals who persecute us desire."

The king's council further required that the publishers issue refunds to subscribers to close accounts. The edict put the publishers at risk of financial insolvency. But through the intervention of Malesherbes, the government allowed the publishers to apply the money to the production of a new book that was, in fact, the plates of the *Encyclopédie* under a different title.

The new book received a *privilège* in September 1759, and the publishers were able to proceed to print the last 10 volumes of text. These volumes appeared all at once in 1765 and 1766 under a false imprint, Chez Samuel Faulche & Compagnie, Neufchastel. The Jesuits, the enemies of the *Encyclopédie*, had been expelled from France in 1764, and powerful figures at court and in the government quietly used their influence to allow distribution of the volumes. The government, recognizing the fait accompli, did not take further action against Diderot.

The *Encyclopédie* became the best-known work of its time and the most formidable instrument for diffusion of the progressive ideas of the Enlightenment. Its 28 volumes were reprinted in Switzerland, Italy, Germany, and Russia, and numerous approved and pirated editions appeared in France—43 in all over a 25-year period. Many of the later printings were inexpensive quarto and octavo editions that reached ordinary readers everywhere in Europe. In all, about 25,000 copies of the *Encyclopédie* were circulated in Europe before 1789, at least 11,500 of them in France.

In 1804, the church placed the entire work on the Index of Forbidden Books, where it remained until the last edition of the Index was published in 1966. It was not an official act of church or state, however, that was most effective in censoring the *Encyclopédie*. In 1764, after the last 10 volumes of text had already been set in type, Diderot discovered that his printer, Le Breton, had secretly deleted text and altered many articles containing liberal opinions. He had, for example, removed from Diderot's article on the Saracens the following passage: "It is a general observation that religion declines as philosophy grows. You may reach what conclusions you like either against the usefulness of philosophy or the truth of religion; but I can tell you that the more philosophers there are in Constantinople, the fewer pilgrims there will be to Mecca." The mutilated articles also included those in which Diderot had eulogized the skeptical philosophy of the 17th-century philosopher Bayle, author of the controversial HISTORICAL AND CRITICAL DICTIONARY.

Diderot was enraged by Le Breton's betrayal. "You have driven a dagger into my heart," Diderot wrote to Le Breton. "I shall bear the wound until I die." For almost 200 years, the expurgated text was the only one available, until a volume turned up containing Le Breton's corrections of the proof and was acquired by an American collector.

FURTHER READING

Darnton, Robert. *The Business of Enlightenment: A Publishing History of the Encyclopédie 1775–1800*. Cambridge, Mass.: Belknap Press of Harvard University Press, 1979.

Diderot, Denis. *Diderot's Selected Writings*. Edited and with an introduction by Lester G. Crocker. Trans. Derek Coltman. New York: Macmillan, 1966.

Durant, Will, and Ariel Durant. *The Age of Voltaire*. New York: Simon and Schuster, 1965.

Garraty, John A., and Peter Gay. *The Columbia History of the World*. New York: Harper and Row, 1972.

Gay, Peter. *The Enlightenment: An Interpretation. The Rise of Modern Paganism*. New York: W. W. Norton, 1995.

Green, Jonathon. *The Encyclopedia of Censorship*. New York: Facts On File, 1990.

Haight, Anne Lyon. *Banned Books: 387 BC to 1978 AD*. Updated and enlarged by Chandler B. Grannis. New York: R. R. Bowker, 1978.

Hornstein, Lillian Herlands, ed. *The Readers' Companion to World Literature*. New York: New American Library, 1956.

Reill, Peter Hanns, and Ellen Judy Wilson, eds. *Encyclopedia of the Enlightenment*. New York: Facts On File, 1996.

AN ESSAY CONCERNING HUMAN UNDERSTANDING

Author: John Locke
Original date and place of publication: 1690, England
Literary form: Philosophical treatise

SUMMARY

The English philosopher John Locke, the intellectual ruler of the 18th century, was the founder of the school of philosophy known as British empiricism. Educated at Oxford, he lectured there in Greek, rhetoric, and philosophy. His familiarity with scientific practice gained through study of medicine had a strong influence on his philosophy. He became a physician and adviser to Anthony Ashley Cooper, first earl of Shaftesbury, and in 1675 went to France, where he became acquainted with French leaders in science and philosophy. In 1679, he retired to Oxford.

Suspected of radicalism by the British government, Locke fled to Holland in 1683. During his six years in Holland, he completed *An Essay Concerning Human Understanding*, one of the most important works in modern philosophy. First published in 1690, it was reissued in expanded editions in 1694, 1700, and 1706.

Through this essay, Locke became known in England and on the Continent as the leading philosopher of freedom. It was the most widely read philosophical book of his generation, written in a lucid style and without technical philosophical terminology. Locke "created metaphysics almost as Newton had created physics," wrote Jean Le Rond d'Alembert in 1751 in the *Preliminary Discourse* to the great monument to Enlightenment thought, the ENCYCLOPÉDIE.

Locke saw the philosopher's primary task as clarification, "to be employed as an under-labourer in clearing the ground a little, and removing some of the rubbish that lies in the way to knowledge." His contribution was to present philosophy as a discipline based on empirical observation and common sense judgments, rather than an esoteric study. He established the connection between philosophy and scientific thought by explaining in a manner that was consistent with 17th-century science how knowledge was acquired.

In the opening "Epistle to the Reader," Locke describes how the *Essay* developed as the fruit of a casual discussion with a few friends: "After we had awhile puzzled ourselves, without coming any nearer a resolution of those doubts which perplexed us, it came into my thoughts that we took a wrong course, and that before we set ourselves upon inquiries of that nature, it was necessary to examine our own abilities, and see what objects our understandings were, or were not, fitted to deal with."

Locke wrote down some "hasty and undigested thoughts on a subject he had never before considered" to bring to the next meeting of his friends. These first notes led to an extensive critical inquiry "into the origins, certainty and extent of human knowledge together with the grounds and degrees of belief, opinion and assent" that was to absorb 20 years of study and writing.

In the *Essay*, Locke examines the nature of knowledge and the basis for judging truth. By observing the natural world, he traces beliefs and states of mind to their psychological origins. He sets out to show that human understanding is too limited to allow comprehensive knowledge of the universe. For Locke, if we insist on certainty we will lose our bearings in the world. "[I]t becomes the Modesty of Philosophy" for us not to speak too confidently where we lack grounds of knowledge and to content ourselves with faith and probability.

He begins by refuting Plato's doctrine of "innate ideas," maintaining, instead, that all knowledge is of empiric origin. The mind at birth is a tabula rasa, a "white paper, void of all characters, without any ideas," Locke believed. Experience in the form of sensations and reflections provides raw materials that the mind analyzes and organizes in complex ways. Because all knowledge is ultimately derived from experience, language—the means by which knowledge is transmitted—has meaning only within the context of experience.

For Locke, even the idea of God is not innate. It can be discovered by a rational mind reflecting on the works of creation. Locke criticizes the innateness doctrine as esoteric and open to exploitation by those in positions of authority who claim to be guardians of hidden truths. "Vague and insignificant forms of speech, and abuse of language, have so long passed for mysteries of science . . . ," Locke writes, "that it will not be easy to persuade either those who speak or those who hear them that they are but the covers of ignorance, and hindrance of true knowledge." Reason must judge the authenticity of religious revelation. To accept an irrational belief as revelation "must overturn all the principles and foundations of knowledge."

Locke's abandonment of the innateness doctrine opened the way for three influential concepts: that knowledge is cumulative and progressive, the necessity of communication, and curiosity about cultural variety. As Voltaire wrote of Locke, "Aided everywhere by the torch of physics, he dares at times to affirm, but he also dares to doubt. Instead of collecting in one sweeping definition what we do not know, he explores by degrees what we desire to know."

CENSORSHIP HISTORY

Locke's *Essay* was widely read in England and on the Continent, where most of his works became known in French translations. His rejection of innate ideas immediately involved him in controversy with theologians who saw his argument as a threat to religious belief and the maintenance of church discipline. It was, however, another aspect of the *Essay*—Locke's comment on "thinking matter"—that became its single most disputed issue.

Locke's statement that one "possibly shall never be able to know, whether any material Being thinks, or no" caused great controversy, particularly in France, where Voltaire quoted it in LETTERS CONCERNING THE ENGLISH NATION and declared it a central concept in Locke's thinking. This remark and Locke's belief that "all the great ends of Morality and Religion, are well enough secured, without philosophical Proofs of the Soul's Immateriality" were held to support materialism and atheism.

These passages became a subject of intense debate between Locke and the bishop of Worcester, Edward Stillingfleet. The bishop read the essay when it first appeared in 1690 and had not seen it as having any dangerous consequences for the doctrines of the Church of England. But with the publication in 1696 of the radical deist John Toland's CHRISTIANITY NOT MYSTERIOUS, a widely banned book positing reason as the only test of faith, Locke came under attack.

Although Toland's rationalistic approach to theology went far beyond anything Locke advocated or believed, Toland adopted Locke's theory of knowledge from the *Essay*. Stillingfleet prefaced a 1696 critique of Toland with a condemnation of Locke. Some of the issues raised by Locke's debate with Stillingfleet appeared in 1699 as material added by Locke to the fourth edition of the *Essay*.

In *The Reasonableness of Christianity,* published in 1695, Locke maintained that knowledge must be supplemented by religious faith. He dismissed the doctrine of Original Sin as unsupported by the Bible and contrary both to reason and to the idea of a benevolent God. He was accused of being anti-Trinitarian and Socinian, a heresy that rejected the divinity of the Holy Trinity.

In 1701, in London, the Latin version of *Essay* was prohibited at Oxford with the instructions "that no tutors were to read with their students" this investigation into the basis of knowledge. In 1700, the Catholic Church placed the French translation of *An Essay Concerning Human Understanding* on the Index of Forbidden Books. It remained listed until 1966. *Essay* was singled out as condemned directly by the pope in a solemn manner, a designation shared by only 144 of the 4,126 works listed on the modern Index and the only distinguished book in that category. Despite the censorship of *An Essay on Human Understanding,* Locke's book exerted a profound influence on its time and in the history of philosophy.

FURTHER READING

Chappell, Vere, ed. *The Cambridge Companion to Locke.* Cambridge: Cambridge University Press, 1994.
Collinson, Diané. *Fifty Major Philosophers: A Reference Guide.* London: Routledge, 1988.
Green, Jonathon. *The Encyclopedia of Censorship.* New York: Facts On File, 1990.
Scott-Kakures, Dion, Susan Castegnetto, Hugh Benson, William Taschek, and Paul Hurley. *History of Philosophy.* New York: HarperCollins, 1993.

ESSAYS

Author: Michel de Montaigne
Original date and place of publication: 1580, France
Literary form: Essays

SUMMARY

Michel de Montaigne was the originator of the personal essay as a literary form and the inventor of a new form of autobiography. In his *essais,* or "trials," he set out to test his judgment on a wide range of subjects of interest to him, revealing his inner life and personality. Written over a period of 20 years, beginning in 1571 when Montaigne was 38 until his death in 1592, the 94 essays trace the evolution of Montaigne's thinking as he added to and changed his earlier writings. Books one and two were published in 1580. Revised and enlarged editions of the first two books appeared with book three in 1588; a final complete edition was published posthumously in 1595.

The earliest essays, which began as notes on Montaigne's reading, are mainly compilations of anecdotes with brief commentary. Over the years the essays became longer and more personal. His most influential philosophical essay was the book-length "Apology for Raymond Sebond," composed in 1576. Montaigne's skepticism, summed up in his famous motto *"Que Sçay-je?"* (What do I know?), is revealed in this essay, a sustained argument on the impotence and vanity of presumptuous human reason. In the later essays his self-portrait emerges as the central theme.

Essays opens with Montaigne's preface, "To the Reader," in which he sets the conversational, personal and modest tone that is characteristic of his writing: "This book was written in good faith, reader. It warns you from the outset that in it I have set myself no goal but a domestic and private one. I have had no thought of serving either you or my own glory. . . . If I had written to seek the world's favor, I should have bedecked myself better, and should have presented myself in a studied posture. I want to be seen here in my simple, natural, ordinary fashion, without straining or artifice; for it is myself that I portray."

Drawing on his own recollections, conversations with neighbors and friends, readings in classical literature, and the narratives of historians and ethnographers, the essays range over a vast array of subjects, from cannibalism to education, politics, friendship, nature, and death. Montaigne reveals himself as intellectually curious, tolerant, skeptical, and unafraid to contradict himself. His aim is to provide an unvarnished picture of his experience and attitudes, for if a man does not know himself, what does he know?

"My sole aim is to reveal myself," he writes, "and I may be different tomorrow if some new lesson changes me. . . . Contradictions of opinion, therefore, neither offend nor estrange me; they only arouse and exercise my mind."

Through his quest for self-knowledge, Montaigne is led to recognize common human traits and values. In his last essay, "On Experience," he concludes, "It is an absolute perfection and virtually divine to know how to enjoy our being rightfully. We seek other conditions because we do not understand the use of our own, and go outside of ourselves because we do not know what it is like inside. . . . The most beautiful lives, to my mind, are those that conform to the common human pattern, with order, but without miracle and without eccentricity."

CENSORSHIP HISTORY

The first attempt to censor the *Essays* took place in 1580–81, shortly after the first publication of books one and two, when Montaigne traveled to Germany, Switzerland, and Italy. Upon his entry into Rome, as Montaigne recounted in his *Travel Journal*, his baggage was thoroughly examined by customs. Although he had passed through Germany and "was of an inquiring nature," he carried no forbidden books. Nevertheless, all the books he had, including a copy of the *Essays*, were confiscated for examination. They included a prayer book (suspect only because it was published in Paris, rather than Rome) and "also the books of certain German doctors of theology against the heretics, because in combatting them, they made mention of their errors."

Though Montaigne had been cordially received by Pope Gregory XIII, he was later summoned to the Vatican's Holy Office and advised that some passages in his *Essays* should be changed or deleted in future editions. The papal censor, theology professor Sisto Fabri, who did not read French, discussed with Montaigne various errors that had been identified upon the report of a French friar. The censor objected to the overuse of the word *fortune;* the defense of the fourth-century Roman emperor Julian, who abandoned Christianity; the praise of heretical poets; the idea that one who prays should be free from evil impulses; the critical comments on torture ("All that is beyond plain death seems to me pure cruelty"); and the recommendation that children should be fit to do either good or evil so that they may do good through free choice. Though Fabri was "content with the excuses I offered," Montaigne commented, "on each objection that his Frenchman had left him he referred it to my conscience to redress what I thought was in bad taste."

Montaigne responded that these were his opinions, which he did not feel were erroneous, and suggested that perhaps the censor had improperly understood his thoughts. He did promise, however, to consider some revisions. Ultimately, he made none of the recommended revisions in the essays.

In 1595, an unauthorized, expurgated edition was published in Lyon by Simon Goulart. As it was produced for Calvinist consumption, the publisher suppressed a number of chapters and omitted passages critical of Protestants. In its complete edition, as edited by Montaigne's literary executor Marie de Gournay and published in 1595, *Essays* remained a best seller in France into the mid-17th century and was reprinted every two or three years. The book was considered a classic and Montaigne a standard author.

Though the Spanish Inquisition prohibited Montaigne's writing in 1640, it was not until 84 years after Montaigne's death, when the *Essays* had been circulating for close to a century, that the Vatican condemned it. In 1676, it was placed on the Index of Forbidden Books and remained there for almost 300 years.

Montaigne was a faithful Catholic, but he felt that the spheres of faith and reason should be separate. He believed that when faith and reason are contradictory, faith must prevail in religious matters. Not even the most important church dogmas, such as the existence of God and the immortality of the soul, can be proved. They must, rather, be accepted on faith. Theology and philosophy were thus separated, and modern scientific discoveries, such as the new astronomy combatted by the church, could be accepted as a matter of reason without challenging religious doctrine.

"No proposition astounds me, no belief offends me," Montaigne wrote, "however much opposed it may be to my own." Montaigne's skepticism, tolerance, and mistrust of dogmatic systems of belief reflected an open-minded humanistic spirit. This attitude was still possible in Montaigne's day while the liberal philosophy of Renaissance humanism prevailed. But as the Counter Reformation gained strength and church traditions were secured against the innovations of Protestant theology, Montaigne's views on the separation of faith and reason were attacked as the heresy of "fideism." The placement of the *Essays* on the Index in 1676 is thought to be the result of criticisms by theologians influenced by the rationalism of Descartes, which declared that faith could appeal to reason.

FURTHER READING

Boase, Alan M. *The Fortunes of Montaigne: A History of the Essays in France, 1580–1669.* New York: Octagon Books, 1970.

Frame, Donald M., trans. and intro. *The Complete Works of Montaigne.* Stanford, Calif.: Stanford University Press, 1967.

———, trans. and intro. *The Complete Essays of Montaigne.* Stanford, Calif.: Stanford University Press, 1958.

Montaigne, Michel de. *Essays.* Ed. and introduction by J. M. Cohen. Middlesex, England: Penguin Books, 1958.

Tetel, Marcel. *Montaigne: Updated Edition.* Boston: Twayne Publishers, 1990.

Toulmin, Stephen. *Cosmopolis: The Hidden Agenda of Modernity.* Chicago: University of Chicago Press, 1990.

ETHICS

Author: Baruch Spinoza
Original date and place of publication: 1677, Holland
Literary form: Philosophical treatise

SUMMARY

The Dutch rationalist philosopher Baruch (Benedict) Spinoza was born in Amsterdam to Portuguese Jewish parents who had fled the Spanish Inquisition. A scholar of Hebrew, he questioned many traditional tenets of Judaism as conflicting with reason and natural science. For his heretical thinking, he was excommunicated from the Jewish community in 1656 at the age of 24. He subsequently made his living as a lens grinder and devoted himself to his philosophical writings, discussing René Descartes's new philosophy with a group of secular Christians. His most important and difficult masterpiece, *Ethics,* was completed in 1665 but not published until after his death in 1677.

Of the rationalist philosophers of the period, Spinoza's ideas have the most in common with modern, secular conceptions of the cosmos. According to Spinoza, all that exists is of this world. The order of the world cannot be explained by appeal to the acts of a transcendent God. The fundamental presupposition of his method is that the structure of the cosmos can be set out in geometrical fashion and understood by appeal to self-evident claims bound by logical relations. Mathematics, which deals not in final causes, but in the essence and properties of forms, offers a standard of truth.

In all of his writing, Spinoza advocated, in opposition to traditional theology, a purely naturalistic and scientific study of all aspects of human thought and behavior free of emotional and moral attitudes, which are reflections of subjective desires and fears. All problems, whether metaphysical, moral, or scientific, can be formulated and solved as if they were geometrical theorems. Thus he wrote *Ethics* in the geometrical manner, as a succession of definitions and propositions with supporting proofs.

The definitions and propositions set out in the first part of *Ethics* can be properly understood only in relation to the mutually supporting propositions that follow. Spinoza introduces definitions for his notions of substance, cause, attribute, freedom, and necessity, successively explaining each in terms of the others. With the aid of these logically connected notions he defines what he means by God or nature.

It is Spinoza's fundamental argument in *Ethics* that there can only be a single substance, God or nature (*Deus sive Natura*), which necessarily exists and is the cause of itself. All other aspects of reality must be explained as attributes of this unique, infinite, and all-inclusive substance. "Hence it follows that God alone is a free cause. For God alone exists from the mere necessity of his own nature." God is not the creator of nature beyond himself. Rather, God *is* nature in its fullness.

Everything that exists has its place in the system of causes in nature, Spinoza believed. Every human choice, attitude, or feeling is the necessary effect of causes in the infinite chain of causes. Nature has no fixed aim in view and all final causes are merely human fabrications.

Spinoza was a determinist. He believed that all actions are determined by past experience and the laws of nature. He was also a relativist, in that he believed that things are not inherently good or bad but take on such properties in relation to circumstances.

CENSORSHIP HISTORY

Spinoza's reputation as a dangerous skeptic and heretic was firmly established when he was excommunicated from the Jewish community of Amsterdam in 1656. Because of his family's prominence, his lapse from orthodoxy caused a scandal that was viewed as a threat to the survival of the community. Jews were not yet citizens in Holland, and their leaders feared that the spread of intellectual dissent in their midst would alarm the Dutch, who were already sheltering many religious sects and schisms within their borders.

Spinoza found biblical doctrine incompatible with natural science and logic. He was uncomfortable with the notion of miracles, found the description of God in the Torah unacceptable to his reason, and regarded its laws as arbitrary. He considered the Bible to have been written by human beings and did not accept it as the "word of God." He also questioned whether the Jews were uniquely God's chosen people.

On July 17, 1656, the ruling council of the community announced that having endeavored for some time without success to deter Baruch de Espinoza [as he was known in the Jewish community] from his evil ways, it was "resolved that the said Espinoza be put in *herem* (ban) and banished from the nation of Israel. . . . We warn that none may contact him orally or in writing, nor do him any favor, nor stay under the same roof with him, nor read any paper he made or wrote."

When *Ethics* was completed in 1665, in view of Spinoza's growing notoriety and criticism of his philosophy as atheistic and subversive, it was clear that its publication, even anonymously, would be too dangerous while he was alive. In 1668, Adrian Coerbach, a doctor of medicine of Amsterdam, was charged with having accepted and defended opinions of Spinoza. Coerbach was sentenced to prison for 10 years and banished from Holland for another decade.

When Spinoza's THEOLOGICAL-POLITICAL TREATISE, a defense of freedom of opinion that laid the foundations for a rational interpretation of the Jewish and Christian religions, was published in 1670, it brought Spinoza fame. It also aroused hostility because of its skepticism about religious doctrine. Although it was published anonymously under a fictitious imprint, Spinoza was known to be the author.

This treatise was the only one that Spinoza was able to publish during his lifetime, except for a 1663 exposition on Descartes's philosophy that included an introduction explaining that the work did not represent his own views. Spinoza spent the last years of his life on the *Political Treatise*, which he intended as a more popular exposition of the principles of tolerance in a rational society.

After Spinoza's death in 1677, his friends published his writing in a single volume, *Opera posthuma*, including *Ethics*, *Political Treatise*, and several other works. *Ethics* was widely condemned as atheistic and morally subversive. Spinoza's pantheism—his identification of God with nature—and his determinism were viewed as particularly offensive.

A series of bans against Spinoza's work in Holland ensued under the authority of the prince of Orange, states of Holland, synods of the church, local magistrates, university authorities, and the burgomaster of Leiden. A total of 50 edicts or judgments against reading or circulating Spinoza's works were issued through 1680. In 1679, the Catholic Church placed all of his writing on the Index of Forbidden Books. The church denounced his *Theological Political Treatise* as a book "forged in hell by a renegade Jew and the devil." His work remained on the Index under the most severe category of *opera omnia*, or all works condemned, through the last edition of the Index in the 20th century.

For about 100 years after his death, Spinoza's name was linked with immorality, and his philosophy was largely neglected. Only at the end of the 18th century, when Johann Wolfgang von Goethe aroused interest in him, was his work studied seriously again.

FURTHER READING

Gerber, Jane S. *The Jews of Spain: A History of the Sephardic Experience*. New York: Free Press, 1992.

Hampshire, Stuart. *Spinoza: An Introduction to His Philosophical Thought*. London: Penguin Books, 1988.

———, ed. *The Age of Reason: The 17th Century Philosophers*. New York: New American Library, 1956.

Putnam, George Haven. *The Censorship of the Church of Rome*. Vol. 2. New York: G. P. Putnam's Sons, 1906–07.

Scott-Kakures, Dion, Susan Castegnetto, Hugh Benson, William Taschek, and Paul Hurley. *History of Philosophy*. New York: HarperCollins, 1993.

THE FABLE OF THE BEES

Author: Bernard Mandeville
Original dates and place of publication: 1714, 1723, 1728, England
Literary form: Satirical essays

SUMMARY

The Fable of the Bees was one of the most controversial and widely read books of early 18th-century England. Its author, Bernard Mandeville, was a Dutch physician who had moved to London, where he practiced medicine and wrote on ethical subjects.

In 1705, he published a satirical poem, "The Grumbling Hive: Or, Knaves Turn'd Honest." It was reprinted in 1714 along with an essay, "An Enquiry into the Origins of Moral Virtue," and a series of remarks elaborating upon ideas expressed in the poem. The new volume was called *The Fable of the Bees: Or, Private Vices, Publick Benefits*.

A moral fable about the symbiotic relationship between vice and national greatness, Mandeville's satire mixed verse with prose, including parables, fables, and anecdotes. Portraying England as a flourishing beehive, he proposed that the prosperity of the hive depended on the evil behavior of its members. The unknowing cooperation of individuals working for their own interests resulted in the satisfaction of society's needs. "Thus every Part was full of Vice, Yet the whole Mass a Paradise."

Mandeville declared that vice, rather than virtue, was the foundation of the emerging capitalist society. Examining virtuous actions taken out of self-interest, he contended that in reality they were only "counterfeited" virtues. The "most hateful qualities of its citizens"—pride, self-interest, and the desire for material goods—represented, in fact, the very basis of the economic well-being of society. Economic prosperity was best maintained when there was least interference by government or charitable organizations.

Commission of crime kept the legal profession employed. The vices of vanity and luxury in the rich, for example, benefited the poor by providing employment for them, creating wants that kept merchants and manufacturers in business. Prostitution was inevitable and socially useful. "Religion is one thing and Trade is another," Mandeville declared. Economics and morality were not natural allies. "The moment Evil ceases, the Society must be spoiled." Therefore, a nation of atheists would probably be healthier, more prosperous, and more powerful than a society of believers.

In a stinging attack on clerical hypocrisy, he also indicted "reverend Divines of all Sects," who lecture on the spiritual benefits of self-denial and then demand for themselves "convenient Houses, handsome Furniture, good Fires in Winter, pleasant Gardens in Summer, neat Clothes and Money enough to bring up their Children. . . ."

Despite its bold ideas, *The Fable of the Bees* attracted little attention until 1723, when Mandeville published a new and enlarged edition of the book, adding two lengthy essays: "A Search into the Nature of Society" and "An Essay on Charity and Charity-Schools."

"A Search into the Nature of Society" provided additional illustrations of the social and economic utility of vice, attacking the optimistic philosophy of Anthony Ashley Cooper, 3rd Earl of Shaftesbury. It was Mandeville's charity-school essay, however, that became notorious.

In 1699, the Society for Promoting Christian Knowledge had organized a movement to establish charity schools for the poor in every parish in Britain. Several hundred such schools were founded, supported by the clergy and the British public. Dedicated to moral improvement of the poor, the schools provided instruction in Bible reading, the catechism, and mathematics. In an attack on the schools, Mandeville contended that to lavish charity on the poor was to remove their incentive to work and foster unrealistic ambitions and desires. Defining charity as "that Virtue by which part of that sincere Love we have for our selves is transferr'd pure and unmix'd to others," Mandeville claimed that no action was genuinely charitable unless it was untainted by any selfish desire. Pity was not a virtue, since it derived from a self-indulgent wish to spare ourselves unpleasant sights and feelings. "Thousands give Money to Beggars from the same Motive as they pay their Corn-cutter, to walk easy," he wrote.

CENSORSHIP HISTORY

In a 1714 preface to *The Fable of the Bees*, Mandeville remarked: "If you ask me, why I have done all this . . . and what Good these Notions will produce? Truly, besides the Reader's Diversion, I believe, none at all. . . ." Rather than a mere diversion for Mandeville's readers, however, *The Fable of the Bees* became the subject of one of the most heated controversies of the time.

After 1723, *The Fable* was the target of attacks in the press, pulpits, and courts that were to last through most of the century. "Vice and Luxury have found a champion and a Defendor, which they never did before," one critic wrote. In the view of one anonymous 18th-century poet, whose sentiments were typical of public reaction to the volume, Mandeville was the anti-Christ. "And if GOD-MAN Vice to abolish came / Who Vice commends, MAN-DEVIL be his name."

By implying that religion was damaging to social welfare, the book seemed to advocate atheism and immorality. In 1723, Mandeville's book was the subject of a presentment by the grand jury of Middlesex, in which the book was declared a public nuisance and the author accused of a blasphemy so "diabolical" that it had "a direct Tendency to the Subversion of all Religion and Civil Government." The jury indicated concern that the continued publication of Mandeville's "flagrant Impieties" would provoke divine retribution, particularly his recommendations that vice was necessary to public welfare.

Mandeville's case never came to trial, however, because he was befriended by a former lord chancellor, Sir Thomas Parker, the earl of Macclesfield. Also, it is assumed that because Mandeville intended his book only for people of "knowledge and education" who could afford the price of five shillings, the book was felt to be a lesser threat to public order.

Undeterred by the grand jury's findings, Mandeville immediately published a six-penny pamphlet containing the grand jury's presentment against the 1723 edition, the text of an attack on the book from the *London Journal*, and his own "Vindication" of the book. The pamphlet's contents were added to a new edition of *The Fable*, published in 1724.

During the next five years, 10 different books were published attacking *The Fable*. In 1728, the work was again presented to the grand jury of Middlesex. The grand jury alleged that Mandeville had undermined the authority of the Bible and advocated "a Freedom of thinking and acting whatever Men please." His book was "atheistical" and had "many blasphemous passages." The grand jury also complained about the new edition's inclusion of the earlier grand jury's condemnation of *The Fable*.

In late 1728, Mandeville issued yet another edition, doubling the book's size with the inclusion of part two, a series of six dialogues in which two characters, Cleomenes and Horatio, debate Mandeville's philosophy.

Attacks on *The Fable* persisted after Mandeville's death in 1733. In 1740, it was translated into French and in 1761 into German. A storm of criticism greeted the book on the Continent. In France it was ordered to be burned by the common hangman. The Catholic Church also placed the book on the Index of Forbidden Books, where it remained through the last edition of the Index, published until 1966.

Described by one critic as "the wickedest cleverest book in the English language," *The Fable of the Bees* today is regarded as a masterpiece of the great English age of satire. Historians also recognize Mandeville's significant contribution to social philosophy and economic theory as a precursor of Adam Smith's 18th-century doctrine of laissez-faire economics and as an influence on the 19th-century philosophy of utilitarianism, the theory that the rightness of an action is determined by its consequences.

FURTHER READING

Cook, Richard I. *Bernard Mandeville*. New York: Twayne Publishers, 1974.
Levy, Leonard W. *Blasphemy: Verbal Offense Against the Sacred, from Moses to Salman Rushdie*. New York: Alfred A. Knopf, 1993.
Mandeville, Bernard. *The Fable of the Bees*. Introduction by Philip Harth. London: Penguin Books, 1970.

THE GUIDE OF THE PERPLEXED

Author: Maimonides
Original date and place of publication: 1197, Egypt
Literary form: Philosophical text

SUMMARY

Maimonides (Moses ben Maimon), the most important Jewish medieval philosopher, was born in Córdoba, Spain, where his father was a judge and rabbi. When Córdoba fell in 1148 to the Almohads, a fundamentalist Islamic regime from North Africa, Maimonides and his family were forced as Jews to flee Spain. They moved to Morocco, then to Palestine, and eventually settled in Egypt. Maimonides became a physician in the court of Saladin and attained wide recognition as a jurist, a philosopher, and the leader of Egypt's Jewish community.

Maimonides's writings include works on law, logic, medicine, and theology. His greatest legal study, the *Mishneh Torah*, an attempt to organize all of Jewish law into a single code, is regarded as one of the most important Jewish works ever written. In his principal philosophical work, *The Guide of the Perplexed*, written in 1197 in Arabic and translated in 1204 into Hebrew, Maimonides sought to reconcile Judaism with the teachings of Aristotle, explaining in a logical way all that could be known about metaphysical problems. He was considered among the most distinguished philosophers of the Islamic world to apply the methodology of Aristotle to difficult conceptual issues.

Maimonides did not write *The Guide* for average readers but for select contemporaries who had studied classical science and philosophy, as well as Jewish scholarship. He addressed it to a pupil who found it difficult to reconcile the letter of Jewish law with the discoveries of natural science and Aristotelian philosophy. The purpose of *The Guide* was, Maimonides wrote, "to give indications to a religious man for whom the validity of our Law has become established in his soul and has become actual in his belief." His aim was to guide such "perplexed" individuals to a deeper insight into philosophical truths without compromising their religious commitments.

Maimonides criticized the lack of logical rigor in the arguments of theologians addressing metaphysical problems. He viewed the world as a complex but comprehensible system of necessary laws. Exploring questions of the immortality of the soul, the basis of morality, the creation of the world, the nature of prophecy and the concept of God, Maimonides contended that Judaism and its traditions could be presented as a rational system. Yet the perplexity of the believer could not be resolved by reason alone.

Basic to Maimonides's thought in *The Guide* was the gap between our limited perspective as human beings and that of God, whose apprehension is unlimited and perfect. He was skeptical of attempted dissolutions of this gap by theologians and philosophers but searched nevertheless for bridges to span it. Maimonides claimed: "He, however, who has achieved demonstration, to the extent that it is possible, of everything that may be demonstrated; and who has ascertained in divine matters, to the extent that that is possible, everything that may be ascertained; and who has come close to certainty in those matters in which one can only come close to it—has come to be with the ruler in the inner part of the habitation."

Maimonides believed that the requirements of religion are both intellectual and moral. Believers should not simply pursue religious rituals and regulations without attempting to investigate and understand their purposes and, ultimately, the divine purpose implicit in the structure of the world. "If however, you pray merely by moving your lips while facing a wall," Maimonides wrote, "and at the same time think about your buying and selling, or if you read the Torah with your tongue while your heart is set upon the building of your habitation and does not consider what you read . . . you should not think that you have achieved the end." Maimonides concluded that we must be content to speculate about the nature of what lies beyond our experience and limit ourselves to deriving conclusions from propositions that can be established only as possible, rather than as actual.

CENSORSHIP HISTORY

Maimonides was recognized as a leading figure in Jewish thought as well as one of the most radical philosophers of the Islamic world. *The Guide of the Perplexed* also exerted profound influence on Christian thinkers. It had been translated into Latin and was well known to medieval Scholastics. However, soon after his death in 1204, *The Guide of the Perplexed* sparked furious controversy. Orthodox Jewish opponents objected to Maimonides's sympathy for Aristotelian thought, which was considered fundamentally incompatible with Hebrew tradition. They stressed the incompatibility of being both a believer and a philosopher, contending that the religion proscribed theoretical inquiry. Teaching infected by Greek philosophy and attempts to reconcile Scripture and secular rationality were condemned as heresy.

In 1232, in Montpellier, France, the learned Talmudist Solomon ben Abraham led an attack on *The Guide* and obtained the support of the rabbis of France and some of the important scholars of Spain. The work was banned from Jewish homes under penalty of excommunication. The rabbis of France approached the Catholic Dominican friars, known for an unexcelled record in "burning your heretics," and appealed to them for help in destroying the study of philosophy among Jews. If the church would burn the books of Maimonides, it would deliver "a warning to the Jews to keep away from them." The monks obligingly confiscated copies of *The Guide* and in 1233 burned them as heretical works. Maimonides is thought to be the first Jewish scholar to have his works officially burned. Three hundred years later *The Guide* was again condemned by the Yeshiva of Lublin, Poland. The work still faced bans as late as the 19th century.

FURTHER READING

Aronsfeld, C. C. "Book Burning in Jewish History." *Index on Censorship* 11, no. 1 (February 1982): 18.

Gerber, Jane S. *The Jews of Spain: A History of the Sephardic Experience.* New York: Macmillan, 1992.

Green, Jonathon. *The Encyclopedia of Censorship.* New York: Facts On File, 1990.

Leaman, Oliver. *Moses Maimonides.* Cairo: American University in Cairo Press, 1993.

HARRY POTTER AND THE SORCERER'S STONE

Author: J. K. Rowling
Original dates and places of publication: 1997, United Kingdom; 1998, United States
Original publishers: Bloomsbury Publishing; Scholastic Press
Literary form: Novel

SUMMARY

Harry Potter and the Sorcerer's Stone (published in the United Kingdom as *Harry Potter and the Philosopher's Stone*) is the first volume of J. K. Rowling's seven-part series chronicling the adventures of young Harry Potter in wizardry school. The story begins on a dull, gray Tuesday outside the home of Vernon and Petunia Dursley and their son, Dudley, at No. 4 Privet Drive. That night a half-giant on a flying motorcycle leaves a baby boy on the Dursleys' doorstep. It is their nephew Harry Potter.

We learn that the evil wizard Lord Voldemort murdered Harry's parents, the renowned wizards Lily and James Potter, and then mysteriously disappeared. Harry survived Voldemort's attack with a lightning bolt–shaped scar on his forehead and is famous in the wizard world as "the boy who lived." Headmaster Albus Dumbledore and Professor McGonagall of the Hogwarts

School of Witchcraft and Wizardry have left Harry with his Muggle (nonwizard) relatives until he is old enough to attend Hogwarts.

Ten years later, Harry is living a miserable life with the odious Dursleys and has been told nothing about his wizardly heritage. One day, a letter arrives addressed to him. Uncle Vernon confiscates it, yet the letters continue to arrive by the dozens. He flees with his family to a shack on an island in the middle of the sea, but the letters follow them there. Finally, Rubeus Hagrid, the half-giant who is keeper of keys and grounds at Hogwarts, appears at the door. He explains to Harry that Voldemort had killed his parents, that Harry, too, has magical powers, and that he has been accepted at Hogwarts.

On September 1, Harry's new life begins, as he takes the Hogwarts Express from Platform Nine and Three-Quarters at King's Cross Station, a platform accessible only to wizards. On the train, Harry meets the students who will become his best friends: Ron Weasley, Hermione Granger, and Neville Longbottom, as well as the school bully, Draco Malfoy. When the students are divided into houses, Harry, Ron, Hermione, and Neville are assigned to the noble house of Gryffindor, and Malfoy to the sinister Slytherin, run by malicious Severus Snape, the teacher of potions.

During Harry's first flying lesson, it is evident that he is a natural talent on the broomstick. He is recruited to be the Seeker, a pivotal position on Gryffindor's Quidditch team, a kind of soccer played in the air on broomsticks.

When Malfoy challenges Harry to a midnight wizard's duel, Harry, while evading the ever-vigilant custodian, Argus Filch, and his cat, Mrs. Norris, discovers an enormous three-headed dog guarding a trap door in a forbidden third-floor corridor. During his first Quidditch game, Harry escapes an attempt on his life by someone using sorcery. He suspects Snape. Hagrid inadvertently reveals that the dog, Fluffy, is guarding a secret and that a certain Nicholas Flamel is involved.

Harry remains at school for the Christmas holidays. Among his Christmas presents is the Invisibility Cloak that had belonged to his father. Hidden beneath his cloak, he explores the deserted school and discovers a magnificent mirror, in which he sees his parents and grandparents for the first time. Though his family appears to be alive, Dumbledore explains that the Mirror of Erised reflects neither knowledge nor truth but rather only the deepest desires of those who look upon it.

After Christmas, Harry and his friends learn that Nicholas Flamel is the only known maker of the Sorcerer's Stone. This stone transforms metal into gold and produces the Elixir of Life, which grants immortality to those who drink it. They realize that Flamel had asked Dumbledore to keep the stone safe and that Fluffy now guards it.

Professor McGonagall catches Harry and his friends at midnight at the top of the tallest astronomy tower, off limits for students, while they are doing a favor for Hagrid. As punishment they are sent into the Forbidden Forest for the night. They come upon a hooded figure drinking the blood of a dead unicorn. A centaur rescues Harry and explains that the hooded man was Voldemort, who seeks the Sorcerer's Stone to achieve immortality.

Harry finds out that Fluffy goes to sleep to the sound of music and that Hagrid has revealed this information to a hooded stranger in a bar. The night after exams end, Harry, Ron, and Hermione, in an attempt to protect the stone, go to the third floor, put the dog to sleep, and pass a series of tests and obstacles to reach the chamber where the stone is kept. Harry is shocked to encounter Quirrell, the timid professor of Defense Against the Dark Arts, who admits that he was the one who had tried to kill him.

Quirrell orders Harry to look into the Mirror of Erised, the final seal protecting the Sorcerer's Stone, and reveal its location. When Harry lies about what he sees, Quirrell's turban falls away. At the back of his head, Harry sees a terrible, snakelike face. It is Voldemort, who is sharing Quirrell's body. Quirrell tries to strangle Harry, but his hands burn when he touches Harry's skin. Harry loses consciousness and then awakens in the school infirmary to find out that Dumbledore had arrived just in time to save him. Dumbledore destroyed the stone, but Voldemort is still out there somewhere, perhaps looking for another body to share.

Quirrell could not touch Harry without burning, Dumbledore explains, because "if there is one thing Voldemort cannot understand, it is love. He didn't realize that love as powerful as your mother's for you leaves its own mark. . . . It is in your very skin."

At the Hogwarts' year-end banquet, the bravery of Harry and his friends wins the House Cup for Gryffindor. Now Harry must return to the Muggle world and face another summer with the Dursleys, but this time, he has magic tools at hand.

CENSORSHIP HISTORY

See HARRY POTTER AND THE DEATHLY HALLOWS.

HARRY POTTER AND THE CHAMBER OF SECRETS

Author: J. K. Rowling
Original dates and places of publication: 1998, United Kingdom; 1999, United States
Original publishers: Bloomsbury Publishing; Scholastic Press
Literary form: Novel

SUMMARY

Harry is at home for the summer with the Dursleys after his first year at the Hogwarts School of Witchcraft and Wizardry. One day he awakens to find Dobby, the house elf, leaning over him. Dobby warns Harry that if he returns to Hogwarts, he will be in danger. In an attempt to convince Harry of his sincerity, Dobby lifts Aunt Petunia's pudding to the ceiling and drops it on the floor. Soon after, an owl arrives with a letter from the Ministry of Magic warning Harry that he risks expulsion for using a Hover Charm outside school. As punishment, Uncle Vernon locks Harry in his room around the clock.

One evening, Harry's friend Ron Weasley appears outside Harry's window. Ron and his twin brothers, Fred and George, have borrowed their father's Ford Anglia and are parked in midair outside. They break Harry out of his room and fly to the Weasleys' home, where Harry will stay until school starts. While buying their school supplies in Diagon Alley, the students meet Gilderoy Lockhart, a famous author of magic books who is their new Defense Against the Dark Arts teacher, and have a run-in with Draco Malfoy and his equally slimy father. When Ron and Harry try to pass through the gateway to platform Nine and Three-Quarters at the station to catch the Hogwarts Express, they find the magical barrier has been sealed. They fly the Weasley's car to Hogwarts and crash-land at the school. Ron's wand is damaged, and they get detention for their escapade.

In Lockhart's class, they find that despite his fame, he is unable to handle even lowly Cornish pixies. While serving detention by helping Lockhart with his fan mail, Harry hears a disembodied venomous voice. "Come to me. . . . Let me kill you," it says.

Nearly Headless Nick, the ghost of Gryffindor Tower, invites Harry, Ron, and Hermione Granger to his deathday party. As they leave the hall, Harry again hears the same voice whisper, "Time to kill." On the second floor, Harry, Ron, and Hermione see shining on the wall the words: "The Chamber of Secrets has been opened. Enemies of the heir, beware." Mrs. Norris, the caretaker Filch's cat, is hanging by her tail, stiff as a board. Filch accuses Harry of killing his cat. Dumbledore says that it has been petrified, something that requires advanced Dark Magic, but that the spell can be reversed.

In History of Magic class, Professor Binns tells the students about the legend of the Chamber of Secrets. A rift grew between Godric Gryffindor and Salazar Slytherin, two of the wizards who founded Hogwarts some thousand years ago. Slytherin was opposed to admitting students of Muggle, or nonwizard, parentage, and left the school. The story goes that Slytherin built a hidden chamber within the castle. He sealed it so that only his true heir could open it, unleash the monster, and purge the school of all who were unworthy to study magic.

Who would want to frighten away all the Muggle-borns and the Squibs, those who, like Filch, were born into a wizard family but have no magical powers? Harry suspects Malfoy, who is prejudiced against half-bloods and whose family has been in Slytherin for generations.

During Harry's Quidditch match against Slytherin, the Bludger, a magical ball designed to aimlessly wreak havoc on the field, targets Harry. It hits him and breaks his arm. But before he crashes to the ground, he catches the Snitch, winning the game for Gryffindor. Dobby visits Harry in the hospital wing and again warns him that he is in danger. Dobby admits that he sealed the barrier at the station and then tampered with the Bludger, hoping Harry would be injured and sent home. He fears that terrible things will happen now that the Chamber of Secrets is open again. Soon, there is another attack and the student Colin Creevy is petrified.

In the school's new dueling club, Malfoy uses his wand to conjure a black snake. As it is about to strike Justin Finch-Fletchley, Harry calls out, "Leave him alone," and the snake obeys him. Harry discovers that he is a Parselmouth; he can talk to snakes in Parseltongue. Many famous Dark Wizards were Parselmouths, including Salazar Slytherin and Lord Voldemort. The other students suspect that Harry was ordering the snake to attack Justin.

Later, Justin and Nearly Headless Nick are found petrified. Hermione prepares a batch of Polyjuice Potion that will allow Harry and Ron to masquerade as Malfoy's henchmen, Crabbe and Goyle, and find out what Malfoy knows. Malfoy says that he is not Slytherin's heir and knows only that the person who had previously opened the chamber was expelled and is probably still in prison at Azkaban. Hermione makes a mistake with her potion and finds that her face is covered in black fur. She is sent to the hospital wing for several weeks.

In the bathroom of the whiny ghost Moaning Myrtle, the students find T. M. Riddle's 50-year-old diary. Its pages are blank, but when Harry writes his name in the diary, it writes back, "Hello, Harry Potter. My name is Tom Riddle." Riddle tells Harry that in his fifth year at Hogwarts, the Chamber of Secrets was opened, and the monster attacked several students, killing a girl. He caught the person who opened the chamber, who was expelled. He was forbidden to tell the truth, and the story was told that the girl had died in a freak accident. The monster and the person with the power to release it lived on.

Through the diary, Harry time-travels and observes Riddle as a student. He sees Riddle confronting Hagrid, who was then a student. Hagrid is protecting a giant spider. Harry realizes that Hagrid was the one who had opened the chamber, released the monster spider, and was expelled.

The diary is stolen from Harry's room. As Harry prepares for his Quidditch match, he hears the threatening voice again. The match is cancelled after Hermione and another girl are found petrified near the library.

The school's governors suspend Dumbledore for failing to protect the students. The magic authorities suspect Hagrid of the attacks. As Hagrid is being taken away to prison, he tells Harry and Ron to follow the spiders. They see a trail of spiders making a beeline for the Forbidden Forest and follow them. There they find the Weasleys' wrecked car and are grabbed by giant arachnids. They explain to the spider Aragog that Hagrid is in trouble. Aragog says that years ago Hagrid was expelled because the authorities believed that Aragog, whom Hagrid had raised, was the monster from the Chamber of Secrets. But, in fact, it was a different creature that even the spiders feared. Hagrid hid Aragog in the forest. He says that the body of the girl who was killed was discovered in a bathroom.

When the other spiders menace them, Harry and Ron escape in the car. They realize that the girl who died might be Moaning Myrtle. The Mandrake plants that will revive those who were petrified are ready. Harry and Ron visit Hermione, still comatose in the hospital wing, and notice that she is clutching a page from an old library book about Basilisk, the King of Serpents. She has written the word *pipes*. They realize that the monster was a basilisk, which kills people by looking at them. Those who were petrified survived because none of them had looked directly at the serpent. The serpent has been entering the school through the plumbing. They suspect that the entrance to the chamber is in Moaning Myrtle's bathroom.

The Heir of Slytherin leaves another message on the wall: "Her skeleton will lie in the Chamber forever." The monster has taken Ginny Weasley, Ron's younger sister, into the Chamber of Secrets. The administration expects Lockhart to use his powers to tackle the monster, but when Harry and Ron go to Lockhart's room to tell him what they know, they find that he is packing to leave. He admits that he is a fraud and cannot employ all the magic he writes about. He tries to use a Memory Charm on the boys so they will not tell. Harry disarms Lockhart and forces him to go with them to the bathroom. With Moaning Myrtle's help, they find the entrance to the chamber in the sink. Harry speaks in Parseltongue, and a large pipe opens.

He and Ron take Lockhart and go down the pipe into a dark tunnel. Lockhart attempts a Memory Charm with Ron's defective wand, but it backfires, knocking him out and causing an avalanche that separates Harry from the others. Ultimately Harry finds Ginny alive and sees a tall, dark-haired boy, Tom Riddle. Riddle says that Ginny had been corresponding with him in the diary, and he had fed his secrets into her. He took control of Ginny, and she opened the chamber, left the messages on the wall, and unleashed the serpent. As a student, Riddle had framed Hagrid. He decided to leave his diary behind so that one day he would be able to lead another in his footsteps. His real target is Harry. Riddle admits that he is Lord Voldemort. We are strangely alike, Riddle tells Harry. Both of us are half-bloods, orphans raised by Muggles and Parselmouths.

Dumbledore's phoenix, Fawkes, appears. He drops the old school Sorting Hat into Harry's lap. Riddle calls out to the giant Slytherin statue in the chamber, and a basilisk uncoils from its mouth. Riddle orders it to kill Harry. Fawkes punctures the eyes of the basilisk. Harry rams the Sorting Hat onto his own head, and a gleaming silver sword, its hilt glittering with rubies, emerges from inside the hat. Harry drives the sword into the serpent's mouth. The serpent's fang sinks into his arm, but Fawkes, using the power of phoenix tears, heals Harry's wound. Harry plunges the basilisk fang into the diary. Riddle screams and writhes, then disappears.

Fawkes flies Harry, Ron, Ginny, and Lockhart back up into the bathroom. Lockhart no longer knows who he is. Dumbledore explains that Tom Riddle was Hogwarts' most brilliant student. He disappeared after leaving the school, sank deeply into the Dark Arts, and resurfaced as Lord Voldemort.

Hermione and the others are revived with Mandrake juice. Harry wonders if he really is like Voldemort. Harry can speak Parseltongue, says Dumbledore, because Voldemort, Slytherin's last remaining descendant, transferred some of his powers to Harry when he gave Harry his scar. The Sorting Hat placed Harry in Gryffindor instead of Slytherin because he chose to go there, which shows how different he is from Voldemort. "It is our choices, Harry," Dumbledore says, "that show what we truly are, far more than our abilities." On the silver sword, Harry sees engraved the name Godric Gryffindor. "Only a true Gryffindor could have pulled *that* out of the hat, Harry," Dumbledore adds.

Hagrid is released from Azkaban, and the governors remove Dumbledore's suspension. At the year-end feast, Gryffindor wins the House Cup for the second year in a row. As the students return home aboard the Hogwarts Express, Harry gives Ron his phone number at the Dursleys. Then together, Harry, Ron, and Hermione walk back through the gateway to the Muggle world.

CENSORSHIP HISTORY

See HARRY POTTER AND THE DEATHLY HALLOWS.

HARRY POTTER AND THE PRISONER OF AZKABAN

Author: J. K. Rowling
Original date and places of publication: 1999, United Kingdom and United States
Original publishers: Bloomsbury Publishing; Scholastic Press
Literary form: Novel

SUMMARY

Harry is spending the summer vacation with his relatives, the Dursleys, after his second year at Hogwarts School of Witchcraft and Wizardry. At breakfast he hears the latest news. A dangerous escaped convict, Sirius Black, is on the loose, and Aunt Marge is coming for a week's visit. On the final evening of Aunt Marge's stay, she disparages Harry's late parents, Lily and James Potter. Harry's loses his temper and accidentally uses magic on her. She inflates like a monstrous balloon and rises to the ceiling. Harry grabs his belongings and runs out of the house.

He is now stranded in the Muggle world. Suddenly, the Knight Bus, emergency transport for stranded wizards, screeches to a halt, picks him up and takes him to Diagon Alley, London. At the entrance to the Leaky Cauldron Inn, he runs into Cornelius Fudge, the Minister of Magic. Fudge says that the Accidental Magic Reversal Department has dealt with the unfortunate blowing-up of Marjorie Dursley.

Fudge tells Harry to stay at the inn, where he meets his school friends Ron Weasley and Hermione Granger again. After dinner with the Weasleys, he overhears Ron's parents talking about him. Sirius Black, the madman, has escaped from the prison of Azkaban, and they fear that he wants to murder Harry to bring the Dark Lord, Voldemort, back to power. Harry will be safe at Hogwarts, under Dumbledore's protection.

The next day, the students catch the Hogwarts Express. On their trip, a dementor, one of the horrifying creatures that guards the prison at Azkaban, enters the doorway of their car. Dementors suck the happiness from those around them and force them to dwell on their worst memories. Professor Lupin, the new Defense Against the Dark Arts teacher, uses a spell to send the dementor away, but Harry faints. When they arrive at Hogwarts, Harry shudders to see two more dementors at the gates. Dumbledore greets the assembled students and explains that the grounds will be guarded by dementors, and no one is to leave without permission.

The half-giant Hagrid has been appointed as Care of Magical Creatures teacher. He introduces the students to hippogriffs, bizarre horse-eagles. Harry is able to fly on the hippogriff Buckbeak. But when Draco Malfoy insults Buckbeak, the hippogriff attacks him. Hagrid fears that he will be fired because his creature has injured a student.

When the students return to Gryffindor Tower and give their passwords to the portrait that guards the entrance, they are shocked to find it has been slashed. Peeves the Poltergeist says that Sirius Black did it. The school is talking of nothing else, and Harry is now being closely watched.

Harry's Gryffindor Quidditch team is playing against Hufflepuff. As Harry flies high on his Nimbus Two Thousand broomstick, he is distracted by the silhouette of an enormous shaggy dog in the topmost row of seats. He continues to play, zooming toward the Snitch, when he sees a hundred dementors beneath him. A woman's voice is screaming inside his head.

Harry comes to in the hospital wing. He has fallen 50 feet to the ground. Gryffindor lost the match, and his broomstick has been shattered beyond repair. He realizes that the screams he heard were those of his dying mother. Lupin explains that the dementors affect Harry so strongly because of the horrors in his past. He agrees to help Harry with antidementor lessons.

George and Fred Weasley have stolen a magical map from the caretaker Filch's office. It is the Marauder's Map of Hogwarts. It tracks the movements of everyone in the castle and shows all its secret passages. Harry uses the map to sneak out to visit the wizard village of Hogsmeade. Because the Dursleys had never signed his permission slip, he was not able to go there in the company of the other students and the professors.

Arriving unobserved at the sweet shop, Harry overhears Professor McGonagall, Fudge, and Hagrid saying that Sirius Black was a student at

Hogwarts and that Harry's father, James, was his closest friend. Black was best man at James and Lily's wedding and was named Harry's godfather. James and Lily had gone into hiding from Voldemort, using a Fidelius Charm. No one could find them unless the chosen person, or Secret-Keeper, divulged the information. Black was the Potters' Secret-Keeper.

Black betrayed the Potters to Voldemort, who killed them, and then Black went on the run. Peter Pettigrew, another friend from Hogwarts, went after Black and cornered him. Black blew Pettigrew to bits along with a group of innocent Muggles. Black was caught and taken to Azkaban. Harry is angry. Why had no one told him that his parents died because their best friend betrayed them?

On Christmas morning, Harry finds a present, a new Firebolt broomstick. Hermione and Professor McGonagall think that Sirius Black may have left it for him, and McGonagall takes it away to be checked for jinxes. Lupin begins to teach Harry the Patronus charm, which acts as a shield against dementors.

The day of the big Gryffindor-Slytherin Quidditch match has arrived, and Harry's Firebolt is returned. Harry captures the Snitch, and Gryffindor wins the coveted Quidditch cup. He is the hero of the moment.

A few weeks later, the Committee for the Disposal of Dangerous Creatures has decided that Buckbeak is to be executed at sunset. Harry, Ron, and Hermione use Harry's Invisibility Cloak to visit Hagrid's cabin. As the executioner approaches, they climb the slope away from the cabin. In the distance, they hear the thud of an ax.

Ron's pet rat Scabbers is in his pocket, and when Hermione's cat Crookshanks appears, the rat runs off. Ron throws off the cloak to chase Scabbers, and an enormous black dog grabs him and drags him away. The dog pulls Ron through a gap in the roots of the Whomping Willow, a vicious limb-swinging tree. Harry and Hermione follow them through a tunnel to the Shrieking Shack. They find Ron there, but it is a trap. The dog is really Sirius Black. He is an Animagus, able to change into a dog at will.

Harry overpowers Black. His wand is pointed straight at Black's heart. "You killed my parents," Harry says. Then Lupin comes hurtling into the room. Harry is astonished when Lupin embraces Black like a brother. Hermione says that Lupin cannot be trusted, as he is a werewolf. He admits that this is true, but that Dumbledore knew of his condition when he hired him.

Until now, he had not been helping Sirius Black. But he has found out that Scabbers, Ron's pet rat, is really the wizard Peter Pettigrew. James, Sirius, and Peter had all become Animagi when they were students at Hogwarts to keep their friend Remus Lupin company when he turned into a werewolf once a month. Everyone thought that Sirius had killed Peter, but Lupin realized that Peter was still alive when he saw his movements at Hogwarts revealed on the Marauder's Map.

Professor Snape arrives and moves to take Sirius into custody and turn him over to the dementors. But Harry stops him. Harry believes Sirius's story. Sirius says he had persuaded James and Lily to make Peter their Secret-Keeper instead of him. Peter betrayed them to Voldemort, faked his own death, and escaped by turning himself into a rat. At Azkaban, Sirius had seen a picture of Ron with his pet rat in the newspaper, recognized the rat as Peter and realized that Peter was at Hogwarts to deliver Harry to Voldemort's allies. Sirius had to escape from Azkaban, as he was the only one who knew that Peter was alive and had betrayed the Potters.

Lupin and Sirius use their wands on Scabbers, and in a blinding flash of light, he changes into Peter Pettigrew. Lupin and Sirius want to kill Peter on the spot, but Harry does not want them to become murderers. Instead, he will deliver Peter to the authorities and send him to Azkaban. As they are escorting Peter to the castle, Lupin begins to turn into a werewolf. Peter grabs Lupin's wand, becomes a rat again and escapes.

After a struggle with Lupin, Sirius is at the lakeshore, threatened by a hundred dementors. Harry and Hermione confront the dementors, using Patronus charms, but their spells are not strong enough. As Harry loses consciousness, through the fog he sees a silvery light. Something is driving the dementors back. Amid the light, an animal is galloping away across the lake. He thinks he sees his father, then passes out.

Harry wakes up in the hospital wing. Snape has captured Sirius and brought him to the castle and will soon turn him over to the dementors. Harry and Hermione cannot persuade Fudge and Snape that Sirius is innocent. Dumbledore says that they need more time. So Hermione pulls out a Time-Turner hourglass that Professor McGonagall had given her to allow her to attend two classes at once. She turns it over three times, and she and Harry go back three hours in time.

They return to Hagrid's cabin and spirit Buckbeak away to the forest before the executioner can find him. Harry returns to the lakeside where he sees himself trying to fight off the dementors. He realizes that he was the one who had saved Sirius and himself earlier with the powerful Patronus charm. Out of his wand bursts a blinding, dazzling silver animal—a stag, the same Animagus form his father had taken. The dementors disappear. Hermione and Harry fly on the hippogriff to the castle and rescue Sirius. He rides away on Buckbeak and is gone.

As the Hogwarts Express takes Harry back to the Dursleys for the summer, an owl drops off a message from Sirius. He and Buckbeak are in hiding; he was the one who had given Harry the new Firebolt; and as his godfather, he can give Harry a permission slip to visit Hogsmeade next term.

Uncle Vernon meets Harry at the station. He stares at the envelope in Harry's hand. Harry explains that it is a letter from his godfather, a convicted murderer who has broken out of prison, is on the run, and will be checking to see if Harry is happy. Harry is delighted by the look of horror on Uncle Vernon's face. They set off for the station exit, for what looks like a much better summer than the last.

CENSORSHIP HISTORY

See HARRY POTTER AND THE DEATHLY HALLOWS.

HARRY POTTER AND THE GOBLET OF FIRE

Author: J. K. Rowling
Original date and places of publication: 2000, United Kingdom and United States
Original publishers: Bloomsbury Publishing; Scholastic Press
Literary form: Novel

SUMMARY

Harry Potter is spending the summer before his fourth year at Hogwarts School of Witchcraft and Wizardry with his relatives, the Dursleys. One night, Harry awakes from a dream with his scar burning. He has had a vision of the Dark Lord, Voldemort, killing a man.

Harry joins his friends Ron Weasley and Hermione Granger to watch the Quidditch World Cup. They meet Bartholomew Crouch, head of the Department of International Magical Cooperation in the Ministry of Magic. Ireland defeats Bulgaria in the match, despite the brilliant play of Bulgarian Seeker Viktor Krum.

That night Harry is awakened by screams and explosions. A group of masked wizards are torturing Muggles, nonwizards. Harry flees to the forest but realizes that his wand is missing. A figure hidden in the shadows casts a spell that sends a constellation-like image of a giant skull with a snake in its mouth into the sky.

Panicked ministry wizards arrive at the scene, searching for the person who cast the spell. Harry's wand is discovered to have cast the spell, but the culprit is not found. The hooded wizards were Death Eaters, supporters of Voldemort, and the image in the sky was the Dark Mark, Voldemort's symbol.

Harry returns to school on the Hogwarts Express. At the opening feast, Headmaster Dumbledore announces that, instead of the Quidditch Cup, this year Hogwarts is hosting the Triwizard Tournament. The tournament is a contest between representatives of three schools of wizardry: Hogwarts, Durmstrang, and Beauxbatons. The champions will be selected at the Halloween feast. Each champion must be at least 17 years old and will be chosen by an impartial judge.

Harry begins his classes. The most gripping is Defense Against the Dark Arts, taught by Mad-Eye Moody. He is a famous Auror, or Dark Wizard catcher. Moody teaches about the three Unforgivable Curses: the Imperius Curse that controls another's actions, the Cruciatus Curse that inflicts terrible pain, and Avada Kadavra, the Killing Curse. Harry learns that

Voldemort had used this curse to kill his parents and that Harry is the only person to have ever survived it.

The Beauxbatons group arrives, led by Madame Maxine, and the Durmstrang party arrives soon after, led by Professor Karkaroff. The impartial judge is the Goblet of Fire, a chalice into which the names of each candidate will be placed. The next night, the goblet will shoot out the papers containing the names of each school's champion. Dumbledore draws an Age Line around the goblet to prevent underage wizards from entering their name.

On Halloween, the champions are announced. Viktor Krum will represent Durmstrang, Fleur Delacour will represent Beauxbatons, and Cedric Diggory will represent Hogwarts. However, the goblet spits out a fourth slip of paper with the name "Harry Potter." Harry is shocked. Moody determines that someone must have entered Harry's name into the Goblet of Fire and tricked it into thinking a fourth school was competing, to put Harry in danger during the perilous tournament.

Hagrid tips off Harry that the first of the three tasks he must complete is to get past dragons. Moody gives Harry the idea of using his Firebolt broomstick. The first task begins. Each contestant must get past a dragon and retrieve a golden egg. Harry goes last, flies past the dragon on his Firebolt, and snags the egg. He receives the highest score.

The golden egg from the first task is a clue for the second, but when opened it makes an incomprehensible wailing noise. The next task is not for several months. Mr. Crouch, a judge in the tournament, stops coming to work, seemingly due to illness. A witch from the ministry, Bertha Jorkins, has been missing for months, and her disappearance is raising eyebrows.

Harry and Ron manage to find dates for the Christmas Yule Ball, although Harry's first choice, Cho Chang, has already been taken by Cedric. They are shocked to see Hermione and Viktor Krum together at the ball.

Time is running out for Harry before the next task when Cedric suggests Harry bring the egg with him into the bath. Underwater, the noise becomes intelligible words. For the second task, something precious will be taken by the merpeople in the lake, and he will have one hour to retrieve it. On the way back from the bathroom, Harry nearly gets into trouble, and when Moody helps him, he gives Moody his secret Marauder's Map of the school.

Harry attempts to find a way to breathe underwater, but by the morning of the second task, he still has not found a solution. Dobby the house elf wakes him up. He has learned by eavesdropping on teachers that a plant called gillyweed will solve Harry's problem. Harry takes the gillyweed and rushes to the lake. The contest begins, and Harry eats the gillyweed. His hands and feet become webbed, and he grows gills. He dives in and eventually finds at the center of the merpeople village the person each champion will miss most. Harry frees his hostage, Ron, but worries about the others.

Soon after, Cedric arrives to take Cho Chang. Viktor Krum shows up and takes Hermione, but Fleur, whose hostage is her little sister, is nowhere to be seen. Harry decides to take both Ron and Fleur's sister with him and swims to the surface. Harry is well outside the time limit and returns last, but the chief merman tells the judges of Harry's bravery and that he had been the first to find the hostages. The judges award Harry nearly full marks.

Harry meets with Sirius Black, his fugitive godfather, at Hogsmeade. He learns that Mr. Crouch has a son who was affiliated with the Death Eaters and whom he sent to Azkaban. Mr. Crouch's son died soon after his arrival, as did his wife.

The champions receive instructions for the final task. They must pass through a maze full of hexes and magical creatures. The first to touch the Triwizard Cup in the center of the maze wins the tournament. Afterward, Harry and Viktor encounter a clearly mad Mr. Crouch. He mentions Bertha Jorkins's death, the Dark Lord's growing strength, and his own guilt. He repeatedly asks for Dumbledore. Harry goes to get Dumbledore, leaving Viktor with Crouch. When they return, Viktor is stunned, and Crouch is gone.

During Divination class, Harry falls asleep and has a vision of Voldemort and his servant, Wormtail. Voldemort uses the Cruciatus Curse on Wormtail, and Harry wakes up screaming, his scar searing with pain. He goes to Dumbledore's office to discuss his vision. When Dumbledore leaves Harry alone in the office, he sees a light coming from a basin filled with liquid. Harry touches the liquid and is sucked in. He finds himself in a chamber full of wizards, including Dumbledore and Moody, but they cannot see him. He realizes he is in a memory.

He observes several trials presided over by Mr. Crouch, then head of the Department of Magical Law Enforcement, including those of Karkaroff, who was a Death Eater, and Mr. Crouch's own son. Harry learns that Professor Snape was once a Death Eater who turned against Voldemort and helped Dumbledore. Dumbledore brings Harry back to reality and discusses the memories with him.

At the end of June, the third task begins. Harry deals with the obstacles in the maze. He hears Fleur scream but moves onward. He later hears Viktor using the Cruciatus Curse on Cedric. Harry arrives in time to stun Viktor and save Cedric. They arrive at the center of the maze together, and after dispatching a giant spider, Cedric is in a position to reach the Triwizard Cup first. They decide to share the victory. When they touch the cup they are transported to a graveyard.

A hooded man kills Cedric. It is Wormtail, carrying an infantlike Voldemort. Wormtail begins a ritual to bring Voldemort back to power. Using a bone from Voldemort's father's grave, Harry's blood, and Wormtail's hand, Voldemort is restored to his old body. With the Dark Mark burned onto Wormtail's forearm, Voldemort calls his Death Eaters to him. Many Death Eaters answer his call and teleport to the graveyard.

Voldemort reveals that his trusted servant at Hogwarts has delivered Harry to him. To prove his power, Voldemort duels with Harry. Harry struggles to survive and launches one last curse at Voldemort as Voldemort uses the Killing Curse. The curses meet in midair, and suddenly a bolt of energy connects the wizards' two wands. They are lifted up into the air as they each try to force the power toward the other. Harry succeeds, and Voldemort's wand suddenly begins spouting traces of each spell it has ever performed. The spectral form of Cedric appears, as do Bertha Jorkins and others Voldemort has killed.

Soon, Harry's parents appear. They counsel Harry to break the connection and run while they hold Voldemort back. Harry wrenches away his wand and starts running to the cup. He avoids the chasing Death Eaters, grabs Cedric's body, and touches the Triwizard Cup, bringing Cedric back to Hogwarts. Someone rushes him away from the surrounding crowd. It is Moody, who brings Harry to his office. Moody reveals that he is in fact Voldemort's loyal supporter and that he had orchestrated the plan for Harry to enter and win the tournament.

He plans to kill Harry, but Dumbledore bursts into the room and stuns Moody. Dumbledore says that this is not the real Moody and that it is someone using Polyjuice Potion to pass as Moody. The potion wears off, and the fake Moody is revealed to be Bartholomew Crouch, Mr. Crouch's son.

Under the effects of truth serum, the young Crouch admits that his parents had helped him escape Azkaban and that his father had controlled him with the Imperius Curse for years. Bertha Jorkins had found out Mr. Crouch's secret, but he edited her memory so she would forget. Wormtail happened to meet her in Albania, and Voldemort extracted this information from her, along with her knowledge of the Triwizard Tournament.

Crouch's son had gone to the Quidditch World Cup and cast the Dark Mark. Voldemort came to Mr. Crouch's house and liberated his faithful servant. Young Barty kidnapped the real Moody and took on his appearance. Mr. Crouch had been under Voldemort's control until one day he broke free and went to Hogwarts, where Harry met him in the woods. Barty saw his father's movements on the Marauder's Map, found him in the woods, stunned Viktor, killed his father, and buried him. During the final task, the fake Moody knocked out Fleur and forced Krum to attack Cedric. He turned the Triwizard Cup into a Portkey, a teleportation device.

Dumbledore mobilizes his allies to counter Voldemort. Harry learns that the core of his wand contains a feather from the same phoenix as the core of Voldemort's, which is why the two wands reacted when brought together. Cornelius Fudge, the Minister of Magic, visits Harry but refuses to believe that Voldemort has returned.

At the year-end feast, Cedric and Harry are honored, and Dumbledore warns the students that Voldemort is back. Harry returns to King's Cross Station and prepares for another summer with the Dursleys.

—Daniel Calvert

CENSORSHIP HISTORY

See HARRY POTTER AND THE DEATHLY HALLOWS.

HARRY POTTER AND THE ORDER OF THE PHOENIX

Author: J. K. Rowling
Original date and places of publication: 2003, United Kingdom and United States
Original publishers: Bloomsbury Publishing; Scholastic Press
Literary form: Novel

SUMMARY

Harry is home for the summer on Privet Drive in Little Whinging with his aunt and uncle, Petunia and Vernon Dursley. In the fall, he will begin his fifth year at the Hogwarts School of Witchcraft and Wizardry. He is feeling bored and isolated, cut off from his friends and the wizard world. Late one evening, as he walks in the neighborhood, he and his cousin, Dudley, are menaced by a towering hooded figure. It is a dementor.

Harry uses his wand and a Patronus charm to send the dementor away and save himself and a shaken Dudley. When they arrive at the Dursleys, Harry receives an owl message from the Ministry of Magic. Because he is an underage wizard who has illegally performed a Patronus charm in a Muggle-inhabited area, he has been expelled from Hogwarts, and the authorities will soon arrive to confiscate his wand. But Dumbledore intervenes, and he receives another letter. The Ministry of Magic has reversed its decision and will instead hold a disciplinary hearing on August 12.

A group of wizards arrives to take him away from the Dursleys. Harry flies off with them to No. 12 Grimmauld Place, London. The house, which formerly belonged to the parents of Harry's godfather, Sirius, is the headquarters of the Order of the Phoenix, a secret society founded years ago by Dumbledore to fight against the Dark Lord, Voldemort. Dumbledore has recalled the society in order to respond to Voldemort's reappearance. Sirius, a wanted man, is in hiding at the headquarters.

The Ministry of Magic refuses to acknowledge Voldemort's return and is working to discredit Dumbledore and portray Harry as an unstable liar for insisting that Voldemort is alive. At Harry's hearing, the Minister of Magic, Cornelius Fudge, says that a dementor could not have attacked Harry in Little Whinging, as all of them guard the prison of Azkaban under the ministry's control. But Dumbledore presents a surprise witness, Harry's batty neighbor, Mrs. Figg. She is revealed to be a Squib who has been watching over Harry. She corroborates his story, and the ministry exonerates him of the charges.

In September, Harry catches the Hogwarts Express back to school. As the school year begins, he is sullen and alienated. Most of the other students believe he is crazy for thinking that Voldemort is back. His pals Ron Weasley and Hermione Granger have been appointed prefects, and he has not. His friend the half-giant Hagrid is not there to greet him, and sitting next to Dumbledore in the Great Hall is a toadlike woman in pink. It is Dolores Umbridge, who works for Fudge at the Ministry of Magic. She is the new Defense Against the Dark Arts teacher and High Inquisitor of the school, sent by the ministry to undermine Dumbledore's authority.

Harry is coping with a heavy course load in preparation for Ordinary Wizarding Levels (O.W.L.) examinations. But Harry's defiance of Umbridge gets him sent repeatedly to detention. When it becomes clear that Umbridge will not teach defensive maneuvers and spells to the students in her class as the Ministry of Magic fears that Dumbledore is forming his own army to take on the ministry, Harry agrees to secretly teach the other students. He is the only one who knows what it is really like to face Voldemort.

But after their first meeting, the High Inquisitor disbands all school organizations and clubs. Any student who gathers in a group of three or more without her permission will be expelled. With the assistance of Dobby, the house elf, the students find a secret room in the school where they can practice. The scar on Harry's forehead is searing more painfully than ever, and he is getting flashes of Voldemort's moods.

Hagrid has returned to the school, beaten and bruised, after a visit to the land of the giants. He brings the students into the forest and introduces them to the thestrals, dragonlike winged horses. Only those like Harry, who have seen death, can see thestrals. To the others, they are invisible.

Asleep in his dorm, Harry dreams that he is a snake who is attacking a man. When he awakes he realizes that the snake has bitten Arthur Weasley, his friend Ron's father, who works at the Ministry of Magic. Dumbledore sends a wizard to check on Weasley and confirms that he has indeed been attacked. Harry fears that he did not merely see the snake, but that he was the snake and Voldemort was using him as a weapon. Ron confirms, however, that Harry could not have injured his father because Harry never left his bed in the dorm during the night.

On Dumbledore's orders, Professor Snape secretly teaches Occlumency, the magical defense of the mind against external penetration, to Harry. The curse that failed to kill Harry in childhood has forged a connection between Harry and the Dark Lord. When Harry's mind is relaxed, he shares Voldemort's thoughts and emotions. Occlumency will teach him to close his mind to the Dark Lord.

Harry realizes that the place where the snake attacked Weasley is the corridor in the Ministry of Magic that he has been dreaming about for months. His scar hurts, and he feels that Voldemort is now happy about something. The next day, Harry learns that there has been a mass breakout from Azkaban, and the Death Eaters, Voldemort's servants, have escaped. Harry's Occlumency lessons are not going well. His scar is almost continuously painful, and he dreams almost every night that he is walking down the corridor in the Ministry of Magic toward the entrance to the Department of Mysteries.

Umbridge discovers that the students are secretly meeting and apprehends them as they flee their secret room. Dumbledore covers for them and says that he had recruited the students for his army and that this was to be their very first meeting. When Fudge moves to take Dumbledore into custody for plotting against Umbridge, Dumbledore uses his magic to disappear.

Umbridge replaces Dumbledore as head of Hogwarts. Hagrid, fearing that he will be sacked, brings Harry, Ron, and Hermione to the forest and introduces them to his giant brother, Gawp. Gawp does not know his own strength and is responsible for the injuries visible on Hagrid's face. Hagrid hopes that Harry and his friends will care for Gawp if he loses his job. Later on, Umbridge attempts to capture Hagrid to expel him. He escapes, but Professor McGonagall, coming to his assistance, is stunned unconscious and taken off to the hospital. The High Inquisitor is now in total control of Hogwarts, and all of Harry's allies are gone.

Harry is taking an exam and closes his eyes. He is walking down the corridor to the Department of Mysteries, where he sees Sirius being tortured. Harry tells Ron and Hermione that he must go there to save Sirius. Hermione warns him that Voldemort may be trying to lure him there and suggests that Harry check to see if Sirius has left the headquarters of the Order of the Phoenix. Using Umbridge's fireplace, Harry employs Floo powder to transport himself to Grimmauld Place. Kreacher, the treacherous house elf, says that Sirius is gone. As Harry returns to Hogwarts through the fireplace, Umbridge appears in her room and captures Harry and his friends.

Hermione lures Umbridge to the forest by confessing that the students have been preparing a weapon for Dumbledore and that she will show it to her. Hermione leads Umbridge on the path toward Gawp's lair. Suddenly they are surrounded by hostile centaurs. Umbridge insults them and is seized by the centaur Bane and borne away through the trees. Gawp appears, and when the centaurs shoot arrows at him, Harry and his friends escape, flying on thestrals to the Ministry of Magic.

Harry follows the corridor familiar to him from his dreams and reaches a room with towering shelves covered with glass orbs. The shelf under one orb is labeled with his name. As Harry touches the orb, he is surrounded by Lucius Malfoy and the other Death Eaters. Malfoy demands that Harry turn over the orb, which contains a prophecy.

Harry and his friends fight the Death Eaters. Just in time, the members of the Order of the Phoenix, including Sirius, burst into the room. The orb falls to the floor and breaks. Dumbledore arrives to dispatch the Death Eaters, but Sirius falls through an ancient doorway, vanishes behind a veil, and is presumed dead. Then Lord Voldemort appears—tall, thin, black-hooded, his face terrible and snakelike. His wand is pointed at Harry. But the strength of Dumbledore's wizardry vanquishes Voldemort. For a few seconds he is visible as a dark, rippling, faceless figure. Then he is gone. Fudge and the other wizards show up. It is now clear that Fudge was wrong about Voldemort. Dumbledore orders Fudge to remove Umbridge from Hogwarts. He is back in charge.

Harry feels responsible for Sirius's death. "It is my fault that Sirius died," says Dumbledore. You should never have believed for an instant that you had to go to the Department of Mysteries to rescue Sirius, he tells Harry. Dumbledore had not been open with him. Dumbledore had realized 15 years ago that Harry's scar might be a sign of a connection between Harry and Voldemort. He had sent Harry to live with the Dursleys because there he would be protected by an ancient magic curse that Voldemort fears, the fact that Harry's mother had died to save him. As long as Harry can still call home the place where his mother's blood dwells in the body of her sister, Aunt Petunia, Harry cannot be touched by Voldemort.

Voldemort tried to kill Harry because of a prophecy told to Dumbledore shortly before Harry's birth, which Voldemort had partly overheard: The person with the only chance of conquering Lord Voldemort for good was born at the end of July nearly 16 years ago, to parents who had already defied Voldemort three times. This child will be marked by Voldemort "as his equal," and one of them will have to kill the other in the end. Voldemort had heard only the first part of the prophecy, which is why he attacked Harry as a child. He wanted to hear the full prophecy to learn how to destroy Harry. Dumbledore had not told Harry about the prophecy because he wanted to protect Harry from this knowledge about himself. After his talk with Dumbledore, Harry feels that an invisible barrier separates him from the rest of the world. He is a marked man.

When Harry arrives at King's Cross Station after his journey home for the summer on the Hogwarts Express, he finds the members of the Order of the Phoenix and the Dursleys waiting for him. Arthur Weasley tells Uncle Vernon that if he mistreats Harry, this time, he will have to answer to the wizards. Harry cannot find the words to tell the members of the order how much their support means to him. He says good-bye and leaves the station, with Uncle Vernon, Aunt Petunia, and Cousin Dudley hurrying along behind him.

CENSORSHIP HISTORY

See HARRY POTTER AND THE DEATHLY HALLOWS.

HARRY POTTER AND THE HALF-BLOOD PRINCE

Author: J. K. Rowling
Original date and places of publication: 2005, United Kingdom;
 United States
Original publishers: Bloomsbury Publishing; Scholastic Press
Literary form: Novel

SUMMARY

As the sixth installment of the Harry Potter series, *Harry Potter and the Half-Blood Prince*, begins, the Ministry of Magic's war against Lord Voldemort is going badly. Ministry officials have lost control of the Dementors, soul-sucking wraiths, and Voldemort is wreaking havoc. Death Eaters are murdering dozens of people.

The scene shifts, and two women—Narcissa Malfoy, the mother of Draco Malfoy, and Bellatrix Lestrange, her sister—arrive at Professor Severus Snape's home. Snape makes an Unbreakable Vow to promise to protect and help the young Malfoy during the school year.

Harry Potter is in the house of his relatives, the Dursleys, awaiting a visit from Professor Albus Dumbledore, who will take him to the Burrow for the summer. Harry has inherited his godfather Sirius Black's possessions, including the house that once served as headquarters for the Order of the Phoenix, and the services of Kreacher, the Black family's house elf. Dumbledore's right hand is blackened and shriveled, and he is wearing a new ring with a cracked black stone.

Dumbledore and Harry convince Horace Slughorn to come to Hogwarts to be the new Potions Master. Alone, Dumbledore and Harry discuss the prophecy that named Harry as the "Chosen One." Dumbledore counsels Harry and tells him that he can share this information with his friends Ron Weasley and Hermione Granger. Harry learns that he will be taking private classes with Dumbledore during the school year.

At the Burrow, Harry finds that Fleur Delacour has recently become engaged to Bill, Ron's older brother. Harry tells Ron and Hermione that the prophecy said, "Neither can live while the other survives." Ron, Hermione, and Harry have passed their Ordinary Wizarding Levels (O.W.L); Harry is named Quidditch Captain.

Harry, Ron, and Hermione proceed to Diagon Alley to buy school supplies and visit Fred and George's joke shop. They see Draco Malfoy hurrying by and decide to follow him. Malfoy goes into Knockturn Alley and enters Borgin and Burkes, a Dark artifacts store. The three overhear him reserving something in the store and talking about mending another. Harry speculates that Malfoy has become a Death Eater, but Ron and Hermione are not so sure.

Professor Slughorn invites Neville Longbottom and Harry to eat with him during the train ride to Hogwarts. The room is full of students connected to influential people. Following this, Harry sneaks into Malfoy's train compartment to spy on him and arrives late to the Great Hall. Snape is named the new Professor for Defense Against the Dark Arts. The sixth-year students become busy with their N.E.W.T-level classes. They are expected to use nonverbal spells, and the classes are more difficult. Harry takes Potions with Professor Slughorn. When the professor learns that Harry has not purchased the required books and supplies at Diagon Alley, he shares a battered-looking copy of *Advanced Potion-Making* with his student. The Potions class makes a Draught of the Living Death, and Slughorn informs them that the best potion will win a tiny bottle of Felix Felicis, liquid luck. Harry finds in the old, borrowed book that someone has written comments in all the margins, and Harry finds them to be helpful instructions. With this assistance, he wins the prize. Later, Harry sees that the book belonged to the "Half-Blood Prince."

Harry has his first private class with Dumbledore and learns they will be investigating Voldemort's past. They enter Dumbledore's collection of memories in the Pensieve and watch Voldemort's mother and grandfather interact. Voldemort's grandfather wears the same ring that Dumbledore now wears and claims that it holds the Peverell coat of arms. In the memory, he also shows off a gold Slytherin locket.

As Captain, Harry has to run Quidditch trials. Ron is nervous, but Ginny and Ron are chosen as members of the team. Harry and Hermione attend Professor Slughorn's parties for bright students, and Ron feels left out.

On the trip to Hogsmeade, Harry catches Mundungus Fletcher, a member of the Order of the Phoenix, with stolen articles from Sirius's house. On the trip home, Katie Bell, a Hogwarts student, is cursed by an opal necklace that Harry had seen earlier at Borgin and Burkes. Harry accuses Draco Malfoy of having given it to Katie, but Professor McGonagall tells him that Malfoy did not go to Hogsmeade.

During Harry's second private class with Dumbledore, they go into the headmaster's memory of his first encounter with Tom Marvolo Riddle, later Lord Voldemort. Tom Riddle was a strange boy, already using his power to torture and hurt those around him.

Ron and Hermione face the loss of their friendship when Ron decides to date Lavender Brown. Hermione sees this as a betrayal, and Harry is caught in the middle. Harry realizes that he has feelings for Ron's sister, Ginny, but worries that he cannot tell Ron. Meanwhile, a number of Hogwarts girls are interested in Harry, and Hermione warns him to be careful of Love Potions.

Harry overhears Malfoy and Snape talking in the passageway. Snape talks of the Unbreakable Vow sworn to Narcissa and pushes Malfoy to let him help with the task Voldemort has given Malfoy, but Malfoy rejects his offer. Harry tells Dumbledore, but he dismisses Harry's suspicions. During the second term, Harry keeps an eye on Malfoy's whereabouts, certain that he is up to something. He gets the house elves Dobby and Kreacher to follow Malfoy, and they report that he is always in the Room of Requirement, but they do not know what he is doing.

At Harry's next private lesson, Harry and Dumbledore enter Dumbledore's memory again. They see first a memory of Voldemort's uncle on the day he met Tom Riddle. Riddle was researching his mother's family, stole away his family's ring, and later killed his Muggle father. Now they enter a memory of Professor Slughorn's, when a teenage Riddle asked him about Horcruxes. The Professor, ashamed of his responses to Riddle's questions, had tampered with this memory. Dumbledore asks Harry to retrieve the true memory. However, when Harry tries to approach Slughorn, the Potions Master panics and leaves the room immediately. Following this, Slughorn avoids Harry.

Ron swallows a love potion meant for Harry, and Harry takes him to Slughorn for an antidote. As a celebratory drink afterwards, Slughorn offers the two boys some mead he had meant to deliver to Dumbledore. Ron drinks his quickly and then almost dies from poison. Harry saves his life by putting a bezoar down his throat. Ron and Hermione make up after his near death, and Ron breaks up with Lavender soon after.

Harry has yet another lesson with Dumbledore, and they continue with Voldemort's story, watching one more memory. Dumbledore and Harry watch Tom Riddle coveting two treasures: the Slytherin necklace that once belonged to Voldemort's family and a cup that belonged to Helga Hufflepuff, a Hogwarts founder. Both treasures disappeared two days after he saw them.

Harry decides to take his Felix Felicis potion to help him get the memory out of Slughorn. He takes Slughorn to Hagrid's to bury Hagrid's pet spider, Aragog, and gets him drunk. Once Slughorn is drunk, Harry convinces Slughorn to give him the memory.

Harry goes straight to Dumbledore's office, and they enter the memory together. Slughorn explains that Horcruxes are pieces of a soul and that when a Horcrux exists, a person cannot be killed, as part of their soul is still alive. One can create a Horcrux only by an act of murder. Riddle asks if one could split a soul into seven Horcruxes, and a disturbed Slughorn tells him that this is a banned subject at Hogwarts.

Once Dumbledore and Harry have left the memory, Dumbledore explains that it confirmed his theory that Voldemort split his soul into seven Horcruxes. One, Tom Riddle's diary, was destroyed in *Harry Potter and the Chamber of Secrets*, and Dumbledore broke the curse on the black ring owned by Voldemort's ancestors. Dumbledore also says that the seventh Horcrux resides in Voldemort's own body, which means that there are four Horcruxes that must be destroyed before challenging Voldemort. Dumbledore guesses that the Hufflepuff cup is one, the Slytherin locket another, and that Nagini, Voldemort's snake, is also a Horcrux. He surmises that the fourth Horcrux probably belonged to one of the four Founders of Hogwarts. Finally, he tells Harry that he is close to finding another Horcrux and promises to take Harry with him when he goes to retrieve it.

Harry and Malfoy begin to duel when Harry surprises him. Harry uses a curse he found in the Prince's potions book and nearly kills Malfoy. He decides that he cannot trust the "Half-Blood Prince." Harry is given Detention and misses the final Quidditch match of the season, but Gryffindor wins anyway. During the celebrations, Ginny and Harry kiss for the first time.

During a conversation with Professor Trelawney, Harry realizes that Snape told Voldemort about the prophecy and brought about his own parents' murder. He runs to Dumbledore and confronts him, but Dumbledore tells him that he trusts Snape absolutely. Now Dumbledore informs Harry that it is time for them to retrieve the third Horcrux.

Harry and Dumbledore Apparate (transport themselves magically) to a dark cliff, surrounded by water. They swim to a cave where Voldemort terrorized two small children during his time in the orphanage. They enter a cavern full of water, with an island in the middle. They take a boat to the island and find a basin with liquid inside it. The liquid cannot be moved or enchanted; it can only be drunk. Dumbledore begins to drink it and orders Harry to make him continue to drink even if he loses consciousness. Harry forces the liquid into Dumbledore's mouth, despite his intense pain, and finds a locket at the bottom of the basin. However, as soon as Harry removes the locket, enchanted dead bodies in the water come to life and begin attacking. Dumbledore, who had passed out, comes to, and saves Harry with a ring of fire. The two of them then escape and return to Hogwarts, where they see a Dark Mark floating in the sky above the castle. They rush back to the castle on brooms and alight in the Astronomy Tower. Dumbledore quickly freezes Harry, ensuring that Harry would remain safe. Malfoy arrives and disarms Dumbledore.

Death Eaters, who entered the castle through a Vanishing Cabinet that Malfoy repaired, confront a wandless Dumbledore. Snape comes out of the castle as well, and Dumbledore pleads with him. In response, Snape uses the Killing Curse, and Dumbledore dies.

Harry chases Snape, but Snape manages to disarm him and informs the boy that he, Snape, is the Half-Blood Prince. Hagrid almost dies as he fights the Death Eaters, but once they have left Hogwarts, the entire campus comes together to grieve Dumbledore's death. A state funeral is held on the Hogwarts campus.

Harry looks at the locket that Dumbledore died to acquire and sees that it is not even the Slytherin locket. A note inside says that someone named R. A. B. had taken the locket and was going to destroy it. Harry decides that he will not be returning to Hogwarts and that, instead, he will set off on his own to find the other four Horcruxes. He breaks up with Ginny, telling her that he must not endanger her life with their relationship. Finally, he tells Ron and Hermione about his decision. To his surprise, they tell him that they will join him. The three friends soberly agree that just after Bill and Fleur's upcoming marriage, they will go off in search of Horcruxes.

—Elizabeth Calvert-Kilbane

CENSORSHIP HISTORY

See HARRY POTTER AND THE DEATHLY HALLOWS.

HARRY POTTER AND THE DEATHLY HALLOWS

Author: J. K. Rowling
Original date and places of publication: 2007, United Kingdom;
  United States
Original publishers: Bloomsbury Publishing; Scholastic Press
Literary form: Novel

SUMMARY

The seventh and final book of the Harry Potter series, *Harry Potter and the Deathly Hallows*, begins as Severus Snape arrives at a Death Eater meeting with information on when Harry Potter will leave the home of his relatives, the Dursleys. The evil wizard Lord Voldemort reveals that he will kill Harry himself.

Harry reads Professor Albus Dumbledore's obituary and realizes that he knows little about his mentor's life. He then sees a review of Rita Skeeter's new scandalous biography of Dumbledore. Stewing, Harry picks up a shard of glass from a broken two-way mirror and sees a flash of blue, which reminds him of Dumbledore's eye. It disappears, and Harry decides that it was his imagination.

Thirteen members of the Order of the Phoenix arrive to escort Harry to a safe location. They plan to create six Potter doubles to confuse any Death Eaters who might be on watch for their departure. Harry will ride with the half-giant Hagrid on Sirius Black's old motorcycle. However, 30 Death Eaters ambush them, and Hedwig, Harry's owl, dies from a stray curse. Harry is able to protect Hagrid and himself against the Death Eaters, but then Voldemort appears out of nowhere. Harry escapes to a safe house. Harry and Hagrid later arrive at the Burrow to find that George Weasley has lost his ear to a curse and that Mad-Eye Moody, the famous Auror, or Dark Wizard catcher, has died.

Harry, along with Hermione Granger and the Weasleys, prepares for the wedding of Fleur Delacour and Bill Weasley, Ron Weasley's brother. Harry, Ron, and Hermione plan to leave quietly the day after the wedding on their brave quest for Horcruxes. Dumbledore had bequeathed three objects to the threesome. For Ron, it is a Deluminator that sucks the light from any source. For Hermione, it is a copy of *The Tales of Beedle the Bard*. For Harry, it is the first Golden Snitch that Harry ever caught at Quidditch. Dumbledore also left him the sword of Godric Gryffindor, but the Ministry of Magic will not release it to him. Harry is still connected to Voldemort's mind and unable to block him out at times. Voldemort seems to seek a specific object, but Harry cannot yet discern what it is.

The following day is Bill and Fleur's wedding. Harry meets Xenophilius Lovegood, Luna Lovegood's father. Viktor Krum tells Harry that Xenophilius is wearing the sign of a famous Dark wizard, Grindelwald.

Later, Harry learns more incriminating information about Dumbledore's past. The party ends when the Ministry of Magic falls to Voldemort.

Harry, Ron, and Hermione escape the party and go to 13 Grimmauld Place, Sirius's old house. In the house, Harry discovers the room of Regulus Arcturus Black, or R. A. B., the owner of the locket found with Dumbledore the previous spring. The three remember seeing a locket hidden around the house two years before and ask Kreacher, the house elf, about its whereabouts. Regulus had asked Kreacher to destroy the locket, but he was unable to do so, and then Mundungus Fletcher stole the locket to sell. Harry asks Kreacher to find Mundungus, which he does. They learn that Dolores Umbridge, the former Ministry-appointed headmistress of Hogwarts, took the locket, and they decide to infiltrate the Ministry to retrieve it.

The Ministry wants to question Harry about Dumbledore's death, and all Muggle-Borns are now required to register with the Ministry, so there is great risk for this mission. Ron, Harry, and Hermione spend the next few weeks preparing and collecting information, disguised as Ministry workers.

On their big day at the Ministry, they immediately run into problems and must separate. Umbridge enlists Hermione to take notes at a hearing for registering Muggle-Borns. At the hearing, Harry sees that Umbridge is wearing the locket. Harry manages to stun her and take the locket, then releases all of the Muggle-Borns under trial. When the three friends Apparate, or magically teleport, away from the Ministry, a Death Eater travels with them, and now their cozy hideout is known. From now on, they must camp out and stay on the move.

They know that the locket it is one of the Horcruxes they seek to eliminate, but they have no way to destroy it. The three travelers continue their search for the other Horcruxes. However, Hermione and, particularly, Ron feel that Harry has too little information. Hearing a conversation between escaped Ministry prisoners, they find that the sword of Gryffindor stored in Bellatrix Lestrange's Gringotts safe is a fake. Harry and Hermione realize that the original, goblin-made sword could destroy the locket or any Horcrux. Later, a tired and impatient Ron becomes enraged with Harry and leaves them. With Ron gone, Harry realizes that it is true—he has no leads. He decides to travel to Godric's Hollow to visit his parents' graves.

At the cemetery, Hermione finds a grave with the same symbol that Xenophilius wore and a sign in her copy of *The Tales of Beedle the Bard*. On their departure, an old woman who says she is Bathilda Bagshot signals that they should follow her home. Following Bathilda upstairs, Voldemort's snake comes from inside her body and attacks. Luckily, Hermione saves Harry, and they escape, breaking Harry's wand in the process. But Voldemort sees a photo that Harry dropped, identifying the owner of the item he seeks.

Hermione manages to steal Bathilda's copy of Rita Skeeter's biography of Dumbledore, where she discovers that Voldemort seeks Gellert Grindelwald, the Dark wizard, and that he was Dumbledore's friend.

The following evening, a silver doe, Patronus, comes to Harry at the tent and draws him to a small frozen pool where he sees the Gryffindor sword at the bottom. He dives to retrieve the sword and nearly drowns, but Ron arrives to save his life. The Deluminator has drawn him back to his friends. Ron destroys the Horcrux and tells Harry and Hermione that Voldemort's name is taboo, which means when someone says his name, protective enchantments disappear and roving bands of wizards appear to capture them.

Hermione decides they must visit Xenophilius Lovegood to decipher the strange symbol he wore. He tells them it represents the three Deathly Hallows: an unbeatable Elder Wand; the Resurrection Stone, which brings back the dead; and an Invisibility Cloak. Then, he reveals that Luna is a prisoner of the Ministry and Death Eaters are on their way to capture Harry, but the three manage to escape.

Harry realizes that Voldemort seeks the Elder Wand to defeat him. However, Voldemort knows of no other Hallows. Harry also discovers that his Invisibility Cloak is the third Hallow and that Dumbledore destroyed the Horcurx on the Resurrection Stone before his death. Moreover, he now realizes that Dumbledore has enclosed it in the Snitch he left him.

Later, Harry accidentally utters Voldemort's name, which brings a gang of Snatchers who capture the three friends and take them to the Malfoy Manor. They also have collected a Goblin prisoner named Griphook.

Bellatrix Lestrange sees the Gryffindor sword in the Snatcher's possessions and believes that her Gringotts safe was broken into. She tortures Hermione and Griphook until they convince her that the sword is a fake. Locked in a cell, Harry retrieves the glass from the two-way mirror, sees Dumbledore's blue eye again, and desperately asks for help. In response, Dobby, the house elf, Apparates into the cell and helps them escape, losing his life as a result.

Harry decides to focus the search on Horcruxes, not Hallows, trusting in Dumbledore's plan for him. In the meantime, Voldemort finds Grindelwald and kills him after discovering that Dumbledore owned the Elder Wand. He opens Dumbledore's tomb and takes possession of the wand.

After Lestrange's panic for her Gringotts vault, Harry realizes that she must keep a Horcrux there. With the help of Griphook, Harry, Ron, and Hermione decide to break into Gringotts to retrieve it. Griphook agrees to help if he can keep the Gryffindor sword, and Harry grudgingly accepts.

For their Gringotts robbery, Hermione transforms into Bellatrix Lestrange. They use the Imperius curse to enter the Lestrange vault and find the Hufflepuff cup Horcrux. They lose the sword to Griphook and fly on a Gringotts dragon to safety.

Voldemort hears of the robbery and now worries about the other Horcruxes. He decides to return to each of his hidden locations. Harry sees him thinking and discovers that the second-to-last Horcrux is at Hogwarts.

Harry, Hermione, and Ron head to Hogsmeade to enter Hogwarts and receive help from Aberforth Dumbledore, Professor Dumbledore's brother and the owner of the blue eye that sent them Dobby. He shows them a secret entrance to Hogwarts into the Room of Requirement.

Harry must find the last Horcrux but knows only that it has a Ravenclaw symbol. He asks students for help, and they mention Rowena Ravenclaw's lost diadem. Meanwhile, members of Dumbledore's Army and the Order arrive to take a stand against Voldemort, preparing for battle. Harry finds Professor McGonagall, and she promises to give Harry time to find the diadem. Harry asks the Gray Lady, Ravenclaw's ghost, for insight into the diadem's whereabouts. Harry realizes he saw the diadem before in the Room of Requirement when he hid his potion book.

Meanwhile, Ron and Hermione destroy the Hufflepuff Horcrux with Basilisk fangs from the Chamber of Secrets. They also finally profess their love for each other. Charmed, the three enter the Room of Requirement in search of the diadem, only to find Draco Malfoy, Vincent Crabbe, and Gregory Goyle, who try to kill them. Crabbe starts a Fiendfyre, or a cursed fire, which destroys the diadem Horcrux, and they all nearly perish. Harry enters Voldemort's mind and finds that he and his snake, which is the last Horcrux, are in the Shrieking Shack. Ron, Hermione, and Harry find him and watch Voldemort kill Severus Snape. Voldemort believes that he must murder Snape for full control of the Elder Wand, as Snape killed Dumbledore. On Voldemort's departure, Harry approaches the dying Snape, who passes him memories.

Harry, distraught after finding Nymphadora Tonks, Remus Lupin, and Fred Weasley dead, goes to Professor Dumbledore's old office and enters the Pensieve with Snape's memories. He discovers that Snape loved Lily Potter, Harry's mother, and had protected Harry from Voldemort his entire life. Harry also sees that Dumbledore and Snape planned the headmaster's death when Dumbledore realized he was terminally ill. Finally, Harry understands that he is a Horcrux and must surrender himself to kill Voldemort.

Harry leaves Ron and Hermione to take care of the final Horcrux on his own. When he reaches the Forbidden Forest where Voldemort waits, he opens the Snitch and retrieves the Resurrection Stone. The ghostly figures of his mother, father, Lupin, and Sirius surround him and help him continue walking, until Voldemort uses the Killing Curse.

Harry awakes in a place that reminds him of King's Cross Station, with Dumbledore next to him. There, Dumbledore explains that because Voldemort has Harry's blood in his body, he tethered Harry to life and could not kill him. Harry learns that he is the true master of the Hallows and that by returning to his body, he could finish Voldemort.

Harry comes to, but plays dead. Voldemort is celebrating his victory, carrying Harry's body to the castle. Neville Longbottom receives the sword of Gryffindor from the Sorting Hat and kills Voldemort's snake, the last Horcrux. Harry finally corners Voldemort. There, he reveals that the Elder

Wand had recognized Draco Malfoy as its new Master when he disarmed Dumbledore, before Snape killed him. So, when Harry disarmed Malfoy on his escape from the Malfoy Manor, Harry became the Elder Wand's new Master. Voldemort refuses to accept this and shoots a killing spell at Harry, but the curse rebounds and Voldemort finally dies.

Rowling completes the epic series with an epilogue, set 19 years later. Harry and Ginny and Ron and Hermione, now two married couples, are sending their children off to Hogwarts, bringing the story full circle.

—Marie Calvert-Kilbane

CENSORSHIP HISTORY

The seven books in the Harry Potter series have been an international publishing sensation, translated into at least 60 languages and sold in more than 200 countries. In June 2008, the number of books sold worldwide had reached 400 million.

But Rowling's series has also achieved a more dubious distinction: According to the American Library Association (ALA), every year from 1999 to 2002, Harry Potter topped the list of titles "challenged," or targeted for censorship, in libraries and schools in the United States because it portrays wizardry and magic. In 2003, it ranked second. The ALA defines a challenge as a formal written complaint filed with a library or a school requesting that materials be removed because of content or appropriateness. The ALA documented 125 attempts during 1999–2003 to restrict access or remove the Potter books from classrooms, curricula, or school or public libraries.

In most cases, the efforts were unsuccessful. However, in Zeeland, Michigan, in November 1999, school superintendent Gary L. Feenstra ordered that *Harry Potter and the Sorcerer's Stone* could not be used in classrooms or displayed on library shelves, that students could check it out or write reports about it only with parental permission, and that no new copies could be purchased for school libraries. Zeeland students, parents, and teachers joined with groups representing booksellers, librarians, publishers, and writers to form an organization to fight the restrictions, Muggles for Harry Potter. The Zeeland Board of Education set up a committee composed of parents and educators from each school in the district to evaluate the superintendent's restrictions. On May 11, 2000, Feenstra accepted the committee's recommendations to rescind the ban, retaining only the restriction on classroom readings in kindergarten to grade 5.

The first legal challenge to a ban on Potter books came in July 2002, when a student and her parents sued the Cedarville, Arkansas, school board. It had restricted access to the books in school libraries by placing them in a section that was off limits to students unless they had their parents' permission, overruling a unanimous decision by the district's library committee to allow unrestricted access. The board acted in response to a parent's complaint that the books show "that there are 'good witches' and 'good magic' and that they teach 'parents/teachers/rules are stupid and something to be ignored.' " The complaining parent said in court depositions that she became concerned about children's exposure to Harry Potter after hearing anti-Potter sermons by the pastor of the Uniontown Assembly of God church, who was also a member of the Cedarville school board.

In April 2003, U.S. District Court judge Jimm L. Hendren in Fort Smith, Arkansas, ordered the Cedarville school district to return the books to the open shelves of its libraries "where they can be accessed without any restrictions other than those. . . that apply to all works of fiction in the libraries of the district." Hendren said there was no evidence to support the school board's claim that the books threatened the orderly operation of the schools and concluded that the majority of the board members voted to "restrict access to the books because of their shared belief that the books promote a particular religion." This violated the First Amendment rights of the students. "Regardless of the personal distaste with which these individuals regard 'witchcraft,' " the judge said, "it is not properly within their power and authority as members of defendants' school board to prevent the students at Cedarville from reading about it."

Conservative groups and Christian fundamentalist organizations such as Focus on the Family, Family Friendly Libraries, Freedom Village USA, and activist Phyllis Schafly's Eagle Forum organized efforts to remove Harry Potter from schools or libraries. They believe that the books are dangerous to children because they promote the occult, Satanism, and antifamily themes and encourage witchcraft and drug use.

On its Web site in 2002, Family Friendly Libraries explained that it promotes book policies it believes "are necessary to protect children, preserve parental rights, re-establish decency as a standard for the classroom, encourage higher educational standards, and uphold Constitutional law as today's courts seem to interpret it."

The group singled out categories of books and other materials that "constitute family sensitive materials that deserve special handling in the public school library setting on special shelves that do not allow general student access." They include "those with religious symbolism and language (Harry Potter and C. S. Lewis' Narnia series falls in this category)."

Family Friendly Libraries also recommended that "a family-friendly attorney send a letter on his/her official stationary [sic] to school officials reminding them that although teacher-led objective discussions about religious history, holidays etc are not forbidden within relevant educational planning, nevertheless . . . the teacher also cannot present Harry Potter or other materials celebrating a pagan religious system."

Other organizations that have targeted Harry Potter cite the Hatch Amendment (the Protection of Pupil Rights Amendment to the General Education Provisions Act), which prohibits federally funded schools from conducting psychological testing or surveys of students on certain subjects and restricts the types of physical exams children can receive without parental consent.

According to form letters made available by Christian fundamentalists on the Internet, the Hatch Amendment gives parents the right to excuse children from classroom activities involving discussion of alcohol and drug education; nuclear issues; education on human sexuality; "globalism"; "one-world government" or "anti-nationalistic curricula"; evolution, including Darwin's theory; and witchcraft, occultism, the supernatural, and mysticism.

Jim Bradshaw, a spokesman for the U.S. Department of Education, told the *South Bend* (Indiana) *Tribune* in April 2004 that the Hatch Amendment is often misinterpreted by the public. "There are many form letters out there created and distributed by parental rights groups that misapply the Protection of Pupil Rights Amendment (PPRA) to certain situations," he said. "PPRA has to do with surveying students, not with what is taught to students. Thus, whether a particular book can be taught is a local issue. The Department of Education is specifically prohibited by law from telling a school what they can or cannot teach." Nevertheless, parents have presented form letters citing the Hatch Amendment to school officials as justification for restricting access to the Harry Potter series and other books in schools.

In an interview with the *Baltimore Sun* in 2000, Rowling commented on the attempts to keep Harry Potter out of the hands of schoolchildren: "I think it's shortsighted in the sense that it is very hard to portray goodness without showing what the reverse is and showing how brave it is to resist that. You find magic, witchcraft, and wizardry in all sorts of classic children's books. Where do you stop? Are you going to stop at *The Wizard of Oz?* Are you going to stop at C. S. Lewis? The talking animals in *Wind in the Willows?*"

During 2001–03, the Potter books were publicly burned or shredded by fundamentalist church groups in the United States in Butler County, Pennsylvania; Lewiston, Maine; Alamogordo, New Mexico; and Greenville, Michigan. Harry Potter books have also been banished from some Christian religious schools in the United States, as well as in Australia, Britain, and Sweden.

Although a few U.S. Catholic schools banned the books, the Vatican informally approved them. In February 2003, Rev. Peter Fleetwood, former official of the Pontifical Council for Culture, introducing a Vatican document on New Age religious beliefs to the press, commented that the books helped children "to see the difference between good and evil." "I don't think there's anyone in this room who grew up without fairies, magic, and angels in their imaginary world," he told reporters. "They aren't bad. They aren't serving as a banner for an anti-Christian ideology."

In July 2005, however, it was revealed that when Pope Benedict XVI was a cardinal (Joseph Cardinal Ratzinger) and head of the Vatican's Congregation for the Doctrine of the Faith, he had criticized the Potter books. In 2003, Ratzinger had written two letters replying to Gabrielle Kuby, a Catholic sociologist from Germany and author of *Harry Potter: Gut oder Böse* (Harry Potter: Good or evil). Kuby's book alleges that the books prevent the young from developing a proper sense of good and evil and harm their relationship with God.

In the first letter, written in German, dated March 7, 2003, Ratzinger thanked Kuby for her "instructive book" and suggested she send a copy to Monsignor Fleetwood. "It is good that you enlighten us in matters relating to Harry Potter," Ratzinger wrote, "for these are subtle temptations, which act imperceptibly and, for that reason, deeply, and subvert Christianity in the soul, before it can really grow properly." Despite the pope's negative assessment of the books in the past, the Vatican has not attempted to bar them from Catholic schools or recommend that Catholics refrain from reading them.

As *Harry Potter and the Half-Blood Prince* hit U.S. bookstores in July 2005, it appeared that some of the steam had gone out of the anti–Harry Potter movement. The ALA announced that in 2004, for the first time in five years, the series did not appear on its list of "most challenged" books. A number of observers noted that the frequency of protests against the books had diminished markedly in 2004 and 2005.

Only a few incidents of attempted censorship of the Harry Potter books were reported to the ALA during 2004–2009. In 2006, trustees of the Wilsona School District in California removed Harry Potter and 23 other books from a reading list recommended by a parent-teacher committee for the Vista San Gabriel elementary school library. Also in 2006, in Gwinnett County, Georgia, a parent asked that the books be removed from school libraries because they promote witchcraft. The county school board rejected the request. The parent appealed, and in December 2006 the Georgia Board of Education supported the school board's decision and ruled that the parent had failed to prove her contention that the books "promote the Wicca religion." In May 2007, a state superior court judge upheld the state board of education's decision. In October 2007, the pastor of St. Joseph's School in Wakefield, Massachusetts, removed the books from the school library, declaring that the themes of the witchcraft and sorcery were inappropriate for a Catholic school.

Though the epicenter of the anti-Harry Potter movement is in the United States, the book has also been targeted abroad. In February 2002, board of education officials in the United Arab Emirates banned 26 books from schools, including the Harry Potter series and George Orwell's *Animal Farm*, because "they have written or illustrated material that contradicts Islamic and Arab values." They nonetheless remained available in bookstores.

In December 2002, a representative of the International Foundation for Slavic Writing and Culture filed criminal hate-crime charges against Rosman Publishing in Moscow for publishing a Russian translation of *Harry Potter and the Chamber of Secrets,* claiming that it "instilled religious extremism and prompted students to join religious organizations of Satanist followers." After an investigation, the Moscow City Prosecutor's Office decided that there were no grounds for a criminal case.

FURTHER READING

American Library Association. *Newsletter on Intellectual Freedom* 54, no. 3 (May 2005).

Blakely, Rhys. "Pope Criticises Harry Potter." *Times* (London) (July 13, 2005). Available online. URL: http://www.timesonline.co.uk/article/0,,1=1692541,00.html.

Chansanchai, Athima. "Darkness and Delight of Potter's Creator." *Baltimore Sun* (October 20, 2000). Available online. URL: http://www.baltimoresun.com. Accessed November 2, 2000.

Churnin, Nancy. "Bible Belt Beware: Harry Potter Isn't So Controversial Anymore." *Dallas Morning News* (July 13, 2005). Available online. URL: http://www.free republic.com/focus/f-news/1443583/posts. Accessed November 15, 2005.

deLuzuriaga, Tania. "Man from Ministry Bans Potter." *Boston Globe* (October 25, 2007). Available online. URL: http://www.boston.com/news/local/articles/2007/10/25/man_from_ministry_bans_potter/. Accessed June 6, 2010.

Doyle, Robert P. *Books Challenged or Banned in 2008–2009.* Chicago: American Library Association, 2009.

———. *Books Challenged or Banned in 2006–2007.* Chicago: American Library Association, 2007.

———. *Books Challenged or Banned in 2005–2006.* Chicago: American Library Association, 2006.

———. *Banned Books: 2004 Resource Book.* Chicago: American Library Association, 2004.

———. "Books Challenged or Banned in 2002–2003." Chicago: American Library Association, 2003.

———. "Books Challenged or Banned in 2001–2002." Chicago: American Library Association, 2002.

———. "2000–2001: Books Challenged or Banned." Chicago: American Library Association, 2001.

Family Friendly Libraries. "Family-Friendly Public School Book Policies." 2002. Available online. URL: http//www.fflibraries.org/Book_Reports/PSBookPolicies.htm.

Kern, Edmund. "Pope Should Spell Out Views on Potter." *The Scotsman* (July 29, 2005). Available online. URL: http://www.scotsman.com/opinion.cfm?id=1700982005.

Meenan, Jim. "Mom: Parental Rights Central to Book Issue." *South Bend Tribune* (April 16, 2004). Available online. URL: http://www.southbendtribune.com. Accessed April 27, 2004.

Rowling, J. K. J. K. Rowling Official Site. Available online. URL: http://www.jk rowling.com.

Scholastic Press. "Harry Potter." Available online. URL: http://scholastic.com/harry potter.

THE HIDDEN FACE OF EVE: WOMEN IN THE ARAB WORLD

Author: Nawal El Saadawi
Original dates and places of publication: 1977, Lebanon; 1980, United States
Publishers: al-Mu'assassat; Zed Books
Literary form: Sociological text

SUMMARY

A physician, sociologist, novelist, and author of nonfiction essays and books on Arab women's issues, Nawal El Saadawi is one of the most widely translated Egyptian writers and an outspoken feminist. In this personal and disturbing account, the author exposes the hidden abuses of girls and women in the Muslim world and the ideologies she holds responsible for their oppressed condition.

Covering a wide range of topics, from female genital mutilation and sexual abuse of girls, to prostitution, sexual relationships, marriage, and divorce, El Saadawi advances the thesis that the problems of Arab women stem not from the substance and values of Islam, but rather from an economic and political system based on male domination. One of the primary weapons used to suppress the revolt of women against patriarchy and its values is the misuse of the doctrines of Islam, the exploitation of religion for social and political ends.

The oppression of women in any society is an expression of an economic structure built on landownership, systems of inheritance and parenthood, and the patriarchal family as a social unit, El Saadawi contends. Arab cultures are not exceptional in having transformed women into commodities. In the very essence of Islam, the status of women is no worse than it is in Judaism or Christianity.

El Saadawi recounts her own genital mutilation at the age of six, a prevalent custom for Egyptian girls when she was growing up. "Society had made me feel, since the day that I opened my eyes on life, that I was a girl, and that the word *bint* (girl) when pronounced by anyone is almost always accompanied by a frown." Recalling her experiences as a doctor working in rural areas of Egypt, she analyzes the psychological and physical damage of genital mutilation, which is aimed at denying sexual pleasure to women in order to ensure their virginity before marriage and chastity throughout.

Society, as represented by its dominant classes and male structure, El Saadawi contends, realized at an early stage the power of female sexual desire. Unless women were controlled and subjugated, they would not submit to moral, legal, and religious constraints, in particular those related to monogamy. An illicit intimacy with another man could lead to confusion in succession and inheritance, since there was no guarantee that another man's child would not step into the line of descendants.

El Saadawi also discusses another taboo subject, sexual molestation of girls by male family members. She cites a study she conducted in 1973, involving 160 Egyptian girls and women from different social classes, from both educated and uneducated families. One of her findings showed that sexual molestation of female children by men was a common occurrence. The increasing number of men unable to marry for economic reasons, the segregation of the sexes, the lack of sexual outlets for men, the convenient proximity of female family members or young domestic servants, and the low status of women are all contributing factors to the problem.

El Saadawi systematically analyzes other abuses against women, including marriage customs and laws that transform women into merchandise to be bought in exchange for dowry and sold for the price of alimony; laws that punish a woman for committing adultery; prohibitions on abortion that result in maternal deaths from illegal abortions; and marriage regulations giving the husband the right to refuse his wife permission to leave the house to work or travel.

Looking back into Egyptian history, she finds in the predominance of the female goddesses of pharaonic Egypt a reflection of the high status of women before the advent of the systems characterized by the patriarchal family, land ownership, and division into social classes. In Islamic history, she points to one of Muhammad's wives, Aisha, as an example of a liberated woman known for her strong will, eloquence, and intelligence. Aisha did not hesitate to oppose or contradict the Prophet; she fought in several wars and battles and was actively involved in politics and cultural and literary activities. The complete emancipation of women, whether in the Arab countries or elsewhere, El Saadawi says, can occur only when humanity does away with class society and exploitation and when the structures and values of the patriarchal system have been erased.

CENSORSHIP HISTORY

El Saadawi has long been a thorn in the side of Egyptian religious and political authorities, whom she has angered by her unyielding demands for women's rights, daring writings on gender and sexuality in 35 books, and questioning of religious and secular foundations of patriarchal authority.

She was the first feminist in the Arab world to publicly confront issues such as female genital mutilation, prostitution, incest, and sexual abuse of Arab girls and women. Her first study of Arab women's problems and their struggle for liberation, *Women and Sex*, published in Egypt in 1972, was a best seller, but it offended religious and government leaders. As a direct result of the book's publication, she was dismissed from her post as director general of health education in the Ministry of Health. She also lost her job as editor of the journal *Health* and was removed as assistant general secretary of the Medical Association. Her publisher was ordered to recall all copies of *Women and Sex* and put them in storage.

The 1977 publication of *The Hidden Face of Eve: Women in the Arab World* in Arabic and its subsequent translation into several languages brought her international attention but also more harassment in Egypt. During the presidency of Anwar Sadat, from 1970 until 1981, despite the absence of official censorship, emergency laws allowed the prime minister to withhold printing permits for publications. When a permit was denied for *The Hidden Face of Eve*, El Saadawi had it published in Beirut, Lebanon. The book was prohibited from entry to many Arab countries, including Egypt, where Egyptian customs and excise authorities barred it under the Importing of Foreign Goods Act. "Islamicists considered its critical examination of the links between the Middle East's three social taboos—religion, sex and the ruling establishment—blasphemous," El Saadawi wrote. "A disobedient woman writer is doubly punished," she contended, "since she has violated the norm of her fundamental obligation to home, husband and children."

When the Center for New Ideas in Tehran, Iran, translated the book into Farsi in 1980, Islamic extremists among followers of the Ayatollah Ruhollah Khomeini burned the book and its publishing house. Despite the bannings, the book, smuggled from Lebanon and sold surreptitiously, has been widely read in Egypt and in many of the other Arab countries where it is prohibited.

El Saadawi's writings and her left-wing political views—she opposed the 1979 Camp David peace treaty between Egypt and Israel—led to her arrest and imprisonment in 1981 under the Sadat regime. Along with many other Egyptian intellectuals, she was jailed for three months for alleged "crimes against the state" and released after Sadat's assassination.

Only in the early 1980s was she able to publish a book in Egypt, though she remained blacklisted from Egyptian television and radio. After her release from prison she founded the Arab Women's Solidarity Association, an international Arab women's network to support women's rights and secularism. In July 1991, the Egyptian government under President Hosni Mubarak banned the Egyptian branch of the association and also closed down its feminist magazine.

El Saadawi has been the target of numerous death threats by Muslim fundamentalists. Sheikh Mohammed al-Ghazzali, a well-known faculty member at Al-Azhar University, Egypt's state-funded religious establishment, called her "an animal." In June 1992, the government posted armed guards outside her home to protect her. "I never trusted them," says El Saadawi. "I did not believe that those in power were so concerned about my life." In 1993, she left Egypt, fearing for her life, and moved to the United States, where she was a visiting professor for four years at Duke University. She returned to Egypt in 1999.

In 2001, El Saadawi faced charges of apostasy in Cairo's Civil Affairs Court brought by an Islamist lawyer who sought to divorce her forcibly from her Muslim husband of 37 years, Dr. Sherif Hetata. The lawyer, Nabih El-Wahsh, claimed that El Saadawi's views, as quoted in a local weekly newspaper, on the veil, Muslim inheritance laws and the pagan aspects of the pilgrimage to Mecca "ousted her from the Muslim community."

El Saadawi said that her statements were taken out of context as "part of a campaign by the political religious trend against me." The lawyer based his case on the claim that Islamic law, or sharia, prohibits Muslims from marrying those who have abandoned their Islamic faith and that the Muslim community is empowered by sharia to defend its tenets against such transgressions through the exercise of *hisba*. *Hisba* allows any Muslim to file a case on behalf of society when the plaintiff feels that great harm has been done to Islam.

In July 2001, the court rejected the lawyer's claim on grounds that under Egyptian law, only a state prosecutor can bring *hisba* cases. A number of Islamist lawyers had brought Egyptian intellectuals and writers to court using *hisba* during the 1990s. A notorious suit in 1995 against university professor Nasr Hamed Abu Zeid, alleging that his writings denied some of the basic teachings of Islam, resulted in a court order for Abu Zeid's separation from his wife, Ibtihal Younes. The couple went into exile in the Netherlands to avoid the forcible divorce and escape death threats by militant Islamists. In the wake of international criticism and embarrassment over the Abu Zeid case, the government asked Parliament in 1998 to amend the law to allow only the state's prosecutor-general to file *hisba* cases.

During the 33rd International Cairo Book Fair in 2001, government censors confiscated four books written by El Saadawi, including her memoirs. In May 2004, the Islamic Research Academy of Al-Azhar, Egypt's leading Muslim religious institution, called on the government to ban El Saadawi's 1987 novel, *The Fall of the Imam*, on the grounds that it offends Islam. "Almost every year," El Saadawi said, "they launch a campaign against me in order to draw people's attention away from crucial issues and to frighten creative writers."

In January 2007, five of her books were again barred from display at the Cairo International Book Fair, including her 2006 play, *God Submits His Resignation from the Summit Meeting*. Later that year, Al-Azhar filed suit against El Saadawi for blasphemy for publishing the play. In January 2008, the owner of Egypt's Madbouli bookstore and publishing company, who had published dozens of El Saadawi's books in the past, destroyed the entire inventory of the play, as well as *The Fall of the Imam*, in the presence of the government's book controller, "once we learnt it offends religion." After Islamists called for revocation of her Egyptian citizenship, El Saadawi fled Egypt for Brussels.

FURTHER READING

Anis, Mona, and Amira Howeidy. " 'I Dream of a Better Future.' " *Al-Ahram Weekly* (June 22–29, 1995). In *World Press Review* (October 1995): 19–21.

Dawoud, Khaled. "Did *Hisba* Ever Go Away?" *Al-Ahram Weekly On-line* 539 (June 21–27, 2001). Available online. URL: http://weekly.ahram.org.eg/2001/539/eg7.htm.

Ehab, John. "Publish and Be Damned." *Daily News Egypt* (April 11, 2008). Available online. URL: http://www.dailystaregypt.com/article.aspx?ArticleID=13056. Accessed June 6, 2010.

Howeidy, Amira. "The Persecution of Abu Zeid." *Al-Ahram Weekly* (June 22–28, 1995). In *World Press Review* (October 1995): 18–19.

Malti-Douglas, Fedwa, and Allen Douglas. "Reflections of a Feminist." In *Opening the Gates: A Century of Arab Feminist Writing*, edited by Margot Badran and Miriam Cooke, 394–404. Bloomington: Indiana University Press, 1990.

El Saadawi, Nawal. "Defying Submission." *Index on Censorship* 19, no. 9 (October 1980): 16.

———. *The Hidden Face of Eve: Women in the Arab World.* Preface by Nawal El Saadawi. Trans. Sherif Hetata. London: Zed Books, 1980.

———. *The Hidden Face of Eve: Women in the Arab World.* Foreword by Irene L. Gendzier. Boston: Beacon Press, 1982.

———. Nawal El Saadawi's official Web site. Available online. URL: http://www.nawalsaadawi.net.

Al-Tahhawi, Amira. "Egypt's 'Woman Rebel' Back in the Line of Fire." *Menassat* (July 2, 2008). Available online. URL: http://www.menassat.com/?q=en/news-articles/4034-egypts-woman-rebel-back-line-fire. Accessed June 6, 2010.

HIS DARK MATERIALS TRILOGY, BOOK I: *THE GOLDEN COMPASS*

Author: Philip Pullman
Original date and places of publication: 1995, United Kingdom; United States
Original publishers: Scholastic Children's Books; Alfred A. Knopf
Literary form: Novel

SUMMARY

The Golden Compass (originally published under the title *Northern Lights* in the United Kingdom) is Book I of Philip Pullman's His Dark Materials trilogy, which follows the adventures of young Lyra Belacqua and her daemon, Pantalaimon (Pan), on a fated quest.

Pullman has, in convincing fashion, created an alternate version of Earth as Lyra's birth-world, where all humans have daemons (animalistic manifestations of the soul's qualities), and the Church has almost absolute control of society. With the abolition of the papacy, the Holy Church has become a hierarchy of courts and councils known as the Magisterium, chief among them being the General Oblation Board. The traditional Church teachings of heaven and hell are threatened by the notion of the existence of other universes in different dimensions and by the alleged presence of mysterious particles known as Dust.

It is in this atmosphere of theological and political intrigue that the tale begins. Lyra, brought up at Jordan College, learns that her uncle, the powerful Lord Asriel, has come to the school with photographic evidence of Dust and of an alternative universe, revealed in the light of an aurora. Lord Asriel persuades the Master and the Scholars of the College to grant his request for further funding and returns to the North to continue his experiments regarding Dust.

Shortly thereafter, children and their daemons from the surrounding area are being kidnapped by what have come to be called Gobblers by the locals. On the day Lyra's friend, Roger, is kidnapped, she is summoned by the Master to meet Mrs. Coulter, a one-time Scholar mounting her own expedition north. Lyra is made Mrs. Coulter's assistant. Before she goes with Mrs. Coulter, the Master gives her an alethiometer, a device for revealing the truth of a situation, telling her she must keep it hidden from Mrs. Coulter. Lyra assumes that the Master wants her to bring the device to Lord Asriel.

Lyra slowly becomes suspicious of Mrs. Coulter and her golden monkey daemon. At a social function, Lyra overhears several startling conversations: She learns that Lord Asriel is being held prisoner by order of the Magisterium in an arctic kingdom called Svalbald, ruled by sapient armored bears; she also learns that the Gobblers are from the General Oblation Board and that Mrs. Coulter herself is the head of the board. When Pan discovers the golden monkey daemon leaving Lyra's quarters, Lyra realizes that Mrs. Coulter must now know about the alethiometer; Lyra gathers her possessions and flees with Pan.

While escaping, Lyra is accosted by two slave traders but is rescued by a group of gyptian men, who know Lyra from Jordan College. The gyptians are a gypsy-like boat people who value loyalty above all else and whose children have been targeted by the Gobblers; when Lyra learns of the gyptian's plan to go North and rescue all the children, she offers to accompany them so that she may use the alethiometer to help find Roger and free her uncle. However, she learns from the gyptians' leaders, John Faa and Farder Coram, that, in actuality, she is the offspring of Lord Asriel and Mrs. Coulter; after the adulterous scandal, both of them shunned the child, and the courts placed her at Jordan College. Despite this emotional shock, Lyra manages to master the alethiometer.

Before the gyptians begin their expedition, they build their supplies and try to gain support from their allies, the witches. Like the gyptians, the witches honor obligations, and Farder Coram, who once saved the life of witch queen Serafina Pekkala, asks for and receives her pledge of aid. John Faa engages itinerant aeronaut Lee Scoresby and his hot-air balloon for the trip, while Lyra enlists Iorek Byrnison, a renegade armored bear who was deposed as king of his clan and exiled from Svalbald. Soon after the expedition sets out, they are attacked by Tartars who are in league with Mrs. Coulter. They kidnap Lyra and Pan and take them to Bolvangar, where the

Oblation Board conducts its own experiments, which, Lyra learns, entail cutting daemons away from their children. Lyra stumbles into one of the operating rooms, where three technicians about to subject her to the procedure are interrupted by the timely arrival of Mrs. Coulter, who has been relentlessly following Lyra.

Mrs. Coulter tells Lyra that Dust is first attracted to people at the time of puberty, when their daemons begin to trouble them with the normal awakenings of sexuality, which is why the Magisterium holds Dust to be the source of Original Sin. The board's attempt to eradicate what they feel is sin results in the depersonalization of the child, incurring a servile attitude. But now that Lord Asriel has given proof of Dust and of alternative universes, the Magisterium can no longer dismiss them as heresies and is now trying to gain control of access to Dust, since Lord Asriel's findings have shown a link between Dust and the ability to cross over into those alternative worlds.

Lyra escapes from Mrs. Coulter and sets a fire in the kitchen, which consumes the whole compound. The Tartars begin to stalk the children, but the gyptian expedition arrives in time to rescue them. Lyra means to continue on with Roger and Iorek Byrnison to find Lord Asriel. Lee Scoresby, accompanied by Serafina Pekkala, takes them farther north by balloon. While en route, they are attacked by bat-like creatures called cliff-ghasts. As the balloon nears the ground, Lyra is thrown from the basket and taken prisoner by the armored bears. Iorek Byrnison and Roger also manage to get off the balloon and arrive in time for Iorek to fight the bear-king to the death and reclaim his throne. The bears now turn and fight Mrs. Coulter and the Tartars, who have come by airship, while Lyra, Roger, and Iorek Byrnison go on to the cabin where Lord Asriel is being held.

They find Lord Asriel, and he affirms to Lyra that there is a connection between Dust and sex and, more important, that there is an energy released when a child is separated from his daemon that, properly conducted, can create a portal into one or more of the alternative universes. This would mean the end of the Magisterium's power. Lord Asriel thinks that Dust comes from these other worlds and is determined to destroy its source. Lyra realizes it was not the alethiometer he wanted but Roger, a child to complete his experiment.

As an aurora reveals a city in the sky, Lord Asriel separates Roger from his daemon, killing them both. The released energy creates an opening in the sky, through which Lord Asriel passes. Lyra and Pan follow him over, determined to locate the source of Dust before he does.

—Philip Milito

CENSORSHIP HISTORY

See THE AMBER SPYGLASS.

HIS DARK MATERIALS TRILOGY, BOOK II:
THE SUBTLE KNIFE

Author: Philip Pullman
Original dates and places of publication: 1997, United Kingdom and
United States
Original publishers: Scholastic Point; Alfred A. Knopf
Literary form: Novel

SUMMARY

The adventures of Lyra Belacqua and her daemon, Pantalaimon (Pan), continue in Book II of Philip Pullman's His Dark Materials trilogy. As the book begins, young Will Parry, an inhabitant of our world, brings his mentally unstable mother to stay with his old piano teacher. Two mysterious agents have been breaking into the Parry household. With his mother out of harm's way, young Will returns home to recover a satchel of letters written by Will's long-lost father to Will's mother. Will is interrupted during another break-in by the agents. As he escapes, Will accidentally kills one of the agents and flees.

Will comes to a roadside, where he sees a cat disappearing into the shrubbery. He follows it and finds a window in the air. He passes through the portal and finds himself in a deserted-looking city in another world. In search of shelter, he comes upon an abandoned café, where he encounters Lyra and Pantalaimon; Will and Lyra marvel at each other's differences, since Will has never before seen a daemon, while Lyra has never seen a human without a daemon. She tells Will that she and Pan found themselves in this world by following Lord Asriel. (At the climax of the trilogy's previous volume, *The Golden Compass*, Asriel forced an opening between parallel worlds by using the energy released by the separation of Lyra's friend, Roger, from his daemon.) Lyra and Will slowly gain each other's trust and support, as Lyra finds out from the truth-telling alethiometer that part of her quest entails helping Will find his missing father.

Back in Lyra's home world, the witch Serafina Pekkala continues her search for the young girl. She comes upon Mrs. Coulter torturing another witch in an effort to discover Lyra's true role in these cataclysmic events. Serafina Pekkala kills the other witch before she can reveal Lyra's purpose and flees to Trollesund, where the witch consul Dr. Lanselius advises her to seek out Lord Asriel's servant, Thorold.

Thorold reveals to Serafina Pekkala Lord Asriel's intention to kill the Authority, the "God" of the Magisterium. The Authority was the first created angel; he convinced all the angels created after him that *he* was God and has ruled tyrannically ever since. Lord Asriel wishes to rid humanity of this oppressive influence once and for all.

Serafina Pekkala returns to her clan to find aeronaut Lee Scoresby and Ruta Skadi, the queen of the Latvian witches, with them. Serafina Pekkala convinces her clan that they must fight alongside Lord Asriel against the Authority. Lee Scoresby pledges to find the explorer Stanislaus Grumman, news that is of interest to a young witch named Juta, who has vowed to kill Grumman for spurning her love. Serafina Pekkala takes Juta with the rest of the clan to continue the search for Lyra, while Ruta Skadi will go to her ex-lover Lord Asriel to find out the status of his war preparations. Ruta travels with the other witches until they encounter angels on their way to Lord Asriel; she joins the angels.

Meanwhile, Lyra and Will meet two children named Angelica and Paolo, who inform them that the city in which they have found themselves is called Cittàgazze, a world that is beset with dark, insubstantial forms called Specters, who devour the souls of adults but show no interest in children. Lyra and Will decide to go to Oxford in Will's world, so that she may find a scholar who can tell her something about Dust (the mysterious force described in *Compass*), while Will can gather more information about his father's disappearance.

Will learns the address of the Institute of Archeology, where he discovers that his father, John Parry, was also studying auroras and looking for windows into alternative worlds and that a journalist is interested in learning about Parry. Will sees the journalist arriving and recognizes him as the surviving agent who had broken into Will's house.

Lyra, meanwhile, encounters Dr. Mary Malone, who is part of a government project that is investigating dark matter. Mary believes that dark matter is conscious and refers to its particles as "Shadows." Lyra uses her alethiometer skills on Mary's computer and contacts "Shadows" with pictures and symbols. Lyra and Mary realize that "Shadows" and Dust are one and the same thing. Lyra suggests that Mary rewire her program so she can speak to "Shadows" in words. Mary asks Lyra to return the next day, and Lyra returns to Cittàgazze with Will.

While Serafina Pekkala and the witches enter Cittàgazze, Lee Scoresby goes north to search for Stanislaus Grumman. On making inquiries, Scoresby inadvertently arouses the suspicions of a Magisterium representative and is forced to kill him. Scoresby learns from his guide that Grumman is well known as a shaman in those parts. Scoresby tracks him down, and Grumman reveals that he is John Parry and that he knows of a unique knife that Lord Asriel needs to win his war. They depart and ride in Scoresby's balloon into Lyra's home world to search for the knife bearer.

Lyra returns to Mary Malone's office, where government officials question her about Will. Lyra flees and is saved by Sir Charles Latrom, who observed Lyra using the alethiometer the previous day. He steals it from her. She and Will confront him afterward, and Sir Charles offers to return it if they can find and bring back to him a unique knife that is being held by a man in the "Tower of Angels" in Cittàgazze.

Lyra and Will go there and find the knife holder, Giacomo Paradisi, bound and Angelica's and Paolo's brother, Tullio, dancing insanely with the knife. Will fights with Tullio and wins, losing two fingers in the process; Tullio flees only to be destroyed by the Specters. Paradisi, also missing two fingers, acknowledges this as a sign of the knife bearer and teaches Will how to use the knife for cutting windows into other worlds.

Lyra and Will cut a window into Sir Charles's house and see Mrs. Coulter arriving. Lyra then recognizes Sir Charles as Lord Boreal, who was depicted at the cocktail party in *The Golden Compass*. He has also traveled between worlds and has established powerful bases in many of them. Will just barely retrieves the alethiometer and closes the window. Lyra and Will return to the center of the city, where they are attacked by a mob of children incited by Angelica and Paolo as revenge for the fate of Tullio. Serafina Pekkala and the witches arrive in time to save them.

Back in our world, Mary Malone contacts the "Shadows" and learns that she has a part to play in Lyra's quest; the "Shadows" urge her to destroy all of her project's data and to leave to find Lyra in the other worlds.

As they sail over Cittàgazze, Lee Scoresby and John Parry realize that they are being followed by the zeppelins of the Magisterium's forces. Scoresby makes a hard landing in a mountainside forest. Parry uses magic to crash three of the zeppelins, but the fourth dispatches its soldiers. Scoresby tells Parry to go on and look for the knife bearer while he holds the soldiers off. Scoresby kills many of the soldiers but is finally slain himself. Before dying, he aims a shot at the zeppelin's engines and manages to destroy the vehicle and the remaining soldiers. Scoresby calls out to Serafina Pekkala for aid as he breathes his last.

Serafina Pekkala hears his cry and goes to find him. In her absence, another witch, Lena, sees a camp in the distance and goes to investigate it. It is the camp of Mrs. Coulter and Lord Boreal. Mrs. Coulter has learned to control the Specters and has one of them torture Lena into revealing Lyra's purpose and whereabouts. Lyra is to be the new Eve in the post-Authority life, to cause a new fall from grace. Mrs. Coulter decides she must kill Lyra to prevent this. She has the Specters kill Lena while she poisons Lord Boreal. She then summons the Specters and goes to Lyra's camp.

Will takes a restless walk and comes upon a man, with whom he fights. The man recognizes Will as the knife bearer and, struggling to a draw, tells Will that his purpose is to bring the knife to Lord Asriel. As Will realizes that the man is John Parry, his father, the young witch Juta, who loved Parry as Stanislaus Grumman, appears and claims her vengeance. When she finds out that Will is Parry's son and that she was spurned because Parry had a family to whom he was loyal, she kills herself in remorse.

On his way back, Will is met by two angels who urge him to go with them to Lord Asriel. They go to the camp to find that Mrs. Coulter and the Specters have killed all the witches and abducted Lyra. Will looks at Lyra's knapsack and, as the book ends, wonders what to do next.

—Philip Milito

CENSORSHIP HISTORY

See THE AMBER SPYGLASS.

HIS DARK MATERIALS TRILOGY, BOOK III: *THE AMBER SPYGLASS*

Author: Philip Pullman
Original dates and places of publication: 2000, United Kingdom and United States
Original publishers: Scholastic Point; Alfred A. Knopf
Literary form: Novel

SUMMARY

The Amber Spyglass, Book III of Philip Pullman's His Dark Materials trilogy, begins as a child named Ama pays a visit to a wise woman living in a cave in the forest with a sleeping child. The woman turns out to be Mrs. Coulter, and the sleeping child is her daughter, Lyra. Mrs. Coulter is actually keeping Lyra drugged. Lyra, in her delirium, is dreaming of speaking to her late friend, Roger, and promising to come to his aid somehow.

Ama decides to find a way to awaken the sleeping Lyra and departs, determined to consult a local magician. In the meantime, Will, at the campsite depicted at the conclusion of *The Subtle Knife*, takes Lyra's knapsack, which holds the truth-telling alethiometer, and persuades the two angels, Balthamos and Baruch, to join him in searching for Lyra. Baruch goes ahead to seek her out while Will and Balthamos return to Lyra's home world, where Balthamos agrees to pose as Will's daemon, so they will not call attention to themselves. Baruch returns, having found Lyra and Mrs. Coulter and having discovered that Mrs. Coulter is now herself hiding from the Magisterium. The three are interrupted by the appearance of Metatron, the Lord Regent who now rules in God's stead. Will cuts a window into another world, and the three escape before Metatron can kill them and take possession of the knife that Will is bearing for Lord Asriel. Baruch flies off to bring word to Lord Asriel of all that has happened.

The witch Serafina Pekkala answers Lee Scoresby's cry for help but arrives too late; she seeks out the bear-king Iorek Byrnison and informs him of his old friend Scoresby's death. Iorek returns to his clan and leads the bears to service in Lord Asriel's army.

Baruch is attacked by Metatron's angels and is severely wounded as he approaches Lord Asriel's fortress. He is brought before Lord Asriel and tells him that God (the Authority) is very old and that Metatron now rules; Metatron no longer trusts the Magisterium and is striving for direct impact on human life in all worlds. Baruch informs Lord Asriel of the whereabouts of Lyra and Will and then dies of his wounds. Lord Asriel gathers his allies, among them two Gallivespians (tiny people with poisonous spurs on their heels who travel on the backs of hawks and dragonflies) who are to find and protect Lyra and Will.

The Consistorial Court of the Magisterium also knows of Lyra's destiny and dispatches a group of soldiers to find and kill her. They also send an assassin, Father Gomez, to track Mary Malone. Mary, in the world of Cittàgazze, has discovered another window and passes through to yet another world, where she is befriended by the *mulefa*, a strange but peaceable people who had developed consciousness 33,000 earlier. She learns how to communicate with them and discovers that the *mulefa* can see Dust, or what Mary referred to as "Shadows." Mary speaks with the wisest of the *mulefa* and learns that 300 years ago, their vegetation began to sicken. If this continues, the *mulefa* will revert to being dumb beasts. Mary pledges to help them.

In Lyra's world, Balthamos senses the death of Baruch and falls into despair. He and Will come upon Iorek Byrnison and his armored bears. Will tells Iorek that he is searching for Lyra, and Iorek agrees to help. Balthamos, in his sorrow over Baruch, abandons them, and Will and Iorek press on, finally arriving at the cave where Mrs. Coulter has hidden Lyra. They meet the girl Ama, who has procured a potion to awaken Lyra. Using the knife to cut their way into the rear of the cave, Will and Ama revive Lyra but are caught by Mrs. Coulter. Seeing Mrs. Coulter, Will is reminded of his own mother; his mind clouded by remorse, he tries to cut another way out of the cave, but the knife is stuck in the air and breaks into several pieces.

Lord Asriel's forces arrive at the cave at the same time as the Church's soldiers. In the ensuing battle, the Gallivespian spies, named Chevalier Tialys and Lady Salmakia, rescue Will and Lyra, as Ama returns to her home and Mrs. Coulter is brought to Lord Asriel's fortress. The two little spies insist that the knife be taken to Lord Asriel, but they are forced to follow Will and Lyra as the latter attempt to travel into the world of the dead. Lyra has pledged to help Roger, while Will needs to find his father.

The broken knife is brought to Iorek Byrnison, who repairs it. Iorek and his clan resume their trek to join Lord Asriel, while Will and Lyra and the two spies use the knife to cut their way into the world of the dead. They encounter harpies, who prey on the dead by reinforcing hopelessness. They evade the harpies and inquire after Roger among the ghosts in this afterlife. The ghosts and the Gallivespians find Roger, to whom Lyra apologizes for leading him to his death. Lyra decides that all of the dead must also be freed, and while a plan of escape from the underworld is determined, Lyra tells stories of her life to the dead and to the harpies. Will and Lyra strike a deal with the harpies: Future ghosts will tell their stories to the harpies, who will then feed off the energy of the stories and lead those dead to an exit, which will be created by Will with the knife.

At Lord Asriel's fortress, Mrs. Coulter learns of Lord Asriel's plan to establish a Republic of Heaven upon the death of the Authority. She escapes in one of Lord Asriel's aircraft and goes to the Consistorial Court, where she meets Father MacPhail. She tells him of Lord Asriel's intention, and MacPhail has her arrested. While she is in confinement, a young priest takes her locket, which contains a lock of Lyra's hair.

Knowing Lyra is meant to be the new Eve, the Court will use Lyra's hair to key a bomb that will find and destroy her. To activate the bomb, the energy released from the parting of a human from his daemon must occur. The Court intends to use Mrs. Coulter to this end, but she evades them. Father MacPhail sacrifices himself and the bomb goes off, while Lord Asriel arrives in his aircraft and takes Mrs. Coulter away.

The ghosts of Lee Scoresby and John Parry return to Lyra and tell her of the bomb and of her need to shave the spot where the lock of hair was cut. Will takes the hair and puts it into another world just as the bomb strikes, creating a massive abyss descending to nothingness. Will and Lyra cut a hole into the world of the *mulefa*, and the emerging dead begin to dissolve and drift away, freed at last to join the rest of the universe in conscious unity.

Back at Lord Asriel's fortress, Mrs. Coulter learns that Lyra is still alive and has freed the spirits of the dead, while Lord Asriel finds that Metatron has moved his domain closer to the fortress to wage direct war on Lord Asriel's forces. Lord Asriel goes to the underworld to look for Will and Lyra, as Mrs. Coulter enters Metatron's domain. She entices him to the abyss in the underworld, where she and Lord Asriel attack him. The three of them fall into the abyss, to be lost forever.

Will and Lyra return to the scene of warfare to find some angels trying to move away the Authority, now old and enfeebled, in a glass case. They release the Authority from the case; he dissolves away; and the reign of the God of the Magisterium is ended. Upon the deaths of the two Gallivespian spies, the ghosts of Lee Scoresby and John Parry bid their children farewell and disperse into the unity of the Universe.

Throughout the trilogy, Dust was seen as evil, or ambivalent at best, but now it is understood that Dust is the very essence of life. Will and Lyra go back to the world of the *mulefa*, where they find Mary Malone. Father Gomez, the lone assassin, has found his way there, unaware of all that has happened. As he is about to close in on the children, Balthamos returns and fights him to the death. Will and Lyra fall in love, losing their childhood innocence and fulfilling Lyra's destiny as the new Eve. Serafina Pekkala the witch and an angel named Xaphania arrive to inform Will and Lyra that all the windows left open by previous world crossers must be closed, since Dust escapes into oblivion through these windows, and each new window creates another Specter. Only one window is to be left opened: the exit from the land of the dead.

Will and Lyra make the painful decision to part, since neither can survive for long in the other's universe. Will and Mary Malone return to their world, where Will breaks the knife. Lyra and Pan go back to Jordan College, to continue the establishment of the Republic of Heaven.

CENSORSHIP HISTORY

Since its publication in 1995, *The Golden Compass* has enjoyed considerable critical acclaim and popular success, as have Books II and III of Pullman's His Dark Materials trilogy, *The Subtle Knife* (1997) and *The Amber Spyglass* (2000). Protest against the books began only in 2007, after a film adaptation of *The Golden Compass* was announced. As the December release date approached, Pullman helped promote the film with provocative interviews, in which he proclaimed his atheism and affirmed that the books of his trilogy were an inverted retelling of John Milton's epic poem *Paradise Lost*, this time with God as the vanquished instead of Satan.

Even though the film of *The Golden Compass* watered down Pullman's references in the novel to abuses of power by a religious institution very much like the Catholic Church, the Vatican condemned the movie. An editorial in the Vatican newspaper, *L'Osservatore Romano*, stated that the film and Pullman's writings showed that "when man tries to eliminate God from his horizon, everything is reduced, made sad, cold and inhumane."

In the United States, William Donohue, president of the ultraconservative Catholic League, called for a boycott of the film and the books of the trilogy. The league felt that if children could not see the film, they would not be enticed to read the trilogy, which a league spokesperson described as "a candy-coated message of atheism." The league sent out pamphlets to hundreds of groups, ranging from Roman Catholic bishops to Protestant and Muslim organizations, as well as to Catholic schools around the country, urging them to pull *The Golden Compass* and its companion volumes from their shelves.

This campaign met with success. In 2007, according to the American Library Association (ALA), *The Golden Compass* was the fourth most-challenged book in the United States, with reports of 420 formally submitted complaints to libraries or schools asking for the book's removal, and in 2008, the His Dark Materials trilogy was listed second on the ALA's list. In some cases, the volumes remained on the shelves; in others, the books were removed but later returned; and in yet other cases, such as at a Christian school library in Montrose, Texas, use of *The Golden Compass* was permanently discontinued, even though it had been on the school's eighth-grade recommended reading list for 10 years.

The Golden Compass was also targeted in Canada. The Catholic School Board of Ontario's Halton district removed it from circulation on the strength of one anonymous complaint that the book was "written by an atheist where the characters and text are anti-God, anti-Catholic, and anti-religion." The Catholic School Board of Calgary followed suit. Board officials said that its decision came in response to concern voiced by parents as well as publicity about the film. In Ontario, the decision was reversed in a matter of days; however, the book was removed from public display and made available only upon request. In Calgary, the book was returned to library shelves two months later.

In 2008, the school board of the publicly funded Dufferin-Peel Catholic School District in Mississauga, Ontario, asked principals to remove the books of the trilogy from school library shelves pending review. They were eventually returned to libraries with a sticker on the inside cover telling readers that "representations of the church in this novel are purely fictional and are not reflective of the real Roman Catholic Church or the Gospel of Jesus Christ."

Commenting on the censorship of *The Golden Compass* in Canada, Lorne Gunter, writing in *The Edmonton Journal*, suggested that Christian parents use the book as a teaching opportunity, rather than demand that it be pulled from library shelves. In the *Boston Globe*, Donna Freitas, a Catholic theologian at Boston University, wrote a vigorous defense of the trilogy. She said that it is a thoroughly Christian work, albeit one that reflects the influence of heterodoxy—the notion of the feminized God of love and mercy, represented by Dust, versus the patriarchal God of judgment and unyielding authority, the false God who dies at the end of the trilogy.

As it happened, the film received mixed reviews and did poorly at the box office. But it did draw attention to the books after all, which saw an enormous spike in sales (15 million copies worldwide as of December 2007).

Writing almost a year later in *The Guardian*, Pullman explained his views about religion and expressed his delight at being listed on the ALA's list of most challenged books. "Religion, uncontaminated by power, can be the source of a great deal of private solace, artistic expression, and moral wisdom," he wrote. "But when it gets its hands on the levers of political or social authority, it goes rotten very quickly indeed. The rank stench of oppression wafts from every authoritarian church, chapel, temple, mosque, or synagogue—from every place of worship where the priests have the power to meddle in the social and intellectual lives of their flocks, from every presidential palace or prime ministerial office where civil leaders have to pander to religious ones." Pullman also said that the controversy about *The Golden Compass* moved interested readers from the library, "where they couldn't get hold of my novel" to the bookstores, "where they could. . . . The inevitable result of trying to ban something—book, film, play, pop song, whatever—is that far more people want to get a hold of it than would ever have done if it were left alone. Why don't the censors realise this?"

—Philip Milito

FURTHER READING

Associated Press. "Ontario Catholic School Board Pulls Fantasy Book following Complaint about Atheist Author." *International Herald Tribune* (November 22, 2007). Available online. URL: http://www.iht.com/bin/printfriendly.php?id=8443713. Accessed June 12, 2009.

Borst, John, et al. "Golden Compass 'Review' Causes Media Firestorm." *Tomorrow's Trust, A Review of Catholic Education*, blog archive (November 26, 2007). Available online. URL: http://tomorrowstrust.ca/?9=1129. Accessed June 12, 2009.

"Calgary Catholic School Board Dumps Golden Compass." *Globe and Mail* (December 5, 2007). Available online. URL: http://www.theglobeandmail.com/servlet/story/RTGAM.20071205.wgoldcompass1205/B. Accessed December 6, 2007.

Freitas, Donna. "God in the Dust." *Boston Globe* (November 25, 2007). Available online. URL: http://www.boston.com/bostonglobe/ideas/articles/2007/11/25/god_in_the_dust

Gunter, Lorne. "Faith Strengthened by a Good Test." *Edmonton Journal* (November 25, 2007). Available online. URL: http://lgunter@shaw.ca. Accessed June 12, 2009.

Pullella, Philip. "Vatican Blasts 'Golden Compass' as Godless and Hopeless." Reuters (December 19, 2007). Available online. URL: www.reuters.com/article/entertainmentNews/idUSL1958884920071219. Accessed November 18, 2009.

Pullman, Philip. "The Censor's Dark Materials." *Guardian* (September 28, 2008). Available online. URL: http://www.guardian.co.uk/books/2008/sep/29/philip.pullman.amber.spyglass.golden.compass. Accessed June 12, 2009.

Viren, Sarah. "Does Film 'Compass' Steer Kids in Wrong Direction?" *Houston Chronicle*, December 7, 2007, A1.

HISTORICAL AND CRITICAL DICTIONARY

Author: Pierre Bayle
Original date and place of publication: 1697, Holland
Literary form: Dictionary

SUMMARY

Pierre Bayle's *Historical and Critical Dictionary* was among the most frequently printed and widely used books of the 18th century. In its innovative form, rationalism, skepticism, and subtle irony, it paved the way for such classic works of the Enlightenment as the ENCYCLOPÉDIE and Voltaire's PHILOSOPHICAL DICTIONARY.

Originally a Protestant, the French philosopher and historian Bayle converted to Catholicism but later returned to the Calvinist faith. A victim of the French monarchy's policy of persecution and banishment of Protestants, he was exiled in 1681 to Holland, where he spent most of the rest of his life.

Bayle established a reputation in Europe as a notable advocate of religious toleration and freedom of thought. His first important work, *Miscellaneous Thoughts on the Comet* (1682), which challenged the prevailing belief that comets were harbingers of evil, introduced the skeptical views found in his *Dictionary*—that tradition and authority are suspect, that morality exists independently of religion, and that superstition should be combatted. In *What Wholly Catholic France under the Reign of Louis XIV Really Is* (1686), he protested the 1685 revocation of the Edict of Nantes, which renewed persecution of French Protestants. *A Philosophic Commentary on Christ's Words,*

"Compel Them to Come In" (1686–87) argued against using a literal interpretation of the Bible to justify forcible conversion of heretics.

Bayle's greatest work was his *Historical and Critical Dictionary*, published in four folio volumes in 1697. A compendium of historical biographies listing important figures of classical and religious history, it included comprehensive marginal notes and commentary by Bayle appended to each article that referred to errors and omissions in the work of the author's literary predecessors. While the articles themselves seemed orthodox, the notes, often longer than the articles themselves, were subversive of religious orthodoxy and provided a mine of information for alert and inquiring readers. Using obscure quotations in Latin and Greek, cross-references, and ironic and humorous digressions, Bayle challenged accepted religious beliefs and exposed conflicting interpretations of historical events.

Only theologians would find his approach dangerous, Bayle wrote in one of his *Dictionary* entries, "for it is not clear why it should seem so to the natural scientist or to the statesman. . . . We need not allow ourselves to be discouraged by the argument that the human mind is too limited to discover anything about the truths of nature, the causes that produce heat, cold, the tides. . . . We can be content to gather data from experiments and seek probable hypotheses."

In Bayle's view, the theological controversies of his time were pointless. If the truths of religion were essentially nonrational, they could not be resolved by argument. Faith is outside the realm of reason, and human reason is better adapted for detecting errors than for discovering positive truth, Bayle believed. He contended further that religious convictions are unnecessary to lead a moral life and that it is possible for a society to be moral and virtuous even if its people do not believe in immortality or even in God.

For the 18th-century philosophes, Bayle was a guiding spirit and his *Dictionary* a seminal influence. The English historian Edward Gibbon— author of THE HISTORY OF THE DECLINE AND FALL OF THE ROMAN EMPIRE— acknowledged that Bayle's "vast repository of facts and opinions" had taught him respect for the facts and the subversive possibilities of historical accuracy. Voltaire described it as the first dictionary that taught men how to think, and he placed Bayle in the ranks of intellectual architects of the critical mentality.

CENSORSHIP HISTORY

After its first publication in 1697, Bayle's *Dictionary* was soon expanded and translated into English and German. The four folio volumes of the *Dictionary* went through nine editions in France in less than 50 years, and despite the large and unwieldy format and expensive price of the original folio editions, it was owned by more educated people in Europe than any other book of its time. No personal library was considered complete without it.

Bayle's views on religious tolerance expressed in his 1696 *Philosophic Commentary* had been denounced by both Catholic and Protestant clergy. A similar reaction greeted the *Dictionary*. In response to criticisms by Protestant theologians, Bayle promised to modify his text in the second edition and remove several items they found offensive. But, with the exception of a few titles, the future editions remained unaltered.

A half-century later, the attacks on Bayle's *Dictionary* increased as religious and civil authorities moved to combat the influence of Enlightenment thinking. Widely circulated both in unabridged additions and in extracts and summaries, such as *The Essential Bayle*, the *Dictionary* was seen to cast doubt on some of the most widely accepted principles of morality and religion. The influential Jesuit publication *Journal de Trévoux*, which devoted a lengthy analysis to the *Dictionary*, declared that Bayle had been a writer of extraordinary talents who had chosen to abuse those talents and become a "great skeptic."

In 1754, the *Dictionary* was publicly burned in France, and in 1757, the Vatican placed all of Bayle's writing on the Index of Forbidden Books in its most severe category, *opera omnia*, or all works condemned. Bayle was still on the Index in its last edition, compiled in 1948 and in effect until 1966.

In 1764, it was discovered that text from articles in the *Encyclopédie* that praised and restated the philosophy of Bayle and criticized his clerical prosecutors had been secretly deleted by its printer, who feared repercussions from government authorities. For almost 200 years, the expurgated text of the *Encyclopédie*, minus the full commentary on Bayle, was the only one available.

FURTHER READING

Dunham, Barrows. *Heroes and Heretics: A Political History of Western Thought*. New York: Alfred A. Knopf, 1964.

Gay, Peter. *The Enlightenment: An Interpretation. The Rise of Modern Paganism*. New York: W. W. Norton, 1995.

Hazard, Paul. *European Thought in the Eighteenth Century: From Montesquieu to Lessing*. Cleveland: World Publishing Co., 1973.

Hollier, Denis. *A New History of French Literature*. Cambridge, Mass.: Harvard University Press, 1989.

Kilcullen, John. *Sincerity and Truth: Essays on Arnauld, Bayle and Toleration*. Oxford, U.K.: Clarendon Press, 1988.

HISTORY OF THE CONFLICT BETWEEN RELIGION AND SCIENCE

Author: John William Draper
Original date and place of publication: 1874, United States
Literary form: Historical and philosophical text

SUMMARY

John William Draper's *History of the Conflict Between Religion and Science* was written as an introduction to the history of science for a mass reading audience. Draper, a scientist and historian, sought to justify the importance of scientific thought at a time when the Catholic Church was expanding its political power and taking a strong stance against scientific thinking, particularly new theories of human evolution. Draper maintained that science brought about advancement and that this was a more practical and useful idea than the retreat from modernity advocated by the Catholic Church. He believed that science promoted tolerance and intelligence, while religion engendered hatred for nonbelievers and submission to one way of thinking.

Draper was born in England and graduated from the newly built University of London in 1831. Unlike the older universities at Oxford and Cambridge, this university stressed practical education over a religion-based liberal arts curriculum. London's strong science program led Draper to pursue a course of study in chemistry. On receiving his degree, he immigrated to Virginia, where he performed chemistry experiments in a makeshift laboratory on his family's farm. He attended the University of Pennsylvania medical school, then returned to Virginia to teach at Hampden-Sydney College. In 1839, he moved to New York City to teach at New York University's medical school. During this time, he worked on experiments in photography, alongside Samuel F. B. Morse, the inventor of the telegraph.

While Draper was teaching physiology to medical students in New York, Charles Darwin was writing ON THE ORIGIN OF SPECIES in England. Darwin's theories of evolution sparked great debate in the mid-19th century scientific community. Draper became fascinated with the application of Darwin's theories of natural selection to human behavior. In pursuing this quest, Draper drifted from physical science to social science. He wrote books on the U.S. Civil War and the intellectual history of Europe and discussed these events as scientific processes, applying evolutionary theory to intellectual, political, and military leaders' motives and actions.

Draper's histories, which first appeared in 1861, were designed to appeal to a popular audience. He published essays in *Harper's Magazine,* a well-known monthly, and served as an American spokesman for the general advancement of science. Unlike some scientists who avoided the glare of publicity in favor of the solitary lab, Draper relished his role as a science popularizer. As scientific thinking became more widely accepted, he became a more outspoken critic of antiscientific forces in intellectual life, especially religious authorities who continued to preach a literal interpretation of Scripture.

History of the Conflict Between Religion and Science, which appeared in 1874, asserted that science was justifiably winning the conflict. By this time, Draper's reputation had spread throughout Europe, as his book was translated into French, Spanish, German, Dutch, Russian, Italian, Portuguese, Polish, and Serbo-Croatian. It was the best-selling volume in the popular science series in which it was published.

Draper believed that Pope Pius IX's increased power and hostility to modern times, papal meddling in French and German politics, and the pope's insistence on a literal interpretation of Genesis had led to an unfortunate split between intellectuals and Christians. He also believed that science, which he broadly defined as freedom of conscience and willingness to question authority, was inevitably growing stronger despite the church's objections.

Throughout his book, Draper contrasts the history of religion with the history of science. He begins by looking at Greek, Persian, Roman, and Egyptian science and how early science developed alongside religion, until the Spanish Inquisition and subsequent reactionary Vatican decrees punished medieval scientists and nonbelievers, pushing scientific thought out of Europe. Draper then traces the histories of several general conflicts between religion and science and finds that scientific explanations win over religious beliefs in each case. Draper ends his book by analyzing the Catholic Church and the scientific method in relation to modern civilization, warning that the church's expansion of power and antimodernism are a threat to civilization and progress.

CENSORSHIP HISTORY

Scientists and other readers who were sympathetic to Draper's optimistic view of science bought his book in great numbers around the world. Some reviewers wondered why he seemed to equate Christianity with Catholicism, especially since evangelical Protestant churches in the United States and England had also spoken against theories of creation that contradicted a literal reading of the first chapter of Genesis. Liberal clergymen writing in religious magazines found fault with Draper's history. Pointing to the great civilizations of Europe, they asserted that Christianity was not an impediment to human progress.

One minister criticized Draper's universal faith in progress, claiming that Draper's blind devotion to the scientific method could lead to a breakdown of traditional ways of life and erosion of moral standards. Religious and secular critics questioned whether the overpopulation, pollution, and mechanization of modern cities, fed by advances in science and technology, constituted the utopia claimed by Draper.

An even more damning criticism came from the Catholic Church. Vatican officials read a Spanish edition of *History of the Conflict Between Religion and Science* and in September 1876 placed it on the Index of Forbidden Books. It was the first American work to be listed, and one of only four that appeared on the Index. Two years after its initial publication, Draper had been given, in the words of a Draper biographer, "an honor which its author has shared with Galileo, with Copernicus, with Kepler, with Locke, and with Mill." He had joined the company of some of the greatest minds in science and philosophy whose works offended the Roman Catholic Church.

Unlike Galileo Galilei or Nicolaus Copernicus, however, Draper suffered no personal punishment for offending the Catholic hierarchy. Instead, the book's sudden notoriety led many to buy the book who might not otherwise have been interested in the history of science. Draper faced no legal consequences for writing his book, even in predominantly Catholic countries. Its appearance on the Roman Index meant little to Draper, as he was not Catholic and had no regard for what the pope thought of his work. Nor did he feel any need to apologize for or revise his book. On the contrary, he considered the continuing existence of the Index of Forbidden Books as just the sort of papal antimodernity and power grabbing that he had railed against in his writings.

History of the Conflict Between Religion and Science remained in print for nearly 60 years, through more than 50 printings, and Draper became a popular public speaker. After his book was placed on the Index, he became president of the American Chemical Society and addressed a national gathering of Unitarian ministers on the topic of evolution. He also became a celebrated professor at New York University, where he continued his teaching and research duties until a few months before his death at age 70.

Draper today is known as one of the most prominent American scientists of the mid-19th century and an important historian and popularizer of the theory of evolution.

—Jonathan Pollack

FURTHER READING

Barker, George F. *Memoir of John William Draper, 1811–1882*. Reprint ed. New York: Garland Publishing, 1974.
Draper, John William. *History of the Conflict Between Religion and Science*. Reprint ed. Westmead, England: Gregg International Publishers, 1970.
Fleming, Donald. *John William Draper and the Religion of Science*. Philadelphia: University of Pennsylvania Press, 1950.

THE HISTORY OF THE DECLINE AND FALL OF THE ROMAN EMPIRE

Author: Edward Gibbon
Original dates and place of publication: 1776–88, England
Literary form: History

SUMMARY

Edward Gibbon's epic and magisterial six-volume history of the Roman Empire from A.D. 180 to 1453 is one of the most widely read historical works of modern times. His history begins in the reign of Trajan, when the empire of Rome "comprehended the fairest part of the earth, and the most civilised portion of mankind," and ends with the fall of Constantinople, when the empire lay in ruins. It was among the ruins of ancient Rome on a visit in 1764 that Gibbon conceived the work that was to occupy nearly 20 years of his life.

Gibbon believed that the propagation of the Gospel and the triumph of Christianity were inseparably connected to the decline of the Roman monarchy. Gibbon was raised as a Protestant and converted to Catholicism as a student at Oxford. Expelled from Oxford because of his conversion, he was sent by his family to Lausanne, Switzerland, where he reconverted to Protestantism under the care of a Calvinistic minister. He became, nevertheless, a skeptic, indifferent to religious dogma and guided by the principles of the French Enlightenment.

Influenced by the ideas of French political thinker Charles-Louis de Secondat, baron de La Brède et de Montesquieu, Gibbon's methodology was to weigh historical evidence impartially, unencumbered by religious prejudice. He examined religions as social phenomena, rather than as received doctrine, and was opposed to superstition and fanaticism, which he saw as destructive of human liberty.

The two chapters of Gibbon's 71-chapter history that offered "a candid but rational inquiry into the progress and establishment of Christianity" became notorious. In chapter 15, "The Progress of the Christian Religion, and the Sentiments, Manners, Numbers, and the Condition of the Primitive Christians," and chapter 16, "The Conduct of the Roman Government towards the Christians, from the Reign of Nero to that of Constantine (180–313 A.D.)," Gibbon set out to explore what he described as the "secondary causes" of the rapid growth of the Christian church.

"While that great body [the Roman Empire] was invaded by open violence, or undermined by slow decay," he wrote, "a pure and humble religion gently insinuated itself into the minds of man, grew up in silence and obscurity, derived new vigour from opposition, and finally erected the triumphant banner of the Cross on the ruins of the Capitol."

Gibbon defines the theologian's duty as "describing Religion as she descended from Heaven, arrayed in her native purity." A more melancholy duty, however, is imposed on the historian, "who must discover the inevitable mixture of error and corruption which she contracted in a long residence upon earth, among a weak and degenerate race of beings."

How did the Christian faith establish so remarkable a victory over the established religions of the Earth? Gibbon asks. While allowing that the primary cause of Christianity's success might be the convincing evidence of the doctrine itself and the "ruling providence of its great Author," Gibbon outlines five secondary reasons: Christian zeal, purified of the narrow and unsocial spirit that had deterred Gentiles from embracing the law of Moses; the promise of eternal happiness after death to those who adopted the faith; the miraculous powers ascribed to the church; the pure and austere morals of the Christians; and the unity and discipline of the Christian republic, which gradually formed an independent state in the heart of the Roman Empire.

In his discussion of miracles, Gibbon uses the term *superstition* to describe how the church, from the time of apostles and their first disciples, claimed an uninterrupted succession of miraculous powers—the gifts of tongues and of vision and prophecy, the power to expel demons, and the ability to heal the sick and raise the dead.

He portrays the early church hierarchy, particularly the bishops, as using executive and arbitrary power "to attack, with united vigour, the original rights of their clergy and people. . . . The prelates of the third century imperceptibly changed the language of exhortation into that of command, scattered the seeds of future usurpations, and supplied by Scripture allegories and declamatory rhetoric, their deficiency of force and of reason."

In chapter 16, Gibbon analyzes the treatment of Christians by the Roman Empire, stating that the worst of the Roman emperors were no less repressive than modern sovereigns who have employed violence and terror against their subjects because of their religious beliefs. "We shall conclude this chapter by a melancholy truth which obtrudes itself on the reluctant mind," Gibbon writes, "that, even admitting, without hesitation or inquiry, all that history has recorded, or devotion has feigned, on the subject of martyrdoms, it must still be acknowledged that the Christians, in the course of their intestine discussions, have inflicted far greater seventies on each other than they had experienced from the zeal of infidels."

The church of Rome, he continues, "defended by violence the empire which she had acquired by fraud; a system of peace and benevolence was soon disgraced by the proscriptions, wars, massacres, and the institution of the holy office." The number of Protestants executed in a single province and a single reign, Gibbon contends, far exceeded that of the primitive martyrs who died at the hands of the Roman Empire over three centuries of its rule.

CENSORSHIP HISTORY

The first volume of Gibbon's history, published in 1776, was immediately successful and highly praised for its learning and literary style. Gibbon wrote in his memoirs: "The first impression was exhausted in a few days; a second and third edition scarcely adequate to the demand. My book was on every table. . . ."

His comments on the early Christians, however, particularly his discussion of institutionalized Christianity as an alien and divisive element in Roman society that contributed to the empire's downfall, offended the Catholic Church and pious believers. Gibbon was assailed by criticism. Nevertheless, he continued his work on the history, commenting on the reception to chapters 15 and 16, "I adhered to the wise resolution of trusting myself and my writings to the cauldron of the public. . . ."

He replied to his theological critics in 1779 with "A Vindication of Some Passages in the Fifteenth and Sixteenth Chapters" and worked on the second and third volumes, which appeared in 1781. In 1783, the Catholic Church placed the book's Italian edition on the Index of Forbidden Books, as being in contradiction to official church history. It remained on the Index through its last edition, compiled in 1948 and in effect until 1966.

Writing in his memoirs, Gibbon declared: "Had I believed that the majority of English readers were so fondly attached even to the name and shadow of Christianity, had I foreseen that the pious and the timid and the prudent would feel or affect to feel such exquisite sensibility, I might perhaps have softened the two invidious chapters, which would create many enemies, and conciliate few friends."

FURTHER READING

Gibbon, Edward. *Memoirs of My Life*. Edited and with an introduction by Betty Radice. London: Penguin Books, 1984.

HOLT BASIC READING SERIES

Senior editor: Bernard J. Weiss
Original date and place of publication: 1973, United States
Original publisher: Holt, Rinehart and Winston
Literary form: Textbook series

SUMMARY

Holt Basic Reading was a series of nine textbooks for use in kindergarten through eighth grade, first published in 1973. Before the controversy began regarding the content of its 1983 edition, it had been adopted by more than 15,000 U.S. school districts and was used by more than 8 million students in all 50 states. The textbooks contained primarily excerpts from literature rather than material written expressly for students and presented writing, spelling, and language as a unified arts program. The 1983 edition reflected revisions to reduce gender stereotypes and provide more multicultural content in response to criticisms of earlier editions by feminists and civil rights activists.

The content of the sixth-grade reader, *Riders on the Earth*, touched off the protest that led to a major legal challenge to the series. "Dear Reader, Welcome to RIDERS ON THE EARTH," the introduction began. "Many adventures and new ideas from around the world can be found in the selections in this book. You will read ancient tales of knights and dragons, and modern-day stories of people all over the world. You will explore the depths of the ocean and meet its fantastic creatures by reading articles written by Jacques Cousteau and Rachel Carson. You will discover secrets of the past through story and legend, myth and folktale. You will venture into the possibilities of the future through science fiction. You will find that no matter when or where the story takes place people have problems to overcome, decisions to make and challenges to meet."

The 51 selections in the 544-page illustrated book included poems by Elinor Wylie, Eve Merriam, Langston Hughes, Walter de la Mare, Alfred Lord Tennyson, and A. A. Milne, as well as Japanese haikus. There were stories by Pearl S. Buck, Jean Craighead George, and Virginia Hamilton; an essay by Rachel Carson; an excerpt from L. Frank Baum's *The Wizard of Oz;* and retellings of Greek myths, Beowulf, Camelot, and African folktales.

The second entry in the text was a short story, "A Visit to Mars" by John Kier Cross, in which astronauts visit Mars and find that Martians communicate by thought transference. The book also included excerpts from biographical sketches of athletes Sandy Koufax, Frank Robinson, Joe DiMaggio, Dorothy Hamill, Wilma Rudolph, and Billy Mills and a newspaper article about baseball player Roberto Clemente's death in a plane crash. There were profiles of undersea explorers Sylvia Earle and Jacques Cousteau and anthropologists Margaret Mead, Ruth Benedict, and Franz Boas. An art portfolio included Picasso's *Guernica* and paintings by Henri Rousseau, J. M. W. Turner, Claude Monet, Leonardo da Vinci, Raphael, El Greco, Mary Cassatt, Winslow Homer, and Jean Renoir. A section on signs and symbols around the world showed internationally understood signs designed for the Olympic Games.

The largest selection in the book—100 pages—was an excerpt from *The Forgotten Door* by Alexander Key, an award-winning science fiction novel for children ages nine to 12, published in 1965. In the story, an alien boy who can talk to animals and read minds finds himself in danger after falling through a door to a strange planet—Earth.

CENSORSHIP HISTORY

In August 1983, Vicki Frost, a mother of four in Church Hill, Tennessee, noticed that her daughter's new sixth-grade textbook mentioned mental telepathy in the story, "A Visit to Mars." This alarmed her, as she believed that the Antichrist would be telepathic. Frost, who described herself as a "born again" and "fundamentalist Christian," believed that the textbook was promoting ideas contrary to her religion. She examined the Holt reading texts used by her children in the first, second, and eighth grades and found that they also contained subject matter that, in her view, taught witchcraft, evolution, disobedience, feminism, one-world government, the breakdown of the family, and the religion of humanism. She concluded that the books should be removed from the schools.

Frost and her friend Jennie Wilson requested a public meeting with the Hawkins County School Board. On September 1, 1983, more than 100 parents, students, teachers, and school administrators met to discuss the textbooks. Wilson said that the readers were saturated with secular humanism and "New Age" religion and taught Hinduism, as telepathy, evolution, and other themes in the books were connected to Hindu beliefs. The international symbols illustrated in *Riders on the Earth* promoted universal language and one-world government. She also objected to stories about cats, because she believed that they were associated with witches, as well as to those involving astral projection, American Indian religions, animal rights, and other concepts that she considered ungodly.

Bob Mozert, a parent and fundamentalist minister, argued that there was educational value in only 20 percent of *Riders on the Earth* because more than 80 percent of its pages were devoted to fictional stories and poems, as opposed to nonfiction. He claimed that inclusion of a poem about future space travel, "Post Early for Space," originally published in Boston's *Christian Science Monitor,* was evidence that the schools were promoting the Christian Science religion.

The parents opposed the use of reading materials in the curriculum that would encourage their children to learn about different ideas and cultures, make critical judgments, or use their imagination. They believed that imaginative thinking denied the primacy of Jesus Christ and would lead their children away from the only source of truth, the Bible.

The school board refused to remove the textbooks. Frost, Mozert, and other parents approached the principal of Church Hill Middle School, who agreed to allow the students whose parents objected to the Holt series to leave classrooms during reading sessions and work on assignments from a different textbook. The principal of the local elementary school attended by Wilson's grandchildren, however, decided not to allow students to use alternative readers.

As the controversy continued, the protesting parents began corresponding with national conservative organizations, including Concerned Women for America (CWA), based in Washington, D.C., and formed a group called Citizens Organized for Better Schools to pursue the campaign against the textbooks. Mozert became the group's director.

In a letter to the editor of a local paper, Mozert explained that the texts were preaching secular humanism, a "lethal religion" that denies God and morality by endorsing "evolution, self-authority, situation ethics, distorted realism, sexual permissiveness, anti-Biblical bias, anti-free enterprise, one world government and death education."

In November, the Hawkins County School Board voted unanimously to eliminate all alternate reading programs and require every student to use the Holt series. The principal of the Church Hill Middle School imposed a series of school suspensions against the children whose parents refused to allow them to attend reading class, including Frost's and Mozert's children.

In late November, Frost appeared at Church Hill Elementary School, where her daughter was a second-grade student, removed her from her classroom, and demanded the right to teach her daughter on school property, using an alternate reader. School administrators refused Frost's request and threatened to have her arrested if she refused to leave school premises.

Frost contacted Michael Farris, the head of the legal department of CWA and former executive director of the state of Washington's branch of Moral Majority. The group had already filed a lawsuit (which was ultimately unsuccessful) in the state of Washington, *Grove v. Mead School District No. 354*, that contended that Gordon Parks's autobiographical novel, *The Learning Tree*, taught the religion of secular humanism and should be removed from schools.

The next day, Frost returned to the school and was arrested for trespassing after refusing to leave the building. On December 2, 1983, the Mozerts, Frosts, and seven other families, represented by Farris and CWA, filed suit in U.S. District Court against the Hawkins County Board of Education, its school superintendent, and four school principals. They asked for injunctive relief and money damages for the violation of their First Amendment rights to free exercise of religion, because the school board did not allow their children to use alternative readers. The Washington, D.C.–based civil liberties organization People For the American Way (PFAW) joined the case on the side of the defendants.

The battle over the textbooks made headlines across the country. The Religious Right and liberal civil liberties and educational organizations lined up on opposing sides of the dispute. "As soon as CWA and PFAW entered the picture with their deep pockets and Washington lawyers," wrote Joan DelFattore in her account of the case, "Mozert turned into a national event reaching far beyond the original dispute between Hawkins County parents and school authorities. The case became a clash between two well-funded and highly politicized national organizations, each fighting to set a legal precedent that would support at least part of its educational agenda."

Mozert v. Hawkins County Public Schools was assigned to U.S. District Court judge Thomas Gray Hull. In February 1984, Hull dismissed eight of the nine counts in the suit, including the allegations that the Holt books taught disrespect for parents, the Bible, and Jesus Christ and that they promoted witchcraft, situation ethics, idol worship, humanism, and evolution. He decided that the free-exercise clause would apply only if the textbooks cast doubt on the validity of Christianity. The judge determined that only one of the plaintiffs' claims merited examination by the court: that the Holt readers taught that any faith in the supernatural is an acceptable means of salvation.

In March 1984, Hull granted summary judgment in favor of the defendants, dismissing the case without trial. He ruled that although the Holt books presented a particular worldview by seeking to instill a "broad tolerance for all of man's diversity, in his races, religions and cultures," they discussed religion in a neutral manner.

Farris and the plaintiffs appealed Hull's decision to the U.S. Court of Appeals for the Sixth Circuit. In June 1985, the appeals court ordered him to try the case. The court found that two disputed issues of fact needed to be examined: whether forcing the plaintiffs' children to use the readers infringed their rights to practice their religion and if so, whether a compelling state interest justified the burden on their rights.

In pretrial depositions, the plaintiffs presented more than 400 specific objections to literature in the Holt readers and testified that reading such material was forbidden by their religion. They objected to the title of the sixth-grade reader, *Riders on the Earth*, and the following quotation from a poem by Archibald MacLeish, "Fitting Parts into a Whole," written on the occasion of the *Apollo 11* Moon landing in 1969: "To see the earth as it truly is, small, blue, and beautiful in that eternal silence where it floats, is to see ourselves as riders on the earth together, brothers on that bright loveliness in the eternal cold—-brothers who know now they are truly brothers." The protesters believed that only "those who have received Jesus Christ as their Savior, who have been born again, are of the Family of God. . . . We are not brothers of every religion."

They criticized the story "The Forgotten Door" in *Riders on the Earth* for promoting belief in evolution by teaching sympathy for animals, encouraging pacifism, mentioning telepathy, suggesting that there are situations when it might be acceptable to lie, and portraying some characters who are thieves and liars as churchgoers. They challenged the retelling of the fairy tale Cinderella and excerpts from Shakespeare's *Macbeth* because they dealt with magic and witchcraft. They were offended by an adaptation of *The Wizard of Oz*, in the sixth-grade reader, because it depicted good witches and implied that courage, intelligence, and compassion, rather than being God-given, could be personally developed.

They found the following excerpt from a dramatized version of *The Diary of Anne Frank*, in the eighth-grade reader, to be unacceptable because it suggested that all religions are equal: "Oh, I don't mean you have to be Orthodox . . . or believe in heaven and hell and purgatory and things. . . . I just mean some religion . . . it doesn't matter what. Just to believe in something."

They objected to any portrayal of nontraditional roles for women, such as "The Revolt of Mother" by Mary Wilkins Freeman, a short story in the seventh-grade reader about a woman who challenges her husband's authority. They also opposed the inclusion in the readers of biographical information about women who were recognized for achievements outside their homes, as well as the poem "I'll Tell Emily," in the second-grade text, because it described a little girl who likes worms, mice, and snakes. They believed that "Raymond's Run" by Toni Cade Bambara in the seventh-grade reader presented a bad example for children because the girl in the story was interested in competitive sports and did not like to wear frilly clothing.

Shel Silverstein's humorous poem "Sarah Cynthia Stout Would Not Take the Garbage Out," in the fourth-grade reader, was one of many selections they cited for promoting disobedience. They objected to the use of imagination to solve problems as depicted in Jack London's "To Build a Fire," in the eighth-grade reader, because it contradicted their belief that absolute reliance on God is necessary for salvation. They claimed that a passage in the short story "Benjamin Franklin Flies His Kite," in the seventh-grade text, taught that Franklin believed in reincarnation and therefore was a Hindu. They challenged many stories in the readers that promoted empathy for animals, including "Freddy Found a Frog" in the second-grade book, and messages that could be construed as antiwar, such as the reproduction of Picasso's painting *Guernica* in *Riders on the Earth*.

The plaintiffs testified that they objected to any readings that would expose their children to religious beliefs and lifestyles other than their own or to attitudes and values that contradicted their religious views. They argued that forcing their children to read the Holt texts was tantamount to making Orthodox Jewish children eat ham sandwiches.

On October 24, 1986, Hull ruled in favor of the plaintiffs. He said that the parents should not have to choose between their religious beliefs and the right to a public school education for their children. They had the right to a partial "opt-out" arrangement, whereby their children would participate in the school curriculum but could be taught reading at home by their parents. By the time of the ruling, the plaintiffs had removed their children from the public schools. Hull awarded them damages of $50,521.29 as reimbursement for their actual expenses of private school tuition, transportation, and books.

The school board appealed Hull's decision. On August 24, 1987, in *Mozert v. Hawkins County Board of Education*, the Court of Appeals of the Sixth Circuit overturned Hull's ruling by a 3-0 vote. The parents had lost the case. The judges decided that "mere exposure" to ideas different from those of the parents' religious faith did not violate the First Amendment's guarantee of free exercise of religion. Chief Judge Pierce Lively wrote for the court: " 'The tolerance of divergent . . . religious views' referred to by the Supreme Court is a civil tolerance, not a religious one. It does not require a person to accept any other religion as the equal of the one to which that person adheres. It merely requires a recognition that in a pluralistic society we must 'live and let live.'. . . The only conduct compelled by the defendants was reading and discussing the material in the Holt series, and hearing other students' interpretations of those materials. . . . What is absent from this case is the critical element of compulsion to affirm or deny a religious belief. . . ."

The parents appealed the decision to the Supreme Court. In 1988, the Supreme Court decided not to review the lower court's decision, and the case against the Holt readers came to an end. Although the plaintiffs had lost in court, the long-term results of their four-year campaign against the textbooks could be seen as a partial victory for them. The national controversy brought about by the Hawkins County case sounded the death knell for the textbook series. In the 1986 edition of the readers, some passages opposed by the Mozert plaintiffs were removed. In 1989, the Hawkins County schools quietly dropped the Holt readers and adopted a series published by Macmillan. The publishing company Harcourt Brace Jovanovich bought Holt, Rinehart and Winston in 1986. That year's edition was the last to be published. The series, once the most popular in the country, was never again updated or promoted by its publisher and eventually went out of print.

FURTHER READING

Bates, Stephen. *Battleground: One Mother's Crusade, the Religious Right, and the Struggle for Control of Our Classrooms.* New York: Poseidon Press, 1993.
DelFattore, Joan. *What Johnny Shouldn't Read: Textbook Censorship in America.* New Haven, Conn.: Yale University Press, 1992.
Foerstel, Herbert N. *Banned in the U.S.A.: A Reference Guide to Book Censorship in Schools and Public Libraries.* Westport, Conn.: Greenwood Press, 2002.
Newsletter on Intellectual Freedom 33, no. 1 (January 1984): 11; 36, no. 1 (January 1987): 1, 36–39.
Ravitch, Diane. *The Language Police: How Pressure Groups Restrict What Children Learn.* New York: Alfred A. Knopf, 2003.

IMPRESSIONS READING SERIES

General editor: Jack Booth
Original date and place of publication: 1984, Canada
Original publisher: Holt, Rinehart and Winston of Canada
Literary form: Textbook series

SUMMARY

Impressions was a literature-based language arts reading series for kindergarten through sixth grade used in schools in the United States and Canada during the 1980s and 1990s. The 59 books of the series contained 822 literary selections followed by suggested learning activities and included excerpts from the works of authors such as C. S. Lewis, Laura Ingalls Wilder, A. A. Milne, Rudyard Kipling, Lewis Carroll, Martin Luther King, Jr., Dr. Seuss, Ray Bradbury, L. Frank Baum, Maurice Sendak, and the Brothers Grimm.

Impressions implemented a "whole language" rather than a phonics-based approach to the teaching of reading and writing through exposure to fiction, poetry, myths, folk tales, and songs. During the early 1990s, the textbook series was at the top of the list of challenged or banned books in the United States. Christian fundamentalists claimed the schoolbooks promoted paganism, satanism, and New Age religion and organized campaigns to remove them from schools.

Among the titles in the series, which consisted of student texts, workbooks, and teacher resource books, were: *Catch a Rainbow, Good Morning Sunshine, Fly Away Home, Ready or Not, How I Wonder, Cross the Golden River,*

Thread the Needle, Under the Sea, Wherever You Are, East of the Sun, and *Run Forever.*

Catch a Rainbow, a beginning reader, for example, included 12 illustrated selections by such noted children's book authors as John Burningham, Elizabeth Bridgman, Pat Hutchins, and Meguido Zola. The book's cover displayed a colorful picture of a unicorn flying over a rainbow. The first selection was "What Will I Wear" by David Booth: "Here is my hat. It is orange. Here is my T-shirt. It is red. Here is my belt. It is yellow. Here are my jeans. They are blue. Here are my socks. They are green. Here are my shoes. They are purple. Here is a rainbow. (Sometimes it hides in my closet.)" Margaret Wise Brown's "Little Black Bug" also appeared: "Little black bug, / Little black bug, / Where have you been? / I've been under the rug, / Said the little black bug. / Bug-ug-ug-ug." One of the poem's illustrations is a green fly buzzing over a rainbow.

The student workbook for *Good Morning Sunshine* contained 63 fill-in-the-blank worksheets, including, for example, "The Chicken and the Princess": "One day the ch_cken was g_ing to town. The chicken g_t l_st, b_t a princ_ess found h_m." Another entry is titled "A Goblin in Our House" and is illustrated by a drawing of a comical ghost: "He knocks and he __ and he rattles at the __."

A small number of the selections in the series—22 of 822 stories—mentioned ghosts, goblins, or witches or included fantasy from fairy tales such as The Gingerbread Man or Beauty and the Beast.

CENSORSHIP HISTORY

"Nightmarish Textbooks Await Your Kids—Concerned Parents Say *Impressions'* Violent and Occultic Content Torments Even Happy, Well-Adjusted Children" read the cover headline of *Citizen Magazine,* published by the Colorado-based conservative Christian group Focus on the Family in 1991. The Impressions reading series had been well reviewed by educators. At the time, it was in use in 1,500 schools in 34 states and was the leading elementary school text in Canada. Some attempts to ban the series occurred during 1987–89 in Washington, Oregon, California, and Idaho after its publisher first began to market the book in the western states. By 1990 the Religious Right had begun a national campaign against Impressions, charging that it taught lessons in the occult, New Age religion, and witchcraft.

Protests against the textbooks sprang up in 400 school districts. More than 30 districts in California alone banned it, and it was challenged in Alaska, Georgia, Illinois, New Mexico, Maine, Maryland, Mississippi, New York, North Carolina, South Dakota, and Tennessee. According to a report by the civil liberties organization People For the American Way (PFAW) in Washington, D.C., it topped the list of books most frequently targeted for banning in the United States between 1990 and 1992.

The source for many complaints appeared to be a packet of materials circulated by several conservative religious groups, including Educational Research Analysts, the Texas-based textbook review organization founded by conservative activists Mel and Norma Gabler, and Citizens for Excellence in Education (CEE), based in Costa Mesa, California. In a letter to its members in 1990, CEE's head, Robert Simonds, called the fantasy tales of supernatural characters and monsters in the books "an affront to all decent people."

The CEE published a manual titled "How to Elect Christians to Public Office" and encouraged Christian conservatives to run for local school board offices. According to PFAW, 31 percent of the Religious Right's candidates were elected in California school board elections in 1992. Focus on the Family, the Rutherford Institute, Concerned Women for America (CWA), and Phyllis Schlafly's Eagle Forum also spearheaded attempts to remove the Impressions series from schools.

While most of the objections focused on witchcraft and the occult, some of the groups opposing the reading series distributed a book called *N.E.A.: Trojan Horse in American Education* (1984) by Samuel L. Blumenfeld, which contends that there is a conspiracy by the National Education Association to create a socialist government and that teachers "have been deliberately trained to produce functional illiterates" by using the whole-language method of teaching reading skills, rather than phonics.

In 1990, parents in Coeur d'Alene, Idaho, and Stockton, California, pressed for the removal of Impressions because the third-grade reader included "A Wart Snake in a Fig Tree" by George Mendoza, a parody of "The Twelve Days of Christmas." In Yucaipa, California, some parents contended that the face of the devil could be seen in the series' illustrations by photocopying them and holding them upside down and up to a mirror.

In Winters, California, parents complained to the school board in 1990 that Impressions emphasized witchcraft and the occult, promoted disrespect for parents and other authorities, and had a Canadian bias. A list of objections presented to the school superintendent and board of trustees said that Impressions promoted drug and alcohol abuse, as the troll princess in Beauty and the Beast puts a sleeping tablet in the prince's wine; cannibalism in The Gingerbread Man; satanic ritual, because it encouraged children to chant rhymes; rainbows as a symbol of New Age religion; and witchcraft and the Wicca religion, because witches appeared in some stories, including in excerpts from C. S. Lewis's *The Lion, the Witch and the Wardrobe*. Despite the protests, the school board unanimously voted to retain the textbooks.

In November 1990, in Wheaton, Illinois, 300 parents attended a school board meeting to urge the removal of Impressions. When the board refused to abandon the series, used in the district since 1988, a group of parents sued, alleging that assignment of the books to their children violated their religious freedom under the First Amendment. The parents claimed that the series "fosters a religious belief in the existence of superior beings exercising power over human beings by imposing rules of conduct with the promise and threat of future rewards and punishments" and focuses on supernatural beings, including "wizards, sorcerers, giants and unspecified creatures with supernatural powers." They also said that it "indoctrinates children in values directly opposed to their Christian beliefs by teaching tricks, despair, deceit, parental disrespect and by denigrating Christian symbols and holidays," and requires students "to prepare and cast chants and spells and to practice being witches."

In October 1992, district judge James B. Moran dismissed the action: "It is not the province of this court . . . to sit as some sort of reviewer of the decisions of local school boards. Plaintiffs must be able to establish that the series fosters a partial religious belief, and a review of the series establishes that it cannot be reasonably concluded that it does so."

The parents appealed to the Court of Appeals of the Seventh Circuit, which on February 2, 1994, in *Fleischfresser v. Directors of School District 200* ruled in favor of the school board. The court declared: "While the parents and their children may be sincerely offended by some passages in the reading series, they raise a constitutional claim only if the use of the series establishes *a religion*. The parents insist that the reading series presents religious concepts, found in paganism and branches of witchcraft and Satanism; this hardly sounds like the establishment of a coherent religion."

In reaching its decision, the appeals court applied the three-pronged *Lemon* test, formulated by U.S. Supreme Court justice Warren Burger in the majority opinion in a 1971 case, *Lemon v. Kurtzman*, to determine whether a law had the effect of establishing religion. Under that test, the school district's choice of texts would violate the Constitution if it did not have a secular purpose, if its principal or primary effect advanced or inhibited religion, or if it fostered an excessive government entanglement with religion.

In *Fleischfresser*, the appeals court determined that fantasy and make-believe did not establish a religion: "The parents would have us believe that the inclusion of these works in an elementary school curriculum represents the impermissible establishment of pagan religion. We do not agree. After all, what would become of elementary education, public or private, without works such as these and scores and scores of others that serve to expand the minds of young children and develop their sense of creativity?"

A few months after the *Fleischfresser* decision, the Court of Appeals of the Ninth Circuit heard a similar challenge to Impressions. In Woodland, California, during the 1989–90 school year, several parents of children in the Woodland Joint Unified School District filed a written complaint asking the school board to remove the reading series. The school board offered to give their children alternate reading assignments but declined to remove the books. In 1991, two parents sued the school district. The Mississippi-based American Family Association, headed by Rev. Donald E. Wildmon, and the American Center for Law and Justice in Virginia, affiliated with Rev. Pat Robertson, supported the parents in their suit. Those who backed the school board's position included PFAW, the American Association of

School Administrators, the American Association of University Women, the Association of American Publishers, the National Congress of Parents and Teachers, the Association for Supervision and Curriculum Development, the California Teachers Association, and the American Library Association's Freedom to Read Foundation.

In *Brown v. Woodland Unified Joint School District*, the parents alleged that the district's use of portions of Impressions endorsed and sponsored the religions of "witchcraft" and "neo-paganism" and thereby had violated federal and state constitutional requirements regarding the separation of church and state. U.S. District Court judge William B. Schubb rejected their claims and ruled that he found no evidence that school officials were seeking to promote any religion: "A school district may incorporate folk traditions into learning exercises. . . . [F]ar from preferring one religion over another, *Impressions* materials were chosen in part to reflect the cultural diversity of North American society." The Woodland parents appealed the ruling to the U.S. Court of Appeals for the Ninth Circuit. The court applied the *Lemon* test and upheld Schubb's decision.

In September 1990, Georgia's state textbook commission decided against adopting the texts in the state's schools by a 13-8 vote. The decision came after parents allied with the local conservative Christian group Family Concerns lobbied the committee, armed with guidelines on how to fight the series published by Focus on the Family's *Citizen Magazine*. Robert Hess, *Citizen*'s editor, acknowledged that the objectionable material in the readers might amount to only 5 percent of their content. But "you find a pattern of darker themes that include witchcraft and fear," he added.

The *Atlanta Journal and Constitution* responded in an editorial: "This is, of course, utter gibberish, just the latest of those occasional damn fool notions that, for obscure reasons, strike a spark that spreads like wildfire through the state's considerable forests of ignorance. . . . Charged with the solemn and, you would think, inspiring task of getting Georgia's children up to educational speed for the 21st century, the state textbook committee has instead brought back the book-burning and witch-hunting of the 16th."

In North Carolina, state representative Connie Wilson (R) led a campaign against the series, and the North Carolina Textbook Commission and the state Board of Education voted against its adoption. It also was rejected by the textbook adoption committee in Mississippi but was adopted in New Mexico after a heated debate.

In 1991, opponents of the series in Coeur d'Alene, Idaho, asserted that the books taught children to disrespect parents, teachers, and authority figures and brought religion into the public schools. They claimed that 52 percent of the series' contents dealt with the occult, as they identified certain words and symbols as occult, including six-pointed stars and rainbows. A local minister of the Nazarene church told the state's textbook committee that illustrations of the Aztec calendar, which contained eight points, subliminally inculcated children into the occult, as each of the points represented a day on which a child was sacrificed.

In November 1990, a group of parents in Willard, Ohio, filed a $1.6 million civil lawsuit in federal court against their school district, charging that Impressions taught their children about witchcraft. PFAW joined the school district's defense team, and the American Family Association backed the parents. In January 1991, U.S. District Court judge Nicholas Walinski rejected a motion that would have halted the use of Impressions in the schools until the lawsuit was settled. That month, the plaintiffs decided to drop their suit.

Impressions was also the subject of protests organized by conservative religious groups in Canada, where the series had been part of the curriculum since 1984. In Manning, Alberta, in September 1991, a group of parents at Rosary Catholic School claimed that an illustration contained a subliminal image of the devil and that the line "In Napanee I'll eat your knee," from a nonsense poem by Dennis Lee, promoted cannibalism. A group of parents entered the school, threatened the staff and the principal, and warned that they would burn the Impressions texts if they were not immediately removed. Within a few days, the Catholic school board instructed the school superintendent to cease using the books. In 1982, the Manning Elementary School also decided to remove them from its first-through third-grade curriculum.

In 1993, a parent group in Burns Lake, Vancouver, petitioned for removal of the books, used since 1985, because the stories were frightening and taught the occult, promoted violence, undermined parental authority, and discredited "basic human morals." The school board voted to remove them from six elementary schools. In 1995, some trustees of the Metropolitan Toronto Separate School Board asked that the series be dropped. As more than three-quarters of the district's schools used Impressions, this would have cost the school system $1 million in replacement texts. The board ultimately decided against replacing the series.

As Diane Ravitch pointed out in her study of textbook censorship, *The Language Police: How Pressure Groups Restrict What Children Learn*, although the Religious Right consistently lost court battles to ban Impressions, its campaign had an impact on educational publishers. "The *Impressions* series, for all its literary excellence, was not republished and quietly vanished," she wrote, and the furor that sank Impressions has made textbook publishers cautious about including material that might anger Christian conservatives.

FURTHER READING

Brown, Ron. "Children's Book Challenges: The New Wave." *Canadian Children's Literature* 68 (1992): 27–32.

Carver, Peter. "Good Impressions—and Bad." *Canadian Children's Literature* 68 (1992). Available online. URL: http://libnt_lib.uoguelph.ca. Accessed September 29, 2004.

Clark, Charles S. "Why Are Complaints about American Schoolbooks on the Rise?" *CQ Researcher* (February 19, 1993). Available online. URL: http://www.college ofsanmateo.edu/library/cqresrre1993021900.htm.

DelFattore, Joan. *What Johnny Shouldn't Read: Textbook Censorship in America.* New Haven, Conn.: Yale University Press, 1992.

Foerstel, Herbert N. *Banned in the U.S.A.: A Reference Guide to Book Censorship in Schools and Public Libraries.* Westport, Conn.: Greenwood Press, 2002.

Institute for First Amendment Studies. "Groups Unite to Ban Textbooks." *Freedom Writer* (March/April 1991). Available online. URL:http://www.publiceye.org/ifas/ fw/9103/textbooks.html.

Junas, Dan. *Report on the Religious Right in Washington State.* Seattle: American Civil Liberties Union of Washington, 1995. Available online. URL: http://www.aclu-wa. org/Issues/religious/3.html.

Newsletter on Intellectual Freedom 39, no. 3 (March 1990): 46; 39, no. 6 (November 1990): 201; 40, no. 1 (January 1991): 16; 40, no. 2 (March 1991): 47; 42, no. 1 (January 1993): 11.

"Parents' Pressure Leads Trustees to Vote to Scrap Reading Series." *Vancouver Sun,* May 10, 1993, p. A-3.

Ravitch, Diane. *The Language Police: How Pressure Groups Restrict What Children Learn.* New York: Alfred A. Knopf, 2003.

"Textbook Panel Goes Witch-Hunting." *Atlanta Journal and Constitution* (September 29, 1990). Available online. URL: http://www.holysmoke.org/wicca/textbook.htm. Accessed November 15, 2005.

INFALLIBLE? AN INQUIRY

Author: Hans Küng
Original dates and places of publication: 1970, Germany; 1971, United States
Original publishers: Benzinger Verlag; Doubleday and Company
Literary form: Theological analysis

SUMMARY

To err is human. To err is also papal, contends Catholic theologian Hans Küng. Küng's rejection of the doctrine of papal infallibility, as expressed in *Infallible? An Inquiry,* embroiled him in conflict with Vatican authorities.

Infallibility is defined by the Roman Catholic Church as exemption from the possibility of error, bestowed on the church by the Holy Spirit. Infallibility is vested in the pope when he speaks as the head of the church on matters of faith and morals. Definitive pronouncements resulting from an ecumenical council, when ratified by the pope, are also held to be infallible. In *Infallible? An Inquiry,* Küng examines papal encyclicals and statements, conciliar pronouncements, Scripture, and church history and concludes that there is no such thing as an infallible proposition. No church teaching is automatically free from error, because the church is composed of human beings. God alone is a priori free from error in detail and in every case.

Küng believes the dogma of papal infallibility should be discarded, as it has been disproved by historical and biblical research. He suggests that it be replaced by the notion of "indefectibility"—the perpetuity of the whole church in the truth of God's word despite the possible errors of any of its parts. In the long run, he believes, in spite of errors by the teaching authority of the church, the truth of the message of God in Jesus Christ will prevail.

Küng contends that the Second Vatican Council (1962–65), for which he served as a theological consultant, despite its efforts to renew the church by broadening ecumenical understanding and opening out toward the modern world, did not go far enough in reforming church structures. The ecclesiastical teaching office is still conceived by the pope and the hierarchy in a preconciliar, authoritarian way.

"The conception of continuity, authority, infallibility of the Church and the Church's teaching has led the Catholic Church into a dangerous tight corner," Küng writes in *Infallible*. He lists numerous and indisputable past errors of the ecclesiastical teaching office, now largely recognized by the church, including the condemnation of Galileo Galilei and the excommunication of the Greek church. "A close scrutiny of the Index of Forbidden Books would be particularly revealing in this respect," he adds, "yet the teaching office found it difficult to admit these errors frankly and honestly."

Küng raises doubts about the authority of Pope Paul VI's 1968 encyclical on birth control, "Humanae Vitae," which reaffirmed the church's traditional prohibition of contraception. In this encyclical, Küng contends, the ecclesiastical teaching office counts for more than the gospel of Christ, and papal tradition is placed above Scripture. Jesus himself did not found a church, Küng says, but rather his life and death set in motion a movement that over the course of time took on increasingly institutional forms.

Küng calls for a new age of leadership, one in which "the pope exists for the Church and not the Church for the pope," in which the pope's primacy is not one of ruling, but of service. Küng writes that he remains for all his criticism a convinced Catholic theologian. But because he is deeply bound to his church, he claims the right and the duty in full awareness of his own human inadequacy and fallibility to raise a protest.

CENSORSHIP HISTORY

When *Infallible? An Inquiry* first appeared in 1970, on the centennial of the First Vatican Council's enunciation of the doctrine of papal infallibility, it sparked an international debate that was unprecedented in recent theology. The assertion of infallibility of the teaching office in the Catholic Church has long been unacceptable to non-Catholic theologians. But Küng was the first major Catholic theologian to question dramatically and forcefully the most basic concept of church authority. The divergence on this issue by a theologian as distinguished as Küng represented the extent to which the doctrine had become questionable.

In his preface to *Infallible? An Inquiry*, Küng wrote: "It is true that the Index has been abolished and another name given to the Roman Inquisition. But there are still inquisitional processes against troublesome theologians. . . ." Küng himself became subject to such processes for his dissident views. In obvious reaction to Küng's ideas, the Vatican's Congregation for the Doctrine of the Faith (CDF) issued on June 24, 1973, a "Declaration Against Certain Errors of the Present Day," which reiterated Catholic teaching on the infallibility of the church and the pope and declared that the pope and bishops are indeed guaranteed immunity from error when they define doctrine.

Küng's best-selling 1974 book, *On Being a Christian*, an effort to make the traditional articles of faith intelligible to modern believers, raised further doubts within the hierarchy about his orthodoxy. In 1975, the Vatican admonished Küng not to advocate two theses drawn from his 1967 book *The Church* and from *Infallible? An Inquiry*: that in case of necessity, the Eucharist might be consecrated by an unordained person and that propositions defined by the church might be erroneous. In addition, church authorities instituted an official process to examine the orthodoxy of his views. They requested repeatedly that he come to Rome for discussions. Küng called for due process, demanded the right to see the full dossier on his case before submitting to any inquiry, and asked to choose his own defense counsel. In 1968, 1,360 theologians had signed a statement calling for such due process for theologians in cases where authorities in Rome objected to their teachings. Claiming he would not receive a fair trial, Küng refused to come to Rome.

When Pope John Paul II succeeded Paul VI in 1978, he moved to confront dissident theologians. On December 18, 1979, the CDF withdrew Küng's *missio canonica*, thereby barring him from teaching "in the name of the Church." The CDF accused him of "causing confusion" among the faithful by casting doubt in his writing and teachings on the dogma of papal infallibility and questioning the doctrine of Christ's divinity. Küng was informed that he could no longer be considered a Catholic theologian. He was forbidden to teach Catholic doctrine, and Catholic institutions were prohibited from employing him.

Küng remained a Catholic priest, however, as well as a tenured professor at the University of Tübingen until his retirement in 1996, a position protected by German law. He founded the Global Ethics Foundation in 1991 and has continued to write and publish.

FURTHER READING

Bokenkotter, Thomas S. *A Concise History of the Catholic Church*. Garden City, N.Y.: Doubleday, 1977.

Collins, Paul. *The Modern Inquisition: Seven Prominent Catholics and Their Struggles with the Vatican.* Woodstock, N.Y.: Overlook Press, 2002.

Küng, Hans. *Infallible? An Unresolved Inquiry.* Preface by Herbert Haag. New York: Continuum, 1994.

AN INQUIRY CONCERNING HUMAN UNDERSTANDING

Author: David Hume
Original date and place of publication: 1748, England
Literary form: Philosophical treatise

SUMMARY

The Scottish philosopher and historian David Hume was among the most influential philosophers of the 18th-century Age of Enlightenment. Hume's profoundly skeptical empiricist philosophy, based on the principle that "nothing is in the mind that was not first in the senses," challenged many of the claims and conclusions of the rationalist philosophers of the 17th century. His method was to employ experience and observation to analyze human nature and the human understanding. "There is no question of importance whose decision is not compriz'd in the science of man," Hume believed.

Hume was educated in Edinburgh and lived in France from 1734 to 1737, where he completed his first philosophical work, *A Treatise of Human Nature.* The first two volumes of the *Treatise,* an empirical investigation of how human beings perceive the world, were published anonymously in 1739. To Hume's disappointment, the *Treatise* failed to make an impression and, as he later wrote, "fell dead-born from the press, without reaching such distinction as even to excite a murmur among the zealots." A third volume, an examination of morals, politics, and criticism, published the following year, also attracted little notice.

Hume believed that the abstract style of the *Treatise* was a barrier to attracting a larger readership. He rewrote portions of it and in 1741 published anonymously a volume of *Essays, Moral and Political.* In 1748, a third, enlarged edition of these essays appeared under the title *Philosophical Essays Concerning Human Understanding.* This was the first volume Hume published under his own name. Another edition was published in 1751 with a new title, *An Inquiry Concerning Human Understanding.* The *Inquiry,* like the previous versions of the essays, restated sections of Hume's *Treatise* in a more accessible form.

In the *Inquiry,* Hume recommends that the experimental, inductive method of the natural sciences should be applied to the study of humanity. The process must begin with empirical data, the observation of psychological processes and behavior, in order to establish principles and causes. Hume doubts the value of unsupported generalizations and a priori propositions that form the basis for much philosophical and religious thought and suggests a new methodology for arriving at conclusions about knowledge and truth.

There are two approaches to the science of human nature, Hume observes. Philosophers who view man "chiefly as born for action" may work to stimulate people to choose virtuous conduct by displaying the beauties of virtue. Alternatively, if philosophers regard human beings as rational, rather than active, their aim may be to increase understanding rather than to improve conduct. The first type of philosophy, in Hume's view, is "easy and obvious" and thus preferred by most people; the second is "accurate and abstruse" but necessary if the first type of philosophy is to be based on any sure foundation.

In two sections of the *Inquiry*, Hume added new material on the application of his philosophy to religious thought. Before publishing the *Treatise* in 1737, he had omitted an essay doubting the reliability of reports of miracles, which he knew would be considered antireligious and feared would detract from consideration of the significance of his work. "I am at present castrating my work, that is, cutting off its nobler parts," he wrote. He decided that publishing it at that time "would give too much offense, even as the world is disposed at present."

A decade later, he included the essay as section 10, "Of Miracles," in the *Inquiry*. He also added a critical examination in dialogue form of the philosophical arguments for God's existence in section 11, "Of a Particular Providence and of a Future State." This section introduced many of the arguments later developed more fully in his final work, published posthumously, more than 30 years later, DIALOGUES CONCERNING NATURAL RELIGION.

In "Of Miracles," Hume states that "a miracle can never be proved so as to be the foundation of a system of religion." He describes the concept of miracles as a violation of the law of nature and asserts that the testimony offered in support of miracles is never totally reliable and always inferior to the testimony of the senses. "The knavery and folly of men are such common phenomena," he writes, "that I should rather believe the most extraordinary events to arise from their concurrence, than admit of so signal a violation of the laws of nature."

Hume treats religious belief as a hypothesis, "a particular method of accounting for a visible phenomena of the universe," from which we can deduce only facts that we already know. He is dubious about religious authority, preferring to put faith in beliefs and values people have developed in the course of their own experiences.

"So that upon the whole, we may conclude," he states in one of the most controversial passages of the *Inquiry*, "that the *Christian Religion* not only was at first attended with miracles, but even at this day cannot be believed by any reasonable person without one."

In his celebrated conclusion to the *Inquiry*, Hume writes: "If we take in our hand any volume; of divinity or school metaphysics, for instance; let us ask, *Does it contain any abstract reasoning concerning quantity or number?* No. *Does it contain any experimental reasoning concerning matter of fact and existence?* No. Commit it then to the flames: For it can contain nothing but sophistry and illusion."

CENSORSHIP HISTORY

Hume's thoughts on religion expressed in the *Inquiry* were the most controversial of the writings published during his lifetime. His skeptical outlook offended not only religious orthodoxy but also the deist critics of organized religion, who held that the reality of God could be established through the use of reason. Hume believed that religion was an impediment to morality, because it encouraged people to act for motives other than love of virtue for its own sake. He saw religious belief as a source of anxiety, as well as persecution, intolerance, and civil strife.

Hume's friends warned him that publication of the *Inquiry* would cause a scandal. But he vowed to proceed, writing to a colleague, "In the first place, I think I am too deep engaged to think of a retreat. In the second place, I see not what bad consequences follow, in the present age, from the character of an infidel." Hume felt that progress in learning and liberty indicated that the time was right for consideration of his ideas. "Most people, in this island, have divested themselves of all superstitious reverence to names and authority," he wrote in an essay first published in 1742. "The Clergy have entirely lost their credit: Their pretensions and doctrines have been ridiculed; and even religion can scarcely support itself in the world."

In the 1748 edition of this essay, Hume changed the phrase "entirely lost their credit" to "much lost," for it became clear that, despite the increasingly receptive climate among the public for the skeptical ideas of the Enlightenment, his comments on religion went far beyond what was considered acceptable.

Hume was rejected for appointments at the Universities of Edinburgh and Glasgow primarily because of the *Inquiry*. He decided in 1755 because of the furor over sections 10 and 11 to remove two essays on the topics of suicide and immortality from a volume of "Five Dissertations" that had already been printed in preparation for publication. The essays were not published until 25 years later, and then anonymously in French translation.

In 1756, Hume's opponents tried to have him formally excommunicated by the General Assembly of the Church of Scotland. But with the help of Hume's friends in the church's moderate party, the resolution was defeated. In 1761, the Vatican placed a French version of *A Treatise of Human Understanding* on the Index of Forbidden Books.

Many attacks on Hume's views on religion were published in the years following publication of the *Inquiry*. George Campbell's book *A*

Dissertation on Miracles: Containing an Examination of the Principles advanced by David Hume, Esq: In an Essay on Miracles, published in Edinburgh in 1762, was typical. "The *Essay on Miracles* deserves to be consider'd as one of the most dangerous attacks that have been made on our religion," the author proclaimed. "The danger results not solely from the merit of THE PIECE; it results much more from that of THE AUTHOR. . . . What a pity it is that this reputation should have been sullied by attempts to undermine the foundations of *natural religion,* and of *reveal'd!*" In 1770, a satirical critique of Hume by James Beattie, *An Essay on the Nature and Immutability of Truth: in Opposition to Sophistry and Scepticism,* was widely read and appeared in five editions from its first publication to the time of Hume's death.

The most significant result of the reception to the *Inquiry* was Hume's decision not to publish during his lifetime his greatest work on the philosophy of religion. *Dialogues Concerning Natural Religion,* completed in draft form in 1751, did not appear until 1779, three years after his death. In 1827, Hume's *History of England* and all his philosophical works were placed on the Index of Forbidden Books. They remained forbidden to Catholics through the last edition of the Index compiled in 1948 and in effect until 1966.

FURTHER READING

Collinson, Diané. *Fifty Major Philosophers: A Reference Guide.* London: Routledge, 1988.

Copleston, Frederick. *A History of Philosophy.* Vol. 5: *Modern Philosophy: The British Philosophers from Hobbes to Hume.* New York: Doubleday, 1994.

Gay, Peter. *The Enlightenment: An Interpretation. The Rise of Modern Paganism.* New York: W. W. Norton, 1995.

Hume, David. *An Inquiry Concerning Human Understanding.* Edited and with an introduction by Charles W. Hendel. Indianapolis, Ind.: Bobbs-Merrill, 1979.

———. *On Human Nature and the Understanding.* Edited and with an introduction by Anthony Flew. New York: Macmillan Publishing, 1975.

Penelhum, Terence. *David Hume: An Introduction to His Philosophical System.* West Lafayette, Ind.: Purdue University Press, 1992.

Price, John V. *David Hume.* New York: Twayne Publishers, 1968.

Scott-Kakures, Dion, Susan Castegnetto, Hugh Benson, William Taschek, and Paul Hurley. *History of Philosophy.* New York: HarperCollins, 1993.

INSTITUTES OF THE CHRISTIAN RELIGION

Author: John Calvin
Original dates and place of publication: 1536–59, Switzerland
Literary form: Theological treatise

SUMMARY

Institutes of the Christian Religion, by John Calvin, the French Protestant theologian of the Reformation, was the first systematic, comprehensive, and logical exposition of reform belief. As both a defense of the reform movement and a handbook for Christian instruction, its influence was profound. Completed in Basel, Switzerland, in 1536 and extensively revised and supplemented in later editions, it was originally written in Latin. In 1541, it was published in French in Calvin's own translation. The first theological treatise in French prose, its lucid and direct style was a major influence in the evolution of the French language from its medieval to its modern form.

In its first edition, the *Institutes* was a relatively small book of six chapters, designed to be carried in the pocket. The first four chapters, on the Ten Commandments, faith, the Lord's Prayer, and the sacraments, followed the order of Martin Luther's catechism. The last two chapters, which discussed the rejection of the Catholic sacraments, Christian liberty, and church and civil government, were more polemical in tone in their arguments on behalf of Reformation thought.

The second edition, which appeared in 1539, was three times larger than the first and more systematic and coherent; it also departed from the form of a catechism in favor of a formal exposition of theology. The final edition (1559) filled four volumes and fully systematized the theological thinking of the time, including discussions of ancient philosophy, the church fathers, the Scholastics, and the contemporary Roman Catholic Church.

In the significant introductory sentence of the *Institutes*, Calvin wrote: "All our wisdom, in so far as it really deserves the name wisdom and is sure and religious, comprises basically two things—the knowledge of God and the knowledge of ourselves." To know ourselves we can observe our own actions and motives. But to know God we must read the Scriptures, where the only true knowledge of God can be found. Calvin placed primary emphasis on study of the Bible and held it as the only authority in matters of belief and observance.

In the *Institutes*, Calvin rejected papal authority. Man is directly responsible to God and must claim salvation directly, guided only by his own conscience and the teachings of the Bible. Denying the Catholic Church's stand that salvation could be merited by good works, Calvin, in agreement with Luther, asserted that it was dependent on faith alone. But Calvin went further, asserting that God has predestined those to be saved. Only the elect, the chosen of God, can achieve salvation.

"In actual fact, the covenant of life is not preached equally among all men," he wrote, "and among those to whom it is preached it does not gain the same acceptance either constantly or in equal degree. . . . As Scripture, then, clearly shows, we say that God once established by His eternal and unchangeable plan those whom He long before determined once and for all to receive into salvation, and those whom, on the other hand, he would devote to destruction."

Calvin believed that man was subject to two kinds of government, the civil law and the rule of God, and that civil government had the duty to establish religion. The state should be subordinate to the church. He approved of "a civil administration that aims to prevent the true religion which is constituted in God's law from being openly and with public sacrilege violated and defiled with impunity. . . ." He would not "allow men to make laws according to their own decision concerning religion and the worship of God."

Indeed, freedom of religion was not allowed under Calvinist administration in Geneva, as was demonstrated in a notorious manner by the execution of the young Spanish theologian Michael Servetus, author of CHRISTIANITY RESTORED. Servetus was arrested under Calvin's orders for heresy and blasphemy and burned at the stake in 1553.

Calvin regarded the church of Rome as no longer the church of God. The gospel was absent under the papacy, he believed, and the Catholic Church had twisted the form and meaning of the sacraments in ways that contradicted their true character. "We had to leave them in order to come to Christ," he said of the Catholic Church.

CENSORSHIP HISTORY

The new Protestant faith as promulgated by Calvin was equated by King Francis I of France with violence and lawlessness. Fearing that he might be arrested for his association with reformers, Calvin fled France for Basel in 1534, where he published *Institutes* two years later. Its entire first edition sold out within a year. Some copies were printed under the pseudonym Alcuin to divert the censors and circulated to Roman Catholic countries.

The persecution that had driven Calvin and many others away from France in 1534, and eventually to Geneva, continued sporadically in the years that followed. Francis's successor, Henry II, upon his accession in 1547, set up special courts to deal with heresy charges against evangelical Christians. After two years, heresy trials were once again taken over by the ecclesiastical courts. But when the church courts were seen as too lenient, the trials were transferred to the civil courts by the Edict of Chateaubriand. A reign of terror against Calvinists ensued.

Calvin and his followers, who had established a local government in Geneva that implemented his doctrines, sent help to the fledgling French congregations by smuggling ministers and books by Calvin into France. One result of the thriving movement of Calvinist books into France from Geneva was that printing became the major industry in Geneva and the sale of books the major export. Despite repression of Calvinism, in 1559, there were as many as 50 churches in France organized according to Calvin's thought.

In England in 1555, Queen Mary issued a proclamation requiring "that no manner of persons presume to bring into this realm any manuscripts, books, papers . . . in the name of Martin Luther, John Calvin . . . or any like books containing false doctrine against the Catholic faith." After 1558 and the accession of the Protestant Queen Elizabeth, Calvin's influence in England became substantial through the widespread circulation of his commentaries, sermons, and *Institutes*, translated into English in 1561.

In the first Index of Forbidden Books published by Pope Paul IV in 1559, the Catholic Church condemned the writings of Calvin as heretical, along with those of Martin Luther, in the Class I category of authors whose works were totally banned. The revised Index issued by the Council of Trent in 1564, which was effective in Belgium, Bavaria, Portugal, Italy, and France, confirmed the banning of the works of Luther and Calvin. In the last Index issued by the church in 1948 and in effect until 1966, Calvin's *Institutes of the Christian Religion* was not specifically listed but was considered banned according to the church's canon law forbidding the reading of books "which propound or defend heresy or schism."

FURTHER READING

Burman, Edward. *The Inquisition: Hammer of Heresy.* New York: Dorset Press, 1992.
Parker, T. H. L. *John Calvin.* Batavia, Ill.: Lion Publishing, 1975.
Simon, Edith. *The Reformation.* New York: Time-Life Books, 1966.
Wilcox, Donald J. *In Search of God and Self Renaissance and Reformation Thought.* Boston: Houghton Mifflin, 1975.

INTRODUCTION TO THEOLOGY

Author: Peter Abelard
Original date and place of publication: 1120, France
Literary form: Theological treatise

SUMMARY

The French theologian, poet, and teacher Peter Abelard is best known for his tragic love affair with Héloïse, his pupil, and for the love letters he wrote to her after he entered a monastery and she became a nun. Abelard also exercised considerable influence on the intellectual life of his times as a philosopher and teacher.

Abelard reported that his love for dialectical disputation of philosophical issues led him to reject a military career and "wander about the various provinces like the peripatetics wherever I heard the pursuit of this art was vigorous." He opened his own school in Paris and attracted large numbers of students drawn by his reputation as a brilliant teacher. He became a Benedictine monk at the monastery of Saint Denis in 1120.

As a Scholastic philosopher, Abelard shifted the theological argument from reliance on authority to analysis by logic and reason, emphasizing the critical method and applying the method of Aristotle's dialectic to faith and dogma. In discussing a thesis, he put forward the views of opposing authorities and suggested the principles that might be useful in deciding a question, leaving the solution of the problem to the reader. The basic approach of Scholasticism was to use reason to deepen the understanding of what was believed on faith, ultimately giving a rational content to faith.

His first theological work, *Introduction to Theology*, was written for his students, Abelard explained in his autobiography, "because they asked for a human and philosophical basis, and preferred something they could understand to mere words. Talk alone is of no use, they said, if it is not accompanied by understanding. . . . Besides, the Lord Himself criticized the blind leading the blind."

In *Introduction to Theology*, Abelard recommended training in logic and the use of logical methods in theology. Reason must be able to understand what is accepted on authority. But reason should not supersede faith. Acceptance of dogma is an act of free will rewarded in the future life by ultimate knowledge of the grounds of faith.

The most important philosophical problem of the 12th century was the question of the relationship between the concepts of the universal and the particular. There were two approaches to the question: realism, which held that universals exist independently of the human mind and particular things, and nominalism, which proposed that the prior notion of an object does not have an independent existence. Abelard taught a doctrine of moderate realism, in opposition both to realism and extreme nominalism. He recognized the universal as a symbol to which human beings have attached significance, based on the similarity perceived in different objects.

In *Introduction to Theology*, he put forth a view of the Trinity in opposition to nominalism, which tended to make three Gods of the Trinity. His analysis was regarded by other theologians as verging on the third-century heresy of monarchianism, or Sabellianism, which challenged the doctrine of the essential Trinity by holding that God was one indivisible substance with three fundamental activities or modes that appeared successively as the Father, Son, and Holy Spirit.

Abelard's analysis of Atonement, the doctrine that Christ by his suffering and death on the cross satisfied God for the sins of man, was that Jesus' sacrifice was unnecessary for the forgiveness of sins, as God had forgiven sin before Christ came. He also rejected Saint Augustine's doctrine of Original Sin, holding that mankind does not share in the guilt of Adam's sin. His most influential work was his treatise *Sic et non*, in which he compared passages in the writings of the church fathers and exposed their contradictions.

CENSORSHIP HISTORY

Abelard did not wish to place dialectics above theology but rather, through its use, to understand revelation. His use of dialectics and his emphasis on the powers of reason revolutionized the traditional method of teaching theology. It also brought him into conflict with Abbot Bernard of Clairvaux, the most powerful theologian in western Europe, declared a saint after his death by the Catholic Church.

Bernard, a protector of tradition, polemicized against those, like Abelard, "who call themselves philosophers" and are no better than "slaves to curiosity and pride." Abelard's belief in the application of logic to faith conflicted with the mysticism of Bernard. Bernard believed that it was not man's concern to explore God's majesty but rather to be eager to know God's will. Abelard's opinions on the Trinity, Atonement, free will, and Original Sin were also regarded as subversive to the faith.

The conflict between Bernard and Abelard exemplified the differences between monasticism and the new Scholastic theology. The monks were not concerned with explaining dogma and drawing conclusions by means of dialectic but rather with prayer and meditation, the seeking of salvation, and the unity of man with God. Scholasticism was characterized by speculation, analysis, abstraction, and a desire to expand the range of understanding.

In 1121, Abelard was called before the Council of Soissons and charged with heresy for his teachings on the Trinity. *Introduction to Theology* was condemned and burned, and he was imprisoned for a short time in the convent of Saint Médard before he was allowed to return to Saint Denis. Abelard viewed the council's actions as contrary to ecclesiastic law, as he had not been allowed to speak in his own defense.

Abelard resumed teaching in Paris in 1136. His popularity and skill as a lecturer led Bernard to regard his continuing influence as dangerous. Referring to Abelard as "an infernal dragon and the precursor of the anti-Christ," Bernard asked the bishops of France to restrain him. The Council of Sens charged Abelard with heresy in 1140. Among the charges against him was the claim that he said "the Father has perfect power, the Son a certain amount, and the Holy Ghost none at all."

In the "Profession of Faith," which Abelard wrote to defend himself against the charges of Sens, he replied: "Such words are more diabolical than heretical. I am in full conformity with justice in detesting them, abhoring them, condemning them as I would condemn anyone who wrote them. If perchance they can be found in my writings, then I admit I am indeed a favorer of heresy."

The verdict of the convocation was to ban all of his writings as heretical. Abelard left for Rome to appeal directly to Pope Innocent II, unaware that Bernard had already persuaded the pope to support the council. En route in Cluny, France, he learned that the pope had confirmed the judgment of Sens and supervised the burning of his works, along with those of Abelard's pupil, the Italian monk Arnold of Brescia. The pope also ordered Abelard confined to a monastery, forbade him to continue writing, and excommunicated all his followers.

Abelard submitted to the pope's judgment as a dutiful son of the church. In a letter to Héloïse he said, "I do not wish to be an Aristotle by separating myself from Christ, since there is no other name under heaven by which I can be saved." Peter the Venerable, the abbot of Cluny, convinced Abelard to seek reconciliation with Bernard, who was able to persuade the pope to mitigate the condemnation.

Abelard did not preach again but remained at the monastery of Cluny, where he died in 1142. Although Abelard reconciled with the church, he remained confident that his theology was in conformity with church doctrine. In his last, unfinished work, *The Dialogue between a Jew, a Philosopher and a Christian*, he proudly referred to his *Introduction to Theology* as an admirable work.

Arnold of Brescia, however, continued to preach Abelard's teachings and his own views opposing the church's possession of temporal property. The pope exiled him and in 1145 summoned him to Rome to do penitence. There Arnold became a leader in the movement on behalf of democratic rights and headed a republican city-state that forced the pope into temporary exile. The Roman Curia eventually tried him, and he was executed as a political rebel by secular authorities at the pope's request.

The first Roman Index of Forbidden Books in 1559 and the Tridentine Index of 1564 prohibited all of Abelard's writings as heretical. Modern editions of the Index, however, did not include Abelard's works.

FURTHER READING

Christie-Murray, David. *A History of Heresy.* Oxford: Oxford University Press, 1976.

Dunham, Barrows. *Heroes and Heretics: A Political History of Western Thought.* New York: Alfred A. Knopf, 1964.

Grane, Leif. *Peter Abelard: Philosophy and Christianity in the Middle Ages.* Translated by Frederick and Christine Crowley. New York: Harcourt, Brace and World, 1970.

Haight, Anne Lyon. *Banned Books: 387 BC to 1978 AD.* Updated and enlarged by Chandler B. Grannis. New York: R. R. Bowker, 1978.

Thilly, Frank. *The History of Philosophy.* Rev. Ledger Wood. New York: Holt, Rinehart and Winston, 1957.

Wippel, John F., and Alan B. Wolter. *Medieval Philosophy: From St. Augustine to Nicholas of Cusa.* New York: Free Press, 1969.

AN INTRODUCTION TO THE PRINCIPLES OF MORALS AND LEGISLATION

Author: Jeremy Bentham
Original date and place of publication: 1789, England
Literary form: Philosophical treatise

SUMMARY

The English jurist, philosopher, and political theorist Jeremy Bentham is known as the founder of utilitarianism, or, as he called it, "the greatest happiness principle." Bentham was an intellectual prodigy who entered Oxford at the age of 12. Though trained as a lawyer, he devoted himself instead to the scientific analysis of morals and legislation and efforts to correct abuses and faults of legal and political systems.

His greatest and best-known philosophical work was *An Introduction to the Principles of Morals and Legislation,* which won him recognition throughout the Western world when it was published in 1789. Bentham was influenced by the work of the French philosopher Claude-Adrien Helvétius, who in DE L'ESPRIT posited self-interest as the motive for all action.

Bentham also held that the greatest happiness of the greatest number is the fundamental principle of morality. Pleasure, which can be intellectual, moral, social, and physical, is synonymous with happiness. The aim of legislation is to increase total happiness in any way possible.

An Introduction to the Principles of Morals and Legislation is a scientific attempt to assess the moral content of human action by focusing on its results and consequences. It includes an exposition of Bentham's ethical positions and an analysis of the aspects of psychology relevant to legislative policy. It begins with a definition of his principle of utility: "Nature has placed mankind under the governance of two sovereign masters, *pain* and *pleasure*. It is for them alone to point out what we ought to do, as well as to determine what we shall do. On one hand the standard of right and wrong, on the other the chain of causes and effects, are fastened to their throne."

Bentham proposes that an action should be judged right or wrong according to its tendency to promote or damage the happiness of the community, or the happiness of those affected by it. He explains his theory of morals as emerging from the observable facts of human nature and from feelings and experience, without recourse to religious or mysterious concepts. He divides motives into three general categories: social, dissocial, and self-regarding. "The motives, whereof the influence is at once most powerful, most constant, and most extensive, are the motives of physical desire, the love of wealth, the love of ease, the love of life, and the fear of pain: all of them self-regarding motives."

He also defines four sanctions of sources of pain and pleasure: physical, political, moral, and religious. In 1814, he added a fifth, the sanction of sympathy. He devises methods to measure and judge the relative value of pleasure or pain, allowing society to determine how to react when confronted with situations requiring moral decision making. He concludes his analysis with a discussion of punishment and the role that law and jurisprudence should play in its determination and implementation.

Bentham devoted much of his life to the work of reforming jurisprudence and legislation in accordance with the principles outlined in the *Introduction*. He and his followers promoted democracy and self-government and sponsored measures relating to public health, insurance, poor laws, and humanitarian prison reform. Legal codes drawn up by Bentham were adopted in whole or part by France, Germany, Greece, Spain, Portugal, India, Australia, Canada, and other countries of Europe and South America, as well as by several U.S. states.

CENSORSHIP HISTORY

The tenor of Bentham's philosophy was frankly secular. In his writings on ethics and legislation he denied the existence of any divinely implanted moral consciousness or norms. He maintained that human knowledge was either positive or inferential and that inferential knowledge, such as that drawn from religious teachings, was inherently uncertain. He believed that religious sanctions, embodied in the fear of punishment after death, were largely ineffective as a means of deterring people from misconduct. He felt also that religion produced repression, unhappiness, and dissension in society among the adherents of different faiths and sects.

In his first published work on religion, *Church of Englandism* in 1818, Bentham made similar references to the church's reliance on authority and obfuscation in propagating its doctrines. Much of Bentham's writing on religion remained unpublished in manuscript form. His most radical attack on religion in general, *Analysis of the Influence of Natural Religion on the Temporal Happiness of Mankind*, appeared in 1822 under a pseudonym.

Some of the most vehement opposition to Bentham's ideas came from the clergy of both the Church of England and the Roman Catholic Church. José Vidal, a Dominican theologian at the University of Valencia, argued in response to Bentham in 1827 that, since the Creator had endowed mankind with free will, it was not true that man had been placed under the "governance" of pain and pleasure. If this principle were accepted, the notion of individual responsibility for actions would be eliminated.

In the 1830s and 1840s, Benthamism came under attack in England by leaders of the Tractarian, or Oxford, movement, a religious movement of Anglican clergymen at Oxford University aimed at renewal of the Church of England by revival of certain Roman Catholic doctrines and rituals.

Between 1819 and 1835, the Catholic Church placed four works of Bentham on the Index of Forbidden Books: *Introduction to the Principles of Morals and Legislation, The Rationale of Judicial Evidence, Deontology*, and *Three Tracts Relevant to Spanish and Portuguese Affairs*. The 1897 Index of Pope Leo XIII confirmed these works as prohibited reading for Catholics. They remained on the Index through its last edition published until 1966.

FURTHER READING

Bentham, Jeremy. *The Principles of Morals and Legislation*. Buffalo, N.Y.: Prometheus Books, 1988.
Collinson, Diané. *Fifty Major Philosophers: A Reference Guide*. London: Routledge, 1988.
Dinwiddy, John. *Bentham*. Oxford: Oxford University Press, 1989.

INTRODUCTORY LECTURES ON PSYCHOANALYSIS

Author: Sigmund Freud
Original dates and places of publication: 1933, Germany; 1935, United States
Original publishers: Kiepenheuer; Liveright
Literary form: Psychological text

SUMMARY

Introductory Lectures on Psychoanalysis is probably Sigmund Freud's most widely read book. As the title suggests, it is a compilation of his lectures on aspects of the psychoanalytic theory that he had been developing for more than 20 years. Originally, Freud delivered these lectures to students at the University of Vienna, where he was an assistant professor. His work in the academy was secondary, however, to his career as an analyst in private practice. Still, the demands of teaching university students forced Freud to condense his ideas and make them comprehensible to a wide audience. Thanks to this lecture format, *Introductory Lectures* is among the easiest of Freud's works to understand.

The 1933 edition of *Introductory Lectures* brings together Freud's 1915–17 Vienna lectures with new talks delivered in 1933. Freud believed that these two series contained his whole psychoanalytic thought. The 1917 *Introductory Lectures* discusses parapraxes (more commonly known as Freudian slips), dream analysis, and neuroses. The 1933 work revises and refines Freud's earlier ideas, especially the analysis of dreams. Freud also adds a look at the creation of femininity and the development of a scientific Weltanschauung, or worldview.

Freud's discussion of parapraxes is his first line of argument in presenting his theory. He uses slips of the tongue and other blunders to show the power of the unconscious mind. Dream analysis became one of the most popular applications of Freud to everyday life. Freud came under fire for treating dream interpretation as a science, because astrologers, fortune-tellers, and other pseudoscientists had been analyzing dreams for centuries. Freud viewed dreams, like parapraxes, as useful avenues for psychoanalysis. As everyday occurrences without apparent purposes, they offered insight into the workings of the subconscious mind. Equally important was the way the patient described dreams. Rather than asking the patient to interpret the dreams, Freud believed that the psychoanalyst, due to rigorous training, was best equipped to unlock the symbols and fears hidden in dreams.

The final chapter of his first *Introductory Lectures* concerns neuroses, the mental disorders and compulsive behaviors that interfere with a person's everyday life. In his lectures on neurosis, Freud discusses such now-famous concepts as the Oedipus complex, the libido, and narcissism. He concludes the chapter with a discussion of anxiety and the "talking cure": months, or even years, of analytic therapy, sharing the implications of the patient's verbal slip-ups, dreams, compulsions, and fears.

The second part of the *Introductory Lectures*, written in 1933, addresses criticism of Freudian methods. Freud discusses arguments with other psycho-analysts and tackles subjects that critics noted he omitted from his earlier works, especially the psychoanalysis of women. While his theories of women's psychosexual makeup have been widely criticized, his idea that some of his female patients' neuroses could be traced to "penis envy" was popularized and detracted from women's efforts to win social equality.

The final chapter of the *Introductory Lectures* concerns the development of a Weltanschauung, or worldview. Freud believed that psychoanalytic theory contributed to a scientific Weltanschauung that was rapidly displacing religious cosmologies. He saw this process as inevitable and desirable, as advancements in science brought order to the otherwise indeterminate workings of the mind. He asserted that religious belief was the main source of resistance to his ideas, especially as most religions were reluctant to acknowledge his thinking on issues of sexuality.

While Freud is interested in the ways that religion provides an ethos and an explanation for the universe, he ultimately finds that the same mental conflicts are at work in religion that operate in the mind of a neurotic patient. He sees religious explanations for the creation of the world as a child's view of his father: The father is idealized, and the religious person's faith and dependence are like a child's dependence on a parent.

CENSORSHIP HISTORY

Religious leaders were among the loudest of Freud's detractors. In earlier works, Freud referred to religion as a neurosis, finding similarities between the rituals of organized faiths and the compulsive behaviors of neurotic patients. By 1933, Freud had written *Totem and Taboo*, in which he examined anthropologists' research on remote pagan cultures and compared their views to modern Christianity, and *The Future of an Illusion*, in which he most forcefully made his case that religion was a kind of mass neurosis.

Although for more than 20 years Freud had argued that religion could be analyzed like a human neurosis, it was not until 1934 that Catholic Church authorities took notice of psychoanalysis and censored psychoanalytic works. Offending the Catholic Church at this time was problematic, as the church's power in Freud's native Austria counterbalanced the nationalistic impulses of Nazism. In 1934, Pope Pius XI forced an Italian psychoanalytical journal to stop publishing, and he released a statement in which he expressed his disagreement with Freud's ideas, especially regarding religious belief.

Freud feared that the church would clamp down on his profession altogether. In a letter to a friend, Freud wrote, "One cannot publish this formula (psychoanalytic theory) without running the risk of the Catholic authorities forbidding the practice of analysis." This would mean more than mere censorship. By the mid-1930s, psychoanalysts had just begun to gain international respectability among scientists and the general public, and the church's ban would be a huge setback for the whole discipline.

In response to his fear of a backlash against psychoanalysis, Freud delayed publishing *Moses and Monotheism*, his analysis of the story of Moses and the birth of Judaism, until 1939, after he had left Austria and the Nazi menace and was safely in England. Freud's books were among the 25,000 volumes by Jewish authors burned by the Nazis in Germany in May 1933. "Against the soul-destroying glorification of the instinctual life, for the nobility of the soul! I consign to the flames the writings of the school of Sigmund Freud," read the declaration announced at the book burning.

The Catholic Church viewed *Introductory Lectures on Psychoanalysis* as especially dangerous because of its widespread popularity. Written in an easygoing style and translated into 16 languages, it used examples from everyday life to explain Freud's complex theories. Freud's idea that sexual activity was natural, though a breeding ground for neuroses, was interpreted as advocating free sexuality and following one's impulses. Traditional moralists saw Freud as just another manifestation of the moral decay brought on by Darwinism and scientific rationality in general.

The last edition of the Index of Forbidden Books, compiled in 1948, did not specifically mention Freud. However, his writings were considered off-limits to Catholics according to canon law, a general prohibition of works that by their nature were considered dangerous to faith or morals. *What Is the Index?*, a guide for American Catholics published in 1952, advised readers, according to canon law provisions, against reading Freud's *Origins and Development of Psychoanalysis* as part of a national Great Books program.

Although the first translation of Freud's writings was into Russian and, after the 1917 Bolshevik revolution, the Soviet government recognized psychoanalysis as a science and awarded its practitioners state funds, Freud's works were banned from bookstores and libraries under Stalin in 1930 as bourgeois ideology. They circulated only in bootleg editions until the mid-1980s.

—Jonathan Pollack

FURTHER READING

Clark, Ronald W. *Freud: The Man and the Cause*. London: Jonathan Cape and Weidenfeld and Nelson, 1980.
Costigan, Giovanni. *Sigmund Freud: A Short Biography*. New York: Macmillan, 1965.
Freud, Sigmund. *The Complete Introductory Lectures on Psychoanalysis*. Ed. and trans. James Strachey. New York: W. W. Norton, 1966.
Gay, Peter. *Freud: A Life for Our Times*. New York: W. W. Norton and Company, 1988.
Ritvo, Lucille B. *Darwin's Influence on Freud: A Tale of Two Sciences*. New Haven, Conn.: Yale University Press, 1990.
Stanley, Alessandra. "Freud in Russia: Return of the Repressed." *New York Times*, December 11, 1996, pp. 1, 10.

THE JEWEL OF MEDINA

Author: Sherry Jones
Original date and place of publication: 2008, United States
Original publisher: Beaufort Books
Literary form: Novel

SUMMARY

The Jewel of Medina is a work of historical fiction based on the story of Muhammad's rise to power, narrated by his child bride and purported favorite wife, A'isha bint Abi Bakr. The story begins in Mecca in 619 c.e., when six-year-old A'isha is beginning purdah, the Islamic custom of secluding women. Sick at heart, the spirited A'isha dreams of marrying her friend Safwan and living as a Bedouin.

A'isha's father, Abu Bakr—Muhammad's friend and one of the first converts to Islam—builds a mosque where he and other "Believers" (Muslims) can pray. At this time, Muhammad has not yet gained full acceptance as God's prophet, nor has his belief in "the one true God," al-Lah (Allah). Muhammad's *qur'an* ("recitations"), proclaiming that the other gods in Mecca's holy shrine are false, angers his kinsmen, the Quraysh, a merchant tribe who depend on the idols to attract worshippers and their money into the city. Among Muhammad's fiercest enemies is his cousin, Abu Sufyan. Abu Sufyan and his men routinely slit the throats of Believers in Mecca, and hundreds—including Muhammad, Abu Bakr, and their families—flee to the Jewish city of Yathrib (called al-Medina, "The City," by Muhammad), where they have been promised asylum.

Shortly after arriving in Medina, nine-year-old A'isha is married to Muhammad. Though she knows and cares for him, she is distraught; he is 43 years her senior, and she loves Safwan. But she does not live with Muhammad until age 12, and even then, he delays consummation of the marriage, teaching her instead how to wield a sword. The novel relates A'isha's maturation from a spoiled, willful girl to become Muhammad's respected adviser and *hatun* (first wife), as well as someone whom his other wives come to love and respect. Alongside her own personal story—of her troubled attraction to Safwan; her impetuousness and her desire to be a warrior; her growing love for Muhammad and her jealousy over each new wife he takes; and, most of all, her wish to control her own destiny—she describes Muhammad's increasing power as more and more people convert to Islam, and the ongoing clashes between the Muslims and the Quraysh.

In 625, the Believers defeat Abu Sufyan and his army in battle at Badr. Their continuing raids on the Qurayshi caravans, along with Muhammad's claim that he is the prophet that the Jewish book foretold, also exacerbate tensions with their Jewish Kaynuqah and Nadr neighbors, who trade with the Quraysh and do not believe that God would send an Arab to minister to Jews. When the Muslims ride into battle at Uhud, A'isha is thrilled to be permitted to join them, if only to carry water and tend the wounded. But the Believers are outnumbered, outsmarted, and nearly massacred, and Muhammad is seriously wounded.

Meanwhile, Muhammad's marriage to the beautiful young widow Hafsa bint Umar, whose father, a former enemy, has become an important member of his circle, inspires the first of A'isha's many jealous rages. After taking two more wives—Zainab bint Khusainah, known as Umm al-Masakin (Mother of the Poor) for her charitable works, and the beautiful widow Umm Salama—Muhammad reminds a jealous A'isha that these "alliances" are important for extending Muslim influence and increasing their chance of survival, for as they grow in power, they acquire more enemies. But Muhammad soon becomes smitten with Zaynab bint Jahsh, the wife of his cousin and adopted son, Zayd. Zaynab leaves Zayd for Muhammad, though she is forbidden to marry him because it would be considered an act of incest—whereupon Muhammad says that Allah has told him in a "revelation" that he may marry her to protect her from the shame of divorce. He defends his decision by observing that since Zayd is not a blood relation, the charge of incest does not hold. At the same time, A'isha fumes at the thought that Muhammad is ignoring his own rule forbidding Muslim men to marry more than four wives. Tongues wag at the wedding reception, and the Prophet is advised to sequester his wives to prevent more gossip. While he stops short of this move, he claims that Allah has said his wives may be addressed only from behind a curtain and that they must be covered "from head to toe, every inch, except for a single eye." Upon his death, his widows will be forbidden to remarry.

A'isha is stung by this seeming change in Muhammad, who had always been gentle and fair to women and had even extended some of their rights. Suffocated by the new restrictions and humiliated because her marriage remains unconsummated, A'isha runs off with Safwan. She soon has misgivings, however, and returns, scandalized, to Medina. She understands that, as a woman, she will always be chained and that resisting those chains will only make things worse for her—yet she knows that women often "found ways to slip those bonds . . . and then return to their so-called captivity before anyone noticed." To be free, she must learn to become politically useful to Muhammad by advising him well. Eventually, Muhammad declares that Allah has revealed that A'isha is innocent of adultery, and the marriage is finally consummated. Now A'isha assumes the role of adviser: Faced with an onslaught from Abu Sufyan's approaching army, which strongly outnumbers the Muslim army, A'isha suggests building a trench around Medina. Muhammad likes her plan. Protected by the trench for nearly a month while Abu Sufyan tries to gain entry to the city via an alternative route, the Believers are spared at the last minute when a sandstorm destroys the enemy camp, and Abu Sufyan flees with his army. In the wake of this news, many people convert to Islam, increasing Muhammad's power. He soon signs a treaty with the Quraysh, which Abu Sufyan later breaks.

A'isha, meanwhile, hatches a plan to help her neglected sister-wives earn some sorely needed cash, for they often go hungry and thinly clothed: They hire themselves out to prepare brides for their wedding ceremonies. Meanwhile, Muhammad takes two more wives—Saffiya bint Huyayy, a traitor's daughter, and Umm Habiba bint Abu Sufyan, Abu Sufyan's daughter—and takes the Christian courtesan Maryam, a gift from Egypt, as his concubine. When another bride-to-be—the exotic Alia—arrives as a gift from Yemen, A'isha learns that Alia is part of a Yemenite plot to assassinate Muhammad on his wedding night, and she tries to stop it by tricking Alia into antagonizing Muhammad in bed. Muhammad, enraged, does not believe A'isha when she explains that she was trying to save his life. Meanwhile, A'isha sees Abu Sufyan slip into his daughter's hut and suspects Umm Habiba of spying, but it turns out that Abu Sufyan has only come to plead mercy, terrified at rumors of a Muslim invasion. Muhammad is merciful and reinstates the treaty with the Quraysh.

Learning that his wives have started a business without consulting him, Muhammad stalks away angrily to pray for one month and decide their fate. At the end of the month, Muhammad tells A'isha that he loves her spirit but that a wife cannot constantly defy her husband. He gives her the choice of following the rules of the *harim* or claiming her freedom. Recognizing his generosity and their love for each other, she chooses to stay. She also defends her sister-wives, quelling Muhammad's anger and securing her permanent position as *hatun*.

A'isha is now 17 years old, and new converts to Islam arrive in Medina every day. Muhammad decides that he must prove his strength by ruling the Quraysh once and for all, which means invading Mecca. He emerges victorious and is proclaimed the Prophet of the One God, becoming the most powerful man in the kingdom.

Maryam, meanwhile, bears a long-awaited son, Ibrahim, to Muhammad, but at the age of two, Ibrahim contracts a fever and dies. With no heir, Muhammad is inconsolable and, within months, he is dying. Infighting begins in Medina, as the people wonder who will take Muhammad's place. But Muhammad refuses to name anyone, saying that Allah must decide. In his final days, Muhammad chooses Abu Bakr to lead the weekly prayers, though he does not name him as his formal successor.

On the day he dies, in June 632, Muhammad gives his sword to A'isha, his "warrior bride." Abu Bakr is poised to become Medina's next leader, though he faces challengers from within. A'isha understands that the jihad of which Muhammad spoke on his deathbed has already begun and that she must fight to preserve what he has built. The book ends with an affirmation that A'isha—a name that has been associated with scandal—means "life."

CENSORSHIP HISTORY

Described by its author, Sherry Jones, as "a book about women's empowerment and the origins of Islam," *The Jewel of Medina* was suppressed before it was ever published. Recalling the events surrounding the publication of Salman Rushdie's THE SATANIC VERSES some 20 years earlier, the story of the suppression and subsequent publication of *The Jewel of Medina* stands as a sobering example of the stranglehold that extremism can have on free expression. Unlike Rushdie, however, this book's author was not threatened or harmed. Neither were any employees of Random House or its imprint, Ballantine Books, the publisher that bought the rights to the book in 2007 in a $100,000, two-book deal. But in spring 2008, shortly before the book's scheduled release, Random House executives told Jones, a veteran, award-winning journalist and first-time novelist, that they wanted to "indefinitely postpone" its publication because they feared terrorist attacks by radical Muslims.

It seems that one Denise Spellberg, associate professor of history and Middle Eastern studies at the University of Texas at Austin, had read the book's galleys at Random House's request and the author's suggestion. Spellberg, the author of *Politics, Gender, and the Islamic Past: The Legacy of A'isha Bint Abi Bakr*—which Jones says she used in her research and originally listed in her novel's bibliography—concluded that it was a "very ugly, stupid piece of work" that "deliberately misinterpret[ed] history" and would offend Muslims. Spellberg contacted Shahed Amanullah, editor in chief of the online newsmagazine altmuslim.com, and asked him to warn Muslims about the book, which, she said, "made fun of Muslims and their history." Amanullah, who had not read the book, sent an e-mail to a listserv of Middle East and Islamic studies graduate students, which appeared out of context the next day on a Web site for Shiite Muslims under the headline, "Upcoming Book, 'Jewel of Medina': A New Attempt to Slander the Prophet of Islam." Things escalated from there, with demands from Muslims that the book be withdrawn and that the author apologize to "all the Muslims across the world."

Meanwhile, Spellberg warned Random House that the book's publication presented a "national security issue" that could cause a backlash of violence from some Muslims. Spellberg and her attorney also sent a letter to Random House stating that she would sue the publisher if her name was associated with the book. Random House, in turn, after consulting with other "credible and unrelated sources," concluded that the book's publication "could incite acts of violence by a small, radical segment," and pulled it from publication, "for the safety of the author, employees of Random House, booksellers and anyone else who would be involved in distribution and sale of the novel." No threats of any attacks had been made at the time, just "threats of terrorist threats," as Jones put it.

Salman Rushdie, reacting to the Random House decision, said, "I am very disappointed to hear that my publishers, Random House, have cancelled another author's novel, apparently because of their concerns about possible Islamic reprisals. This is censorship by fear and it sets a very bad precedent indeed."

Jones reported that she was stunned by the news. In many interviews following Random House's decision, Jones said that she emphasized her "respect for Islam; about what a gentle, wise, and compassionate leader Muhammad really was; Muhammad's respect for women, especially his wives; and women's crucial roles in the formation of the early Islamic community"—themes that she hoped her book would make plain, if anyone ever got the chance to read it.

Determined to see the book published elsewhere, she terminated her contract with Random House. In August 2008, the *Wall Street Journal* published an opinion piece about the incident ("You Still Can't Write about Muhammad") by Asra Nomani, a Muslim-American who had read *Jewel* in galleys. "The series of events that torpedoed this novel are a window into how quickly fear stunts intelligent discourse about the Muslim world," Nomani wrote, giving a detailed account of the events that had occurred and placing Spellberg at the center of the maelstrom. "I don't have a problem with historical fiction," Spellberg told Nomani in an interview. "I do have a problem with the deliberate misinterpretation of history. You can't play with a sacred history and turn it into soft core pornography."

With regard to that characterization, two brief sections in particular were quoted most often in the press accounts of the controversy. In one, A'isha expresses her anxiety about the impending consummation of her marriage to Muhammad: "Soon I would be lying on my bed beneath him, squashed like a scarab beetle, flailing and sobbing while he slammed himself against me." In another, A'isha describes the actual consummation: "Desire burned like a fire in Muhammad's loins, unquenchable in one night, or two, or three. As for me, the pain of consummation soon melted away—Muhammad was so gentle, I hardly felt the scorpion's sting. To be in his arms, skin to skin, was the bliss I had longed for all my life."

Responding to both Nomani's piece and the uproar caused by Random House's decision, Spellberg sent a letter to the *Wall Street Journal*, denying that she was the "instigator" of Random House's decision and refuting the book jacket's claim that the novel was "extensively researched." She also wrote, "As an expert on A'isha's life, I felt it was my professional responsibility to counter this novel's fallacious representation of a very real woman's life . . . . I felt it my duty to warn the press of the novel's potential to provoke anger among some Muslims. . . . I do not espouse censorship of any kind, but I do value my right to critique those who abuse the past without regard for its richness or resonance in the present. . . ." In her letter, Spellberg also charged that *Jewel* "follows in the oft-trodden path" of "anti-Islam polemic that uses sex and violence to attack the Prophet," a bewildering statement given the mildness of this book's contents by almost any standards.

The Jewel of Medina was soon sold to independent publisher Beaufort Books in the United States and Gibson Square Books in Britain. In August 2008, the book was published in translation in Serbia. When the Muslim community there protested, the novel's Serbian publisher withdrew it from bookstores but quickly restored it upon learning that pirated copies were being sold, and it soon became a best seller in that country. Shortly before the book's scheduled October 2008 release, the North London home of Jones's British publisher, Martin Rynja—which doubles as the office of Gibson Square—was fire-bombed. Three Islamic extremists—Ali Beheshti, 40; Abrar Mirza, 22; and Abbas Taj, 30—were arrested, later found guilty of conspiracy to recklessly damage property and endanger life (Beheshti and Mirza pleaded guilty to conspiracy to commit arson), and sentenced to four and a half years in jail. Beheshti's attorney said that "it was an act of protest born of the publication of a book felt by him and other Muslims to be disrespectful, provocative and offensive."

Following the incident, Jones postponed a planned publicity tour, and Gibson Square Books announced that she had decided to delay publication. Jones denied this and said that the decision was the publisher's alone. As of mid-2010, the book had not been published in the United Kingdom. Soon after the firebombing, radical Muslim clerics warned of further attacks, and on October 6, 2008, a Muslim organization run by Anjem Choudhary and Omar Bakri released an article that called the book "blasphemous" and Jones "an enemy of Islam." Beaufort Books, however, proceeded with its plans and released the book in the United States in October 2008. No new incidents of violence relating to its publication have been reported.

Many of those who had opposed the book's release consistently side-stepped the fact that *Jewel* is a work of fiction or echoed Spellberg's comment that "even historical fiction should take some responsibility for the past." But others, such as writer and poet Marwa El-Naggar of IslamOnline.net, who criticized the book for its "inaccuracies, its faults, and its biases," nonetheless supported its publication. So did Shahed Amanullah, the journalist whom Spellberg had first contacted about the book: "The best response to free speech is simply more speech in return," he wrote. "Anyone should have the right to publish whatever they want about Islam or Muslims—even if their views are offensive—without fear of censorship or retribution. Muslims, however, shouldn't be expected to be passive consumers of these views. An offended Muslim has the right—indeed, the responsibility—to vigorously critique anything written about them or their religion, provided they do not cross the line into intimidation and coercion. In an ideal world, both parties would open their minds enough to understand the other point of view."

Still other critics were concerned mostly with what they say was Jones's poor scholarship and the quality of her prose ("lamentable" and "purple"), and the *Los Angeles Times* went so far as to describe the book as "a second-rate bodice ripper," though that characterization seems overstated. In her *New York Times* review, Lorraine Adams referred to Jones as "an inexperienced, untalented author" who had written a book that does not "qualify as art."

Ethar El-Katatney, writing in *Egypt Today*, called Jones to task for using mostly English books and Arabic books translated by Western authors to do her research, adding, "Jones has taken great literary license in depicting history in a manner that fits best with how she wanted her novel to develop." But Katatney also observed, "While there is plenty of sexuality, there are no sex scenes," and concluded, "Rather than alienating her [Jones], Muslims should aim to win her over as an ally and use her novel to teach non-Muslims about the true history of Islam."

Literary theorist Stanley Fish wrote in his blog for the *New York Times* that Random House's decision did not constitute censorship, and that, rather, it was "a minor business decision," arguing that the term *censorship* should only be used in relation to a government's interference with free expression. Linguist Bill Poser, writing in the linguistics blog Language Log, disagreed and observed that "A free society cannot permit anyone, government, corporation, church, or individual, to decide what may and what may not be published. That a publisher should cancel publication of a novel out of fear of violence by religious fanatics has everything to do with the Western tradition of free speech." And in a widely circulated editorial that appeared in the *New Republic*, Álvaro Vargas Llosa wrote, "Any time, any place in which the threat of violence inhibits the exercise of free expression, the imperfect freedoms of Western civilization that so many people around the world struggle to imitate are in danger. . . . The problem is not whether Random House was entitled to its decision, but what the decision to go against its own desire to publish the book tells us about the fear that fanaticism has instilled in Western countries through systematic acts of intolerance."

Readers who objected to the book's portrayal of Muhammad were most likely, as suggested by Lorraine Adams in the *New York Times*, put off by Jones's portrayal of his sexuality, the potentially self-serving nature of his revelations, his decision that Muslim women must speak from behind a curtain (which, Adams says, is "the basis for the veiling of Muslim women"), and his marriage to 12 women, despite his decree that Muslim men be forbidden to take more than four wives—the latter two being "among the most contested criticisms of Muhammad," according to Adams.

As far as its historical accuracy is concerned, Jones notes openly, in a Q&A at the back of the book, that she took literary license with the facts—in particular, A'isha wielding a sword, her near-adulterous encounter with her childhood sweetheart Safwan, her obsessive struggle to become *hatun* (first wife), and, mostly, details about Muhammad's other wives. She attempted, she explained, to use fiction to symbolize an individual trait or suggest a characteristic of the times: The sword both represents A'isha's strength and demonstrates that some women fought in early Islamic battles under Muhammad, for instance, and the stories about the other wives were invented to explore the reasons for their behavior. A'isha's struggle to become *hatun* (which is rooted in Turkish, but not Islamic, tradition) is emblematic of harem behavior at that time, Jones has said. "I had to invent motives, which, as a fiction writer, I appreciated being able to do," she noted.

By late 2009, *The Jewel of Medina* had been published in translation in some 20 countries. A sequel to the book, *The Sword of Medina*, was published in the United States by Beaufort Books in October 2009.

—Alice Tufel

FURTHER READING

Adams, Lorraine. *"Thinly Veiled." New York Times Sunday Book Review* (December 12, 2008). Available online. URL: http://www.nytimes.com/2008/12/14/books/review/

Adams-t.html?_r=1&scp=1&sq=publisher%20of%20O.J.%20book%20to%20 handle%20Muhammad%20novel&st=cse. Accessed November 16, 2009.

Allen, Nick, and Aislinn Simpson. "Mohammed Novel: Academic Faces Calls to Apologise Over 'Pornographic' Remarks." *Daily Telegraph* (September 29, 2008). Available online. URL: http://www.telegraph.co.uk/news/3102416/Mohammed-novel-Academic-faces-calls-to-apologise-over-pornographic-remarks.html. Accessed October 12, 2009.

Bingham, John. "Radical Islamic Clerics Warn of Further Attacks after Publisher Is Firebombed." *Daily Telegraph* (September 28, 2008). Available online. URL: http://www.telegraph.co.uk/news/uknews/3097350/Radical-Islamic-clerics-warn-of-further-attacks-after-publisher-is-firebombed.html. Accessed November 14, 2009.

Bone, James. "Salman Rushdie Attacks 'Censorship by Fear' over The Jewel of Medina." *Times* (London) (August 16, 2008). Available online. URL: http://entertainment. timesonline.co.uk/tol/arts_and_entertainment/books/article4543243.ece. Accessed June 2, 2009.

El-Katatney, Ethar. "Flawed Jewel." *Egypt Today* (October 2008). Available online. URL: http://www.egypttoday.com/article.aspx?ArticleID=8171. Accessed October 12, 2009.

Fish, Stanley. "Crying Censorship." Think Again blog *New York Times*. (August 24, 2008). Available online. URL: http://fish.blogs.nytimes.com/2008/08/24/crying-censorship/index.html. Accessed August 27, 2008.

Flood, Alison. "Publication of Controversial Muhammad Novel Delayed." *Guardian* (October 10, 2008). Available online. URL: http://www.guardian.co.uk/books/2008/ oct/10/jewel-of-medina-sherry-jones-aisha/print. Accessed July 9, 2009.

Fresno, Adam. "Radical Muslims Guilty of Firebomb Plot on Publisher of Prophet Mohammed Book." *Times* (London) (May 15, 2009). Available online. URL: http://www.timesonline.co.uk/tol/news/uk/crime/article/article6295795.ece. Accessed November 14, 2009.

Goldenberg, Suzanne. "Novel on Prophet's Wife Pulled for Fear of Backlash." *Guardian* (August 9, 2008). Available online. URL: http://www.guardian.co.uk/ books/2008/aug/09/fiction.terrorism/print. Accessed July 9, 2009.

Hogan, Ron. "Judge for Yourself: *Jewel of Medina* in U.S. Bookstores." GalleyCat (October 6, 2008). Available online. URL: http://www.mediabistro.com/ galleycat/authors/judge_for_yourself_jewel_of_medina_in_us_bookstores_96577. asp. Accessed October 12, 2009.

Hume, Mick. "A Festival of Grovelling to Terrorists." *Times* (London) (August 12, 2008). Available online. URL: http://www.timesonline.co.uk/tol/comment/colum-nists/article4509698.ecc?print=yes&rand... Accessed July 23, 2009.

Jones, Sherry. Afterword to *The Jewel of Medina*. New York: Beaufort Books, 2008.

———. "Censoring 'The Jewel of Medina.'" PostGlobal: Islam's Advance. Posted by Jack Fairweather (August 11, 2008). Available online. URL: http://newsweek. wash-ingtonpost.com/postglobal/islamadvance/2008/08/censoring_islam.htm. Accessed October 12, 2009.

———. "Our Own Worst Enemy." *New Humanist* 124, no. 6 (November/December 2009). Available online. URL: http://newhumanist.org.uk/2163/our-own-worst-enemy. Accessed June 6, 2010.

———. "Q&A with 'The Jewel of Medina' Author Sherry Jones." In *The Jewel of Medina*, 355–358. New York: Beaufort Books, 2008.

Llosa, Álvaro Vargas. "The Freedom to Publish." *New Republic* (September 10, 2008). Available online. URL: http://www.tnr.com/story_print.html?id=6c96c81a-63d0-4bcd-8d06-fcfb9b84fccd. Accessed June 6, 2010.

Nomani, Asra Q. "You Still Can't Write about Muhammad." Op-Ed. *Wall Street Journal* (August 6, 2008). Available online. URL: http://online.wsj.com/public/article_print/SB1217979790078815073.html. Accessed October 12, 2009.

Poser, Bill. "Rushdie 1, Fish 0." Language Log (August 25, 2008). Available online. URL: http://languagelog.ldc.upenn/edu/nll/?p=525. Accessed August 27, 2008.

Spellberg, Denise. "I Didn't Kill 'The Jewel of Medina'." Letters. *Wall Street Journal* (August 9, 2008). Available online. URL: http://online.wsj.com/article/SB121824366910026293.html#printMode. Accessed October 12, 2009.

Trachtenberg, Jeffrey A. "Bride of the Prophet." *Wall Street Journal* (October 4, 2008). Available online. URL: http://online.wsj.com/article/SB122306918228703347.html#. Accessed October 12, 2009.

Walker, Peter. "Three Jailed for Arson Attack over Muhammad Bride Novel." *Guardian* (July 7, 2009). Available online. URL: http://www.guardian.co.uk/2009/jul/07/muslims-jailed-arson-book-protest. Accessed July 9, 2009.

Washington Post. "Random Error." Editorial. (August 22, 2008). Available online. URL: http://www.washingtonpost.com/wp-dyn/content/article/2008/08/21/AR2008082103104.html. Accessed October 12, 2009.

Willis, Simon. "The Jewel of Medina." *Granta* (September 20, 2008). Available online. URL: http://www.granta.com/Online-Only/The-Jewel-of-Medina. Accessed November 14, 2009.

Wilson, G. Willow. "Sherry Jones Has the Right to Offend Me." Red Room (August 13, 2008). Available online. URL: http://www.redroom.com/blog/g-willow-wilson/sherry-jones-has-the-right-to-offend-me. Accessed November 14, 2009.

THE KORAN (QUR'AN)

Original date and place of composition:　Seventh century A.D., Arabia
Literary form:　Religious text

SUMMARY

The Koran, or Qur'an (Recitation), is the earliest and the finest work of classical Arabic prose and the sacred book of Islam. Muslims believe that it was revealed by God to the prophet Muhammad, transmitted over time by the angel Gabriel, beginning in A.D. 619 until the Prophet's death in 632. To Muslims, the Koran is an unalterable reproduction of original scriptures that are preserved in heaven. Originally committed to memory and recited by Muhammad's followers, the Koranic revelations were written down during the Prophet's lifetime on palm leaves, stones, bones, and bark. The verses of the Koran were collected by the caliph Umar, and the canonical text was established in 651–652 under the caliph Uthman by Arabic editors following the instructions of the Prophet's secretary.

The Koranic revelations are divided into 114 suras, or chapters, each beginning with the phrase, "In the Name of Allah, the Compassionate, the Merciful." Excepting the brief first chapter that is included in Muslim daily prayers, the suras are arranged generally by length, with the longest first and the shortest last. The longest suras relate to the period of Muhammad's role as head of the community in Medina. The shorter ones, embodying mostly his ethical teachings, were revealed earlier during his prophethood in Mecca.

The Koran preaches the oneness of God; God's omnipotence and omniscience are infinite. He is the creator of heaven and earth, of life and death. The Koran also emphasizes God's divine mercy and compassion. As his omnipotence is tempered with justice, he is forgiving to the sinner who repents. In the Koran, God speaks directly in the first person and makes known his laws. The Koran provides the basic rules of conduct fundamental to the Muslim way of life. Believers must acknowledge and apply both beliefs and acts in order to establish their faith as Muslims. The religion took on the title of Islam because Allah decreed in the Koran: "Lo the religion with Allah is *al-Islam* (the Surrender) to His will and guidance."

Duties in Islam are incumbent on all the faithful, regardless of status in society. "Verily there is no preference for any of you except by what ye enjoy in good health and your deeds of righteousness," says the Koran. The most important duties for the believer, known as the Five Pillars of Islam, are the profession of faith in Allah and his apostle, daily prayer at appointed hours, almsgiving, fasting in the month of Ramadan and, if possible, the pilgrimage to Mecca. "Lo! Those who believe and do good works and establish worship and pay the poor-due, their reward is with their Lord and there shall no fear come upon them, neither shall they grieve," the Koran says.

For Muslims, the Koran is the living word of God, "the Scripture whereof there is no doubt," and, as such, contains not only eternal Truth but also the most perfect representation of literary style.

CENSORSHIP HISTORY

Around 1141, Peter the Venerable, the abbot of Cluny, translated the Koran into Latin. During the period of the medieval Crusades, Christian hostility toward Arabs and their religion mounted. The church fathers regarded Islam as a heresy, Muslims as infidels, and Muhammad as a "renegade bishop, an imposter" who rebelled against the central mission of Christ. By 1215, the church had introduced legislation severely restricting Muslims in Christendom.

The Arabic text of the Koran was not published in Europe until 1530, in Venice. The pope ordered the burning of this edition. Latin translations of the Koran were prohibited by the Spanish Inquisition, a ban that remained in effect until 1790.

In 1541, Johannes Oporinus, a printer in Basel, Switzerland, began printing Robert of Ketton's 12th-century Latin translation of the Koran. City authorities confiscated the entire edition. Protestant reformer Martin Luther argued that the edition should be released because knowledge of the Koran would work to "the glory of Christ, the best of Christianity, the disadvantages of the Moslems, and the vexation of the Devil." The edition was allowed to appear in 1542 with prefaces by both Luther and Protestant reformer Philipp Melanchthon.

The first English edition of the Koran and a new Latin translation were produced in the 17th century. The Koran had still not been printed in the Islamic world; it could be reproduced only in the original handwritten format used by the Prophet's disciples. In the late 17th century, a Turkish printer in Istanbul, Ibrahim Müteferrika, secured the sultan's permission to set up the first printing press in a Muslim country. In 1727, despite protests by calligraphers, he was granted an imperial edict to print books. But the printing of the Koran itself was still expressly forbidden. It was not until 1874 that the Turkish government gave permission to print the Koran, but only in Arabic. In modern times an English translation was tolerated. In the rest of the Muslim world, printing of the Koran was still prohibited.

The first printed edition of the Koran in Egypt appeared in 1833 under Muhammad Ali Pasha, credited with having laid the foundations of modern Egypt. His Bulaq Press became the first and most distinguished publisher in the Arab world. But on his deathbed, religious leaders persuaded his successor, Abbas Pasha, to lock up all printed copies and ban their circulation. Only under Said Pasha, who ruled from 1854 to 1863, were they released.

The Egyptian government published the first official printed version of the Koran in 1925. But this version and other late 20th-century editions of the Koran published in other Muslim countries were reproduced in block printing or lithography, considered closer to handwritten script, rather than movable type. Although Islamic law prohibits only the liturgical use of the Koran in a language other than Arabic, some Muslim theologians today believe that it is a sacrilege to translate the Koran because Allah declared to Muhammad, "We have revealed unto thee an Arabic Koran." Yet, despite such objections, unauthorized translations have been made into 43 different languages.

In 1995, the government of Malaysia banned *Bacaan*, a Malay translation of the Koran by Othman Ali, published in Singapore. The banning was part of an official policy aimed at outlawing "deviant" Islamic sects. *Bacaan* was labeled as "deviational" because it offered an interpretation that differed from the official government-approved version and did not include the original text in Arabic.

Modern government censorship of the Koran has been recorded in socialist countries. In 1926 in the Soviet Union, government directives to libraries stated that religiously dogmatic books such as the Gospels, the Koran, and the Talmud could remain only in large libraries, accessible to students of history, but had to be removed from the smaller ones. Such restrictions were lifted after a modus vivendi was worked out between Muslims and the state during World War II.

In China during the Cultural Revolution of the 1960s and 1970s, study of the Koran and its reading in mosques were prohibited. The Koran had been printed in China since the 19th century and translated into Chinese since the 1920s. The Communist government had published an authorized Chinese translation in 1952.

In 1986 in Ethiopia, under the socialist military government, it was reported that copies of the Koran were destroyed or confiscated by the army, Koranic schools and mosques were closed or razed, Muslims were prohibited from praying, and some were ordered to convert to Christianity and burn the Koran. Ethiopia's ruling military council, the Derg, feared that a resurgence of Islamic fundamentalism would provide moral and financial aid to Muslims who opposed the Marxist-Leninist revolution.

In March 2001, a group of right-wing Hindus in New Delhi, India, burned copies of the Koran to protest the destruction of ancient Buddhist statues in Afghanistan by the Taliban.

The Koran is today the most influential book in the world after the BIBLE and, with the Bible, is the most widely read of sacred texts. More portions of it are committed to memory than those of any other similar body of sacred writings.

FURTHER READING

Boorstein, Daniel J. *The Discoverers: A History of Man's Search to Know His World and Himself.* New York: Random House, 1983.

Dawood, N. J., trans. and intro. *The Koran.* Baltimore: Penguin Books, 1968.

Farah, Caesar E. *Islam: Belief and Observances.* New York: Barron's Educational Services, 1987.

Lippman, Thomas W. *Understanding Islam: An Introduction to the Muslim World.* New York: Penguin Books, 1990.

Nugent, Philippa. "Of Such Is Reputation Made." *Index on Censorship* 25, no. 2 (March/April 1996): 160.

LAJJA (SHAME)

Author: Taslima Nasrin
Original dates and places of publication: 1993, Bangladesh; 1994, India
Publishers: Ananda Publishers; Penguin Books
Literary form: Novel

SUMMARY

Taslima Nasrin, a former physician from Bangladesh, is a poet, novelist, and journalist and an outspoken feminist. *Lajja* (*Shame*) is a documentary novel about the plight of a Hindu family in Bangladesh persecuted by Muslim fundamentalists during an outbreak of anti-Hindu violence in 1992. On December 6, 1992, Hindu extremists demolished the Babri Masjid, a 16th-century mosque in Ayodha, India. The incident set off weeks of mob violence in India during which more than 1,200 people were killed. In Bangladesh, Muslims terrorized Hindus and ransacked and burned Hindu temples, shops, and homes in retaliation. Hindus are a minority in Bangladesh, which has an Islamic constitution.

The novel traces the events of 13 days in the life of a fictional family, the Duttas—Sudhamoy Dutta, a physician, his wife Kironmoyee and their grown children Suranjan and Maya—in the aftermath of the razing of the Babri mosque. It also reflects Hindu complaints of persistent violation of their rights.

Many Hindu friends of the Dutta family crossed the border into India to settle with relatives, particularly after a 1990 wave of anti-Hindu violence. But Sudhamoy, now an invalid, had long ago moved from the countryside to the capital, Dhaka, after being forced from his house and land. He chooses to stay, though his wife wants to flee to India.

Sudhamoy, an atheist who fought for the independence of Bangladesh from Pakistan, believes with a naive mix of optimism and idealism that his country will not let him down. His son, Suranjan, rebels against the prospect of having to flee his home as they had in 1990, when the family took shelter in the home of Muslim friends.

"After independence the reactionaries who had been against the very spirit of independence had gained power," Suranjan thinks, "changed the face of the constitution and revived the evils of communalism and unbending fundamentalism that had been rejected during the war of independence." Unlawfully and unconstitutionally, Suranjan recalls, Islam became the national religion of Bangladesh.

Suranjan catalogs the hundreds of violent incidents representing the heavy toll that communalism—chauvinism and prejudice based on religious identity—and religious fundamentalism have taken in Bangladesh over the years. He remembers the looting and burning by Muslims in Hindu communities in October 1990. Women were abducted and raped, people were beaten and thrown out of their houses, and property was confiscated. Suranjan is critical of the failure of the government to protect Hindus.

"Why don't we work to free all State policies, social norms and education policies from the infiltration of religion?" he asks. "If we want the introduction of secularism, it does not necessarily mean that the Gita must be recited as often as the Quran is on radio and TV. What we must insist on is the banning of religion from all State activities. In schools, colleges and universities all religious functions, prayers, the teachings of religious texts and the glorifying of lives of religious personae, should be banned."

The terror finally reaches the Dutta family when a group of seven young men invade the house and abduct 21-year-old Maya. Suranjan and his Muslim friend, Haider, search the streets of Dhaka for Maya but can find no sign of her. Maya is never found and is presumed dead. In the end Suranjan and his family decide to flee to India, their lives and their hopes for their country in ruins. "There was absolutely no one to depend upon," Nasrin writes. "He was an alien in his own country."

CENSORSHIP HISTORY

Nasrin is an uncompromising critic of patriarchal religious traditions that she sees as oppressive to women and an outspoken advocate of women's social, political, and sexual liberation. In her crusading syndicated newspaper columns, collected and published in two books, she protested religious intolerance and increasing incidents of violence against women by local *salish*, or Islamic village councils in Bangladesh, as well as the failure of the government to take adequate measures to stop them. According to Amnesty International, *salish* have sentenced women to death by stoning, burning, or flogging for violating the councils' interpretation of Islamic law.

Nasrin's newspaper columns, her bold use of sexual imagery in her poetry, her self-declared atheism, and her iconoclastic lifestyle aroused the fury of fundamentalist clerics. By early 1992, angry mobs began attacking bookstores that sold her works. They also assaulted Nasrin at a book fair and destroyed a stall displaying her books. That year, en route to a literary conference in India, her passport was confiscated by the Bangladeshi government, ostensibly because she listed her employment as a journalist rather than a doctor. (Nasrin is a gynecologist and at the time was employed by the Ministry of Health.)

Lajja (*Shame*) was published in Bangladesh in the Bengali language in February 1993, three months after the razing of the Babri mosque in India that touched off a wave of violence against Hindus in Bangladesh. Nasrin states in a preface to the English-language edition of the novel that she wrote the book in seven days soon after the demolition of the mosque because "I detest fundamentalism and communalism. . . . The riots that took place in 1992 in Bangladesh are the responsibility of us all, and we are to blame. *Lajja* is a document of our collective defeat."

During the first six months after its publication, the novel sold 60,000 copies in Bangladesh. Though panned by some critics as a didactic political tract, it was a commercial success in both Bangladesh and neighboring Bengali-speaking Calcutta, India. Pirated copies of the novel were widely circulated in India by militant Hindus. In 1994, the novel was published in English in New Delhi. (It was published in the United States in October 1997.)

After protests by Muslim fundamentalists in Bangladesh, in July 1993 the Bangladeshi government banned *Lajja* on the grounds that it had "created misunderstanding among communities." On September 24, 1993, Nasrin opened the daily newspaper and saw a prominently displayed notice calling for her death. A fatwa, or death decree, had been issued by a mullah, or Muslim cleric, of the Council of Soldiers of Islam, a militant group based in Sylhet, Bangladesh. It called for her execution for blasphemy and conspiracy against Islam.

The group offered a $1,250 bounty for her death. In the following weeks, additional bounties were promised. Thousands of Muslim fundamentalists attended mass rallies and marched through the streets of Dhaka, hanging and burning Nasrin in effigy. Nasrin was able to obtain police protection only after suing the government, which, in response to international pressure, posted two police officers outside her home.

The International PEN Women Writers' Committee organized a campaign on Nasrin's behalf, enlisting the support of human rights and women's organizations around the world. It called on Bangladesh's government to protect Nasrin, prosecute those who sought her death, lift the ban on her book, and restore her passport. The governments of Sweden, Norway, the United States, France, and Germany lodged official protests. Sweden and Norway ultimately threatened to cut off all economic assistance.

Almost overnight, Nasrin, who was unknown outside Bangladesh and India, became a symbol in the Western world of freedom of expression and women's rights. The government of Bangladesh returned Nasrin's passport, but no arrests were made, even though making a death threat and offering a reward for it is a crime in Bangladesh.

At the time, Bangladesh was governed by the Bangladesh Nationalist Party under Prime Minister Khaleda Zia, the widow of President Ziaur Rahman, an army general assassinated in 1981. Prime Minister Zia was elected with the support of the Muslim party, Jamaat-e-Islami, which held 20 seats in Parliament. Critics of the government contended that she capitulated to fundamentalist demands in the Nasrin case to preserve her electoral coalition.

In April 1994, after the return of her passport, Nasrin traveled to France, where she spoke at a meeting marking International Press Freedom Day. Returning to Bangladesh through India, she gave an interview to the English-language daily the *Calcutta Statesman*, which quoted her as saying, "The Koran should be revised thoroughly." In an open letter to the Bangladeshi and Indian press, Nasrin denied making the reported remarks, but in her denial she wrote that "the Koran, the Vedas, the Bible and all such religious texts" were "out of place and out of time."

In Bangladesh, fundamentalists took to the streets by the tens of thousands in daily demonstrations calling for her death. Mobs attacked the offices of newspapers that showed sympathy for her and ransacked bookstores carrying her books. Religious groups pressed the government for her arrest. On June 4, 1994, the Bangladeshi government brought charges against her under a rarely used 19th-century statute dating from the era of British colonialism that proscribes statements or writings "intended to outrage the religious feeling of any class by insulting its religion or religious believers." The crime carries a maximum penalty of two years in prison.

When a warrant was issued for her arrest, Nasrin left her apartment and went underground. In an interview given just before going into hiding, Nasrin explained, "So many injustices are carried out here in the name of Allah. I cannot stop writing against all these simply to save my own skin. . . . The Koran can no longer serve as the basis of our law. . . . It stands in the way of progress and in the way of women's emancipation. . . . The problem is the intolerance of the fundamentalists. I fight with my pen, and they want to fight with a sword. I say what I think and they want to kill me. I will never let them intimidate me."

On August 3, after protracted negotiations among her legal advisers, Western ambassadors, and the government of Bangladesh, Nasrin was granted bail and ordered to appear for trial at a later, unspecified date. She fled to Stockholm, Sweden, and remained in exile in Europe and the United States. (In 1998, she returned to Bangladesh to care for her critically ill mother and was again forced to go into hiding because of threats and demonstrations against her.) In 2005, Nasrin moved to Kolkata, India, where she hoped to obtain permanent residency. The Indian government, instead, granted her a series of temporary visas. After violent protests by Muslim groups in Kolkata in 2007, the government moved her to Jaipur, then to a safe house in Delhi, and restricted her movements. In March 2008, Nasrin, protesting her confinement in Delhi, left India for Europe and the United States.

"The mullahs who would murder me will kill everything progressive in Bangladesh if they are allowed to prevail," Nasrin wrote in her preface to *Lajja*. "It is my duty to try to protect my beautiful country from them, and I call on all those who share my values to help me defend my rights. I am convinced that the only way the fundamentalist forces can be stopped is if all of us who are secular and humanistic join together and fight their malignant influence. I, for one, will not be silenced."

More than a 16 years after the first efforts to censor Nasrin, she still faced bans of her writing and threats against her life. All four volumes of her autobiography published in 1999–2004, including MEYEBELA: MY BENGALI GIRLHOOD (1999), were banned in Bangladesh.

FURTHER READING

Crossette, Barbara. "A Cry for Tolerance Brings New Hatred Down on a Writer." *New York Times*, July 3, 1994, p. 7.

Dhar, Sujoy. "Bangladeshi Author's New Book Upsets Prurient Fans." Inter Press Service (November 27, 2003).

Irvine, Lindesay. "Taslima Nasrin to Leave India." *Guardian* (March 17, 2008). Available online.URL: http://www.guardian.co.uk. Accessed June 6, 2010.

Nasrin, Taslima. Taslima Nasrin's official Web site. Available online. URL: http://taslimanasrin.com

Riaz, Ali. "Taslima Nasrin: Breaking the Structured Silence." *Bulletin of Concerned Asian Scholars* 27, no. 1 (January–March 1995): 21–27.

Tax, Meredith. "Taslima Nasrin: A Background Paper." *Bulletin of Concerned Asian Scholars* 25, no. 4 (October–December 1993): 72–74.

Weaver, Mary Anne. "A Fugitive from Justice." *New Yorker*, September 12, 1994, 47–60.

Whyatt, Sara. "Taslima Nasrin." *Index on Censorship* 23, nos. 4–5 (September/October 1994): 202–207.

THE LAST TEMPTATION OF CHRIST

Author: Nikos Kazantzakis
Original dates and places of publication: 1953, Greece; 1960, United States
Publishers: Athenai; Simon & Schuster
Literary form: Novel

SUMMARY

The Last Temptation of Christ by the Greek novelist, poet, dramatist, and translator Nikos Kazantzakis, best known for his novel *Zorba the Greek*, retells the life story of Jesus of Nazareth, imagining the human events of the gospel accounts in a vivid mosaic colored by extravagant imagery. Kazantzakis's Jesus is not the self-assured son of God following a preordained path but a Christ of weakness, whose struggles mirror those of human beings who face fear, pain, temptation, and death. Though Jesus is often confused about the path he should choose, as the story proceeds his sense of mission becomes clear. When he dies, it is as a hero who has willed his own destiny.

Though the story follows the gospel narrative, its setting and atmosphere derive from the peasant life of Kazantzakis's native Crete. The novel was written in the rich, metaphor-laden vocabulary of demotic Greek, the everyday language of modern Greece.

In the 33 chapters of *The Last Temptation of Christ*, corresponding to the number of years in Jesus' life, Kazantzakis portrays what he describes as "the incessant, merciless battle between the spirit and the flesh," a central concern explored in his novels and philosophical writings. Jesus is tempted by evil, feels its attractiveness, and even succumbs to it, for only in this way can his ultimate rejection of temptation have meaning.

The novel opens with the scene of a young man in the throes of a nightmare, dreaming that hordes are searching for him as their savior. Jesus of

Nazareth, the village carpenter, has been gripped since childhood by strange portents and has felt the hand of God clawing at his scalp. He shrinks from these signs and visions, hoping that, if he sins, God will leave him alone.

Jesus has loved Mary Magdalene, the daughter of the village rabbi, since childhood. He had wished to marry her but had been mercilessly forced by God to reject her. She has become a prostitute in order to forget Jesus. Overwhelmed by remorse, Jesus seeks refuge in a desert monastery. A reluctant Messiah, he cries out to God, "I love good food, wine, laughter. I want to marry, to have children. . . . Leave me alone. . . . I want Magdalene, even if she's a prostitute. I want you to detest me, to go and find someone else; I want to be rid of you. . . . I shall make crosses all my life, so that the Messiah you choose can be crucified."

During his stay in the desert, Jesus finds the courage and determination to embark on his public ministry. The central chapters of the novel trace the familiar episodes of the Gospel, leading to the moment of the Crucifixion, where the last temptation comes to Jesus in his delirium on the cross in the form of a dream of erotic bliss and a worldly life: His guardian angel snatches him away from the Crucifixion, and Jesus takes the smooth, easy road of men. He has at last married Magdalene. Upon Magdalene's death, he marries Martha and Mary, the sisters of Lazarus, and fathers children. Now, as an old man, he sits on the threshold of his house and recalls the longings of his youth and his joy to have escaped the privations and tortures of the cross.

He comes face to face with his former disciples, led by Judas, who accuses him of being a traitor, a deserter, and a coward. "Your place was on the cross," Judas says. "That's where the God of Israel put you to fight. But you got cold feet and the moment death lifted its head, you couldn't get away fast enough." Jesus suddenly remembers where he is and why he feels pain. Though temptation captured him for a split second and led him astray, he has stood his ground honorably to the end. The joys of marriage and children were lies, illusions sent by the devil. He has not betrayed his disciples, who are alive and thriving, proclaiming his gospel. "Everything had turned out as it should, glory be to God."

CENSORSHIP HISTORY

Critics recommended Kazantzakis's unorthodox portrait of Jesus as a powerful and important novel, an extraordinary and original work of art, which in the deepest sense celebrates the spiritual struggles of humankind. It was widely acknowledged, however, that from an orthodox point of view, his interpretation might be considered as heretical or blasphemous.

Kazantzakis's primary motive in writing *The Last Temptation of Christ* was not, however, to disagree with the church. He wanted, rather, to lift Christ out of the church altogether, to portray Jesus as a figure for a new age, in terms that could be understood in the 20th century. In a 1951 letter, Kazantzakis explained his intentions: "It's a laborious, sacred creative endeavour to reincarnate the essence of Christ, setting aside the dross—false-hoods and pettiness which all the churches and all the cassocked representatives of Christianity have heaped up on His figure, thereby distorting it."

"That part of Christ's nature which was profoundly human helps us to understand him and love Him and pursue his passion as if it were our own," Kazantzakis wrote in the prologue of the novel. "If he had not within him this warm human element, he would never be able to touch our hearts with such assurance and tenderness; he would not be able to become a model for our lives. . . . This book was written because I wanted to offer a supreme model to the man who struggles; I wanted to show him that he must not fear pain, temptation or death—because all three can be conquered, all three have already been conquered."

The Eastern Orthodox Church excommunicated Kazantzakis in 1954 as a result of publication in Greece of *The Last Temptation of Christ*. Kazantzakis wrote, "The Orthodox Church of America convened and damned *The Last Temptation* as extremely indecent, atheistic and treasonable, after admitting they hadn't read it. . . ." Kazantzakis wrote to Orthodox church leaders, quoting the third-century Christian thinker Tertullian: "At Thy Tribunal, Lord, I make my appeal," adding, "You have execrated me, Holy Fathers; I bless you. I pray that your conscience may be as clear as mine and that you may be as moral and as religious as I am."

The same year, the Catholic Church placed the novel on its Index of Forbidden Books. Kazantzakis commented, "I've always been amazed at the narrow-mindedness and narrow-heartedness of human beings. Here is a book that I wrote in a state of deep religious exaltation, with a fervent love of Christ; and now the Pope has no understanding of it at all. . . ."

The furor over the novel, however, had the result of increasing its sales. "I have ended up by becoming famous in Greece," Kazantzakis wrote in 1955. "All the newspapers, except two, have declared themselves on my side, and from all over Greece telegrams are being sent in protest over the priests' wanting to seize my books. . . . And the books are sold out the moment they are printed and certain booksellers buy up a number of copies and sell them at very high black market rates. What a disgrace! How medieval!"

Ultimately the Greek Orthodox Church was pressured to halt its anti-Kazantzakis campaign. Princess Marie Bonaparte read the book and recommended it to the queen of Greece. The queen "kept the Greek Orthodox church from making itself ridiculous," wrote Helen Kazantzakis in her biography of her husband.

In 1962–65 in Long Beach, California, the novel, in the company of Jessica Mitford's *The American Way of Death* and poetry by Langston Hughes, was the target of a three-year campaign by a right-wing group aimed at removing it from the public library. The campaign was unsuccessful.

A 1988 film of the novel directed by Martin Scorsese caused worldwide controversy and was banned in several countries mainly because of the sequence drawn from the novel in which a delirious Jesus on the cross imagines that he has loved, married, and fathered children. Scorsese and the director of the Venice Film Festival were prosecuted for blasphemy in Rome but were acquitted. In the U.S., Roman Catholic authorities criticized the film as blasphemous. Three Republican congressmen introduced a resolution to force the withdrawal of the film. The Dallas, Texas, city council passed a resolution condemning it. Blockbuster Video announced that it would not carry the film. In Escambia County, Florida, the board of county commissioners passed an ordinance to prohibit the showing of the movie in the county at risk of 60 days in jail and $500 fine, or both. U.S. District Court judge Roger Vinson issued a restraining order against the ban as an unconstitutional violation of the First Amendment.

Director Scorsese's response to the film's censorship echoed that of Kazantzakis 34 years earlier. "My film was made with deep religious feeling. . . . It is more than just another film project for me. I believe it is a religious film about suffering and the struggle to find God." In December 1988, the novel was banned in Singapore as a result of pressure from fundamentalist Christians related to the controversy over the film.

In 2005, another story of the life of Jesus, the satirical *Das Leben des Jesus* (*The Life of Jesus*) by Austrian cartoonist Gerhard Haderer, fell afoul of Greek censors. It was the first book to be banned there in more than 20 years. The best-selling illustrated book, which was published in Germany and Austria in 2002, depicts Jesus as a binge-drinking friend of Jimi Hendrix and a naked surfer high on marijuana.

Haderer did not realize that his book had been translated and published in Greece until he received a summons in late 2003 to appear before an Athens court. The Greek Orthodox Church had filed a complaint against the author. The book was confiscated and Haderer, his Greek publisher, and four booksellers were tried for blasphemy. The publisher and booksellers were acquitted, but Haderer was convicted and given a six-month suspended sentence in absentia. Artists and writers in the European Union rallied around Haderer and raised concerns that the European arrest warrant system instituted in 2002 as an antiterrorist measure was being used to curtail freedom of expression. Haderer appealed his conviction and ultimately the court of appeals in Athens overturned the lower-court ruling, describing the case as "daft," and ordered that the book could be sold openly again.

In 2006, Iran's Ministry of Culture banned *The Last Temptation of Christ*, which had been published in Iran four times previously.

FURTHER READING

"Court Laughs at Cartoonist's Trial." *Kathimerini* (April 4, 2005). Available online. URL: http://www.ekathimerini.com/4dcgi/_w_articles_politics_100014_14/04/2005_55187.

Diver, Krysia. "Cartoonist Faces Greek Jail for Blasphemy." *The Guardian* (March 23, 2005). Available online. URL: http://www.guardian.co.uk/arts/news/story/0,11711,1443908,00.html.

Heins, Marjorie. *Sex, Sin, and Blasphemy: A Guide to America's Culture Wars.* New York: New Press, 1993.

Kazantzakis, Helen. *Kazantzakis: A Biography Based on His Letters.* Translated by Amy Mims. New York: Simon and Schuster, 1968.

Kazantzakis, Nikos. *The Last Temptation of Christ.* Translation and afterword by P. A. Bien. New York: Simon and Schuster, 1960.

Levy, Leonard. *Blasphemy: Verbal Offense against the Sacred, from Moses to Salman Rushdie.* New York: Alfred A. Knopf, 1993.

Sarkouhi, Faraj. "Iran: Book Censorship the Rule Not the Exception." Radio Free Europe / Radio Liberty (November 26, 2007). Available online.URL: http://www.vferl.org/articleprintview/1079193.html. Accessed July 8, 2009.

Thompson, David, and Ian Christie, eds. *Scorsese on Scorsese.* London: Faber and Faber, 1989.

LETTER ON THE BLIND

Author: Denis Diderot
Original date and place of publication: 1749, France
Literary form: Philosophical essay

SUMMARY

The versatile French writer and reformer Denis Diderot, who was responsible for the production of the ENCYCLOPÉDIE, the greatest single work of the French Enlightenment, was also the author of essays, works of dramatic and art criticism, novels, and plays. Among his most notable philosophical writings is his first mature work, *Letter on the Blind, for the Use of Those Who See,* an essay containing the most complete statement of his materialism.

Published in 1749, *Letter on the Blind* presented an original analysis of the impact of the senses on moral and metaphysical ideas. The *Letter* began with an account of Diderot's visit to a blind widower. He was struck by the man's sense of order, the keenness of his surviving senses, and the differences in his values accountable to his blindness. His sense of beauty was confined to tactile qualities. He had no shame in nudity and considered theft a major crime, since he was so helpless against it. Diderot concluded that the ideas of right and wrong are derived from sensory experience. "I have never doubted that the state of our organs and of our senses has a great influence on our metaphysics and our ethics," Diderot explained, "and that our most purely intellectual ideas, if I may express it thus, are very much dependent on the structure of our body. . . ."

In *Letter on the Blind,* Diderot investigated the psychology of the blind, the effect of the absence of one sense on the human view of morality and the universe, and the blind person's reaction to proofs of God and the origin and information of ideas. Far in advance of his time, Diderot also envisioned the possibility of teaching the blind to read by the sense of touch. The Braille system of reading was not invented by French professor Louis Braille until the 19th century.

Taking issue with the idea that nature's marvels are an argument for God's existence, he used as an example the case of a blind man who has never seen such marvels and declares, " 'For these things are proofs only to those who can see, like you. If you desire me to believe in God, then you must make me touch and feel him. . . . And even if the physical mechanism of animals is as perfect as you claim—and I am certainly willing to believe it, for you are an honest man and incapable of any attempt to deceive me—what has that to do with a sovereignly intelligent being?' "

Diderot was particularly critical of the tendency to regard everything that is beyond human comprehension as a miracle or "the work of God." "Can we not reason with a little less pride and a little more philosophy?" he asked. "If nature presents us with a knot that is difficult to untie, then let us leave it as it is; let us not insist in cutting it there and then and on employing for the task the hand of a being who thereupon becomes a knot even more difficult to untie than the first."

CENSORSHIP HISTORY

In 1746, Diderot published his first original work, *Philosophic Thoughts*, an attack on Christianity and a defense of deism, combining cosmological speculations with moral considerations. The volume was highly successful and sold in several editions. The boldness of Diderot's thoughts on religion in the essay attracted vocal criticism. The book was burned by order of the Parlement of Paris, and from that time on, Diderot was subject to investigation by the authorities. "A very bright young fellow, but extremely dangerous," was the description of him found in police records. In 1747, in a surprise visit to his apartment the police found another antireligious manuscript, *Skeptic's Stroll*, which was not published until 1830.

When *Letter on the Blind* appeared in 1749, its philosophical speculation was considered a flagrant challenge to government authorities. Its conclusion that human spiritual and moral concepts depend on the senses rather than on the received doctrine of the church, was viewed as an attack on orthodox religious ideas. On July 24, 1749, the police searched Diderot's home and confiscated a few copies of *Letter on the Blind* and boxes of material he was preparing for the *Encyclopédie*. Diderot was arrested and imprisoned in the dungeon of Vincennes, a few miles east of Paris. After a month in solitary confinement, he was persuaded under threat of life in prison to admit his guilt in a formal confession. He acknowledged his authorship of three books that were "intemperances of intellect which escaped me" and promised never again to write on religion.

He was then transferred to a neighboring chateau and given freedom to walk in the park and write. On November 3, 1749, after 102 days in confinement, he was released. Diderot did not keep his promise to hew to orthodoxy. His next great project was the *Encyclopédie*, the epitome of Enlightenment rationalism.

FURTHER READING

Diderot, Denis. *Diderot's Selected Writings*. Ed. and introduction by Lester G. Crocker. Trans. Derek Coltman. New York: Macmillan Company, 1966.

Durant, Will, and Ariel Durant. *The Age of Voltaire*. New York: Simon and Schuster, 1965.

Garraty, John A., and Peter Gay. *The Columbia History of the World*. New York: Harper and Row, 1972.

Green, Jonathon. *The Encyclopedia of Censorship*. New York: Facts On File, 1990.

Haight, Anne Lyon. *Banned Books: 387 BC to 1978 AD*. Updated and enlarged by Chandler B. Grannis. New York: R. R. Bowker, 1978.

Reill, Peter Hanns, and Ellen Judy Wilson. *Encyclopedia of the Enlightenment*. New York: Facts On File, 1996.

LETTERS CONCERNING THE ENGLISH NATION

Author: Voltaire
Original date and place of publication: 1733, England
Literary form: Essays

SUMMARY

The French philosopher and author François-Marie Arouet, known as Voltaire, personified the 18th-century Enlightenment and did more to popularize the new science and philosophy of rationalism and empiricism than any other thinker of his age. Voltaire was an implacable enemy of intolerance and despotism and a foe of institutional Christianity, particularly the Catholic Church. His polemical genius made him the most admired and feared writer of his time.

At a young age Voltaire began a battle with institutional authority and censorship that continued throughout his long life. In 1717, at age 23, he spent 11 months in the Bastille under suspicion of writing satirical verses insulting to the regent Philippe II of Orléans. In 1726, he was imprisoned again when a young nobleman, the chevalier de Rohan-Chabot, took offense at a joke by Voltaire at his expense. He had Voltaire beaten and then, through the influence of Rohan-Chabot's powerful family, sent to the Bastille. Voltaire was released after two weeks only upon his promise to leave France for England.

During the three years Voltaire spent in exile in England, he was impressed by the greater freedom of thought and influenced by the scientific discoveries of Isaac Newton and the philosophy of Francis Bacon and John

Locke. Bacon's and Locke's application of the scientific method to philosophy, based on empirical observation and common sense judgment, appealed to Voltaire.

He returned to France full of enthusiasm for England's more tolerant form of government and the intellectual movement that fostered confidence in human reason and a rational and scientific approach to religious, social, economic, and political issues. The chief literary fruit of this sojourn was *Letters Concerning the English Nation*, also known by the title *Philosophical Letters*. His *Letters*, called "the first bomb hurled against the old regime," launched the interest in English philosophy and science that was to characterize the literature of the Enlightenment on the Continent.

In 24 letters to a friend in France, Voltaire discussed the English Parliament, constitution, commerce, and other issues, such as the benefits of inoculation against disease and motivations for suicide, criticizing by comparison French institutions. France had a single monarch, a single church, and a feudal economy. In England, the monarchy was constitutional, commerce thrived, and almost all religions were acceptable. "The English are the only people on earth who have been able to prescribe limits to the powers of kings by resisting them," he wrote, "and who, by a series of struggles, have at length established that wise and happy form of government where the prince is all-powerful to do good, and at the same time is restrained from committing evil; where the nobles are great without insolence or lordly power, and the people share in the government without confusion."

Voltaire praised England's progress in extending religious tolerance: "An Englishman, like a free man, goes to heaven by the path he prefers." He celebrated Newton, Bacon, and Locke in glowing terms. Instead of those who promote brute force and violence, a man such as Newton should be revered and admired, he declared, "who sways our minds by the prevalence of reason and the native force of truth" and "who by the vigor of his mind is able to penetrate into the hidden secrets of nature's vast frame of the universe."

He commended Bacon as the father of experimental philosophy and Locke as the genius who, in his modest way, had done for the human mind what Newton had done for nature. "Mr. Locke has laid open to man the anatomy of his own soul, just as some learned anatomist would have done that of the body," he declared. "Everything contributes to prove that the English are greater philosophers, and possessed of more courage than we. It will require some time before a true spirit of reason and a particular boldness of sentiment will be able to make their way over the Straits of Dover."

CENSORSHIP HISTORY

Before publishing the *Letters*, Voltaire attempted to negotiate with the abbé de Rothelin, a confidante of André-Hercule Cardinal Fleury, the state censor. Voltaire was told that he might receive permission to publish the book, except for those passages commenting on Locke's philosophy. The church held that Locke supported materialism and atheism and had listed the French translation of his AN ESSAY CONCERNING HUMAN UNDERSTANDING on the Index of Forbidden Books in 1700. Rather than accepting the censor's suggestions, he decided to publish the *Letters* in London in English.

The English edition appeared in 1733. Voltaire negotiated the book's underground publication in France through a printer in the city of Rouen, Claude-François Jore, who was willing to issue it without a *privilège*, or official permit. Before any book could be published in France, the king had to grant permission, usually given upon recommendation of a censor who testified that the book contained nothing contrary to religion, public order, or sound morality. Even after publication with a *privilège*, the censor's verdict could be superseded by the police, other government officials, the Sorbonne, or ecclesiastical authorities. Thousands of books appeared without the *privilège*. In some cases a tacit permission could be received from the censor allowing a book's publication without fear of prosecution.

Voltaire warned Jore not to circulate the book right away, but in 1734, several clandestine copies reached Paris. News of the London and Rouen editions attracted the interest of the underground printers of Paris, and a pirate publisher printed a large edition without Voltaire's knowledge.

Everywhere in France clandestine printing presses, sometimes secretly protected by the police, reproduced smuggled copies or printed original manuscripts. Along the French frontier, relay stores were established for forbidden books destined to be smuggled into the capital. The public was eager to buy forbidden books such as Voltaire's and there was a lucrative underground trade.

A French parliamentary decree on June 10, 1734, declared the book "scandalous and against religion" and "likely to inspire the most dangerous license toward religion and the civil peace." It ordered the burning of the book by the public executioner and the prosecution of its author. Several printers were sent to the Bastille for the publication of the *Letters*. Voltaire took refuge at the home of Madame Gabrielle-Émilie du Châtelet at Cirey, near the frontier of Lorraine, where he could slip out of the country, if necessary, to escape arrest. He remained there for 10 years. Though the book's sale was forbidden in France, it was distributed underground and widely read. Its notoriety served only to increase its fame and influence.

Two years later, however, the government, recognizing a fait accompli, agreed to rescind the order for Voltaire's arrest if he would disavow authorship of the book. Voltaire agreed to these conditions as part of the game of cat and mouse he played with the censors. "They say I must retract," he wrote to the Duchess d'Aguillon. "Very willingly I will declare that Pascal is always right; . . . that all priests are gentle and disinterested; . . . that monks are neither proud nor given to intrigue nor stinking; that the Holy Inquisition is the triumph of humanity and tolerance." Voltaire's order of arrest was withdrawn with the proviso that he remain at a respectful distance from Paris.

In 1752, the Catholic Church placed the *Letters* on the Index of Forbidden Books, where it remained through the last 20th-century edition of the

Index, published until 1966. Between 1758 and 1800, the church placed practically all of Voltaire's books on the Index, individually listing a total of 38, including the PHILOSOPHICAL DICTIONARY. The Spanish Index also prohibited all of his writings.

FURTHER READING

Bachman, Albert. *Censorship in France from 1715–1750: Voltaire's Opposition*. New York: Burt Franklin, 1971.

Durant, Will, and Ariel Durant. *The Age of Voltaire*. New York: Simon and Schuster, 1965.

Gay, Peter. *The Enlightenment: An Interpretation. The Rise of Modern Paganism*. New York: W. W. Norton, 1995.

Haight, Anne Lyon. *Banned Books: 387 BC to 1978 AD*. Updated and enlarged by Chandler B. Grannis. New York: R. R. Bowker, 1978.

Redman, Ben Ray, ed. and intro. *The Portable Voltaire*. New York: Penguin Books, 1977.

LEVIATHAN

Author: Thomas Hobbes
Original date and place of publication: 1651, England
Literary form: Political philosophy

SUMMARY

The greatest work of the English philosopher Thomas Hobbes was *Leviathan or the Matter, Forme, and Power of a Commonwealth Ecclesiastical and Civil*. Published in 1651, it represented Hobbes's contribution to what he called "a science of politics," a body of knowledge on how human beings live in society that would offer solutions to the problems of government.

Hobbes was deeply concerned about social anarchy, "the dissolute condition of masterless men," resulting from the English Civil War, the execution of King Charles I, and religious disputes. In *Leviathan*, he proposed a system of rules for society, a political structure, and authority that would end such anarchy.

He believed that the Commonwealth, which he called Leviathan, is created as a result of a social contract. Man in the state of nature is a selfish animal motivated by appetites, desires and fears, "a perpetual and restless desire of power after power, that ceaseth only in death." Human life is "solitary, poor, nasty, brutish, and short." The passions that incline human beings to live peacefully are "fear of death; desire of such things as are necessary to commodious living; and a hope by their industry to obtain them."

For self-preservation and to obtain peace and order, people agree to relinquish their freedom, submitting to the authority of the state. For "where there is no common power, there is no law; where no law, no justice." In his Commonwealth, order is secured by the sovereign, who is responsible for the administration of both civil and ecclesiastical law. The sovereign is the "supreme pastor," who is the best interpreter of God's will and whose authority supersedes that of the Catholic Church and the pope.

Although his recommendation of absolutism as the price for obtaining peace in society was unexceptional, the method he used to arrive at his political theory was innovative. Hobbes was inspired by recent developments in physical sciences and mathematics to apply the deductive reasoning of geometry and physics to analysis of the organization and conduct of society.

Just as Galileo Galilei used the deductive method to study the physical universe, Hobbes applied it to the study of human activities. "Reasoning from authority of books. . . ," he wrote, "is not knowledge, but faith." Only the use of logic, proceeding from a basic premise and moving step by step to conclusions, as opposed to speculation and opinion, could produce incontrovertible conclusions about the organization and conduct of political society.

CENSORSHIP HISTORY

The frank materialism of *Leviathan* offended many of Hobbes's contemporaries. He was regarded as an atheist and blasphemer for viewing human beings as no more than bits of matter in motion whose motivations were crude and animalistic, for his skeptical attitude toward Christianity, and for his advocacy of state control over the church. *Leviathan* was regarded as one of the most damaging and systematic attacks ever made upon revealed religion. The book had been published during Oliver Cromwell's reign as lord protector of England. After the restoration of the monarchy and militant Anglicanism, Hobbes came under attack in Parliament.

In October 1666, as a solution to eliminate the influence of blasphemers such as Hobbes, the House of Commons discussed the revival of the 15th-century writ that sentenced heretics to burning. The great fire that had devastated London that year and the plague of the previous year were seen as evidence of divine wrath for Hobbes's sins. The House of Commons established a committee to which it submitted for consideration a bill "touching such books as tend to atheism, blasphemy, and profaneness, or against the essence and attributes of God, and in particular. . . the book of Mr. Hobbes called the Leviathan." The bill failed to pass in Parliament.

Hobbes was the last eminent writer to fear the application of the writ against heretics. Parliament permanently abolished it in 1677. However, Hobbes was forbidden from publishing his philosophical opinions thereafter and turned to the writing of history. *Leviathan*, along with the works of the Dutch philosopher Baruch Spinoza, was also widely condemned throughout Holland during the period 1650 to 1680.

In 1703, the Catholic Church in Rome placed *Leviathan* on the Index of Forbidden Books. In 1709, 30 years after his death, Hobbes's complete works were included on the Index. They remained listed through the last edition of the Index published until 1966.

FURTHER READING

Collinson, Diané. *Fifty Major Philosophers: A Reference Guide*. London: Routledge, 1988.
Curtis, Michael, ed. and intro. *The Great Political Theories*. Vol. 1. New York: Avon Books, 1981.
Jordan, W. K. *The Development of Religious Toleration in England*. Vol. 4. Gloucester, Mass.: Peter Smith, 1965.
Levy, Leonard W. *Blasphemy: Verbal Offense Against the Sacred, from Moses to Salman Rushdie*. New York: Alfred A. Knopf, 1993.
Putnam, George Haven. *The Censorship of the Church of Rome*. Vol. 1. New York: G. P. Putnam's Sons, 1906–07.

THE LIFE OF JESUS

Author: Ernest Renan
Original date and place of publication: 1863, France
Literary form: History

SUMMARY

Ernest Renan was a French historian, philologist, critic, and essayist who studied religion from a historical, rather than a theological, perspective. Although educated for the priesthood, he rejected orthodox Catholicism and turned to faith in science. His historical studies of the Old and New Testaments, explaining their origins in their geographic, social, and political environments, popularized the use of scientific and historical methods in biblical study.

The first volume in Renan's series of religious histories was *The Life of Jesus*. Renan had traveled to Syria in 1860–61 to direct the first large-scale archaeological expedition ever conducted there. During this scientific mission he went to Galilee, visiting Jerusalem, Hebron, and Samaria. Tracing Jesus' footsteps, he was deeply moved and resolved to devote himself to a work on the life of Jesus that would make the Savior more real historically.

In his introduction, Renan described his plans for four books on the origins of Christianity. "On the whole, I admit as authentic the four canonical Gospels. All, in my opinion, date from the first century, and the authors are, generally speaking, those to whom they are attributed; but their historic value is very diverse." The duty of the historian, Renan wrote, is to explain supernatural accounts, rather than accepting them.

When Renan first conceived the idea of a history of the origins of Christianity, he had intended to write a history of doctrines. "But I have learned since that history is not a simple game of abstractions; that men are more than doctrines." To write the history of a religion, Renan contended, it is necessary first to have believed it and, in the second place, to believe it no longer, "for absolute faith is incompatible with sincere history."

Jesus cannot belong solely to those who call themselves his disciples, as he is the common honor of all who share a common humanity, Renan wrote. "His glory does not consist in being relegated out of history; we render him a truer worship in showing that all history is incomprehensible without him."

Renan began his biography of Jesus: "At that time there lived a superior personage, who, by his bold originality, and by the love which he was able to inspire, became the object and fixed the starting-point of the future faith of humanity." He described Jesus' birth in humble circumstances in Nazareth and his upbringing and education in the tradition and culture of Judaism. The perusal of the books of the Old Testament made a great impression upon Jesus. He never attached much importance to the political events of his time and probably knew little about them. Jesus never once gave utterance to the sacreligious idea that he was God, Renan claimed. He did, however, believe himself to be the Son of God and in direct communication with God.

Renan described Jesus as a sweet, amiable, and gentle character, a perfect idealist with a dream of a great social revolution, in which rank would be overturned and all worldly authority would be humiliated. Renan denied the supernatural nature of the miracles Jesus is said to have performed, asserting that a miracle, understood as the specific intervention of superhuman power in the operation of nature, is an impossibility.

Jesus is miraculous only in the sense that he was governed by a fresh and powerful religious instinct. In the opinion of Jesus' contemporaries, two means of proof—miracles and the accomplishment of prophecies—could verify a supernatural mission. Jesus, and especially his disciples, employed these two processes of demonstration in perfect good faith, as miracles were regarded as the indispensable mark of the divine and the sign of the prophetic vocation.

Almost all the miracles Jesus thought he performed appear to have been those of healing, particularly exorcism or the expulsion of demons, Renan explained. Scientific medicine was unknown to the Jews of Palestine at the time. The presence of a superior man, treating the diseased with gentleness and assuring them of their recovery, was often viewed as a decisive remedy. "Healing was considered a moral act; Jesus, who felt his moral power, would believe himself specially gifted to heal." Jesus was not a founder of dogmas or a maker of creeds; he infused into the world a new spirit of perfect idealism. The faith, enthusiasm, and constancy of the first Christian generation is inexplicable, Renan claimed, unless Jesus was a man of surpassing greatness.

According to Renan, the transformation of a great religious leader into a God is a recurring pattern of religious history. Jesus' death on the cross gave further impetus to his deification, a process already begun during his lifetime. Jesus' character condensed all that is good and elevated in human nature, Renan believed. Jesus was not sinless, however, and he conquered the same passions that all human beings combat. "But whatever may be the unexpected phenonemona of the future," Renan concluded, "Jesus will not be surpassed. His worship will constantly renew its youth, the tale of his life will cause ceaseless tears . . . all the ages will proclaim that, among the sons of men, there is none born who is greater than Jesus."

CENSORSHIP HISTORY

When *The Life of Jesus* was published in France in 1863 it caused a sensation. The success of the biography, the first to use modern historical methods to recount the life of Jesus, was immediate and unprecedented for a scholarly work on a religious subject. "It was one of the world-shaking books of a world-shaking epoch," Renan's English-language translator declared. "Like [Thomas Babington] Macaulay's *History of England*, it lay on every library table, and was the subject of universal discussion."

Only five months after its first publication, it had gone through 11 editions, and 60,000 copies had been sold. In the next year, it was translated into all the major European languages, and Renan became one of the best-known writers of his time. In 1864, Renan published a low-cost edition for the poor under the title *Jesus*, which was also a best seller.

While *The Life of Jesus* elevated Renan's literary reputation, it also plunged him into controversy. He firmly believed that his critical approach restored greater dignity to Jesus by humanizing him. Renan's intention was to preserve the religious spirit while dispelling superstitions and historical inaccuracies, which he felt were opposed to science and common sense. "If the Gospels are like other books," he wrote in the preface to the 13th edition of *The Life of Jesus*, "I am right in treating them in the same manner as the student of Greek, Arabian or Hindu lore treats its legendary documents which he studies. Criticism knows no infallible texts; its first principle is to admit the possibilities of error in the text which it examines."

However, Renan's rationalistic and skeptical perspective, his denial of the divinity of Christ, and his attempts to explain in purely human terms such fundamental tenets of Christianity as the Resurrection of Jesus scandalized the devout. The year before the publication of *The Life of Jesus*, he had realized his great ambition to succeed a former professor in the chair of Hebrew, Chaldaic, and Syriac languages at the Collège de France. In earlier essays he had introduced his theory that the life of Jesus represented an extraordinary historical event, rather than a supernatural one, which human reason could explain in psychological terms. In the course of his inaugural lecture, he made clear his philosophical position of denial of

Jesus' divinity. Quickly, anti– and pro–clerical student factions created noisy disturbances centered around his views. Soon afterward *The Life of Jesus* came off the press.

In the atmosphere of controversy surrounding the publication of the book, Renan was expelled from his professorship in 1864, becoming a central figure in debates on the moral and political issues of academic freedom. In exile from academia, he was appointed assistant director of manuscripts in the imperial library. With the advent of the Third Republic (1870–1940), marking the end of imperial rule, Renan regained his academic position. In 1876, *The Life of Jesus* was republished in revised form as part of an eight-volume work, *History of the Origins of Christianity* (1876–81). Renan was elected to the French Academy and in 1883 appointed director of the Collège de France. Until his death in 1892 and for decades after, he was regarded as among the most influential literary figures of his age, particularly on the development of modern views of religious history.

Beginning in the 1860s, the Catholic Church and the French government became engaged in a bitter struggle. Pope Pius IX condemned the liberal trends that reflected modern scientific thinking in his 1864 encyclical, "Quanta Cura," and in 1870 defined papal infallibility as a dogma. The French state, on the other hand, was moving toward the complete secularization of government and education, a movement that gained momentum under the Third Republic and culminated in the official separation of church and state in the Separation Law of 1905. It was in this context that in 1897, the Catholic Church placed *The Life of Jesus* on the Index of Forbidden Books along with 19 other works by Renan.

Despite its condemnation by the Catholic Church, many more editions of the book appeared in France and other countries. Though the furor over *The Life of Jesus* had long since subsided by the 1920s, Renan's work remained on the Index through its last edition compiled in 1948 and in effect until 1966. Once regarded as one of the most controversial authors in the Western world, Renan is not widely read today, and *The Life of Jesus*, despite its impressive blend of scholarship and art, has been superseded by more modern works, such as Nikos Kazantzakis's THE LAST TEMPTATION OF CHRIST.

FURTHER READING

Chadbourne, Richard M. *Ernest Renan.* New York: Twayne Publishers, 1968.
———. *Ernest Renan as an Essayist.* Ithaca, N.Y.: Cornell University Press, 1957.
Putnam, George Haven. *The Censorship of the Church of Rome.* Vol. 2. New York: G. P. Putnam's Sons, 1906–07.
Renan, Ernest. *The Life of Jesus.* Introduction by John Haynes Holmes. New York: Modern Library, 1955.

MARY AND HUMAN LIBERATION

Author: Tissa Balasuriya
Original dates and places of publication: 1990, Sri Lanka; 1997, United States
Original publishers: Centre for Society and Religion; Trinity Press International
Literary form: Theological text

SUMMARY

Tissa Balasuriya, a Roman Catholic theologian and social activist, is a member of the Oblates of Mary Immaculate, the largest order of priests in Sri Lanka. In *Mary and Human Liberation*, as Balasuriya explains in the book's preface, he intends "to reflect on the meaning of Mary, especially for our times, and in the circumstances of an unjust world."

In contrast to the traditional portrayal of Mary, the mother of Jesus, Balasuriya sees her as a mature adult woman who supported the struggle of her son in a search for human liberation. She was "a woman of real life involved in the day-to-day struggles of ordinary people at individual and community levels."

Mary has a special place in Catholic devotion. Churches, shrines, hymns, and prayers are dedicated to her, and Marian feasts mark the liturgical year. Yet most of the popular hymns and prayers do not express or appreciate Mary's strength of character and adult womanly qualities. Balasuriya examines 19 hymns sung by English-speaking congregations in Sri Lanka. In most of them, Mary is presented as a humble virgin mother who is insulated from the normal trials and temptations of life. She is shown as tender and loving but not concerned with removing the societal causes of poverty, injustice, and the exploitation of women. This is quite different from the Mary portrayed in the Gospels and the Acts of the Apostles.

Balasuriya contends that this view of a "domesticated and passive" Mary corresponds to a traditional theology built around the hypothesis of humanity's fall in Original Sin. It derives from a spirituality that has stressed sins of sexual relations and neglected other sins, such as selfishness, injustice, exploitation, and male domination. Christians are encouraged to be dependent on Mary for resolving their individual concerns but not for bringing about the radical change expressed in the hymn the "Magnificat": "He casts the mighty from their thrones and raises the lowly. He fills the starving with good things and sends the rich away empty . . . and scatters the proud-hearted."

Prayer is influenced by the prevailing theology, which, in turn, is influenced by the concerns of those who hold power in the church community. Hail Mary, the most commonly recited personal and public Marian prayer, suggests a concept of salvation in which the socially liberative aspects of the transformation of values, relationships, and structures are absent. This has the effect of "tranquilizing" Catholics, Balasuriya argues. "The male-dominated, patriarchal, salvation-oriented theology of the period from Augustine to Vatican II still pervades much of the Marian piety of Sri Lanka," he writes. In this "top-down Mariology," Mary embodies the message that the powerful want to hear.

Many elements of Marian theology, especially the defined dogmas, are not found explicitly in the Gospels. Rather, Mariology is an evolution of the church's thinking in subsequent centuries. Since Jesus the God-Man could never be under Satan's dominion, even through Original Sin, the church argued that he was not born of a human father. Hence it developed the view that Jesus was conceived in the womb of Mary through the "overshadowing" of the Holy Spirit. It was not enough that Jesus should be born without a human father; it was necessary that his mother be without Original Sin, otherwise she would transmit sin to Jesus through procreation. The teaching gradually evolved that Mary was conceived in the womb of her mother, Anne, without the stain of Original Sin. Mary's Assumption into heaven was asserted on the basis that her body would not bear corruption, as it did not have to pay the "wages of sin which is death."

While Marian spirituality is historically deep-rooted among Sri Lankan Catholics, its impact is of an individualistic and even otherworldly nature. The faithful think of Mary as a heavenly being rather than a human mother of a human son who confronted situations similar to those faced by millions of contemporary mothers and children.

This perspective has not contributed adequately to the understanding and growth of new dimensions of mission and ministry required today. Catholics had to develop their theological reasoning against the background of the dominant theology, within a framework of European domination and of the popular religion of the colonized peoples themselves. This theology, when concerned with Mariology, elaborated teachings and religious practices that related more to angels, shepherds, and the garden of Eden, than to earthly sociopolitical realities, such as Mary's flight into Egypt, her exile, and the later challenge by her son of the local religious establishment and the foreign rulers and their false values. Now that a new approach to Christology is being derived from the Gospel, witness of the commitment of Jesus to human life and social justice, a new Mariology is also emerging. If the church does not rethink its theology and spirituality in a manner relevant to the present population and their needs, Balasuriya contends, it will be bypassed as irrelevant.

As the church bars women from the priesthood and the clergy controls power in the church, women have less access to theological education, decision making, financial resources, and the freedom that flows from those powers. Yet women shared fully in the mission of Jesus. "If the church is to be the continuation of this community of Jesus, I do not see why women cannot offer the sacrifice and announce the message of Jesus," Balasuriya writes. "The papacy is a function in which gender is not significant."

Balasuriya argues that a theology or doctrine should be analyzed with a "hermeneutic of suspicion" in order to evaluate the impact of myth, ideology, imagination, and prejudice in the evolution of dogma. "Ideological taint" should be expected in all theology, including his own, Balasuriya writes. "In Mariology we should keep in mind the suspicion that it is possible, likely and even probable, that male clergy would foster a theology that would preserve their interests and power in the religious community."

From a Catholic perspective, the sources of Christian theology are the Bible and tradition. Both of these should be subject to critical evaluation. The Bible's core teaching of love and unselfish service is truly meaningful and redeeming for all humanity. "But many elements in the Bible are less praiseworthy, or even indefensible, especially when they impinge on the rights of human beings." Likewise, in church tradition, the teachings of the church have been intolerant and harmful to others, particularly other religions and women.

"When we find that some Christian teachings have been harmful, injurious and degrading to human beings, or have given legitimacy to grave injustice, we should institute a critical re-examination of such theology," asserts Balasuriya. Christian theology "may have to be rethought when the Church finds itself in a plural context of different religions and social systems."

Balasuriya states that he has no difficulty with the dogma of Original Sin in the sense of a human proneness to evil, the concept of the collective sinfulness of a society, or an environment that has a corrupting influence. "What I question is the hypothesis of original sin as propounded in traditional theology, according to which human beings are born into a situation of helpless alienation from God, because of the primary original sin of the first parents." The traditional doctrine of Original Sin, he believes, has several drawbacks in its sources, in its lack of internal coherence, and in its consequences.

One of its consequences is discrimination against women, as the church fathers, especially after Augustine, interpreted the Genesis story to blame a woman for humanity's fall. Other consequences are negativity toward nature and discrimination against people of other religions or no religion and a wrong emphasis on the conversion of individuals and countries.

"[T]he dogma of the Immaculate Conception has its roots in the interpretation of original sin, and requires critical rethinking," according to Balasuriya. There is no convincing evidence for the doctrine, he says, except that it is traditional belief in the Catholic Church. Again, it is a doctrine related to Original Sin and the ideology of male domination.

In the last chapter, Balasuriya proposes "a Marian Way of the Cross." The Way of the Cross is the principal Catholic devotion during the six weeks of Lent, in which the faithful meditate upon 14 scenes from the Passion of Christ. The more traditional interpretation emphasizes personal sins and an individualistic path to salvation. Balasuriya contends that this spirituality does not question the social and structural causes of many of the evils of our time and encourages passivity and conformism. Mary participates in the redemptive action of Jesus by sharing his life and risks and his arrest, torture, and death. Her own Way of the Cross could be understood in relation to the suffering of the poor and women.

The book ends with a quote from Pope Paul VI: "The modern woman will note with pleasant surprise that Mary of Nazareth, while completely devoted to the will of God, was far from being a timidly submissive woman or one whose piety was repellent to others; on the contrary, she was a woman who did not hesitate to proclaim that God vindicates the humble and the oppressed, and removes the powerful people of the world from their privileged positions."

CENSORSHIP HISTORY

Mary and Human Liberation was first published in 1990 in a double issue of *Logos*, the quarterly review of the Centre for Society and Religion in Colombo, Sri Lanka, with a print run of 600 copies. More than two years later, Sri Lankan bishop Malcolm Ranjith raised the first objection to the book. On December 1, 1992, an ad hoc theological commission of the Bishops Conference in Sri Lanka met to review Balasuriya's writing. Later that month, Balasuriya received a letter from the archbishop of Colombo, Nicholas Fernando, saying that the commission wished to discuss his publication with him.

Balasuriya met with the members of the commission in Colombo in January 1993. Bishop Ranjith read from a document that listed the erroneous beliefs Balasuriya had expressed in his publication: that there is no Original Sin; no redemption or savior is necessary, Jesus Christ is not the Savior, and he is not God. The commission did not discuss its concerns with Balasuriya at the meeting but asked him to respond in writing.

A year later, Balasuriya sent the bishops his reply, pointing out what he viewed as their falsifications and distortions of his text. In June 1994, the bishops published a statement in the *Catholic Messenger*, saying the book contained "four glaring errors" and recommended that Catholics not read it. Balasuriya's reply to the charges was not published.

On July 27, 1994, Balasuriya received a letter from his superior-general in Rome, Father Marcello Zago, informing him that the Vatican's Congregation for the Doctrine of the Faith (CDF) had discussed his book and requested that he withdraw his opinions. The CDF said that the book contained statements regarding the existence and nature of Original Sin, the divinity of Christ, the need for redemption, Christ as the only Savior, the nature and mission of the church, and Mariology that are incompatible with the faith of the church. Zago was asked "to take the necessary measures as he shall see fit, which include eventually a request for public withdrawal, and within a reasonable time he shall let the Congregation know the author's answer." Accompanying the letter was an anonymous document, "Some Observations on the Book *Mary and Human Liberation*."

On March 14, 1995, Balasuriya sent a lengthy response to the CDF that pointed out 58 specific instances in the anonymous document where the observations contained "unproved generalizations, misunderstandings, misrepresentations, distortions and falsifications." In late 1995, he received a brief letter from the CDF. It said only that his detailed response of March was "unsatisfactory" and enclosed a "Profession of Faith," prepared especially for him, which he was required to sign. His superior-general was told that if Balasuriya decided otherwise, "besides the disciplinary provisions [of] Canon 1364, consideration will be given to an eventual public declaration by this Congregation that Fr. Balasuriya is no longer a Catholic theologian."

Church canon law 1364 allows excommunication *latae sententiae*, or automatic excommunication, of an "apostate from the faith, a heretic, or a schismatic." *Latae sententiae* means that the subject is considered to be self-excommunicated by persisting in his or her errors. There is, therefore, no need for a formal trial that might result in excommunication by actual judgment (*ferendae sententiae*).

"In the profession of faith," Balasuriya explained, "the CDF demanded that I profess under oath: 'Every man is born in sin. Therefore I hold that original sin is transmitted with human nature by propagation, not by imitation, and that it is in all men, proper to each; it cannot be taken away by the powers of human nature.' " He also was asked to swear: "I firmly accept and hold that the Church has no authority whatsoever to confer priestly ordination on women."

In May 1996, Balasuriya received a fax from the CDF, informing him that if he did not sign the profession of faith by the 15th of the month, he would be excommunicated. On May 14, Balasuriya instead signed the "Credo of the People of God" of Pope Paul VI, with the added statement that he did so "in the context of theological development and Church practice since Vatican II, and the freedom and responsibility of Christians and theological researchers under Canon Law." The key difference between Paul VI's profession of faith and the one drafted specifically for Balasuriya was that the Vatican had subtracted a clause on salvation outside the Church and added a clause forbidding women's ordination.

On December 7, 1996, Balasuriya was summoned to the residence of the papal nuncio and was again told that if he did not sign the profession of faith, he would be excommunicated. Balasuriya again refused. On January 2, 1997, the notification, dated December 8 and signed by Joseph Cardinal Ratzinger, the prefect of the CDF (who succeeded Pope John Paul II as Pope Benedict XVI in April 2005), was published in the Vatican newspaper. Balasuriya heard the news of his excommunication on the BBC. He was 72 and had been a member of the Oblates order for more than a half-century and a priest for 44 years.

Balasuriya appealed to the Apostolic Signatura, the supreme court of the Catholic Church, on the grounds that the procedures in his case violated canon law, which requires a trial unless precluded by just causes and grants the accused the right of self-defense. The Signatura agreed to hear his appeal but the papal secretary of state informed the body that it had no competence to try the case. Pope John Paul II had personally approved the procedures and the excommunication, and such a papal decision could not be appealed.

Balasuriya's excommunication created a worldwide furor and made him an international cause célèbre. It was the harshest sanction levied in recent times against a Catholic theologian. The church previously had barred dissident theologians, such as the Swiss theologian Hans Küng and the American Charles Curran, from teaching Catholic theology but had not stripped them of their right to remain within the church. An excommunicated priest may not participate in public worship or administer or receive the sacraments, though he remains a priest unless formally dismissed.

The excommunication occurred in the context of the Vatican's campaign to stem the tide of religious "relativism." The CDF viewed Balasuriya as a relativist who equated all religions and philosophies and reduced Christian spirituality to social action.

The severity of the penalty and the lack of due process for Balasuriya were widely criticized, including by many Catholics who agreed with the Vatican's reservations regarding his views. "The main issue of the whole affair is not the rightness or wrongness of Fr. Balasuriya's theology," commented Edmund Hill, a Dominican priest and teacher of theology, in an introduction to Balasuriya's book, "but the appropriateness or otherwise of the reaction to it by the ecclesiastical authorities, both in Sri Lanka . . . and in Rome."

"Where is the due process of law? Without that process, there is tyranny," asked the lead article on January 11, 1997, in the influential London-based Catholic newspaper *The Tablet*. "Balasuriya's writings may call for challenge," said the *National Catholic Reporter*, an independent Catholic weekly based in Kansas City, "but threat of excommunication? It has no place here. And should Balasuriya be ousted, history would undoubtedly prove it to be one more sad and serious abuse of authority in a church that professes the God of love."

In what was seen as a response to such criticisms, in August 1997 the Vatican issued new guidelines on doctrinal debates within the church, bowing to what it called "the heightened sensitivity" of contemporary thinking in this area. The new rules gave Catholic scholars and theologians investigated by the church the right to a Vatican-appointed defender. They could also select their own adviser to take part in doctrinal examinations and involve their local bishops in the process. The Vatican described these changes as a step toward greater openness, but critics within the church said that they did not go far enough, as the Vatican maintained the right to select both the defender of the accused and the experts called in to judge the work.

"My book was essentially a simple one, which suggested that we need to change the accent of Marian devotion," Balasuriya explained in an interview with author Paul Collins. "It also implicitly questioned the fundamental traditional understanding of the Bible and the myths developed around the concept of original sin that resulted in the exclusion of the rest of humanity from salvation, except through Jesus Christ and the Church." This view, he continued, "would imply that the vast majority of the people of Asia were not saved. The point has dawned on us that this is not acceptable."

In a statement distributed after his excommunication, Balasuriya maintained that what he had written was within the bounds of Catholic orthodoxy and that he was prepared to correct any errors that were proved to him through "an objective and fair evaluation of my views at the level of accepted contemporary Catholic scholarship. . . . Many other writers, especially in the West, have expressed similar or identical views. None of them, as far as we know, has been treated so severely."

A year later, on January 15, 1998, in a stunning reversal, the Vatican announced that it had rescinded Balasuriya's excommunication. His reconciliation with the church was the result of a compromise that came about after six days of negotiations involving Balasuriya, Oblate theologians from Sri Lanka chosen by him, and a delegation of Oblate officials from Rome. The Vatican dropped its earlier demand that Balasuriya sign its custom-made profession of faith that asserted the church cannot ordain women. Balasuriya signed the same profession of faith by Pope Paul VI he had proffered in 1996 but without the caveat he had added. In his signed statement of reconciliation, Balasuriya noted: "I realize that serious ambiguities and doctrinal errors were perceived in my writings and therefore provoked negative reactions from other parties, affected relationships, and led to an unfortunate polarization in the ecclesial community. I truly regret the harm this has caused."

"The phrase 'perceived error' is very crucial to my statement," Balasuriya told South African Catholic weekly the *Southern Cross*. "I accept that there was some perceived error in my writings, . . . but no errors were proved. So, there is no confession and no punishment."

The Vatican's turnaround was "very significant," Curran told the *National Catholic Reporter*. "To my knowledge, this is the first time they have backed away from anything so quickly and publicly. Obviously they gave in to the *sensus fidelium* (the sense of the faithful)," referring to an international clamor from bishops, clergy, theologians, and lay groups for Balasuriya's reinstatement. Balasuriya said that he attributed his reconciliation "first of all to the grace of God and the Spirit operating" and secondly, "to immense pressure from all over the world. . . . Human rights groups, the mass media, the Internet, E-mail—these are ways in which the Holy Spirit operates today. This is a new reality in the life of the church."

FURTHER READING

Akkara, Anto. " 'Don't Hijack the Pope.' " *The Southern Cross* (March 8, 1998). Available online. URL: http://www.southerncross.co.za. Accessed December 16, 2004.

Balasuriya, Tissa. *Mary and Human Liberation: The Story and the Text*. Harrisburg, Pa.: Trinity Press International, 1997.

Bohlen, Celestine. "Heresy Brings Hint of Martyrdom to Sri Lanka Priest." *New York Times* (January 15, 1997). Available online. URL: http://www.newyorktimes.com. Accessed December 16, 2004.

———. "A Sri Lankan Priest Is Excommunicated for His Relativism." *New York Times* (January 7, 1997). Available online. URL: http://www.newyorktimes.com. Accessed December 16, 2004.

———. "Vatican Sets Rules for Doctrinal Debates." *New York Times* (August 30, 1997). Available online. URL: http://www.newyorktimes.com. Accessed December 16, 2004.

Burkeman, Oliver. "'Heretic' Priest Defies Inquisitors in Rights Battle." Gemini News Service (October 10, 1997).

Collins, Paul. *The Modern Inquisition: Seven Prominent Catholics and Their Struggles with the Vatican.* Woodstock, N.Y.: Overlook Press, 2002.

"Excommunication Is an Inordinate Threat." *National Catholic Reporter* (December 27, 1996). Available online. URL: http://findarticles.com/p/articles/mi_m1141/is_n9_v33/ai_19013597#continue. Accessed November 16, 2005.

Schaeffer, Pamela. "Condemned Priest Is Restored to Church." *National Catholic Reporter* (January 30, 1998). Available online. URL: http://natcath.org/NCR_Online/archives/013098/bala1.htm.

MEDITATIONS ON FIRST PHILOSOPHY

Author: René Descartes
Original date and place of publication: 1641, France
Literary form: Philosophical essays

SUMMARY

The 17th-century French philosopher and scientist René Descartes is the founder of modern philosophy and mathematics. His *Meditations on First Philosophy* contains the most thorough exposition and defense of his philosophical ideas.

In six meditations, Descartes attempted to apply the scientific method to philosophical concepts, approaching philosophy through analysis of experience rather than assertion of faith. He began his meditations with a letter addressed to the Sacred Faculty of Theology of Paris. "I have always thought that the two questions, of God and of the soul, were the principal questions among those that should be demonstrated by [rational] philosophy rather than theology," he wrote. "For although it may suffice us faithful ones to believe by faith that there is a God and that the human soul does not perish with the body, certainly it does not seem possible ever to persuade those without faith to accept any religion, nor even perhaps any moral virtue, unless they can first be shown these two things by means of natural reason."

In his first meditation, Descartes introduced the concept of universal doubt, examining the principles underlying his opinions. He intended to base his theories only on what could be proven to be true and began his search for truth by doubting everything he had been taught. Doubt delivers the mind from prejudices and makes available a method of accustoming the mind to independence from the senses, he believed. Though the sense sometimes mislead, there are some ideas that cannot reasonably be doubted.

The first certainty is that I am thinking about these matters, Descartes declared. And if I am thinking, I must exist. And, as Descartes wrote in DISCOURSE ON METHOD, his earlier essay on the scientific method, "*Cogito ergo sum*" (I think, therefore I am).

From the certainty of the existence of a thinking being, Descartes moved to consider the existence of God. He asserted that in order for an idea to contain a particular objective reality, it must obtain from some cause, a first idea or archetype. If there is something that could not have come from himself, it must come from an infinite, omniscient entity that created all things. Descartes could not conceive of an infinite substance unless the idea had been placed in him by some substance which was, in fact, infinite. Therefore, he must conclude that God exists.

The existence of God leads to the reality of perception of the physical world. God could not deceive the thinking mind by illusory perceptions because it is impossible for God to deceive, as in all fraud and deception there is some kind of imperfection. Therefore, man cannot err if volition is restricted to the boundaries of knowledge. Everything that we perceive clearly and distinctly is wholly true. Though we should not rashly admit everything that the senses seem to teach us, neither should we doubt them in general.

Descartes describes the physical world as mechanistic and entirely divorced from the mind, the only connection between the two being by intervention of God. In Descartes's concept of dualism, mind and body exist independently, even though they happen to coincide here on Earth. There is no doubt that what nature teaches contains some truth. Yet human life is often subject to error in particular matters. God made human beings perfect in their potential, rather than in actuality. They must use their perceptions wisely by restricting the will only to accept clear and distinct perceptions.

CENSORSHIP HISTORY

See DISCOURSE ON METHOD.

FURTHER READING

Descartes, René. *Meditations on First Philosophy*. Trans. and introduction by Laurence J. Lafleur. New York: Bobbs-Merrill Co., 1960.

Green Jonathon. *The Encyclopedia of Censorship*. New York: Facts On File, 1990.

Jolley, Nicholas, "The Reception of Descartes' Philosophy." In *The Cambridge Companion to Descartes*, edited by John Cottingham, 393–423. Cambridge: Cambridge University Press, 1992.

THE MERITORIOUS PRICE OF OUR REDEMPTION

Author: William Pynchon
Original date and place of publication: 1650, England
Literary form: Religious text

SUMMARY

The Meritorious Price of Our Redemption was the first work to be burned publicly in North America. Its author, William Pynchon, was a prominent British merchant and colonizer of the Connecticut River valley in western Massachusetts. After sailing to New England with John Winthrop in 1630, he founded the city of Roxbury, Massachusetts. History does not record exactly why Pynchon left the Boston area for the sparsely populated western edge of the Massachusetts Bay Colony. Historians speculate that he moved for economic reasons: Demand for beaver pelts was increasing, and there was a huge beaver population in the Connecticut River valley. He may also have been motivated to move by his disagreements with the growing Puritan orthodoxy in the Boston area. Whatever his reasons, Pynchon moved to Springfield in 1636 and immediately became one of the town's most powerful citizens.

Until 1650, it appears that Pynchon was content running his fur-trading business and serving as a local magistrate. He first appeared in Massachusetts court records as the judge in an early witchcraft case, which he dismissed for lack of evidence. Witchcraft cases were just beginning to appear in Massachusetts in the late 1640s, and if it were for this case alone, he would have remained a footnote to legal history. However, Pynchon's spare-time writings were the subject of Massachusetts's first case of public book burning.

In *The Meritorious Price of Our Redemption*, Pynchon set out to refute the Calvinist idea that Christ had suffered for humankind's sins. It seemed illogical to Pynchon that God would have punished Christ with the eternal damnation that would have been the result of dying for all the sins of humankind. Rather, Pynchon believed, Christ achieved a perfect atonement for all Christians' misdeeds. Through his obedience of the divine plan for him, he avoided undergoing the punishments of hell. If Christ had suffered these torments, then God would have punished him twice.

As Pynchon pointed out, "I never heard that any Tyrant did require [the payment of] full price for their Galley-slaves, and to bear their punishment of their curse and slavery in their stead. . . . [Calvinist doctrine] makes God the Father more rigid in the price of our Redemption than ever a Turkish Tyrant was. . . ." In Pynchon's opinion, theologians who maintained that Christ did suffer in hell were portraying God as a merciless tyrant.

The Meritorious Price also questioned the era's thinking about who killed Jesus. Most theologians blamed the Crucifixion on Roman soldiers, but Pynchon was convinced that the Jews had persuaded the Romans to kill Jesus. Pynchon's anti-Semitism reappeared in *The Jewes Synagogue: or a Treatise Concerning the ancient Orders and manner of Worship used by the Jewes in their Synagogue-Assemblies,* published in 1652. Pynchon's toleration for free thought was in fact quite narrow, not extending beyond more rights for Presbyterians.

Pynchon was no defender of broad definitions of religious liberty or freedom of conscience, as was fellow wilderness-dweller Roger Williams. Pynchon believed that only Presbyterians should have been allowed to vote for office in Massachusetts along with the majority Congregationalists. He shared this belief with a dissident group called the Remonstrants but did not share the Remonstrants' desire to see a British-appointed governor of the Massachusetts Bay Colony. While Pynchon believed that "a world of good hath been done by ministers that haue no certaine forme of discipline," he feared the radical movements that had come to power during the English Civil War and subscribed to mainstream Presbyterianism.

Toward the end of his life, Pynchon returned to England, where he bought a large estate on the Thames and continued to produce theological tracts, though none brought him as much attention as *The Meritorious Price.* He was buried in an Anglican churchyard, apparently proof that he had rejoined the Church of England shortly before his death.

CENSORSHIP HISTORY

The Meritorious Price of Our Redemption was published in England in June 1650 and quickly found its way to Boston. Pynchon's book was a literary sensation in England. British readers took great interest in the religious feuds of their day and were particularly interested to hear how interdenominational battles were fought in the colonies. Pynchon satisfied this demand by signing his book "William Pinchon, Gentleman, in New England."

Once Pynchon's book reached Boston that October, local religious and civil authorities were furious. By including his place of residence, Pynchon implied that his opinions were representative of other respectable New Englanders. If Parliament thought that a majority of Massachusetts landholders held such unorthodox views, colonial leaders feared that they might well be tempted to cut off financial support for the colony. The document also confused colonial leaders, as Pynchon had been a respectable landholder, town founder, and fur merchant for nearly 20 years. No one had suspected that he held such unorthodox and possibly blasphemous views.

On October 15, 1650, Boston's general court, the judicial body charged with approving new books, decided that *The Meritorious Price* was "erronious and daingerous" and ordered an Anglican theologian to prepare a response to it. The court summoned Pynchon to appear before its next session to answer its questions and declared that the book would be burned in the Boston market the next day.

In all likelihood, Pynchon had never intended to offend the authorities. It seems more likely that he had merely committed to paper the ideas he had held for several decades and provoked an unforeseen rebuke from Boston. He appeared in court on May 7, 1651, and over the course of the next two weeks he made a partial apology and retraction of the statements that inflamed the general court. Pynchon spent his days conversing with theologians, explaining his justification for his ideas while listening to the elders' objections. Finally, Pynchon admitted that he had not "spoken in my booke so fully of the prize and merit of Christs sufferings as I should have done." He never did recant his statement that Christ could not have been sentenced to suffer in hell, however.

On May 13, 1651, Pynchon was allowed to return to Springfield to write a book that would correct the objectionable ideas in *The Meritorious Price.* The general court asked Pynchon to have the book ready for its October meeting. Pynchon did not appear at the October session. But the judges ruled that he should be given more time to finish his book in order to fully repent for his offenses and so that he had a chance to read the official rebuttal to *The Meritorious Price.* If Pynchon did not show up at the May 1652 session, the court decided, he would be fined £100 and would be subject to other penalties.

In late 1651, the court received letters from prominent Englishmen asking that it treat Pynchon lightly because he had not intended to create controversy by publishing his book. The members of the general court responded politely but firmly. Pynchon's book had lent credence to false images of New England religious life, and the book's blasphemous passages had to be burned and recanted. The court informed Pynchon's English supporters that his sentence would be carried out, though the court agreed that Pynchon had been an important New England leader.

Pynchon had returned to England by April 1652. He never published a refutation of his own work; rather, he responded with a counterattack on the Boston Puritans. In his British theological writings he continued to insist that Christ could not have suffered torment in hell and generally argued fine doctrinal points with Massachusetts clergy. While his writings caused some controversy in England, the official censor approved them for printing, and Pynchon never again had his books publicly burned.

Unlike other religious dissenters of this period, Pynchon had not arrived at his ideas through involvement with a radical dissenting sect. Rather, he evidently formulated them while living in the wilderness of early Springfield, Massachusetts. Pynchon was no young hothead when he wrote *The Meritorious Price of Our Redemption:* He was a well-connected, well-respected entrepreneur and colonist. For these reasons he escaped the harsher punishments heaped on Williams for his publication of THE BLOUDY TENENT OF PERSECUTION and William Penn for THE SANDY FOUNDATION SHAKEN.

—Jonathan Pollack

FURTHER READING

Armytage, Frances, and Juliette Tomlinson. *The Pynchons of Springfield: Founders and Colonizers (1636–1702).* Springfield, Mass.: Connecticut Valley Historical Museum, 1969.

Burt, Henry M. *The First Century of the History of Springfield: The Official Records from 1636 to 1736.* Springfield, Mass.: self-published, 1898.

McIntyre, Ruth A. *William Pynchon: Merchant and Colonizer.* Springfield, Mass.: Connecticut Valley Historical Museum, 1961.

Smith, Joseph H., ed. *Colonial Justice in Western Massachusetts (1639–1702): The Pynchon Court Record.* Cambridge, Mass.: Harvard University Press, 1961.

THE METAPHYSICS

Author: Aristotle
Original date and place of publication: Fourth century B.C., Greece
Literary form: Philosophical treatise

SUMMARY

Aristotle, one of the greatest of the ancient Greek philosophers, was born in Macedonia in 384 B.C. and studied for 20 years under Plato at the academy in Athens. In 335, he founded his own school, the Lyceum, which attracted large numbers of scholars. Though much of his writing was lost, almost 50 works survived, mainly in the form of notes or summaries of his lectures made by his students and edited in the first century B.C. Aristotle's work included almost every field of study known in his time; biology, physics, politics, ethics, economics, grammar, rhetoric, poetry, metaphysics, and theology. He created the study of logic, the science of reasoning, which he regarded as the necessary tool of any inquiry.

The Metaphysics is a collection of lectures written at different dates during the late development of his thought. Their subject is what he called first philosophy, the study of the first causes of things. Aristotle considered first philosophy to be the discerning of the self-evident changeless first principles that form the basis of all knowledge, the true nature of reality. "All men by nature desire to know," *The Metaphysics* begins. But there are different degrees of knowledge. "Sense perception is common to all and therefore easy and no mark of wisdom," Aristotle declares. The highest wisdom is the pursuit of knowledge for its own sake, the science of first principles or first causes. Though metaphysics is the most abstract science, the most removed from the senses, it is the most exact.

All things, whether they are changing or unchanging, quantitative or nonquantitative, fall within the purview of first philosophy. The universe, which is constantly moving and changing, can best be understood through the doctrine of the four causes: the material cause (the substance of which the thing is made), the formal cause (its design), the efficient cause (its maker or builder), and the final cause (its purpose or function).

Aristotle depicts a hierarchy of existence, a ladder of nature proceeding from formless matter at the bottom to pure form, which is the Unmoved Mover, at the top. There is one unchangeable perfect being, which causes motion while remaining itself unmoved. This Prime Mover, or God, energizes the whole, so that each thing strives to attain its complete or perfect form. Thus study of first philosophy culminates in theology, or the study of God.

Differing with Plato, Aristotle believed that a form, with the exception of the Prime Mover, has no separate and independent existence but rather is immanent in matter. Instead of inhabiting separate worlds of their own, forms exist materially in the individual things they determine.

CENSORSHIP HISTORY

In the ninth century A.D., Arab and Jewish scholars reintroduced Aristotle to the West. His works became the basis of medieval Scholasticism, particularly through the writing of Saint Thomas Aquinas. During the 12th and 13th centuries, Aristotle's writings, accompanied by the work of the masterful Arabic commentators Avicenna and Averroës, profoundly influenced European thought, dominating the intellectual life of the University of Paris, the Christian world's center of learning.

For the first time, Christian thinkers were confronted with a completely rationalistic interpretation of human experience and a powerful metaphysical system that analyzed the world without reference to the tenets of Christian orthodoxy. The interpretation of Aristotle by Averroës in his COMMENTARIES, which was thought to imply rejection of the reality of individual intellect, denial of personal immortality, and the eternal and noncreated nature of the universe, was viewed as opposing Christian doctrine.

In 1210, the bishops of the Provincial Council of Paris forbade the public or private teaching of the natural philosophy and metaphysics of Aristotle. The ban, which applied to instruction of the arts faculty of the University of Paris, was imposed under penalty of excommunication and confirmed in 1215 by the papal legate, Robert de Curzon. In 1231, Pope Gregory IX prohibited the reading of the works of Aristotle until they had been purged of heresy, and he appointed a commission of theologians to correct them. The prohibition was extended to Toulouse in 1245 by Pope Innocent IV.

The bans on Aristotle were impossible to enforce and were gradually lifted. During the same period, study of Aristotle was widespread at Oxford and at the theological faculty of the University of Paris, where his writings were not forbidden. Between 1241 and 1247, Roger Bacon lectured on Aristotle at the arts faculty of the University of Paris, and by mid-century all the known works of Aristotle and the commentaries on them were part of the curriculum of the university. By the mid-14th century, the Legates of Urban V required that all candidates for the Licentiate of Arts at Paris prove their familiarity with Aristotle's works.

FURTHER READING

Bokenkotter, Thomas. *A Concise History of the Catholic Church*. New York: Doubleday, 1977.

Copleston, Frederick. *A History of Philosophy.* Vol. 1: *Greece and Rome, Part II.* New York: Doubleday, 1962.

———. *A History of Philosophy.* Vol. 2: *Medieval Philosophy.* New York: Doubleday, 1993.

Wippel, John F., and Alan B. Wolter, eds. *Medieval Philosophy: From St. Augustine to Nicholas of Cusa.* New York: Free Press, 1969.

MEYEBELA: MY BENGALI GIRLHOOD

Author: Taslima Nasrin
Original dates and places of publication: 1999, India; 2002, United States
Original publishers: People's Book Society; Steerforth Press
Literary form: Autobiography

SUMMARY

Taslima Nasrin is a feminist writer from Bangladesh and an uncompromising critic of Islam as a religion that oppresses women. She became world famous in 1994 when her novel LAJJA (SHAME) was banned in Bangladesh and a death sentence issued against her by fundamentalist Islamic clerics forced her into exile.

Meyebela: My Bengali Girlhood (Amar Meyebela) is the first volume of Nasrin's memoirs. It recounts incidents from her life to the age of 14 growing up in a middle-class Muslim family in rural Bangladesh (then East Pakistan) during the 1960s and 1970s. Her story is set against the backdrop of Bangladesh's war for independence from Pakistan. *Meyebela,* or "girlhood," is a term coined by the author because no word for a girl's childhood exists in her native Bengali.

Nasrin's father, Rajab Ali (Baba), was an ambitious and extraordinarily handsome doctor, the son of a poor farmer from a remote village. Her mother, Idulwara Begum (Ma), was a painfully thin and plain woman from a more affluent family. She was married off to her husband when she was 12 and was never able to finish school. Nasrin, then called Nasrin Jahan Taslima, had two older brothers—Noman (Dada) and Chotda (Kamal). When she was born, her parents lived with Ma's family, much to Ma's embarrassment and discontent. Ma tried to return to school when her oldest son began his studies, but her own father convinced Baba that there was no need for her to be educated.

"Baba rose higher and higher in life, but Ma remained where she was, in the same dark corner, stuck at the seventh standard. All she could do was open Baba's fat medical books and leaf through them before dusting and putting them away, fully aware that compared to her husband she was totally insignificant. One day he just might leave her."

Baba was having an affair with a beautiful woman, Razia Begum. When Nasrin was 11 months old, Baba was transferred to Pabna to work at the prison hospital, where the family had their own house and there was no

Razia Begum. But Ma's happiness was short-lived. A year later Baba was transferred back to Mymensingh. He bought some rooms from his wife's parents, so at least the family's residence was partly separated, but now Ma felt that she was really in prison. Baba resumed his relationship with Razia Begum. "All the dreams and desires of a small dark woman were blown away as if by a sudden dust storm."

Baba left the family for two years to obtain an advanced medical degree in Rajshahi. Nasrin had been his favorite child, yet when he returned, when Nasrin was four, she failed to recognize him. "I stopped calling him Baba. In fact, I stopped speaking to him. Even today, I do not address him directly. His two years in Raj ruined the closeness we once had. . . . An invisible wall separated us, even when he held me close to his heart."

Nasrin recalls her joy as a very young child spending most of her time outdoors playing with her young maternal uncles. She was a curious and bright child, and Baba, who believed strongly in the value of educating his children, sent her to school. There she felt lonely and foolish, too shy to stand in front of the blackboard, to raise her voice and recite a poem.

Ma became increasingly despondent and distracted, as she had found more letters from Razia Begum in Baba's shirt pockets. While Ma escaped her troubles at the cinema, Nasrin visited the courtyard of her grandparents' house. Her Uncle Sharaf promised to show her something interesting, and when she followed him, he molested her and threatened to kill her if she told.

From that time on, Nasrin refused to go to her grandmother's house to sleep but could not tell her mother why. Ma taught her to say her prayers, *namaz*, and told her that if she prayed to Allah she would get whatever she wanted. Nasrin's prayers were not answered. "I couldn't possibly pray any harder. Perhaps I was being punished for some sin. At any rate, I started thinking of myself as a sinner. When Uncle Sharaf took me to that empty room and stripped me naked, was that some how *my* fault, *my* sin? Was that why Allah hated me? Perhaps."

One day, Ma sent Nasrin to the room of her Uncle Aman, her father's brother, to borrow matches. He raped her. "Suddenly, at the age of seven, I was filled with a new awareness. What had happened was shameful, and it would not be right to talk about it. . . . After that, I felt myself split in two. One half went out with all the other children, played games, and ran around. The other half sat alone and depressed. . . . When she stretched her arm, she could not touch anyone, not even her mother."

In 1969, the family left the grandparents' compound and moved to a large house in Amlapara. When Baba continued seeing Razia Begum, Ma took to her bed. Then she became a devotee of Peer Amirullah, an Islamic teacher with a cultlike following, and began to give money and food to him "to clear the path to heaven." She neglected her children and her housework to visit the peer and began to follow a strict Muslim way of life; she could not wear a sari or follow other "Hindu" customs.

In a Bengali translation of the Koran, Nasrin read the words: "The moon has its own light. The earth always stands still. If it does not lean on one side, it is because all the mountains, acting like nails, are holding it in place."

"How was this possible?" she asked. "How could anyone say such things? As far as I knew, the earth did *not* stand still. It moved around the sun. . . . What the Koran said was wrong. Or was what I had been taught in school wrong? I felt very confused."

She read that man's female companion was created from one of his ribs. Women are like a field of growing crops; men are totally free to cultivate whenever they like. If a woman remains disobedient, her husband may beat her. When acting as a witness to an event, two women are counted as one witness. Men can take four wives. Men can divorce their wives by uttering the word *talaq* three times. "How could the Koran—a book so holy . . . speak of such discrimination?"

"The Koran lay open on my knee. . . . I felt as if I had chanced upon a hidden treasure. I had seen, secretly, a pitcher full of gold coins, and a snake was curled around it to guard its contents. At least, I thought that the pitcher was full of gold. But was it? What if it was empty? An empty pitcher made more noise that a full one, didn't it?"

Nasrin's brother Chotda, now a college student, eloped with a Hindu girl. Baba and his uncle captured Chotda, tied him up with iron chains, and whipped him. He was locked in his room for four days without food but refused to leave his wife. Chotda left home and did not look back.

Nasrin's classmate Dilruba, who had taught her to write poetry, was married off to a total stranger, a much older man. Two days before her wedding she came to Nasrin's house for help. Baba sent her away, and Nasrin never saw her again. "Her notebook of poems would be burned, and she would be forced into a life of peeling, grinding, cooking, and serving, as well as bearing a child almost every year. And what would happen to me? . . . Would I go on writing poetry?"

Uncles Tutu and Sharaf became followers of the peer. Aunt Fajli's daughter Mubashwera was chosen to give *naseehat*, or religious instruction and guidance, to her Uncle Sharaf. It had to be given in a dark room in complete privacy, stroking the chest of the recipient. Eventually, Mubashwera became severely ill, and Baba was sent for, but by morning, she was dead. She had been pregnant and had tried to abort the fetus using the root of some plant. She died of septicemia.

"Many times I was warned that if I did not follow the precepts laid down in the Koran and the hadith, there would be hell to pay on the day of judgment," Nasrin writes. "However, until now, I had no idea what *hadith* meant. Now that I knew, I did not wish to delve any deeper. I knew that it was useless to search for pears or diamonds in a pot of shit. . . . What I couldn't understand was why I was supposed to turn to Allah because Mubashwera was dead. . . . I thought that the Koran was written by a greedy, selfish man like Uncle Sharaf, or the man who grabbed my breasts by the river. If the hadith was the words of Prophet Muhammad, then he was definitely like Getu's father: nasty, cruel, an abuser, insane."

Nasrin continued to study, reading a lot, hiding "unsuitable" books under "suitable" ones. "Baba continued to dream: One day his daughter would finish her studies, be a brilliant success, and stand on her own two feet. . . . And I, in my corner, continued to grow."

CENSORSHIP HISTORY

Nasrin's 1993 novel, *Lajja* (*Shame*), about attacks on the Hindu minority in Bangladesh by Muslim mobs, was banned in Bangladesh on charges of disturbing religious harmony. Islamist clerics in Bangladesh issued a fatwa, or death decree, against her, demanding her arrest and execution for blasphemy and insults to Islam. She went into hiding, fearing for her life, and in 1994 was granted political asylum in Sweden. Since that time, Nasrin has remained in exile in Europe, the United States, and India.

In early 1999, a poem written in memory of Nasrin's mother, who died of cancer, was published in an Indian Bengali-language weekly magazine. The government of Bangladesh banned the poem and blocked imports of the magazine.

In August 1999, the Bangladeshi government banned the importation, sale, and distribution of *Meyebela*, contending "that its sentiments might hurt the existing social system and religious sentiments of the people." The little-known People's Book Society in Kolkata, India, had published the book in Bengali. The ban in Bangladesh sent sales of the book soaring on the other side of the border. The publishers announced that they had sold out its first edition.

In April 2000, Nasrin was awarded the prestigious Ananda Puraskar prize for Bengali literature in Kolkata for *Meyebela*. As she received the prize, Nasrin said of her exile from Bangladesh: "I'm not allowed to live in my own country. The place where I live now has no similarity with my childhood environment. My writings now completely depend on my memory and it is, indeed, a painful experience for me that I cannot write something [while] being at the centre of it."

The second volume of her autobiography, *Utal Hawa* (Wild wind, 2002), published in Kolkata, also was banned in Bangladesh. According to an order issued by the Home Ministry, it proscribed the book because it "contains anti-Islamic sentiments and statements that could destroy religious harmony in Bangladesh." That year, Nasrin was convicted in absentia by a court in Gopalgani, Bangladesh, of writing derogatory comments about Islam and was sentenced to one year in prison. The case was filed by a hardline Islamic leader, Mohammad Dabiruddin, who heads a religious school.

In November 2003, the government of Bangladesh banned the third installment of her autobiography, *Dwikhandita* (Split in two), published in

Bangladesh under the title *Ka*. The government acted after writer Syed Shamsul Haque filed a defamation suit charging that the book falsely portrayed him as a philanderer. In February 2004, a Bangladeshi businessman was arrested at Dhaka's international airport for carrying 15 copies of *Ka* in his luggage. The penalty for possessing the book is six months in jail, yet contraband copies were reported to be selling in Dhaka at three times the cover price.

The left-wing government of West Bengal State in India also banned *Dwikhandita* in April 2004 and confiscated copies of the book from the publisher and book sellers. The government cited two paragraphs in the book that appeared to "promote, or attempt to promote, enmity between different groups on grounds of religion." The High Court in Kolkata issued the ban after the poet Syed Hasmat Jalal filed a defamation suit, complaining that the autobiography contained references to him that were "false and frivolous." In response to a petition filed challenging the ban, the government said the earlier ban was "improper" and proscribed the book again under a fresh notification. The earlier notification had said the book could create tensions between two communities. The grounds for the new ban was that it hurt the feelings of a particular community. In September 2005, the Kolkata High Court declared that the ban was "unjustified and untenable" and ordered the return of the confiscated books.

When Nasrin came to Kolkata in January 2004 to promote the fourth volume of her autobiography, *Sei Shob Andhakar* (Those dark days), demonstrators burned two effigies of her, and Islamic clerics announced a cash award of 20,000 rupees to anyone who would insult her by blackening her face or garlanding her with shoes. In February 2004, the government of Bangladesh prohibited the import, printing, and sale of the book in Bangladesh because it contains "grave and objectionable comments about Islam and Prophet Muhammad" and "may cause hatred in the society."

To sidestep the censorship of her autobiographical volumes, Nasrin has made them available in Bengali at no cost on her Web site. "Is it wrong to expose the deep, sacred truths of life as you have lived it?" Nasrin asked in an essay in *SaraiReader*. "The unwritten rule of every autobiography is—'Nothing will be hidden, everything shall be written about.' "

FURTHER READING

Ahmed, Kamel. "Bangladesh Bans New Taslima Book." BBC News (August 13, 1999). Available online. URL: http://news.bbc.co.uk/2/hi/south_asia/419428.stm.

Bhaumik, Subir. "Indian State Lifts Ban on Writer." BBC News (September 22, 2005). Available online. URL: http://news.bbc.co.uk/1/hi/world/south_asia/4272858.stm.

Davis, Thulani. "Taslima Nasrin Speaks (Still)." *Village Voice* (November 13–19, 2002). Available online. URL: http://www.villagevoice.com/news/0246,davis,39832,1.html.

Dhar, Sujoy. "Bangladeshi Author's New Book Upsets Prurient Fans." Inter Press Service (November 27, 2003).

Gupta, Tilak D. "Autobiography of a Controversial Writer." *Tribune* (September 5, 1999). Available online. URL: http://www.tribuneindia.com/1999/99sep05/sunday/head10.htm.

"Jail Term Surprises Bangladeshi Author." BBC News (October 14, 2002). Available online. URL: http://news.bbc.co.uk/1/hi/world/south_asia/2327329.stm.

Nasreen Taslima. "Homeless Everywhere: Writing in Exile." *SaraiReader04* (February 2004). Available online. URL: http://www.sarai.net/journal/04_pdf/59taslima.pdf.

Nasrin, Taslima. *Meyebela: My Bengali Girlhood.* Royalton, Vt.: Steerforth Press, 2002.

————. Taslima Nasrin's official Web site. Available online. URL: http://taslimanasrin.com.

Tax, Meredith. "Taslima's Pilgrimage." *The Nation* (November 18, 2002). Available online. URL: http://www.thenation.com/doc/20021118/tax.

THE NEW ASTRONOMY

Author: Johannes Kepler
Original date and place of publication: 1609, Germany
Literary form: Scientific treatise

SUMMARY

The brilliant German mathematician and astronomer Johannes Kepler developed the first significant improvement of the astronomical theories of the 16th-century astronomer Nicolaus Copernicus. Kepler was convinced of the truth of the Copernican heliocentric hypothesis—that the Earth and the planets revolve around the Sun. His aim, he explained in 1605, was "to show that the celestial machine is to be likened not to a divine organism, but rather to a clockwork." Relying on the astronomical calculations of Mars's orbit by Danish astronomer Tycho Brahe, which were much more accurate than any earlier work, Kepler found that the positions of the planets differed from those calculated in Copernican theory.

In the Copernican theory of planetary motion, as in the geocentric Ptolemaic theory that had dominated astronomy since the second century A.D., planetary orbits were described as perfect circles. Many complex circular motions had to be combined to reproduce variations in the planets' movements. After attempting to combine circular motions in a way that would generate the observed planetary paths, it occurred to Kepler that the planets might move in oval, or elliptical, paths.

In *The New Astronomy* (1609), considered one of the most important books on astronomy ever published, Kepler stated the first of his three laws of planetary motion: that the planets move in elliptical orbits. While Copernicus took the revolutionary step of describing a change in the relations of the heavenly bodies, he had not altered the view of their movements as circles or the circular shape of the whole system. Kepler was the first to abandon the Aristotelian circular perfection of celestial movements.

In *Harmonies of the World* (1619), Kepler stated his second and third laws: that the speeds of the planets in their orbits are greatest when nearest the Sun and that there is a mathematical proportion between the square of the time it takes a planet to travel around the Sun and the cube of its distance from the Sun. The modern era in astronomy is commonly dated from the discovery of what became known as Kepler's laws. Kepler's laws paved the way for the development of celestial mechanics and the development by the British physicist Sir Isaac Newton of the law of universal gravitation.

CENSORSHIP HISTORY

In 1616, the Catholic Church denounced the Copernican system as dangerous to the faith and summoned Galileo Galilei, who had recently declared his belief in Copernicus's theory in *Letters on the Solar Spots*, to Rome. Pope Paul V warned him not to "hold, teach or defend" Copernican theories. Then, in 1619, the Vatican prohibited Kepler's *The New Astronomy* and his textbook of Copernican astronomy, *The Epitome of Copernican Astronomy* (1618), under a general prohibition covering all books teaching the heliocentric theory. According to the papal bull accompanying these bans, to teach or even to read the works of Copernicus or Kepler was forbidden.

Kepler was informed by a colleague that, in fact, his *Epitome*, a low-cost textbook prepared for students with an easily understood analysis, could be read in Italy, but not by those for whom it was intended. Only learned people and those with scientific training, who had received special permission, could legally have access to the book.

In a 1619 "Memorandum to Foreign Booksellers, Especially in Italy," regarding the publication of *Harmonies of the World*, Kepler wrote, "The greater the freedom of thought the more will faith be awakened in the sincerity of those who are devoted to scientific research. . . . You booksellers, if it is true, will act according to law and order if, considering the judgment, you will not openly offer copies of my book for sale. But you must realize that you have to serve philosophy and the good writers. . . . Therefore, please sell the book only to the highest clergy, the most important philosophers, the experienced mathematicians, to whom I, personally, as the advocate of Copernicus have no other approach. These men may decide whether one should make these immeasurable beauties of the divine works known to the common people or rather diminish their glory and suppress them by censures."

Kepler was undeterred by the censorship of his work. As Albert Einstein later wrote of Kepler: "Neither by poverty, nor by incomprehension of the contemporaries who ruled over the conditions of his life and work, did he allow himself to be discouraged. In addition, he dealt with a field of knowledge that immediately endangered the adherent of religious truth. He belonged, nevertheless, to those few who cannot do otherwise than openly acknowledge their convictions on every subject." After 1619, Kepler published eight additional treatises before his death in 1630.

The Roman Index of Forbidden Books of 1664 confirmed the condemnation of the works of Copernicus, Kepler, and Galileo and any other writings affirming the movement of the Earth and the stability of the Sun. This prohibition remained in effect up to the Index of Benedict XIV in 1753, which omitted the general prohibition.

It was not until 1824, however, when Canon Settele, a professor of astronomy in Rome, published a work on modern scientific theories, that the church finally announced its acceptance of "the general opinion of modern astronomers" and granted formal permission for the printing in Rome of books reflecting the theories of Copernicus, Kepler, and Galileo. In the next Index, published in 1835, the names of Copernicus, Kepler, and Galileo were finally omitted.

FURTHER READING

Baumgardt, Carola. *Johannes Kepler: Life and Letters*. Introduction by Albert Einstein. New York: Philosophical Library, 1951.

Boorstein, Daniel J. *The Discoverers: A History of Man's Search to Know His World and Himself*. New York: Random House, 1983.

Garraty, John A., and Peter Gay. *The Columbia History of the World*. New York: Harper and Row, 1972.

Green, Jonathon. *The Encyclopedia of Censorship*. New York: Facts On File, 1990.

O'Connor, James. *Kepler's Witch: An Astronomer's Discovery of Cosmic Order Amid Religious War, Political Intrigue and the Heresy Trial of His Mother*. San Francisco: HarperSanFrancisco, 2004.

THE NEW TESTAMENT

Translator: William Tyndale
Original date and place of publication: 1526, Germany
Literary form: Religious text

SUMMARY

The English Protestant reformer and linguist William Tyndale was the first person to translate THE BIBLE into English from the original Greek and Hebrew and the first to print it in English. Many scholars consider his influence on English literature comparable to William Shakespeare's.

In 1524, when Tyndale, an Oxford graduate and Catholic priest, resolved to translate the Bible, England was the only European country without a printed vernacular version. The 1408 synod of Canterbury had forbidden translation into English of any portion of the Scriptures by an unauthorized individual. Only the fifth-century Latin Vulgate edition of the Bible translated by Saint Jerome was considered acceptable.

Translation of the Bible into the vernacular remained illegal in England for fear that anarchy and schism would be brought about by the spread of Lutheranism. Lutheran books had been publicly burned in Cambridge and London in 1520. Martin Luther's doctrine of *sola scriptura*, Scripture alone, which emphasized the ability of believers to read and understand the Bible themselves without church intervention, was considered to defy church authority. Scripture could be interpreted only by the infallible pope and the hierarchy.

Tyndale could find no religious authority in London who would support his work. "And so in London I abode for almost a year, and marked the course of the world . . . ," he later wrote, "and saw things whereof I defer to speak at this time and understood at the last not only that there was no room in my lord of London's palace to translate the New Testament, but also that there was no place to do it in all England, as experience doth now openly declare."

In 1524, Tyndale left England for Germany. The following year in Cologne, he began printing his translation of the New Testament from the Greek. The printing had reached Matthew 22 when it had to be suspended. His translation was violently opposed by the clergy, who, fearing Lutheranism, saw it as "pernicious merchandise." When the Cologne authorities moved to arrest him and his assistant and impound their work, they fled to Worms, where publication of the 700 pages of the New Testament was completed clandestinely and anonymously at the press of Peter Schoeffer in 1526. Six thousand copies of Tyndale's New Testament were smuggled into England the following year and widely distributed. For the first time, all 27 books of the New Testament were available in clearly printed portable form in a language that every reader could understand.

The primary source for Tyndale's New Testament was the original Greek, although he drew from both the Latin Vulgate and Martin Luther's German translation. Because he believed that the word of God should speak directly to the reader in an understandable way, his first aim was clarity, to write in everyday spoken English. "If God spare my life, ere many years, I will cause a boy that driveth a plough shall know more of the Scripture than thou dost," he told a learned man before leaving England.

His ability to write in simple, direct, and rhythmic prose and, as his biographer David Daniell says, "to create unforgettable words, phrases, paragraphs and chapters, and to do so in a way that . . . is still, even today, direct and living" had an indelible impact on both the language of the Bible and English prose.

"Am I my brother's keeper?" "Blessed are the pure of heart; for they shall see God." "No man can serve two masters." "Ask and it shall be given to you." "There were shepherds abiding in the fields." These and hundreds of proverbial phrases such as "the signs of the times," "the spirit is willing," and "fight the good fight" come from Tyndale's New Testament.

Tyndale's 1534 revision of the New Testament, published in Antwerp under his own name, was carried forward into later Renaissance Bibles and formed the basis of the Authorized, or King James, Version of the Bible published in 1611.

Living in concealment in the Low Countries, Tyndale also translated the first half of the Old Testament from the original Hebrew. His masterly translation of the Pentateuch appeared in 1530, beginning with Genesis: "In the beginning God created heaven and earth. . . . Then God said: let there be light and there was light." The Book of Jonah was completed in 1536. Tyndale's Old Testament books were published in pocket volumes and smuggled into England. His Old Testament was also adopted in large part into the King James Version of the Bible.

CENSORSHIP HISTORY

Church dignitaries in England immediately denounced Tyndale's 1526 edition of the New Testament. In the summer of 1526, the English bishops met and agreed that "untrue translations" should be burned, "with further sharp corrections and punishment against the keepers and readers of the same." The Catholic cardinal Thomas Wolsey, who controlled domestic and foreign policy for Henry VIII, instructed the English ambassador to the Low Countries to act against printers or booksellers involved in the production and distribution of the English New Testament. Tyndale's New Testament was the first printed book to be banned in England. Wolsey ordered Tyndale to be seized at Worms, but Tyndale found refuge with Philip of Hesse at Marburg.

Although Henry VIII was to break with Rome in the early 1530s, he had no sympathy with Protestant views and saw Tyndale's New Testament as Lutheran in its influence. Tyndale had translated the Greek word *ekklesia*, for example, as "the congregation," which is the body of Christ, rather than "the church." The English bishops saw this as heretical in that the word *congregation* implied equality of the gathering of believers. They believed that this idea was Lutheran and denied the church's authority. Copies of the book were publicly burned at Saint Paul's Cathedral in 1526. In May 1527, church authorities ordered all copies to be bought up and destroyed. But despite the ban, reprints continued to be distributed, many imported clandestinely from the Low Countries.

Tyndale, in hiding in Antwerp, continued to publish polemics from abroad in defense of the principles of the English reformation, including *The Obedience of a Christian Man* and *The Parable of the Wicked Mammon* in 1528, an exposition of the New Testament teaching that faith is more important than works. When *Wicked Mammon* began to circulate in England, the church, viewing it as containing Lutheran heresies, moved to suppress it. Those who were found with it were arrested and severely punished. *Wicked Mammon*, like the New Testament translation, was widely read, nevertheless, and continued to be influential, even years later when it was still prohibited.

The English ambassador to the Low Countries was instructed to demand that the regent extradite Tyndale and his assistant, William Roye, to England, but they could not be found. In 1530, Tyndale further enraged King Henry VIII by publishing *The Practice of Prelates*, which condemned the king's divorce. In May 1535, Tyndale, working in Antwerp on his translation of the Old Testament, was arrested as the result of a plot masterminded by English authorities. He was imprisoned in Vilvoorde Castle near Brussels, charged with Lutheran heresy and disagreeing with the Holy Roman Emperor. Tyndale was put on trial, formally condemned as a heretic, degraded from the priesthood, and handed over to the secular authorities for punishment. In early October 1536, he was strangled at the stake, and his body was burned with copies of his Bible translation. His last words were "Lord, open the king of England's eyes."

At the time of Tyndale's death, about 50,000 copies of his Bible translations in seven editions were in circulation in England. A small portion of Tyndale's translation was included in a complete English Bible published illegally in Germany by his colleague Miles Coverdale. In 1537, Matthew's Bible appeared in England under the pseudonym John Matthew. Its editor, John Rogers, was a Catholic priest who converted to Protestantism and Tyndale's friend. Two-thirds of Matthew's Bible contained Tyndale's translations.

Matthew's Bible was the first Bible in English to be licensed by the government. Despite its inclusion of Tyndale's translations, it was approved by Henry VIII. His break with the Catholic Church had been completed by the Act of Supremacy in 1534, which established the Church of England. Tyndale's and Coverdale's translations were also included in Henry VIII's Great Bible of 1539, which was declared the official Bible of the Church of England.

In 1546, the Catholic Church's Council of Trent said that the Latin Vulgate of Saint Jerome was the sole canonical text of the Bible. Catholics were forbidden to read any translation, such as Tyndale's, without special permission of the pope or the Inquisition. This restriction remained in effect until the late 18th century.

During the reign of the Catholic queen Mary I in England from 1553 to 1558, the ban on Protestant Bibles was reinstated. In 1555, a royal proclamation commanded "that no manner of persons presume to bring into this realm any manuscripts, books, papers . . . in the name of Martin Luther, John Calvin, Miles Coverdale, Erasmus, Tyndale . . . or any like books containing false doctrines against the Catholic faith."

The committee assembled in 1604 by King James I to prepare the Authorized Version of the Bible—often acclaimed as the greatest work ever produced by a committee and ranked in English literature with the work of Shakespeare—used as its basis Tyndale's work. Nine-tenths of the Authorized Version's New Testament is Tyndale's. Many of its finest passages were taken unchanged, though unacknowledged, from Tyndale's translations.

The tragedy of Tyndale's execution at the age of 42 is compounded by the knowledge that he was cut down before having completed his life's work. Tyndale was unable to go on to translate the poetic books and prophecies of the Old Testament or revise again his New Testament translation. As his biographer Daniell laments, it is as though Shakespeare had died halfway through his life, before his greatest tragedies had been written.

In 2000, Tyndale's New Testament was given its first complete reprint after more than 400 years by the British Library in a pocket-sized edition that mirrors the original.

FURTHER READING

Daniell, David. *Let There Be Light: William Tyndale and the Making of the English Bible.* London: British Library, 1994.
———. *William Tyndale. A Biography.* New Haven, Conn.: Yale University Press, 1994.
Haight, Anne Lyon. *Banned Books: 387 B.C. to 1978 A.D.* Updated and enlarged by Chandler B. Grannis. New York: R. R. Bowker, 1978.

NINETY-FIVE THESES

Author: Martin Luther
Original date and place of publication: 1517, Switzerland
Literary form: Theological tract

SUMMARY

Martin Luther, a German monk of the Augustinian order, was the founder of the Protestant Reformation in Europe. He was a doctor of divinity and town preacher of Wittenberg, where he taught theology at the university. A visit to Rome had convinced him of the decadence and corruption of the Catholic pope and clergy. In 1516, he began to question the efficacy of indulgences in a series of sermons.

In 16th-century Roman Catholic doctrine, the pope could transfer superfluous merit accumulated by Christ, the Virgin Mary, or the saints to an individual sinner in order to remit temporal penalties for sin later to be suffered in purgatory. Such transfers of indulgences could benefit both the living and the dead. Luther's evangelical emphasis on the complete forgiveness of sins and reconciliation with God through God's grace alone led him to question the doctrine of indulgences and the pervasive ecclesiastical practice of selling them.

The following year, Johann Tetzel, a Dominican monk, hawked indulgences to pay a debt that Albert of Brandenburg had incurred to purchase the Bishopric of Mainz and to help pay for the new basilica of Saint Peter in Rome. Luther resolved to voice his pastoral concern about the spiritual dangers of indulgences as an obstacle to the preaching of true repentance and interior conversion.

On October 15, 1517, Luther challenged his academic colleagues to debate the subject. Luther issued his challenge in the traditional manner—by posting a placard written in Latin on the door of the castle church in Wittenberg. Luther's notice contained his 95 theses on indulgences. To his surprise, the theses were circulated in Latin and German throughout Germany and within a few weeks to much of Europe, unleashing a storm of controversy that was to lead to the Protestant Reformation.

In his *Ninety-five Theses or Disputation on the Power and Efficacy of Indulgences,* Luther argued that the pope could remit only those penalties he had imposed himself and denied the pope's authority to remit sin. Luther rejected the idea that the saints had superfluous merits or that merit could be stored up for later use by others.

The pope has no control over the souls in purgatory, Luther asserted. "They preach only human doctrines who say that as soon as the money clinks into the money chest, the soul flies out of purgatory." If the pope does have such power, Luther asked, "why does not the pope empty purgatory for the sake of the holy love and the dire need of all the souls that are there if he redeems an infinite number of souls for the sake of miserable money with which to build a church?"

He branded indulgences as harmful because they gave believers a false sense of security. By implying that the payment of money could appease the wrath of God, the sale of indulgences impeded salvation by diverting charity and inducing complacency. "Christians should be taught that he who gives to the poor is better than he who receives a pardon. He who spends his money for indulgences instead of relieving want receives not the indulgence of the pope but the indignation of God." Those who believe that their salvation is assured because they have indulgence letters will face eternal damnation, "together with their teachers," who preach unchristian doctrine.

Luther objected to the church's intent to raise money for a basilica by sale of indulgences. "Why does not the pope, whose wealth is today greater than the wealth of the richest Crassus, build this one basilica of St. Peter with his own money rather than with the money of poor believers?" Luther asked. Luther believed that to repress by force the objections of the laity to the sale of indulgences, rather than resolving them reasonably, "is to expose the church and the pope to the ridicule of their enemies and to make Christians unhappy."

Luther's theses were directed toward church reform. He did not see them as an attack on the pope's authority or as the beginnings of a schism. But the church's response to Luther's proposals pushed him toward a more radical stance that led ultimately to a break with Rome and the founding of a new church.

CENSORSHIP HISTORY

At first Pope Leo X did not take serious notice of Luther's theses, viewing them instead as a reflection of the rivalry between Luther's Augustinian order and the Dominicans, who were Luther's most vociferous critics. But the theses, rapidly distributed in Germany, found active support among the peasantry and civil authorities, who objected to Rome's siphoning of local funds. The hierarchy became convinced that the abuses of indulgences should be corrected and Luther silenced.

In 1518, the pope asked Hieronymus, bishop of Ascoli, to investigate Luther's case. Luther was summoned to Rome to answer charges of heresy and contumacy, or insubordination. Frederick III, elector of Saxony, stepped in to demand that Luther's hearing be held on German soil. When the hearing before the papal legate was transferred to Augsburg, where the imperial diet (the legislative assembly) was unsympathetic to papal claims, Luther refused to retract any of his theses. In a debate in Leipzig in 1519 with the German professor Johannes Eck, Luther argued that because the authority of the pope was of human origin, rather than rooted in divine right, he could be resisted when his edicts contravened the Scriptures.

Johannes Froben of Basel had published the Ninety-five Theses in an edition with Luther's sermons. In February 1519, Froben reported that only 10 copies were left and that no book from his presses had ever sold out so quickly. Taking full advantage of the new potential of the printing press, the book had been distributed not only in Germany, but in France, Spain, Switzerland, Belgium, England, and even in Rome. The same year, the theological faculties of the Universities of Louvain and Cologne ordered copies of the theses to be burned for heresy.

The pope appointed commissions to study Luther's writings. On June 15, 1520, the pope proclaimed in the papal bull "Exsurge Domine," "Rise up O Lord and judge thy cause. A wild boar has invaded thy vineyard." The bull pronounced 41 errors of Luther as "heretical, or scandalous, or false, or offensive to pious ears, or seductive of simple minds, or repugnant to Catholic truth, respectively." In his preface the pope wrote, "Our pastoral office can no longer tolerate the pestiferous virus of the following forty-one errors. . . . The books of Martin Luther which contain these errors are to be examined and burned. . . . Now therefore we give Martin sixty days in which to submit." It was forbidden to print, distribute, read, possess, or quote any of Luther's books, tracts, or sermons.

Then in August, October, and November of 1520, Luther published three revolutionary tracts that dramatically raised the stakes of his disagreement with the church: ADDRESS TO THE CHRISTIAN NOBILITY OF THE GERMAN NATION, which attacked the claim of papal authority over secular rulers; THE BABYLONIAN CAPTIVITY OF THE CHURCH, which rejected the priesthood and the sacraments; *The Freedom of Christian Man*, which reiterated his doctrine of justification by faith alone. The first edition of 4,000 copies of the *Address* sold out within a week. Riding the crest of a wave of public support, Luther in his sermons, debates, and writings proposed a radical alternative to the Catholic Church.

On October 10, the papal bull reached Luther in Germany. Luther wrote a stinging reply to the bull: *Against the Execrable Bull of Antichrist.* "They say that some articles are heretical, some erroneous, some scandalous, some offensive," Luther wrote. "The implication is that those which are heretical are not erroneous, those which are erroneous are not scandalous, and those which are scandalous are not offensive." Calling on the pope to "renounce your diabolical blasphemy and audacious impiety," he concluded, "It is better that I should die a thousand times than that I should retract one syllable of the condemned articles."

Luther's books were burned in Louvain and Liège during October and the following month in Cologne and Mainz. On December 10, 1520, Luther and his followers publicly burned the papal bull at Wittenberg, along with copies of canon law and the papal constitutions. "Since they have burned my books, I burn theirs," Luther said. In January 1521, the pope issued a new bull, "Decet Romanum Pontificum," which affirmed the excommunication of Luther and his followers and the burning of his works.

Luther's enormous popularity, bolstered by his appeal to German nationalist objections to Roman intervention in their affairs, saved him from the fate of other heretics. Elector Frederick III of Saxony, Luther's temporal ruler, refused to give him over for trial to Rome. The only power in Europe capable of suppressing Luther was the Holy Roman Emperor Charles V, a devout Catholic determined to root out the heresy.

On April 18, 1521, Luther was called before the Diet of Worms. Before the emperor and the assembled princes of the empire he refused to recant or disown his writings. "Should I recant at this point," he said, "I would open the door to more tyranny and impiety, and it will be all the worse should it appear that I had done so at the instance of the Holy Roman Empire." He continued, "Unless I am convicted by Scripture and plain reason—I do not accept the authority of popes and councils, for they have contradicted each other—my conscience is captive to the Word of God."

On May 26, 1521, Charles V decreed in the Edict of Worms that Luther was "a limb cut off from the Church of God, an obstinate schismatic and manifest heretic. . . . [N]o one is to harbor him. His followers are also to be condemned. His books are to be eradicated from the memory of man." The edict included a Law of Printing, which prohibited printing, sale, possession, reading, or copying Luther's work or any future works he might produce.

Though the emperor had persuaded most of the princes of Germany to sign the condemnation, few strongly supported it. Though the edict called for Luther's arrest, his friends were able to harbor him at the castle in Wartburg of Elector Frederick III of Saxony. There he translated the New Testament into German and began a 10-year project to translate the entire Bible. He returned to Wittenberg in March 1522 at considerable risk and spent the rest of his life spreading his new gospel.

Censorship of Luther's writing was pervasive throughout Europe. His works and those of his disciples were destroyed and banned in England,

France, Spain, and the Netherlands. In 1524, the Diet of Nürnberg declared that "each prince in his own territory should enforce the Edict of Worms in so far as he might be able." As the edict implied, it could not be enforced in most of northern Germany. Cities in southern Germany and elsewhere in northern Europe joined the Lutheran reform. "Lutheran books are for sale in the marketplace immediately beneath the edicts of the Emperor and the Pope who declare them to be prohibited." a contemporary commented.

In 1555, Charles V signed the Peace of Augsburg, giving up further attempts to impose Catholicism on the Protestant princes. The peace allowed each prince to choose the religion of his state and declared that people could not be prevented from migrating to another region to practice their own religion. Lutheranism had taken hold.

Luther's works remained on the Vatican's Index of Forbidden Books until 1930. They were still prohibited, however, according to the church's canon law barring Catholics under penalty of mortal sin from reading books "which propound or defend heresy or schism."

FURTHER READING

Bainton, Roland H. *Here I Stand: The Life of Martin Luther.* New York: Penguin, 1995.

Bokenkotter, Thomas S. *A Concise History of the Catholic Church.* Garden City, N.Y.: Doubleday, 1977.

Christie-Murray, David. *A History of Heresy.* Oxford: Oxford University Press, 1989.

Haight, Anne Lyon. *Banned Books: 387 B.C. to 1978 A.D.* Updated and enlarged by Chandler B. Grannis. New York: R. R. Bowker, 1978.

Putnam, George Haven. *The Censorship of the Church of Rome.* Vol. 1. New York: G. P. Putnam's Sons, 1906–07.

Spitz, Lewis W., ed. *The Protestant Reformation.* Englewood Cliffs, N.J.: Prentice Hall, 1966.

Wilcox, Donald J. *In Search of God and Self: Renaissance and Reformation Thought.* Boston: Houghton Mifflin, 1975.

Zagorin, Perez. *How the Idea of Religious Toleration Came to the West.* Princeton, N.J.: Princeton University Press, 2003.

OF THE VANITIE AND UNCERTAINTIE OF ARTES AND SCIENCES

Author: Henricus Cornelius Agrippa
Original date and place of publication: 1530, Belgium
Literary form: Theological treatise

SUMMARY

Of the Vanitie and Uncertaintie of Artes and Sciences is the most significant work of German scholar Henricus Cornelius Agrippa, best known for his earlier writings on the occult sciences. His treatise on magic, *De occulta philosophia*, written in 1510 but not published until two decades later, studied occult traditions found in long-neglected ancient writings. Agrippa contended that the metaphysical Hermetic writings on magic, astrology, and alchemy and the esoteric system of Scripture interpretation found in the writings of the Kabbalah provided new insights into the meaning of Biblical texts. His aim in *De occulta* was to redeem the sacred tradition of magic, purging it of dangerous and superstitious elements.

Of the Vanitie and Uncertaintie of Artes and Sciences (*De incertitudine et vanitate scientarum declamatio inuectiua*), a satire on the state of religion, morals, and society, appeared to disavow his own earlier studies on the occult. He attacked the occult sciences and their authorities, appealing to the Bible and the grace of God as the only real source of truth. He stressed the superiority of the Christian gospel to human learning, denying the power of reason to know reality.

Of the Vanitie was also a bitter denunciation of ecclesiastical abuses in contemporary society—the corruption of monks, the intrusion of pagan customs into worship, and the worldliness and immorality of the papacy. Agrippa was particularly critical of the papacy as having excessive power over the clergy and faithful and temporal affairs outside the spiritual realm. Though he regarded the basic power and authority of the pope as legitimate, because it came from God, Agrippa recognized papal jurisdiction only when it did not conflict with Scripture.

He regarded the claim that the pope can release souls from purgatory as heretical and implied that the pope could err. Yet he believed it was dangerous and unwise to oppose the pope, at the risk of martyrdom as a heretic, "just as Jerome Savanarola, theologian of the Order of Preachers and also a prophetic man, was formerly burned at Florence."

Agrippa also argued that the path to God and the ultimate good of man was found neither in pursuit of knowledge nor by participating in external acts of worship. "Those carnal and external ceremonies are unable to profit men with God, to whom nothing is acceptable except faith in Jesus Christ, with ardent imitation of Him in charity, and firm hope of salvation and reward. . . . The path to God and the ultimate good of man is not found in knowledge, but in a good life."

CENSORSHIP HISTORY

Agrippa was a Catholic allied with the humanists and reformers in Germany, France, and Italy who pressed for changes in what they regarded as a corrupt church. Though he was hostile to the Catholic conservatives who dominated the theology faculty of the Sorbonne in Paris, he was not fully associated with the Protestant reformers who moved to break away from the Catholic Church. Nevertheless, the view that Agrippa was a covert supporter of the Protestant Reformation appeared in many attacks on his writings.

Of the Vanitie was published in Latin in Antwerp, Belgium, by imperial license, and in Paris and Cologne in 1530. The following year, book one of *De occulta* appeared in the same cities. In 1531, the theological faculty of the University of Louvain denounced and banned *Of the Vanitie* as scandalous, impious, and heretical. Agrippa, instead of recanting the charges against him, wrote two defenses, a *Querela* attacking the "theosophists" who charged him, and an *Apologia*, in which he refuted them point by point. "I have replied to the Louvain slanders modestly, of course, but not without salt and vinegar and even mustard," he wrote.

That same year, the theology faculty of the Sorbonne prohibited the French edition and charged it with favoring Lutheran doctrine and being "against the worship of images, temples, feasts, and ceremonies of the church and . . . also blasphemous against the writers of the holy canon; and so must be publicly burned. . . ."

In 1532, publication of the second part of *De occulta* was under way in Cologne, but the Dominican inquisitor of Ulm denounced Agrippa's books as suspect of heresy and unfit to be printed. The city council forced the printer to suspend work and impounded the completed parts. Agrippa wrote a defense of his book in a long letter to the city council denouncing the theology faculty at Cologne for having impeded publication of the book. In 1533, the attention of the Inquisition in Rome was drawn to *De occulta* and book one was banned on charges of magic and conjury.

Of the Vanitie was reprinted and translated in many editions in the 16th and 17th centuries. It was an important source for the skeptical thought of Michel de Montaigne's ESSAYS. Montaigne drew from Agrippa's work extensive passages of his influential philosophical essay, "Apology for Raymond Sebond," composed in 1576, in which he argued against the impotence and vanity of presumptuous human reason.

FURTHER READING

Nauert, Charles G., Jr. *Agrippa and the Crisis of Renaissance Thought*. Urbana: University of Illinois Press, 1965.

OLIVER TWIST

Author: Charles Dickens
Original date and place of publication: 1838, United Kingdom
Literary form: Novel

SUMMARY

The publication of *Oliver Twist*, Dickens's second novel, the story of an orphan who falls into the hands of a group of thieves in the slums of London, firmly established the literary eminence of its 25-year-old author. Within a few years, Dickens was the most popular and widely read writer of his time. Beginning in 1837, *Oliver Twist* appeared in monthly installments in a London magazine. The following year it was published in three volumes in book form. *Oliver Twist* offers the first glimpse of the genius of Dickens that would reach full flower in his later novels. It is among the most powerful works of fiction portraying the misery of daily life for the urban poor and the uncaring bureaucracies that sustain an oppressive system.

When Dickens was 12, his father was taken to debtors' prison. While the rest of the family accompanied his father to the workhouse, Dickens was sent to paste labels on bottles in a blacking factory. This experience left him with a bitter and passionate opposition to child labor and inhumane treatment of the poor and is reflected in the biting sarcasm that animates the early chapters of *Oliver Twist*.

When Oliver's destitute mother, found lying in the street, dies giving birth to him in a nearby workhouse, the infant becomes the ward of the local parish overseers. He is dispatched to a parish institution where he and other orphans are brought up under cruel conditions, "without the inconvenience of too much food or too much clothing."

At age nine, Oliver is returned to the workhouse by Mr. Bumble, the unctuous parish beadle. The workhouse boys are fed three meals of thin gruel a day, with an onion twice a week and half a roll on Sunday. "Please, sir, I want some more," Oliver says. In punishment for the "impious and profane offence of asking for more," Oliver is ordered into instant solitary confinement.

He is then apprenticed by Mr. Bumble to the undertaker, Mr. Sowerberry, where he lives and works in mean circumstances. After fighting with his bullying coworker, Noah, Oliver is beaten and runs away to London. There he unwittingly falls into the hands of Fagin, the nefarious leader of a gang of thieves, whose other chief members are the burglar Bill Sikes, Sikes's companion, Nancy and the pickpocket known as the Artful Dodger. When the Dodger picks the pocket of an elderly gentleman, Oliver is caught and brought to the police magistrate. Injured and ill, Oliver is rescued by the benevolent Mr. Brownlow, who takes him into his household. But Nancy finds Oliver and brings him back to the gang. When Oliver is made to accompany Sikes on a burgling expedition and is shot and wounded, he comes into the hands of Mrs. Maylie and her protégée, Rose, who treat him kindly.

A sinister person named Monks, who is known to Fagin, appears to have a special interest in Oliver. Nancy, who overhears a conversation between Fagin and Monks, goes to Rose and reveals to her that Monks is Oliver's older half brother, knows the secret of Oliver's parentage, and wishes all proof of it destroyed. When Nancy's betrayal is discovered by the gang, she is brutally murdered by Sikes.

While trying to escape capture by a mob, Sikes accidentally hangs himself. Fagin is arrested and sentenced to execution. Monks confesses that he pursued Oliver's ruin so that he could retain the whole of his late father's property. Upon the death of his mother, Oliver was to have inherited the estate, as long as he had in his minority never stained the good name of his family. Fagin had received a reward from Monks for turning Oliver into a thief. It turns out that Rose is the sister of Oliver's late mother. In the end Oliver is adopted by Mr. Brownlow. Mr. Bumble ends his career as a pauper in the very same workhouse over which he formerly ruled.

In Dickens's preface to the third edition of the novel, he wrote, "I wished to show, in little Oliver, the principle of Good surviving through every adverse circumstance and triumphing at last." All ends happily in *Oliver Twist*, yet the haunting memory of the evils that beset Oliver in the poorhouses and streets of London remains.

CENSORSHIP HISTORY

"The walls and ceiling of the room were perfectly black with age and dirt. . . . Some sausages were cooking; and standing over them, with a toasting fork in this hand, was a very old shriveled Jew, whose villainous-looking and repulsive face was obscured by a quantity of matted red hair." The sinister and evil Fagin is introduced to readers of *Oliver Twist* with an archetypal anti-Semitic image dating back many centuries in Western culture, that of the Satanic and fiendish Jew. Dickens's caricature of Fagin has been the subject of protest and debate since the time of the novel's publication.

Dickens shaped the character of Fagin, referred to as "the Jew" hundreds of times throughout the novel, according to a traditional pattern commonly employed to portray Jews in literature and on the stage in the 19th century. Fagin's red hair and beard were commonly associated with ancient images of the devil. He has a hooked nose, shuffling gait, a long gabardine coat, and broad-brimmed hat and is a dishonest dealer in secondhand clothes and trinkets. Fagin is portrayed, like Satan, as serpentlike, gliding stealthily along, "creeping beneath the shelter of the walls and doorways . . . like some loathsome reptile, engendered in the slime and darkness through which he moved. . . ."

Though literary critics believe that Dickens did not intend to defame or injure Jews in his creation of the character of Fagin, Dickens was a product of the anti-Semitic culture of his time. Reflected in laws, public discourse, literature, and popular entertainment, prejudice against Jews was a part of the early Victorian heritage. In the 1830s, Jews were barred from owning stores within the city of London, could not work as attorneys, receive a university degree, or sit in Parliament. Because they were confined to certain occupations, the majority of England's 20,000 to 30,000 Jews made their living by buying and selling old clothes, peddling, and moneylending.

In a letter to a Jewish woman who had protested the stereotypical treatment of Fagin, Dickens wrote, "Fagin is a Jew because it unfortunately was true, of the time to which the story refers, that class of criminal almost invariably was a Jew." The 1830 trial of Ikey Solomons, a Jewish fence, who, like Fagin, dealt in stolen jewelry, clothing, and fabrics, had been extensively publicized and was one of the influences on Dickens's portrayal of Fagin.

The years 1830 to 1860 saw a rise in the status of Jews in England. Legal barriers and commercial restrictions were removed, Jews were elected to posts in local and national government, and many became socially prominent. Social attitudes also changed, reflected in Dickens's increased awareness of and sensitivity to anti-Semitism in the years that followed the initial publication of *Oliver Twist*. "I know of no reason the Jews can have for regarding me as inimical to them," Dickens wrote in 1854.

In 1867–68, a new edition of Dickens's works was published. Dickens revised the text of *Oliver Twist*, making hundreds of changes, most in relation to Fagin. He eliminated the majority of the references to Fagin as "the Jew," either cutting them or replacing them with "Fagin" or "he." Nevertheless, "Fagin remains 'the Jew,'" literary critic Irving Howe commented, "and whoever wants to confront this novel honestly must confront the substratum of feeling that becomes visible through Dickens's obsessive repetition of 'the Jew.'" A critical reading of the novel can lead to a better understanding of the anti-Semitic stereotypes that were part of the popular culture of early 19th-century England. "There is nothing to 'do' [about Fagin]," wrote Howe, "but confront the historical realities of our culture, and all that it has thrown up from its unsavory depths."

In 1949, a group of Jewish parents in Brooklyn, New York, protested that the assignment of *Oliver Twist* in senior high school literature classes violated the rights of their children to receive an education free of religious bias. Citing the characterization of Fagin in *Oliver Twist* and Shylock in William Shakespeare's play *The Merchant of Venice*, they sued the New York City Board of Education. They asked that both texts be banned from New York City public schools "because they tend to engender hatred of the Jew as a person and as a race."

In *Rosenberg v. Board of Education of City of New York*, the Kings County Supreme Court decided that the two works should not be banned from New York City schools, libraries, or classrooms, declaring that the Board of Education "acted in good faith without malice or prejudice and in the best interests of the school system entrusted to their care and control, and, therefore, that no substantial reason exists which compels the suppression of the two books under consideration."

In denying the plaintiffs' bid to ban the books, the presiding judge stated, "Except where a book has been maliciously written for the apparent purpose of fomenting a bigoted and intolerant hatred against a particular racial or religious group, public interest in a free and democratic society does not warrant or encourage the suppression of any book at the whim of any unduly sensitive person or group of person, merely because a character described in such book as belonging to a particular race or religion is portrayed in a derogatory or offensive manner." Removal of the books "will contribute nothing toward the diminution of anti-religious feeling," the court said.

FURTHER READING

Dickens, Charles. *Oliver Twist*. Introduction by Irving Howe. New York: Bantam Books, 1982.

Doyle, Robert P. *Banned Books: 2004 Resource Guide*. Chicago: American Library Association, 2004.

Kaplan, Fred, ed. *Oliver Twist: A Norton Critical Edition*. New York: W. W. Norton, 1993.

Veidmanis, Gladys. "Reflections on 'the Shylock Problem.'" In *Censored Books: Critical Viewpoints*, edited by Nicholas J. Karolides, Lee Burress, and John M. Kean, 370–378. Metuchen, N.J.: Scarecrow Press, 1993.

ON CIVIL LORDSHIP

Author: John Wycliffe
Original date and place of publication: 1376, England
Literary form: Theological treatise

SUMMARY

The religious scholar and reformer John Wycliffe, who studied and taught theology at Oxford, was the most eminent English heretic to challenge the Catholic Church before the 16th-century Protestant Reformation. In his Latin treatise *On Civil Lordship*, read to his students at Oxford in 1376, in his sermons in English in Oxford and London, and through the preaching of the itinerant "poor priests" who spread his views, he attacked orthodox church doctrines. He claimed that the Scriptures rather than the church were the supreme authority on matters of faith.

Going beyond criticism of the abuses of the church hierarchy, Wycliffe came to the radical conclusion that the church was incapable of reforming itself and must be brought under secular supervision by the king, as God's vicar on Earth.

He transferred salvation from the agency of the church to the individual. "For each man that shall be damned shall be damned by his own guilt," he wrote, "and each man that is saved shall be saved by his own merit." He believed that the popes of the period were Antichrists and that the pope and the hierarchy, having abdicated their rights to lead the church by their displays of greed, cruelty, and lust for power, should not be obeyed. Power within the church should be a function of grace rather than of entitlement.

Anticipating fundamental convictions of the Protestant Reformation, Wycliffe opposed the sale of indulgences, image worship, auricular confession, and the cult of saints, relics, and pilgrimages. He also refused to acknowledge the doctrine of transubstantiation, by which the bread and wine of the Eucharist are held to be transformed into the Body and Blood of Christ. He developed the doctrine of the priesthood of all elected believers, proposing that in certain circumstances, laymen could conduct the sacrament of the Eucharist. He also advocated the translation of the Bible into English on the theory that Christians could read and understand Scripture without intervention by the clergy. His followers were the first to translate the Latin Vulgate Bible into English.

CENSORSHIP HISTORY

The church hierarchy viewed Wycliffe's deviations from orthodoxy as a serious danger. For the first time, a learned church scholar of brilliant intellect had questioned the church's authority and, further, had endeavored to spread his heretical ideas among ordinary people.

In 1377, Pope Gregory XI issued five bulls attacking Wycliffe's doctrines as expressed in *On Civil Lordship,* condemning him for "heretical pravity, tending to weaken and overthrow the status of the whole church, and even the secular government." Gregory XI commanded Wycliffe's prosecution by secular authorities as a heretic. Despite the hostility of the archbishop of Canterbury and the bishop of London, Wycliffe was protected by John of Gaunt, the duke of Lancaster, one of the most influential nobles in England and a supporter of Wycliffe's movement.

In 1381, a council at Oxford pronounced eight of Wycliffe's theses as unorthodox and 14 as heretical and prohibited him from further lecturing or preaching. The following year, a council at Blackfriars repeated the condemnation, and in 1383, his disciples, known as the Lollards, were barred from Oxford. Though he was condemned as a heretic and the Lollards were persecuted, Wycliffe was not disturbed in his retirement and died peacefully in his rectory in 1384.

By 1386, the spread of Lollardy provoked Parliament to outlaw heretical writings and to make their teaching a crime, punishable by forfeiture of properties and imprisonment. In 1401 under the orthodox Henry IV, burning at the stake became the legal penalty for heresy. Parliament passed the act known as De Haeretico Comburendo ("On the Desirability of Burning Heretics"). The act recommended that convicted heretics be burned in a prominent place so "that such punishment may strike fear to the minds of others." Wycliffe's writings were further proscribed in 1408 by the Convocation of Canterbury. Lollards were ruthlessly persecuted, hanged, or burned at the stake, and the heresy was extirpated from England.

The marriage of Richard II to Anne of Bohemia in 1382 opened a channel for the transmission of Wycliffe's ideas when many Bohemians visited England during the excitement caused by Wycliffe's controversies. These Bohemians carried his writings back to Prague, where they found fertile ground through the efforts of Wycliffe's disciple, Jan Hus. Church and secular authorities moved to stem the heresy. In 1403, the University of Prague formally condemned 45 articles extracted from Wycliffe's writing.

A papal bull ordering the surrender of Wycliffe's works was carried out in 1409 under the instructions of Archbishop Sbynko of Prague. Two hundred volumes of Wycliffe's writings were burned in the palace courtyard. In 1413, the council of Rome pronounced an authoritative condemnation of Wycliffe. Two years later a church council at Constance, Germany, proclaimed Wycliffe a heresiarch, or arch-heretic, condemning him on 260 different counts, and ordered his bones exhumed and removed from sacred ground. Wycliffe's bones were burned and his ashes thrown into a running stream. Hus, whose treatise DE ECCLESIA reflected Wycliffe's heresies, was burned at the stake upon order of the council on July 6, 1415.

FURTHER READING

Christie-Murray, David. *A History of Heresy*. Oxford: Oxford University Press, 1989.

Dunham, Barrows. *Heroes and Heretics*. New York: Alfred A. Knopf, 1964.

Green, Jonathon. *The Encyclopedia of Censorship*. New York: Facts On File, 1990.

Haight, Anne Lyon. *Banned Books: 387 BC to 1978 AD*. Updated and enlarged by Chandler B. Grannis. New York: R. R. Bowker, 1978.

Lea, Henry Charles. *History of the Inquisition of the Middle Ages*. Vol. 2. New York: Russell and Russell, 1955.

Levy, Leonard W. *Blasphemy: Verbal Offense Against the Sacred, from Moses to Salman Rushdie*. New York: Alfred A. Knopf, 1993.

ON JUSTICE IN THE REVOLUTION AND IN THE CHURCH

Author: Pierre-Joseph Proudhon
Original date and place of publication: 1858, France
Literary form: Political theory

SUMMARY

The French social theorist, anarchist philosopher, and reformer Pierre-Joseph Proudhon achieved notoriety with a series of incendiary pamphlets and books in which he condemned the abuses of private property and the absolutism of church and state. In his first notable work, *What Is Property?*—described by Karl Marx as "the first decisive, vigorous, and scientific examination of property"—Proudhon claimed that property was not a natural right and that its attributes of profit, rent, and interest represented exploitation of labor and a denial of the fundamental principles of justice and equality. Workers had the right to own the products of their labor, as well as houses, land for subsistence, and the tools of trade, Proudhon maintained, but the means of production should be held in common. His answer to the question, "What is property?"—"Property is theft"—became the most famous revolutionary phrase of the 19th century.

The key to Proudhon's revolutionary thought was his hostility to the state. He proposed to replace government by a system of voluntary contracts, or associations between free individuals. According to his theory of "mutualism," small, loosely federated groups would bargain with one another over economic and political matters within the framework of a consensus on fundamental principles. Proudhon rejected the use of force to impose any system, however, hoping that ethical progress would eventually make government unnecessary. He believed that the victory of the proletariat, which was to be brought about gradually through the establishment of a system of free credit, would inaugurate a just order of mutuality and cooperation.

Though he is most often remembered today for his claim that property is theft, Proudhon was an uncommonly prolific writer, with 20,000 published pages of writing to his credit and nearly 2,000 more pages left in unpublished manuscripts. Among his most important books were *System of Economic Contradictions; or the Philosophy of Poverty*, published in 1846, and his three-volume masterwork, *On Justice in the Revolution and in the Church*, published in 1858 and enlarged and revised in 1860.

From his early years, Proudhon, as an anarchic individualist, was hostile to conventional organized religion. Under the rule of Emperor Napoléon III, who expanded his powers after an 1852 coup d'état, Proudhon became more intensely anticlerical, convinced that the Catholic clergy were allied with the government to suppress liberty and that the church was a reactionary force. In *On Justice*, Proudhon describes justice as "the central star which governs society . . . the principal and regulator of all transactions." The Catholic Church and the state, as absolutist institutions, are the enemies of justice, as the balance between interests of the individual and those of the community is upset by centralization of government and authority.

Proudhon recognizes no external authority as the appropriate source of societal norms. The rules guiding society must stem from the internal, rational faculties of individuals. Justice is *"Logos,"* he writes, "the common soul of humanity, incarnate in each one of us." Proudhon repudiates any absolute and inflexible system of thought based on a priori reasoning as a negation of morality. Because the church is inaccessible to rational faculties, is based on dogmatic ideas and suppresses individuality, it is immoral. The Christian doctrines of the fall of man, Original Sin, and the authority of revelation are stultifying to conscience and therefore to justice. Proudhon sees the annihilation of the individual conscience as "the fatal stumbling block of every church and every religion."

Proudhon rejects the absolute idea of God as all-powerful and infinite. He neither affirms nor denies the existence of God, but believes that theology should be supplanted by secular philosophy and that the religious spirit, or transcendental justice, should be replaced by a human sense of justice, or immanent justice. Religion's ultimate weapon is intimidation, Proudhon asserts. By means of its "dogmas, its mysteries, its sacraments, its discipline, its terror, its promises," religion frightens the socially inferior into staying in their place. The moral sense can develop only by "the cessation of myth, by the return of the soul to itself. . . [and by] the end of the reign of God." For progress to occur, individual reason must replace myth, miracles, and mystery.

CENSORSHIP HISTORY

Proudhon found it difficult to find a publisher for his important pamphlet, *What Is Property?*, because it was a provocative work by an unknown author. It was published, unannounced and unadvertised, only after he agreed to cover the cost of the printing and to sell copies to his friends and acquaintances at his own risk. He escaped public prosecution, recommended by the law officers of the crown, when the minister of justice, impressed with the quality of Proudhon's mind, sent the book to the Academy of Moral Sciences for evaluation. The academy asked one of its distinguished fellows, the economist Adolfe Blanqui, brother of the militant communist Auguste Blanqui, to report on the book. He recommended to the academy that, despite some inflammatory language, its scientific and scholarly character was undeniable and worthy of respect and it should not be banned.

The government's tolerance did not extend, however, to Proudhon's next revolutionary pamphlet, *Warning to the Proprietors*, published in 1842. The police raided his printer and confiscated 500 copies of the pamphlet by order of the public prosecutor in Besançon, France. Proudhon was summoned to appear before the Doubs assize court to answer to nine charges. The public prosecutor contracted the list of charges to four: attack on the constitutional right of property, incitement of hatred of government, incitement to hatred of several classes of citizens, and offense to religion. Proudhon was acquitted of all charges when the jury returning the verdict admitted that his ideas were too difficult to understand. "It is impossible to be sure that he is guilty and we cannot condemn at random," the jury stated.

In 1848, Proudhon founded a newspaper, *Representative of the People*, to propagate his ideas. When it was suppressed by the government, he started another newspaper, *The People*. He was charged with sedition for denouncing the newly elected president Louis-Napoléon Bonaparte (later to become emperor) for "conspiring to enslave the people" and escaped to Belgium.

He returned secretly to France to liquidate the people's bank he had founded and continued to edit his newspaper in hiding. He was finally caught and spent three years in prison, where he continued to write. He founded *The Voice of the People*, which was repeatedly suspended and finally prohibited.

When *On Justice in the Revolution and in the Church* appeared in April 1858 under the Catholic empire of Napoléon III and the Empress Eugénie, it immediately became a best seller, selling thousands of copies within a few days. In November 1857, while the book was in press, the police commissioner of the Interior Ministry's press licensing department had visited its printer and publisher and demanded to know the contents of the book Proudhon was about to publish. The publisher did not cooperate, and as there was no statute allowing for prepublication censorship, publication went forward.

Within five days of its publication, however, the government ordered its seizure and the remaining stock was confiscated. Proudhon was put on trial and charged with offenses against church and state. His derogatory criticism of the Catholic Church and its authoritarian position in French society was perceived as an outrage against public and religious morality and a threat to the status quo. Proudhon was convicted and received the maximum sentence—a fine of 4,000 francs and three years in prison.

Proudhon appealed his conviction but while awaiting the appeals court's decision, took refuge in Brussels, where his book was printed. The appeals court confirmed his sentence, and he was later informed that in the future, no work of his would be allowed into France. Proudhon remained in exile in Belgium for four years. When the French government extended an amnesty in 1859 to all those convicted under the press laws, only one person was excluded by name—Proudhon. However, the emperor later pardoned him, and he returned to France in 1862, three years before his death. Because of his prosecution for *On Justice*, he met with great difficulty finding French firms to publish his subsequent books. Though two publishers offered to guarantee him large sums if he would moderate his writings to avoid further prosecution, he refused, despite his poverty.

During Proudhon's lifetime, the Catholic Church placed all of his writing on the Index of Forbidden Books in the most severe category of *opera omnia*, or all works condemned; his works remained proscribed through the last edition of the Index.

In the 1860s, groups of French working-class men began to found mutual credit and other cooperative movements based on Proudhon's ideas. The great mass of Proudhon's writing was an influential legacy to later political theorists in many countries, notably the syndicalists and anarchic socialists in the later 19th century in France, Italy, and Spain.

FURTHER READING

Hall, Constance Margaret. *The Sociology of Pierre Joseph Proudhon (1809–65)*. New York: Philosophical Library, 1971.

Hoffman, Robert L. *The Social and Political Theory of P.-J. Proudhon*. Urbana: University of Illinois Press, 1972.

Hyams, Edward. *Pierre-Joseph Proudhon: His Revolutionary Life, Mind and Works*. New York: Taplinger Publishing, 1979.

ON MONARCHY

Author: Dante Alighieri
Original dates and place of publication: 1310–13, Italy
Literary form: Political treatise

SUMMARY

The Florentine poet Dante Alighieri—author of *The Divine Comedy*, among the greatest literary classics—argued in *On Monarchy*, his treatise on political philosophy, against papal claims of control over secular authority. Dante claimed that the emperor ruled by divine right, just as the pope did, and that the emperor was supreme in secular matters, while the pope oversaw the spiritual realm.

Dante saw the emperor and the pope as dual guardians of the welfare of society, each dependent on God for their separate powers. He challenged the papal analogy that spiritual power is the Sun and secular power is the Moon, receiving its light from the Sun and thus subordinate to it. He believed that lack of cooperation between the two leaders prevented the achievement of peace and justice in his time, in which politics was dominated by the struggle for domination between the empire and the papacy.

The cause of conflict was the papacy's claim to temporal power, which it justified by a document known as the Donation of Constantine, later proven to be an eighth-century forgery. The document maintained that in the year 312, when Emperor Constantine I shifted the seat of his empire to Constantinople, he transferred to Pope Sylvester I, the bishop of Rome, political dominion over Italy and the Western Roman Empire. The papacy's desire for temporal power, Dante believed, was based on spurious premises and weakened both civil government and the church's mission of spiritual guidance.

Two warring political parties, the Guelphs and Ghibellines, had arisen in Italy in the 12th century, their party lines originally drawn over the dispute between the papacy and the emperor. The Guelph party had split into two factions, the White and the Black. Dante was a passionate supporter of the White Guelphs and the return of imperial rule to Italy. After the victory of the Black Guelphs, assisted by Pope Boniface VIII, Dante was dispossessed and banished from Florence in 1302 and sentenced to be burned alive if he ever returned. In exile he served various princes but supported Emperor Henry VII as the potential savior of Italy.

Dante's position in the conflict is reflected in *On Monarchy*. For the well-being of the world, he believed, a single temporal government should rule. The betterment of humankind depends upon the unity of the will of its members. This is impossible unless there is one will that dominates all others. "But the human race is most one when all are united together, a state which is manifestly impossible unless humanity as a whole becomes subject to one Prince and consequently comes most into accordance with that divine intention which we showed is the good, nay, the best disposition of mankind."

If the church had received power from God, it would have been by divine or natural law, he wrote. God does not approve anything contrary to nature's intentions. "It is indisputable that nature gave not this law to the Church. . . . In the bosom of the two Testaments, wherein is embodied every divine law, I am unable to discover any command for the early or later priesthood to have care or solicitude in temporal things." Because he knew that his argument would be offensive to religious leaders, he supported his position with quotations from the Old and New Testaments, Aristotle, and the church fathers. Church traditions, he argued, while worthy of respect, were subordinate to the Scriptures.

CENSORSHIP HISTORY

Dante, as an orthodox Catholic, accepted church dogma without reservation. Although he criticized individual popes, particularly his bitter enemy, Boniface VIII, who exiled him from Florence, Dante revered the office of the pope as vicar of Christ. The church, though, had declared as dogma that the authority of kings derived from the pope, rather than directly from God. Dante was aware that his position that the Roman prince ruled by divine right would generate controversy. In Book Three of *On Monarchy*, he writes: "Since the truth about it can scarcely be brought to light without putting certain people to shame, it may give rise to anger against me. . . . But I take courage from the words of Daniel, quoted above, assuring us that the defenders of the truth are shielded by divine power. . . ."

In 1329, *On Monarchy* was publicly burned in the marketplace of Bologna by order of Pope John XXII. The pope, in the throes of a struggle with Holy Roman Emperor Louis IV, whose throne the pope claimed, feared the influence of Dante's work. More than two centuries later, *On Monarchy* was still anathema to the papacy on the same grounds. The 16th-century papacy was concerned with the threat to its temporal power and independence posed by the domination of Italy by Holy Roman Emperor Charles V. *On Monarchy* was among the books that Pope Paul IV placed on the church's first Index of Forbidden Books in 1559. The Tridentine Index of 1564, which consolidated and expanded the earlier Roman Index, ordered the excision of the passages in *On Monarchy* that argued that imperial authority derives from God rather than from the pope. The Spanish Inquisition placed *On Monarchy* on its Index of Forbidden Books in 1558 and 1612.

Although in his epic masterpiece, *The Divine Comedy*, Dante had placed corrupt popes in the eighth circle of hell and engaged in invective against Pope Boniface VIII, *The Divine Comedy* was not prohibited in Italy. The Inquisition in Portugal and Spain, however, found such sentiment in *The Divine Comedy* to be offensive. In 1581, authorities in Lisbon called in all copies for expurgation and the Spanish Index of 1612 eliminated three short passages from the poem.

On Monarchy remained on the Roman Index for 400 years, until it was finally removed in the 19th century. In 1921, Pope Benedict XV issued an encyclical in praise of Dante's works.

FURTHER READING

Burman, Edward. *The Inquisition: Hammer of Heresy.* New York: Dorset Press, 1992.

Curtis, Michael, ed. and intro. *The Great Political Theories.* Vol. 1. New York: Avon Books, 1981.

Dante. *On Monarchy and Three Political Letters.* Translated and with an introduction by Donald Nicholl. London: Weidenfeld and Nicholson, 1954.

Putnam, George Haven. *The Censorship of the Church of Rome.* Vol. 1. New York: G. P. Putnam's Sons, 1906–07.

ON THE INFINITE UNIVERSE AND WORLDS

Author: Giordano Bruno
Original date and place of publication: 1584, France
Literary form: Philosophical treatise

SUMMARY

The Italian philosopher Giordano Bruno entered the Dominican order at a young age and was expelled in 1576 at the age of 28 when he was charged with heresy. He traveled throughout Europe for 15 years, one step ahead of the censors, teaching at Toulouse, Paris, Oxford, Wittenberg, and Frankfurt. In *On the Infinite Universe and Worlds*, his major metaphysical work, published in 1584, he refuted the traditional cosmology of Aristotle and its limited conceptions of the universe. Instead, Bruno asserted that the physical universe is infinite and includes an indefinite number of worlds, each with its own sun and planets. He pictured the world as composed of individual, irreducible elements of being, called monads, governed by fixed laws of relationship.

Bruno's philosophy prefigured modern cosmic theory. He accepted Nicolaus Copernicus's hypothesis that the Sun, rather than the Earth, is the center of our world. But he went further than Copernicus in arguing that the Sun is simply one star among others. All judgments about position are relative, since there are as many possible modes of viewing the world as there are possible positions. Therefore, no one star or planet can be called the center of the universe. Human beings cannot conclude that they are unique, because the presence of life, even that of rational beings, may not be confined to Earth. There is no absolute truth, and there are no limits to the progress of knowledge.

The infinite universe is the product of a pantheistic infinite divine power or cause whose work is manifest in human beings and in all of nature. "The Divine one extols his own glory and sets forth the greatness of his sway, not in one sun, but in uncountable suns; not in one earth, but in worlds without end."

Because God's power is infinite, his creation must also be infinite. The agent would be imperfect if his works did not fulfill his power. Bruno believed that understanding of the universe as the manifestation of God would free the human spirit. "[It] opens the senses, contents the soul, enlarges the mind and brings true blessed news to man. . . . For deeply considering the Being and substance in which we are fixed, we find that there is no such thing as death, not for us alone, but for the true substance."

CENSORSHIP HISTORY

"I wish the world to possess the glorious fruits of my labor," Bruno wrote in *On the Infinite Universe and Worlds*, "to awaken the soul and open the understanding of those who are deprived of that light, which, most assuredly, is not mine own invention. Should I be in error, I do not believe I willfully go wrong."

In the view of his contemporaries, Bruno had indeed gone wrong. His assault on Aristotelian views of the universe and his construction of a "new philosophy" challenged the Scholasticism that dominated the universities. It ran counter to the beliefs held by all the ecclesiastical institutions, whether Catholic, Lutheran or Calvinist. His speculation about an endless number of celestial worlds was viewed as heretical pantheism.

In 1577, the Inquisition in Naples initiated proceedings against him, and Bruno fled Italy. In 1592, he rashly returned and, denounced by a Venetian nobleman, was delivered to the Inquisition in Venice. He was imprisoned and tried on charges of blasphemy, immoral conduct, and heresy. On May 26, 1592, the Holy Tribunal met to consider his case. Bruno told the judges: "I have ever expounded philosophically and according to the principles of Nature and by its light . . . although I may have set forth much suspicious matter occasioned by my own natural light . . . never have I taught anything directly contrary to the Catholic religion. . . ." When asked whether he believed that the Father, Son, and Holy Spirit were one in essence but distinct persons, he admitted "I have never been able to grasp the three being really Persons and have doubted it. . . ." Bruno offered to submit to all church doctrines, but he refused to abjure his philosophy.

Bruno remained in prison for months awaiting the decision of the Venetian Inquisition. Because he was regarded as a "heresiarch," an originator and leader of heresy, the chief inquisitor at the Holy Office in Rome demanded that he be delivered there for trial. He was extradicted to Rome and on February 27, 1593, was imprisoned for seven years. He was allowed neither books nor writing material, and his only visitors were officials of the Inquisition and priests sent to urge him to repent. In 1559, several cardinals interrogated him regarding heresies extracted from his books. At a final interrogation he declared he would recant nothing. In January 1660, at a meeting presided over by the pope, it was decreed that he would be burned at the stake for "many various heretical and unsound opinions." He was executed in Rome on February 17, 1600.

On August 7, 1603, all of Bruno's writings were placed on the Index of Forbidden Books, where they remained through the last edition of the Index, in effect until 1966. Robert Cardinal Bellarmino, who had overseen Bruno's trial and punishment, was declared a saint by the Catholic Church in 1930. Bruno's works had never been popular in England or on the Continent and were scarce in Catholic countries because of their suppression. John Toland, the 17th-century English deist and author of CHRISTIANITY NOT MYSTERIOUS, recognized Bruno as a forerunner of the freethinkers of his own era; Toland translated part of *On the Infinite Universe and Worlds* and wrote an account of the book. Bruno's philosophy also had an important influence on the philosophers Baruch Spinoza and Gottfried Wilhelm Leibniz.

In 2000, on the 400th anniversary of the execution of Bruno, the Vatican's secretary of state, Angelo Cardinal Sodano, said that his death was "a sad episode of modern Christian history" but that his writing was "incompatible" with Christian thinking and that he therefore remains a heretic.

FURTHER READING

Boulting, William. *Giordano Bruno: His Life, Thought and Martyrdom*. New York: Books for Libraries Press, 1972.

Copleston, Frederick. *A History of Philosophy*. Vol. 3: *Late Medieval and Renaissance Philosophy*. New York: Doubleday, 1993.

George, Leonard. *Crimes of Perception: An Encyclopedia of Heresies and Heretics*. New York: Paragon House, 1995.

Green, Jonathon, and Nicholas J. Karolides, reviser. *The Encyclopedia of Censorship, New Edition*. New York: Facts On File, 2005.

Jaspers, Karl. *The Great Philosophers*. Vol. 3. New York: Harcourt Brace, 1993.

Levy, Leonard W. *Blasphemy: Verbal Offense Against the Sacred, from Moses to Salman Rushdie*. New York: Alfred A. Knopf, 1993.

ON THE LAW OF WAR AND PEACE

Author: Hugo Grotius
Original date and place of publication: 1625, France
Literary form: Legal treatise

SUMMARY

The Dutch statesman, jurist, and theologian Hugo Grotius (Huig de Groot) was the most renowned man of letters of 17th-century Holland and is regarded as the father of modern international law. *On the Law of War and Peace* is the first definitive text on the subject.

Grotius was a civil servant who studied law at Orléans and Leiden. He became a leader of the bar at The Hague, then Dutch ambassador to England, and later chief magistrate of Rotterdam. He was a political ally of Johann van Oldenbarneveldt, the chief policymaker of the United Provinces, of which Holland was a prominent member. Oldenbarneveldt was a leader of the Remonstrants, or Dutch Arminians, a dissenting Protestant sect opposed to strict Calvinism.

Doctrinal disputes between the Calvinists and the Remonstrants led to a constitutional crisis. The local government of Holland, led by Maurice (Maurits) of Nassau, prince of Orange and commanding general of the Dutch army, who was obliged by oath to uphold the tenets of Calvinism, came into conflict with the central government of the United Provinces led by Oldenbarneveldt. Maurice of Nassau, determined to crush the Remonstrants, ousted Oldenbarneveldt in a coup d'état and in 1618 convoked the Synod of Dort to condemn the Remonstrants' doctrine. Oldenbarneveldt was arrested, convicted of treason, and executed. Grotius, as a supporter of Oldenbarneveldt and a Remonstrants leader, was sentenced to life imprisonment in the castle of Loevestein.

In 1621, he escaped from prison, hidden in a large chest of books, and fled to Paris. He was warmly received in France, where he published several important books on politics, law, and religion. These included *Defense of the Lawful Government of Holland* (1622), which was banned in the Netherlands; *On the Law of War and Peace* (*De jure belli ac pacis*) (1625); and *On the Truth of the Christian Religion* (1627), a Christian epic written in simple verse, which was translated into 12 languages and spread Grotius's fame worldwide. He later returned to Rotterdam but was forced into exile again and went to Sweden. From 1635 to 1645 he represented Sweden at the French court. In addition to his writing on law, Grotius also published major works of theological and biblical criticism.

Grotius's theory of international law, as expressed in his influential treatise *On the Law of War and Peace*, was based on natural law common to all men and nations. Natural law, he believed, prescribed rules of conduct both for nations and individuals that were reasonable, universal, and binding. "Natural law," he wrote in a famous passage, "is so unalterable that God himself cannot change it." Assuming that God did not exist, he proposed in another controversial passage, the rules of natural law would retain their validity. The primary rule of natural law is that whatever is necessary is lawful.

The treatise defined the legal obligations of human societies and recommended procedures for enforcing rules and punishing violations. Grotius drew the specifics of his proposed international law from both the Bible and the Roman classics. The central tenet of his legal theory was that a nation may use armed force against another only in defense of rights or property or to punish criminal acts, and if no tribunal had been authorized to settle the dispute. His legal provisions were directed toward making conditions of warfare more humane by inducing respect for noncombatants and their property.

His own experience of imprisonment and exile led Grotius to criticize the tendency within Protestantism to adopt rigid doctrinal systems and to secure or maintain dominance by force. He saw these practices as destructive of the spiritual nature of religion and particularly dangerous when enforced by the power of the state. Inflexible church structures had provoked nations to war and impeded unity of Christians based on common acceptance of fundamental truths.

In *On the Law of War and Peace*, he proposed a policy of toleration. Religion may not be imposed on individuals or nations through coercion. "From the kind of evidence on which Christianity rests," he wrote, "it is plain that no force should be used with nations to promote its acceptance." Christ taught that only reason and persuasion, rather than force, could be used to disseminate the Gospel. Grotius warned against the disastrous results of "the zealous attachment of every one to his own tenets; an evil which Galen says is more difficult to be eradicated than any constitutional disease."

CENSORSHIP HISTORY

The first of Grotius's books to be censored was *Defense of the Lawful Government of Holland* (1622), written after his escape from Loevestein castle to defend both his innocence and the concepts of religious tolerance and to protest the illegality of the procedures that condemned him to prison. When Dutch authorities discovered that the book was being printed in Amsterdam, they seized the manuscript at the printer's house. Published instead in 1622 in another city in the Netherlands and in Paris, the book was widely read in Holland.

In November 1622, the States-General of the Netherlands declared the book to be notorious, seditious, and scandalous libel. It was declared illegal to print, distribute, possess, read, give to others, or otherwise handle the book. In response to a request from Grotius, Louis XIII of France replied to the decree of the States-General in 1623 by taking Grotius under his special protection and forbidding persons "of every quality, nation, or condition" from harming him. Grotius contended that, since the book's publication in France was authorized by the king, the Dutch decree was an infringement of the laws of France.

The publication history of Grotius's masterpiece, *On the Law of War and Peace*, was unaffected by the political censorship of his *Defense*. *On the Law of War and Peace* became a definitive work on international law that maintained its influence for centuries after its publication. Grotius's work was read and debated by the educated people of Europe, particularly in the Netherlands, Germany, England, and France. By the late 18th century, the book had appeared in 77 editions in its original Latin, as well as in Dutch, French, German, English, and Spanish. Enlightenment philosophes, such as Edward Gibbon and Charles-Louis de Secondat, baron de La Brède et de Montesquieu, expressed their admiration for his thinking. It was consulted by generations of statesmen and diplomats, including the founding fathers of the American nation.

Although Grotius was a Christian who championed the doctrine of free will against the Calvinist belief in predestination and who wrote influential annotations on the Old and New Testaments, he considered all church systems as detrimental to both religious and civil life. He felt that the clergy should be restrained by civil authority because, if unchecked, they would seek to exercise religious tyranny and interfere in temporal affairs. Though he did not intend in his hypothetical construction of a natural law without God to cast doubt on God's existence, his natural law existed outside scriptural revelation or the teachings of Christianity.

In his last major ecclesiastical treatise, *A Vote for Peace in the Church*, published in 1642, Grotius wrote a justification for the ecumenical unity of Protestantism and Catholicism. He proposed that both branches of Christianity be reunited under the Roman pope, with reduced ecclesiastical powers. Calvinist writers bitterly attacked him, and the rumor spread that Grotius had secretly become a Catholic. The Vatican sent a Jesuit theologian to meet with Grotius, who decided that Grotius was "not sufficiently Catholic." This view led the Spanish Inquisition to place all of Grotius's main works, including *On the Law of War and Peace*, on the Spanish Index of Forbidden Books.

It took the Catholic Church in Rome another century to decide that his writings were dangerous enough to warrant condemnation. When the church moved in the 18th century to do battle with the rationalist and anticlerical philosophy of the Enlightenment, it placed Grotius's writings on theology on the Roman Index of Forbidden Books in 1757 in the most severe category of *opera omnia*, or all works condemned. They remained on the Index through its last edition published until 1966.

FURTHER READING

Durnbauld, Edward. *The Life and Legal Writings of Hugo Grotius*. Norman: University of Oklahoma Press, 1969.

Gay, Peter. *The Enlightenment: An Interpretation. The Rise of Modern Paganism*. New York: W. W. Norton, 1966.

Gellinek, Christian. *Hugo Grotius*. Boston: Twayne Publishers, 1983.

Jordan, W. K. *The Development of Religious Toleration in England*. Vol. 2. Gloucester, Mass.: Peter Smith, 1965.

ON THE ORIGIN OF SPECIES

Author: Charles Darwin
Original date and place of publication: 1859, United Kingdom
Literary form: Scientific text

SUMMARY

The British naturalist Charles Darwin published his groundbreaking work, *On the Origin of Species*, 22 years after he initially wrote it, in response to competition from other scientists who were preparing to publish similar ideas. In this book, Darwin outlines the observations he made while sailing around South America on the HMS *Beagle* from 1831 to 1836.

Darwin believed in "descent with modification," that generations of organisms changed over time, and those that best withstood climatic and other changes were most likely to survive and multiply. Darwin stated that these changes occurred through natural selection, controlled by the organisms themselves, over millions of years. *On the Origin of Species* discussed these broad concepts through specific examples of evolution in pigeons and ants, as well as in discussion of embryology and morphology. Though his theory was based on careful measurements and observations, Darwin understood that it would be seen as radically at odds with prevailing ideas about the design of nature. Attempting to head off criticism, Darwin acknowledged that "nothing at first may be more difficult to believe than that the more complex organs and instincts should have been perfected . . . by the accumulation of innumerable slight variations, each good for the individual possessor."

Most readers of Darwin's book had been taught that God created the world according to an orderly plan, placing humans on Earth with dominion over nature. Darwin's ideas provided much less certainty than traditional, biblical-based explanations of nature. Popular impressions of Darwinism, however, differed from Darwin's actual writings. Social scientists summed up his concept of descent with modification through natural selection as "survival of the fittest" and used this term to explain relations between social classes. To so-called Social Darwinists, wealthier, more powerful people deserved to hold on to their advantages because they were the "fittest" human beings. Under Social Darwinism, any aid to the disadvantaged became an unnatural act, needlessly prolonging the lives and traits of the "unfit." Social Darwinists shortened Darwin's ideas by using the term *evolution* and added a belief that evolution always resulted in progress.

Darwin never intended this linear approach to the study of nature. He was most interested in the mutations that occurred over generations of organisms, whether the mutations resulted in progress or not. Further, Darwin never wished to explore his theories in the realm of human behavior and social organization. When he discussed his ideas in relation to humans, he focused on the development of organs and systems in the body, not in society.

Darwin was part of a movement in science toward reliance on empirical data. He was a contemporary of scientists such as John William Draper, author of HISTORY OF THE CONFLICT BETWEEN RELIGION AND SCIENCE, who questioned religious-based models for scientific observation. While Darwin was careful not to attack religion directly, as Draper did, his quiet, measured arguments did not include any mention of a divine power ordering the universe.

CENSORSHIP HISTORY

Historians of science believe that one of the reasons Darwin delayed publishing his work for so long was his fear that his ideas were too radical for the time and would be greeted with hostility. In 1844, he wrote to a friend that to publish his thoughts on evolution woud be akin to "confessing a murder." Seeing himself as a scientist, he refused to comment on the wider importance of his ideas. Near the end of his life, after publishing several other works in which he affirmed his belief in natural selection, he continued to think only in terms of advancing science and hoped that his quiet example would win people to his ideas.

On the Origin of Species by means of Natural Selection, or the Preservation of Favoured Races in the Struggle for Life was published on November 24, 1859, in an edition of only 1,250 copies by the reluctant John Murray, who did not anticipate much interest in the book. The first edition was sold out on the day of publication and a second edition of 3,000 copies soon after. The book appeared in six editions through 1872. An American edition appeared in May 1860 and was greeted with widespread controversy.

"Sixteen thousand copies have now (1876) been sold in England," Darwin wrote in his autobiography, "and considering how stiff a book it is, it is a large sale. It has been translated into almost every European tongue." He counted more than 265 reviews and numerous essays. Darwin's ideas gained wide currency in academic scientific circles almost immediately and became the foundations of modern evolution theory.

However, the publication of *On the Origin of Species* also unleashed one of the most dramatic controversies of the Victorian era. Darwin was accused of "dethroning God," as one critic put it, by challenging the literal interpretation of the Book of Genesis. Clergy railed against him from pulpits all over Britain. His book was barred from Trinity College at Cambridge, even though Darwin was a graduate. Darwin, referring to occasions when he was "contemptuously criticised," declared that "I could not employ my life better than in adding a little to natural science. This I have done to the best of my abilities, and critics may say what they like, but they cannot destroy this conviction."

Unlike Zoonomia, a scientific treatise written by Darwin's grandfather, Erasmus Darwin, in the late 18th century, which was banned by the Catholic Church because it expressed a theory of evolution, *On the Origin of Species* was never placed on the Roman Index of Forbidden Books.

A resurgence of opposition to Darwinism began in the 1920s in the United States. By the early 20th century, American high school science textbooks had begun to incorporate Darwinian evolution in discussing human origins and biology. In 1919, the World Christian Fundamentals Association (WCFA) was founded to oppose teaching of evolution in American public schools. Local school boards and state boards of education in areas with large fundamentalist Christian populations were pressured to reject the new textbooks and legislatures around the country were lobbied to pass antievolution resolutions. More than 20 state legislatures considered such measures.

In 1925, in the most famous example of antievolutionary sentiment, Tennessee passed a law prohibiting teachers from teaching the theory of evolution in state-supported schools. A combination of factors compelled the Tennessee state legislature to pass such a sweeping measure. The 1920s were an era of pleasure-seeking in popular culture, especially among teenagers; at the same time, fundamentalist religion and nativism were on the increase as a reaction to these "modern" ideas. Fundamentalist Christians feared that a materialistic philosophy such as natural selection would send a damaging, nihilistic message to schoolchildren. They believed that schools would produce more orderly students if they taught the biblical account of Creation, with a God designing nature according to a set plan. Local leaders in the small town of Dayton, Tennessee, welcomed the chance to put their town on the map in the context of this battle.

John T. Scopes, a science teacher in Dayton, volunteered to be the test case for Tennessee's antievolution law. Representing the state was William Jennings Bryan, a populist leader and three-time Democratic presidential candidate who had served as Woodrow Wilson's secretary of state and was popular among fundamentalists for his biblically inspired rhetoric and his devotion to maintaining traditional, rural ways of life. Clarence Darrow, a noted defense lawyer and avowed agnostic, defended Scopes, arguing that academic freedom was being violated and that the legislation violated the separation of church and state. Members of the American Civil Liberties Union (ACLU), at that time a new organization devoted to defending free speech, also contributed to Scopes's side.

The Scopes "monkey trial," as it became known, was an event of national importance during the summer of 1925. Newspapers from around the country sent correspondents to Dayton to cover the proceedings, and Dayton merchants sold souvenirs of the trial, including stuffed monkeys to represent the idea that Darwin claimed humans were descended from apes. Reporters from big-city newspapers reported on the trial with amusement, while fundamentalist observers saw the proceedings as a crucial battle against the forces of modernism.

Both sides claimed victory. Scopes was found guilty of violating Tennessee's statute prohibiting the teaching of evolution. As a state employee, the judge ruled, Scopes could not disobey state laws. His backers were also pleased, as the decision gave them the chance to appeal the matter to a higher court, where the case for evolution and freedom of expression could get even more publicity. The Scopes case, however, was thrown out on a technicality. In the original case the judge, rather than the jury, had fined Scopes $100. This procedural error reversed the verdict that found Scopes guilty.

Antievolution efforts did not end with the conclusion of the Scopes trial. The Tennessee antievolution law remained on the books until 1967, and grassroots fundamentalists in the United States launched efforts to remove Darwin's ideas from public school textbooks. In 1968, the U.S. Supreme Court considered a case similar to Scopes's. Susan Epperson, a high school biology teacher, challenged the constitutionality of the Arkansas Anti-Evolution Statute of 1928, which provided that teachers who used a textbook that included Darwin's theory of evolution could lose their jobs. The Supreme Court ruled that the law was unconstitutional and conflicted with the First and Fourteenth Amendments. Government power could not be used to advance religious beliefs.

Having been defeated in the courts, antievolutionists shifted their focus to requiring instruction in "creationism" as an alternative to evolutionary theories. They defined creationism as the theory that all life forms came into existence instantaneously through the action of a single intelligent creator. In the early 1980s, Arkansas and Louisiana state boards of education required the teaching of both creationism and evolution in public schools. These laws were ruled unconstitutional in 1987 by the U.S. Supreme Court in *Edwards v. Aguillard* as advocating a religious doctrine and violating the establishment clause of the First Amendment. However, battles about the teaching of evolution still rage on, especially at the local school board level.

In 2002, the Cobb County, Georgia, school system decided to place stickers in science textbooks that said "evolution is a theory not a fact" and should be "approached with an open mind, studied carefully and critically considered." The stickers were added after more than 2,000 parents complained that the textbooks presented evolution as fact, without mentioning rival ideas about the beginnings of life, such as the biblical story of the Creation.

Five parents sued the school district, claiming that the stickers were unconstitutional. In January 2005, a federal judge in Atlanta ordered the schools to remove them, as they send "a message that the school board agrees with the beliefs of Christian fundamentalists and creationists," "convey a message of endorsement of religion," and violate the First Amendment's separation of church and state, as well as the Georgia Constitution's prohibition against using public money to aid religion.

The case was only one of many battles waged around the country since 2000 over the teaching of evolution in science classes. In 2004, Georgia's education chief proposed a science curriculum that substituted "changes over time" for the word "evolution." The idea was dropped after teachers protested. The same year, a school district in Dover, Pennsylvania, became the first in the nation to mandate that science students be told about "intelligent design," the concept that the universe is so complex that it must have been created by a higher power. Teachers were to read students a brief statement introducing intelligent design in ninth-grade biology class and referred students for more information to an intelligent design textbook, *Of Pandas and People*. The ACLU of Pennsylvania and 11 parents filed suits in federal court, saying that teaching intelligent design in public school classrooms violated their religious liberty by promoting particular religious beliefs.

In December 2005, after a six-week trial in federal district court in Harrisburg, Pennsylvania, U.S. District Judge John E. Jones III ruled that it was unconstitutional for the school district to present intelligent design as an alternative to evolution in high school biology courses. He declared that intelligent design is "a religious alternative masquerading as a scientific theory" and that evidence at the trial proved that it was "creationism relabeled." "We find that the secular purposes claimed by the Board amount to a pretext for the Board's real purpose, which was to promote religion in the public school classroom in violation of the establishment clause," Jones wrote in his ruling. The ruling was unlikely to be appealed by the school board, because the board members who supported intelligent design were unseated in elections in November 2005 and replaced by a slate that opposed intelligent design.

In the first seven months of 2005 alone, 17 pieces of antievolution legislation were introduced in 12 states, according to the National Center for Science Education in Oakland, California, a group that advocates teaching evolution in public schools. Most of the bills were efforts to limit teaching of evolution and include alternate theories in science classes.

In November 2005, a creationist majority on the Kansas Board of Education voted to include criticism of evolution in the school science standards used to develop statewide tests in the fourth, seventh, and 10th grades. The most significant change was in the definition of science. Instead of "seeking natural explanations for what we observe around us," the new standards describe it as a "continuing investigation that uses observation, hypothesis testing, measurement, experimentation, logical argument, and theory building to lead to more adequate explanations of natural phenomena."

Board member Kathy Martin, who supported the new standards, told the *Kansas City Star* that she hoped the changes would encourage teachers and students to look at "all the scientific research and data and evidence and whether it supports or refutes evolution because evolution is not a sacred cow." The majority of the 26-member committee that had originally drafted the standards objected to the changes made by the Board of Education. The changes include "intelligent design–inspired language," the committee wrote in a reply to the board, and "intelligent design has no scientific basis."

In 2006, the makeup of the Kansas Board of Education shifted to a pro-science majority, and new standards were approved that ended the requirement to include antievolution concepts.

In August 2009, the National Center for Science Education reported that there was currently no explicit requirement in any of the states' science standards that creationism be taught or evolution not be taught. However, creationists and proponents of intelligent design have reduced their advocacy of state-level legislation and policies that explicitly endorse creationist claims or attack evolution. Having been struck down by the courts, "blanket bans of evolution and policies requiring 'balanced treatment' of evolution and creationism have given way to more innocuous language," the center reported, "such as 'teaching the controversy,' 'critical analysis,' 'strength and weaknesses,' 'academic freedom,' and 'discussing the full range of scientific views.' " Creationists are using such language to justify the use of teaching material that casts doubt on the theory of evolution.

In 2009, the Texas Board of Education approved a science curriculum that opened the door for teachers and textbooks to present creationists' claims. Although the board voted to remove a long-standing requirement that students analyze the "strengths and weaknesses" of evolutionary theory, it approved standards requiring students to analyze and evaluate the completeness of the fossil record and the complexity of the cell. Social conservatives on the board, the *Wall Street Journal* reported, "have made clear that they expect books to address those topics by raising questions about the validity of evolutionary theory." As Texas represents the largest single publishing market for high school textbooks, scientists and educators said that they feared the decision in Texas would have deleterious effects on the teaching of science in other states.

Living Waters, an antievolution evangelical group, announced plans in October 2009 to distribute on American university campuses 175,000 copies of a special edition of *On the Origin of Species* with an introduction promoting creationism. The group's fund-raising materials said that the introduction "gives a timeline of Darwin's life, and his thoughts on the existence of God. It lists the theories of many hoaxes, exposes the unscientific belief that nothing created everything, points to the incredible structure of DNA, and notes the absence of any undisputed transitional forms. To show the dangerous fruit of evolution, it also mentions Hitler's undeniable connections to the theory, Darwin's racism, and his disdain for women. In addition, it counters the claim that creationists are 'anti-science' by citing numerous scientists who believed that God created the universe."

It was reported in March 2005 that the controversy over evolution had gone beyond the schools to affect Imax theaters. Some dozen theaters, particularly in the South, including some in science museums, had refused to show movies that mention evolution, the big bang, or the geology of Earth, as they feared protests from people who believe that evolution contradicts the Bible. Because only a few dozen Imax theaters routinely show science documentaries, barring such films from even a few cinemas could affect a film's bottom line and ultimately a producer's decision in the future to make similar documentaries.

Opponents of evolution have made significant inroads among the American public. In 2004, a national Gallup poll found that only 35 percent of those asked were confident that Darwin's theory was "supported by evidence," and 37 percent of those polled by CBS News said creationism should be taught in schools instead of evolution.

On the 200th anniversary of Darwin's birth in 2009, a Gallup poll found that only 39 percent of Americans said they "believe in the theory of evolution." A quarter said that they did not believe in the theory, and 36 percent had no opinion.

There have been some reports from abroad of censorship of *On the Origin of Species* in the 20th century. In 1935, it was prohibited in Yugoslavia, and in 1937 it was banned under the right-wing Metaxas regime in Greece. In Malaysia, in 2006, an Indonesian translation of *On the Origin of Species* was among 56 books banned by the Internal Security Ministry. But unlike other cases of book censorship, the book was generally not removed from bookstore or library shelves in the United States. It was, rather, the ideas expressed in the book that were censored.

—with Jonathan Pollack

FURTHER READING

Alter, Alexandra. "Decades after the 'Monkey Trial,' Creationists Turn to Science." *Miami Herald* (August 15, 2005). Available online. URL: http://www.centredaily. com/mid/centredaily/news/12424164.htm.

"Anti-Evolution Teachings Gain in U.S. Schools." *Newsletter on Intellectual Freedom* 54, no. 1 (January 2005).

Boorstein, Daniel J. *The Discoverers: A History of Man's Search to Know His World and Himself.* New York: Random House, 1983.

Carroll, Diane. "Evolution Issue Again Gets Look from Board." *Kansas City Star* (August 9, 2005). Available online. URL: http://www.kansascity.com/mld/kansascity/ news/local/12336247.htm.

DelFattore, Joan. *What Johnny Shouldn't Read: Textbook Censors in America.* New Haven, Conn.: Yale University Press, 1992.

Demac, Donna A. *Liberty Denied: The Current Rise of Censorship in America.* New York: PEN American Center, 1988.

Goodstein, Laurie. "Judge Rejects Teaching Intelligent Design." *New York Times* (December 21, 2005). Available online. URL: http://www.nytimes.com. Accessed December 27, 2005.

Gould, Stephen Jay. *Ever Since Darwin: Reflections on Natural History.* New York: W. W. Norton, 1977.

Hart, Ariel. "Judge in Georgia Orders Anti-Evolution Stickers Removed from Textbooks." *New York Times* (January 14, 2005). Available online. URL: http://www.nytimes.com. Accessed January 14, 2005.

Jaschik, Scott. "Darwin, From the Creationists." *Inside Higher Ed* (October 7, 2009). Available online. URL: http://www.insidehighered.com/news/2009/10/07/darwin. Accessed June 6, 2010.

Larson, Edward J. *Trial and Error. The American Controversy over Creation and Evolution.* New York: Oxford University Press, 1985.

Mead, Louise S., and Anton Mates. "Why Science Standards Are Important to a Strong Science Curriculum and How States Measure Up." National Center for Science Education (August 7, 2009). Available online. URL: http://springerlink.com/content/9u0610162rn51432/fulltext.html. Accessed June 6, 2010.

Newport, Frank. "On Darwin's Birthday, Only 4 in 10 Believe in Evolution." *Gallup Daily News* (February 11, 2009). Available online. URL: http://www.gallup.com/poll/114544/darwin-birthday-believe-evolution.aspx. Accessed June 6, 2010.

Numbers, Ronald L., ed. *Creation-Evolution Debates.* New York: Garland, 1955.

Raffaele, Martha. "Controversial Step Taken in Rural Pennsylvania District." Associated Press (November 12, 2004).

Rogers, Donald J. *Banned! Book Censorship in the Schools.* New York: Julian Messner, 1988.

Simon, Stephanie. "Texas Opens Door for Evolution Doubts." *Wall Street Journal* (March 28, 2009). Available online. URL: http://www.wsj.com/article/SB123819751472561761.html. Accessed June 6, 2010.

Southeast Asian Press Alliance/International Freedom of Expression eXchange. "Authorities Ban Films, Books, Television Talk Show; Film Director Appeals Ban" (March 1, 2007). URL: Available online: http://www.ifex.org/malaysia/2007/03/01/authorities_ban_films_books_television/. Accessed June 6, 2010.

ON THE REVOLUTION OF HEAVENLY SPHERES

Author: Nicolaus Copernicus
Original date and place of publication: 1543, Germany
Literary form: Scientific treatise

SUMMARY

The celebrated Polish astronomer Nicolaus Copernicus was the first to propose the heliocentric theory—that the planets, including the Earth, move in orbits around the Sun. The geocentric Ptolemaic theory of the universe, which had held sway since antiquity and was considered authoritative in philosophy, science, and church teaching, placed the Earth at the center of the universe, with the Sun and other planets moving around it.

Copernicus developed his revolutionary theory from a study of ancient astronomical records. He understood that it was the turning of the Earth on its axis that gave the impression that the Sun was moving. By liberating astronomy from the geocentric viewpoint, Copernicus laid the foundations of modern astronomy, paving the way for the work of Johannes Kepler, Galileo Galilei, and Sir Isaac Newton.

Copernicus was a cathedral canon in the city of Frauenburg, East Prussia, and had studied canon law, mathematics, and medicine. He developed his heliocentric theory as an avocation. His friends and disciples, including a Catholic cardinal and a bishop, urged him to have it published. "They insisted," Copernicus wrote, "that, though my theory of the Earth's movement might at first seem strange, yet it would appear admirable and acceptable when the publication of my elucidatory comments would dispel the mists of paradox."

A brief popular account of his theory was circulated in manuscript from 1530. In 1540, Copernicus granted permission to one of his disciples, Georg Joachim, known as Rheticus, to publish an initial report about his ideas. When the demand for Rheticus's report required a second edition in 1541, and hearing no objections from the church, Copernicus began preparing for publication the manuscript of his great work, *On the Revolution of Heavenly Spheres*. Copernicus asked Rheticus to supervise its publication. When Rheticus was unable to complete the task, he entrusted it to an acquaintance, Andreas Osiander, a militant Lutheran theologian. Copernicus was on his deathbed when *On the Revolution of Heavenly Spheres* was published in 1543.

The book, dedicated to Pope Paul III, contained a lengthy unsigned preface stating that the heliocentric theory was not an account of the actual physical organization of the heavens, but rather a mere hypothesis, a convenient device for simplifying astronomical calculations. "For these hypotheses need not be true nor even probable," the preface claimed.

Later it was discovered that this introduction had not been written by Copernicus at all. In the cause of Lutheran orthodoxy, Osiander had suppressed Copernicus's introduction and substituted one he had written himself. The German mathematician Kepler uncovered Osiander's deception and defended the integrity of Copernican theories. "He thought that his hypotheses were true," Kepler wrote, "no less than did those ancient astronomers. . . . He did not merely think so, but he proves they are true."

CENSORSHIP HISTORY

During Copernicus's lifetime and for a half-century after his death in 1543, *On the Revolution of Heavenly Spheres* was not opposed by Catholic Church authorities. Although Copernicus was attacked by Martin Luther, who referred to him as "an upstart astrologer" who "wishes to reverse the entire science of astronomy," Copernicus's book, read at some of the best Catholic universities, was not seen as a threat to prevailing scientific and religious concepts.

The early 17th-century astronomical writings of Kepler and Galileo, which demonstrated, proved, and popularized Copernican theory, led the church to see it as a challenge to orthodoxy. In 1616, the church placed *On the Revolution of Heavenly Spheres* on the Index of Forbidden Books. It raised particular objection to passages representing the heliocentric hypothesis as a certainty. Kepler's writings on Copernican theory, including THE NEW ASTRONOMY, were also placed on the Index, and Galileo was warned not to teach or write on the heliocentric theory.

In 1633, Galileo was put on trial by the Inquisition for heresy for his defense of Copernican theories in DIALOGUE CONCERNING THE TWO CHIEF WORLD SYSTEMS. The *Dialogue* was formally condemned and banned along with all of Galileo's works, and in 1644, the Index of Forbidden Books confirmed the condemnation of the works of Copernicus and Galileo.

It was not until the 18th century that the Index of Benedict XIV in 1753 omitted the general prohibition against Copernican theory. Finally, in 1835, it removed the names of Copernicus, Galileo, and Kepler. On October 31, 1992, more than four centuries after the publication of *On the Revolution of Heavenly Spheres*, Pope John Paul II formally rehabilitated Galileo and his defense of Copernicus's heliocentric theory.

FURTHER READING

Boorstein, Daniel J. *The Discoverers: A History of Man's Search to Know His World and Himself.* New York: Random House, 1983.

Garraty, John A., and Peter Gay. *The Columbia History of the World.* New York: Harper and Row, 1972.

Green, Jonathon. *The Encyclopedia of Censorship.* New York: Facts On File, 1990.

OPUS MAJUS

Author: Roger Bacon
Original date and place of publication: 1268, England
Literary form: Philosophical treatise

SUMMARY

The 13th-century English scientist and philosopher Roger Bacon, known as "Doctor Mirabilis," was a Franciscan friar who came under suspicion of heresy for advocating the experimental method in science. Bacon had an extensive knowledge of the sciences, was an accomplished Greek scholar, and knew Hebrew and Aramaic. Among his accomplishments in practical science were the invention of spectacles and a unique understanding of how a telescope might be constructed. He was the first European to describe in detail the manufacture of gunpowder and to suggest that it would be possible in the future to have boats, coaches, and flying machines powered by the Sun's energy.

Bacon studied in Paris, where he was among the first scholars to lecture on Aristotle's natural philosophy and metaphysics. He wrote several works on Aristotelian thought and on Aristotle's Arab commentators. In 1247, disenchanted with the rise of Scholasticism in Paris, he returned to Oxford, where he called for a return to the study of the Scriptures and the biblical languages. He devoted the next 10 years to the study of science and languages and to scientific experimentation. In 1257, the Franciscan order sent Bacon back to Paris, where he was confined for 10 years. He was forbidden to write for publication because it was believed that he experimented with the "black arts" of magic and had adopted mystical interpretations of history. Bacon's interest in alchemy may have led his contemporaries to suspect him of dabbling in magic.

Bacon was critical of methods of contemporary academic learning and conceived a plan to reform science to better place it at the disposal of theology. At the request of his friend, Pope Clement IV, who had met Bacon when Clement was a church cardinal, he outlined his ideas in three Latin works, completed in 1268. *Opus majus*, his great encyclopedic work, included discussion of grammar, logic, mathematics, physics, and modern philosophy. *Opus secundum* and *Opus tertium*, which summarized and expanded the content of the first opus, followed shortly after.

In *Opus majus*, Bacon expressed his distinctive philosophic ideas. The work is divided into seven parts: the causes of error, philosophy as an aid to theology, the study of languages, mathematics, optics, experimental science, and moral philosophy. Bacon asserts that all wisdom stems from God through three channels of revelation: the Scriptures, the works of nature, and the interior illumination of the soul achieved in seven stages of internal experience. Knowledge of foreign languages, mathematics, and the moral and spiritual disciplines are needed to decipher these revelations. But the truth can be found only by appeal to experience or the use of the deductive scientific method. Reason may guide the mind to a right conclusion, but it is only confirmation by experience that removes doubt.

Bacon began *Opus majus* by stating that the chief causes of error and failure to attain truth are "submission to faulty and unworthy authority, influence of custom, popular prejudice, and concealment of our own ignorance accompanied by an ostentatious display of our knowledge." Where these impediments hold sway, "no reason influences, no right decides, no law binds, religion has no place, nature's mandate fails, the complexion of things is changed, their order is confounded, vice prevails, virtue is extinguished, falsehood reigns, truth is hissed off the scene."

Bacon asserted that although the Scriptures contain all truth, both canon law and philosophy are needed to lead man to the knowledge and service of God. Philosophy and the use of reason cannot be condemned, because reason is of God. Pagan philosophy—that is, the philosophy of the ancient

Greeks—should be consulted in an intelligent manner and should neither be ignorantly rejected nor blindly followed.

He emphasized the importance of studying languages in order to understand both the Scriptures and the Greek and Arab philosophers, and mathematics, which he saw as the "door and key" to other sciences. In the concluding section of *Opus majus*, Bacon said that all other human sciences are subordinate to moral philosophy, which is closely related to theology, as it instructs people about their relations with God, their fellow human beings, and themselves. God is the illuminating active intellect.

CENSORSHIP HISTORY

Bacon's thought blended traditional medieval ideas with a scientific outlook that was foreign to the thinking of the majority of contemporary theologians and philosophers. He fought for years to have the teaching of science recognized as part of the university curriculum. Although it is commonly assumed that *Opus majus* was sent to Bacon's protector, Pope Clement IV, the pope died in 1268, the year of its publication, and it is not known for certain if he received it or how he reacted to it. The death of Pope Clement put an end to Bacon's plans to expand scientific study. For the rest of his life Bacon remained unpopular with his fellow intellectuals.

Bacon's Franciscan order regarded the ideas expressed in *Opus majus* as heresy. In 1277, he wrote another work, the *Speculum astronomiae*, in which he defended his ideas on astronomy against charges of determinism and asserted that the influence and movements of the heavenly bodies affected earthly and human events. According to a 14th-century work, the *Chronicle of the Twenty-four Generals*, in 1278 Bacon was accused of "certain suspect novelties" by Jerome de Ascoli, general of the Franciscan order, who later became Pope Nicholas IV, and was sent to prison. He may have spent as many as 14 years behind bars, though some reports say that he was imprisoned for only two years. It is known that when he died in 1292 he was in the process of writing a new work, a compendium of theological studies.

FURTHER READING

Boorstein, Daniel J. *The Discoverers: A History of Man's Search to Know His World and Himself.* New York: Random House, 1983.

Copleston, Frederick. *A History of Philosophy.* Vol. 2: *Medieval Philosophy.* New York: Doubleday, 1994.

Green, Jonathon, and Nicholas J. Kavolides, reviser. *The Encyclopedia of Censorship, New Edition.* New York: Facts On File, 2005.

Haight, Anne Lyon. *Banned Books: 387 BC to 1978 AD.* Updated and enlarged by Chandler B. Grannis. New York: R. R. Bowker, 1978.

Manguel, Alberto. *A History of Reading.* New York: Viking, 1996.

Wippel, John F., and Alan B. Wolter, eds. *Medieval Philosophy: From St. Augustine to Nicholas of Cusa.* New York: Free Press, 1969.

PENGUIN ISLAND

Author: Anatole France
Original dates and places of publication: 1908, France; 1909, United States
Original publishers: Calmann-Lévy; Dodd, Mead and Company
Literary form: Novel

SUMMARY

Anatole France (Jacques-Anatole Thibault) was one of the most popular and influential French authors in his lifetime. In *Penguin Island* he presents a satirical history of France, telling the story of the Penguins from mythological prehistory through the present and into the future. Throughout *Penguin Island* the author attacks the hypocrisies of organized religion and the French Socialist Party of the early 20th century.

In the first section of the novel, France indulges his interest in myths and religion of the Middle Ages by creating a detailed Penguin world that alludes to and spoofs early French history. The Penguins at the start of the novel are actual birds, but after a monk baptizes them and a conference of saints agrees to give them souls, they take on human form and behavior. The Penguins' humble beginnings and France's description of Penguin Island as an area south of Brittany poke fun at nationalist myths about early France and French prejudices against Bretons. The Penguins' transformation into humans also reflects the author's interest in human evolution.

The present-day section of *Penguin Island* focuses largely on an allegory of the Dreyfus Affair, which rocked France at the turn of the century. Alfred Dreyfus, a French Jew, was wrongly accused of stealing from the French army and was sent to Devil's Island penal colony off the coast of French Guiana. Leftist intellectuals such as France took up Dreyfus's case and persuaded the French government to grant him another trial, in which Dreyfus was cleared of wrongdoing.

Penguin Island's Pyrot, accused of stealing 80,000 bales of hay, is a stand-in for Dreyfus. The Penguin socialists initially take Pyrot's side in the controversy, but their pacifism compels them to oppose Pyrot, following an argument that "if Pyrot is a good soldier, then his duties consist of shooting the people." The socialist debate over supporting or opposing Pyrot mirrored the debate within French Socialist Party circles about Dreyfus.

In the final section of his novel, France depicts a grim future for Penguinia. He is skeptical of progress defined solely by the accumulation of wealth, demonstrating his socialist conviction that capitalism inevitably leads to concentration of wealth among a few people and that charity, art, and scholarship will suffer as a result. This last chapter begins and ends with the same paragraph, showing France's belief that a decline of civilization is inevitable and would occur time and again, as fallen capitalist societies are rebuilt in the same image.

CENSORSHIP HISTORY

Penguin Island touched off controversy among Anatole France's socialist colleagues as well as among religious groups. The Dreyfus case had split the French Socialist Party, as some members doubted Dreyfus's innocence and attempted to speak for all socialists against him. By 1908, the socialists who had opposed Dreyfus wanted to patch up their differences and saw France's satire as prolonging the conflict. Some thought the author's vision of the future was nihilistic, as they espoused a belief in a perfect, socialist future, rather than Anatole France's flawed capitalist one.

Religious readers disliked his mixture of pagan and Christian allusions in the early history of the Penguins. With this tactic, France implied that the two beliefs were interchangeable. He pointed out churchgoers' fondness for lavish displays of wealth in the name of religious piety. He made a connection between holy pilgrimage sites and vacation spots for the wealthy. Further, the book's references to the Dreyfus case were found offensive by the church, in view of the church's position against Dreyfus and the strongly anticlerical elements within the pro-Dreyfus movement.

In 1922 in Rome, the Index of Forbidden Books placed its most stringent prohibition on Anatole France's writing by designating *opera omnia*, or all of his works, as condemned. France remained on the Index through its last edition revised in 1948 and in effect until 1966. Despite these criticisms and the church's censorship, France's work sold well in his homeland and around the world. He was awarded the Nobel Prize in literature in 1921. While his works are seldom read today, 100 years ago he was widely admired as an independent-thinking skeptic, and his books enjoyed popular and critical success.

—Jonathan Pollack

FURTHER READING

Dargan, Edwin Preston. *Anatole France*. New York: Oxford University Press, 1937.
Jefferson, Carter. *Anatole France: The Politics of Skepticism*. New Brunswick, N.J.: Rutgers University Press, 1965.

THE PERSIAN LETTERS

Author: Charles-Louis de Secondat, baron de La Brède et de Montesquieu
Original date and place of publication: 1721, Holland
Literary form: Novel

SUMMARY

In his epistolary novel *The Persian Letters*, the French political philosopher Charles-Louis de Secondat, baron de La Brède et de Montesquieu, satirized and criticized French institutions through the imaginary correspondence of Persians traveling in Paris and Venice. The letters, commenting with wit and irony on contemporary events and issues, included pungent observations of politics, religion, government, law, agriculture, economics, and philosophy. Many of the perspectives Montesquieu attributed to the Persian travelers were drawn from his own experiences when, in 1709, he moved from the French provinces to the world of Parisian high society.

The first edition, published anonymously in 1721, contained 150 letters exchanged during a nine-year period between two engaging Persian travelers, Usbek and Rica, and their friends, servants, and wives in Persia. Their accounts of life in Persia were gleaned by Montesquieu from a contemporary translation of *The Thousand and One Nights* and from travelers' writings. Montesquieu revised *The Persian Letters* several times; the final edition, published as part of his complete works three years after his death, had expanded Rica and Usbek's correspondence to 161 letters.

The Persian Letters was a comedy of Parisian manners, but it also addressed serious issues of political and religious abuses in 18th-century France in an irreverent and entertaining style. Among the targets of Montesquieu's satire were royal absolutism and the Catholic Church, particularly the pope, the Jesuit order, and the church's suppression of dissent. "I see here people who dispute endlessly about religion," Usbek writes from Venice, "but who at the same time apparently compete to see who can at least observe it. These people are not better Christians than others; they are not even better citizens."

Discussing the Jesuits, Usbek observes, "These dervishes make three vows, of obedience, poverty, and chastity. It is said that the first is the best observed; as for the second, I assure you it is certainly not; I leave it to you to judge the third." The "dervishes" hold in their hands most of the state's wealth, Usbek continues, "and they are an avaricious lot, always taking and never giving, constantly hoarding their revenue so as to acquire capital."

Usbek describes to his correspondent the "magician" called the pope: "Sometimes he makes the prince believe that three is only one, or that the bread he eats is not bread, or that the wine drunk is not wine, and a thousand similar things." Those who publicize a novel proposition are at first called heretics, writes Rica. "But no one is a heretic unless he wishes to be, for he needs only to split the difference and to offer some subtle distinction to his accusers, and no matter what the distinction is, or whether it is intelligible or not, it renders a man pure as snow and worthy of being called orthodox." This is the case in France and Germany, but "I have heard in Spain and Portugal that there are dervishes who do not understand a joke, and who have a man burned as if he were straw."

Transposing the situation to Persia, Montesquieu criticized the revocation of the Edict of Nantes by Louis XIV in 1685, which denied religious freedom to the Protestant minority in France. Usbek concludes that a strong state should have several religions since "those who practice the tolerated religion are usually more useful to the state than those in the majority religion" and that war and conflict come from the intolerance engendered by a single dominant religion.

Beyond the particular social criticisms that Montesquieu expressed through the observations of his Persian travelers, his fundamental purpose was to explore the idea of cultural relativity. "How can you be a Persian?" an incredulous Frenchman asks Rica in one of the most memorable sentences in the novel. Montesquieu makes this question a tool for cultural inquiry. Using the empirical and inductive method of the early Enlightenment, Montesquieu sought to understand how ideas and institutions varied and to discover amid diversity the absolutes in human society.

CENSORSHIP HISTORY

In 1720, Montesquieu brought a completed manuscript of *The Persian Letters* to Pierre-Nicholas Desmolets, a priest, librarian, and literary critic, to seek his opinion on whether it should be published. As a priest, Desmolets argued that the book's publication would show disrespect for religion and disregard for the obligations of Montesquieu's aristocratic social position. He predicted it would cause a scandal. But as a critic, he said that if Montesquieu disregarded his advice and published the book, it could not fail "to sell like bread."

Montesquieu did not take Desmolets's advice. Published anonymously in Amsterdam with the imprint of a fictitious Cologne publisher, *The Persian Letters* was smuggled into France early in 1721. The publisher applied for a "tacit permission" to distribute the book in France, but the censor neither granted nor denied the request. Although the book was allowed into the country without danger of prosecution, it was not listed in the catalogs of French booksellers until some 10 years later.

As Desmolets had warned, *The Persian Letters* caused a sensation and, in some political and religious circles, a scandal. During its first year of publication it sold out in multiple printings and attracted widespread notice throughout Europe. Although Montesquieu did not formally acknowledge his authorship of *The Persian Letters* until years later, it was widely known that he had written it, and he became instantly famous. A new edition was published annually for the next eight years, and there were many unsuccessful imitations. In "Some Reflections on *The Persian Letters*," a commentary added to the 1754 edition, Montesquieu wrote that "*The Persian Letters* had such a prodigious sale when they first appeared that publishers made every effort to obtain sequels. They buttonholed everyone they met. 'Sir,' they would say, 'write me some more *Persian Letters*.'"

Despite the book's success, clerical disapproval of the book was responsible for a delay of seven years in Montesquieu's acceptance to the prestigious

French Academy. According to Montesquieu's son, Montesquieu himself met with the prime minister, André-Hercule Cardinal Fleury, who opposed his election to the academy. Fleury's primary objection was to *The Persian Letters;* he had never read the work, but what he had heard about it through an abstract given to him "made the hair on his head stand up."

Montesquieu replied that he neither admitted nor denied being the author and that he preferred to give up a seat in the academy rather than disavow the book. He challenged Fleury to read the entire book. The cardinal did so and subsequently withdrew his opposition. Montesquieu was finally admitted to the academy in 1728. Despite the cardinal's approval, *The Persian Letters* and Montesquieu's masterpiece of political theory, THE SPIRIT OF LAWS, were listed by the Catholic Church in 1752 on the Index of Forbidden Books, where they remained through the last edition of the Index compiled in 1948 and in effect until 1966.

Commenting on the criticisms of the books, Montesquieu wrote in "Some Reflections on *The Persian Letters*": "Some people have found certain remarks excessively bold, but they are advised to regard the nature of the work itself. . . . Far from intending to touch upon any principle of our religion, he did not even suspect himself of imprudence. The remarks in question are always found joined to sentiments of surprise and astonishment, never to a sense of inquiry, and much less to one of criticism. . . . Certainly the nature and the design of *The Persian Letters* are so obvious that they can deceive only those who wish to deceive themselves." Despite the church's ban, *The Persian Letters* remained popular throughout the rest of the century.

FURTHER READING

Conroy, Peter V., Jr. *Montesquieu Revisited.* New York: Twayne Publishers, 1992.
Haight, Anne Lyon. *Banned Books: 387 BC to 1978 AD.* Updated and enlarged by Chandler B. Grannis. New York: R. R. Bowker, 1978.
Montesquieu. *The Persian Letters.* Translated and with an introduction by George R. Healy. Indianapolis, Ind.: Bobbs-Merrill, 1964.
Shklar, Judith N. *Montesquieu.* Oxford: Oxford University Press, 1987.

PHILOSOPHICAL DICTIONARY

Author: Voltaire
Original date and place of publication: 1764, France
Literary form: Essays

SUMMARY

Voltaire (François-Marie Arouet), perhaps the most famous individual of the 18th century and among the greatest of its writers, was the chief standard-bearer of the Enlightenment. In the name of rationalism and tolerance, he declared war on dogmatic religion, especially Catholicism and its traditions. As a deist, Voltaire affirmed his personal belief in God but rejected the doctrines of institutionalized religion. In a 1762 letter to Jean Le Rond d'Alembert, an editor of the famous ENCYCLOPÉDIE, to which Voltaire was a contributor, he attacked persecution, torture, and other abuses of religious freedom carried out by the church with the phrase *"Écrasez l'infâme"* ("Stamp out the infamous thing"). Voltaire's denunciation of Christianity became his most repeated watchword and the militant battle cry of the Enlightenment.

Theological religion is "the source of all imaginable follies and discords; it is the mother of fanaticism and civil discord; it is the enemy of mankind," Voltaire wrote in his *Philosophical Dictionary*. A series of alphabetical essays on a variety of subjects, the *Dictionary* is regarded as Voltaire's anti-Christian *summa*. It collected short articles on a wide range of subjects, including religion, government, war, friendship, beauty, and love. The articles were written with the elegant irony, clarity, and uncompromising frankness characteristic of Voltaire's style. First published in a pocket edition in 1764, it was gradually enlarged to six volumes, becoming a compendium of Voltaire's philosophical writings.

In a sentence that at first glance seemed innocuous, Voltaire gave his readers a taste of the iconoclastic nature of the book in the opening entry in the *Dictionary*'s first edition. "Abraham is one of the names famous in Asia Minor and in Arabia," he wrote, "like Toth among the Egyptians, the first Zoroaster in Persia, Hercules in Greece, Orpheus in Thrace, Odin among the northern nations, and so many others whose fame is greater than the authenticity of their history." Voltaire had in a matter-of-fact manner ranked the biblical personage of Abraham among pagan or mythological figures whose historical origins were doubtful. Voltaire's skeptical approach to the Bible was to inquire into the veracity of the events of Scripture and if he determined that a particular event really occurred, to ask whether it was good and conformed to the idea of justice.

Jesus taught no metaphysical dogma at all, Voltaire claimed. "He abandoned to the Franciscans and the Dominicans, who were to come 1,200 years after him, the trouble of arguing whether his mother had been conceived in original sin. . . . He instituted neither monks nor inquisitors. He commanded nothing of what we see today." In the article "Religion," Voltaire analyzed the qualities that in his view determined the "least bad" religion. He asked whether it might be the simplest, the one that taught morality and very little dogma and "that which did not order one to believe in things that are impossible, contradictory, injurious to divinity, and pernicious to mankind, and which dared not menace with eternal punishment anyone possessing common sense?"

Voltaire reserved his most scathing and impassioned comments for what he described as religious fanaticism leading to persecution and injustice, which he viewed as a thousand times worse than atheism. As the most detestable example of the disease of fanaticism, he cited the St. Bartholomew's Day Massacre, when French Catholics butchered 70,000 French Protestants on August 24, 1572, and subsequent days. "There is no other remedy for this epidemic illness than the spirit of free thought, which, spreading little by little, finally softens men's customs, and prevents the renewal of the disease."

In "Torture," an article added to the 1769 edition, he commented on the case of the chevalier de Barre, a promising young man in Abbeville, France, who, according to Voltaire, was convicted of blasphemy for singing impious songs and passing a procession of Capuchin monks without removing his hat. He was tortured and burned to death in 1766. Barre's personal copy of the first edition of the *Philosophical Dictionary* went to the flames with him. "Foreign nations judge France by her theatre, her novels, her charming verse, the girls of her opera, whose morals are very agreeable . . . ," Voltaire declared. "They do not know that there is no nation more cruel at bottom than the French."

In "Japanese Catechism," Voltaire asked, "If there are a dozen caterers, each of whom has a different recipe, must we on that account cut each other's throats instead of dining? On the contrary every man will eat well in his fashion with the cook who pleases him best." The *Philosophical Dictionary* is full of such bons mots on the subject of tolerance. From "Freedom of Thought": "It's shameful to put one's mind into the hands of those whom you wouldn't entrust with your money. Dare to think for yourself."

CENSORSHIP HISTORY

"The greatest misfortune of a writer is not perhaps to be the object of his colleagues' jealousy, the victim of intrigue, to be despised by the powerful of this world—it is to be judged by fools," wrote Voltaire in the *Philosophical Dictionary*, predicting the reception of censors to his book. "Fools sometimes go far, especially when ineptitude is added to fanaticism, and vengefulness to ineptitude."

Voltaire's "alphabetic abomination" was immediately condemned by religious and civil authorities throughout Europe. It was banned and burned in France, Geneva, the Netherlands, and Rome. When Geneva's public prosecutor, Jean Robert Tronchin, was asked in 1764 by the city council to give his opinion of the book, he described it as indecent, scandalous, and destructive of revelation, a contagious poison and "a deplorable monument of the extent to which intelligence and erudition can be abused." One of the prosecutor's most vehement and puzzling objections was that Voltaire quoted passages from the Bible which "taken literally would be unworthy of Divine Majesty."

Comparing his *Dictionary* with the monumental ENCYCLOPÉDIE, Voltaire wrote, "Twenty folio volumes will never make a revolution. It is the little portable volumes of thirty *sous* that are to be feared." Indeed, Voltaire's alphabetical essays became enormously popular and influential and, despite their banning, were published clandestinely in numerous editions, some prepared under Voltaire's supervision, but more often pirated by underground printers. On numerous occasions Voltaire felt obliged to deny that he had written the book. In the absence of proof to the contrary, he was able to avoid prosecution.

Because Voltaire had planned the *Dictionary* as a deliberately revolutionary book, in which he would express liberal ideas in accessible form, its banning did not come as a surprise; nor did its placement on the Catholic Church's Index of Forbidden Books, ultimately in the company of 37 other works by Voltaire, including LETTERS CONCERNING THE ENGLISH NATION.

The Catholic Church's antipathy to Voltaire was again demonstrated in 1938 when Alfred Noyes, a British Catholic writer, was denounced to the Vatican for having written a biography of Voltaire that was regarded as sympathetic. The second edition of *Voltaire*, which had earlier received favorable reviews in both the Catholic and Anglican press in England, was about to be published when an anonymous letter writer reported it to the Vatican.

According to Noyes, the purpose of his book was to show that atheists and skeptics were unaware of Voltaire's support for the central principles and beliefs of religious faith. The Supreme Congress of the Holy See issued a temporary suspension of the book. As a Catholic, Noyes was compelled to consider the church's views of the book or face excommunication. The archbishop of Westminster, Arthur Cardinal Hinsley, wrote to Rome to inquire about the Vatican's specific objections; in response, the matter was referred back to him for settlement. In April 1939, Cardinal Hinsley issued a public letter that was prominently published in major newspapers and in the Catholic press, stating that the competent authorities desired no alteration in the book's text. Noyes, by agreement with the church, wrote a new preface, clarifying his thoughts on Voltaire, and there was no further objection to the biography.

FURTHER READING

Bachman, Albert. *Censorship in France from 1715–1750: Voltaire's Opposition.* New York: Burt Franklin, 1971.

Gay, Peter. *The Enlightenment: An Interpretation. The Rise of Modern Paganism.* New York: W. W. Norton, 1995.

Noyes, Alfred. *Two Worlds for Memory.* Philadelphia: J. B. Lippincott, 1953.

Voltaire. *Philosophical Dictionary.* Edited, translated, and with an introduction by Theodore Besterman. New York: Penguin Books, 1972.

THE POLITICAL HISTORY OF THE DEVIL

Author: Daniel Defoe
Original date and place of publication: 1726, England
Literary form: Religious history

SUMMARY

The English writer Daniel Defoe, author of more than 500 works of journalism and pamphlets, including the censored THE SHORTEST WAY WITH THE DISSENTERS, and novels such as *Robinson Crusoe* and *MOLL FLANDERS,* devoted three long books during the prolific last decade of his life to supernatural matters. *The Political History of the Devil* and *A System of Magick; or, A History of the Black Art* in 1726 and *An Essay on the History and Reality of Apparitions* in 1727 reflected Defoe's lifelong interest in the occult, in common with many intellectuals of his time. Though these books have puzzled modern readers, they were of great interest during the 1720s in plague-ridden London, when superstition, folklore, and magic proliferated. Even clergymen who wrote books combatting superstition admitted the possibility of the appearance in the world of devils, apparitions, and omens.

Defoe's aim in these books was to separate legitimate consideration of the supernatural from superstition. In *The Political History of the Devil,* Defoe, blending the serious and the comic, explores the evidence for the actions and influence of Satan in the world. He ridicules faith in wizards, witches, and astrologers but affirms that those who believe in God cannot deny the existence of Satan. The devil, as a spirit, however, lacks the power to take human form and interfere with the natural order of things. Satan's power lies, rather, in his influence on human inclinations and passions, in "mischief, seducing and deluding mankind, and drawing him in to be a rebel like himself."

The devil cannot be used as an excuse: "Bad as he is, the Devil may be abus'd, / Be falsely charged; and causelessly accus'd, / When men Unwilling to be blam'd alone, / Shift off those Crimes on Him which are their own." Defoe dismisses as profane and ridiculous popular belief that the devil is a person or that hell is a physical location. Hell is, rather, "Absence from . . . all Beatitude," despair and lack of hope, redemption or recovery. This "devilish spirit," he writes, "forms a hell within us, and . . . imperceptibly . . . transforms us into devils." Hell is a state of mind and the "devilish spirit" is evil as visibly manifest in history through human actors. The power of the devil is limited. "He can only bark, but cannot bite."

CENSORSHIP HISTORY

Though they are little read today, all three of Defoe's books on the supernatural were popular in the early 18th century. *The Political History of the Devil* went into a second edition in 1727 and before Defoe's death was translated into French and German. *The Political History of the Devil,* the only one of the three to be censored by the Catholic Church, was placed on the

Index of Forbidden Books in 1743. In the book, Defoe refers to the church's Inquisition as the "perfection of devilism," and imputes the presence of evil in the actions of the church hierarchy. "[T]yranny of the worst sort crept into the pontificate," he wrote, "errors of all sort into the profession, and they proceeded from one thing to another, till the very popes . . . professed openly to confederate with the Devil, and to carry on a personal and private correspondence with him."

Though Defoe's novels have faced various bans for obscenity and *Robinson Crusoe* was placed on the Spanish Index of Forbidden Books in 1720, *The Political History of the Devil*, among the most obscure of Defoe's hundreds of works, stands out as the only one to be placed on the Roman Index. Its presence on the Index was reconfirmed by Pope Leo XIII in 1897, and it remained forbidden reading for Catholics through the last edition compiled in 1948 and in effect until 1966. Defoe's book again emerged from obscurity when a quotation from it was selected by Salman Rushdie as the epigraph of the most censored book of the 20th century, THE SATANIC VERSES.

FURTHER READING

Backschneider, Paula R. *Daniel Defoe: His Life*. Baltimore: Johns Hopkins University Press, 1989.
Earle, Peter. *The World of Defoe*. New York: Atheneum, 1977.
Levy, Leonard W. *Blasphemy: Verbal Offense Against the Sacred, from Moses to Salman Rushdie*. New York: Alfred A. Knopf, 1993.
Richetti, John J. *Daniel Defoe*. Boston: Twayne Publishers, 1987.

POPOL VUH

Original date and place of composition: ca. 1000–1550, Guatemala
Literary form: Religious text

SUMMARY

The Popol Vuh, the sacred book of the Quiché Maya, is the most important text in the native languages of the Americas and the greatest Mesoamerican mythological work. It is considered to be among the world's masterpieces of religious writing. Blending myth, legend, and history, it recounts the cosmology, migratory tradition, and history of the Quiché Maya of Guatemala's highlands. The Quiché, who number more than 500,000 today, live in the same land and among the same landmarks whose ancient history is described in the Popul Vuh, or "Council Book," consulted by the lords of Quiché when they sat in council.

The narrative in part one of the Popol Vuh begins in the primeval darkness before creation, in an empty world of only sky and sea and the gods who live in the waters. The Heart of Sky (a tripartite being also called Hurricane) and the Sovereign Plumed Serpent, who resides in the primordial sea, resolve to create the world. They say "Earth," and it suddenly comes into being, rising like a cloud or a mist. The gods begin their efforts to create human beings. On the first try they create beings who can only squawk, chatter, and howl. Because they cannot speak properly to worship their gods, they are condemned to be killed for food. Their descendants are the birds and animals.

A second experiment creates a being of mud that dissolves into nothing, incapable of speaking or worshipping. Before their third attempt, the younger gods consult the elderly divinities—the matchmaker, Xpiyacoc, and the midwife, Xmucané, both daykeepers or diviners who can interpret the auguries of the calendar cycle. They approve the creation of human beings made of wood. Because the wooden mannequins are empty-headed, with no memory of their creators, Heart of Sky brings a great flood down upon them. They are crushed and destroyed, and their only descendants are the monkeys of the forests.

Before telling of their fourth attempt to create human beings, the narrators recount in parts two and three the three-part cycle of the exploits of the hero twins. First Hunahpú and Xbalanqué, the twin grandsons of Xpiyacoc and Xmucané, in a series of adventures, vanquish Seven Macaw (the Big Dipper) and his offspring, Zipacna and Earthquake.

Then the story flashes back to an earlier story of the exploits in Xibalbá, the underworld, of another set of twins—One Hunahpú and Seven Hunahpú, the father and uncle of Hunahpú and Xbalanqué and the sons of Xpiyacoc and Xmucané. They are summoned to the underworld and fail a series of tests and traps set by their hosts. They are sacrificed in Xibalbá by the lords of death.

The final segment relates the adventures in the underworld of the first set of hero twins, Hunahpú and Xbalanqué. They are successful in escaping from the traps that had caused the demise of their father and uncle and plan a way to die that will allow them to come back to life. The twins then ascend from Xibalbá into the heavens to become the Sun and the Moon.

The stage is now set for the fourth creation. In part four, as the Sun, Moon, and stars are about to rise, Xpiyacoc and Xmucané find yellow and white corn in a mountain. Xmucané grinds it together nine times. Mixed with water, the corn provides the material for the first human beings: Jaguar Quitzé, Jaguar Night, Mahucutah, and True Jaguar, the first mother-fathers of the Quiché people. But as the new men are too perfect, the gods worry that their creations will compete with them in greatness. The gods weaken the men's eyes so that they can see only nearby things clearly, limiting their powers of knowing and understanding. Then the gods make a wife for each new man and the leading Quiché lineages descend from these pairs. Finally, after much sacrifice and prayer, the Sun appears for the first time. "There were countless peoples, but there was just one dawn for all tribes."

The creation myth recounted in the Popol Vuh is an actual map of the sky that replays creation in the pattern of its yearly movements. The actions of the gods, the heroes, and their enemies correspond to the movements of the Sun, Moon, planets, and stars. Creation is not a single act but a process through which the essence of divinity continually creates and maintains life. The Popol Vuh concludes in part five with a lengthy migration story that recounts episodes in the mythological and actual history of the Quiché people and their Maya neighbors. It lists the names of 14 generations of the rulers of Quiché up to the time when this version of the Popol Vuh was written. In the 12th generation, the names of Three Deer and Nine Dog are followed by two sentences. "And they were ruling when Tonatiuh (Pedro de Alvarado) arrived. They were hanged by the Castilian people."

CENSORSHIP HISTORY

The Popol Vuh was originally written in Mayan hieroglyphics by Quiché Maya nobles during the Postclassic period (A.D. 1000 to 1500) and was in use by the Quiché at the time of the Spanish conquest in the 16th century. Illustrations on painted pottery and inscriptions carved on stone monuments indicate that the myths and legends told in the Popol Vuh are much older, dating at least to the Classic period (A.D. 250 to 900), the time of the highest flourishing of Maya art and culture.

After 1523, when the Spanish conquistador Pedro de Alvarado was sent by Hernán Cortés to subdue the Maya peoples of Guatemala, Spanish missionaries burned thousands of hieroglyphic books. The original Popol Vuh is assumed to have been among them. Hieroglyphic books were regarded by the Spanish as superstitious works of the devil. Their destruction was part of a sustained campaign to eradicate Maya religion and culture and impose European Catholicism.

In the 1550s, a text of the Popol Vuh was secretly rewritten in the Roman alphabet in the town of Santa Cruz del Quiché, Guatemala, by descendants of the lordly lineages who once ruled the Quiché Kingdom. Its anonymous authors had been taught by missionaries to write their language in the alphabet. In 1701–03, the book was translated into Spanish by a Dominican friar, Francisco Ximénez, the parish priest of the nearby town of Chichicastenango, who was shown the document and recognized its importance. He also made what is now the only copy of the Quiché Mayan text.

The original Popol Vuh would have been fully illustrated, a folding-screen manuscript painted on bark paper thinly coated with lime plaster. It would have included astrological tables and ritual almanacs used for divination, similar to the pages of the only four Maya hieroglyphic books or fragments, called codices, that survived the depredations of the Spanish conquest. Three codices from Yucatán, Mexico, were taken to Europe in colonial times and bear the names of the cities where they were found in museums or libraries: the Dresden, Paris, and Madrid Codices. A fourth fragment, known as the Grolier

Codex, now in Mexico City, was found in a cave in Chiapas, Mexico, in 1971. The Popol Vuh of the 16th century presented an expanded version of the original hieroglyphic book, telling the full story behind the charts and pictures.

According to the writers of the alphabetic version, the hieroglyphic codex was among the most precious possessions of the Quiché rulers because "they knew whether war would occur; everything they saw was clear to them. Whether there would be death or whether there would be famine. . . . [T]hey knew it for certain, since there was a place to see it, there was a book." The Council Book allowed the Quiché lords to recover the vision lost by the first four humans.

The highly praised first unabridged English-language translation of the Popol Vuh by Dennis Tedlock, published in 1985, incorporates the insight of a contemporary Quiché Maya daykeeper and head of his patrilineage, Andrés Xiloj. It is engaging and readable, despite the complexity of the mythology it contains, and has brought the Popol Vuh to a larger audience.

FURTHER READING

Freidel, David, Linda Schele, and Joy Parker. *Maya Cosmos: Three Thousand Years on the Shaman's Path*. New York: William Morrow, 1993.

Gallenkamp, Charles. *Maya: The Riddle and Discovery of a Lost Civilization*. New York: David McKay, 1976.

Markman, Roberta, and Peter Markman. *The Flayed God: The Mythology of Mesoamerica*. New York: HarperCollins, 1992.

Stuart, Gene S., and George E. Stuart. *Lost Kingdoms of the Maya*. Washington, D.C.: National Geographic Society, 1993.

Tedlock, Dennis, trans. *Popol Vuh: The Definitive Edition of the Mayan Book of the Dawn of Life and the Glories of Gods and Kings*. New York: Simon and Schuster, 1985.

THE POWER AND THE GLORY

Author: Graham Greene
Original date and places of publication: 1940, United Kingdom and United States
Literary form: Fiction

SUMMARY

The Power and the Glory, widely regarded as Graham Greene's finest novel, tells the story of a dissolute fugitive priest pursued by a fanatical police lieutenant during an anticlerical purge in Mexico in the 1930s. In 1938, Greene visited Mexico to research a report commissioned by the Catholic Church on religious persecution under the new revolutionary regime. His journey took him through the southern states of Chiapas and Tabasco, where Catholic churches had been destroyed and priests banished or executed. Greene wrote a nonfiction account of his trip, *The Lawless Roads*, and drew on his experiences for the setting and theme of *The Power and the Glory*.

The unnamed priest of the novel, sometimes known as Montez, more commonly as "the whiskey priest," is the last surviving priest in the state. He defies the government ban on administering the sacraments, moving from village to village, keeping one step ahead of the police and certain arrest on charges of treason. The whiskey priest, an alcoholic who has fathered a child by a parishioner in a tiny village, is troubled by guilt and the knowledge of his own weakness and sinfulness.

Montez's relentless pursuer, a young policeman, is an ardent and upright revolutionary who believes that only when Mexico is rid of the Catholic Church and its clergy will the poor find liberation. His fervent atheism is described by Greene as a kind of mysticism. "There are mystics who are said to have experienced God directly. He was a mystic, too, and what he had experienced was vacancy—a complete certainty in the existence of a dying, cooling world, of human beings who had evolved from animals for no purpose at all."

The priest has come to the coast to board a boat that will take him to safety in the port of Veracruz. But a boy pleads with him to administer the last rites to his dying mother, several miles inland. Now in the interior, he is at risk of capture by the revolutionary Red Shirts, who shoot priests on sight. He finds temporary refuge in a remote banana plantation run by an Englishman, Captain Fellows.

The priest eventually makes his way to the village where his daughter, Brigida, and her mother, Maria, live. Before dawn he conducts a secret mass for the villagers, interrupted by the arrival of the police. Maria pretends the priest is her husband, and although a hostage from the village is taken, no one informs on him.

In the company of a poor and wily mestizo, whom he fears will betray him for a reward, he travels to a town where he is able to elude his companion, but he is arrested for illegal possession of liquor and thrown into jail overnight. His fellow prisoners, who realize he is a priest, protect his identity. He is released by the police lieutenant, who does not recognize him as the priest he seeks.

On his way to safe territory in the city of Las Casas, he again encounters the Judas-like figure of the mestizo, who tells him that an American bandit has been wounded by the police and wishes to receive the last rites. Fully suspecting that he will walk into a police trap, the priest embraces his duty and accompanies the mestizo into the mountains. He is captured by the police lieutenant, tried for treason, and sentenced to be shot.

He spends his last night in despair and regret at his own uselessness and failures. "The eight hard hopeless years seemed to him to be only a caricature of service: a few communions, a few confessions, and an endless bad example. He thought: If I only had one soul to offer, so that I could say, Look what I've done. . . . People had died for him, they had deserved a saint, and a tinge of bitterness spread across his mind for their sake that God hadn't thought to send them one."

Yet, while he was without sin in his early years as a priest, he was bereft of the love he has come to feel for his daughter and compassion for the poor whose squalid existence he now shares. The night after his death, a young boy who has been moved by his quiet bravery spurns the lieutenant he once admired and welcomes another fugitive priest who has come secretly to town. The corrupt whiskey priest has been vindicated, for the work of the church has gone forward, and in his flawed and wretched life he has attained a kind of saintliness.

CENSORSHIP HISTORY

The first British edition of *The Power and the Glory*, in 1940 (published the same year in the United States as *The Labyrinthine Ways*), was printed in only 3,500 copies. Published during the "phony war" period of World War II, a month before Hitler invaded the Low Countries, it was overshadowed by public crisis; despite favorable reviews and its receipt of the Hawthornden Prize for 1940, there was little public interest in Greene's story of remote Mexico. The book did not sell well during the war, but immediately after, its English publisher released a pocket edition of 18,650 copies and, in 1949, another 23,450 for a uniform edition of Greene's work. Interest in the novel was revived, especially in France, where it was published with a sympathetic introduction by the Nobel laureate François Mauriac.

Mauriac has described Greene's novels as being about "the utilization of sin by Grace." In Greene's fictional world, God's grace is often bestowed on sinners, the wretched who are close to despair. Many of his most sympathetically drawn characters, such as the whiskey priest in *The Power and the Glory*, are those in a state of doubt or unbelief.

Greene had converted to Catholicism in 1926 but preferred to be known as a writer who was a Catholic, rather than as a Catholic writer. "I always considered myself a protestant inside the Church rather than being a protestant outside," he said. In a 1948 essay, *Why Do I Write?*, Greene defended his right to be "disloyal" to the church. To preserve his artistic integrity, he wrote, he must be able to write "from the point of view of the black square as well as from the white," for if his writing merely conformed with official dogma, the result would be propaganda.

Greene recounted that the story of the drunk priest was partly inspired by his irritation at "the smug Protestant treatment of the erring priest. It always seemed to me a very superficial kind of condemnation. I wanted to show that the man's office doesn't depend on the man. A priest in giving a sacrament believes he is giving the body and blood of Christ, and it doesn't matter whether he himself is a murderer, an adulterer, a drunkard." The priest in the novel says, "I can put God into a man's mouth just the same—and I can give him God's pardon. It wouldn't make any difference to that if every priest in the Church was like me."

Greene's sympathetic portrayal of the whiskey priest led two Catholic bishops in France to denounce the book to Rome on two different occasions. Fourteen years after the book's publication, it was condemned by Giuseppe Cardinal Pizzardo, of the Vatican's Holy Office, on the grounds that it was "paradoxical" and "dealt with extraordinary circumstances." In 1953, Greene was summoned by Bernard William Cardinal Griffin, the archbishop of Westminster, and told of Cardinal Pizzardo's action. Griffin read Greene a letter from the Holy Office in which Pizzardo requested that changes be made in the text, "which I naturally—though I hope politely—refused to make," Greene wrote in his memoirs. He used the excuse that the copyright was in the hand of his publisher.

Griffin added that he would have preferred that Rome had condemned another of Greene's novels, *The End of the Affair*, rather than *The Power and the Glory*. "You and I receive no harm from erotic passages, but the young . . . ," he said. When the interview ended, Griffin provided a copy of his pastoral letter, which was read in the churches of his diocese during Advent of 1953. His letter condemned not only *The Power and the Glory* but also, by implication, *The Heart of the Matter* and *The End of the Affair*, both among Greene's most highly regarded novels.

"It is sadly true that a number of Catholic writers appear to have fallen into this error," the letter said. "Indeed, novels which purport to be the vehicle for Catholic doctrine frequently contain passages which by their unrestrained portrayal of immoral conduct prove a source of temptation to many of their readers. . . . The presentation of the Catholic way of life within the framework of fiction may be an admirable object but it can never be justified as a means to that end the inclusion of indecent and harmful material."

Despite this rebuke, the church took no further action against the novel. "The affair was allowed to drop into that peaceful oblivion which the Church wisely reserves for unimportant issues," Greene wrote. Greene did not dwell on the church's attempts to censor his writings when he recounted the incident in his memoirs, and the censorship had little effect on the book's reputation or its sales. But his authorized biographer, Norman Sherry, reported that Greene was deeply troubled by the incident.

In later years, Greene had an audience with Pope Paul VI in Rome. The pope told Greene that he had read *The Power and the Glory*. Greene responded that it had been condemned by the Holy Office. "Who condemned it?" the pope asked. "Cardinal Pizzardo," Greene responded. The pope repeated the name with a smile and added, "Mr. Greene, some parts of your books are certain to offend some Catholics, but you should not worry about that."

Four of Greene's books—*The Heart of the Matter*, *The End of the Affair*, *England Made Me*, and *The Quiet American*—did offend Catholics on the Irish censorship board and were banned by the Eire government. In each case the ban was successfully reversed upon an appeal by his publishers. In the case of *The Heart of the Matter,* prohibited in 1948 for being "indecent in tendency," Greene remarked that the banning helped to sell copies.

FURTHER READING

Donaghy, Henry J., ed. *Conversations with Graham Greene.* Jackson: University Press of Mississippi, 1992.
Greene, Graham. *A Sort of Life.* New York: Simon and Schuster, 1971.
———. *Ways of Escape.* New York: Simon and Schuster, 1980.
O'Prey, Paul. *A Reader's Guide to Graham Greene.* New York: Thames and Hudson, 1988.
Sherry, Norman. *The Life of Graham Greene.* Vol. 2: *1939–1955.* New York: Viking Penguin, 1994.

THE PRAISE OF FOLLY

Author: Desiderius Erasmus
Original date and place of publication: 1511, France
Literary form: Satirical essay

SUMMARY

The Dutch humanist Desiderius Erasmus, a proponent of reform within the Catholic Church, was among the best-known and influential men of his time. Through the new technological advances of printing, his work became known throughout Europe. He produced dozens of volumes on a wide range of subjects, including scholarly editions of the writing of the church fathers and translations of classical authors, a ground-breaking translation of the Greek New Testament into Latin, numerous commentaries and homilies, moral, religious and political essays, books on education, and a dictionary of proverbs.

Erasmus's original works, written in Latin, the language of the 16th-century scholar, were mainly satirical and critical. In advocating moderation and tolerance, Erasmus's writing combined erudition with sharp wit and style. *The Praise of Folly* is a light satire suggested by Sir Thomas More, at whose home in England Erasmus wrote the book while resting from an Italian journey in 1509. In the preface he declared, "We have praised folly not quite foolishly," for *The Praise of Folly* had the same serious purpose as all of his writing: to criticize abuses in the church and in society and to promote a purer spirituality in religion.

In *The Praise of Folly,* Folly is presented as a person who offers an oration of praise to herself. She claims as her own all human activity except that which is governed by reason. She exalts the life of instinct, proclaiming her superiority over wisdom. The followers of Folly are devotees of self-love and ignorance in every trade and profession. By ironically praising stupidity and corruption, Erasmus exalts the Christian humanist way of life and the values that Folly, or the fool, disdains. He targets for ridicule superstitious practices within Catholicism, castigates insincere monks, "who make a good living out of squalor and beggary," and church authorities who betray their high offices by leading unchristian lives.

Erasmus reserves his most scathing criticism for the "tortuous obscurities" of quibbling Scholastic theologians, "a remarkably supercilious and touchy lot. I might perhaps do better to pass over them in silence without stirring the mud of Camarina or grasping that noxious plant, lest they marshal their forces for an attack and force me to eat my words. If I refuse they'll denounce me as a heretic on the spot, for this is the bolt they always loose on anyone to whom they take a dislike."

Delving into theological minutiae, the theologians interpret hidden mysteries to suit themselves. Erasmus suggests that there are many more worthy questions to be considered: "Could God have taken on the form of a woman, a devil, a donkey, a gourd, or a flintstone? If so, how could a gourd have preached sermons, performed miracles, and been nailed to the cross? . . . Shall we be permitted to eat and drink after the resurrection? We're taking due precaution against hunger and thirst while there's time."

Such is the erudition and complexity displayed by the theologians, Erasmus writes, "that I fancy the apostles themselves would need the help of another Holy Spirit if they were obliged to join issue on these topics with our new breed of new theologian. . . . Who *could* understand all this unless he has frittered away 36 whole years over the physics and metaphysics of Aristotle and Scotus?" The apostles refuted the philosophers with whom they disagreed but did so more by the example of their way of life than by syllogisms.

CENSORSHIP HISTORY

At the time of Erasmus's death in 1536, 36 Latin editions of *The Praise of Folly* had been published. It was translated into Czech, French, German, Italian, and English. Published in more than 600 editions over the centuries, it remains his most popular work today. Upon its appearance in 1511, it was well received by humanists but was sharply criticized in clerical circles as heretical. In *The Praise of Folly*, Erasmus lambastes theologians who appoint themselves as the world's censors and "demand recantation of anything which doesn't exactly square with their conclusions. . . ." This was an apt description of his satire's reception.

Though Erasmus wrote that he thought so little of the work that he was unsure if it was worth publishing, "hardly anything of mine has had a more enthusiastic reception, especially among the great. A few monks only, and those the worst, took offense at its freedom; but more were offended when Listrius added notes, for before that moment it had gained from not being understood." Erasmus said that he had originally conceived the idea of writing three simultaneous declamations, in praise of Folly, Nature, and Grace. "But some people I could name proved so difficult that I changed my mind."

The theologian Maarten van Dorp of Louvain, Belgium, was among those who reproached Erasmus for his hostility toward professional theologians. Erasmus replied to Dorp in the form of an apologia addressed to all conservative theologians. "First then, to be perfectly frank," he wrote, "I am almost sorry myself that I published my Folly. That small book has earned me not a little reputation coupled with ill will. My purpose was guidance and not satire; to help, not to hurt; to show men how to become better and not to stand in their way."

Erasmus declared that anyone who claims that he was injured by his satire "betrays his own guilty conscience, or at any rate his apprehensions." Dorp was later converted to Erasmus's position, but such was not the case with other theologians. Though the pope was said to be delighted with *The Praise of Folly*, it was prohibited at the universities of Paris, Louvain, Oxford, and Cambridge.

Despite bans of the book, Erasmus enjoyed great popularity and was hailed as a hero among humanists. "Every day I receive letters from learned men which set me up as the glory of Germany and call me its sun and moon," he wrote in 1515. He was given benefices, offered teaching posts, and in 1515 appointed councilor to Prince Charles. By the 1520s, however, his situation had changed. "There is no party that does not hate me bitterly," he reflected.

The turning point in Erasmus's career had come with the publication in 1516 of his magnum opus, his translation into Latin of the Greek New Testament, and with the rise of Martin Luther. Already unpopular with theologians because of his sharp criticism of the profession in *The Praise of Folly*, his pursuit of biblical studies was considered meddling.

Conservative theologians challenged Erasmus's authority to translate the Bible; his version revised and corrected errors that had crept into the standard Vulgate text over the years. Although he dedicated his translation to Pope Leo X, who praised him for "exceptional service to the study of sacred theology and to the maintenance of the true faith," Erasmus was unable to quell the controversy that arose over his translation.

But it was the conflict over Luther's views that brought about a definitive change in Erasmus's fortunes. In a "Brief Outline of His Life," an autobiographical sketch composed in 1524, Erasmus explained that "[t]he sad business of Luther had brought him [Erasmus] a burden of intolerable ill will; he was torn in pieces by both sides, while aiming zealously at what was best for both." Luther had looked upon Erasmus as an ally in attacking clerical abuses in the church. Eager for church reform, Erasmus at first welcomed Luther's initiatives. However, powerful Catholic friends urged Erasmus to declare himself against Luther. He refused, preferring to engage in debates with the Protestant reformers while remaining a loyal Catholic.

Erasmus eventually withdrew his support for Luther, attacking his position on predestination and free will. But conservative Catholics thought he had done too little too late. Both sides in the dispute assailed Erasmus. The Lutherans and Calvinists called him a traitor to their cause, and Catholics, who viewed him as a Lutheran sympathizer, denounced him for heresy. In

1524, the university of the Sorbonne in Paris forbade the sale or reading of Erasmus's COLLOQUIES, a book designed to teach schoolchildren good Latin, because of "its Lutheran tendencies." In 1527, the Spanish inquisitor general convened a conference to examine his writings. Four years later, the prestigious faculty of theology at Paris also reviewed his works and condemned a number of passages as scandalous and unorthodox.

After Erasmus's death in 1536, the onslaught continued. In 1544, his works were forbidden at the Sorbonne. *The Praise of Folly* and most of his other works were banned in Spain. The Index of Forbidden Books published by the Inquisition of Toulouse, France, in 1548 included the work of Erasmus along with Luther's. In 1550, all of his works were placed on the Spanish Index of Forbidden Books. In 1551, the Parlement of Paris forbade the printing or sale of his books. The following year the Louvain theologians joined their colleagues at the Sorbonne and described condemned passages from his writings as erroneous, scandalous and heretical. In 1555, Mary, Queen of Scots, forbade the reading of his works in Scotland.

The papacy in Rome, however, had not yet seen Erasmus as an enemy, having been friendly toward him during his lifetime. But as the Counter-Reformation intensified, Erasmus's work came under attack with the publication of the first Index of Forbidden Books by Pope Paul IV in 1559. He condemned Erasmus as harshly as Luther and Calvin as a major influence on the Protestant Reformation. Erasmus's name was placed in the Index's Class I, the list of authors whose works were totally banned. "All of his Commentaries, Remarks, Notes, Dialogues, Letters, Criticisms, Translations, Books and writings, including even those which contain nothing concerning religion," stated the Index, were prohibited.

Among the new features of the 1559 Index, evident in its full title, Index auctorum et librorum prohibitorum, was the simultaneous banning of books and authors. In some cases a single book was chosen to be suppressed, but, in other cases, notably that of Erasmus, all the author's works were banned. This blanket condemnation was slightly modified by the Tridentine Index of 1564, issued by the Council of Trent. In the revised Index some of Erasmus's works were permitted in expurgated form. Others, such as *The Praise of Folly* and *Colloquies*, remained suppressed. Apart from Spain, which had its own Index, the Tridentine Index was effective in Belgium, Bavaria, Portugal, Italy, and France.

Subsequent Indexes, both in Rome and Spain, maintained the bans on Erasmus. A list of his forbidden works took up 55 quarto pages in the Index of Quiroga, Spain, in 1583. The list had increased to 500 double-columned folio pages by 1640. Erasmus was consigned to the ranks of incorrigible heretics, and the words *auctoris damnati* (of a condemned author) were inserted after his name on all title pages.

Erasmus's reputation recovered only when the intellectual climate changed in the 18th century, as the progressives of the Enlightenment discovered a kindred spirit in his values of reason and tolerance. Erasmus's works, nevertheless, remained on the Roman Index of Forbidden Books for four centuries, until his name was finally removed in 1930.

FURTHER READING

Burman, Edward. *The Inquisition: Hammer of Heresy.* New York: Dorset Press, 1992.
Erasmus, Desiderius. *The Praise of Folly.* Translated by John Wilson. Ann Arbor: University of Michigan Press, 1958.
Rummel, Erika, ed. *The Erasmus Reader.* Toronto: University of Toronto Press, 1990.
Wilcox, Donald J. *In Search of God and Self: Renaissance and Reformation Thought.* Boston: Houghton Mifflin, 1975.

PRINCIPLES OF POLITICAL ECONOMY

Author: John Stuart Mill
Original date and place of publication: 1848, United Kingdom
Literary form: Economics treatise

SUMMARY

The British philosopher, economist, and social reformer John Stuart Mill was one of the leading intellectual figures of the 19th century. His treatise on toleration, entitled *On Liberty* and published in 1859, celebrated the primacy of the individual and opposed repression of individual rights by church, state, or the "tyranny of the majority." "Whatever crushes individuality is despotism, by whatever name it may be called, and whether it professes to be enforcing the will of God or the injunctions of men," he wrote.

In his philosophical writings, such as *System of Logic*, published in 1843, which became the standard philosophical text of the time, he maintained that knowledge was derived from experience and attacked the theory that knowledge and behavior were governed by innate ideas. His most influential contribution in philosophy was his advocacy of the moral theory of utilitarianism, espoused by his father, the philosopher James Mill, and by the political theorist Jeremy Bentham.

Utilitarianism assessed the value of human actions by evaluating their consequences in experience and the general welfare of those affected by them. The aim of the utilitarians was to test institutions in the light of reason and common sense in order to determine whether they contributed to the happiness of the greater number of people. Believing that concern for human emotions was lacking in their system, John Stuart Mill sought to temper the utilitarian doctrines of his father and Bentham with humanitarianism.

In his essay *Utilitarianism*, published in 1861, he introduced into the utilitarian calculus a principle that suggested weighing not only the quantity but also the quality of pleasure in determining the rightness of an action. Mill's utilitarianism suggested that the right thing to do in a given situation was the action that brought about "the best state of affairs."

In *Principles of Political Economy*, an earlier work published in 1848, Mill applied his views to the study of economics, using economic theory to explain how men could affect the moral progress of society. Mill built on the classic economic theories of his predecessors Adam Smith and David Ricardo. Smith, in his 1776 *Wealth of Nations*, identified self-interest as the basic economic force. Ricardo's "iron law of wages" asserted that wages tended to stabilize at the subsistence level. In addition to self-interest, Mill introduced habit and custom as economic motives and challenged the classical economic theory of the immutability of natural law by demonstrating that wages, rent, and profit could be controlled by human intervention.

Mill asserted that the province of economic law was confined to production, rather than distribution. Though man cannot change the modes and conditions under which production must take place, society can decide to distribute what has been produced as it pleases. There is no correct form of distribution, and natural law does not determine how society should share what is produced. "The things once there," Mill wrote, "mankind, individually or collectively, can do with them as they please. They can place them at the disposal of whomsoever they please, and on whatever terms. . . ." The distribution of wealth depends on the laws and customs of society and the opinions and feelings of the ruling portion of the community. Mill argued further that if economic growth caused the population to increase and if, as economist Thomas Malthus argued, population would eventually outstrip the means of subsistence, perhaps economic growth should be relinquished in order to build a better society.

In place of the wage system, Mill advocated cooperative societies in which the employees would collectively own the capital and control the managers. While maintaining the right of workers to retain what they gained by their own efforts, he suggested heavy taxation of unearned rents and inheritances. Under this system, the formation of new capital would cease, thereby preventing growth of industry and maintaining population at a more stationary level. In this static, no-growth society, he hoped that leisure time would increase and create enhanced opportunities for educational pursuits and the solution of social problems. Because a static population would require less social care, there would be a reduced need for government interference and a decreased danger that a bureaucracy would make political decisions.

CENSORSHIP HISTORY

Heated criticism of Mill's theories came from both conservatives and liberals who believed that there were much narrower limits than Mill recognized on the freedom of societies to structure their distribution. Nevertheless, *Principles of Political Economy* was an enormous success, published in seven editions during Mill's lifetime. Mill also had it printed at his own expense in a compact edition that would be affordable to the working class.

This edition sold out in five separate printings. Mill was regarded as the great economist of his day.

The Catholic Church, however, generally opposed Mill's secular philosophical perspective; his utilitarianism, which denied the existence of any divinely implanted moral consciousness or norms; his empiricism, which posited experience rather than religious authority as the source of all knowledge; and his defense of the rights of the individual as being more important than the institutions of church or state.

Earlier in the century, the church had already condemned Jeremy Bentham's utilitarian works, including AN INTRODUCTION TO THE PRINCIPLES OF MORALS AND LEGISLATION. In 1856, the Vatican placed on the Index of Forbidden Books the major works published by Mill up to that time, *System of Logic* and *Principles of Political Economy*. The prohibition of Mill's writing, as well as works such as Auguste Comte's THE COURSE OF POSITIVE PHILOSOPHY, which had influenced Mill, reflected the church's battle against the trends in philosophy and political and economic theory that reflected the modern scientific thinking of the 19th century. In 1864, Pope Pius IX issued an encyclical, "Quanta cura," accompanied by a "Syllabus of Errors," listing erroneous modernist statements and condemning toleration and "progress, liberalism and civilization as lately introduced." The advanced thinkers of the time, according to the pope, were "evil men, who. . . endeavored by their fallacious opinions and most wicked writings to subvert the foundations of Religion and of Civil Society, to remove from our mind all virtue and justice, to deprave the hearts and minds of all." Six years later at the First Vatican Council, the church confirmed the papal denunciations of modernity and liberalism by defining papal infallibility as a doctrine.

However, the Catholic Church's instructions on appropriate reading material for Catholics had little influence in England, a predominantly Protestant country. The Vatican's condemnation of Mill's work had no discernible impact on his standing as a philosopher and social theorist or on the popularity of his writings. Despite the fact that Mill's economic theories had long since been superseded, his works remained on the Index of Forbidden Books until 1966, when the Index was abolished after the reforms of the Second Vatican Council.

FURTHER READING

Christie-Murray, David. *A History of Heresy*. Oxford: Oxford University Press, 1976.

Heilbroner, Robert. *The Worldly Philosophers: The Lives, Times and Ideas of the Great Economic Thinkers*. New York: Simon and Schuster, 1986.

Mill, John Stuart. *Essential Works of John Stuart Mill*. Ed. and introduction by Max Lerner. New York: Bantam Books, 1971.

Scott-Kakures, Dion, Susan Castegnetto, Hugh Benson, William Taschek, and Paul Hurley. *History of Philosophy*. New York: HarperCollins, 1993.

Van Hollthoon, F. L. *The Road to Utopia: A Study of John Stuart Mill's Social Thought*. Assem, Netherlands: Van Gorcum, 1971.

THE PROVINCIAL LETTERS

Author: Blaise Pascal
Original dates and place of publication: 1656–57, France
Literary form: Satire

SUMMARY

The French scientist, mathematician, and religious philosopher Blaise Pascal was a convert to Jansenism, a reform movement within the Catholic Church. Following the ideas of Cornelius Jansenius (Cornelis Jansen), Catholic bishop of Flanders, and of Jean Du Vergier de Hauranne, of the abbé de Saint-Cyran of France, Jansenism advocated a return to greater personal holiness and strictness in morals, stressing the corruption of human nature, the weakness of the will, and the need for divine grace to convert the soul to God.

Reacting against the pessimism and dour piety of Calvinism, the prevailing form of Protestantism in France, the influential Jesuit order promoted an opposing doctrine known as Molinism. Rather than stressing human corruption and dependence on divine grace, the Jesuits held that free will and good works played the major role in effecting human salvation. Jansenism, seen as reflecting Protestant beliefs, was regarded by the church as heresy.

In 1653, Pope Innocent X declared that five propositions found in Jansenius's *Augustinius*, a commentary on the works of Saint Augustine, published posthumously in 1640, were heretical in that they emphasized predestination of salvation for the elect. Though Jansenius was loyal to the Catholic Church and rejected the Calvinist doctrine of justification by faith alone, he emphasized personal religious experience and the direct contact of man with God in sudden conversion.

Jansenius's disciple, Antoine Arnauld, based at the Jansenist religious community at Port-Royal, near Paris, denied that the condemned propositions were found in Jansenius's work. He admitted the pope's right to pronounce on questions of faith, but claimed that the pope was not infallible in factual matters. Accused of Calvinism, Arnauld was condemned by the theologians of the Sorbonne, and the Jesuits moved to expel him from the university.

At the request of Jansenists, Pascal came to Arnauld's defense, writing a series of *Provincial Letters*, published individually over an 18-month period during 1656 and 1657. Using a pseudonym, Pascal assumed the character of a puzzled bystander explaining in letters to a friend the course of events at the Sorbonne.

"Sir, How wrong we were!" he wrote in his first letter. "I only had my eyes opened yesterday. Until then I thought that the arguments in the Sorbonne were about something of real importance and fraught with the gravest consequences for religion. So many meetings of a body as famous as the Faculty of Paris, at which so much has occurred that is extraordinary and unprecedented, raise expectations so high that it seems incredible that the subject should be anything but extraordinary."

Using the techniques of modern journalism, Pascal interviewed the various parties to the dispute to clarify the theological issues at stake in the debate. Quoting from Jesuit statements, he trapped the experts into contradictory statements on questions of fact and faith, demonstrating the absurdity of the Jesuit position. The 11th through 18th letters were addressed directly to Jesuit fathers. Arnauld had already been expelled from the Sorbonne, and Pascal's tone became more indignant and impassioned as he moved from a defense of Arnauld to an attack on what he considered to be Jesuit hairsplitting, hypocrisy, and dishonesty. "I have told you before, and I tell you again, violence and truth have no power over each other," he wrote. "You strain every effort to make people believe that your disputes are over points of faith, and it has never been more evident that your whole dispute is simply over a point of fact."

Like Arnauld, Pascal questioned the pope's authority to decide questions of fact, asserting that his infallibility extended only to supernatural matters. "It was in vain, too," he wrote, addressing his Jesuit correspondents, "that you obtained from Rome the decree against Galileo, which condemned his opinion regarding the earth's movement. It will take more than that to prove that it keeps still, and if there were consistent observations proving that it is the earth that goes round, all the men in the world put together could not stop it from turning, or themselves turning with it."

CENSORSHIP HISTORY

The success of *The Provincial Letters* was immediate. The work was distributed clandestinely in major cities of France, translated into Latin and English, and circulated throughout Europe. The clarity and wit of Pascal's style and his use of French, rather than Latin, made the theological debates accessible to a wider audience, expanding them beyond the narrow circle of clerics.

The anti-Jesuit flavor of the *Letters* aroused a storm of criticism. Pascal was attacked for not having written in Latin, the language of theological discussion; for having used the satirical dialogue form, deemed inappropriate for religious discussion; and for having made a mockery of Jesuit theological disputes.

On February 9, 1657, the Parlement of Aix condemned the first 16 letters. Jesuit influence at court resulted in an order by Louis XIV that the *Letters* be torn up and burned at the hands of the high executioner, "fulfillment of which is to be certified to His Majesty within the week; and that meanwhile all printers, booksellers, vendors and others, of whatever rank or station, are explicitly prohibited from printing, selling, and distributing, and even from having in their possession the said book under pain of public (exemplary) punishment."

Publication of new letters ended in March 1657, as it had become too dangerous for Pascal to continue. The suppression of *The Provincial Letters*, however, did not impede the work's growing popularity. Despite police raids and arrests of publishers, the book was reprinted in France in numerous editions. Pascal stayed out of sight, moving from place to place to avoid arrest. Though among the Jansenists at Port-Royal it was an open secret that

Pascal was the author, Pascal's anonymity was officially retained until after his death. On September 6, 1657, the Catholic Church placed *The Provincial Letters* on the Index of Forbidden Books.

When Pascal was asked later in his life if he regretted having written *The Provincial Letters*, he replied that "far from regretting it, if I had to write them at the present time I would make them even stronger. . . . People ask why I used a pleasant, ironic and amusing style. I reply that, if I had written in a dogmatic style, only scholars would have read it, and they did not need to, because they knew as much about it as I."

The popularity and influence of *The Provincial Letters* endured, both as a polemical work and, later, when the religious controversies of the 17th century had long been forgotten, as a masterpiece of French classicism. *The Provincial Letters* was reprinted repeatedly in France in the first half of the 18th century as anti-Jesuit propaganda and was cited as prime evidence in the trial of Jesuits in parlement that ended with their expulsion from France in 1762. Later in the century, the *Letters* became a favorite work of the writers of the Enlightenment. Both Charles-Louis de Secondat, baron de La Brède et de Montesquieu's PERSIAN LETTERS and Voltaire's LETTERS CONCERNING THE ENGLISH NATION were indebted to Pascal. The introduction by Voltaire, the scourge of Catholicism, to the 1776 edition of *Pensées*, Pascal's book of thoughts in defense of Christian belief, not previously regarded by the church as dangerous to the faith, caused it also to be placed on the Index in 1789. Both *The Provincial Letters* and the 1776 edition of *Pensées* remained on the Index until the 20th century.

FURTHER READING

Pascal, Blaise. *The Provincial Letters*. Ed. and introduction by J. Krailsheimer. Middlesex, England: Penguin Books, 1967.
Rex, Walter. *Pascal's Provincial Letters: An Introduction*. New York: Holmes and Meier Publishers, 1977.

THE RAPE OF SITA

Author: Lindsey Collen
Original dates and places of publication: 1993, Mauritius; 1995, United States
Original publishers: Ledikasyon pu Travayer; Heinemann Educational Books
Literary form: Novel

SUMMARY

The Rape of Sita, a complex and lyrical novel by the South African–born feminist writer Lindsey Collen, who lives in Mauritius, won the 1994 Com-

monwealth Writers Prize for the best novel from Africa. Sita, the novel's protagonist, is a political activist, trade unionist, feminist, and champion of the
oppressed in Mauritius. Her namesake, the goddess Sita, a model of virtue,
was abducted and rescued in the Sanskrit epic the *Ramayana*. The story of the
contemporary Sita, told by the narrator Iqbal the Umpire, a male friend of
Sita's, echoes ancient myths, folk tales, and religious prophecies. Yet Sita must
unearth her own past, buried not in myth and legend, but in the recesses of
her memory.

On April 30, 1982, while on an overnight visit to the French colony
of Réunion, in transit between Mauritius and the Seychelles, Sita loses
12 hours, time that she cannot account for. As she plumbs her memory for
clues to what happened on that date—more than eight years previous—she
bumps into a heavy, dense presence, like the big hole in the universe. It is
anger, rage, and fury. "Closely knotted into that anger was imprisonment.
The hands that were hers and that wanted to perpetrate an act of murder,
were trapped. She saw herself trapped, or was it locked up, or tied down
physically, or handcuffed, or ball-and-chained, or paralyzed, or perhaps with
a rock on her chest under water. Or being buried alive."

She has only a few clues to the mystery. First there were the missing
hours. Then there was her reaction on a visit to Réunion with her husband in
1987, five years after the day of lost hours. She had become violently ill at the
thought of phoning their acquaintances Rowan Tarquin, a probation officer,
and his wife, Noella, the only people she knows in Réunion.

On the eve of the declaration of war against Iraq in 1991, Sita is diving
into her past and comes up with the buried memory of what happened to her
in 1982. She had taken a plane to the Seychelles to go to a women's conference. She had called Tarquin asking if she could stay overnight on her way.
At her arrival at the airport in Réunion, she learned that Tarquin and his
wife had separated. Though alarmed by the news, she had gone to his apartment, where he raped her. Fearing she would never win a rape case, Sita
returned home without reporting the crime. Not knowing what she should
say, or how to say it, she never spoke of the rape. It was incised from her
memory, yet a knot of murderous anger remained.

Why, the narrator asks, are women blamed for the violence perpetrated
against them by men? "Should a woman never accept to go into the same
house as a man is in on his own, even a man she knows? Should a woman
never accept an invitation for a cup of tea? And what about the lift?. . . And
what about the stairway? . . . Should a woman take a taxi? What should she
do if she misses the last bus? . . . What time is trespass for woman? What
place?"

The novel addresses not only Sita's rape but also the social, religious, and
political conditions that support and condone violence against women. Sita's
rape comes to symbolize all rapes, all violations, all colonizations. Addressing an open letter to "God, or god, Sir or Madam," Sita writes, "Why have

you forsaken me?" God will not answer. "Wait for the silence, girls," Sita says. "For the gods if they ever spaketh in the past, hath stopped in the present."

CENSORSHIP HISTORY

On December 7, 1993, four days after *The Rape of Sita* was published in Mauritius, as its author Collen describes, it was "plunged into a strange limbo." It was driven from circulation by Hindu fundamentalists, banned by the Mauritian government, and temporarily withdrawn by the author and her publishers. "Hindu fundamentalists whipped up hysteria within 72 hours of publication," Collen wrote, "and I started to get anonymous rape and death threats." As no one had yet read the book, though 250 people had already ordered copies, Collen and her publisher withdrew it from bookstores to create an opportunity for an open debate and to decide whether to change the title.

Hindu fundamentalists regard the name of the Hindu deity Sita, revered as a prototype of noble womanhood and virtue, as sacred. The suggestion that she might be raped was considered blasphemous. Collen chose the name, which is common in Mauritius, to create a contrast between the story of the Hindu goddess, who was rescued by armies sent by the gods, and the contemporary Sita in the book, who is bereft of protection. Collen says she used the name of Sita to be "evocative, not provocative," and considers the book to be a defense "of women's rights and women's struggles."

A few hours after the book's withdrawal, but apparently unaware of it, Mauritian prime minister Aneerood Jugnauth halted the proceedings of Parliament to make a statement attacking the book and its author. Jugnauth said, "A glance at the back page of the book suffices to indicate that this publication may constitute an outrage against public and religious morality" under Section 206 of the Criminal Code. Jugnauth, referring to his own decree to ban Salman Rushdie's SATANIC VERSES, gave instructions for the police to act against Collen.

"The prime minister acted under pressure from what we call 'communal' lobbies," Collen wrote. "I am known not only as a writer, but also as a feminist. Feminists generally annoy fundamentalists of all ilk, and I have been no exception." Collen also believes the book was targeted because of her activism in the left-wing political party, Lalit.

The following day the police arrived with orders to confiscate all copies of the books and to take a statement from Collen as part of an official inquiry. Collen and her publisher informed the police that they had no legal right to confiscate the books, as the books were not exhibited for sale as required by the law. Cohen refused to give a statement, kept the books, and distributed them. The case was referred by the police to the director of public prosecutions.

Though *The Rape of Sita* was widely reviewed in the press in Mauritius and caused literary and social debate on a national scale, as of 2005, the book remained banned. Those who supported the banning made it clear that they did not read the book. The book was published in Britain and North America, and there was an outpouring of both international and local support in Mauritius for Collen.

FURTHER READING

Atwood, Margaret. Untitled. *The Women's Review of Books* 12, nos. 10–11 (July 1995): 28.
Collen, Lindsey. "The Rape of Fiction." *Index on Censorship* 12, nos. 4–5 (September/
    October 1994): 210–212.
Moore, Celia. "Banned in Mauritius." *Ms.*, November/December 1995, 89.
Piggott, Jill. "Rage Deferred." *The Women's Review of Books* 12, nos. 10–11 (July 1995): 28.

THE RED AND THE BLACK

Author: Stendhal
Original date and place of publication: 1831, France
Literary form: Fiction

SUMMARY

Stendhal—the pseudonym of Marie-Henri Beyle—was among the greatest French novelists of the 19th century. *The Red and the Black*, the story of Julien, an ambitious small-town youth who is executed for shooting his wealthy mistress, is regarded as one of the most boldly original masterworks of European fiction.

In *The Red and the Black*, Stendhal portrays a vivid tableau of French society and politics during the 1820s, the final years of the Restoration of the Bourbon monarchy. "Everywhere hypocrisy, or at least charlatanism, even among the most virtuous, even among the greatest," says Julien, echoing Stendhal's view of the times. The ultraroyalist partisans of absolute monarchy, found among the nobility, the wealthy, and the clergy, had from 1815 waged a struggle to restore the ancien régime, the political state that existed before the 1789 revolution. Upon his accession to the throne in 1824, Charles X initiated antiliberal, pro-Catholic policies that, after 20 years of exile, returned the government and the army to the control of the nobility and passed measures increasing the power of the clergy. Hostility to his policies culminated in the July Revolution of 1830, which ended the rule of the elder branch of the Bourbons.

The subject of the novel was also provided by a newspaper article about a young man, Antoine Berthet, who was guillotined in 1828 for an attempt to kill his former mistress, Madame Michoud, whose children he had tutored. The story of Julien Sorel closely parallels the Berthet case. Verrières, the fictional town in which the story takes place, is much like the provincial city of Grenoble, where Berthet lived and where Stendhal spent his childhood.

Julien Sorel is an intelligent young man of peasant origins who is eager to attain a social position beyond his station in life. Under the rule of Napoléon, his most likely path to success would have been through the military. Now that the country is at peace under Bourbon rule, which has restored the political influence of the clergy, the road to advancement leads him to the Catholic Church. Julien studies Latin and theology to prepare for entrance into a seminary and attains a position as a tutor for the children of Monsieur de Rênal, the wealthy mayor of Verrières.

He becomes involved in an affair with the mayor's wife, a relationship that for Julien is fueled by the thrill of conquering a woman of a higher social class, rather than by affection. When Rênal receives an anonymous letter exposing the affair, Julien leaves the household and enters the seminary at Besançon. The seminary, however, proves not to be a refuge from the provincial life of Verrières, which Julien sees as mired in greed and petty politics. The church's institution for training future leaders is a haven of hypocrisy and mediocrity, rife with political intrigue as sordid as that of the outside world. The motivation of the young seminarians is neither spiritual nor intellectual but, rather, strictly economic.

"Almost all were the sons of peasants," Stendhal writes, "who preferred to gain their daily bread by repeating a few Latin words instead of swinging a pickax." Their religious vocation is based in the desire to have a good dinner and a warm suit of clothes in winter. "Learning counts for nothing here," Julien observes. "The church in France seems to have understood that books themselves are its real enemy. In the eyes of the church, inward submission is all. . . ."

Julien admires two of the priests at the seminary—the elderly Curé Chélan and the seminary's director, the devout Jansenist Abbé Pirard, who is finally ousted by the pro-Jesuit faction led by the vice principal. When Pirard resigns, he takes Julien with him to Paris, where he becomes private secretary to a nobleman, the Marquis de la Mole. Julien embarks on an affair with the marquis's daughter, Matilde, who is fascinated by Julien's daring and ambition. When Matilde becomes pregnant, her father reluctantly consents to her marriage to Julien and agrees to provide him with a private income and a title. But when the marquis makes inquiries about Julien in Verrières, he receives a denunciatory letter from Madame de Rênal, dictated by her confessor. After the marquis cancels the wedding plans, Julien shoots and wounds Madame de Rênal as she kneels at church attending Mass. He is immediately arrested.

Julien is put on trial but refuses to defend himself. Despite attempts by the local clergy to manipulate the jury on his behalf, he is convicted. As

Julien awaits death by the guillotine, he searches for meaning, finding it only in his belated affection for Madame de Rênal. "My word, if I find the God of the Christians, it's all up with me," he thinks. "He's a despot and, as such, full of vengeful ideas; his Bible talks of nothing but frightful punishments. I never liked him; I never could believe that anyone sincerely loved him. He is merciless (and he recalled several scriptural passages). He will punish me in some abominable way. . . . I have loved truth. . . . Where is it?"

CENSORSHIP HISTORY

Stendhal's literary reputation was slow to develop. His contemporaries found the detachment and psychological realism of his novels difficult to comprehend, as his work did not fit any of the literary stereotypes of the day. Some readers were scandalized by what was viewed as Stendhal's indifference to morality and his unapologetic and understanding portrayal of a character who was seen as an unscrupulous monster. "I have been ambitious, but I have no intention of blaming myself for that; I was acting in those days according to the code of the times," Julien explains from his prison cell.

Stendhal said that he wrote "for the happy few" and correctly predicted that he would not be appreciated until 50 years later. Indeed, only one edition of *The Red and the Black* was published during his lifetime. The complete absence of a religious worldview in his novels, his portrayal of the God of the Bible as a "petty despot," and his anticlericalism led the Catholic Church to censor his writing. Stendhal's anticlericalism reflected the intellectual inheritance of the antireligious spirit of Voltaire. It also had its origins in Stendhal's unhappy childhood education at the hands of Jesuit priests.

The church portrayed in *The Red and the Black* is torn between two factions—the Jesuits, the wily and worldly agents of international reaction and proponents of the ancien régime, and the austere Jansenists. Stendhal's bitterly critical attitude toward the Jesuits was common to many in France at the time. The Jesuits had been banished from the country in 1764 but continued to function in secret until 1814. Under the Bourbon regime their influence was restored. In *The Red and the Black*, Stendhal portrays the political manipulations of a powerful secret Jesuit society known as the Congregation (patterned after an organization of the time called the Knights of Faith), dedicated to advancing ultraroyalist views and the agenda of the Vatican to the detriment of France's sovereignty and the liberal agenda.

In 1897, the Vatican placed *The Red and the Black* and all of Stendhal's "love stories" on the Index of Forbidden Books. They remained on the list through the last edition compiled in 1948 and in effect until 1966. In Russia, *The Red and the Black* was banned in 1850 by Czar Nicholas I, whose motto in a campaign to suppress liberal thought was "autocracy, orthodoxy, and nationality." In a similar campaign in Spain in 1939, the novel was purged from Spanish libraries by the dictatorship of Francisco Franco.

FURTHER READING

Brombert, Victor, ed. *Stendhal: A Collection of Critical Essays.* Englewood Cliffs, N.J.: Prentice Hall, 1962.

Haight, Anne Lyon. *Banned Books: 387* B.C. *to 1978* A.D. Updated and enlarged by Chandler B. Grannis. New York: R. R. Bowker, 1978.

Stendhal. *Red and Black: A Norton Critical Edition.* Translated and edited Robert M. Adams. New York: W. W. Norton, 1969.

Talbot, Emile J. *Stendhal Revisited.* New York: Twayne, 1993.

RELIGIO MEDICI

Author: Sir Thomas Browne
Original date and place of publication: 1643, England
Literary form: Religious commentary

SUMMARY

Religio Medici, "A Doctor's Faith," was written in 1635 by Thomas Browne, an Oxford-educated physician who practiced as a country doctor in Norwich, England. A confession of his religious faith and a collection of his opinions on a vast range of subjects generally connected to religion, it was not intended for publication but was composed during his leisure time for his "private exercise and satisfaction." The manuscript had circulated among his friends for several years when a pirated edition was published without his knowledge or consent in 1642. Browne felt bound to issue a "full and intended copy" to correct errors in the unauthorized edition and had an authorized edition published in 1643.

Browne's eclectic reflections on faith reveal a scientific, rational, and skeptical thinker, but one whose temperament is essentially religious. He is unable to give full intellectual allegiance to secularism. "For my Religion," Browne wrote, "though there be several Circumstances that might perswade the World I have none at all, (as the general scandal of my Profession, the natural course of my Studies, the general indifferency of my Behaviour and Discourse in matters of Religion, neither violently Defending one, nor with that common ardour and contention Opposing another;) yet, in despight thereof, I dare without usurpation assume the honourable Stile of a Christian."

In an informal and memorable prose style, commenting on vices and virtues, science, the Scriptures, the classics, miracles, and common superstitions, Browne offered a carefully crafted balance between skepticism and belief. His firm allegiance to the Church of England, a church "whose every part so squares unto my Conscience," did not deter him from exercising his wide-ranging intellectual curiosity or tolerance of the beliefs of others.

In the famous opening sentences of the second part of *Religio Medici*, Browne told his readers "I am of a constitution so general that it consorts and sympathizeth with all things. . . . All places, all airs, make unto me one Countrey; I am in England every where, and under any Meridian." As an enlightened skeptic, Browne could not accept completely any dogma, including the dogma of skepticism. "Many things are true in Divinity, which are neither inducible by reason, nor confirmable by sense; and many things in Philosophy confirmable by sense, yet not inducible by reason."

Browne concluded *Religio Medici* with a prayer that succinctly expressed both his profession of faith and his appeal to reason: "Bless me in this life with but peace of my Conscience, command of my affections, the love of Thy self and my dearest friends, and I shall be happy enough to pity Caesar. . . . Dispose of me according to the wisdom of Thy pleasure; Thy will be done; though in my own undoing."

CENSORSHIP HISTORY

Soon after its authorized publication, *Religio Medici* became popular in England. When a Latin translation appeared in Paris and Leiden in 1644, its resounding success placed Browne among the intellectual elite of Europe. The book went through a dozen reprints during his lifetime. Browne was attacked, however, for his tolerance of "heretics and papists" in an age of religious controversy and his serene exposition of a faith remote in temperament from the contending creeds of the day.

"I borrow not the rules of my Religion from Rome or Geneva, but the dictates of my own reason," Browne wrote. Though Browne professed to be free of heretical opinions, he insisted upon his right to his own views when no specific guidance was proffered by church or Scripture. He considered himself to be "of that Reformed new-cast Religion" that required "the careful and charitable hands of these times to restore it to its primitive Integrity."

The popularity of *Religio Medici* brought the book to the attention of the Vatican, which placed the Latin translation on the Index of Forbidden Books in 1645, where it remained listed through the Index's last edition published until 1966. As a skeptical, rationalist work, despite its deeply felt religious motivation, *Religio Medici* contradicted Roman Catholic doctrine. Further, because Browne professed allegiance to the Anglican Church, which had broken with the Roman Catholic Church in the 16th century, his ideas were not acceptable reading for Catholics.

Browne published several other books, notably *Pseudodoxia Epidemica*, known as *Vulgar Errors* (1646), and *Hydriotaphia: Urn Burial* (1658), a solemn reflection on death and immortality. He was knighted in 1671 by King Charles II. Browne is remembered today as an important figure in the literature of the baroque age.

FURTHER READING

Browne, Sir Thomas. *The Religio Medici and Other Writings of Sir Thomas Browne.*
Introduction by C. H. Herford. New York: E. P. Dutton, 1906.
Haight, Anne Lyon. *Banned Books: 387 BC to 1978 AD.* Updated and enlarged by Chandler B. Grannis. New York: R. R. Bowker, 1978.

RELIGION WITHIN THE LIMITS OF REASON ALONE

Author: Immanuel Kant
Original date and place of publication: 1793, Prussia
Literary form: Philosophical treatise

SUMMARY

The philosophical system of Immanuel Kant, one of the most important philosophers in Western culture, was designed to lay a firm foundation for the entire range of scientific, moral, and aesthetic experience. In THE CRITIQUE OF PURE REASON, published in 1781, Kant offered a radical new approach to fundamental issues of epistemology and metaphysics. Mediating between rationalist claims of knowledge of what lies beyond sense perception and the opposing philosophy of skepticism, which denied the possibility of any real knowledge, Kant defined the boundaries of valid thought.

Kant's philosophy of religion is principally contained in *Religion within the Limits of Reason Alone.* Kant asserts that the existence of God can neither be affirmed nor denied on theological grounds and that all proofs derived from pure reason are invalid. Religion is outside the province of reason, as the divine cannot be an object of thought and knowledge is limited to the world of phenomena.

Kant nevertheless supports the legitimacy of religious belief. Though the existence of God cannot be scientifically demonstrated, Kant's moral philosophy shows the necessity of God's existence. For Kant, religion resides "in the heart's disposition to fulfill all human duties as divine commands." Kant's conception of religion can be described as ethical theism. He argues that moral law requires that people should be rewarded in proportion to their virtue. Since this does not always occur, he infers that there must be another existence where they are rewarded. This leads him to the conclusion that there is an eternal life and a God.

For Kant, a valid religious belief can derive only from the implications of moral principles and the nature of the moral life. Morality, however, does not require the idea of a supreme being and "thus in no way needs religion for its own service . . . but in virtue of pure practical reason, it is sufficient unto itself." In contrast to religious systems that relate doing good to securing a reward, the basis of religion should be the doing of good for its own sake.

Kant divides all religions into those that are *"endeavors to win favor (mere worship)* and *moral religions,* i.e., religions of *good life-conduct."* In the first type, Kant declares, "man flatters himself by believing either that God can make him eternally happy (through remission of his sins) without his having *to become a better man,* or else, if this seems to him impossible, that God can certainly *make him a better man* without his having to do anything more than to *ask* for it. Yet since, in the eyes of a Being who sees all, to ask is no more than to *wish,* this would really involve doing nothing at all; for mere improvements to be achieved simply by a wish, every man would be good."

According to Kant, man's growth begins not in the improvement of his practices but rather in the transformation of his cast of mind and in the grounding of character. Kant describes as a peculiar "delusion of religion" that man supposes that he can do anything, apart from the good actions of his life, to become acceptable to God. "Man *himself* must make or have made himself into whatever, in a moral sense, whether good or evil, he is or is to become. Either choice must be an effect of his free choice; for otherwise he could not be held responsible for it and could therefore be *morally* neither good nor evil."

CENSORSHIP HISTORY

As the Prussian state moved to prosecute the battle against the freethinkers of the 18th-century Enlightenment, it stepped up censorship of printed matter. A government edict allowed toleration of views divergent from Lutheranism "so long as each quietly fulfills his duties as a good citizen of the state, but keeps his particular opinion in every case to himself, and takes care not to propagate it or to convert others and cause them to err or falter in their faith."

Because Kant was a prominent author who enjoyed the confidence of the king, his earlier works of critical philosophy not intended for general readers, such as *The Critique of Pure Reason,* were spared censorship. In 1791, a proposal to prohibit Kant's literary activity was submitted to the king by the high ecclesiastical councillor but was not acted upon.

In 1792, Kant's essay "On the Radical Evil in Human Nature," which was to become the first part of *Religion within the Limits of Reason Alone,* was approved by the government censor for appearance in the publication *Berlinische Monatsschrift.* But because it dealt with biblical matters, the continuation of Kant's treatise, "On the Struggle of the Good Principle with the Evil for Mastery over Mankind," was handed over for approval to a theological censor, who refused permission to publish.

Kant supplemented the two essays with two additional pieces and prepared a book, *Religion within the Limits of Reason Alone,* which he brought for approval to the theological faculty of the University of Königsberg, where he was a professor. The theologians at Königsberg regarded the book as being outside their purview to censor because it did not deal with biblical theology. Kant received, instead, an imprimatur from the philosophical faculty at the University of Jena, and the book was published in 1793.

In October 1794, King Frederick William II (successor to Frederick the Great on the throne of Prussia), who was offended by the book, wrote to Kant accusing him of having "misused" his philosophy over a long period of time and of "the destruction and debasing of many principal and basic teachings of the Holy Scripture of Christianity." He warned Kant not to write or publish any similar works on religion, or "otherwise you can unfailingly expect, on continued recalcitrance, unpleasant consequences." The Lutheran Church in Prussia banned *Religion within the Limits of Reason Alone*.

Kant wrote to the king in his own defense that his book was not directed toward the general public but rather exclusively intended for discussion among scholars, and that, further, it could not have contained a "debasing of Christ and the Bible, for the reason that the sole theme was the evolution of pure rational religion, not the critique of historical forms of belief."

Though Kant refused to retract his opinions, he promised "thus to prevent even at least suspicion on this score . . . cheerfully to declare myself Your Royal Majesty's most faithful subject: that I will refrain entirely in the future from all public discourse concerning religion, natural or revealed, in lectures and in writing alike." Kant kept his promise to the king but considered it binding only during the king's lifetime. After the king's death, in 1798 Kant published *The Conflict of the Faculties*, in which he discussed the relation between theology and critical reason and made public his correspondence with the king about the censorship of *Religion within the Limits of Reason Alone*.

Kant's philosophy did not attract the attention of the Catholic Church until 1827, when an Italian translation of *The Critique of Pure Reason* was published. Kant's contention that the existence of God can be neither confirmed nor denied through the use of reason caused the church to place it on the Index of Forbidden Books, where it remained through the last edition in effect until 1966.

Although *Religion within the Limits of Reason Alone* offered a more direct critique of institutionalized religion that conflicted with the church's doctrine, the Vatican never banned it. It was, however, prohibited in the Soviet Union in 1928, along with all of Kant's writing, presumably because the metaphysical and transcendental themes of Kant's works were thought to conflict with Marxist-Leninist ideology. All of the works of "such disgraceful writers" as Kant and Johann Wolfgang von Goethe were also purged from the libraries of Spain under the dictatorship of Francisco Franco in 1939.

FURTHER READING

Appelbaum, David. *The Vision of Kant*. Rockport, Mass.: Element Books, 1995.

Cassirer, Ernst. *Kant's Life and Thought*. Trans. James Hader. Introduction by Stephan Korner. New Haven, Conn.: Yale University Press, 1981.

Collinson, Diané. *Fifty Major Philosophers: A Reference Guide.* London: Routledge, 1988.

Copleston, Frederick. *A History of Philosophy.* Vol. 6: *Modern Philosophy: From the French Enlightenment to Kant.* New York: Doubleday, 1994.

Green, Jonathon. *Encyclopedia of Censorship.* New York: Facts On File, 1990.

Kant, Immanuel. *The Philosophy of Kant: Immanuel Kant's Moral and Political Writings.* Edited and with an introduction by Carl J. Friedrich. New York: Modern Library, 1993.

Popkin, Richard, and Avrum Stroll. *Philosophy Made Simple.* New York: Doubleday, 1993.

THE RIGHTS OF THE CHRISTIAN CHURCH ASSERTED

Author: Matthew Tindal
Original date and place of publication: 1706, England
Literary form: Religious treatise

SUMMARY

Matthew Tindal was one of the most prominent deists of the 18th century. A convert to Catholicism who returned to the Church of England, and a onetime law fellow at All Souls College, Oxford, Tindal sought to reconcile rationalism with religious belief. Deists held that the natural religion of reason, which sought evidence of God in his creation in the external world, was superior to any alternative form of truth and accessible to all people, regardless of their education and social standing. Biblical revelation was superfluous to natural religion.

In such works as John Toland's CHRISTIANITY NOT MYSTERIOUS (1696) and Tindal's best-known work, *Christianity as Old as the Creation* (1730), regarded as the "Bible" of deism, reason was held to be the only arbiter of religious truth. In *Christianity*, Tindal effectively expressed the deist position as a coherent theory.

While all deists subordinated revelation to reason, Tindal welcomed revelation as providing alternative popular proofs of doctrine. He viewed the gospel as a "Republication of the Religion of Nature." The teachings of Christianity and the discoveries of reason had to agree. He wrote in *Christianity:* "If Christianity is found contradictory to any thing the Light of Nature makes manifest, or should require of us to believe any thing of which we could form no Ideas, or none but contradictory ones, we should be forced so far to acknowledge is faulty and false." Only those parts of Christianity that honored God and served man were true, he maintained.

The Rights of the Christian Church Asserted, an earlier work, published in 1706, first established Tindal's notoriety as a freethinker. In *Rights,* Tindal expressed uncompromising Erastian views of the subordination of church to state authority. Erastianism, which achieved its definitive expression in the 17th century in Thomas Hobbes's LEVIATHAN, held that civil authorities should control punitive measures and that all authority, including ecclesiastical authority, derived from the king and Parliament.

Government is based on agreement, founded on the consent of the parties governed, Tindal explained in *Rights*. If the church is a part of the organized community and the magistrate is responsible for everything affecting the public interest, his power must extend to the church and those who serve it. "There's no branch of spiritual jurisdiction which is not vested in him [the king] and . . . all the jurisdiction which the archbishop, bishops, or any other inferior ecclesiastical judges have, is derived from him," Tindal wrote. The church has no independent jurisdiction and the clergy cannot claim any rights that exempt it from state control.

"The clergy's pretending to be an independent power has been the occasion of infinite mischief to the Christian world," Tindal declared, "as it is utterly inconsistent with the happiness of human society." Those who try to extend priestly rights are binding the church in "ecclesiastical tyranny." Persecution for disagreement on questions of belief cannot be allowed.

CENSORSHIP HISTORY

In 1707, the grand jury of Middlesex, England, made a presentment against Tindal, his printer, and his bookseller, characterizing *The Rights of the Christian Church Asserted* and its Erastian views as a blasphemous attack on the established church and a public nuisance. The book was proscribed by Parliament and burned by the public hangman in 1710. In response to the grand jury presentment, in 1708 Tindal published two important defenses of *Rights*, in which he proclaimed the necessity of press freedom, elevating it to the status of a natural right. "There is no freedom either in civil or ecclesiastical [affairs], but where the liberty of the press is maintain'd," he wrote. Everyone has a right to hear views "on all sides of every subject, including civil and governmental matters, even if antiministerial." Tindal's defenses of *Rights* were also banned and burned.

FURTHER READING

Burne, Peter. *Natural Religion and the Nature of Religion: The Legacy of Deism*. London: Routledge, 1991.

Cragg, G. R. *Reason and Authority in the Eighteenth Century*. Cambridge: Cambridge University Press, 1964.

Gay, Peter. *The Enlightenment: An Interpretation. The Rise of Modern Paganism*. New York: W. W. Norton, 1995.

Levy, Leonard W. *Blasphemy: Verbal Offense Against the Sacred, from Moses to Salman Rushdie*. New York: Alfred A. Knopf, 1993.

Sullivan, Robert E. *John Toland and the Deist Controversy: A Study in Adaptations*. Cambridge, Mass.: Harvard University Press, 1982.

THE SANDY FOUNDATION SHAKEN

Author: William Penn
Original date and place of publication: 1668, England
Literary form: Religious text

SUMMARY

The Society of Friends, or Quakers, was among the most controversial of the religious groups of the mid-17th century. In addition to the visible emotion they displayed in their services, they were also notorious for allowing equality between men and women, for their plain dress and abstinence, and for their pacifism.

William Penn was not born a Quaker, but from the time he heard a Quaker preacher at the age of 13, he began to question his upbringing in the Church of England. He studied theology at Oxford and was expelled in 1662 for religious nonconformity. After attending a French seminary, he returned to England to become a lawyer. By late 1667, he had officially joined the Society of Friends and was thrown into jail for his beliefs. One year later, following a series of arguments with the Presbyterian theologians Thomas Danson and Thomas Vincent, Penn wrote *The Sandy Foundation Shaken* as a damning critique of Presbyterianism.

The Sandy Foundation Shaken refutes Presbyterian views of the Holy Trinity. In his introduction to his attack on three Presbyterian doctrines, Penn addresses "the Unprejudiced READER," asking that the reader consider how Presbyterianism has "adulterated from the Purity both of Scripture Record, and Primitive Example." Penn contends that Presbyterians have strayed from the true word of God. He goes on to describe how prominent Presbyterian theologians visited a Quaker meeting and mocked it by pretending to pray and by condemning the members of the congregation.

In the first section of his theological argument, Penn disputes the view that one God exists in the Father, Son, and Holy Ghost. Penn believed that this notion of the Trinity was too abstract. To support his argument, he refers to more than a dozen New Testament references to one God, without any mention of a Trinity. Under the heading "Refuted from Right Reason," Penn extrapolates that "if each Person [of the Trinity] be God, and that God subsist in three persons, then each Person are three Persons or Gods, and from three, they will increase to nine, and so *ad infinitum*." Penn believed the Presbyterians' ideas absurd, and he minced no words in saying so.

The second argument of the book points to a contradiction at the heart of the moralistic temper of Penn's time. Penn explains that, according to Scripture, it is impossible to satisfy God if a person has committed a sin. First, Penn notes the passages where the Bible says that God will forgive sinners. Next, he points out passages where the Bible mentions that Christ died for all mankind's sins. Clearly, this creates a paradox; people are unable to erase their debt to God because Christ has already died, thus forgiving their sins. Penn outlines nine "Consequences Irreligious and Irrational" that stem from this paradox. In concluding this second section, Penn cautions readers that he does not believe in these principles. He still holds that people should repent for their sins, for instance. But the existence of these absurdities should show people that a more "primitive" form of worship and belief, such as the Quakers practiced, is the true road to salvation.

Penn asserts further that Presbyterian doctrine allows wicked people to be forgiven by merely attending Presbyterian church services, without necessarily altering their behavior and seeking forgiveness. Penn ends this third, complex section with a direct refutation of the Presbyterian theologian Theodore Vincent's lecture "For whatsoever is Born of God, Overcometh the World." Penn concludes his treatise by foreseeing the controversy his views will arouse. Fearing misunderstanding by rival denominations eager to harass and imprison Quakers, he reaffirms the Quaker's faith in one God, in the virgin birth of Jesus Christ, and in the truth of Jesus' teachings.

CENSORSHIP HISTORY

William Penn's frequent asides to the reader, cautioning against misreading his ideas as anti-Christian, did nothing to prevent his imprisonment or his book's censorship. Penn's enemies misinterpreted his work as an attack on all Protestant beliefs. In December 1668, Penn and his printer, John Darby, were jailed in the Tower of London. The stated reason for their imprisonment was their failure to get permission from London's archbishop to print the book. Yet most printers and authors customarily did not consult the archbishop. Many Londoners of the time thought the real reason for their incarceration was a plan to charge them with the crime of blasphemy, which had been made a capital offense only a few months previous to the publication of *The Sandy Foundation Shaken.*

From jail, Darby petitioned the authorities, protesting his innocence. He claimed that Penn's haphazardness in transmitting the manuscripts for the book prevented him from understanding how dangerous the ideas were. Penn had sent Darby his copy in small installments and occasionally improvised passages as he stood over Darby's shoulder. Darby persuaded the court that, given the hurried way he had to print it, he was unable to comprehend Penn's message, and he was set free. It became obvious that Penn was being held in prison for blasphemy.

The archbishop of London gave Penn an ultimatum on Christmas Eve 1668: "Recant or stay in prison until you die." Penn responded with an appeal to the idea of freedom of conscience: "My prison shall be my grave before I will budge a jot, for I owe my conscience to no mortal man." Despite the attempts of the archbishop's negotiators to convince Penn to recant, a stalemate ensued.

While Penn languished in prison, his father, the well-connected Admiral William Penn, mulled over what to do about his 24-year-old nonconformist son. The elder Penn was an Anglican, though not a follower of the era's detailed theological disputes. His military background led him to believe that some discipline would serve his son well, so at first he did not use his connections to intervene on the younger Penn's behalf. After five months, however, the elder Penn wrote the privy council asking for his son's release. In his letter he ascribed the younger Penn's nonconformity to "a great affliction" and reassured the authorities that he had not taught his son his blasphemous ideas.

At about the same time, Penn showed some signs of moderating his views. He continued his discussions with the archbishop's emissary, though Penn wanted to show the British king and other followers of his case that he was not about to recant. Penn wrote, "The Tower is the worst argument in the world to convince me. Whoever is in the wrong, those who use force in religion can never be in the right." Through months of imprisonment on vague charges, Penn held to his belief in liberty of conscience and freedom of religion.

Having taken his stand, Penn still wanted to get out of jail. He petitioned a court secretary to set him free on the grounds that he had never received a fair trial. In addition, he wrote a follow-up to *The Sandy Foundation Shaken*, titled *Innocency with Her Open Face*. He called this new pamphlet an "Apology for the Book entitled, *The Sandy Foundation Shaken*." A Penn biographer calls Penn's strategy "the first of a series of arrangements . . . whereby conscience accommodated itself to irresistible official pressure." Penn's plan allowed both sides to claim a victory.

Innocency with Her Open Face reaffirms his cautions to the readers of *The Sandy Foundation Shaken*. Penn tried to clear his name with Londoners who had been following the controversy. After all, *The Sandy Foundation Shaken* was intended primarily to show the righteousness of Quakerism and only secondly to attack Presbyterianism. In *Innocency with Her Open Face*, he states that he had no quarrel with the existence of a Trinity; rather, he merely disputed the Presbyterians' notions of it. By extension, Penn was reaffirming the Anglican Church's ideas and trying again to discredit the Presbyterians. Penn was released from prison in 1669, after nearly eight months locked in the Tower of London. He did not stay in England long enough to see if his campaign was successful but traveled to Ireland for business and missionary work.

At first glance, Penn's brush with censorship looks like an obscure matter of interdenominational squabbling among British Protestants. Yet Penn continued to hold beliefs in freedom of conscience and religious tolerance and made those ideas law in the colony he founded—Pennsylvania.

—Jonathan Pollack

FURTHER READING

Dunn, Mary Maples, and Richard S. Dunn, eds. *The Papers of William Penn*. Vol. 1: *1644–1679*. Philadelphia: University of Pennsylvania Press, 1981.

Dunn, Richard S., and Mary Maples Dunn, eds. *The World of William Penn*. Philadelphia: University of Pennsylvania Press, 1986.

Endy, Melvin B., Jr. *William Penn and Early Quakerism.* Princeton, N.J.: Princeton University Press, 1973.

Wildes, Harry Emerson. *William Penn.* New York: Macmillan, 1974.

THE SATANIC VERSES

Author: Salman Rushdie

Original dates and places of publication: 1988, United Kingdom; 1989, United States

Original publishers: Penguin Books; Viking Penguin

Literary form: Fiction

SUMMARY

The Satanic Verses, by the Indian-born British author Salman Rushdie, holds a unique place in the history of literary censorship. In 1989, Iran's leader, Ayatollah Ruhollah Khomeini, condemned the book for blasphemy against Islam and issued an edict calling for its author's execution. The death threat drove Rushdie into hiding, and the furor over the novel escalated to become an unprecedented event of global dimensions.

Rushdie's complex and challenging novel is a surreal and riotously inventive mixture of realism and fantasy. In a cycle of three interconnected tales set in present-day London and Bombay, an Indian village, and seventh-century Arabia, it explores themes of migration and dislocation, the nature of good and evil, doubt and loss of religious faith. "It is a migrant's-eye view of the world," Rushdie explained, commenting on the intentions of his novel. "It is written from the experience of uprooting, disjuncture and metamorphosis (slow or rapid, painful or pleasurable) that is the migrant condition, and from which, I believe, can be derived a metaphor for all humanity."

The novel opens at 29,000 feet in the air as two men fall toward the sea from a hijacked jumbo jet that has blown up over the English Channel. The two—both Indian actors—mysteriously survive the explosion and wash up on an English beach. Gibreel Farishta, formerly Ismail Najmuddin, is a legendary star of Indian movies; Saladin Chamcha, formerly Salahuddin Chamchawala, is an urbane Anglophile who makes a successful living in London doing voiceovers for television commercials.

As Rushdie describes his protagonists, "*The Satanic Verses* is the story of two painfully divided selves. In the case of one, Saladin Chamcha, the division is secular and societal; he is torn, to put it plainly, between Bombay and London, between East and West. For the other, Gibreel Farishta, the division is spiritual, a rift in the soul. He has lost his faith and is strung out between his immense need to believe and his new inability to do so. The novel is 'about' their quest for wholeness."

To their surprise and puzzlement, Gibreel and Saladin find after their fall from the sky that they have undergone a metamorphosis, acquiring characteristics alien to their own personalities. Gibreel, the womanizer, develops a halo, assuming the appearance of the archangel Gibreel (Gabriel), while the mild and proper Saladin grows horns, hooves, and a tail in the image of Satan. The fantastic adventures in England and India of these two walking symbols of good and evil form the central thread of the narrative.

The second tale, told in alternating chapters, evokes the historical origins of Islam in narratives dealing with the nature and consequences of revelation and belief. It takes place in the dreams of Gibreel Farishta, in which he becomes the archangel Gibreel, and in a film based on his imaginings in which he plays the role of the archangel. The dream-film sequences, which parallel the story of the prophet Muhammad in Mecca, tell the story of Mahound. He is a businessman turned prophet of Jahilia, the city of sand, who receives divine revelation through the intercession of the angel Gibreel and founds a religion called Submission (the literal English translation of the Arabic word *Islam*).

In the third tale, also dreamed up by Farishta, a charismatic holy woman cloaked in butterflies leads the faithful of a Muslim village in India on a pilgrimage to Mecca. As they walk toward Mecca, they perish when the waters of the Arabian Sea do not part for them as expected.

The parts of the novel recounting Gibreel's painful visions, set in Mahound's city of Jahilia, are the primary focus of the controversy about the book. They allude to a legendary episode in the Prophet's life in which Muhammad added verses to the Koran that elevated to angelic status three goddesses worshipped by the polytheistic citizens of Mecca. Later, Muhammad revoked these verses, realizing that they had been transmitted to him not by Allah but by Satan posing as the angel Gabriel.

In contrast to the version of the incident recounted in Islamic history, Gibreel in his dream says that he was forced to speak the verses by "the overwhelming need of the Prophet Mahound," implying that Mahound, rather than Satan, put the false verses into Gibreel's mouth for opportunistic reasons. "From my mouth," Gibreel says, "both the statement and the repudiation, verses and converses, universes and reverses, the whole thing, and we all know how my mouth got worked."

In another dream passage alluding to an incident drawn from Islamic historical accounts, a scribe called Salman alters the text of the book dictated to him by Mahound. "Mahound did not notice the alterations," the scribe says, "so there I was, actually writing the Book, or re-writing anyway, polluting the word of God with my own profane language. But, good heavens, if my poor words could not be distinguished from the Revelation by God's own Messenger, then what did that mean?" Salman notices that the angel Gibreel's revelations to Mahound are particularly well timed, "so that when the faithful were disputing Mahound's views on any subject, from the possibility of space travel to the permanence of Hell, the angel would turn up with an answer, and he always supported Mahound."

Another provocative episode from Gibreel's dreams is a cinematic fantasy about a brothel in Jahilia called The Curtain (a translation of the Arabic word *hijab*, the Muslim women's veil), where business booms after 12 prostitutes assume the names and personalities of Mahound's 12 wives. A line of men awaiting their turns circles the innermost courtyard of the brothel, "rotating around its centrally positioned Fountain of Love much as pilgrims rotated for other reasons around the ancient Black Stone."

Hearing the news of the prostitutes' assumed identities, "the clandestine excitement of the city's males was intense; yet so afraid were they of discovery, both because they would surely lose their lives if Mahound or his lieutenants ever found out that they had been involved in such irreverences, and because of their sheer desire that the new service at The Curtain be maintained, that the secret was kept from the authorities."

Rushdie prefaces the story of the brothel with a statement that proved to be prescient in view of the events that engulfed his novel: "Where there is no belief, there is no blasphemy." Only because the men of Jahilia had accepted the tenets of their new faith could they find illicit pleasure in patronizing a brothel serviced by prostitutes impersonating the wives of the Prophet.

As the novel ends, Saladin Chamcha has become reintegrated into Indian society. He has completed a process of renewal and regeneration in his embrace of love and death and his return to his roots in India. Gibreel Farishta, tormented by his epic dreams and visions of doubt and skepticism, has lost his faith and failed to replace it by earthly love. Unable to escape his inner demons, he is driven mad and commits suicide.

CENSORSHIP HISTORY

The Satanic Verses was published in the United Kingdom on September 26, 1988. Rushdie's eagerly awaited fourth novel received laudatory reviews in the British press. It was hailed as "a masterpiece," "truly original" and "an exhilarating . . . extraordinary contemporary novel . . . a roller coaster ride over a vast landscape of the imagination."

Even before its publication, however, the controversy about the novel had already begun. Syed Shahabuddin and Khurshid Alam Khan, two Muslim opposition members of India's Parliament, alerted to the book's content by articles in Indian publications, launched a campaign to have it banned.

"Civilization is nothing but voluntary acceptance of restraints," Shahabuddin wrote in defense of censorship. "You may hold whatever private opinions you like but you do not enjoy an absolute right to express them in public." Expressing a view that was echoed by many opponents of the book as the controversy continued, Shahabuddin admitted that he had not read *The Satanic Verses* and did not intend to. "I do not have to wade through a filthy drain to know what filth is," he declared.

India's government, fearing civil disorder among the country's Muslim population, was the first to censor the book. On October 5, 1988, only nine days after its publication in Britain, the importation of the British edition was prohibited under a ruling of the Indian Customs Act. Muslims in India contacted Islamic organizations in Britain, urging them to take up the protest campaign. Two London publications sponsored by the Saudi Arabian government prominently featured stories denouncing the novel. At his home in London, Rushdie began to receive death threats.

The U.K. Action Committee on Islamic Affairs released a statement demanding withdrawal and destruction of the book, an apology, and payment of damages to an Islamic charity. "The work, thinly disguised as a piece of literature," the statement read, "not only greatly distorts Islamic history in general, but also portrays in the worst possible colours the very characters of the Prophet Ibrahim and the Prophet Mohamed (peace upon them). It also disfigures the characters of the Prophet's companions . . . and the Prophet's holy wives and describes the Islamic creed and rituals in the most foul language."

The British-based Union of Muslim Organisations called for Rushdie's prosecution under rarely enforced British laws prohibiting blasphemy against the doctrines of the Church of England. The British government declined to consider expansion of the laws to include transgressions against the Islamic faith. On November 11, Prime Minister Margaret Thatcher announced that "there are no grounds on which the government could consider banning the book." On November 21, the grand sheik of Egypt's Al-Azhar, the mosque and university that is considered the seat of Islamic authority, called on all Islamic organizations in Britain to join in taking legal steps to prevent the book's distribution.

In the United States, where the novel had not yet appeared, its publisher, Viking Penguin, received bomb threats and thousands of menacing letters. On November 24, 1988, *The Satanic Verses* was banned in South Africa, even though it had not yet been published there. A planned visit by Rushdie was canceled when its sponsors feared that his safety could not be guaranteed. Within weeks, the book was also banned in several countries with predominantly Muslim populations: Pakistan, Saudi Arabia, Egypt, Somalia, Bangladesh, Sudan, Malaysia, Indonesia, and Qatar.

In November 1988 in England, *The Satanic Verses* received the Whitbread literary prize for best novel. In December and again in January 1989, Muslims in Bolton, near Manchester, and in Bradford, Yorkshire, held public book burnings. A large group of demonstrators marched in London to protest the book. The Islamic Defence Council in Britain presented a petition to Penguin Books, demanding that the publisher apologize to the world Muslim community, withdraw the book, pulp the remaining copies, and refrain from printing future editions.

The petition listed as insulting to Muslims the fact that Abraham was referred to in the books as "the bastard"; that the prophet Muhammad was given the archaic medieval name of Mahound, meaning "devil" or "false prophet"; that the text states that revelations the Prophet received were well timed to suit him when "the faithful were disputing"; that the Prophet's companions were described in derogatory terms and the namesakes of his wives were depicted as prostitutes; and that the Islamic holy city of Mecca was portrayed as Jahilia, meaning "ignorance" or "darkness."

Penguin Books refused to comply with the petitioners' demands. On January 22, 1989, Rushdie published a statement in defense of his novel. *The Satanic Verses* is not an antireligious novel, he said. "It is, however, an attempt to write about migration, its stresses and transformations, from the point of view of migrants from the Indian subcontinent to Britain. This is for me, the saddest irony of all; that after working for five years to give voice and fictional flesh to the immigrant culture of which I am myself a member, I should see my book burned, largely unread, by the people it's about, people who might find some pleasure and much recognition in its pages."

Rushdie's repeated efforts throughout the controversy to clarify the intentions and meaning of his book had little impact on the fervent opposition to it. Few of those who protested against the book had read it, and for many, the very title of the novel, which seemed to imply that the Koranic verses were written by the devil, was sacrilegious and sufficient to condemn it.

It is never stated within Gibreel Farishta's dreams that Satan wrote the sacred book. However, the passages in which Gibreel claims to have received the verses directly from Mahound, rather than from God, imply that the book was written without divine intervention. Attributing the KORAN (Qur'an) to human composition is considered blasphemous in Muslim belief.

Rushdie explained that Gibreel's blasphemous visions were intended to dramatize the struggle between faith and doubt, rather than to insult the Muslim religion. "Gibreel's most painful dreams, the ones at the center of the controversy," Rushdie wrote, "depict the birth and growth of a religion something like Islam, in a magical city of sand named Jahilia (that is 'ignorance,' the name given by Arabs to the period before Islam). Almost all of the alleged 'insults and abuse' are taken from these dream sequences. The first thing to be said about these dreams is that they are *agonizingly painful to the dreamer.* They are a 'nocturnal retribution, a punishment' for his loss of faith. . . . The first purpose of these sequences is not to vilify or 'disprove' Islam, but to portray a soul in crisis, to show how the loss of God can destroy a man's life."

The novel's would-be censors frequently cited the tale of the brothel as particularly offensive to Muslims. Rushdie pointed to a distinction often ignored by his critics, that the prostitutes only take the names of the Prophet's wives. The real wives are "living chastely in their harem." "The purpose of the 'brothel sequence,' then," Rushdie explained, "was not to 'insult and abuse' the Prophet's wives, but to dramatize certain ideas about morality; and sexuality, too, because what happens in the brothel . . . is that the men of 'Jahilia' are enabled to act out an ancient dream of power and possession. . . .

That men should be so aroused by the great ladies' whorish counterfeits says something about *them*, not the great ladies, and about the extent to which sexual relations have to do with possession."

Critics also noted Rushdie's use of the name "Mahound," the Satanic figure of medieval Christian mystery plays, for the Muhammad-like character in the novel, as evidence of his invidious intentions. Rushdie described his choice of the name as an example of how his novel "tries in all sorts of ways to reoccupy negative images, to repossess pejorative language." "Even leaving aside the obvious fact that my Mahound is a dream-prophet and not the historical Muhammad," Rushdie wrote, "it may be noted that on page 93 of the novel there is this passage: 'Here he is neither Mahomet nor Moehammered; has adopted, instead, the demon tag the farangis hung around his neck. To turn insults into strengths, whigs, tories, blacks all chose to wear with pride the names that were given in scorn. . . .'"

Rushdie's view that "there are no subjects that are off limits and that includes God, includes prophets" was clearly not shared by those who urged banning of the novel. "The use of fiction was a way of creating the sort of distance from actuality that I felt would prevent offence from being taken," Rushdie declared. "I was wrong."

On February 12, 1989, during violent demonstrations against the book in Islamabad, Pakistan, six people died and 100 were injured. The next day in Srinigar, India, rioting led to the death of another person and the injury of 60. On February 14, Iran's leader, Ayatollah Ruhollah Khomeini, issued a fatwa, or religious edict, against the book.

Khomeini's edict stated: "I inform all zealous Muslims of the world that the author of the book entitled *The Satanic Verses*—which has been compiled, printed, and published in opposition to Islam, the Prophet, and the Qur'an—and all those involved in its publication who were aware of its contents, are sentenced to death. I call on all zealous Muslims to execute them quickly, wherever they find them, so that no one else will dare to insult the Islamic sanctities. God willing, whoever is killed on this path is a martyr. In addition, anyone who has access to the author of this book, but does not possess the power to execute him, should report him to the people so that he may be punished for his actions."

The 15 Khordad Foundation, an Iranian charity, offered a reward for Rushdie's murder: $1 million if the assassin were non-Iranian and 200 million rials (approximately $750,000) for an Iranian. The reward was later raised by the foundation to $2.5 million. During the days following Khomeini's edict, several Middle East terrorist organizations sponsored by the Iranian government publicly declared their determination to execute Rushdie. Demonstrations were held outside the British embassy in Tehran, and all books published by Viking Penguin were banned from Iran.

On February 16, Rushdie went into hiding under protection of the British government. Two days later, he issued a public statement regretting that some Muslims might have been offended by his book. "As author of *The Satanic Verses*," he said, "I recognize that Muslims in many parts of the world are genuinely distressed by the publication of my novel. I profoundly regret the distress that the publication has occasioned to sincere followers of Islam. Living as we do in a world of many faiths, this experience has served to remind us that we must all be conscious of the sensibilities of others." Khomeini responded with a statement refusing the apology and confirming the death sentence. "Even if Salman Rushdie repents and becomes the most pious man of [our] time," he declared, "it is incumbent on every Muslim to employ everything he has, his life and his wealth, to send him to hell."

On February 22, *The Satanic Verses* was published in the United States. Hundreds of threats against booksellers prompted two major bookstore chains temporarily to remove the book from a third of the nation's bookstores. On February 28, two independently owned bookstores in Berkeley, California, were firebombed.

Violent demonstrations continued to occur in India, Pakistan, and Bangladesh during the month after Khomeini's edict. On February 24, 12 people died during rioting in Bombay. Nonviolent protests against the book also took place in Sudan, Turkey, Malaysia, the Philippines, Hong Kong, and Japan. On March 7, Britain broke off diplomatic relations with Iran. Later that month, two moderate Muslim religious leaders in Belgium who had publicly expressed opposition to the death sentence against Rushdie were shot dead in Brussels.

In mid-March, the Organization of the Islamic Conference, while it refused to endorse the death threat, voted to call on its 46 member governments to prohibit the book. Most countries with large Muslim populations banned the sale or importation of *The Satanic Verses*. The Revolutionary Government of Zanzibar, for example, threatened a sentence of three years in prison and a fine of $2,500 for possession of the book. In Malaysia, the penalty was set at three years in prison and a fine of $7,400. In Indonesia, possession of the book was punishable by a month in prison or a fine. Turkey was the only country with a predominantly Muslim population where it remained legal. Several countries with Muslim minorities, including Bulgaria, Papua New Guinea, Thailand, Sri Lanka, Kenya, Tanzania, and Liberia, also imposed bans.

In some cases, countries with negligible Muslim populations took steps to suppress the book. In Venezuela, owning or reading it was declared a crime under penalty of 15 months' imprisonment. In Japan, the sale of the English-language edition was banned under threat of fines. The government of Poland also restricted its distribution. Many countries banned the circulation of issues of magazines, such as *Time, Newsweek, Asiaweek*, and *Far Eastern Economic Review*, that had published articles about the controversy.

Despite the bannings, the book was imported and circulated clandestinely in countries where it was forbidden, such as Kuwait, Senegal, Egypt,

India, and even Iran, where a few copies were smuggled in and passed from hand to hand. As a result of its notoriety, *The Satanic Verses* became a best seller in Europe and the United States. By the end of 1989, more than 1.1 million copies of hardcover English-language editions had been sold.

On June 3, 1989, the Ayatollah Khomeini died. The edict against Rushdie, however, remained in force, reaffirmed by Iranian government officials. Acts of terrorism related to protests against the book continued to occur. During 1990, five bombings targeted booksellers in England. In July 1991, in separate incidents, Hitoshi Igarashi, the Japanese translator of *The Satanic Verses*, was stabbed to death, and its Italian translator, Ettore Capriolo, was seriously wounded. In July 1993, Turkish publisher Aziz Nesin, who had printed translated excerpts from the novel in a newspaper, was attacked by Islamist rioters in the city of Sivas. They cornered him in a hotel and set it on fire, killing 37 people, but Nesin escaped. In October 1993, William Nygaard, its Norwegian publisher, was shot and seriously injured.

For a total of nine years, Rushdie was in hiding in 30 safe houses in Britain under Scotland Yard's protection. In 1998, the Iranian government, headed by President Mohammad Khatami, publicly disassociated itself from the fatwa against Rushdie and assured the British government that Iran would do nothing to implement it. Though Rushdie remained under partial protection, he began to travel and appear in public again.

Possession or distribution of *The Satanic Verses* remained illegal in Iran. In 2000, a U.S. federal appeals court halted the deportation to Tehran of Abbas Zahedi, an Iranian businessman, after he provided documentary evidence that he faced torture or death for distributing copies of *The Satanic Verses*. Zahedi had fled Tehran for the United States in 1996, when a warrant was issued for his arrest because he had asked a colleague to translate the book, which he had obtained in Turkey, into Farsi. The translator, Moshen, was tortured to death in the custody of Iranian security forces.

Although Rushdie has been able to resume the normal life of a literary celebrity, dividing his time between New York and London, he remains shadowed by the fatwa. In January 2004, he was threatened on a visit to his native city of Bombay by demonstrators outside his hotel calling for his death. Islamic groups in India offered to pay 10,000 rupees to anyone who succeeded in shaming Rushdie by blackening his face with boot polish or soot.

Despite the Iranian government's renewed disavowal of the fatwa, in January 2005, just before its 16th anniversary, Iran's supreme spiritual leader, Ayatollah Ali Khameini, reiterated that Rushdie was an apostate and that killing him remained an act authorized by Islam. Religious authorities in Iran maintain that the only person who can lift the death sentence against Rushdie is the man who imposed it, Ayatollah Khomenei, and as he is dead, the fatwa is permanent. In February 2005, Iran's Revolutionary Guards renewed calls for Rushdie's death, stating, "The day will come when they [Muslims] will punish the apostate Rushdie for his scandalous acts and insults against the Koran and the Prophet." The head of the Khordad

Foundation was quoted in 2003 as saying that the reward for killing Rushdie had risen to $3 million. In February 2004, the foundation declared that a new "committee for the glorification of the martyrs of the Muslim world" was offering an additional bounty of $100,000 for Rushdie's assassination.

In June 2005, a reporter for the *Times* (London) uncovered evidence of how serious the threat against Rushdie had been. In the Behesht Zahra cemetery in Tehran, in an area dedicated to foreign terrorists or "martyrs," stands a shrine bearing the words: "Mustafa Mahmoud Mazeh, born Conakry, Guinea. Martyred in London, August 3, 1989. The first martyr to die on a mission to kill Salman Rushdie." According to Scotland Yard, on that date in the Beverley House Hotel, Paddington, in London, an explosion that leveled two floors of the building killed Mazeh in his room. Antiterrorist squad detectives said he had died while trying to prime a bomb hidden in a book. At the time, British authorities said that there was a "hint" that he had belonged to a terrorist group but had not publicly linked the bombing to Rushdie.

When the British government announced in 2007 that Rushdie would be awarded a knighthood, protests and demonstrations erupted in Pakistan and Malaysia. A hard-line Pakistani cleric called for the author's death, and Pakistan's religious affairs minister, Mohammed Ejaz ul-Haq, said it would now be justified for suicide bombers to kill Rushdie. After the British government protested, ul-Haq explained that his comments were a statement of fact and not intended to incite violence. Rushdie received his knighthood in June 2008.

On the 20th anniversary of the publication of *The Satanic Verses* in October 2008, Sir Salman Rushdie told the *Times* (London) that he did not regret writing his book. "The question I'm always asking myself is: are we masters or victims? Do we make history or does history make us? Do we shape the world or are we just shaped by it? The question of do we have agency in our lives or whether we are just passive victims of events is, I think, a great question and one that I have always tried to ask. In that sense I wouldn't not have wanted to be the writer that asked it."

FURTHER READING

Appignanesi, Lisa, and Sara Maitland, eds. *The Rushdie File*. Syracuse, N.Y.: Syracuse University Press, 1990.

Barnes, Julian. "Staying Alive." *New Yorker* (February 21, 1994): 99–105.

Campbell, Duncan, and Julian Borger. "Rushdie Furore Stuns Honours Committee." *Guardian* (June 20, 2007). Available online. URL: http://www.guardian.co.uk/uk/2007/jun/20/books.pakistan. Accessed June 6, 2010.

For Rushdie: Essays by Arab and Muslim Writers in Defense of Free Speech. New York: George Braziller, 1994.

Harrison, James. *Salman Rushdie*. New York: Twayne, 1992.

Hoyle, Ben. "Salman Rushdie Unrepentant About Satanic Verses." *Times* (London) (October 1, 2008). Available online. URL: http://entertainment.timesonline.co.uk/tol/arts_and_entertainment/books/clive_james/article4856150.ece. Accessed June 6, 2010.

"Iran Adamant over Rushdie Fatwa." BBC News (February 17, 2005). Available online. URL: http://news.bbc.co.uk/2/hi/middle_east/4260599.stm.

Levy, Leonard W. *Blasphemy: Verbal Offense Against the Sacred, from Moses to Salman Rushdie.* New York: Alfred A. Knopf, 1993.

Lloyd, Anthony. "Tomb of the Unknown Assassin Reveals Mission to Kill Rushdie." *Times* (London) (June 8, 2005). Available online. URL: http://www.timesonline.co.uk/article/0,,3-1645223,00.html.

Pipes, Daniel. *The Rushdie Affair: The Novel, the Ayatollah, and the West.* New York: Carol Publishing Group, 1990.

Rushdie, Salman. *Imaginary Homelands: Essays and Criticism 1981–1991.* New York: Penguin Books, 1991.

Ruthven, Malise. *A Satanic Affair: Salman Rushdie and the Wrath of Islam.* London: Hogarth Press, 1991.

Weatherby, W. J. *Salman Rushdie: Sentenced to Death.* New York: Carroll and Graf Publishers, 1990.

SHIVAJI: HINDU KING IN ISLAMIC INDIA

Author: James W. Laine
Original date and place of publication: 2003, United States
Publisher: Oxford University Press
Literary form: History

SUMMARY

Shivaji: Hindu King in Islamic India by James W. Laine, a professor of religious studies at Macalester College in St. Paul, Minnesota, is a scholarly work about the 17th-century Hindu warrior and king Shivaji (1627–80). In 1674, Shivaji established an independent Hindu kingdom in western India, in what is now Maharashtra state, in defiance of the Muslim Mughal Empire, which controlled much of what is now India. The stories of Shivaji's life are legendary among the Marathi-speaking Hindu population of western India, who revere him as a hero of nearly divine status. He is also an icon for Hindu nationalists, who see him as the standard-bearer of opposition to Muslim domination.

Laine's book explores the Shivaji legend, analyzing the way various texts and stories have been woven into a commonly known narrative. He traces its development from the 17th century to the present, noting the different ways the story has been told. His primary interest is to examine critically the growth of Shivaji's legend as it relates to narratives of Maharashtrian Hindu identity.

"Good history is rarely about good guys and bad guys," Laine writes. A simplistic reading of Shivaji's story "leaves Maharashtrians with history in which Muslims (12 percent of the current population of Maharashtra) can only play the role of aggressors, usurpers and oppressors. The modern descendants of those Muslims are thus vilified as outsiders to a society which, though founded on secular principles, is easily swayed by the rhetoric of Hindu chauvinism." His aim is to be "a disturber of the tranquility with which synthetic accounts of Shivaji's life are accepted" and to rescue Shivaji's biography "from the grasp of those who see India as a Hindu nation at war with its Muslim neighbors."

Laine begins his study with early accounts of Shivaji's life at the end of the 17th century, composed by balladeers, court poets, and chroniclers patronized by Shivaji and his immediate descendants. The best-known tales of Shivaji from this period are intimately familiar to Maharashtrians today: his first great act of heroism, the killing of the general Afzal Kahn who had been dispatched by the Muslim sultan Adil Shah to conquer Shivaji; the raid against the Muslim noble Shaista Khan; Shivaji's escape from house arrest at the imperial court in Agra; and the conquest of Simhagad, a fort that had been ceded to the Mughals. The stories also tell of Shivaji's crowning in 1674 as *chatrapati* of an independent Hindu kingdom in an orthodox ceremony that had fallen out of favor in Islamicate (meaning the culture and society associated with Islam) India.

In these heroic texts, Laine sees a complex articulation of ideas and values that construct a Hindu identity. But it would be a misrepresentation to picture Shivaji in 17th-century Maharashtra as leading a band of united Hindu liberationists against a united Muslim oppressor, Laine writes. Elite Hindus were able to participate in the Islamicate world of 17th-century Deccan politics, Laine explains, and elite Muslims often accommodated themselves to Hindu social structures. Though Muslims were different in their beliefs and practices, they were not alien, nor were they a uniform group.

Some Maratha nobles supported Shivaji; others served Adil Shah or the Mughals. Shivaji himself began as a nominal servant of Adil Shah. He later made an alliance with the general Jai Singh and fought as a Mughal general. At that time, it was clear that religious identity was not a major factor for Maratha nobles in determining how they forged military and political alliances. Yet Shivaji stood apart. He attempted to rule as an independent Hindu monarch, to be faithful to his religious traditions, and to challenge the hegemony of the Islamicate world.

In the 17th century, Shivaji's legend was as an epic and martial hero. But in the 18th century, when the complexities of Hindu and Muslim interaction had receded in memory, Shivaji's story became wedded to that of the prominent 17th-century saints of Maharashtra—Tukaram and Ramdas—and he was transformed into a religious figure.

A primary preoccupation of 18th-century chroniclers was the warrior Shivaji's desire to renounce the world of wealth, power, and violence. He became a character who embodied the core values of an "essentialized, universalist Hinduism" in opposition to a single monolithic Islam. The complex picture of cross-religious alliances and internal differences within the Hindu and Muslim communities was replaced by "a picture of mythic clarity." "[S]uch universalism is the necessary precursor to the ideology of nationalism,"

Laine writes, "for nationalism presumes that all the members of the 'imagined community' participate equally in the common cultural tradition."

From the mid-19th century to the present, the retelling of the Shivaji story has reflected awareness of European culture and power. In 1900, Shivaji was portrayed not only as the father of a Maharashtrian nation but also as the leader of an independence movement with significance for all of India.

By the end of the 20th century, Shivaji's legend had become standardized as the patriotic tale of a great man whose kingdom represented a golden age, who lifted up the oppressed common man and gave him freedom. He is brave, fair-minded, compassionate, and pious and a devoted son who is without vice. Shivaji's life story is currently governed by the dictates of neo-Hindu nationalism, Laine says, "and the story has become so naturalized that it is difficult to imagine the story in any other way."

Laine concludes his study with a chapter examining what he describes as the "cracks" in the Shivaji narrative, "the places where we see efforts to construct a meaningful tale against corrosive forces of disharmony, contradiction and hypocritical compromise," where the writers of Shivaji's story seem to have avoided saying something. "Such a pursuit will allow us not to see the 'real' Shivaji but to better appreciate the ideological concerns of the many authors who have shaped the narrative tradition of Shivaji's legendary life. The real issue is what the authors are saying about themselves, about the dreams they hold, the dreams they see expressed in the tales of their hero."

Laine considers some "unthinkable thoughts, carefully held at bay by the narrators who have shaped the Shivaji legend": that Shivaji might have had an unhappy family life, that he had a harem, that he was uninterested in the religion of bhakti saints, that his personal ambition was to build a kingdom rather than liberate a nation, and that he lived in a cosmopolitan Islamicate world and did little to change that fact. It was Laine's expression of the "unthinkable thought" about Shivaji's family life that led to the controversy about his book.

The traditional accounts describe Shivaji's family life in positive terms, Laine writes, but Shivaji's parents lived apart for most if not all of his life. "Perhaps he was born at a time when his parents were already estranged? How would the narrative look in light of such a supposition?" Laine asks. "The repressed awareness that Shivaji had an absentee father is also revealed by the fact that Maharshtrians tell jokes naughtily suggesting that his guardian Dadaji Konddev was his biological father. In a sense, because Shivaji's father had little influence on his son, for many narrators it was important to supply him with father replacements, Dadaji and later Ramdas."

In an epilogue, Laine sums up the trajectory of the Shivaji story. "The narrative of Shivaji's life, already reshaped by *bhakti* writers by 1800, was thoroughly overtaken by the nationalist narrative in 1900 and has been sustained as a grand narrative of Hindu nationalist identity, despite all the inner inconsistencies, anachronisms, and communalism that imaginative enterprise has entailed."

CENSORSHIP HISTORY

An Indian edition of *Shivaji: Hindu King in Islamic India* was published in June 2003 by Oxford University Press India. The book was an English-language best seller in Pune, Maharashtra's second-largest city after Mumbai (Bombay) and the traditional center of Maharashtrian culture, and there were some positive reviews in national newspapers. But later that year, Laine began to receive e-mails, phone calls, and letters referring to the section of his book where he discusses Shivaji's parentage, demanding that he apologize for defaming a national hero.

Shivaji is a highly symbolic figure and a rallying point for Hindu nationalist groups, which include the Bharatiya Janata Party (BJP), the ruling party in India when Laine's book was published, and the Maharashtra-based right-wing Shiv Sena party. Hindu fundamentalists have been particularly vocal in their opposition to any criticism of Shivaji, his father, Shahji, and his mother, Jijabai, all of whom are highly revered.

On November 10, 2003, a group of Indian historians sent a letter to Oxford University Press India, calling for the book's withdrawal. "Though we do believe in freedom of expression," the scholars wrote, "we cannot subscribe to the practice of maligning the life and character of any person, especially of one who commands the love, respect and admiration of crores [tens of millions] of people and is a source of inspiration to them, by casting baseless aspersions." Ten days later, the publisher withdrew the book from the Indian market.

Laine had conducted some of his research at the venerable Bhandarkar Oriental Research Institute (BORI) in Pune. On December 22, activists from Shiv Sena confronted scholars attached to the institute. Sanskrit scholar Shrikant Bahulkar, whom Laine thanked in his preface, was assaulted and his face tarred. Bahulkar had helped Laine to translate Sanskrit and Marathi texts. On December 28, Shiv Sena leader Raj Thackeray apologized to Bahulkar and promised that Sena activists would have to get clearance from their leaders before embarking on "such aggressive campaigns" in the future.

In late December, Laine faxed a statement to Indian newspapers, apologizing for causing offense. "It was never my intention to defame the great Maharashtrian hero," he wrote. "I had no desire to upset those for whom he is an emblem of regional and national pride and I apologize for inadvertently doing so. I foolishly misread the situation in India and figured the book would receive scholarly criticism, not censorship and condemnation."

On January 5, 2004, a mob of some 150 people led by a little-known group called the Sambhaji Brigade stormed and ransacked BORI, destroying books, valuable manuscripts, and artifacts. Four days later, Maharashtra's state government filed charges against Laine and his publishers under Section 153 and 153A of the Indian penal code ("wantonly giving provocation with intent to cause riot;" "promoting enmity between different groups on grounds of religion, race, place of birth, residence, language, etc., and doing acts prejudicial to maintenance of harmony"). Even though the book was no longer being sold in India, the Maharashtra state government proceeded to ban it. The Oxford University Press showroom in Pune was forced to close by Maratha organizations supporting the Sambhaji Brigade.

On January 16, India's prime minister, Atal Bihari Vajpayee, regarded as a moderate within the BJP, spoke out against the book ban while unveiling a statue of Shivaji in Mumbai. "If you do not like anything in a particular book, then sit and discuss it. Banning a book is not a solution. We have to tackle it ideologically," he said. Hindu nationalist groups allied to his party swiftly denounced his comments. By March 20, when Vajpayee was launching the BJP general election campaign in Maharashtra, he had changed his position. "We are prepared to take action against the foreign author," he said. "This was a warning to all foreign authors that they do not play with our national pride." It was clear that the book had become fodder for politicians jockeying for the support of Maharashtra voters during a high-stakes national election campaign.

On March 22, Maharashtra home minister R. R. Patil confirmed that the state was pursuing criminal charges against Laine and his publisher and said that he wished to bring Laine in for interrogation. "If he does not show up on his own, then we will seek the assistance of Interpol to bring him, as a criminal offense has been registered against him for the book, which contains alleged slanderous remarks against Shivaji and his mother Jijamata." The next day Pune police commissioner D. N. Jadhav told reporters that he would write to Laine to summon him to India for questioning. If Laine ignored the summons, he said, the police would go to India's Central Bureau of Investigation and Interpol for help in extraditing him to India.

In fact, it was highly unlikely that Laine could be extradited, as the charges he faced are not crimes under U.S. law and the extradition would have to be ordered by a U.S. court. Days later, the police commissioner said that the police would not be sending a letter to Laine after all, as a petition had been filed by Laine and his publishers in the Bombay High Court challenging the charges.

In April, Laine submitted a formal apology to the high court. "It was never my intention to denigrate Shivaji or outrage sentiments," he wrote. "It is obvious that there can be no historical basis for jokes. Historical evidence suggests that Shahji was Shivaji's biological father and that is also my view. In writing the book, I had hoped to contribute in some way to a rich understanding of this great man. I forthwith direct my publishers to henceforth delete the offending paragraph on page 93 from all future publications of the book worldwide."

Nevertheless, on May 6 the Bombay High Court decided to allow Maharashtra police to proceed with their criminal investigation. On May 20, Laine and his publishers were granted relief when India's Supreme Court overruled the high court. It stayed further investigation or arrests pending the Supreme Court's consideration at a later date of the petition filed by the publishers and author to quash the case against them. At the end of 2005, no further legal action had been taken against Laine and his publishers, but the book remained banned in Maharashtra.

In 2007, India's Supreme Court quashed the criminal proceedings against Laine, declaring that he had no "intention to cause disorder or incite the people to violence," which is an essential element to prove offense under the law. In the meantime, yet another book by Laine, *The Epic of Shivaji*, was banned in Maharashtra. *The Epic of Shivaji*, Laine's first book on the subject, had been published by Orient Longman in 2001 without protest. It is a translation of the Sanskrit poem *Shivbharat*, written in 1674 by Kavindra Paramananda and commissioned by Shivaji himself to celebrate his life. In July 2006, a descendant of Shivaji and former BJP legislator filed a case against Laine for the use of the term *Oedipal rebel* in his introduction to the translation to refer to Shivaji's relationship with his father. The state government banned the book and seized 24 copies from its publisher on the grounds that it may hurt "public sentiments" and threaten law and order.

In an interview in 2004 with the Macalester College student newspaper, Laine, who has received death threats, expressed concern for the chilling effect on scholarship in India. "Storytellers have gone to great lengths to preserve the popular image of their hero," Laine said. "The purpose of academics is not to support the heroes of the state. There is no way scholarship can function under the restriction [of upholding] an ideal portrait as some kind of moral standard."

The events surrounding Laine's books are consonant with a pattern of violence, threats, and censorship against authors, artists, and filmmakers in India who offend the sensibilities of Hindu militants. "Today's new intimidating social censorship knows no limits," wrote Rajeev Dhavan in the Indian daily *The Hindu*, echoing the comments of the Indian journalists and scholars who decried the attacks on Laine and those connected to his book. "Direct threats are handed out by lumpen elements. Powerful informal censorship systems have crippled performance, films, shows and publications. Faced with this barrage, state censorship has retreated or capitulated. Governance has been abandoned to mob intimidation at the price of free speech."

Laine is not the only American scholar to be targeted. Paul Courtright, a professor of religion at Emory University in Atlanta, was threatened with death in 2004 by Hindu militants who were offended by a book he wrote in 1985, *Ganesa: Lord of Obstacles, Lord of Beginnings*. Courtright's Indian publishers recalled the book, which draws on psychoanalytical theories to study the stories of the Hindu god, Ganesha, after U.S.-based Hindus mounted a campaign on the Internet against it.

FURTHER READING

Baldauf, Scott. "How a U.S. Historian Sparked Calls for His Arrest—in India." *Christian Science Monitor* (March 29, 2004). Available online. URL: http://www.csmonitor.com/2004/0329/p01s04-wosc.html.

Barnes, Michael "Warrant for Professor's Arrest Issued in India." *The MAC Weekly*, (April 2, 2004). Available online. URL: http://www.macalester.edu/weekly. Accessed October 2, 2004.

Courtright, Paul. "Studying Religion in an Age of Terror: Internet Death Threats and Scholarship as a Moral Practice." The Academic Exchange, Emory University (April 15, 2004). Available online. URL: http://www.emory.edu/ACAD_EXCHANGE/2004/aprmay/courtright.html.

Dhavan, Rajeev. "Ban, Burn, Destroy." *The Hindu* (January 23, 2004). Available online. URL: http://www.hindu.com/2004/01/27/stories/2004012701571004.htm.

Engineer, Asghar Ali. "The Politics of Attack on Bhandarkar Institute." Centre for Study of Society and Secularism (February 1–5, 2004). Available online. URL: http://www.csss-isla.com/archive/archive.php?article=http://www.css-isla.com/archive/2004/feb 1_15.htm.

"James Laine's *Shivaji: Hindu King in Islamic India* and the Attack on the Bhandarkar Oriental Research Institute." *The Complete Review* (February 2004). Available online. URL: http://www.complete-review.com/quarterly/vol5/issue1/laine0.htm.

Katakam, Anupama. "The Politics of Vandalism." *Frontline* (January 17–30, 2004). Available online. URL: http://www.flonet.com/fl2102/stories/20040130003802800.htm.

Katakam, Anupama, and Nandagopal R. Menon. "Politics of a Ban." *Frontline* (February 11–24, 2006). Available online. URL: http://www.hinduonnet.com/fline/fl2303/stories/20060224002609300.htm. Accessed June 6, 2010.

Laine, James W. "In India, 'the Unthinkable' Is Printed at One's Peril." *Los Angeles Times*, January 12, 2004, p. B-13.

"Laine to Be Summoned to India, Says Police Chief." Express News Service, Mumbai, India (March 23, 2004). Available online. URL: http://cities.expressindia.com/fullstory.php?newsid=79728.

Nandgaonkar, Satish. "Author Explains Oedipus Parallel—Not Derogatory, Says Laine." *Telegraph* (January 12, 2006). Available online. URL: http://www.telegraphindia.com/1060112/asp/nation/story_5711098.asp. Accessed June 6, 2010.

"Pune Institute's Desecration Shocks Author." *Mid Day* (January 6, 2004). Available online. URL: http://ww1.mid-day.com/news/nation/2004/january/73060.htm.

Singh, Vijay. "Bringing Laine Back: Easier Said Than Done." Rediff.com (March 27, 2004). Available online. URL: http://us.rediff.com/news/2004/mar/27laine.htm.

Vedantam, Shankar. "U.S. Scholars' Writings Inspire Hatred in India." *Washington Post*, April 10, 2004, p. A-1.

A SHORT DECLARATION OF THE MISTERY OF INIQUITY

Author: Thomas Helwys
Original date and place of publication: 1612, Holland
Literary form: Theological treatise

SUMMARY

Thomas Helwys was an English Separatist who, with John Murton, founded the first permanent Baptist church in England. *A Short Declaration of the*

Mistery of Iniquity, published in Holland in 1612, was the first work printed in English to advocate religious liberty for all subjects and is an outstanding contribution to the literature of toleration.

Separatists were Christians who withdrew from the Church of England because they desired freedom from church and civil authority over their religious beliefs, control of congregations by their membership, and changes in ritual. Because Helwys held a prominent position in the Separatist movement, he became a target for persecution. He and the other Separatists fled to Amsterdam. His wife, who chose to remain, was arrested and for some time was imprisoned in York Castle.

In Holland, under the leadership of John Smyth, a nonconformist clergyman and early believer in adult baptism, they formed in 1608 the first English Baptist congregation. This was the first of the churches known as the General Baptists, as its members held that the Atonement of Christ is not limited only to the elect but, rather, applies in general to all believers. The Baptists believed that baptism as administered by the Anglican Church was unlawful because infant baptism was not authorized by the Scriptures. They maintained the right of any group of Christians to baptize and to ordain their own ministers and officers.

The earliest publication by Helwys in 1611 contained the first Confession of Faith of the Church of English Baptists. It consisted of 27 brief articles asserting the equality of every church member in knowledge of spiritual and religious matters. Next he published a small volume on Baptist opposition to Calvinist doctrines of particular election and redemption.

Helwys and others broke with Smyth over doctrinal disputes. About the time of Smyth's death in 1612, Helwys became convinced that it was wrong to flee from persecution and that he and the other Baptists should have remained in England to proclaim their message. In *A Short Declaration of the Mistery of Iniquity,* published in 1612, he wrote of the Separatist leaders, "How much better had it been that they had given their lives for that truth they profess in their own Countries." Helwys, John Murton, and a handful of followers returned to London to establish their church there.

Helwys sent King James I a copy of his book, personally inscribed. "The King is a mortal man and not God," he wrote in *A Short Declaration,* and "therefore hath no power over the immortal soules of his subjects to make lawes and ordinances for them to set spiritual Lords over them." No state had lawful authority to force conscience or foster religion. Church and state should be separated, as the world has long suffered from a confusion of temporal and spiritual powers. Earthly crimes should be punished by earthly penalties and spiritual errors by spiritual penalties.

Helwys lamented the "general departing from the faith and an utter desolation of all true religion" that he had observed in the Roman Catholic Church, the Church of England, and other Christian denominations. He attacked those Separatists who had retained as valid the baptism of the Church of England. He also indicated a deep concern about the salvation of the king. Only the king could free the truth to make its way in his kingdom without persecution.

Every individual is responsible to God for his own salvation, Helwys asserted. Erroneous opinions on religion are of no concern to the state and its established church. "For man's religion to God, is betwixt God and themselves; the King shall not answer for it, neither may the King be judge betweene God and man. Let them be heretikes, Turcks, Jewes, or whatsoever it apperteynes not to the earthly power to punish them in the least measure."

Though Helwys detested Roman Catholicism, he extended his principles of religious liberty to Catholics and believed that they should be accorded the same tolerance he requested for himself. Helwys asked, "Whether there be so unjust a thing and of so great cruel tyranny under the sun as to force men's conscience in their religion to God, seeing that if they err they must pay the price of their transgression with the loss of their souls?"

Helwys pleaded to the king: "Do not when a poor soul by violence is brought before you to speak of his conscience in the profession of his religion to his God—do not first implore the oath *ex officio*. Oh, most wicked course! And if he will not yield to that then imprison him close. Oh, horrible severity! . . . Let these courses be far from you, for there is no show, of grace, religion nor humanity in these courses." The right to seek truth in one's own way is the most necessary and sacred of all rights.

CENSORSHIP HISTORY

Helwys tried to forestall the charge that he was promoting sedition against the state in *A Short Declaration* by pointing out to King James that he ascribed to the doctrine of nonresistance. "If the King or any in authority under him shall exercise their power against any, they are not to resist by any way or means, although it were in their power, but rather to keep their consciences to God. . . ."

Helwys referred to the passage in the Scriptures in which Jesus rebuked those who would have called down fire upon his opponents. "Christ will have no man's life touched for his cause. . . . The King's understanding heart will easily discern this," Helwys wrote. The king's heart, however, was not understanding. He was determined to enforce his Anglican preferences in religion, and the result of Helwys's approach to him was a term in Newgate Prison. It is recorded that Helwy's colleague, Murton, was imprisoned in 1613, and it is assumed that Helwys was behind bars that year and possibly the next. By 1616 he was dead.

The cause of religious freedom made little headway during the reign of King James. But despite the suppression of the English Baptists, they won converts. At the close of King James's reign, the first Baptist church in London counted about 150 members, and several other Baptist churches had been established in southeastern England.

Helwys's book was notable and influential as the first work in England to advocate freedom for all religions. Neither Sebastian Castellio's CONCERNING HERETICS (1554) nor Acontinius's *Satan's Stratagems* (1565), pathbreaking books on toleration that were published in Latin and translated into Dutch, had appeared in English. The advocates of civil and religious liberty at the time of the mid-17th-century Commonwealth found in Helwys's writing an important storehouse of arguments in favor of religious freedom.

FURTHER READING

Burgess, Walter H. *John Smith, Thomas Helwys and the First Baptist Church in England*. London: James Clarke, 1911.

Jordan, W. K. *The Development of Religious Toleration in England*. Vol. 2. Gloucester, Mass.: Peter Smith, 1965.

Levy, Leonard W. *Blasphemy: Verbal Offense Against the Sacred, from Moses to Salman Rushdie*. New York: Alfred A. Knopf, 1993.

THE SHORTEST WAY WITH THE DISSENTERS

Author: Daniel Defoe
Original date and place of publication: 1702, England
Literary form: Parody

SUMMARY

The English novelist and journalist Daniel Defoe was one of the most prolific writers in the English language, with more then 500 works to his credit. His work includes newspaper articles, essays, pamphlets, and novels, notably *Robinson Crusoe, MOLL FLANDERS, Journal of the Plague Year*, and *Roxana*.

A turning point in Defoe's career came in 1702 with his publication of a notorious pamphlet, *The Shortest Way with the Dissenters: Or Proposals for the Establishment of the Church*. The pamphlet was a parody of the intolerant views of High Church extremists within the Tory party, who favored the restriction of the rights of Dissenters, or non-Anglicans, who were members of other Protestant sects. These Tories supported legislation that would, in effect, disqualify Dissenters like Defoe from holding political office by ending the practice of "occasional conformity." This practice allowed non-Anglicans to receive the sacraments occasionally at an Anglican church while preserving their allegiance to their own religions.

Henry Sacheverell, a High Church preacher, urged approval of the legislation in inflammatory sermons laced with biblical metaphors. In a parody written in pitch-perfect, though exaggerated, imitation of Sacheverell, Defoe put forth a diatribe favoring total and violent repression of Dissenters. Defoe intended the anonymous pamphlet, published in December 1702, to be read as the work of a Tory zealot.

"This is the time to pull up this heretical weed of sedition that has so long disturb'd the peace of our church and poisoned the good corn," the anonymous writer declared. The Church of England could best be served "by extirpating her implacable Enemies." He proposed the "shortest way" to vanquish the Dissenters: "If one severe law were made, and punctually executed, that whoever was found at a conventicle shou'd be banish'd the nation and the preacher be hang'd, we shou'd soon see an end of the tale; they wou'd all come to church, and one age wou'd make us one again."

For the sake of future generations, the writer urged his readers to imitate Moses, "a merciful meek man, and yet with what fury did he run thro' the camp, and cut the throats of three and thirty thousand of his dear Israelites, that were fallen into idolatry; what was the reason? t'was mercy to the rest, to make these be examples, to prevent the destruction of the whole army." The pamphlet concluded, "*Now let us Crucifie the Thieves.* . . . [L]et the Obstinate be rul'd with the Rod of Iron."

Once the pamphlet was praised by anti-Dissenters, Defoe intended to admit its authorship and expose them as the intolerant fanatics he believed they were. Recalling years later his motivation in publishing it, Defoe wrote that he intended to "speak in the first person of the party, and then thereby not only speak their language, but make them acknowledge it to be theirs, which they did so openly that [it] confounded all their attempts afterwards to deny it, and to call it a scandal thrown upon them by another."

CENSORSHIP HISTORY

Though *The Shortest Way with the Dissenters* must be counted as a successful parody, it has been described as a spectacular failure as a work of irony. Defoe was undone by his great talent for impersonation and mimicry that caused almost everyone who read the pamphlet to believe it was genuine. As Defoe explained three years after its publication, to the "High Church Men the piece in its outward figure, look'd so natural, and was as like a brat of their own begetting, that like two apples, they could not know them asunder."

When it was discovered that Defoe, a prominent Dissenter, was the pamphlet's author, the High Church Tories, many of whom undoubtedly agreed with the sentiments it expressed, condemned it as "a blasphemous attack on Mother Church." The government viewed Defoe's pamphlet as seditious libel because it implied that the government's policy of religious toleration was a sham.

On January 23, 1703, Daniel Finch, second earl of Nottingham, the secretary of state, issued a warrant for Defoe's arrest. Defoe was apprehended but escaped. After a reward of £50 was offered, he was betrayed by an informer and rearrested in May 1703. A complaint lodged against him in the House of Commons charged that the pamphlet was "full of false and scandalous Reflections upon this Parliament, and tending to promote sedition." The House ordered the burning of the pamphlet by the public hangman.

In July, Defoe was tried at Old Bailey for having written a "Seditious, pernicious, and Diabolical Libel" whose purpose was "to Disunite and set at variance the Protestant Subjects of . . . the Queen, and to alarm All her Protestant Subjects Dissenting from the Church of England with the Fear of being deprived of the Exemption. . . ." Defoe pleaded guilty, admitting that he had written and caused *The Shortest Way* to be published but asked for mercy because his intent was not seditious. He had written the work ironically, and his aim was neither to stir up Dissenters nor to encourage others to persecute them.

In spite of the intercession of the Quaker William Penn, Defoe received no mercy; rather, he was meted an unusually severe punishment. He was sentenced in July 1703 to stand three times in the pillory, pay the large fine of 200 marks (about £135 pounds), and remain in Newgate Prison "during the Queen's pleasure," or indefinitely.

As part of his sentence he was ordered to find securities for his good behavior during the next seven years, which precluded publication of anything that could be construed as inflammatory. The harshness of Defoe's sentence has been explained by the personal resentment of the Old Bailey judges whom he had satirized in scathing terms in *Reformation of Manners*, a pamphlet published the previous year. Public exposure in the pillory was considered to be the most humiliating punishment in English law and was potentially fatal. By the time Defoe stood in the pillory, however, he had become a hero for many Dissenters. Rather than pelting him with stones or garbage, the mob threw flowers.

Through the influence of the moderate Tory Robert Harley, an astute politician who was speaker of the House of Commons and had recently become a secretary of state, Defoe was released from Newgate in November 1703. He had spent more than six months behind bars. Harley had obtained a pardon for him and ensured the payment of his fine and court costs. However, while Defoe had languished in prison, his brick-and-tile factory had failed, and his debts had mounted. He was forced to declare bankruptcy.

Defoe's arrest and public humiliation is regarded by biographers as the most significant event of his life. The residue of bitterness and anger over the incident colored Defoe's attitudes and beliefs. He was never again able to free himself from debt. For the next 11 years Defoe served his benefactor Robert Harley secretly as a political spy and confidential agent, and he wrote in Harley's support for the rest of Harley's political career.

Despite the threat of further action against him if he offended the government, while imprisoned at Newgate, Defoe defiantly published *More Reformation*, a satire lambasting two of his judges, and a poem "A Hymn to the Pillory." While he stood in the pillory, the poem was circulated on the streets below: "Let all Mankind be told for what: / Tell them t'was because he was too bold, / And told those Truths which shou'd not ha' been told." Defoe wrote in 1705 that the poem "was the Author's declaration, even when in the cruel hands of a merciless as well as unjust ministry, that the treatment he had from them was unjust, exorbitant, and consequently illegal."

FURTHER READING

Backscheider, Paula. *Daniel Defoe: His Life*. Baltimore: Johns Hopkins University Press, 1989.

Earle, Peter. *The World of Defoe*. New York: Atheneum, 1977.

Levy, Leonard W. *Blasphemy: Verbal Offense Against the Sacred, from Moses to Salman Rushdie*. New York: Alfred A. Knopf, 1993.

Moore, John Robert. *Defoe in the Pillory and Other Studies*. New York: Octagon Books, 1973.

Richetti, John J. *Daniel Defoe*. Boston: Twayne Publishers, 1987.

Sutherland, James. *Daniel Defoe: A Critical Study*. Cambridge, Mass.: Harvard University Press, 1971.

THE SOCIAL CONTRACT

Author: Jean-Jacques Rousseau
Original date and place of publication: 1762, Holland
Literary form: Political-philosophical treatise

SUMMARY

The Social Contract outlines the influential political theories of the Swiss-French philosopher Jean-Jacques Rousseau. One of the most quoted remarks in political philosophy is the opening sentence of its first chapter: "Man is born free and everywhere he is in chains." The chains Rousseau refers to are those of government. His concern is to explain why people should submit to the bondage of government. "What can render it legitimate?" he asks.

To Rousseau, government is a social contract that determines distribution of power along lines dictated by the general will and for the common good. It is law rather than anarchy that makes people free. Freedom consists of voluntary submission by the individual to the general will, which is what rational citizens would choose for the common good. The government exists only to carry out the general will of the people.

The act of association "produces a moral and collective body, composed of as many members as the assembly contains votes, and which receives from this same act its unity, its common identity, its life and its will." This public person is the republic, or body politic.

The contract between a ruler and the people is just in that it entails reciprocal rights and obligations. Because citizens in association constitute the sovereign ruler, the social contract works only if every individual gives up all rights. "That which man loses by the social contract is his natural liberty and an unlimited right to everything he attempts to get and succeeds in getting; that which he gains is civil liberty and the proprietorship of all he possesses."

However, might does not create right, and people are obliged to obey only legitimate powers. "The undertakings binding us to the social body are obligatory only because they are mutual and their nature is such that in fulfilling them we cannot work for others without working for ourselves." When the social compact is violated, people regain their original rights and natural liberty. "There is in the State no fundamental law that cannot be revoked, not excluding the social compact itself; for if all the citizens assembled of one accord to break the compact, one cannot doubt that it would be very legitimately broken." At the heart of Rousseau's political philosophy is a moral theory, which begins with the assumption that human beings are by nature good. By substituting justice for instinct in their conduct, people pass from the state of nature to the civil state.

Among the most controversial elements of *The Social Contract* was Rousseau's promotion of a "civil religion" that would support the idea of the common good and provide one basic faith for everyone. For citizens to live peacefully there can be only one source of authority; the church should be subordinate to the state. Because Christianity "preaches only servitude and dependence," it should not be a state religion. If there is no longer an exclusive national religion, tolerance can be granted to all religions that tolerate others so long as their dogmas contain nothing contrary to the duties of citizenship.

Although Rousseau hoped that *The Social Contract* would be "a book for all times," he did not expect to reach a wide audience. In a letter to his printer in Holland, he admitted that it was "difficult material, fit for a few readers." Because it was published in Holland, censors were able to refuse its entry and impede its circulation in France. But at the time of the French Revolution, it became well known and exerted a profound influence. As one of Rousseau's contemporaries wrote in 1791, "Formerly it was the least read of Rousseau's works. Today all the citizens think about it and learn it by heart."

CENSORSHIP HISTORY

See ÉMILE.

FURTHER READING

Collinson, Diané. *Fifty Major Philosophers: A Reference Guide.* London: Routledge, 1988.
Green, Jonathon. *The Encyclopedia of Censorship.* New York: Facts On File, 1990.

Haight, Anne Lyon. *Banned Books: 387 BC to 1978 AD*. Updated and enlarged by Chandler B. Grannis. New York: R. R. Bowker, 1978.

Mason, John Hope. *The Indispensable Rousseau*. London: Quartet Books, 1979.

Reill, Peter Hanns, and Ellen Judy Wilson. *Encyclopedia of the Enlightenment*. New York: Facts On File, 1996.

Scott-Kakures, Dion, Susan Castegnetto, Hugh Benson, William Taschek, and Paul Hurley. *History of Philosophy*. New York: HarperCollins, 1993.

THE SORROWS OF YOUNG WERTHER

Author: Johann Wolfgang von Goethe
Original dates and place of publication: 1774, 1787, Germany
Literary form: Novel

SUMMARY

The Sorrows of Young Werther is the first novel of the great German poet, playwright, and novelist Johann Wolfgang von Goethe. This epistolary romance about a hopeless love affair and young man's suicide achieved immediate and lasting success and won fame for its 25-year-old author. First published in German in 1774 and translated into every major European language, it was one of the literary sensations of the century. The novel's romantic sensibilities struck a chord among the youth of Europe, who admired it with a cultlike fervor.

The story is told in the form of letters sent by a young man named Werther to a friend, Wilhelm, over the 18 months between May 1771 and December 1772. Book One collects Werther's letters over an idyllic spring and summer in the rural hamlet of Wahlheim. He describes his pleasure at the natural beauties of the area, his peaceful existence in a secluded cottage surrounded by a garden and his delight in the simple folk he meets.

"I am experiencing the kind of happiness that God dispenses only to his saints," he writes on June 21. At a ball he has met a young woman named Charlotte (Lotte), the beautiful and charming daughter of a judge. Though he realizes that she is engaged to be married to Albert, who is away, Werther becomes deeply infatuated with Lotte, to the point of obsession. He visits her daily and begins to object to the time she spends with other acquaintances. At the end of July, Albert returns and the joyous idyll with Lotte must come to an end.

Werther spends a miserable six weeks in the couple's company in the throes of a hopeless and frustrating passion. In August he writes: "My full, warm enjoyment of all living things that used to overwhelm me with so much delight and transform the world around me into a paradise has been turned into unbearable torment. . . ." In early September he leaves the area to escape the tensions of the situation.

Book Two covers the remaining 13 months of Werther's life. He becomes a secretary to an ambassador whom he dislikes. Expressing his boredom at the social aspirations of the "horrible people" with whom he must associate, he chafes at the responsibilities of his position. When he hears the news that Lotte and Albert have married, he resigns his post to become companion to a prince at his country estate but remains discontented. Returning to Wahlheim, he begins to see Lotte and Albert again. His letters become more depressed, speaking of feelings of emptiness and the wish that he might go to sleep and not wake up again.

After Werther's letter of December 6, 1772, an unnamed editor takes over to fill in the account of the last weeks in Werther's life, referring to letters and notes left behind. Werther had become more depressed, exhausted, and anxious. Lotte suggested that he visit her less frequently. One night when Albert was away, Werther went to Lotte's house. After he seized her in a wild embrace, she fled in fear and locked herself in her room. The next day he sent his servant to Albert to borrow a brace of pistols to take on a journey. After writing in a final letter to Lotte that "it has been given to only a few noble beings to shed their blood for those they love, and by their death to create a new life a hundred times better for their friends," Werther shot himself in the head. He died the next day without regaining consciousness. The workmen of the village carried his body to its resting place under the trees at Wahlheim, and "no priest attended him."

Goethe once remarked on the autobiographical nature of much of his fiction, saying that all his works were "fragments of a great confession." *The Sorrows of Young Werther* was inspired by two incidents in Goethe's life. Werther's relationship with Lotte is based on Goethe's unhappy infatuation with Charlotte Buff, the fiancée of his friend G. C. Kestner. Suffering from depression over the unfulfilled relationship with Charlotte, Goethe was also deeply affected by the suicide of Karl Wilhelm Jerusalem, a friend from Wetzlar who was secretary to the Brunswick ambassador. Snubbed by aristocratic society and in love with the wife of a colleague, Jerusalem shot himself.

Goethe wrote in his memoirs, *My Life: Poetry and Truth*, "Suddenly I heard of Jerusalem's death and hot upon the general rumors, an exact and involved description of the entire incident. In that moment, the plan of Werther was found, the whole thing crystallized, like water in a glass that is on the point of freezing and can be turned to ice immediately with the slightest motion." Goethe said that he breathed into the work all the passion that results when there is no difference between fact and fiction.

CENSORSHIP HISTORY

Upon its publication in 1774, readers throughout Europe greeted *The Sorrows of Young Werther* with enthusiasm. The 20th-century German writer Thomas Mann, whose novel *Lotte in Weimar* was based on the central situation of *The Sorrows of Young Werther*, wrote, "As for Werther, all the riches of [Goethe's] gift were apparent. . . . The extreme, nerve-shattering sensitivity of the little book . . . evoked a storm of applause which went beyond all bounds and fairly intoxicated the world." It was "the spark that fell into the powder keg causing the sudden expansion of forces that had been awaiting release."

By proclaiming the rights of emotion, the book expressed the creed of youth protesting against the rationalism and moralism of the older generation. Goethe became the spokesman for his generation. The novel was a grand expression of the spirit of the Age of Sentiment and the first great achievement of what would later be called confessional literature.

The knowledge that Goethe's story was based on real events, particularly the suicide of young Karl Wilhelm Jerusalem, added to the "Werther fever" that swept the continent and was to last for decades after the novel's publication. There were sequels, parodies, imitations, operas, plays, songs, and poems based on the story. Ladies wore Eau de Werther cologne, jewelry, and fans. Men sported Werther's blue dress jacket and yellow vest. Figures of Werther and Lotte were modeled in export porcelain in China. Within 12 years, 20 unauthorized editions were issued in Germany. In England by the end of the century, there were 26 separate editions of a translation from French. Napoléon told Goethe that he had read the novel seven times. Pilgrims came from all over Europe to visit Jerusalem's grave, where they made speeches and left flowers. A 19th-century English travel book guided visitors to the spot.

Werther's suicide inspired some young men and women in Germany and France to take their own lives, with copies of Goethe's novel in their pockets. Though it is not clear whether the suicides would have occurred anyway, Goethe was assailed by critics who saw the novel as having a corrupting influence and encouraging a morbid sensibility. Clergy preached sermons against the book. The Leipzig theological faculty applied for a ban of the novel on the grounds that it recommended suicide. Within two days, the city council imposed the prohibition. In Denmark in 1776, a proposed translation was forbidden as not being in accordance with Lutheran doctrine, established by the crown as the orthodox faith of the nation.

Goethe wrote of the novel in his memoirs: "I had saved myself from a situation into which I had been driven through my own fault. . . . I felt like a man after absolute confession, happy and free again, with the rights to a new life. But just as I had felt relieved and lighthearted because I had succeeded in transforming reality into poetry, my friends were confusing themselves by believing that they had to turn poetry into reality, enact the novel and shoot themselves! What actually took place among a few, happened later *en masse*, and this little book that had done me so much good acquired the reputation of being extremely harmful!"

During the years 1783–87, Goethe revised the novel. In the definitive text of 1787, he added material intended to emphasize Werther's mental disturbance and dissuade readers from following Werther's example of suicide. The note to readers that precedes Book One reads "And you, good soul, who feel a compulsive longing such as his, draw consolation from his sorrows, and let this little book be your friend whenever through fate or through your own fault you can find no closer companion."

The Sorrows of Young Werther was censored again 163 years after its publication. In 1939, the government of Spanish dictator Francisco Franco ordered libraries purged of works by "such disgraceful writers as Goethe."

FURTHER READING

Friedenthal, Richard. *Goethe: His Life and Times.* New York: World Publishing, 1963.

Goethe, Johann Wolfgang von. *The Sorrows of Young Werther.* Translated and with an introduction by Michael Hulse. London: Penguin Books, 1989.

———. *The Sorrows of Young Werther and Selected Writings.* Translated by Catherine Hutter. Foreword by Hermann J. Weigand. New York: New American Library, 1962.

———. *The Sufferings of Young Werther.* Translated and with an introduction by Bayard Quincy Morgan. New York: Frederick Ungar Publishing, 1957.

THE SPIRIT OF LAWS

Author: Charles-Louis de Secondat, baron de La Brède et de Montesquieu

Original date and place of publication: 1748, Switzerland

Literary form: Political treatise

SUMMARY

The Spirit of Laws is generally considered the greatest work of the French jurist and political philosopher Charles-Louis de Secondat, baron de La Brède et de Montesquieu. The fruit of more than 20 years of research and writing, *The Spirit of Laws* was dictated to secretaries after Montesquieu had become blind in his old age. It became a fundamental guide to political thinking in the 18th century. Montesquieu's political theories influenced moderate leaders in the early days of the French Revolution, as well as the framers of the U.S. Constitution, who adopted Montesquieu's recommendations on the separation of legislative, executive, and judicial powers in government.

"Laws in their widest meaning are the necessary relations which derive from the nature of things," Montesquieu declared in the famous first sentence of *The Spirit of Laws.* The law cannot be considered as the result of the arbitrary will of one man or of a nation. All beings have their laws. All laws are relative and vary according to the type of government, whether democracy, monarchy, or tyranny, and the material and geographical conditions, cultural context, and historical experience of each society. The guiding spirit of each type of political system is different. In a democracy it is virtue; in an aristocracy, moderation; in a monarchy, honor; and under despotism, fear.

Attempts to discover laws must begin with the study of facts, the "nature of things," rather than in the realm of ideas or abstractions, Montesquieu believed. In *The Spirit of Laws*, Montesquieu studied three types of government: republic, monarchy, and despotism. A republic can be either a democracy, in which the body of the people possess supreme power, or an aristocracy, in which only a part of the people hold power. In a monarchy, a prince governs in accordance with fundamental laws, while under despotism, the ruler governs without law. Denouncing the abuses of the French monarchy, Montesquieu determined that the powers of government should be separated to guarantee freedom of the individual.

"Power should be a check to power," Montesquieu recommended. When the legislative and executive powers are united in the same person or the same body of magistrates, there can be no liberty. The same monarch or senate could enact tyrannical laws and execute them in a tyrannical manner. If the judiciary power is not separated from the legislative and executive, the life and liberty of subjects would be exposed to arbitrary control. If the judiciary is joined to the executive power, a judge might behave with violence and oppression. "A government may be so constituted, as no man shall be compelled to do things to which the law does not oblige him, nor forced to abstain from things which the law permits."

Montesquieu warned of the dangers of despotism and encouraged humanization of the law. The rules governing the structure and powers of government should be separated from the civil and criminal law applying to private citizens. If the government interferes with the civil law, it endangers the person and property of citizens. Likewise, religious law should be kept entirely separate from politics and secular law. Religious belief cannot be compelled by force.

CENSORSHIP HISTORY

Fearing French censorship, Montesquieu had *The Spirit of Laws* published in Geneva in 1748. It was distributed in France with neither the consent nor the interference of the state censor. Though it was published anonymously, Montesquieu was known to be its author. By the end of 1749, at least 22 editions, some in translation, were in print. The volume was widely read and well received throughout Europe. Most of the world's constitutional governments are indebted to it.

Montesquieu's spirit of moderation and toleration, his rejection of absolutism, denunciation of the abuses of the French monarchial system, and advocacy of the use of reason and the empirical method in his analysis of political theory were seen as challenges to ecclesiastical authority. Though *The Spirit of Laws* was soon recognized as a work of major importance, both Jesuits and their enemies, the Jansenists, attacked it as expressing profound indifference to Christianity and urged secular authorities to take action against the book.

The Jansenist *Ecclesiastical News* wrote: "The parenthesis that the author inserts to inform us that he is a Christian gives slight assurance of his Catholicism; the author would laugh at our simplicity if we should take him for what he is not." Jesuit critics accused Montesquieu of following the pernicious materialistic philosophy of Baruch Spinoza and Thomas Hobbes. By assuming laws in history as in natural science, he left no room for freedom of the will. Truth and justice are absolute and based on God-given universal principles, the Jesuits argued, rather than on diversities of climate, soil, custom, or national character.

Many of Montesquieu's Enlightenment colleagues, such as Voltaire and Claude-Adrien Helvétius, on the other hand, attacked the book as being too conservative, moderate in its reforms, and halfhearted in its concept of religious toleration.

Responding publicly to his critics, in 1750 Montesquieu published his *Defense of the Spirit of Laws*, in which he reaffirmed his Christianity and disclaimed atheism, materialism, and determinism. Religious authorities in Paris and Rome, however, unconvinced by his defense, began investigations of the book. A government order forbade its distribution in France until Chrétien-Guillaume de Lamoignon de Malesherbes, the director of the book trade, removed the prohibition in 1750.

From July 1750 until July 1754, the Sorbonne, the theological faculty of the University of Paris, formally considered its condemnation. Five different accusations were drawn up and made public, but none was ratified. In 1751, the book, like his satirical novel THE PERSIAN LETTERS, was placed on the Catholic Church's Index of Forbidden Books. *The Spirit of Laws* remained on the Index through its final edition, in effect until 1966.

The censorship of *The Spirit of Laws* served only to enhance Montesquieu's fame. In 1753, he was named director of the French Academy. When Montesquieu died in 1755, he was regarded internationally as one of the most important writers of the century. *The Spirit of Laws* continued to be praised as a masterpiece and recognized as a seminal influence on political thinking that has lasted for more than two centuries.

FURTHER READING

Conroy, Peter V., Jr. *Montesquieu Revisited*. New York: Twayne Publishers, 1992.

Curtis, Michael. *The Great Political Theories*. Vol. 1. New York: Avon Books, 1981.

Durant, Will, and Ariel Durant. *The Age of Voltaire*. New York: Simon and Schuster, 1965.

Haight, Anne Lyon. *Banned Books: 387 BC to 1978 AD*. Updated and enlarged by Chandler B. Grannis. New York: R. R. Bowker, 1978.

Shklar, Judith N. *Montesquieu*. Oxford: Oxford University Press, 1987.

SPIRITS REBELLIOUS

Author: Kahlil Gibran
Original dates and place of publication: 1908, United States (in Arabic); 1947, United States (in English)
Original publisher: The Philosophical Library (in English)
Literary form: Short stories

SUMMARY

Spirits Rebellious is a collection of short stories by the Lebanese-American writer and artist Kahlil Gibran. Gibran is better known for *The Prophet,* a book of 28 poetic essays that has sold millions of copies worldwide since its publication in 1923. A Maronite Christian, Gibran was a leader of the Arab-American community and published several periodicals that influenced literary development in the Arab world. Gibran's short stories about oppressive social conditions in 19th-century Lebanon originally appeared in a New York Arab-language newspaper, *Al-Mohajer.*

In "Madame Rose Hanie," the narrator visits his friend Rashid Bey Namaana in Beirut, finding him depressed because the woman whom he had rescued from poverty and made wealthy, and to whom he was a sincere companion and faithful husband, has left him for another man. A few days later the author meets the woman, Madame Rose Hanie, living in a hovel surrounded by flowers and trees. She recounts her involvement with her husband, who married her when she was 18 and he was 40. The husband brought her to his magnificent home, where he exhibited her as a strange rarity. Though she was at first seduced by the material wealth she acquired through the marriage, she felt imprisoned in his mansion. She fell in love with a poor young intellectual. "I comprehended the secrets of her protest against the society which persecutes those who rebel against confining laws and customs," Gibran writes. "For the first time in my life I found the phantom of happiness standing between a man and a woman, cursed by religion and opposed by the law."

In the allegorical story "The Cry of the Graves," Gibran recalls the brutal and ruthless injustice of 19th-century Lebanon. The narrator observes as the malevolent emir sentences three prisoners to death. As the background of each criminal is revealed, the crimes are shown to be society's responsibility. A murderer sentenced to be decapitated turns out to be a man who had protected a woman's honor by killing a rapacious tax collector. A woman stoned to death for committing adultery is revealed to have been wrongly accused. A thief sentenced to hang was a poor man who had stolen two sacks of flour from a monastery's overflowing granaries to feed his starving family. "When a man kills another man, the people say he is a murderer," Gibran writes, "but when the Emir robs him of his life, the Emir is honorable." After the three are executed, they are secretly buried by their loved ones. Above their graves are placed a sheathed sword, flowers, and a cross, symbols of human salvation by courage, love, and the words of Christ.

"Khalil the Heretic" is set in a village in North Lebanon, where Sheik Abbas lives in luxury in a mansion amid the huts of the poor. The huts and the fields the poor peasants till belong to him. In reward for their toil, the farmers are compensated with only a small portion of the crop, which keeps them on the brink of starvation. Rachel, a widow, and her daughter find a youth lying outside in the cold, bring him to their hut, and care for him. He has been expelled from the monastery because he could not rest easy in the comfortable rooms built with the money of poor farmers. "Since the beginning of the creation and up to our present time, certain clans, rich by inheritance, in cooperation with the clergy, had appointed themselves the administrators of the people. . . . The Clergyman erects his temple upon the graves and bones of the devoted worshippers," Gibran writes.

Sheik Abbas arrests the youth, who defends his rebellion against the monastery. "The monks deceived your ancestors and took all the fields and vineyards," he says. "Your souls are in the grip of the priests and your bodies are in the closing jaws of the rulers." Khalil, the youth, reminds the villagers of their usurped rights and the greed of their rulers and monks. The villagers stage a bloodless rebellion, creating a utopian community free of oppression.

A fourth short story, "The Bridal Couch," was included in the Arabic edition but did not appear in the 1947 English-language edition. It tells the story of a desperate bride who kills her lover and herself on the eve of a forced marriage to a man she does not love.

CENSORSHIP HISTORY

Spirits Rebellious is a denunciation of political and religious injustice in 19th-century Lebanon suffering under oppressive Turkish rule. Gibran's impassioned defense of the right of women to marry freely, his attacks on corrupt clergy, and his incitement to resistance against unjust tyranny were met with fury by church and state officials in Lebanon. The book was termed poisonous and dangerous to the peace of the country. The story "Khalil the Heretic," in particular, offended the sultan and his emirs. Soon after its publication, the book was publicly burned in the Beirut marketplace. The book was also suppressed by the Syrian government, although 200 copies were smuggled into the country.

Gibran was exiled from Lebanon and excommunicated from the Maronite Church. He escaped harm because he was in Paris at the time of the book's publication. When he learned of the destruction of the book, he said merely that it was a good reason for the publication of a second edition. In 1908, the government rescinded his exile from Lebanon, and he was ultimately embraced by the Maronite Church.

Though *Spirits Rebellious* was never again targeted, Gibran's most famous book, *The Prophet*, fell afoul of censors in Egypt. In March 1999, Egyptian government censors reviewed 500 books available in the bookstore or library of the American University in Cairo and decided that some 90 of them should be removed. Among them was an English-language edition of *The Prophet*. On the frontispiece of the book was a sketch of a man with a broad forehead and a small moustache. The censors claimed that the sketch was a portrait of Mohammad and that his image could not be portrayed. Word of the censorship reached Beirut, where protestors mounted demonstrations against the Egyptian government and called for a ban in Lebanon on Egyptian books, films, and plays until the restriction on *The Prophet* was rescinded. In September 1999, responding to complaints from the American University in Cairo, the Egyptian information minister removed the ban on *The Prophet* along with several other books. The remaining bans, he stated, were justified, as the books were offensive for religious or sexual reason or because they rendered Egypt vulnerable to "harmful foreign influences."

FURTHER READING

Abou El-Magd, Nadia. "The Prophet Is Back." *Al-Ahram Weekly* (August 5–11, 1999). Available online. URL: http://weekly.ahram.org.eg/1999/441/eg8.htm. Accessed June 6, 2010.

Fisk, Robert. "'The Prophet' Falls Foul of Egyptian Thought Police." *Independent* (July 28, 1999). Available online. URL: http://www.independent.co.uk/news/world/the-prophet-falls-foul-of-egyptian-thought-police-1109157.html?cmp=ilc-n. Accessed June 6, 2010.

Gibran, Jean, and Kahlil Gibran. *Kahlil Gibran: His Life and Work*. New York: Interlink Books, 1981.

Gibran, Kahlil. *Spirits Rebellious*. Translated by Anthony Rizcallah Ferris. New York: Philosophical Library, 1947.

THE STORY OF ZAHRA

Author: Hanan al-Shaykh
Original dates and places of publication: 1980, Lebanon; 1994, United States
Original publishers: Dar al-Nahar; Anchor Books
Literary form: Novel

SUMMARY

The Story of Zahra is a highly praised novel by Hanan al-Shaykh, a Lebanese writer who lives in London, about a young woman's struggle to find personal fulfillment in a society that undervalues and constricts her. Zahra, the novel's memorable protagonist, is a Shiite Muslim from a middle-class Muslim family in Beirut, Lebanon, in the late 1970s. She is haunted by harrowing childhood memories in which sex, fear, guilt, and love are tangled together. From a young age, Zahra had accompanied her mother to secret assignations with a lover. Her tyrannical father, suspecting his wife's affair, had beaten both Zahra and her mother.

When the reader meets Zahra, she has arrived in West Africa to stay with her uncle Hashem, a political exile. As she recounts the story of her ill-fated sojourn, the details of the life she fled in Beirut emerge. She had drifted into an unsatisfying affair with a manipulative married man and had had two abortions, a surgical "repair" of her virginity, and a nervous breakdown treated with electric shock therapy.

With emotional problems, plain looks, and a face scarred by acne, Zahra is not a particularly good marriage prospect. Her parents, fearing she will be an old maid, pressure her to marry a friend of her brother's. But she refuses, swearing to remain single forever. Deeply depressed, in a state of passive rebellion against the limitations of her existence, she escapes into sleep and silence.

Zahra's flight to Africa provides no solution to her alienation. Her uncle Hashem is lonely and stranded, almost forgotten by his political party. His correspondence with Zahra was the only link with his homeland, and her arrival breathes life into his fading sense of connection to his family and culture. His longings are expressed as a powerful attraction for Zahra. When he begins to make sexual advances, the feelings of disgust or fear that mark Zahra's relationships with all the men in her life are transferred to her uncle.

To escape, Zahra suddenly agrees to marry her uncle's friend Majed, a fellow Lebanese whom she barely knows. Eager to save the trouble of returning to Lebanon to find a wife, Majed welcomes this ready-made bride. "Here I was, married at last," he says, "the owner of a woman's body that I could make love to whenever I wished." Revolted by her husband, Zahra realizes her terrible mistake. "I wanted my body to be mine alone," she cries. "I wanted the place on which I stood and the air surrounding me to be mine and no one else's." She leaves her husband and returns to Beirut, now in the throes of civil war.

As rockets shriek and street battles rage, Zahra sleeps too much and overeats. She dreads cease-fires, since they deprive her of an excuse to stay in bed. In war-torn Beirut, normalcy and sheer terror are coupled. Yet Zahra hopes the war will go on. The traditional order of things has been upset, and a new kind of personal freedom has emerged.

After her parents flee to the south, Zahra embarks on an erotic adventure with a rooftop sniper whom she meets on the landing of an abandoned apartment building. In this semi-anonymous relationship she approaches her lover on her own terms and feels sexual pleasure for the first time. When she becomes pregnant, her sniper lover offers to marry her. On her way home, however, she is shot down in the street, most likely at the hands of her lover.

CENSORSHIP HISTORY

Thirty years after its publication, *The Story of Zahra* is still banned in Saudi Arabia and other Arab countries because of its explicit portrayal of women's sexuality and its unsparing indictment of social and political hypocrisy in a contemporary Arab society. Premarital and extramarital sex, masturbation, incest, illegal abortion, fake repair of virginity, and domestic violence are the forbidden subjects that scandalized the religious authorities in Saudi Arabia and the conservative Persian Gulf states where the novel was censored.

Al-Shaykh's work is considered by Islamic authorities to be antireligious in its subversion of patriarchy and its rejection of social and religious strictures that limit women's rights. Despite its censorship, the book has received wide circulation in the Middle East. Critics in Egypt and Lebanon, as well as in the United States and Britain, have praised the book for its strength, sensitivity, and lyrical realism, as well as for its penetrating portrayal of aspects of sexuality as they relate to social and political problems. Al-Shaykh is recognized as a forerunner among writers expanding the scope of the contemporary Arab novel.

FURTHER READING

Accad, Evelyne. "Rebellion, Maturity and the Social Context: Arab Women's Special Contribution to Literature." In *Arab Women: Old Boundaries, New Frontiers*, edited by Judith Tucker, 240–245. Bloomington: Indiana University Press, 1993.

A TALE OF A TUB

Author: Jonathan Swift
Original dates and place of publication: 1704–10, England
Literary form: Satire

SUMMARY

A Tale of a Tub: Written for the Universal Improvement of Mankind is the first important work of the Anglo-Irish satirist Jonathan Swift, author of *GULLIVER'S TRAVELS*. Written in about 1696 but not published until 1704, when it appeared anonymously, *A Tale of a Tub* is a buoyant and good-humored prose satire on "corruptions in religion and learning." Regarded as among the greatest satires in the English language, it burlesques the historical development of the major contemporary Christian denominations: the Roman Catholic, Lutheran, and Anglican Churches and the various Protestant Dissenters.

Though its main theme is the allegory satirizing the abuses of religion, Swift added to later editions several "Digressions" discussing critics, the prevailing dispute between the respective merits of ancient and modern learning, and madness. In its fifth edition, published in 1710, the digressions represented two-thirds of the book.

Swift explains in the preface the meaning of his title. The custom of sailors upon encountering a whale is to throw out an empty tub to divert it from attacking the ship. "The wits of the present age being so very numerous and penetrating," he writes, "it seems the grandees of church and state begin to fall under horrible apprehensions lest these gentlemen during the intervals of a long peace should find leisure to pick holes in the weak sides of religion and government." Swift's satire is the tub intended to divert the wits of the age from "tossing and sporting with the commonwealth."

The allegory traces the story of a father who leaves a legacy to his three sons: Peter (Saint Peter), Martin (Martin Luther), and Jack (John Calvin). Each receives a new coat with directions that the coats are to be kept clean and unaltered. The father further commands that the brothers live together in one house as friends. The sons disobey the injunctions, adding decorations to their coats according to the latest fashion. They fall in love with three ladies: the duchess of money, the madame of grand titles, and the countess of pride. Finally Martin and Jack quarrel with the arrogant Peter and then with each other, and finally separate.

A Tale of a Tub offers a critique of hypocrisy, fanaticism, superstition, priestly greed, and corruption. Swift, who was a loyal Anglican clergyman, reserves his most scathing comments for the Roman Catholic Church, its papal bulls and dispensations, the doctrine of transubstantiation, the use of holy water or "universal pickle," and its devotion to rites and relics. Catholics, like the Protestant Dissenters, were regarded as enemies of the established Anglican Church and threats to the British government.

"In short Peter grew so scandalous that all the neighborhood began in plain words to say he was no better than a knave," Swift writes. "And his two brothers, long weary of his ill usage, resolved at last to leave him, but first they humbly desired a copy of their fathers' will, which had now lain by neglected time out of mind. Instead of granting this request he called them damn'd sons of whores, rogues, traytors, and the rest of the vile names he could muster up."

Swift characterizes Protestant Dissenters as excessively devoted to Holy Scriptures. "He had a way of working it into any shape he pleased, so that it served him for a night-cap when he went to bed and for an umbrella in rainy weather. He would lap a piece of it about a sore toe; or when he had fits, burn two inches under his nose. . . ."

Swift's own Anglican Church is also treated irreverently. In the fifth edition, he makes particular sport of the criticisms of William Wotton, scholar and notable Church of England clergyman whose pedantry he had satirized. In his digressions it becomes clear that Swift regarded his book as more than a satire of corruptions in religion. He is criticizing the abandonment of practical reality and common sense in favor of false learning—the conflict between "right reason" and blind allegiance to one's own private illusions.

"But when a man's faculty gets astride on his reason; when imagination is at cuffs with the senses, and common understanding, as well as common sense, is kicked out of doors; the first proselyte he makes is himself; and when that is once compassed, the difficulty is not so great in bringing over others; a strong delusion always operating from without as vigorously as from within."

CENSORSHIP HISTORY

The first edition of *A Tale of a Tub* was published in 1704 anonymously, as were most of Swift's writings. The book contained irreverent and bawdy passages to which Swift, a clergyman, "could not becomingly put his name," as one critic observed. It soon became known, however, that Swift was the author. The book was well received by the public, and two new editions were printed during its first year alone. Wotton, an object of the book's satire, admitted that it was "greedily bought up and read," and another contemporary declared that it "has made as much noise, and is as full of wit, as any book perhaps that has come out these last hundred years."

However, *A Tale of a Tub* offended powerful Church of England prelates such as Wotton, a notable church rector and chaplain to the earl of Nottingham, Daniel Finch. He saw the book as sacrilegious and lewd, espousing a contemptible opinion of Christianity. "The rest of the book which does not relate to us is of so irreligious a nature, is so crude a banter upon all that is esteemed as sacred among all sects and religions among men," Wotton declared.

In his *Apology* defending the work, Swift wrote: "Why should any clergyman of our church be angry to see the follies of fanaticism and superstition exposed, tho' in the most ridiculous manner, since that is perhaps the most probable way to cure them or at least to hinder them from farther spreading?" Swift "solemnly protests he is entirely innocent" of "glancing at some tenets in religion." Swift insisted the *Tale* celebrated "the Church of England as the most perfect of all others in Discipline and Doctrine."

After the publication of the *Tale*, Swift said, he was suspected within his church of "the sin of wit." One of Swift's great disappointments was his failure to be appointed a bishop in England. He was awarded, instead, the deanship of Saint Patrick's cathedral in Dublin in 1713. The widely shared opinion of Queen Anne that *A Tale of a Tub* was blasphemous was reputedly instrumental in dashing his chances for further advancement within the Church of England.

Two decades later, in 1734, the Catholic Church made known its disapproval by placing *A Tale of a Tub* on the Index of Forbidden Books. It remained listed until 1881, when the ban was lifted by Pope Leo XIII.

FURTHER READING

Haight, Anne Lyon. *Banned Books: 387 BC to 1978 AD*. Updated and enlarged by Chandler B. Grannis. New York: R. R. Bowker, 1978.

Swift, Jonathan. *The Portable Swift*. Edited and with an introduction by Carl Van Doren. New York: Penguin Books, 1978.

———. *A Tale of a Tub and Other Satires*. Introduction by Lewis Melville. New York: E. P. Dutton & Co. 1955.

———. *A Tale of a Tub: Written for the Universal Improvement of Mankind*. Foreword by Edward Hodnett. New York: Columbia University Press, 1930.

THE TALMUD

Original date and place of publication: Ca. A.D. 200–500, Palestine and
Mesopotamia
Literary form: Religious text

SUMMARY

The Talmud, a collection of teachings set down by the Jewish scholars of
antiquity, is the compendium of the oral law and tradition of Judaism. The
word *Talmud* comes from the Hebrew word meaning "instruction." The collection has two main components: the Mishnah, the book of law written in
Hebrew, and the commentaries on the Mishnah, known as the Talmud or
Gemarah, written in Aramaic. Talmudic sages believed that God revealed
two Torahs to Moses. One was the Scriptures, or written books. The other,
the Mishnah, was preserved in oral traditions handed down through many
centuries and compiled toward the end of the second century A.D. The material of the Mishnah is arranged in six groups, called orders, that deal with
agriculture, the sabbath and festivals, marriage, civil and criminal law, ritual
sacrifices, and cleanliness. The orders are subdivided into 63 tracts or books.

Oral explanations and commentaries that developed around the Mishnah
over the centuries were later put into written form and called the Gemarah.
The Mishnah serves as text and the Gemarah as a series of comments and
notes. Two versions of the Gemarah exist: one compiled in the fourth century by the scholars of Palestine, and the other in the fifth century by the
scholars of Babylonia, which became the authoritative work. The Talmud is
considered, with the Hebrew Bible, as the central pillar of Judaism and the
most important book in Jewish culture. It is the accepted religious authority
among all Orthodox Jews.

CENSORSHIP HISTORY

The history of suppression of the Talmud is many centuries long. Early
attempts to ban it date at least to the seventh and eighth centuries. During
the Middle Ages, with the revival of learning and the appearance of books of
theological speculation, the Catholic Church began to adopt a more severe
attitude toward suspect books. It began to examine Jewish literature and the
Talmud more intensively.

In 1144 in Paris, the Catholic Church ordered the burning of the Talmud
on charges of blasphemy and immorality. Other incidents of censorship
were recorded during the next hundred years. The anti-Talmudic campaign
reached its height in 1239, when Pope Gregory IX ordered all Jewish books
to be burned. He acted on allegations of heresy in the Talmud brought by
Jewish converts to Christianity. Gregory sent letters to the kings and prelates of England, France, Navarre, Aragon, Castile, and Portugal, ordering
that on a sabbath during the following Lent, while Jews worshiped in their

synagogues, the books should be seized and delivered to the mendicant friars for examination, and that these books, deemed heretical, should be destroyed. The order was carried out fully only in France.

In 1244, Pope Innocent IV ordered Louis IX of France to burn all copies of the Talmud. This order was repeated in 1248, when 20 wagonloads of books were burned in Paris, and again in 1254. In 1264 in Rome, Pope Clement IV appointed a committee of censors to expunge all passages from the Talmud that appeared derogatory to Christianity, allowing Jews to keep only expurgated versions. Three years later, Clement IV instructed the king of Aragon to force Jews to deliver Talmuds to inquisitors.

Numerous instances of official burnings of the Talmud were recorded in France in the 14th century, as the anti-Jewish polemic continued. In 1415, Pope Benedict XII ordered all copies of Talmudic books delivered to bishops for preservation subject to papal instructions. Jews themselves were forbidden to possess copies of any material considered antagonistic to Christianity and could not read or study the Talmud. A church synod in Basel in 1431 reaffirmed the stringent ban.

Because so many copies of the Talmud had been lost over the centuries, there was great interest among Jews in the new 15th-century technology of the printing press. The first printed edition of the Talmud appeared in Guadalajara, Spain, in 1482. But the Talmud soon became a target of the Spanish Inquisition. In 1490 in Spain, the grand inquisitor, Tomás de Torquemada, burned Hebrew books by order of Ferdinand and Isabella; he later conducted at Salamanca an auto-da-fé, or burning, of more than 6,000 volumes described as books of magic or infected with Jewish errors. When the Jews were expelled from Spain and Portugal, in 1492, all Jewish books were confiscated.

In 1509, Johannes Pfefferkorn, a priest and Jewish convert to Christianity, advocated destruction of Hebrew books in all countries under the rule of the Holy Roman Emperor. Emperor Maximillian requested the opinion of another priest, Johann Reuchlin. Reuchlin, who had published the first Hebrew grammar for Christians, argued that to understand the Old Testament it was necessary to collect and study Hebrew manuscripts rather than destroy them. He suggested that Jews be required to furnish books for the universities and that chairs of Hebrew learning be instituted in every university in Germany. His recommendation was met by intense opposition, to which he responded with *Augenspiegel* (Mirror of the eye) in 1511. He distinguished anti-Christian polemics from classical works in Hebrew, which he believed should be preserved. A sustained controversy developed between the humanists who supported Reuchlin and the clerics and leaders of the Inquisition who supported Pfefferkorn. In 1521, the Roman curia suppressed Reuchlin's writings against Pfefferkorn.

In 1520, Pope Leo X gave permission for the publication and printing of the Talmud in Venice, and several editions appeared in the next few decades. In the 1530s, Martin Luther, convinced that Christians in Moravia were being induced to convert to Judaism, urged that Jews be deported to Palestine and forbidden to practice usury, and that their synagogues be burned and their books destroyed. German principalities expelled Jews from certain localities and suppressed their books. In other German cities, such as Frankfurt and Worms, Jews were tolerated.

As the Counter-Reformation and the church's battle against heresy and the power of the printing press intensified, Pope Julius III in 1553 halted the printings of the Talmud allowed by Pope Leo X. In 1555, the houses of Jews were searched, and Jews were ordered under pain of death to surrender all books blaspheming Christ. Princes, bishops, and inquisitors were instructed to confiscate the Talmud. The books were collected and burned on the first day of Rosh Hashanah, the Jewish New Year. Christians were forbidden under threat of excommunication to possess or read Jewish books or to aid Jews by producing copies in script or by printing. Jewish books, including rare rabbinic manuscripts, were burned by the thousands in Italian cities. Some 12,000 volumes of Hebrew texts were burned after the inquisitor Sixtus of Siena destroyed the library of the Hebrew school at Cremona. The Talmud was not published again in Renaissance Italy.

The harshness of Julius III's decree was somewhat alleviated by Pope Pius IV in 1559, who allowed distribution of the Talmud only if those sections that offended Christianity were erased. As a result of this decision, a truncated and expurgated edition was printed in Basel under the supervision of Catholic monks. Subsequent editions were often similarly expurgated. In many European countries, where the Talmud could be printed only with official permission, licensing was confined to Christian printers.

The church's first Index of Forbidden Books, in 1559, included the Talmud. Under the revised Index prepared by the Council of Trent in 1564, all works of Jewish doctrine were banned, except those permitted by the pope after the Jewish community offered a substantial financial "gift."

In 1592, Pope Clement VIII issued a bull forbidding either Christians or Jews from owning, reading, buying, or circulating "impious talmudic books or manuscripts" or writings in Hebrew or other languages that "tacitly or expressly contain heretical or erroneous statements against the Holy Scriptures of the Old Law and Testament." Any such work, whether expurgated or not, was to be destroyed. In 1596, this ruling was modified when the publication of the Machsor, the basic Hebrew prayer book, was permitted, but only in Hebrew.

Active suppression of the Talmud by the Catholic Church lasted through the 18th century. In 1629, an Italian cardinal boasted of having collected 10,000 outlawed Jewish books for destruction. As late as 1775, Pope Clement XIV confirmed the prohibitions of previous papal bulls. No Hebrew books could be bought or sold until examined and approved by the church.

In the 20th century, the most extensive censorship of the Talmud was reported in Europe under the Communist Party in the Soviet Union and under the Nazis during the Holocaust. In 1926, the government of the Soviet Union ordered that religiously dogmatic books such as the Talmud could be left in the large libraries but must be removed from the small ones. Virtually no printing of the work was allowed after that time. A Russian translation, the first in any language to be permitted since the 1917 revolution, was undertaken during the 1990s under the sponsorship of the Russian Academy of Sciences.

In 1939, most of the schools of Jewish learning in Europe were totally destroyed by the Nazis. Innumerable copies of Jewish religious texts were lost during the Holocaust.

The Second Vatican Council in 1965 brought about a change in attitude toward the Talmud. It deplored anti-Semitism and the persecution of Jews, emphasizing the church's biblical connection to Judaism and the common religious heritage of Christians and Jews.

FURTHER READING

Bainton, Roland. *Here I Stand: A Life of Martin Luther.* New York: Penguin, 1995.

Burman, Edward. *The Inquisition: Hammer of Heresy.* New York: Dorset Press, 1992.

Green, Jonathon. *Encyclopedia of Censorship.* New York: Facts On File, 1990.

Haight, Anne Lyon. *Banned Books: 387 B.C. to 1978* Updated and enlarged by Chandler B. Grannis. New York: R. R. Bowker, 1978.

Hertzberg, Arthur. "Swimming without Drowning: New Approaches to the Ocean of the Talmud." *New York Times Book Review*, March 27, 1994, pp. 12–14.

Lea, Henry Charles. *History of the Inquisition of the Middle Ages.* Vol. 1. New York: Russell and Russell, 1955.

Levy, Leonard W. *Blasphemy: Verbal Offense Against the Sacred, from Moses to Salman Rushdie.* New York: Alfred A. Knopf, 1993.

Peters, Edward. *Inquisition.* New York: Free Press, 1988.

Putnam, George Haven. *The Censorship of the Church of Rome.* Vol. 1. New York: G. P. Putnam's Sons, 1906–07.

Steinsaltz, Adin. *The Essential Talmud.* New York: Basic Books, 1976.

THEOLOGICAL-POLITICAL TREATISE

Author: Baruch Spinoza
Original date and place of publication: 1670, Holland
Literary form: Philosophical treatise

SUMMARY

Theological-Political Treatise is the only work expressing the philosophical ideas of the eminent Dutch rationalist Baruch (Benedict) Spinoza to be published during the writer's lifetime. Spinoza was already notorious for his radically skeptical views and had been excommunicated from the Jewish community of Amsterdam in 1656. He published the work anonymously under a fictitious imprint in 1670.

In the preface to *Theological-Political Treatise*, Spinoza declares the purpose of his book to be the defense of freedom of opinion. Freedom of thought is not only compatible with public order, it is necessary to it. "Everyone should be free to choose for himself the foundation of his creed, and that faith should be judged only by its fruits; each would then obey God freely with his whole heart; while nothing would be publicly honored save justice and charity," writes Spinoza. A rational government requires enlightened and tolerant citizens, he believed, just as free men require an enlightened and tolerant government.

Spinoza proposed that political and social problems should be studied scientifically and dispassionately and that moral and religious exhortations have no place in political science. Appeals to supernatural causes are expressions of ignorance. The natural light of reason, for those skillful in its use, is sufficient to show "the true way of salvation."

Unlike his contemporaries, who insisted that revelation provided knowledge inaccessible and superior to reason, Spinoza held that reason alone was a sufficient path to truth. The Bible cannot be accepted as a reliable source of knowledge, because it contains many contradictions. It is "faulty, mutilated, tampered with and inconsistent." Moreover, Spinoza observed, the authors, circumstances or dates of many biblical books are unclear: "We cannot say into what hands they fell, nor how the numerous varying versions originated; nor, lastly, whether there were not other versions, now lost."

Belief in the Bible "is particularly necessary to the masses whose intellect is not capable of perceiving things clearly and distinctly," who must learn morality from easily understood stories or examples. Spinoza contended that there is no special revelation, or knowledge revealed directly from God to man. The Ten Commandments "were not intended to convey the actual words of the Lord, but only his meaning," and the story of the Ten Commandments itself is questionable because it implies that God has a form.

According to Spinoza, the acceptance of prophetic reports and stories of miracles as sources of knowledge represents superstition and is an "utter mistake." "I care not for the girdings of superstition," he wrote, "for superstition is the bitter enemy of all true knowledge and true morality." To Spinoza, religious superstition was a dangerous and all too real cause of prejudice and violence. Not only had it disrupted his own life and prevented the publication of his works, but it had also devastated Europe with religious wars and persecutions.

The free man, Spinoza believed, should criticize any religious dogma when it is represented as philosophical truth or when it leads to intolerance. "What greater evil can there be for a republic," he wrote, "than that honorable men be thrust into exile like criminals, because they hold dissenting views and know not how to conceal them?" In his view of the primacy of individual liberty, freedom of opinion, and religious tolerance, Spinoza was a precursor of the liberal thinkers of later centuries.

CENSORSHIP HISTORY

See Ethics.

FURTHER READING

Gerber, Jane S. *The Jews of Spain: A History of the Sephardic Experience*. New York: Free Press, Macmillan, 1992.

Hampshire, Stuart. *Spinoza: An Introduction to His Philosophical Thought*. London: Penguin Books, 1988.

———, ed. *The Age of Reason: The 17th Century Philosophers*. New York: New American Library, 1956.

Scott-Kakures, Dion, Susan Castegnetto, Hugh Benson, William Taschek, and Paul Hurley. *History of Philosophy*. New York: HarperCollins, 1993.

THREE-PART WORK

Author: Meister Eckhart
Original date and place of publication: 1311, Germany
Literary form: Theological treatise

SUMMARY

Johannes Eckhart, known as Meister Eckhart, was an influential medieval German theologian and preacher and the founder of German mysticism. He studied and taught in Paris, Strasbourg, and Cologne and held administrative positions in the Dominican order of friars. In his writings, Eckhart for the first time used German as a vehicle for religious ideas that before had been expressed only in Latin.

In 1311, he began an ambitious project, a systematic theological treatise in Latin, the *Three-Part Work*, which was never completed and survives only in fragments. Eckhart had planned the treatise to consist of a Work of Propositions, a Work of Questions, and a Work of Commentaries. The first part was to include 1,000 propositions divided into 14 sections in which synthesis was presented through axioms, or propositions organized according to opposed terms. The only part of the *Three-Part Work* that remains is the general prologue to the Work of Propositions. Eckhart completed other parts, but these were lost over the centuries.

In the *Three-Part Work*, Eckhart attempted to awaken Scholastic theology to the possibility of direct and unmediated experience of God, incorporating personal revelation into systematic religious life. Eckhart accepted Thomas Aquinas's views that God is known through both reason and revelation. But he added a third means of knowledge: God's direct revelation to the inner soul. His first proposition in the *Three-Part Work* is that God and existence are the same, alluding to the words of the Book of Exodus: "I am who am." All essence is God, and apart from God there is no being.

Because God is outside all experience, he cannot be known within nature or described in any terms available to human beings: "God is nameless; his Infinity cannot be expressed or conveyed by words, as everything touching the human soul can be recognized but in finite terms. . . . God is inexpressible, because all Being in him is infinite."

In a formulation that was regarded with suspicion by church censors as implying that God was not good, Eckhart declared: "If anyone said that God was good, he would do him as great an injustice as if he had said that the sun was black." Ecclesiastical investigators also suspected that by claiming that "every distinction is alien to God, whether in Nature or in Persons," Eckhart was challenging the correct interpretation of the doctrine of the Holy Trinity.

Eckhart proposed that God is present everywhere and in the human soul, but human beings in their sinful state are unaware of the divine presence. To prepare oneself for mystical insight, the mind should be emptied of all content by withdrawing as much as possible from experience. Only in this way can the soul be made ready for mystical union with God, the ultimate aim of human existence.

CENSORSHIP HISTORY

In 1323, the general chapter of the Dominican order in Venice received complaints about sermons in the German provinces that might lead simple people astray. During the following year the archbishop of Cologne, referring to the immense popularity of Eckhart's sermons, filed a formal complaint against Eckhart with the papal court in Avignon, France, charging that he had "incited ignorant and undisciplined people to wild and dangerous excesses." The archbishop was unfriendly to the Dominicans and targeted Eckhart, the order's most distinguished and respected member.

The Dominican order's own investigation ended with a declaration of Eckhart's innocence. Without waiting for the papal investigator's verdict, the archbishop set up an independent investigating commission consisting of two Franciscan monks, who were avowed enemies of the Dominicans. They assembled 100 propositions taken from Eckhart's Latin treatises and German sermons, which they viewed as evidence of heresy. They suspected him of connection with the Beghards, a heretical religious association condemned by the church for teaching that those who gain perfection in this life cannot commit sin.

On September 26, 1326, Eckhart submitted a detailed defense of his work, declaring his loyalty to the church. "They think that everything they do not understand is an error and that every error is a heresy," he wrote, "when only obstinate adherence to error makes heresy and a heretic. . . ." The commission summoned both the papal investigator and Eckhart to appear before the archbishop's court in January 1327. Eckhart proclaimed his innocence and requested permission to make a direct appeal to Pope John XXII, challenging the authority of the archbishop and his inquisitors. On February 13, 1327, Eckhart declared in a public sermon that he was prepared to refute any errors the judges might find in his writings and sermons and that he had not deliberately departed from the faith on any point. A week later the archbishop's court refused permission for a direct appeal to the pope.

The official documents of the archbishop's court were forwarded to the pope, who ordered an investigation of their heretical character. Twentieth-century scholars who compared the condemned statements with the original works from which they were extracted found that the Cologne commission had distorted decisive points in Eckhart's writings.

The papal investigation affirmed the verdict of Cologne, and on March 27, 1329, the pope issued a bull condemning as heresy 28 statements from Eckhart's works. The bull was sent to the archbishop of Cologne, bidding him to publicize the condemnation in all his parishes and to instruct the faithful that they could not consider themselves obedient children of the church if they continued to maintain Eckhart's false teachings. By the time the bull was issued, however, Eckhart had died.

The pope's decree said that Eckhart had been deceived "by the Father of Lies who often turns himself into an angel of light in order to replace the light of truth with a dark and gloomy cloud of the senses . . . and presented many things as dogma that were designed to cloud the true faith in the hearts of many . . . ," particularly uneducated people. The pope also stated that Eckhart had retracted his errors on his deathbed, "insofar as they could generate in the minds of the faithful a heretical opinion or one erroneous and hostile to the true faith." Eckhart did not admit, however, that he accepted the church's judgment that his writings were heretical.

Eckhart's disciples tried in vain to have the pope's decree set aside. In 1330, his works were condemned by the University of Heidelberg. Though he had a considerable influence on the piety of the 14th and 15th centuries, by the end of the Middle Ages Eckhart was almost forgotten, condemned to obscurity by the stigma of heresy attached to his work and by the abstract and difficult nature of his writings. Though his disciples passed on his spiritual doctrine, most of his original works had disappeared. Only a handful of men were aware of the existence of his theological works written in Latin, among them the 15th-century German cardinal, papal legate, and humanist philosopher Nicholas of Cusa. He found some of Eckhart's writings and in 1444 preserved them by having them copied for his own use.

Five centuries later, in the early 19th century, Eckhart's writings were rediscovered thanks to a revived interest in mysticism and pre-Reformation religious history. Twentieth-century editions of Eckhart's writings have been published under the Catholic Church's imprimatur, indicating church approval of the religious doctrine contained in them.

FURTHER READING

Christie-Murray, David. *A History of Heresy.* Oxford: Oxford University Press, 1989.

Colledge, Edmund, and Bernard McGinn, eds. *Meister Eckhart: The Essential Sermons, Commentaries, Treatises, and Defense.* New York: Paulist Press, 1981.

Copleston, Frederick. *A History of Philosophy*. Vol. 3: *Late Medieval and Renaissance Philosophy*. New York: Doubleday, 1993.

Eckhart, Meister. *Meister Eckhart: A Modern Translation*. Translated by and with an introduction by Raymond Bernard Blakney. New York: Harper and Row, 1941.

———. *Meister Eckehart Speaks*. Trans. Elizabeth Strakosch. Edited by and with an introduction by Otto Karrer. New York: Philosophical Library, 1957.

Wilcox, Donald J. *In Search of God and Self: Renaissance and Reformation Thought*. Boston: Houghton Mifflin, 1975.

TOUBA AND THE MEANING OF NIGHT

Author: Shahrnush Parsipur
Original dates and places of publication: 1989, Iran; 2006, United States
Original publishers: Esperak; The Feminist Press at the City University of New York
Literary form: Novel

SUMMARY

Shahrnush Parsipur, a woman born of educated, liberal-minded parents in Tehran, showed a strong interest in literature when she was young. Encouraged by her parents, she pursued this vocation, influenced by both Persian and Western writers, exemplified, respectively, by such as Sadegh Hedayat and Charles Dickens. Coming of age in the sociopolitical upheavals of Iran in the last half of the 20th century, Parsipur was part of a small but growing group of women writers finding their voices within the male-dominated culture and, after the Islamic Revolution of 1979, very often against it.

Touba, the protagonist of *Touba and the Meaning of Night (Tuba va ma'na-yi shab)*, is a complex character whose life distills a century of Iranian history that witnessed the warring effects of modernity versus tradition. Her story unfolds in four long chapters that follow her through the advancing stages of her life. The novel is written in a dense style of magic realism that is imbued with rich allusions to classical Persian literature and that unifies character, plot, vision, and historic process into a unique aesthetic whole. But, more deeply, Touba is a seeker of God. According to Persian folklore, Touba is the name of a tree in paradise whose branches shade the house of Mohammad and the domiciles of all the faithful.

Touba's father is a wise man who understands this conflict between old beliefs and the new knowledge that is shaping the contemporary world. He begins Touba's education. Upon his death, Touba, being the only other member of the family with any education, takes over the running of the household. However, at the age of 14, she sacrifices her aspiration to be a spiritual seeker to spare her illiterate mother from marrying an elder relative who is supporting the family by offering to marry the man herself.

After several joyless years, Touba wearies of being belittled by the man and demands a divorce, which is granted. Before she can to determine how she will proceed with her quest, she is married off to a wastrel prince of the Qajar dynasty, a serial philanderer who, nonetheless, offers Touba exposure to Western influences at the time of Iran's Constitutional Revolution. This revolution replaced the monarchy with a constitutional government, which occasioned turmoil, as the shah, with help from Russia, sought to retrieve power from the parliament.

Touba discovers that her husband's long absences are caused by his involvement with the effort to overturn the constitutional government. But when she finds that he has taken a young peasant girl as a second wife, she divorces him.

At this time, the Qajar dynasty falls in a successful coup perpetrated by Reza Shah Pahlavi, who continues the rapid modernization of Iran under his dictatorial regime. At the beginning of World War II, the shah forges friendly relations with the Third Reich, which leads to the occupation of Iran by Russian, British, and American forces and the shah's abdication. His son, Mohammad Reza Pahlavi, succeeds him, and Iran enjoys a decade of freedom of expression. When his prime minister, Mohammad Mosaddeq, attempts to nationalize Iran's oil industry in 1951, British intelligence and the U.S. Central Intelligence Agency depose him, sowing the seeds that a generation later would reach fruition in the expulsion of the Western-backed shah by the Islamic revolution of 1979. As Touba grows older, these events form the backdrop against which her daughter, Moones, and the succeeding generation endure their temporal and spiritual struggles, which are no different in kind or character than those Touba and her generation endured.

While the external events of history are reflected by the other characters' engagement with the world, Touba herself is exemplified by the walls of her house and by the pomegranate tree that grows in her courtyard. Touba's house is an extension of Touba herself. The house and the walls around it hold the content of her life. They are the manifestation of the traditional world into which Touba was born and in which her mystic yearning took root. As Touba nears her final earthly days, the house reaches such a point of deterioration that it begins to collapse. However, it is the pomegranate tree that focuses Touba's being on the realization of metaphysical truth. Though old and withered, the tree bears fruit, leading Touba to the realization that the tree symbolizes the stages of her quest and affirms her state of womanhood (the pomegranate is a classic symbol of femininity.)

As Houra Yavari explains in the book's afterword, "The essence of [Touba's] quest and of her often conflicted personal struggle—is both mystical and worldly, religious and political, spiritual and intellectual. In this sense her deeply personal story reveals also the history of a society in the throes of modernity, with the status of women as a focal point and a touchstone."

—Philip Milito

CENSORSHIP HISTORY

In the summer of 1981, Parsipur, who had written novels and short stories, was imprisoned along with her mother and two brothers because one of her brothers had attempted to create an archive of political publications. In prison, she decided to commit to paper an outline for a historical novel on the conditions of women in Iran, the novel that was to become *Touba and the Meaning of Night*. She set aside a time at night for writing and wrote half the novel, which filled 10 notebooks. When she and her mother were transferred to another prison, their jailers searched their possessions and confiscated Parsipur's notebooks. A year later, a more liberal ayatollah took over management of the prisons and her notebooks were returned, but with some pages torn out. She decided that continuing to write in prison would lead her to censor herself, and she burned all her notebooks.

In 1986, after more than four years, she was released from prison and rewrote her book. In 1989, she found a publisher for *Touba* in Iran. The book was celebrated as a literary landmark and became a best seller. The novel's popularity did not escape the attention of the religious authorities of the Islamic Republic. The historical figure upon whom the novel was based, Tahereh Qorratol'Ayn, was a literate, outspoken woman who was executed in 1852 at the age of 36 for heresy and promotion of the Babi (Baha'i) faith. The novel discusses religion and portrays Touba as finding fault with orthodox and Sufism, as well as nationalism and other forms of thought.

Just after *Touba*'s publication in 1989, Parsipur was also able to find a publisher for her novel, WOMEN WITHOUT MEN. She was arrested twice and detained on both occasions for more than a month. Her publisher, Mohammad Reza Aslani, was also arrested and his publishing house, Nogreh Publishing, was shut down. The government banned *Women Without Men*, as well as all of Parsipur's other novels, including *Touba*, as un-Islamic. Parsipur commented: "Their chief goal was to intimidate me because they couldn't do much else. After the critical success of *Touba*, they didn't know what to do with me. So they harassed me, told me to desist from such writing and they attacked the man who published the book." In 1994, Parsipur obtained refugee status in the United States and now lives in exile from Iran. All 11 of her novels remain remained banned in Iran.

FURTHER READING

Karim, Persis M. "Biography of Shahrnush Parsipur." In *Touba and the Meaning of Night*. New York: The Feminist Press at the City University of New York, 2006.

Parsipur, Shahrnush. "A Prelude to 'Touba and the Meaning of Night.'" Seattle Art Museum (October 7, 2006). Available online. URL: http://www.shahrnushparsipur.com/article9.htm. Accessed June 6, 2010.

Talattof, Kamran. "Translating Women's Experience: A Note on Rendering the Novel." In *Touba and the Meaning of Night*. New York: The Feminist Press at the City University of New York, 2006.

Yavari, Houra. Afterword in *Touba and the Meaning of Night*. New York: The Feminist Press at the City University of New York, 2006.

THE VEIL AND THE MALE ELITE: A FEMINIST INTERPRETATION OF WOMEN'S RIGHTS IN ISLAM

Author: Fatima Mernissi
Original dates and places of publication: 1987, France; 1991, United States
Original publishers: Éditions Albin Michel; Addison Wesley Publishing
Literary form: Religious history

SUMMARY

The Moroccan sociologist, Koranic scholar, and feminist Fatima Mernissi is the author of 14 highly regarded books, including *The Veil and the Male Elite* (*Le Harem politique*), a study of women's status within the Muslim religion. Examining the foundations of Islam, Mernissi advances the thesis that Muslim tradition does not oppose women's emancipation. If some Muslim men block women's rights it is not because of the teachings of the KORAN (Qur'an) or the prophet Muhammad. It is because those rights conflict with the interests of a male elite.

The motivation of those who are against women's rights in Muslim societies, Mernissi writes, is profit. But to find a source to justify exploitation of women it is necessary to go back to the shadows of the past. There are no grounds for the claim that women in Muslim states cannot be granted full enjoyment of human rights because their religion forbids it, Mernissi says, rather "They are simply betting on our ignorance of the past, for their argument can never convince anyone with an elementary understanding of Islam's history."

She cites historical evidence that the quest for women's full participation stems not from imported Western values but from Muslim tradition. Women fled tribal Mecca by the thousands to enter seventh-century Medina, the prophet Muhammad's city. Islam promised equality and dignity for all—men and women, masters, and servants. Every woman who came to Medina while the Prophet was political leader could gain access to full citizenship. Muhammad revolutionized life for women, granting them the right to divorce, to pray in mosques, and to participate in the management of military and political affairs.

How did the schism come about between the egalitarian origins of Islam and the misogynistic practices of Muslim societies today? Islam broke with pre-Islamic practices, calling into question the customs that ruled relations between the sexes. New laws of inheritance deprived men of privileges, and women entered into competition with men for the sharing of fortunes. The Prophet's companions reacted negatively to these new laws and during his lifetime unsuccessfully pressured him to change them. In desperation, Mernissi says, they took to manipulating the interpretation of sacred texts.

In the opening chapter of the book, Mernissi recounts an encounter with her grocer. "Can a woman be a leader of Muslims?" she asked. Another customer responded with a hadith, or saying of the Prophet: "Those who entrust their affairs to a woman will never know prosperity." This hadith is the definitive argument used to exclude women from politics.

The hadith collections record in minute detail what the Prophet said and did and, along with the Koran, constitute both the source of law and the standard for distinguishing the permitted from the forbidden. The science of verifying a hadith consists of investigating both its content and those who first recorded it, so that the reader can judge whether they are credible.

In investigating the origins of this particular hadith, Mernissi went directly to texts usually probed only by religious authorities and found that its veracity had been hotly disputed. She found that other well-known misogynistic hadith were equally suspect. Mernissi contends that the sacred texts were distorted and that "their manipulation is a structural characteristic of the practice of power in Muslim societies." Less than two centuries after the death of the Prophet, more than 500,000 false hadith were already in circulation.

The skepticism that guided the work of the founders of religious scholarship has disappeared today, Mernissi says. Mernissi sees the phobic attitude toward women represented by the *hijab*, or segregation of the sexes and veiling of women, as a violation of the Prophet's beliefs. He encouraged his adherents to renounce it as representing the superstitious attitudes of the *jahiliyya*, the pre-Islamic mentality. Sukayna, one of the Prophet's great-granddaughters through his daughter Fatima, resisted the *hijab*. She attended meetings of the Qurayshi Tribal Council, had a successive total of five or six husbands, stipulated in her marriage contracts that she would not obey her husband, and refused to acknowledge his right to practice polygamy. The image of the Muslim woman will change, writes Mernissi, when the Muslim man "feels the pressing need to root his future in a liberating memory," such as that of Sukayna. Women can help him to do this through daily pressure for equality.

CENSORSHIP HISTORY

Critics and scholars have praised *The Veil and the Male Elite* for its original and scrupulous research, wit, and clarity. In *Islam and Democracy: Fear of the Modern World* (1992), Mernissi commented on the censorship of the book. "In *The Veil and the Male Elite*, I explained that in the course of its egalitarian revolution Islam allowed women to emerge as subjects, whereas in the *jahiliyya* they had the status of objects inherited and passed on like live-stock. . . . With the advent of the Umayyad despotism, however, women sank back into a slavelike status like that which they had in the *jahiliyya*. This theory is apparently disputed because the book was banned in Morocco several months after its publication in French." It was also prohibited in the Persian Gulf states and Saudi Arabia. Nevertheless, the book has been translated into eight languages and is widely read in Muslim countries. An Arabic translation was published illegally in Syria in 1991.

Authorities in theocracies such as Saudia Arabia regarded as particularly threatening Mernissi's contention that the sacred texts were manipulated as political weapons and that commonly accepted hadith are based on falsehood. Saudi Arabia is ruled by Muslim religious law, or sharia, which encompasses the hadith. Moroccan legal family codes at the time were also based on sharia.

"Delving into memory, slipping into the past, is an activity that these days is closely supervised, especially for Muslim women," Mernissi writes. "The sleeping past can animate the present. That is the virtue of memory. Magicians know it and the imams know it too."

"The [Moroccan] state can stop me," Mernissi told an interviewer in 1993. "They stopped *The Veil and the Male Elite*. But I made such *un grand scandale*, that they've never bothered me since." Mernissi lives in Morocco and is a senior researcher at Mohammed V University in Rabat.

In 2003, the book was translated for the first time into Farsi and published in Tehran by Ney Publications. In August 2003, its translator, Maliheh Maghazei, its publisher, Jafar Homayei, and the culture director for the Ministry of Culture and Islamic Guidance, Majid Sayadi, who had officially authorized the book's publication, were convicted by the Criminal Court of Tehran of "insulting and undermining the holy tenets of Islam," "sullying the person of the Prophet Muhammad," and "distorting Islamic history" by "publishing false, slanderous and fabricated texts." Maghazei and Sayadi were sentenced to one year in prison and Homayei to 18 months. Parts of the sentences were suspended, and at the end of 2003, all three were free pending appeal. The court also ordered that copies of Mernissi's book be shredded.

Iran's president Mohammed Khatami criticized the judiciary, which is considered to be one of the pillars of conservatism in Iran, for interfering in cultural affairs by prosecuting those involved in publishing the book. "It is regrettable to see the principles of culture contravened and matters unfold through a faulty grasp of culture and cultural rights," Khatami wrote in a letter to the cultural minister that was released by IRNA, Iran's official news agency.

FURTHER READING

Bardach, Ann Louise. "Tearing off the Veil." *Vanity Fair*, August 1993, 123.
Mernissi, Fatema. Fatema Mernissi's official Web site. Available online. URL: http://www.mernissi.net.

Mernissi, Fatima. *Islam and Democracy: Fear of the Modern World.* Translated by Mary Jo Lakeland. Reading, Mass.: Addison-Wesley, 1992.

———. *The Veil and the Male Elite: A Feminist Interpretation of Women's Rights in Islam.* Translated by Mary Jo Lakeland. Reading, Mass.: Addison-Wesley, 1991.

The Middle East Studies Association of North America, Committee for Academic Freedom in the Middle East and North Africa. Letter to Ayatollah Ali Khamenei, December 23, 2003. Available online. URL: http://fpo.arizona.edu/mesassoc/CAFMENAletters.htm.

VOODOO & HOODOO: THEIR TRADITIONAL CRAFTS AS REVEALED BY ACTUAL PRACTITIONERS

Author: Jim Haskins
Original date and place of publication: 1978, United States
Original publisher: Stein and Day
Literary form: Nonfiction

SUMMARY

Voodoo & Hoodoo by Jim Haskins, who was an English professor at the University of Florida at Gainesville and an award-winning author of more than 100 books for adults and young people, describes the spiritualistic and magical folk traditions that came to the Americas from West Africa via the slave trade. The book traces the origins of hoodoo and voodoo in African tribal religions, their transmission and evolution in the New World, and their survival in black communities. It also includes a collection of spells, tricks, hexes, and recipes provided by practitioners.

In his introduction, Haskins recounts his own experiences with hoodoo growing up in small-town Alabama, which were shared by most black children with roots in the South. The local hoodoo doctor or root worker was a figure of respect in the community. Though Haskins's grandmother was not a practitioner herself and was skeptical about certain methods and claims, she had respect for hoodoo and the people who practiced it. She warned him to avoid passing near the houses of known practitioners and not to aggravate them or eat anything at their homes or the homes of people who visited them, as much conjuring was accomplished by the use of food. Shortly after his birth, Haskins was given a secret "basket name," known only to family and close friends. He learned that if a stranger or even a casual friend knew that "basket name," it could be used against him.

When Haskins went away to school and lived elsewhere, his contact with blacks from different backgrounds and geographical areas led him to realize that there was a universality about many beliefs and superstitions. "Whatever our geographical, social, economic, or educational backgrounds," Haskins writes, "most of us black Americans share either a direct experience or an orally handed-down knowledge of the black mystical-magical tradition."

To obtain the information in his book, which was collected in the 1970s, Haskins interviewed hoodoo and voodoo practitioners, as well as people who knew some of their formulas and methods. His informants, given anonymity, were willing to share their knowledge, though he suspects that they may have protected their secrets by leaving out ingredients in a potion or failing to include an accompanying chant or mystical pronouncement.

Voodoo, hoodoo, and spiritualism as they are practiced today are a survival of West African religions and practices. The coastal slave-gathering areas of West Africa included a large number of different tribes, but they were all related by language and shared similar religious and magic beliefs. An individual needed the help of an intermediary to address the gods, and only the priest or priestess knew the proper rites and ceremonies attendant to the sacrifice, one of the most important religious activities. Sacrifices were offered to pacify deities, to avert disaster or misfortune, to purify, and to offer a substitute for what the deity desired. An intermediary, or priest, was also necessary to facilitate possession by a deity that occurred during a ritual or celebration.

An intermediary was also needed to counteract evil forces; in this case, it was the medicine man. Next to priests, medicine men were the most important people in the community and had years of training in the properties of herbs and roots. Just as the lines were blurred between religion and magic, the functions of the priest and the medicine man overlapped. In addition to prescribing potions, the medicine man knew methods to invoke magic for healing. Herbal mixtures, taboos, sacrifices, chants, and incantations were often necessary to exorcize illness, and the medicine man was far more knowledgeable in these matters than was the priest.

In the African belief system, for every good there was a corresponding evil. The medicine man's counterpart was the sorcerer. His task was to attack a person's vitality by casting spells or by poisoning. In times of peace or prosperity, he was likely to be killed or banished if identified. But in times of war or other threatening situations, a sorcerer would be relied upon to help assure the tribe's safety and victory.

When African slaves arrived in the New World, they faced a culture clash that threatened to uproot or alter their beliefs. Yet many of these beliefs survived in one form or another, especially in the southern states and in the Caribbean. Slaves living on large plantations had more opportunities than those on small farms or in towns to regroup and maintain some of their traditions and social organizations. Medicine men and sorcerers also came to the New World as slaves and were far more successful at plying their crafts than were the priests, whose influence depended on kinship ties and religious institutions that did not exist in the New World. Medicine men found in their new homes, particularly in the Caribbean islands, plants whose properties were similar to those used for their medicines in Africa. Slaves suffering from confusion and disorientation turned increasingly to sorcerers' magic.

After a few generations, the distinctions between priests, medicine men, and sorcerers diminished. Out of this blurring came *voodoo*, a term that can be related to the Dahomean word for spirit, *vodun*. Voodoo became a fairly systematized body of mystical-magical practice and lore, an amalgamation of European Catholic and African religion and magic. Black refugees from Saint Domingue (Haiti), who were steeped in knowledge about the practices of voodoo, found their way to New Orleans in the early 19th century and had a considerable impact on the city and its environs.

A different situation existed in the Protestant areas of the New World, where there was little impetus to convert the slaves. Denied opportunities to practice their religion, slaves in British areas turned increasingly to their magic. It was a situation ripe for the ascendancy of the sorcerer. Outside New Orleans, magical practices were subsumed under the general term *hoodoo*. By most accounts, the word *hoodoo*, called *obeah* in Jamaica, is derived from the word *juju*. meaning "conjure," but some theorize it may also be an adulteration of the term *voodoo*. *Hoodoo* is a more generalized term than *voodoo* and can refer not only to complex, magical practices but also to simple medicinal procedures or superstitions.

"Restricted from the practice of so many other cultural and social forms, blacks found a kind of socio-cultural release in the practice of magic and the maintenance of supernatural beliefs," Haskins writes. "And since the larger white society either did not know about, did not understand or depreciated those practices and beliefs, these forms constituted one of the only areas of black life in which they could find privacy. In sum, voodoo, hoodoo, and their allied phenomena allowed for their own kind of cohesion, a perverse kind perhaps, but a cohesion, nevertheless."

In the second section of the book, Haskins documents the folklore by presenting a collection of recipes for spells and potions. "Even if one is not very religious," Haskins writes, "one has to believe in the efficacy of conjure in order for it to work, either for good or evil, and if the recipes presented in the following chapters seem at times comical, or at least hard to take seriously, you would do well to bear in mind that hoodoo and voodoo are no laughing matter—to those who believe."

A note to the reader after the introduction says: "Some of the procedures and techniques reported here, if put into practice, would be dangerous to one's health and safety. The author and publisher want you not to implement them." Of the more than 200 recipes in the book, several use human bones, dirt from fresh graves, excrement, or urine. A few require the killing of frogs, cats, or snakes or involve potions that contain potentially dangerous or unhealthy ingredients.

The chapter "To Do Ill" contains spells or hexes to kill someone, cause live creatures to appear in the body, make someone ill, affect childbirth and labor, cause insanity, cause disturbance or confusion, or make someone go away. To kill, for example, "Obtain a lock of the intended victim's hair as well as his or her photograph. Bury the two together, preferably in mud or in a moist area where the objects will disintegrate quickly. As they disintegrate, the victim will disintegrate, too—visibly and in like manner." To cause headaches, "put some graveyard dust in a small bag and hide it in the person's pillow."

"To Do Good" includes remedies related to the large body of spiritual practices that are aimed at protection, luck, peace, good fortune, and happiness. "In Matters of Law" contains "court spells" that involve the circumventing of legal sanctions by means of conjuration. "In Matters of Love," a topic that occupies a prominent place in voodoo and hoodoo lore, includes potions to keep a man at home or a woman happy or to get revenge.

Voodoo and hoodoo served an important function of social cohesion for blacks and acted as a vehicle for the preservation of the African heritage. However, Haskins writes, it is unclear whether these practices will continue to survive as a distinct black cultural phenomenon, as black Americans have more access to mainstream American life. But "whenever earthly, secular, non-mystical life becomes too hard to handle, whenever social upheaval occurs, whenever religion and mysticism enjoy a renaissance," Haskins believes, "voodoo and hoodoo will re-emerge as well, if indeed they are fully eclipsed."

CENSORSHIP HISTORY

In early 1992, the parent of a fourth-grade student at Clearwood Junior High School in Slidell, Louisiana, discovered a copy of *Voodoo & Hoodoo* in her daughter's possession. The book was part of the Louisiana collection in the school library for eighth graders, who study the state's history and folklore, and her daughter had taken the book home without checking it out of the library. The parent phoned the assistant principal of the school to complain and also gave the book to a friend who was a member of the Louisiana Christian Coalition. She then filed a formal complaint with the school principal, claiming that the book heightened children's infatuation with the supernatural, promoted antisocial and criminal behavior, and incited students to try the spells in the book, which she believed to be potentially dangerous. She obtained 1,650 signatures on a petition asking for the book's removal from the library.

In response to the complaint, the principal asked a school-level library committee to review the book. The committee recommended that the book remain in the library, as it served an educational purpose and supplied information on a topic in the eighth-grade curriculum, but should be restricted with parental permission to students in the eighth grade.

Without voting on the committee's recommendations, St. Tammany Parish School Board voted 12-2 on June 11 to remove the book from all libraries in the school district, calling it dangerous and without educational value.

The American Civil Liberties Union of Louisiana sued the board in federal court on behalf of two St. Tammany Parish families, who said the ban violated their First Amendment rights. U.S. District Court judge Patrick Carr first ruled in October 1993 that the case should go to trial but later reversed his decision. On October 6, 1994, in *Delcarpio v. St. Tammany Parish School Board*, he granted summary judgment in favor of the parents. He ruled that the book's censorship violated the First Amendment as well as the constitution of Louisiana and ordered the book returned to the schools. He said that the board could not limit students' access to ideas that board members considered dangerous, namely the descriptions of voodoo practices and religious beliefs. He based his decision on the U.S. Supreme Court's 1982 ruling in *Board of Education, Island Trees Union Free School District No. 26 v. Pico*. The Supreme Court declared in its plurality opinion: "Local school boards may not remove books from school library shelves simply because they dislike the ideas contained in those books and seek by their removal to prescribe what shall be orthodox in politics, nationalism, religion, or other matters of opinion."

Judge Carr rejected the school board's defense that its decision rested on a discretionary judgment regarding school curricula. The record belied that claim, the court found. The board opposed the book because ideas in it conflicted with members' religious views. It did not restrict the book's circulation among younger students whose safety it purported to be concerned about but rather entirely removed it. There was no evidence that any student sought to replicate the voodoo spells contained in the book.

The school board voted 8-5 to appeal the decision. In 1995, the Court of Appeals of the Fifth Circuit in *Campbell v. St. Tammany Parish School Board* reversed Judge Carr's decision of summary judgment. It ordered the case sent back to his court for a full trial at which all board members could be questioned about their reasons for removing the book in order to ascertain "the true, decisive motivation behind the School Board's decision." "Our de novo review of the summary judgment evidence leads us to conclude that a genuine issue of material fact exists regarding whether the School Board removed the book for constitutionally impermissible reasons," the court said.

The appeals court was relying on the Supreme Court's plurality opinion in *Pico*, which stated that whether removing a book from a school library infringes First Amendment rights "depends upon the motivation behind petitioners' actions. If petitioners intended by their removal decision to deny respondents access to ideas with which petitioners disagreed, and if this intent was the decisive factor in petitioners' decision, then petitioners have exercised their discretion in violation of the Constitution."

The appeals court noted that "many of the School Board members had not even read the book, or had read less than its entirety, before voting as they did." There was evidence that some members had read only excerpts provided by the Christian Coalition. The court also noted that the fact that the school board's decision was not curricula-based and its refusal to consider its own committees' recommendations suggested that the board's decision might have been an attempt to "strangle the free mind at its source."

A trial was set for April 22, 1996. But on April 1, the school board agreed to a settlement. Its chances of winning the case seemed slim, and momentum for a settlement had been building on the board after two conservative members left in 1994. Additionally, the board's insurer said it might not pay its legal expenses if the board continued to fight the suit.

After a four-year legal battle, the board agreed to the same compromise recommended by the library review committee in 1992. The book would be returned to all school libraries in the district but would be kept on reserve shelves and restricted to students in the eighth grade or above who bad parental permission to read it. The school board also agreed to pay the plaintiffs' attorney fees and costs.

FURTHER READING

Baldwin, Gordon B. "The Library Bill of Rights: A Critique." *Library Trends* 45, no. 1 (Summer 1996): 7–21.

Doyle, Robert P. *Banned Books: 2004 Resource Book*. Chicago: American Library Association, 2004.

Newsletter on Intellectual Freedom 41, no. 5 (September 1992): 137; 44, no. 1 (January 1995): 19–20; 45, no. 4 (July 1996): 134.

VOYAGES TO THE MOON AND THE SUN

Author: Savinien Cyrano de Bergerac
Original dates and place of publication: 1657, 1662, France
Literary form: Fiction

SUMMARY

Savinien Cyrano de Bergerac is most often remembered today as the dueling libertine with a long nose, the legendary protagonist of the romantic drama written in the 19th century by Edmond Rostand. The real Cyrano was a 17th-century writer, playwright, scientist, and soldier, well known as a wit and a freethinker. He satirized the customs and beliefs of his time in two science fiction narratives about imaginary journeys: *Voyage to the Moon* and *Voyage to the Sun*. In the modern English translation of the two books, they are published together as *Voyages to the Moon and the Sun*.

In his fanciful *Voyages*, Cyrano speculated on the possibility of life on other planets and on the eternal nature of the Earth. His purpose was both to entertain and to comment on philosophical, social, and political issues that could not easily be discussed in other formats. Although his imaginary travels are sometimes described as utopian, Cyrano does not offer for consideration an ideal political system. Like Jonathan Swift's *GULLIVER'S TRAVELS*, which was influenced by Cyrano's work, *Voyages* uses the device of a traveler's tales to satirize existing institutions and prejudices and to expose to ridicule fundamental flaws in the human character.

In *Voyages*, Cyrano is propelled to the Moon by means of little bottles filled with dew strapped to his body. The heat of the Sun draws the bottles into the clouds, but he falls to ground in New France, Canada, rather than on the Moon. He then uses rockets to boost himself to the Moon, where he lands in a garden of Eden populated by giant beast-men with human faces and bodies who walk on four legs. The opening sections of his first voyage parody the Old Testament and mock literal belief in the Scriptures.

On the Moon, Cyrano meets a philosopher who originally came from the Sun and was sent to colonize Earth. The philosopher had left the Earth for the kingdom of the Moon and decided to remain there, because the Moon's beast-men are lovers of truth, and there are no pedants among them. "The philosophers allow themselves to be convinced by reason alone and neither the authority of a learned man or numbers can overwhelm the opinion of a corn-thresher if the corn-thresher reasons powerfully."

The royal court of the beast-men detains Cyrano as an entertaining curiosity. The queen believes that Cyrano is the female partner of her little animal, who turns out also to be a man from Earth, a native of Spain. He tells Cyrano that the real reason he was obliged to wander the Earth and abandon it for the Moon was that he could not find a single country where even the imagination was free. "Observe," he says, "unless you wear a square cap, a chaperon or a cassock, whatever excellent things you may say, if they are against the principles of those diplomated doctors, you are an idiot, a madman or an atheist." He fell into the queen's hands because she had taken him for a monkey, for all the monkeys on the Moon are dressed in Spanish clothes.

When they hear that Cyrano, who is thought to be an animal, can talk, the clergy on the Moon publish a decree forbidding anyone to believe that he has the faculty of reason and commanding, instead, that any intellectual thing Cyrano does be regarded as a product of instinct. The quandary over the definition of Cyrano's being—Is he man or animal?—divides the town into two factions. An assembly of the Estates of the realm is called to resolve the religious dispute.

The court of justice examines Cyrano and finally declares that he is indeed a man; as such, he is set free on the proviso that he must make "shameful amends." He must publicly disavow having taught that the Moon was a world, "and this on account of the scandal the novelty of the opinion might have caused the souls of the weaker brethren."

Cyrano meets two philosophers in the town who discuss with him theories of the origin of the universe and the immortality of the soul. "When we try to go back to the origin of this Great All," one of the philosophers says, "we are forced to run into three or four absurdities. . . . The first obstacle that stops us is the Eternity of the World. Men's minds are not strong enough to conceive it and, because they are not able to imagine that so vast, so beautiful, so well regulated a Universe could have made itself, they take refuge in Creation. . . . This absurdity. . . ."

Back on Earth, Cyrano is harassed by critics of the tale of his first voyage to the Moon. The parson of Colignac, in particular, circulates ridiculous tales of Cyrano's sorceries. Cyrano is dragged into jail by a mob and eventually imprisoned in a tower. One day his tower rises high into the sky above Toulouse, transporting him after four months of travel to one of the little worlds that fly around the Sun. He perceives on his trip that it is indeed the Earth that turns around the Sun from east to west, and not the Sun that turns about the Earth.

He eventually arrives at the Sun, a luminous land like burning snowflakes, a weightless world with no center. He comes into the kingdom of the birds, where he is indicted and put on trial in the parliament of birds, charged with being a man. Cyrano's indictment lists various criticisms of man, including his disturbing of peace, lack of equality and barbarity in his conduct. "They are so inclined to servitude," the indictment reads, "that for fear of failing to serve, they sell their liberty to each other. . . ."

Cyrano is sentenced to death for man's crimes but is saved by turtledoves at the request of Caesar, his cousin's pet parrot. He then passes through the land of talking trees and the Kingdom of Love. Here the book ends abruptly, before Cyrano's return to Earth.

CENSORSHIP HISTORY

Voyage to the Moon was written in 1648; *Voyage to the Sun* was begun in 1650 but left unfinished. Cyrano privately circulated *Voyage to the Moon* in manuscript form but did not dare publish it during his lifetime because of ideas in it that would have been viewed as subversive and antireligious and could have exposed him to imprisonment or exile.

In 1654, a collection of Cyrano's works that included a theatrical tragedy, *The Death of Agrippina*, and his *Letters* was printed in two quartos. His *Letters*, which were popular for a half-century after their publication, were heavily censored by their publisher, who eliminated philosophical or satirical arguments directed against government or the church.

After Cyrano's death in 1655, *Voyage to the Moon* was prepared for publication by his friend, Henry Le Bret. However, fearing punishment by the authorities, Le Bret expurgated the manuscript of material that could be construed by the church as offensive. The version that was published in 1657 eliminated many of the most daring passages, notably the pages satirizing the Book of Genesis, with some of the omissions marked with ellipsis or the word *hiatus*. The censored version of *Voyage to the Moon* was the only one available in French until the discovery of the original manuscript in the late 19th century. Until 1962, English translations were also based on the expurgated edition.

Fourteen of the 96 pages that appeared in the first unexpurgated French edition had been deleted by Le Bret. In many cases, the effect of the deletions of essential words, sentences, paragraphs, or whole pages was not only to blunt Cyrano's sarcasm but also to make Cyrano's writing sound nonsensical and absurd. *Voyage to the Sun* was published separately in 1762, but because the original manuscript was never found, the extent of its deletions cannot be estimated.

Cyrano's posthumous reputation as insane, or, at the least, eccentric, was due in part to the impression created by the non sequiturs in his writing. But "he was not mad," his modern English translator claims, "he was simply heavily censored." Though the Catholic Church condemned his writing as pagan heresy, his reputation as a madman had a more significant impact on suppressing interest in his work.

"What wretched works are those of Cyrano de Bergerac!" a 17th-century critic commented. "When he wrote his *Voyage to the Moon*, I think he had one quarter of the moon in his head." The 18th century saw a further decline in his reputation. The influential Voltaire, standard-bearer of the Enlightenment, referred to him as "a madman." No new editions of *Voyages to the Moon and the Sun* appeared in France between 1699 and 1855. Cyrano was virtually forgotten until he was revived as a legendary figure by Edmond Rostand in 1897.

FURTHER READING

Cyrano de Bergerac. *Voyages to the Moon and the Sun*. Translated and with an introduction and notes by Richard Aldington. New York: Orion Press, 1962.
Harth, Erica. *Cyrano de Bergerac and the Polemics of Modernity*. New York: Columbia University Press, 1970.

THE WITCHES

Author: Roald Dahl
Original date and places of publication: 1983, United Kingdom and United States
Original publishers: Jonathan Cape; Farrar, Straus and Giroux
Literary form: Novel

SUMMARY

The Witches by Roald Dahl, the award-winning British author of 19 children's books, is the story of a seven-year-old boy and his Norwegian grandmother who together battle a plot by witches to exterminate the world's children.

In fairy tales, witches wear black hats and cloaks and ride on broomsticks. "But this is not a fairy tale," the author warns his readers in "A Note about Witches." "This is about REAL WITCHES. . . . *REAL WITCHES dress in ordinary clothes and look very much like ordinary women. They live in ordinary houses and they work in ORDINARY JOBS*. That is why they are so hard to catch." Real witches hate children. They are particularly dangerous because they don't look dangerous. "She might even be your lovely school-teacher who is reading these words to you at this very moment."

Twice a year, a boy goes to Norway from England with his family to visit his grandmother. Shortly after his seventh birthday, during a Christmas visit, his parents are killed in a car accident. The day after the accident, the grandmother, an expert on witches, begins telling stories about children who were kidnapped by witches and vanished off the face of the Earth.

How do you recognize a witch? Grandmother explains that a real witch always wears gloves, because witches have thin curvy claws instead of fingernails. Witches never have toes, and their feet have square ends. They are always bald and wear a wig. The wigs make their scalp itch and cause nasty sores on the head. They also have slightly larger nose holes than ordinary people and keen powers of smell. But the dirtier a child is, the less he smells to a witch. A clean child smells to a witch like dog droppings.

One of their favorite tricks is to mix up a powder that will turn a child into a creature that all grown-ups hate. Once a year in each country, the witches meet secretly to hear a lecture by the Grand High Witch of All the World. Grandmother says that when she was younger, she traveled the world trying to track down the Grand High Witch.

The boy and his grandmother move back to his family house in England. One day, he is in his tree house when a peculiar woman appears below, wearing a small black hat and long black gloves. She says that if he comes down she will give him a present, a small green snake. He refuses, and the woman leaves. When his grandmother arrives, he realizes that he has seen a witch for the first time. "It is hardly surprising," he says, "that after that I became a very witch-conscious boy."

Grandmother gets pneumonia, and when she recovers, the doctors recommend that she go to a nice hotel on the south coast of England. She books rooms at the Hotel Magnificent in the seaside town of Bournemouth. Looking for a place to play with his two pet mice, the boy finds an empty ballroom, reserved for the annual meeting of the Royal Society for the Prevention of Cruelty to Children, and settles behind a large folding screen. The ladies from the Royal Society stream in. The boy notices that many of the women are scratching their heads and are wearing wigs and gloves.

A pretty young woman in a long black dress appears on the platform. Her gloved fingers unhook something behind her ears, and the whole of her face comes away in her hands, revealing her real face, a fearsome and ghastly sight. The boy knows immediately that she is none other than the Grand High Witch. As the women remove their wigs, he sees a sea of red and itchy-looking naked scalps. The Grand High Witch gives her orders: Every child in the country "shall be rrrubbed out, sqvashed, sqvirted, sqvittered and frrritered before I come here again in vun year's time. . . . Vee vill vipe them all avay! Vee vill scrub them off the face of the earth. Vee vill flush them down the drain!"

The Grand High Witch instructs the other witches to return to their hometowns and buy the best sweet shops in England. They are to announce a gala grand opening with free sweets and chocolates for every child. The sweets will be filled with the latest magic formula: Formula 86 Delayed Action Mouse-Maker. When the children arrive at school the next day, they will turn into mice. "Down vith children! Do them in! Boil their bones and fry their skin!" sings the Grand High Witch.

The boy realizes that he is in danger and that his only hope of avoiding discovery is that he has not washed for days. The Grand High Witch announces that she has already given a dose of Formula 86 in a chocolate bar to a smelly boy in the hotel lobby and has promised to give him more chocolate if he will meet her in the ballroom at 3:25 P.M. Bruno Jenkins, who is staying in the hotel with his parents, arrives to collect the chocolate bars. As the witches and the boy watch, Bruno is changed into a mouse.

Then the witches smell dog droppings and begin to sniff the air. The boy is discovered. The Grand High Witch pours the entire contents of a little bottle down his throat and he, too, turns into a mouse. While the witches are getting a mousetrap, he runs away. "I was feeling remarkably well," the boy thinks. Perhaps it isn't so bad being a mouse. "Little boys have to go to school. Mice don't. Mice don't have to pass exams. Mice don't have to worry about money. . . . My grandmother is a human, but I know that she will always love me whoever I am."

The boy finds Bruno, and the two mouse-boys make their way to his grandmother's room. There the boy vows to stop the witches. He will go to the Grand High Witch's room, steal a bottle of her Delayed Action Mouse-Maker, give the witches a dose, and turn them into mice. Grandmother lowers the boy over the balcony in a sock into the Grand Witch's bedroom, and he escapes with 500 doses of the mouse-maker.

Grandmother hides the mice-boys in her purse and goes to the dining room. She gives Bruno's parents the bad news that Bruno has been altered. Meanwhile, the boy sneaks into the kitchen and pours the mouse-maker dose into the soup. But before he can escape to the dining room, a cook chops off the tip of his tail with a carving knife.

In the dining room, the Grand High Witch screams and goes shooting up into the air. Suddenly all the other witches begin to scream and jump up out of their seats. Then, all at once, they become still, stiff, and silent. They shrink and turn into mice. Waiters smash the mice with chairs, wine bottles, and frying pans, and behind them comes the cook with his carving knife. Grandmother exits the hotel with her grandson safe in her purse and returns to Norway.

Back in grandmother's fine old house, the boy asks how long he can expect to live as a mouse-person. Grandmother estimates that he will survive about nine years. "Good," the boy says. "It's the best news I ever had. . . . Because I would never want to live longer than you." "Are you sure you don't mind being a mouse for the rest of your life?" Grandmother asks. "I don't mind at all," he says. "It doesn't matter who you are or what you look like so long as somebody loves you."

Grandmother calls the chief of police in Bournemouth and gets the name and address of the lady who disappeared from room 454 in the hotel (the Grand High Witch). Her home is a castle in the mountains above a small village. There the grandmother expects to find the names and addresses of all the rest of the witches in the world. The boy and his grandmother plot to use the doses to destroy the new Grand High Witch and the other witches in the castle. They will turn them into mice and send in cats to destroy them. Then the boy and his grandmother will travel the world, leaving deadly drops of Mouse-Maker in the food of witches. "It will be a triumph, my darling!" says the grandmother. "A colossal unbeatable triumph. We shall do it entirely by ourselves, just you and me! That will be our work for the rest of our lives."

CENSORSHIP HISTORY

Dahl's books for children are among the most frequently targeted for removal from school classrooms and libraries in the United States. His most popular books, including *The BFG, Charlie and the Chocolate Factory, James and the Giant Peach,* and *Matilda,* have all been challenged or banned. Their detractors say the books do not teach moral values or a good philosophy of life, contain rude or offensive language, or encourage children to disrespect adults. Because of its theme of witchcraft, *The Witches* is at the top of the list of censored Dahl books. It ranked number nine among the books most frequently challenged or removed from school curricula and libraries during 1990–92, according to a study by Herbert N. Foerstel. It was number 27 on the American Library Association's (ALA) list of most frequently challenged books during 1990–2000.

A witch's potion in a children's book is a recipe for censorship. Christian fundamentalists who believe that portrayal of magic and witchcraft is dangerous or incompatible with their beliefs have objected to the presence in schools of fantasy fiction with references to sorcery, wizardry, incantation, spells, or witchcraft, such as J. K. Rowling's Harry Potter books, or even fairy tales.

Educators and critics who have evaluated *The Witches* agree that, although the book is macabre and grotesque, it is more than just a scary story. It is a tale of heroism, in which good triumphs over evil, and the unmistakable message of the book is one of love and acceptance. As novelist Erica Jong commented in her review of the book in the *New York Times*, "Children love the macabre, the terrifying, the mythic," and stories that allow them to confront their own fears. *The Witches* is "a parable about the fear of death and separation and a child's mourning for the loss of his parents. . . . It is a curious sort of tale but an honest one, which deals with matters of crucial importance to children: smallness, the existence of evil in the world, mourning, separation and death."

Since 1990, *The Witches* has been challenged in at least 10 school districts in the United States, according to reports collected by the ALA. The ALA estimates that for every challenge about which it receives information, four or five go unreported.

In 1990, parents attempted to remove *The Witches* from the Amana, Iowa, first-grade curriculum because the book was "too sophisticated and did not teach moral values," and from the Goose Lake (Iowa) Elementary School because it had violent content and used the word *slut* and because the boy was turned into a mouse. In 1991, it was challenged at the Dallas (Oregon) Elementary School library because it might entice impressionable or emotionally disturbed children into becoming involved in witchcraft or the occult.

In 1992, Escondido Union Elementary School in Escondido, California, placed the book on the library's restricted list after four parents filed a complaint contending that it would cause "desensitization to violence" and "increased interest in the practice of witchcraft." The restriction requiring a parent's written permission before a child under 12 could check out the book was the first ever imposed in the district. In 1993, the Escondido school district board voted to lift the restriction and return the book to open library shelves. The district still retained bans on four other books that parents charged were promoting the occult, including poet Eve Merriam's *Halloween ABC*, which has frequently been targeted for "satanic" content.

In 1992, in La Mesa, California, a group of parents argued that *The Witches* should be banned from school libraries because it included horrifying depictions of witches as ordinary-looking women and promoted the religion of Wicca or witchcraft. The school board declined to remove the book from libraries. In Spencer, Wisconsin, in 1993, parents objected to the book's presence in a fourth-grade classroom, as they believed it could desensitize children to crimes related to witchcraft. The Spencer school board voted 3-2 to concur with a citizen-teacher committee that recommended its continued use and decided to leave the decision on what books to read in the classroom to faculty and school administrators.

In May 1994, the Lakeview Board of Education in Battle Creek, Michigan, voted to keep *The Witches* on elementary library school shelves despite protests from parents who said it was "satanic." The school board's president said it was inappropriate to debate the book's religious connotations. In Stafford, Virginia, in 1995, the book was removed from classrooms and restricted to school libraries because protesting parents said it contained crude language and encouraged children to disobey their parents and other adults.

In 1997, the librarian at Kirby Junior High School in Wichita Falls, Texas, announced that *The Witches* and three other books had been removed from the library and were in the possession of a parent who was a member of the First Assembly of God Church. The parent asked trustees to ban books with "satanic" themes and said the books would not be returned to library shelves until the school board approved them. A school board member said it was unlikely that *The Witches* and other books would be returned unless there was more academic value to them than he could see from the excerpts he had read.

In February 1998, a parent presented a complaint signed by eight people demanding that *The Witches* be removed from classrooms and libraries in the Dublin, Ohio, school district because it was derogatory toward children, harmful to their self-esteem, and conflicted with the family's religious and moral beliefs. "I find this type of material extremely objectionable and cannot understand why an educator, librarian or parent would knowingly choose this type of reading material for their students or children," the parent said. The complainant objected particularly to passages on how to recognize witches when they are "demons in human shape" and that would encourage children to avoid baths so witches couldn't smell them.

In response to the complaint, the school superintendent recommended discontinuing classroom use but leaving the book in school libraries. In June 1998, the Dublin Board of Education overruled the superintendent and voted 3-2 to allow the book to be read aloud in classrooms and to remain in libraries.

Dahl, who died in 1990, commented in 1989 on an attempt by parents to remove *The Witches* from a school library in Billings, Montana. "This book is a fantasy and an enormous joke," he told the Associated Press. "We all know that witches don't exist, not the way I've written about them. They are parents without any sense of humor at all." Dahl suggested that the school district let the children help decide the book's fate in the school library. "The banning of any book, you know, especially a children's book, is unforgivable."

The Associated Press saw the protest against Dahl's book in the context of a campaign by religious fundamentalists against Halloween. The incident in Montana came a week after parents in Maryland and Texas urged school officials to limit observance of Halloween because they said the holiday is linked to devil worship. Several Maryland school officials canceled traditional Halloween costume parties, opting to hold fall and harvest celebrations instead, while officials in that state and in Texas said they would take a look at the role of Halloween in the schools.

FURTHER READING

Associated Press. "Ban on 'The Witches' Sought." (October 19, 1989).

Doyle, Robert P. *Banned Books: 2004 Resource Book.* Chicago: American Library Association, 2004.

Foerstel, Herbert N. *Banned in the U.S.A.: A Reference Guide to Book Censorship in Schools and Public Libraries*, Revised and expanded edition. Westport, Conn.: Greenwood Press, 2002.

Jong, Erica. "The Boy Who Became a Mouse." *New York Times Book Review* (November 13, 1983). Available online. URL: http://roalddahlfans.com/books/witcrev1.php.

Newsletter on Intellectual Freedom 41, no. 3 (May 1992): 78; 41, no. 6 (November 1992): 196; 42, no. 4 (July 1993): 127; 42, no. 5 (September 1993): 157; 43, no. 3 (May 1994): 200; 47, no. 5 (September 1998): 156.

WOMEN WITHOUT MEN:
A NOVEL OF MODERN IRAN

Author: Shahrnush Parsipur
Original dates and places of publication: 1989, Iran; 1998, United States
Original publishers: Noghreh Publishing; Syracuse University Press
Literary form: Novel

SUMMARY

Shahrnush Parsipur's *Women Without Men: A Novel of Modern Iran* (*Zanan-e-Bedoon-e-Mardan*), drawing on Persian and Islamic mythology and the fantastic elements of tales such as *The Thousand and One Nights*, weaves together stories of five women in contemporary Iran whose lives intersect in a mystical garden in the city of Karaj.

Mahdokht, a teacher, sits in the garden of her brother's house in Karaj, a city 25 miles west of Tehran known for its gardens, river, and cool climate, where she is spending the summer. She knits sweaters for children and, in her interest in performing charitable acts for children, compares herself to Julie Andrews's character in the film *The Sound of Music*. She witnesses a sexual encounter in the gardener's greenhouse between the gardener and a 15-year-old girl. Both the gardener and the girl disgust her. When the girl begs her not to tell anyone, Mahdokht secretly hopes the girl's brothers will find out and beat her to death.

"My virginity is like a tree," Mahkokht thinks. "I'm a tree. I must plant myself." She decides to stay in the garden and plant herself at the beginning of winter. She wants to grow on the riverbank, sprout new leaves, and give them to the wind. She will become thousands of branches and cover the entire world.

Faizeh's story begins on August 25, 1953 (when Mohammad Mosaddeq, the prime minister of Iran, was overthrown in a U.S.-backed coup). That evening, Faizeh puts on her chador and leaves the house in a taxi. There is rioting in the streets. Faizeh arrives at her friend Munis's house. Faizeh's brother's wife, Parvin, has separated from him, and Faizeh recounts a comment that Parvin once made to her: "A woman who spends half her time making out with Farid [Parvin's brother] in the hall should do something about the curtain of virginity, not waste all her time cooking."

"First I thought of slapping her so hard upside the head that her eardrum would break," Faizeh tells Munis. "Besides, virginity is not a curtain, it's a hole." Munis replies, "Virginity is a curtain, my mother says. If a girl jumps down from a height she'll damage her virginity. It's a curtain, it can be torn." Faizeh insists that it is a hole. "It's narrow, and then it becomes wide." Munis's brother, Amir, arrives and agrees to take Faizeh home before nightfall.

On August 27, Munis is standing on the roof looking down at the street. Amir has said she must not go out, as there is fighting in the streets. It has been three days and two nights since she found out that virginity is a hole, not a curtain. She is filled with rage, recalling her childhood fear of climbing a tree lest she tear the curtain of her virginity. As she watches a man staggering in the alley below, Munis bends forward, then falls to the pavement. The man in the alley says he is dead and that she must go away.

Munis leaves and spends a month walking the streets. One day she sees a book in a stall, *The Secrets of Sexual Satisfaction or How to Know Our Bodies*, and after the 13th day of passing the bookstall, she buys the book. After reading it for three days, she looks up. The trees and sunshine and streets have new meaning for her. "She had grown up."

Munis returns home. Amir says that she has destroyed the family's reputation. He takes the fruit knife from the lunch table and stabs her to death. When Faizeh arrives in search of news about Munis and sees that Amir has killed his sister, she feels that the hand of fate has finally showed her the way. "You're a brother, you upheld your family's honor," she says. "You killed her? You did the right thing. Why not? A girl who disappears for a month is as good as dead."

Faizeh helps Amir bury Munis in the garden. Faizeh tells Amir, "Now after this incident, you must get married as soon as possible so that people will forget about Munis. Anyway you need a partner in life who can take care of you." A few days later Amir announces his intention to get married, not to Faizeh, but to the 18-year-old daughter of Haj Mohammad Sorkhchehreh. She is "very beautiful, soft and quiet, modest, shy, kind, diligent, hardworking, dignified, chaste, elegant, and neat. She wears a chador, always looks down when she's in the street, and blushes constantly." When Faizeh hears the news, she bangs her head against the wall and hits the window with her fist, breaking the glass.

On the night of Amir's wedding, Faizeh appears at his house. The servant, Alia, who suspects that Amir has killed Munis, lets her in. Faizeh goes straight to the garden to bury a talisman at the foot of Munis's corpse to bring bad luck for Amir. Suddenly, she hears Munis's voice saying, "Faizeh dear! I can't breathe." Faizeh digs in the dirt until Munis's face appears. She brings water to Munis, who comes to life, gets dressed, and sits down in her usual place by the radio.

Now that Munis has risen from the dead, she can read minds. Munis accuses Faizeh of conspiring with her brother to kill her. After the members of the household arrive, Munis goes to the bridal chamber and tells Amir that his new wife had become pregnant by a cousin and had an abortion. But Amir will have to get along with his bride anyway, or she will punish him. Then Munis announces that she will live with Faizeh, and the two women walk out the door and disappear into the night.

Mrs. Farrokhlaqa Sadraldivan Golchehreh, age 51, is sitting in a rocking chair on the terrace. Her domineering husband of 30 years, Golchehreh, is in the living room tying his tie. Farrokhlaqa is patiently waiting for him to go out. Since he has retired, Golchehreh is home more often, and his presence is suffocating. Fakhredin, a young man Farrokhlaqa had loved, who left for America when she was 13, appears in her memory. He always told her that she looked like Vivien Leigh in *Gone With the Wind*.

Farrokhlaqa tells her husband that she wishes they had a garden in Karaj. "Do you think that after menopause you can still enjoy a garden?" her husband asks. Farrokhlaqa becomes frightened by the strange way her husband is looking at her. She punches him in the stomach. He trips and dies falling down the terrace stairs. Three months later, Farrokhlaqa sells the Tehran house, buys a house and garden in Karaj, and moves there.

Zarrinkolah is a 26-year-old prostitute, working at Golden Akram's house. She has 20 to 30 customers a day and is tired of working but sees no way out of her life of prostitution. One day a customer comes in. It is a man without a head. From that day on, all Zarrinkolah's customers are headless. Zarrinkolah goes to the bathhouse, performs ablutions 50 times, and prays at a shrine. She asks the owner of a diner where to go to drink cool water. He suggests Karaj, and she sets off for the city.

Two girls are on the road to Karaj. One is Faizeh, age 28, and the other is Munis, 38. They are both virgins. They meet a truck driver and his assistant, who rape them. The truck driver leaves the scene, but further down the road he loses control of the truck and crashes. The rapists are killed. A passenger in the truck, a gardener, survives and heads for Karaj.

Farrokhlaqa arrives at the house and garden she has bought in Karaj. She is planning a busy social life and envisions turning her house into a literary salon. She sees a tree on the riverbank. It is Mahdokht, the sister of the garden's former owner, who had lost her mind and planted herself in the earth. A man arrives who offers to work as a gardener. Zarrinkolah is with him. They had met on the road to Karaj. She said he was the first person she had seen in six months who had a head.

Then two tired women in dusty chadors, Munis and Faizeh, knock on the door. They tell of their rape by the truck drivers. Faizeh cries that she was a virgin and that the disgrace has ruined her reputation. Munis says, "Well, Faizeh dear, I was a virgin too. To hell with it. We were virgins, now we're not. It's nothing to cry over." Farrokhlaqa invites them to stay, and they tell one another about their lives.

The women help the gardener repair the main house, and Zarrinkolah and the gardener feed the tree with morning dew. When the house is finished Farrokhlaqa prepares a party room and invites journalists, poets, painters, writers, and photographers, who come every Friday and stay until late at night. Zarrinkolah and the gardener marry, and she becomes pregnant. As she grows fatter, she changes color and becomes transparent. She and the gardener feed her breast milk to the tree. Farrokhlaqa leaves the women in the house and returns to Tehran.

In midwinter, as Mahdokht is nourished by human milk, she has an explosive feeling. In midspring, her body explodes. The tree turns into seeds that blow into the water. Mahdokht travels with the water all over the world.

Faizeh has been traveling to Tehran to meet Amir. Amir and Faizeh marry secretly, and Amir finds a better job and is able to buy a new house. "Their life is neither good nor bad. It just goes on." Munis decides to become light. She flies off into the sky and spends seven years passing through seven deserts. After seven years, she arrives at the city, puts on a clean dress, and becomes a simple schoolteacher.

Farrokhlaqa stays in Tehran, where a young painter paints her portrait day after day. Eventually she gives him money to go to Paris to paint. She meets Mr. Marikhi, an old friend of her childhood love, Fakhredin. They marry, and when Marikhi is stationed in Europe, Farrokhlaqa goes with him. "Their relationship is satisfactory, neither warm or cold."

Zarrinkolah gives birth to a lily, which grows up in a small hole on the riverbank in Karaj. She and her husband sit on the lily together, become smoke, and rise into the sky.

CENSORSHIP HISTORY

Parsipur published her first novel, *The Dog and the Long Winter*, in 1974. While attending college in Tehran, she worked as a producer for Iranian National Radio and Television. After she resigned her position in 1974 to protest the execution of two poets by the shah's regime, she was arrested by the shah's notorious intelligence agency, SAVAK, and imprisoned for a short period.

In 1976, she traveled to France to attend the Sorbonne. During her four-year stay there, she completed her second novel, *The Simple and Small Adventures of the Tree Spirit*. Shortly after her return from Paris to Iran, she was arrested, along with her mother and two brothers, and imprisoned without formal charges by the revolutionary regime as a result of one of her brother's attempt to create an archive of political publications.

Parsipur spent a total of four years, seven months, and seven days in prison. Under the Ayatollah Ruhollah Khomeini's regime, hundreds of writers and journalists were arrested. According to the London-based human rights organization Article 19, by early 1983 at least 39 writers, translators, and journalists had been executed after summary trials.

Parsipur was released from prison in 1986 and, in 1989, her novel, TOUBA AND THE MEANING OF NIGHT, the story of a young girl's coming of age in 19th-century Iran, was published and became a national best seller. The same year, she found a publisher for *Women Without Men*. The novel received a great deal of attention in Iran and was widely discussed by literary critics.

Soon after its publication, the government banned it as un-Islamic and subsequently banned all of her other writings. Censorship laws prohibit the publication of material contrary to the principles of Islam and the authorities reserve the right to ban any work postpublication and take legal action against the author and publisher.

The censors took issue with Parsipur's treatment in the novel of the topics of virginity, rape, prostitution, and failed marriages, as well as references to Western culture, such as the films *The Sound of Music* and *Gone with the Wind*.

Parsipur was arrested twice in connection with the banning of *Women Without Men* and jailed each time for more than a month. Mohammad Reza Aslani, the book's publisher, was also arrested, and his publishing house, Noghreh Publishing, was closed.

As Parsipur was unable to make a living in Iran as a writer, she sought political refugee status and moved to the United States in 1994. All eight of her novels and a prison memoir continue to be banned in Iran. Yet her books continue to circulate underground and are widely read there.

FURTHER READING

Article 19. "Iran: Press Freedom Under the 'Moderates.' " *Censorship News* no. 15 (August 17, 1992).

Parsipur, Shahrnush. *Women Without Men: A Novel of Modern Iran.* Afterword by Persis M. Karim. Translator's note by Kamran Talattof. New York: The Feminist Press at the City University of New York, 2004.

ZHUAN FALUN: THE COMPLETE TEACHINGS OF FALUN GONG

Author: Li Hongzhi
Original dates and places of publication: China, 1994; United States, 2001
Publisher: Fair Winds Press (United States)
Literary form: Spiritual text

SUMMARY

Zhuan Falun (Revolving of the law wheel) is the main book of teachings of a philosophy of spiritual cultivation introduced by Li Hongzhi in China in 1992. Falun Gong, or Falun Dafa, stresses the integration of high ethical standards and physical well-being and the cultivation of one's inner nature by upholding the three principles of truth, compassion, and forbearance.

Falun Dafa reflects the Buddhist and Taoist traditions of Chinese culture and is based in *qigong:* a form of traditional Chinese exercise that cultivates qi (chi), or vital energy. It prescribes a set of five exercises involving routines of physical movements and meditation. Its adherents regard it as a powerful mechanism for healing and health and believe that it is different from other *qigong* techniques in having a higher objective of spiritual enlightenment.

Zhuan Falun: The Complete Teachings of Falun Gong is composed of nine lectures originally given by Li during the period 1992–94. It provides the body of fundamental knowledge essential to the task of undertaking proper cultivation toward higher stages of attainment.

"The BUDDHA FA [meaning law, way, or principles] is most profound," the book begins. "It is the most intricate and extraordinary science of all the theories in the world. In order to explore this domain, people must fundamentally change their conventional human notions. Failing that, the truth of the universe will forever remain a mystery to humankind, and everyday people will forever crawl within the boundaries set by their own ignorance."

Li believes that there were human beings on Earth millions of years ago and that many scientists have already publicly recognized the existence of a prehistoric culture and civilization that was exterminated. The practices of *qigong* were inherited from this remote prehistoric culture.

A nuclear reactor was discovered in Gabon, he says, that was constructed 2 billion years ago and was in operation for 500,000 years. "I made a careful investigation once and found that humankind has undergone complete annihilation eighty-one times," Li writes. "We have found that whenever human societies in prehistoric times experienced periodical destruction, it always took place when humankind was morally corrupt to the extreme."

Li claims that he is the only person genuinely teaching *qigong* "toward higher levels at home and abroad." He states: "The human moral standard is declining tremendously, and human moral values are deteriorating daily. . . . As a practitioner, one must then conduct oneself by following this nature of the universe rather the standards of everyday people."

The book includes discussions of the origins of *qigong*, the roots of illness, and the fundamental *qigong* method of healing. "I do not talk about illness here, nor will we heal illness." Li writes "As a genuine practitioner, however, you cannot practice cultivation with an ill body. I will purify your body. . . . To really dispel such tribulations, karma must be eliminated."

"It is known that what actually causes people to be ill is seventy percent psychological and thirty percent physiological. Once you improve your *xinxing* [mind or heart nature, moral character], your body will undergo a great change."

Li also describes supernormal abilities that he believes "will naturally emerge" through future cultivation practice. Six supernormal abilities are recognized in the world today, he says, including clairvoyance, precognition, and retrocognition. "Yet they are not limited to these alone. I would say that over ten thousand genuine supernormal abilities exist." He cites occasions when Falun Gong practitioners were protected from injury because of their high level of cultivation: One practitioner was struck by a car but was not injured because she had "a very high *xinxing* level" and another was about to be hit by a car when it stopped suddenly. "It was Teacher who protected me," the practitioner said.

Li recommends integrating Falun Dafa practice into ordinary daily life and warns against zealotry. "The fundamental enlightenment that we talk about refers to this: In one's lifetime, from the outset of cultivation practice, one will constantly move up and let go of human attachments and various desires, and one's *gong* will also grow until the final step in cultivation practice. . . . His Third Eye will reach the highest point of its level, and he can see at his level the truth of different dimensions, the forms of existence or different lives and matter in different space-times, and the truth of our universe."

CENSORSHIP HISTORY

Li began to teach the practice of Falun Gong in China in 1992. It was one of many *qigong* groups that sprang up after Cultural Revolution–era restrictions were lifted during the 1980s. Li set up his first study center in Beijing and toured the country between 1992 and 1994 to lecture about his beliefs, often speaking at police and army educational institutions.

In January 1994, *Falun Zhuan* was published in Beijing and assigned an official publishing number. The book became a best seller, reflecting the widespread appeal of Falun Gong. The movement claimed a membership of 70 million in China and 30 million in 40 other countries. But because Falun Gong is a loose network of practitioners with no membership requirements, the number of its adherents is difficult to verify. Clearly Falun Gong's followers numbered in the millions in China and included many Communist Party members and officials. In 1998, the Chinese government estimated that Falun Gong had 40 million adherents; in 2001, after several years of government repression, official Chinese sources cited 2.1 million. The group set up thousands of teaching centers and practice areas in China and abroad and an extensive network of Web sites.

China's officially approved religions are Taoism, Buddhism, Christianity, Confucianism, and Islam. The government condemns any other religious activity as superstition. Falun Gong adherents, however, contend that the movement is not a religion but rather a network for transmitting information and practices.

Li was a member of China's government-approved Qigong Research Society, a body that oversees the various *qigong* groups. After three years of teaching, Li withdrew from the society and became estranged from the official structure. In 1996, the Chinese government's Press and Publications Administration issued a notice banning five Falun Gong publications, including *Falun Zhuan*, for propagating ignorance and superstition. But copies of the book produced in Hong Kong continued to be widely circulated in China. That year, Li announced that he had completed his teachings in China. He traveled in Europe and Asia and then settled in New York.

On April 25, 1999, Chinese officials were stunned when more than 10,000 Falun Gong adherents appeared outside the Chinese government leadership compound in Beijing and stood for 12 hours in a silent protest against government harassment and denigration of their movement. This was the largest mass demonstration since the Tiananmen Square prodemocracy demonstrations in 1989, and it marked a change in the official attitude toward Falun Gong. The government now saw it as a threat to authority and social order.

On July 22, the government declared that Falun Gong, as "an evil cult" that advocated superstition and jeopardized social stability, was now an illegal organization. The government accused the group of causing the deaths of more than 1,600 followers by encouraging them to avoid modern medical care or to commit suicide. It was prohibited "to distribute books, video/audio tapes or any other materials that propagate Falun Dafa (Falun Gong)," "to hold gatherings or demonstrations that uphold or propagate Falun Gong, such as sit-ins or appeals," and "to organize, coordinate or direct any activities that go against the government."

Security forces arrested Falun Gong leaders, ordering that senior members of the movement be "punished severely," and an arrest order was issued for Li. Nearly 30,000 participants nationwide were rounded up, detained, and questioned, many for days in open stadiums with inadequate food, water, and sanitary facilities. Practitioners who refused to renounce the movement were expelled from schools or fired. More than 1,200 government officials who had practiced Falun Gong were compelled to break their ties to the movement.

The police closed Falun Gong instruction centers and exercise areas, raided bookstores and homes of Falun Gong practitioners, and seized and destroyed videotapes and million of books. They arrested booksellers on charges of "illegal business practices" for selling Falun Gong publications. The government shut down or blocked Falun Gong Web sites and filtered Internet search engines such as Google to block access to information on the group.

As Falun Gong demonstrations continued around the country during the summer and fall of 1999, thousands of people were sent to labor camps, psychiatric wards, or prison. International human rights organizations reported abuse, torture, and deaths of practitioners in police custody. Falun Gong claims that more than 900 people have died in custody.

On October 31, 1999, Chinese authorities announced a new anticult law, which specified prison terms of three to seven years for cult members who "disturb public order" or distribute publications. "Banning cult organizations and punishing cult activities goes hand in hand with protecting normal religious activities and people's freedom of religious belief," the law stated. "The public should be exposed to the inhuman and anti-social nature of heretic cults, so that they can knowingly resist influences of the cult organizations, enhance their awareness of the law and abide by it."

In August 2001, the government said that it would summarily close down publications that reported on taboo topics, including press reports that "advocate murder, violence, obscenity, superstition or pseudo-science."

Ten years after the Chinese government began its crackdown on Falun Gong, the repression against the group's adherents continued unabated. In April 2009, the *New York Times* reported that as many as 8,000 practitioners had been detained in the previous year, and at least 100 had died in custody. Scores of practitioners had received long prison terms.

Although the Chinese government has succeeded in suppressing the distribution of Falun Gong publications in China, *Falun Zhuan* has been translated and published in more than 30 languages and is available without cost on the Internet.

FURTHER READING

Beaumont, Peter. "China's Falun Gong Crackdown: 'The Persecution Is Almost Underground.' " *Guardian* (July 18, 2009). Available online. URL: http://www.guardian. co.uk/world/2009/jul/18/china-falun-gong-crackdown. Accessed June 6, 2010.
Country Reports on Human Rights Practices—2003. Washington, D.C.: U.S. Department of State, 2004.
The Crackdown on Falun Gong and Other So-Called Heretical Organizations. London: Amnesty International, 2000.
Dangerous Meditations: China's Campaign Against Falungong. New York: Human Rights Watch, 2002.
Jacobs, Andrew. "China Still Presses Crusade against Falun Gong." *New York Times* (April 28, 2009). Available online. URL: http://www.nytimes.com/2009/04/28/ world/asia/28china.html. Accessed June 6, 2010.
Schechter, Danny. *Falun Gong's Challenge to China.* New York: Akashic Books, 2001.

ZOONOMIA

Author: Erasmus Darwin
Original dates and place of publication: 1794–96, England
Literary form: Scientific treatise

SUMMARY

The English physician and poet Erasmus Darwin was among the most eminent literary figures of his time. Sixty-five years before his grandson Charles Darwin wrote ON THE ORIGIN OF SPECIES and revolutionized biological science, Erasmus Darwin formulated an evolutionary system of world order in *Zoonomia*, his treatise on animal life.

Darwin ran a successful practice as a family physician but was more prominent as a scientific poet. His book-length poem, *The Botanic Garden*, published in two parts—*The Loves of the Plants* in 1789 and *The Economy of Vegetation* in 1792—was immensely popular and influenced the English Romantic poets William Blake, William Wordsworth, Samuel Taylor Coleridge, Percy Bysshe Shelley, and John Keats.

In 1794, Darwin published the first volume of *Zoonomia*, a voluminous and difficult 1,400-page prose work directed to a professional medical audience, which reiterated in technical detail the theories on the physical nature of human life expounded in his poems. The second volume, a medical casebook with treatments for all known diseases, appeared in 1796. Four years later, he published *Phytologia, or the Philosophy of Agriculture and Gardening*, the counterpart to *Zoonomia* on plant life.

In *Zoonomia*, Darwin described the laws of organic life and analyzed the mechanism of all aspects of animal life. He posited a force or phenomenon in nature possessed by all living matter: "animal motion," or the spirit of animation. He divided animal motion into four different types: irritative, sensitive, voluntary, and associative, each with its own definition and description. He then explained how "all our ideas are animal motions of the organs of sense."

The most important section of *Zoonomia* was the long chapter "Of Generation," in which he described descent with modification and expounded his theory of what is now called biological evolution. Darwin had been convinced of the truth of evolution for more than 20 years. In the preface to *Zoonomia*, he wrote: "The great CREATOR of all things has infinitely diversified the works of his hands, but at the same time stamped a certain similitude on the features of nature, that demonstrates to us, that *the whole is one family of one parent.*"

He argued that animals were able to pass on physical changes to their offspring and that such continual regeneration had produced all varieties of life from one original life source. He pointed to changes produced in animals through domestic breeding and naturally, "as in the production of the butterfly with painted wings from the crawling caterpillar; or of the respiring frog from the subnatant tadpole." He also noted that "monstrosities," or mutations, are often inherited.

Discarding the traditional biological notion of fixed species, he replaced it with a description of continual generation over time. "Would it be too bold to imagine," he asked, "that in the great length of time since the earth began to exist, perhaps millions of ages before the commencement of the history of mankind, would it be too bold to imagine that all warm-blooded animals have arisen from one living filament."

Darwin also proposed that a struggle for existence related to the generation and the survival of the fittest: "The final cause of this contest amongst the males seems to be, that the strongest and most active animal should propagate the species, which should thence become improved." Though Erasmus Darwin's account of evolution was incomplete and, unlike the work of Charles Darwin, based on speculation rather than observation, he did define the theory associated with his grandson and considered many of the subjects that were later studied more intensively by Charles Darwin.

CENSORSHIP HISTORY

Darwin began his work on *Zoonomia* in 1771 but did not publish it until more than 20 years later. He had considered delaying its publication until after his death, for fear of the negative reaction it might arouse from religious quarters. However, encouraged by the change in the intellectual climate in Europe after the French Revolution, he went forward with his project.

In *Zoonomia*, Darwin stressed that evolution proceeds "by its own inherent activity," or without divine intervention. He had considered the concept of adaptation without the bias common in 18th-century scientific investigation, which saw a purpose in all the creator's works for the immediate benefit of humankind. The response to *Zoonomia* was similar to that faced by Charles Darwin upon the publication of *On the Origin of the Species* two generations later. Although Erasmus Darwin's work was lauded by many for its great contribution to scientific thought, his theories were immediately denounced by the religious establishment and others who were shocked by the implications of a self-generated, godless universe. Darwin discards "all the authority of revelation in favour of the sports of his own imagination," one critic wrote. "He dwelt so much and so exclusively on secondary causes, he forgot that there is a first," wrote another.

A 560-page book, *Observations on the Zoonomia of Erasmus Darwin*, written by Thomas Brown, lambasted Darwin's medical and philosophic ideas. A government minister, George Canning, wrote a parody, "The Loves of the Triangles," ridiculing both Darwin's style and his belief that humans evolved from lower animals. The poet Coleridge described Darwin's philosophy in *Zoonomia* as the "State of Nature or the Orang Outang theology of the human race, substituted for the first chapters of the Book of Genesis."

Zoonomia's notoriety caused the Catholic Church to place it on the Index of Forbidden Books in 1817. Despite the fact that it was rarely read after the late 19th century, the work remained on the Index through the last edition, in effect until 1966. Ironically, while the ponderous and difficult work of Erasmus Darwin, long ago superseded by that of his grandson, was forbidden to Catholics, Charles Darwin's *On the Origin of Species*, which firmly established evolutionary theories dealt with by his grandfather in embryonic form and aroused even greater controversy, was never listed on the Index.

—Jonathan Pollack

FURTHER READING

Browne, Janet. *Charles Darwin: Voyaging, Volume I of a Biography*. New York: Alfred A. Knopf, 1995.

Darwin, Charles. *The Autobiography of Charles Darwin: 1809–1882*. Edited by Nora Barlow. New York: W. W. Norton, 1993.

Hassler, Donald M. *Erasmus Darwin*. New York: Twayne Publishers, 1973.

King-Hele, Desmond. *Erasmus Darwin and the Romantic Poets*. New York: St. Martin's Press, 1986.

CENSORED WRITERS ON RELIGIOUS CENSORSHIP

I have replied to the Louvain slanders modestly, of course, but not without salt and vinegar and even mustard.

—Henricus Cornelius Agrippa

But I take courage from the words of Daniel . . . assuring us that the defenders of the truth are shielded by divine power.

—Dante Alighieri

I am of a constitution so general that it consorts and sympathizeth with all things. . . . All places, all airs, make unto me one Countrey; I am in England every where, and under any Meridian.

—Sir Thomas Browne

I borrow not the rules of my Religion from Rome or Geneva, but the dictates of my own reason.

—Sir Thomas Browne

I have ever expounded philosophically and according to the principles of Nature and by its light . . . although I may have set forth much suspicious matter occasioned by my own natural light . . . never have I taught anything directly contrary to the Catholic religion.

—Giordano Bruno

[W]e regard those as heretics with whom we disagree . . . so that if you are orthodox in one city or region, you must be held for a heretic in the next.

—Sebastian Castellio

To kill a doctrine is not to protect a doctrine, but it is to kill a man. When the Genevans killed Servetus, they did not defend a doctrine, but they killed a man.

—Sebastian Castellio

I would have made the book more amusing, had it not been for the Holy Office.

—Miguel de Cervantes Saavedra

I am known not only as a writer, but also as a feminist. Feminists generally annoy fundamentalists of all ilk, and I have been no exception.

—Lindsey Collen

Observe, unless you wear a square cap, a chaperon or a cassock, whatever excellent things you may say, if they are against the principles of those diplomated doctors, you are an idiot, a madman or an atheist.

—Savinien Cyrano de Bergerac

I could not employ my life better than in adding a little to natural science. This I have done to the best of my abilities, and critics may say what they like, but they cannot destroy this conviction.

—Charles Darwin

Let all Mankind be told for what: Tell them t'was he was too bold, and told those Truths which shou'd not ha' been told.

—Daniel Defoe

Some men, who produced a silly work which imbecile editors botched further, have never been able to pardon us for having planned a better one. These enemies to all good have subjected us to every kind of persecution. We have seen our honor, our fortune, our liberty, our life endangered within a few month's time.

—Denis Diderot

To abandon the work is to turn one's back on the breach, and do what the rascals who persecute us desire.

—Denis Diderot

They think that everything they do not understand is an error and that every error is a heresy, when only obstinate adherence to error makes heresy and a heretic. . . .

—Meister Eckhart

A disobedient woman writer is doubly punished, since she has violated the norm of her fundamental obligation to home, husband and children.

—Nawal El Saadawi

I might perhaps do better to pass over them [quibbling Scholastic theologians] in silence without stirring the mud of Camarina or grasping that noxious plant, lest they marshal their forces for an attack and force me to eat my words. If I refuse they'll denounce me as a heretic on the spot, for this is the bolt they always loose on anyone to whom they take a dislike.

—Desiderius Erasmus

Had I believed the majority of English readers were so fondly attached even to the name and shadow of Christianity, had I foreseen that the pious and the timid and the prudent would feel or affect to feel such exquisite sensibility, I might perhaps have softened the two individious chapters, which would create many enemies, and conciliate few friends.

—Edward Gibbon

To prohibit the reading of certain books is to declare the inhabitants to be either fools or slaves.

—Claude-Adrien Helvétius

The King is a mortall man and not God, [and] therefore hath no power over the immortall soules of his subjects to make lawes and ordinances for them to set spirituall Lords over them.

—Thomas Helwys

Do not when a poor soul by violence is brought before you to speak his conscience in the profession of his religion to his God—do not first implore the oath ex officio. *Oh, most wicked course! And if he will not yield to that then imprison him close. Oh, horrible severity! . . . Let these courses be far from you, for there is no show of grace, religion, nor humanity in these courses.*

—Thomas Helwys

In the first place, I think I am too deeply engaged to think of a retreat. In the second place, I see not what bad consequences follow, in the present age, from the character of an infidel.

—David Hume

At Thy Tribunal Lord, I make my appeal. You have execrated me, Holy Fathers; I bless you. I pray that your conscience may be as clear as mine and that you may be as moral and religious as I am.

—Nikos Kazantzakis

I've always been amazed at the narrow-mindedness and narrow-heartedness of human beings. Here is a book I wrote in a state of deep religious exaltation, with a fervent love of Christ; and now the Pope has no understanding of it at all.

—Nikos Kazantzakis

The greater the freedom of thought the more will faith be awakened in the sincerity of those who are devoted to scientific research.

—Johannes Kepler

It is true that the Index has been abolished and another name given to the Roman Inquisition. But there are still inquisitional processes against troublesome theologians.

—Hans Küng

They say that some articles are heretical, some erroneous, some scandalous, some offensive. The implication is that those which are heretical are not erroneous, those which are erroneous are not scandalous, and those which are scandalous are not offensive. . . . It is better that I should die a thousand times than that I should retract one syllable of the condemned articles.

—Martin Luther

427

Heretics should be vanquished with books, not with burnings.

—Martin Luther

One idea can only be opposed by another idea.

—Naguib Mahfouz

Delving into memory, slipping into the past, is an activity that these days is closely supervised, especially for Muslim women. The sleeping past can animate the present. That is the virtue of memory. Magicians know it and the imams know it too.

—Fatima Mernissi

If all mankind minus one were of one opinion, and only one person were of the contrary opinion, mankind would be no more justified in silencing that one person, than he, if he had the power, would be justified in silencing mankind.

—John Stuart Mill

No proposition astounds me, no belief offends me, however much opposed it may be to my own.

—Michel de Montaigne

To forbid us anything is to make us have a mind for it.

—Michel de Montaigne

Those who publicize a novel proposition are at first called heretics. But no one is a heretic unless he wishes to be, for he needs only to split the difference and to offer some subtle distinction to his accusers, and no matter what the distinction is, or whether it is intelligible or not, it renders a man pure as snow and worthy of being called orthodox.
—Charles-Louis de Secondat, baron de La Brède et de Montesquieu

Some people have found certain remarks excessively bold, but they are advised to regard the nature of the work itself. . . . Far from intending to touch upon any principle of our religion, he did not even suspect himself of imprudence. The remarks in question are always found joined to sentiments of surprise and astonishment, never to a sense of inquiry, and much less to one of criticism. . . .
—Charles-Louis de Secondat, baron de La Brède et de Montesquieu

The problem is the intolerance of the fundamentalists. I fight with my pen, and they want to fight with a sword. I say what I think and they want to kill me. I will never let them intimidate me.

—Taslima Nasrin

I am convinced that the only way the fundamentalist forces can be stopped is if all of us who are secular and humanistic join together and fight their malignant influence. I, for one, will not be silenced.

—Taslima Nasrin

My own mind is my own church.

—Thomas Paine

It was in vain, too, that you obtained from Rome the decree against Galileo, which condemned his opinions regarding the earth's movements. It will take more than that to prove it keeps still, and if there were consistent observations proving that it is the earth that goes round, all the men in the world put together could not stop it from turning, or themselves turning with it.

—Blaise Pascal

My prison shall be my grave before I will budge a jot, for I owe my conscience to no mortal man.

—William Penn

Criticism knows no infallible texts; its first possibility is to admit the possibilities of error in the text which it examines.

—Ernest Renan

Neither the burning nor the decrees will ever make me change my language. The theologians, in ordering me to be humble, will never make me false and the philosophers, by taxing me with hypocrisy, will never make me profess unbelief.

—Jean-Jacques Rousseau

You find magic, witchcraft, and wizardry in all sorts of classic children's books. Where do you stop? Are you going to stop at The Wizard of Oz? *Are you going to stop at C. S. Lewis? The talking animals in* Wind in the Willows?

—J. K. Rowling

What is freedom of expression? Without the challenge to offend, it ceases to exist. Without the freedom to challenge, even to satirize all orthodoxies, including religious orthodoxies, it ceases to exist. Language and the imagination cannot be imprisoned, or art will die, and with it, a little of what makes us human.

—Salman Rushdie

Everyone should be free to choose for himself the foundation of his creed, and that faith should be judged only by its fruits; each would then obey God freely with his whole heart; while nothing would be publicly honored save justice and charity.

—Baruch Spinoza

What greater evil can there be for a republic than that honorable men be thrust into exile like criminals, because they hold dissenting views and know not how to conceal them?

—Baruch Spinoza

There is no freedom either in civil or ecclesiastical [affairs], but where the liberty of the press is maintain'd.

—Matthew Tindal

429

Lord, open the King of England's eyes.

—William Tyndale

There is no other remedy for this epidemic illness [religious fanaticism] than the spirit of free thought, which, spreading little by little, finally softens men's customs, and prevents the renewal of the disease.

—Voltaire

If there are a dozen caterers, each of whom has a different recipe, must we on that account cut each other's throats instead of dining? On the contrary every man will eat well in his fashion with the cook who pleases him best.

—Voltaire

It is shameful to put one's mind into the hands of those whom you wouldn't entrust with your money. Dare to think for yourself.

—Voltaire

Those churches cannot be truly Christian . . . which either actually themselves, or by the civil power of kings and princes . . . doe persecute such as dissent from them or be opposite against them.

—Roger Williams

BIOGRAPHICAL PROFILES

PIERRE ABELARD (1079–1142)

French theologian, poet, and teacher who shifted the theological argument from reliance on authority to analysis by logic and reason. The church condemned and burned his *Introduction to Theology* (1120) in 1121. In 1140, he was charged with heresy, confined to a monastery and forbidden to continue writing. In the first Roman Index of Forbidden Books in 1559 and in the Tridentine Index of 1564, all of his writings were prohibited.

HENRY CORNELIUS AGRIPPA (1486–1535)

German Catholic scholar, allied with the humanists and reformers in Europe. *Of the Vanitie and Uncertaintie of Artes and Sciences* (1530), a satire on religion, morals, and society, was denounced and banned by the theological faculties of Louvain and the Sorbonne. His book on the occult, *De occulta philosophia* (1531), was banned in Cologne and Rome.

JEAN LE ROND D'ALEMBERT (1717–1783)

French mathematician and philosopher, coeditor with Denis Diderot until 1758 of the most important literary endeavor of the Enlightenment, the *Encyclopédie* (1751–72), which was censored repeatedly during the 21 years of its publication and placed on the Catholic Church's Index of Forbidden Books. He wrote the encyclopedia's *Preliminary Discourse* (1751) and contributed articles on mathematics, philosophy, and literature.

DANTE ALIGHIERI (1265–1321)

Florentine poet and author of the literary classic *The Divine Comedy*. In *On Monarchy* (1310–13), his treatise on political philosophy, Dante argued against papal control over secular authority. The pope condemned the book, and it was publicly burned in the marketplace of Bologna. In the 16th century, the Spanish Inquisition banned it, and it was listed on the Catholic Church's first Index of Forbidden Books, where it remained until the 19th century.

ARISTOTLE (384–322 B.C.)

One of the greatest of the ancient Greek philosophers. Born in Macedonia, he studied for 20 years under Plato at the Academy in Athens. In 335 B.C., he founded his own school, the Lyceum. Fifty of his works survived as notes or summaries of his lectures made by his students. In the 13th century, the provincial council of Paris and the pope forbade reading or teaching the natural philosophy or metaphysics of Aristotle as heretical. The bans on Aristotle were impossible to enforce and were gradually lifted.

KAREN ARMSTRONG (1944–)

British author of more than 20 books on comparative religion, including *Islam: A Short History* (2002) and *The Case for God* (2009). Armstrong, a former Catholic nun, is one of the world's leading commentators on religious affairs. *The Battle for God* (2000), which examines the foundations of religious fundamentalism in Christianity, Judaism, and Islam, was banned in Malaysia in 2006.

AVERROËS (IBN RUSHD) (1126–1198)

Spanish-Arab philosopher and physician from Córdoba who was among the outstanding figures of medieval philosophy. His extensive *Commentaries* (1168–90) on the works of Aristotle influenced the development of medieval Scholasticism. Church authorities banned his writings between 1210 and 1277 for proposing that philosophy could claim truth outside established religious sources. Nevertheless, his interpretation of Aristotle remained influential throughout the later Middle Ages and Renaissance.

FRANCIS BACON (1561–1626)

English philosopher, scientist, and statesman. Educated at Trinity College in Cambridge, he practiced law and served in Parliament. The Vatican placed on the Index of Forbidden Books *The Advancement of Learning* (1605), which advocated the inductive method of modern science. The Spanish Inquisition condemned all of his works.

ROGER BACON (CA. 1214–1294)

Franciscan friar and English scientist and philosopher who came under suspicion of heresy for advocating the experimental method. His great encyclopedic work, *Opus majus* (1268), was regarded as heretical. He was sent to prison and may have spent as many as 14 years behind bars.

TISSA BALASURIYA (1924–)

A Dominican priest and theologian. He is founder and director of the Centre for Society and Religion in Colombo, Sri Lanka, and a founding member of the Ecumenical Association of Third World Theologians. Balasuriya was excommunicated from the Catholic Church in January 1997 for his interpretation of church dogma in his book *Mary and Human Liberation*. A year later, the Vatican rescinded his excommunication.

PIERRE BAYLE (1647–1706)

French historian and philosopher, a notable advocate of religious toleration. His greatest work was his four-volume *Historical and Critical Dictionary* (1697), a compendium of historical biographies with comprehensive marginal notes viewed as subversive of religious orthodoxy. In the 18th century, as authorities fought the influence of Enlightenment thinking, the *Dictionary* was censored. It was burned in Germany and placed by the Vatican on the Index of Forbidden Books, where it remained through the first two-thirds of the 20th century.

JEREMY BENTHAM (1748–1832)

English jurist, philosopher, and social reformer, known as the father of utilitarianism. His *Introduction to the Principals of Morals and Legislation* (1789), a scientific attempt to assess the moral content of human action by focusing on its results and consequences, won him recognition throughout the Western world. His writing was placed by the Catholic Church on the Index of Forbidden Books, remaining listed through its last edition in effect until 1966.

HENRI BERGSON (1859–1941)

French philosopher and Nobel Prize winner, among the most influential thinkers of his time. In *Creative Evolution* (1907), he proposed a dynamic vision of the universe to reconcile evolutionary theory with Christian traditions of creation. In 1907, the Vatican condemned "modernist" views, and in 1914, it placed *Creative Evolution* on the Index of Forbidden Books. Bergson died of pneumonia in German-occupied Paris after standing in line to be registered as a Jew.

GEORGE BERKELEY (1658–1753)

Anglo-Irish philosopher and Anglican bishop, regarded as among the outstanding British classical empiricists. *Alciphron, or the Minute Philosopher* (1732), aimed at vindicating Christianity against the views of freethinkers and atheists, was placed on the Catholic Church's Index of Forbidden Books for anti-Catholic views. It remained listed through the Index's last edition in effect until 1966.

LEONARDO BOFF (1938–)

Brazilian Catholic theologian and former Franciscan priest, a leading exponent of liberation theology. In 1985, Boff was interrogated and censured by the Vatican for his views regarding the church's abuse of hierarchical power expressed in *Church: Charism and Power: Liberation Theology and the Institutional Church* (1981). Boff was sentenced to an "obedient silence," forbidding him to write, publish, or teach, which was lifted after 10 months. In 1991, Boff resigned from the priesthood.

DAN BROWN (1964–)

American novelist, author of many best-selling thrillers. His most successful novel, *The Da Vinci Code* (2003), has sold more than 80 million copies worldwide. His other novels include *Angels and Demons* (2000), *Deception Point* (2001), and *The Lost Symbol* (2009). *The Da Vinci Code*, which was viewed as offensive by the Vatican, was banned in Lebanon, Pakistan, Egypt, Iran, and several states in India.

SIR THOMAS BROWNE (1605–1682)

English Oxford-educated physician and writer. He expressed views of religious tolerance in *Religio Medici* (1643), a popular collection of his reflections on faith. In 1645, the Catholic Church placed it on the Index of Forbidden Books for its skeptical, rationalist perspective and its allegiance to the Anglican Church. The book remained listed until 1966.

GIORDANO BRUNO (1548–1600)

Italian philosopher, expelled from the Dominican religious order when he was charged with heresy. His major metaphysical work, *On the Infinite Universe and Worlds* (1584), refuted the traditional cosmology of Aristotle. He was arrested by the Inquisition in Venice and tried on charges of blasphemy and heresy. After seven years in prison, he was executed in 1600. The Catholic Church placed all his writings on the Index of Forbidden Books, where they were listed through the first two-thirds of the 20th century.

JOHN CALVIN (1509–1564)

French Protestant theologian of the Reformation. He wrote the first systematic and logical exposition of reform belief in *Institutes of the Christian Religion* (1536–59). Calvin's own translation of the work from the original Latin into French was the first theological treatise written in French prose. Calvin's writing was banned from England in 1555 and condemned on the Catholic Church's first Index of Forbidden Books in 1559 and on the Tridentine Index in 1564.

SEBASTIAN CASTELLIO (1515–1563)

French Protestant theologian, wrote the most important book favoring religious toleration to be published on the Continent during the 16th century, *Concerning Heretics* (1554). Prompted by the execution by Calvinists of Spanish heretic Michael Servetus, Castellio protested persecution by Christians carried out in the name of doctrine. In 1563, he was put on trial for heresy but died during the proceedings.

MIGUEL DE CERVANTES SAAVEDRA (1547–1616)

Self-educated son of a Spanish apothecary-surgeon who created one of the greatest and most enduring classics of European literature, *Don Quixote*

(1605, 1615), a burlesque of the popular romances of chivalry. In 1640, the novel was placed on the Spanish Index of Forbidden Books for a single sentence: "Works of charity performed negligently have neither merit nor value." In 1981, the Chilean military junta banned the novel for supporting individual freedom and attacking authority.

LINDSEY COLLEN (1948–)

A novelist and feminist political activist from South Africa who lives in Mauritius. Her second novel, *The Rape of Sita* (1993), won a 1994 Commonwealth Writers Prize for the best book from Africa but was banned by the Mauritian government and temporarily withdrawn by its publisher after protests by Hindu fundamentalists. She won her second Commonwealth Writers Prize for *Boy* (2004).

AUGUSTE COMTE (1798–1857)

French philosopher and social reformer, founder of the school of philosophy known as positivism. His six-volume *Course of Positive Philosophy* (1830–42) substituted a new religion of humanity and sociological ethics for metaphysics and revealed religion. The Catholic Church placed it on the Index of Forbidden Books. It remained banned through the last edition of the Index in effect until 1966.

CONFUCIUS (551–479 B.C.)

China's greatest philosopher, founder of the ethical and religious system of Confucianism, which was influential in China for millennia. *The Analects*, a collection of sayings and short dialogues compiled by his disciples during the third and fourth centuries B.C., was burned by Emperor Shi Huangdi in 221 B.C. During the Cultural Revolution in China in 1966–74, possession of Confucian writings again became dangerous.

NICOLAUS COPERNICUS (1473–1543)

Celebrated Polish astronomer. In *On the Revolution of Heavenly Spheres* (1543), he was the first person to propose the theory that the Earth moves around the Sun. The church viewed the Copernican theory as a challenge to orthodoxy. In 1616, the Catholic Church placed the book on the Index of Forbidden Books. The general prohibition against Copernicus's theories remained in effect until 1753, and his name was not removed from the Index until 1835.

THOMAS CRANMER (1489–1556)

English religious reformer. He was appointed archbishop of Canterbury by King Henry VIII in 1533 and shaped the doctrine and liturgical transformation of the Church of England during the reign of Edward VI. He was responsible for the writing of most of the first Book of Common Prayer in 1549, brought into compulsory use in the Church of England by act of Parliament, and for the 1552 revision of the book. In 1553, the Catholic Queen Mary banned the use of the Prayer Book. Cranmer was convicted of treason and heresy and executed.

SAVINIEN CYRANO DE BERGERAC (1619–1655)

French writer, playwright, scientist, and soldier, later the protagonist of Edmond's Rostand's 19th-century romantic drama. Cyrano satirized the customs and beliefs of his times in two science fiction narratives, *Voyage to the Moon* (1657) and *Voyage to the Sun* (1662). It was considered too dangerous to publish the material during his lifetime. After Cyrano's death his publisher expurgated the manuscripts so that his writing sounded nonsensical, lending credence to his posthumous reputation as insane or eccentric.

ROALD DAHL (1916–1990)

Award-winning British writer of 19 novels for children. His best-selling books, including *The BFG, Charlie and the Chocolate Factory, James and the Giant Peach,* and *Matilda,* are among the most frequently targeted for removal from school classrooms and libraries in the United States. *The Witches* tops the list of censored Dahl books because its theme of witchcraft offends Christian fundamentalists.

CHARLES DARWIN (1809–1882)

British naturalist, who in his *On the Origin of Species* (1859) introduced the concept of "descent with modification" to science. His book unleashed one of the most dramatic controversies of the era. A resurgence of opposition to Darwin's theories began in the 1920s in the United States and led to laws prohibiting the teaching of evolution in schools. Battles about the teaching of evolution have continued, especially at the local school board level. In the 1930s, the book was banned in Yugoslavia and in Greece.

ERASMUS DARWIN (1731–1802)

British physician and poet, one of the most eminent literary figures of his time. Sixty-five years before his grandson Charles Darwin revolutionized biological science, Darwin formulated an evolutionary system in his treatise on animal life, *Zoonomia* (1794–96). *Zoonomia*'s notoriety caused the Catholic Church to place it on the Index of Forbidden Books, where it remained listed until 1966.

DANIEL DEFOE (1660?–1731)

English novelist and journalist. He was one of the most prolific writers in the English language, with more than 500 works to his credit. In 1703,

Defoe was jailed, fined, and pilloried for his parody of religious intolerance, *The Shortest Way with the Dissenters* (1702). His *Political History of the Devil* (1726), about the influence of Satan in the world, was the only one of Defoe's works to be placed on the Index of Forbidden Books. It remained listed until 1966.

RENÉ DESCARTES (1596–1650)

French philosopher and scientist, the founder of modern philosophy and mathematics. By applying the methods and concepts of mathematical and natural sciences to philosophic inquiry in his *Discourse on Method* (1637) and *Meditations on First Philosophy* (1641), he launched an intellectual revolution. Descartes's philosophy was condemned by church, state, and universities in both France and Holland. The Catholic Church placed all of his writing on the Index of Forbidden Books in 1663. They remained listed until 1966.

CHARLES DICKENS (1812–1870)

British author, the most popular and most widely read writer of his time. Dickens's portrayal of the Jewish character Fagin, in his novel *Oliver Twist* (1838), has been the object of protest since the time of the novel's publication. In 1949, Jewish parents in Brooklyn, New York, contending that the book violated their children's rights to an education free of religious bias, sued to prevent study of the novel in public high schools. The Kings County Supreme Court ruled against the banning of the book.

DENIS DIDEROT (1713–1784)

French philosopher, dramatist, and critic, the primary editor of the *Encyclopédie* (1751–72), the greatest single work of the Enlightenment. Diderot was imprisoned for more than three months for flagrant disregard of religious orthodoxy in *Letter on the Blind* (1749), an analysis of the impact of the senses on moral and metaphysical ideas. The *Encyclopédie* was censored repeatedly during the 21 years of its publication. In 1804, the Catholic Church placed it on the Index of Forbidden Books, where it remained listed until 1966.

JOHN WILLIAM DRAPER (1811–1882)

One of the greatest American scientists of the 19th century. He worked on early experiments in photography, taught physiology to medical students, and spoke out in favor of the theory of evolution. In the last 20 years of his life, he sought to apply Charles Darwin's theories of biological evolution to human history and politics. His *History of the Conflict Between Religion and Science* (1874) was the first American book to be listed on the Index of Forbidden Books.

MEISTER (JOHANNES) ECKHART (ca. 1260–ca. 1328)

Influential German mystical theologian and preacher. He studied and taught at Paris, Strasbourg, and Cologne and held administrative positions in the Dominican order of friars. His systematic theological treatise, *Three-Part Work* (1311), never completed, was declared heretical by the pope.

JOHN ELIOT (1604–1690)

Puritan clergyman. He was among the first settlers to minister to the Indian tribes in Massachusetts. In *The Christian Commonwealth* (1659), Eliot laid out his plans for running a society according to the precepts of Mosaic law. The Algonquian Indians of Natick, Massachusetts, welcomed Eliot's ideas and governed their town according to his principles. In 1661, Eliot's book was banned in Massachusetts for stating that even royal authorities owed their power to higher source.

DESIDERIUS ERASMUS (1466?–1536)

Dutch writer, Catholic priest, and biblical scholar. He was an influential proponent of Christian humanism and a critic of abuses within the Catholic Church. His *Colloquies* (1518–33) and *The Praise of Folly* (1511) were condemned by the Sorbonne and the Parlement of Paris for allegedly heretical sympathies with Lutheranism. All of Erasmus's works were listed on the first Index of Forbidden Books established in 1559, a ban that remained until the 1930s.

ANATOLE FRANCE (JACQUES-ANATOLE THIBAULT) (1844–1924)

One of the most popular and influential French authors in his lifetime, awarded the Nobel Prize in literature in 1921. His novel *Penguin Island* (1908), a satirical history of France attacking the hypocrisies of organized religion and the Socialist Party, was placed on the Catholic Church's Index of Forbidden Books, along with all of his works. They remained on the Index until 1966.

SIGMUND FREUD (1856–1939)

The creator of psychoanalysis. He brought the scientific method into the study of everyday mental life. *Introductory Lectures on Psychoanalysis* (1933) was Freud's most widely read book, considered dangerous by the Catholic Church, which opposed psychoanalysis. In 1934, Pope Pius XI published a statement criticizing psychoanalysis and Freud's ideas on religious belief. Freud's writings were considered off-limits to Catholics as dangerous to faith and morals according to canon law. Freud's works were censored in the Soviet Union after 1930 and were among those burned by the Nazis in 1939.

GALILEO GALILEI (1564–1642)

Italian astronomer, mathematician, and physicist who laid the foundations for the development of modern experimental science. His *Dialogue Concerning the Two Chief World Systems* (1632) supported the Copernican Sun-centered system, determining that the Earth was not the center of creation. In 1663, Galileo was put on trial by the Inquisition in Rome for heresy. He was convicted to an indefinite prison sentence and ordered to abjure formally his errors. *Dialogue* was banned along with all of his work. In 1824, the church announced its acceptance of modern astronomy, and in 1992 Pope John Paul II formally rehabilitated Galileo.

EDWARD GIBBON (1737–1794)

English historian and Enlightenment thinker. His epic six-volume *History of the Decline and Fall of the Roman Empire* (1776–88) was one of the most widely read historical works of modern times. The Catholic Church viewed the two chapters on the rise of Christianity as contradicting official church history and placed the work on the Index of Forbidden Books. It remained listed through the last edition of the Index.

KAHLIL GIBRAN (1833–1931)

Lebanese-American writer and artist, best known for *The Prophet*, a book of poetical essays that has sold millions of copies worldwide. Gibran was a leader in the Arab-American community and published periodicals that influenced literary development in the Arab world. His *Spirits Rebellious* (1908), a collection of short stories protesting religious and political tyranny, was publicly burned in the Beirut marketplace and suppressed by the Syrian government. Gibran was exiled from Lebanon and excommunicated from the Maronite Church.

JOHANN WOLFGANG VON GOETHE (1749–1832)

German poet, dramatist, novelist, and scientist. He achieved lasting fame at the age of 25 when he published *The Sorrows of Young Werther* (1774, 1787), an epistolary romance about a young man's hopeless love affair and suicide. His novel became the literary sensation of the century. The Leipzig city council banned the book on the grounds that it recommended suicide. In Denmark, a proposed translation was forbidden for conflicting with Lutheran doctrine. In 1939, the dictatorship of Francisco Franco in Spain ordered libraries purged of Goethe's work.

GRAHAM GREENE (1904–1991)

English novelist and author of short stories, essays, and reviews. Greene, a convert to Catholicism, often portrayed sinful and despairing characters with sympathy and understanding. In 1953, after protests about his portrayal of the whiskey priest in his novel *The Power and the Glory* (1940), the Vatican requested that he change the book's text. Greene refused. A pastoral letter was read to churches in Britain condemning the book. Four other Greene novels were banned in Ireland as offensive to Catholics.

HUGO GROTIUS (1583–1645)

Dutch statesman, jurist, and theologian, regarded as the founder of modern international law. His *On the Law of War and Peace* (1625), which proposed a policy of religious toleration, was the first definitive text on the subject. In 1662, the States-General of the Netherlands banned the book. All of his books were condemned by the Spanish Inquisition, and in the 18th century his complete works were placed on the Index of Forbidden Books, where they remained until 1966.

JIM HASKINS (1941–2005)

Award-winning author of more than 100 books. Many of his books written for young people highlight the achievements of African Americans and illuminate the history and culture of Africa. Haskins was professor of English at the University of Florida, Gainesville. In 1992, St. Tammany Parish School Board in Louisiana, acting under pressure by Christian conservatives, voted to remove his *Voodoo & Hoodoo: Their Traditional Crafts as Revealed by Actual Practitioners* from all libraries in the school district because of its occult content, calling the book dangerous and without educational value. After a four-year legal battle, a federal appeals court ordered that the book be returned to the libraries.

SADEGH HEDAYAT (1903–1951)

The leading fiction writer of modern Iran. Hedayat's novel *The Blind Owl* (1937) is the most important and influential work of 20th-century Iranian literature. He was unable to publish the book in Iran until the 1940s. It remained in print until 1979, when it was banned by the Islamic Republic. During the presidency of reformist Mohammad Khatami from 1997 to 2005, *The Blind Owl* was again published in Iran. In 2005, with the ascension to power of Mahmoud Ahmadinejad's hard-line government, the book was once again banned, along with most of Hedayat's other major writings.

CLAUDE-ADRIEN HELVÉTIUS (1715–1771)

French Enlightenment philosopher and contributor to the *Encyclopédie*. He held the lucrative post of farmer-general, or tax collector. His utilitarian theories, as expressed in his first major work, *De l'esprit* (1758), influenced the British philosophers Jeremy Bentham, James Mill, and Adam Smith.

Banned by the archbishop of Paris, the pope, the Parlement of Paris, and the Sorbonne, the book became an underground best seller.

THOMAS HELWYS (?–1616)

English Separatist who withdrew from the Church of England and founded with John Murton the first permanent Baptist church in England. His *Short Declaration of the Mistery of Iniquity* (1612) was the first work published in English to advocate tolerance of all religions. Helwys was imprisoned on the orders of King James I for defending the ideas of religious freedom.

THOMAS HOBBES (1588–1679)

English philosopher, among the greatest 17th-century philosophers. His most important work, *Leviathan* (1651), was placed on the Catholic Church's Index of Forbidden Books and banned in Holland because of its frank materialism. Hobbes was forbidden thereafter by the English government from publishing his philosophic opinions. His complete works were listed on the Roman Index until 1966.

DAVID HUME (1711–1776)

Scottish philosopher and historian, one of the great empiricists of the Enlightenment. His *Inquiry Concerning Human Understanding* (1748) recommended the application of the scientific experimental method to the study of man and cast doubt on the veracity of miracles. Because of the furor over his writing, Hume's *Dialogues Concerning Natural Religion* (1779) did not appear until after his death. In 1827, all of his historical and philosophical works were placed on the Index of Forbidden Books, where they remained until 1966.

JAN HUS (1369?–1415)

Czech priest, theologian, religious reformer, and forerunner of the 16th-century Protestant Reformation. He was influenced by the views of English heretic John Wycliffe. In *De ecclesia* (1413), he denied the pope's infallibility and proposed that the state should supervise the church. Put on trial at the church Council of Constance, he was convicted of heresy. His books were destroyed, and he was burned at the stake.

SHERRY JONES (1961–)

American journalist and novelist. Publication of her historical novel *The Jewel of Medina* (2008), was canceled by Ballantine Books, an imprint of Random House, when the publishers became concerned about the potential of terrorist attacks by Muslim extremists. The novel is the story of Muhammad's rise to power, narrated by his child-bride and favorite wife, A'isha. In October 2008, the home and office of the book's British publisher was firebombed.

IMMANUEL KANT (1724–1804)

German philosopher, considered to be among the most important philosophers in Western culture. *The Critique of Pure Reason* (1781) marked the birth of the critical philosophy of transcendental idealism. In *Religion within the Limits of Reason Alone* (1793), he proposed a philosophy of ethical theism. He was forbidden by the king to write on religion, and *Religion* was banned by the Lutheran Church. The Vatican placed *The Critique* on the Index of Forbidden Books. All of Kant's writing was banned in the Soviet Union in 1928.

NIKOS KAZANTZAKIS (1883–1957)

Greek novelist, poet, dramatist, and translator. Born on Crete, he studied in Paris under the philosopher Henri Bergson. The Catholic Church placed his novel *The Last Temptation of Christ* (1953), an unorthodox portrait of Jesus, on the Index of Forbidden Books, and Kazantzakis was excommunicated from the Eastern Orthodox Church. A 1988 film of the novel by Martin Scorsese was censored in many countries, including in parts of the United States.

JOHANNES KEPLER (1571–1630)

German astronomer and mathematics professor who developed the first significant improvement of the astronomical theories of the 16th-century astronomer Nicolaus Copernicus. His *New Astronomy* (1609) is considered the most important book on astronomy ever published. The Vatican banned this book and his astronomy textbook under a general prohibition on reading or teaching heliocentric theory. The ban on his theories remained in effect until 1753.

JYTTE KLAUSEN (1954–)

Danish scholar of politics who teaches at Brandeis University in Massachusetts. She is the author of *The Cartoons That Shook the World*, published by Yale University Press in 2009, a scholarly study of the controversy that arose when a Danish newspaper published caricatures of the prophet Muhammad in 2005. Yale University Press, fearing violence by Muslim protestors, decided to expunge from the book reproductions of the cartoons involved in the Muhammad cartoons controversy, along with other historical images of Muhammad.

HANS KÜNG (1928–)

Swiss priest, prominent Catholic theologian, and retired professor of ecumenical theology at the University of Tübingen in Germany. He rejected the doctrine of papal infallibility in *Infallible? An Inquiry* (1970). In 1979, the Vatican withdrew his permission to teach in the name of the church and prohibited Catholic institutions from employing him.

JAMES W. LAINE (1952–   )

Professor of religious studies at Macalester College in St. Paul, Minnesota. He is the author of *Shivaji: Hindu King in Islamic India*. In 2003, Hindu fundamentalists, contending that he had insulted the reputation of Shivaji, the 17th-century Hindu king and warrior, ransacked the institute in Pune, India, where he had conducted research for his book. The book was banned in Maharashtra State in India, which brought criminal charges against Laine and his publisher and threatened to extradite him to India. A high court in Bombay stayed the criminal charges against him.

LI HONGZHI (1951–   )

Leader of Falun Gong, a philosophy of spiritual cultivation. Li introduced Falun Gong in China in 1992, and *Zhuan Falun* (Revolving of the law wheel), his main book of teachings, was published in 1994. In 1999, the Chinese government banned all Falun Gong publications for propagating ignorance and superstition. Thousands of Falun Gong adherents have been arrested. Li now lives in the United States.

JOHN LOCKE (1632–1704)

English philosopher known as the intellectual ruler of the 18th century and a founder of the school of philosophy known as British empiricism. Suspected of radicalism by the English government, he fled to Holland in 1683, where he completed *An Essay Concerning Human Understanding* (1690), one of the most important works in modern philosophy. The Latin version was prohibited at Oxford, and in 1700, the Catholic Church placed a French translation of the essay on the Index of Forbidden Books, where it remained until 1966.

MARTIN LUTHER (1483–1546)

German theologian and monk, the founder of the Protestant Reformation. His *Ninety-five Theses* (1517) challenged Catholic Church doctrine on indulgences and was banned by the pope in 1520. His writings attacking papal authority and rejecting the priesthood and the sacraments led to his excommunication and the destruction and banning of his works throughout Europe.

NAGUIB MAHFOUZ (1911–2006)

Egyptian author of 33 novels and many collections of short stories. In 1988, Mahfouz was the first Arab writer to win the Nobel Prize. His novel *Children of the Alley* (1959) was banned until after his death in 2006 for blasphemy against Islam. Since 1959, Mahfouz had been threatened by religious fundamentalists offended by his novel. In October 1994, he was stabbed by an Islamist terrorist.

MOSES MAIMONIDES (1135–1204)

Court physician, jurist, and leader of Egypt's Jewish community; the most important Jewish medieval philosopher. In his principal philosophical work, *The Guide of the Perplexed* (1197), he sought to reconcile Judaism with Aristotle's teaching. In 1232 in France, the work was banned from Jewish homes under penalty of excommunication. At the request of French rabbis, friars confiscated and burned copies of the book. Three hundred years later, it was condemned by the yeshiva of Lublin, Poland, and it still faced bans in the 19th century.

BERNARD MANDEVILLE (1670–1733)

Dutch physician who lived in London; his *Fable of the Bees* (1714–28) was one of the most controversial and widely read books of the time. His moral fable about the symbiotic relationship between vice and national greatness was the target of attacks in the press, pulpits, and courts that lasted through most of the century. The book was presented twice by an English grand jury for blasphemy, and in France it was ordered burned. The Vatican listed it on the Index of Forbidden Books, where it remained until 1966.

FATIMA MERNISSI (1941–   )

Moroccan sociologist and Koranic scholar, author of highly regarded books on Islam. She teaches at Mohammed V University in Rabat, Morocco. Her study of women's status under Islam, *The Veil and the Male Elite* (1987), was banned in Morocco, Saudi Arabia, and the Persian Gulf States. The translator and publisher of an edition of the book published in Iran were arrested and convicted of insulting Islam.

JOHN STUART MILL (1806–1873)

British philosopher, economist, and social reformer. Mill was one of the leading intellectual figures of the 19th century. The Catholic Church placed his *System of Logic* (1843), the standard philosophical text of the time, and *Principles of Political Economy* (1848), his treatise on economic theory, on the Index of Forbidden Books for reflecting modernist and liberal theories. They remained listed until 1966.

MICHEL DE MONTAIGNE (1533–1592)

French humanist writer, the originator of the personal essay as a literary form. In his *Essays* (1580), he set out to test his judgment on a wide range of subjects, revealing his inner life and personality. His book was confiscated on a trip to Rome, and a papal censor ordered revisions in the *Essays*. In 1595, an unauthorized Protestant version expurgated the book. The Spanish Inquisition condemned it, and in 1676 the Catholic Church placed it on the Index of Forbidden Books, where it remained for almost 300 years.

CHARLES-LOUIS DE SECONDAT, BARON DE LA BRÈDE ET DE MONTESQUIEU (1689–1755)

French novelist, jurist, and political philosopher. His best-selling satirical novel on French institutions, *The Persian Letters* (1721), and his influential treatise on political theory, *The Spirit of Laws* (1748), circulated underground in France. Both were condemned by the Catholic Church and remained on the Index of Forbidden Books until 1966.

TASLIMA NASRIN (1962–)

Bangladeshi physician, novelist, journalist, and poet. She is the author of more than 20 books. Her novel *Lajja* (*Shame*) (1993), about the persecution of Hindus by Muslims in Bangladesh, was banned in Bangladesh, and a death decree was proclaimed against her by a Muslim cleric. When a warrant was issued for her arrest, she went into exile in Europe. Four volumes of her autobiography also have been banned in Bangladesh.

THOMAS PAINE (1737–1809)

Anglo-American political theorist and revolutionary pamphleteer. He was indicted by the British government on the charge of seditious libel for *The Rights of Man* (1791–92), a work defending the French Revolution. British authorities banned *The Age of Reason* (1794–95), an attack on Christianity based on the principles of deism and rationalism. For 25 years, the British government pursued publishers and booksellers of *The Age of Reason*, prosecuting and imprisoning them on blasphemy charges.

SHAHRNUSH PARSIPUR (1946–)

Iranian writer in exile. She is the author of 11 books of fiction and a memoir. Parsipur was jailed three times under the Islamic Republic for her writing. Her novels *Women Without Men: A Novel of Modern Iran* and *Touba and the Meaning of Night* were banned after their publication in Iran as "un-Islamic." She now lives and writes in the United States.

BLAISE PASCAL (1632–1662)

French scientist, mathematician, and religious philosopher. He was a convert to Jansenism, a reform movement within Catholicism. His defense of Jansenism in *The Provincial Letters* (1656–57) made a mockery of Jesuit theological disputes. King Louis XIV ordered *Letters*, an underground best seller, to be burned, and it became too dangerous to continue its publication. The Catholic Church placed both *Letters* and a 1776 edition of *Pensées*, his thoughts in defense of religious belief, with an introduction by Voltaire, on the Index of Forbidden Books. They remained listed until 1966.

WILLIAM PENN (1644–1718)

English-born religious reformer and founder of Pennsylvania. He was an early convert to the Society of Friends, also known as Quakers. His frequent pleas for religious tolerance and freedom of conscience earned him the enmity of English religious and secular authorities. After publishing *The Sandy Foundation Shaken* (1668), which refuted Presbyterian views of the Trinity, he was imprisoned for eight months in the Tower of London on charges of blasphemy.

PIERRE-JOSEPH PROUDHON (1809–1865)

French social theorist, anarchist philosopher, and reformer. He became notorious with a series of pamphlets and books in which he condemned abuses of private property and church and state absolutism. Proudhon's books were seized, and he fled to Belgium to avoid arrest. The Catholic Church placed all of his works on the Index of Forbidden Books, where they remained until 1966.

PHILIP PULLMAN (1946–)

British author of the award-winning His Dark Materials trilogy of young adult fantasy novels. His trilogy includes *The Golden Compass* (1995), *The Subtle Knife* (1997), and *The Amber Spyglass* (2000). A campaign against the books by a conservative Catholic organization led to hundreds of requests to remove them from school libraries and curricula in the United States and Canada. In 2007, according to the American Library Association (ALA), *The Golden Compass* was the fourth most-challenged book in the United States, and in 2008 the His Dark Materials trilogy was listed second.

WILLIAM PYNCHON (1590?–1662)

English colonist and fur merchant. After arriving in Massachusetts in 1630, he founded the cities of Roxbury and Springfield. He began writing theology in 1650, and his long-hidden unorthodox religious ideas surprised and angered his Puritan neighbors. His *Meritorious Price of Our Redemption* (1650) was the first book to be burned publicly in the British colonies in North America. Facing punishments for his writings, he returned to England.

ERNEST RENAN (1823–1892)

French historian, critic, and philologist. Renan studied religion from a historical, rather than a theological, perspective. The Catholic Church condemned his *Life of Jesus* (1863), the first biography of Jesus to use modern historical methods. It was placed on the Index of Forbidden Books, along with 19 other works by Renan, and remained listed until 1966.

JEAN-JACQUES ROUSSEAU (1712–1778)

Swiss-French philosopher and novelist who expressed the visionary theories that generated the romantic movement in literature. His two most influential works were *Émile* (1762), a novel about his ideas on education, and *The Social Contract* (1762), about his political philosophy. *Émile* was condemned by the archbishop and Parlement of Paris, the Sorbonne, and the Inquisition. Rousseau fled France to avoid arrest. In 1763, *Émile* and *The Social Contract* were banned in Geneva. Both books were placed on the Spanish and Roman Indexes of Forbidden Books and remained proscribed to Catholics until 1966.

J. K. ROWLING (1965–)

Author of the Harry Potter series of novels for young readers. The Harry Potter books, which chronicle the adventures of a boy in wizardry school, have sold more than 400 million copies worldwide. The novels have topped the list of books targeted for banning from school curricula and libraries in the United States because they deal with themes of wizardry and witchcraft.

SALMAN RUSHDIE (1947–)

British writer who was born in India; the most censored author of the 20th century. His fourth novel, *The Satanic Verses* (1988), was banned in many countries throughout the world for its perceived offenses against the Islamic faith. In 1989, Iran's clerical leader, Ayatollah Ruhollah Khomeini, issued a death decree against Rushdie, forcing him to go into hiding under protection of the British government. Acts of terrorism against publishers and translators of the book continued through 1993. Only in 1995 was Rushdie able to make public appearances, still under police protection.

NAWAL EL SAADAWI (1931–)

Egyptian physician, sociologist, novelist, and author of essays and books on women's issues. She is one of the most widely translated Egyptian writers and a prominent feminist. After publishing *Women and Sex* (1972), she was dismissed from the Egyptian Ministry of Health and her book was recalled by its publisher. The Egyptian government refused a permit to publish *The Hidden Face of Eve* (1977). A Lebanese edition was barred from Egypt and many Arab countries. She was blacklisted from Egyptian radio and television and has been the target of death threats by fundamentalists.

GIROLAMO SAVONAROLA (1452–1498)

Dominican monk, Italian religious reformer, and charismatic preacher. He became the spiritual leader of Florence after the fall of the Medici in 1494 and organized the censorious "bonfires of the vanities." In his *Compendium revelationum* (1495), he claimed a divine calling to convert Florence to the life of the spirit. The pope excommunicated him and forbade him from preaching. In 1498, he was convicted of heresy and schism, hanged, and burned with all of his writings.

MICHAEL SERVETUS (1511–1533)

Spanish theologian and physician. He became notorious at the age of 20 for *On the Errors of the Trinity* (1531). His book was banned, and he was hunted by the Spanish and French Inquisitions as well as by the Protestants. In *Christianity Restored* (1552), published secretly, Servetus attacked the doctrine of the Trinity and the practice of infant baptism. He was arrested in Geneva on John Calvin's orders and burned at the stake for heresy. Servetus's death sparked the first important controversy over the issue of toleration within Protestantism.

HANAN AL-SHAYKH (1943–)

Novelist born in Lebanon and educated in Egypt; she worked as a journalist in Beirut and now lives in London. Her novel *The Story of Zahra* (1980) is still banned in Saudi Arabia and other Arab countries for offending religious authorities by its explicit portrayal of sexuality and its indictment of social hypocrisy in contemporary Arab society.

BARUCH (BENEDICT) SPINOZA (1632–1677)

Dutch rationalist philosopher who was expelled from Amsterdam's Jewish community for questioning traditional tenets of Judaism. His *Theological-Political Treatise* (1670), setting out foundations for a rational interpretation of religious doctrine, was the only book he could publish during his lifetime. Spinoza's writing, including his masterpiece, *Ethics* (1677), was widely banned in Holland as atheistic and subversive, and in 1679, the Catholic Church placed all of his work on Index of Forbidden Books. They remained listed until 1966.

STENDHAL (MARIE-HENRI BEYLE) (1783–1842)

French author, considered among the greatest French novelists of the 19th century. His novel *The Red and the Black* (1831), which lacked a religious worldview and was bitterly critical of the Jesuits, was placed by the Vatican on the Index of Forbidden Books, listed until 1966. In 1850, the novel was banned in czarist Russia, and in 1939, it was prohibited by the dictatorship of Francisco Franco in Spain.

EMANUEL SWEDENBORG (1688–1772)

Swedish scientist and theologian whose writings form the doctrine of the Church of the New Jerusalem. His most notable scientific volume, *Principia* (1721), which proposed a rational mathematical explanation of the universe, was placed on the Catholic Church's Index of Forbidden Books and remained listed for more than two centuries. The Swedish government banned his mystical theological works, including *Arcana coelestia* (1747–58), as heretical for contradicting Lutheran doctrine.

JONATHAN SWIFT (1667–1745)

Anglo-Irish satirist, novelist, and Anglican clergyman. Swift burlesqued the historical development of the Christian religions in *A Tale of a Tub* (1704–10). The controversy over the book dashed his chances for further advancement in the Anglican Church. In 1734, the Catholic Church placed it on the Index of Forbidden Books. It was listed until 1881.

MATTHEW TINDAL (1655–1753)

English deist who belonged to the Church of England. His *Rights of the Christian Church Asserted* (1706), which favored the subordination of the church to state authority, established his notoriety as a freethinker. In 1707, an English grand jury made a presentment against the book, and in 1710, it was proscribed by Parliament and burned.

JOHN TOLAND (1670–1722)

Irish deist who earned his living as a writer and publicist for radical Whig causes. He wrote some 200 works, including *Christianity Not Mysterious* (1696), asserting that neither God nor revelation is above the comprehension of human reason. The book was presented by an English grand jury and ordered burned for heresy by the Irish parliament. Toland escaped arrest by fleeing to Holland.

WILLIAM TYNDALE (1494?–1536)

Protestant reformer and linguist. He was the first person to translate the Bible into English from the original Greek and Hebrew and the first to print the Bible in English. Tyndale's 1526 translation of the New Testament was burned in England. Arrested in Belgium in 1535, he was convicted on charges of heresy and executed. Tyndale's translations were incorporated in later Bible editions, including the Authorized King James Version begun in 1604 and completed in 1611.

POLYDORE VERGIL (VIRGIL) (ca. 1470–1555)

Italian humanist. Vergil lived in England, where he served as the archdeacon of Wells. His three-volume *De inventoribus rerum* (1499), a reference book tracing the inventions of civilization, was among the most popular books of the 16th and 17th centuries. It was condemned by the Sorbonne and listed on the Spanish, Liège, and Roman Indexes of Forbidden Books. The Catholic Church published an expurgated edition in 1576 removing criticisms of the church, and an English translator rewrote another edition of the book to give it a more Protestant flavor.

VOLTAIRE (FRANÇOIS-MARIE AROUET) (1694–1778)

French author and philosopher, the chief standardbearer of the Enlightenment. His *Letters Concerning the English Nation* (1733) was printed clandestinely, banned by the French Parlement, burned by the public executioner, and placed on the Catholic Church's Index of Forbidden Books, along with 38 other books by Voltaire. His *Philosophical Dictionary* (1764) was banned and burned in France, Geneva, the Netherlands, and Rome.

ROGER WILLIAMS (1603–1682)

Puritan minister and founder of the Massachusetts Bay Colony. Williams was exiled from Salem to the wilderness of Rhode Island for his belief in freedom of worship. His tract, *The Bloudy Tenent of Persecution* (1644), favoring separation of church and state and denouncing religious repression, was burned by order of the English parliament in 1644.

JOHN WYCLIFFE (1328–1384)

English religious scholar and reformer. Wycliffe studied and taught theology at Oxford. He was the most eminent heretic to challenge the Catholic Church before the 16th-century Protestant Reformation. The pope condemned his treatise *On Civil Lordship* (1376). A council at Oxford prohibited his work as heretical and forbade him from preaching or lecturing. In 1415, a church council in Germany ordered his bones exhumed and burned and his ashes thrown into a running stream.

LAURENCE YEP (1948–)

Author and university professor from San Francisco who has written more than 20 books. His novels about Chinese Americans for children and young adults have won numerous prizes. The Newbery Honor winner *Dragonwings* (1975), about a boy who emigrates from China to San Francisco in 1905, was the target of censorship in Pennsylvania in 1992. A Pentecostal minister who objected to allusions to Eastern religion in the book brought suit to prevent it from being used in the eighth-grade curriculum of a public school. The county court denied the request to ban the book.

BIBLIOGRAPHY

BOOKS

Accad, Evelyne. "Rebellion, Maturity and the Social Context: Arab Women's Special Contribution to Literature." In *Arab Women: Old Boundaries, New Frontiers*, edited by Judith Tucker, 240–245. Bloomington: Indiana University Press, 1993.

Appelbaum, David. *The Vision of Kant.* Rockport, Mass.: Element Books, 1995.

Appignanesi, Lisa, and Sara Maitland, eds. *The Rushdie File.* Syracuse, N.Y.: Syracuse University Press, 1990.

Armstrong, Karen. *The Battle for God.* New York: Ballantine Books, 2000.

Armytage, Frances, and Juliette Tomlinson. *The Pynchons of Springfield: Founders and Colonizers* (1636–1702). Springfield, Mass.: Connecticut Valley Historical Museum, 1969.

Bachman, Albert. *Censorship in France from 1715–1750: Voltaire's Opposition.* New York: Burt Franklin, 1971.

Bachschneider, Paula R. *Daniel Defoe: His Life.* Baltimore: Johns Hopkins University Press, 1989.

Bacon, Francis. *Francis Bacon: A Selection of His Works.* Edited by Sidney Warhaft. Indianapolis, Ind.: Odyssey Press, 1981.

Bahr, Lauren S., editorial director, and Bernard Johnston, editor in chief. *Collier's Encyclopedia.* New York: Macmillan Educational, 1992.

Bainton, Roland. *Here I Stand: A Life of Martin Luther.* New York: Penguin Group, 1995.

———. *Hunted Heretic. The Life and Death of Michael Servetus.* Gloucester, Mass.: Peter Smith, 1978.

Balasuriya, Tissa. *Mary and Human Liberation: The Story and the Text.* Harrisburg, Pa.: Trinity Press International, 1997.

Barker, George F. *Memoir of John William Draper, 1811–1882.* Reprint ed. New York: Garland Publishing, 1974.

Bates, Stephen. *Battleground: One Mother's Crusade, the Religious Right, and the Struggle for Control of Our Classrooms.* New York: Poseidon Press, 1993.

Baumgardt, Carola. *Johannes Kepler: Life and Letters.* Introduction by Albert Einstein. New York: Philosophical Library, 1951.

Bentham, Jeremy. *The Principles of Morals and Legislation.* Buffalo, N.Y.: Prometheus Books, 1988.

Berkeley, George. *The Works of George Berkeley.* Vol. 2: *Philosophical Works, 1732–33.* Preface by Alexander Campbell Fraser. Oxford: Clarendon Press, 1931.

Boase, Alan M. *The Fortunes of Montaigne: A History of the Essays in France 1580–1669.* New York: Octagon Books, 1970.

Boff, Leonardo. *Church: Charism and Power: Liberation Theology and the Institutional Church.* New York: Crossroad, 1985.

Bokenkotter, Thomas. *A Concise History of the Catholic Church.* New York: Doubleday, 1977.

The Book of Common Prayer. New York: Seabury Press, 1977.

Boorstein, Daniel J. *The Discoverers: A History of Man's Search to Know His World and Himself.* New York: Random House, 1983.

Booth, Jack, ed. *Catch a Rainbow.* Impressions Reading Series. Toronto: Holt, Rinehart and Winston of Canada, 1984.

———. *Good Morning Sunshine.* Impressions Reading Series. Toronto: Holt, Rinehart and Winston of Canada, 1984.

Boulting, William. *Giordano Bruno: His Life, Thought and Martyrdom.* New York: Books for Libraries Press, 1972.

Boyle, Kevin, ed. *Article 19: World Report 1988.* New York: Times Books, 1988.

Brombert, Victor, ed. *Stendhal: A Collection of Critical Essays.* Englewood Cliffs, N.J.: Prentice Hall, 1962.

Brown, Dan. *The Da Vinci Code.* New York: Doubleday, 2003.

Browne, Janet. *Charles Darwin: Voyaging, Volume I of a Biography.* New York: Alfred A. Knopf, 1995.

Browne, Sir Thomas. *The Religio Medici and Other Writings of Sir Thomas Browne.* Introduction by C. H. Herford. New York: E. P. Dutton, 1906.

Burgess, Walter H. *John Smith, Thomas Helwys and the First Baptist Church in England.* London: James Clarke, 1911.

Burke, Redmond A. *What Is the Index?* Milwaukee: Bruce Publishing, 1952.

Burman, Edward. *The Inquisition: Hammer of Heresy.* New York: Dorset Press, 1992.

Burne, Peter. *Natural Religion and the Nature of Religion: The Legacy of Deism.* London: Routledge, 1991.

Burress, Lee. *Battle of the Books: Library Censorship in the Public Schools, 1950–1985.* Metuchen, N.J.: Scarecrow Press, 1989.

Burt, Henry M. *The First Century of the History of Springfield: The Official Records from 1636 to 1736.* Springfield, Mass.: privately printed, 1898.

Cassirer, Ernst. *Kant's Life and Thought.* Trans. James Hader. Introduction by Stephan Korner. New Haven, Conn.: Yale University Press, 1981.

Castellio, Sebastian. *Concerning Heretics, Whether They Are to Be Persecuted and How They Are to Be Treated.* Trans. and introduction by Roland H. Bainton. New York: Columbia University Press, 1935.

Chadbourne, Richard M. *Ernest Renan.* New York: Twayne Publishers, 1968.

———. *Ernest Renan as an Essayist.* Ithaca, N.Y.: Cornell University Press, 1957.

Chappell, Vere, ed. *The Cambridge Companion to Locke.* Cambridge: Cambridge University Press, 1994.

Christie-Murray, David. *A History of Heresy.* Oxford: Oxford University Press, 1976.

Clark, Ronald W. *Freud: The Man and the Cause.* London: Jonathan Cape; Weidenfeld and Nelson, 1980.

Colledge, Edmund, and Bernard McGinn, eds. and intro. *Meister Eckhart: The Essential Sermons, Commentaries, Treatises, and Defense.* New York: Paulist Press, 1981.

Collen, Lindsey. *The Rape of Sita.* Portsmouth, N.H.: Heinemann Educational Books, 1995.

Collins, Paul. *The Modern Inquisition: Seven Prominent Catholics and Their Struggles with the Vatican.* Woodstock, N.Y.: Overlook Press, 2002.

Collinson, Diané. *Fifty Major Philosophers: A Reference Guide.* London: Routledge, 1988.

Conroy, Peter V., Jr. *Montesquieu Revisited.* New York: Twayne Publishers, 1992.

Cook, Richard I. *Bernard Mandeville.* New York: Twayne Publishers, 1974.

Copleston, Frederick. *A History of Philosophy.* 6 vols. New York: Doubleday, 1993–94.

Costigan, Giovanni. *Sigmund Freud: A Short Biography.* New York: Macmillan Company, 1965.

Covey, Cyclone. *The Gentle Radical: A Biography of Roger Williams.* New York: Macmillan, 1966.

Cox, Harvey. *The Silencing of Leonardo Boff: The Vatican and the Future of World Christianity.* Oak Park, Ill.: Meyer Stone Books, 1988.

Cragg, G. R. *Reason and Authority in the Eighteenth Century.* Cambridge: Cambridge University Press, 1964.

Craig, Alec. *Suppressed Books: A History of the Conception of Literary Obscenity.* Cleveland: World Publishing, 1963.

Curtis, Michael, ed. and introduction. *The Great Political Theories.* Vol. 1. New York: Avon Books, 1981.

Cyrano de Bergerac, Savinien. *Voyages to the Moon and the Sun.* Translated and with an introduction and notes by Richard Aldington. New York: Orion Press, 1962.

Dahl, Roald. *The Witches.* New York: Farrar, Straus and Giroux, 1983.

Daniell, David. *Let There Be Light: William Tyndale and the Making of the English Bible.* London: British Library, 1994.

———. *William Tyndale: A Biography.* New Haven, Conn.: Yale University Press, 1994.

Dante. *On Monarchy and Three Political Letters.* Translated and with an introduction by Donald Nicholl. London: Weidenfeld and Nicholson, 1954.

Dargan, Edwin Preston. *Anatole France.* New York: Oxford University Press, 1937.

Darnton, Robert. *The Business of Enlightenment: A Publishing History of the Encyclopédie 1775–1800.* Cambridge, Mass.: Belknap Press of Harvard University Press, 1979.

Darwin, Charles. *The Autobiography of Charles Darwin: 1809–1882.* Ed. Nora Barlow. New York: W. W. Norton, 1993.

Defoe, Daniel. *The Political History of the Devil, as Well Ancient as Modern.* Reprint ed. New York: AMS Press, 1973.

DelFattore, Joan. *What Johnny Shouldn't Read: Textbook Censorship in America.* New Haven, Conn.: Yale University Press, 1992.

Demac, Donna A. *Liberty Denied: The Current Rise of Censorship in America.* New York: PEN American Center, 1988.

Descartes, René. *Discourse on Method.* Translated and with an introduction by Laurence J. Lafleur. Indianapolis, Ind.: Bobbs-Merrill, 1956.

———. *Meditations on First Philosophy.* Translated and with an introduction by Laurence J. Lafleur. New York: Bobbs-Merrill, 1960.

Dickens, Charles. *Oliver Twist.* Introduction by Irving Howe. New York: Bantam Books, 1982.

Diderot, Denis. *Diderot's Selected Writings.* Edited and with an introduction by Lester G. Crocker. Trans. Derek Coltman. New York: Macmillan, 1966.

Dinwiddy, John. *Bentham.* Oxford: Oxford University Press, 1989.

Djebar, Assia. *Algerian White.* New York: Seven Stories Press, 2000.

Donaghy, Henry J., ed. *Conversations with Graham Greene.* Jackson: University Press of Mississippi, 1992.

Doyle, Robert P. *Books Challenged or Banned in 2008–2009.* Chicago: American Library Association, 2009.

———. *Books Challenged or Banned in 2006–2007.* Chicago: American Library Association, 2007.

———. *Books Challenged or Banned in 2005–2006.* Chicago: American Library Association, 2006.

Doyle, Robert P. *Banned Books: 2004 Resource Book.* Chicago: American Library Association, 2004.

———. *Books Challenged or Banned in 2001–2002.* Chicago: American Library Association, 2002.

———. *Books Challenged or Banned 2002–2003.* Chicago: American Library Association, 2003.

———. *2000–2001: Books Challenged or Banned.* Chicago: American Library Association, 2002.

Draper, John William. *History of the Conflict Between Religion and Science.* Reprint, Westmead, England: Gregg International Publishers, 1970.

Dunham, Barrows, *Heroes and Heretics: A Political History of Western Thought.* New York: Alfred A. Knopf, 1964.

Dunn, Mary Maples, and Richard S. Dunn, eds. *The Papers of William Penn.* Vol. 1: *1644–1679.* Philadelphia: University of Pennsylvania Press, 1981.

Dunn, Richard S., and Mary Maples Dunn, eds. *The World of William Penn.* Philadelphia: University of Pennsylvania Press, 1986.

Durant, Will, and Ariel Durant. *The Age of Voltaire.* New York: Simon and Schuster, 1965.

Durnbauld, Edward. *The Life and Legal Writings of Hugo Grotius.* Norman: University of Oklahoma Press, 1969.

Earle, Peter. *The World of Defoe.* New York: Atheneum, 1977.

Eckehart, Meister. *Meister Eckehart Speaks.* Translated by Elizabeth Strakosch. Edited and with an introduction by Otto Karrer. New York: Philosophical Library, 1957.

Eckhart, Meister. *Meister Eckhart: A Modern Translation.* Translated and with an introduction by Raymond Bernard Blakney. New York: Harper and Row, 1941.

Eliot, John. *The Christian Commonwealth: Or, the Civil Policy of the Rising Kingdom of Jesus Christ.* Reprint, New York: Arno Press, 1972.

Endy, Melvin B., Jr. *William Penn and Early Quakerism.* Princeton, N.J.: Princeton University Press, 1973.

Erasmus, Desiderius. *The Colloquies of Erasmus.* Translated and with an introduction by Craig R. Thompson. Chicago: University of Chicago Press, 1965.

———. *The Praise of Folly.* Translated by John Wilson. Ann Arbor: University Michigan Press, 1958.

———. *Ten Colloquies of Erasmus.* Translated and with an introduction by Craig R. Thompson. New York: Liberal Arts Press, 1957.

Erlanger, Rachael. *The Unarmed Prophet: Savonarola in Florence.* New York: McGraw Hill, 1988.

Farah, Caesar E. *Islam: Belief and Observances.* New York: Barron's Educational Services, 1987.

Fleming, Donald. *John William Draper and the Religion of Science.* Philadelphia: University of Pennsylvania Press, 1950.

Foerstel, Herbert N. *Banned in the U.S.A.: A Reference Guide to Book Censorship in Schools and Public Libraries.* Revised and expanded ed. Westport, Conn.: Greenwood Publishing, 2002.

Foner, Eric. *Tom Paine and Revolutionary America.* London: Oxford University Press, 1976.

For Rushdie: Essays by Arab and Muslim Writers in Defense of Free Speech. New York: George Braziller, 1994.

Frame, Donald M., trans. and intro. *The Complete Essays of Montaigne*. Stanford, Calif.: Stanford University Press, 1958.

———. *The Complete Works of Montaigne*. Stanford, Calif.: Stanford University Press, 1967.

France, Anatole. *Penguin Island*. Translated by A. W. Evans. New York: Dodd, Mead, 1909.

Freidel, David, Linda Schele, and Joy Parker. *Maya Cosmos: Three Thousand Years on the Shaman's Path*. New York: William Morrow, 1993.

Freud, Sigmund. *The Complete Introductory Lectures on Psychoanalysis*. Edited and translated by James Strachey. New York: W. W. Norton, 1966.

Friedenthal, Richard. *Goethe: His Life and Times*. New York: World Publishing, 1963.

Gallenkamp, Charles. *Maya: The Riddle and Discovery of a Lost Civilization*. New York: David McKay, 1976.

Garraty, John A., and Peter Gay. *The Columbia History of the World*. New York: Harper and Row, 1972.

Garlow, James L., and Peter Jones. *Cracking Da Vinci's Code*. Wheaton, Ill.: Victor Books, 2004.

Gaustad, Edwin S. *Liberty of Conscience: Roger Williams in America*. Grand Rapids, Mich.: Wm. B. Eerdmans Publishing, 1991.

Gay, Peter. *Freud: A Life for Our Times*. New York: W. W. Norton, 1988.

———. *The Enlightenment: An Interpretation. The Rise of Modern Paganism*. New York: W. W. Norton, 1995.

Gellinek, Christian. *Hugo Grotius*. Boston: Twayne Publishers, 1983.

George, Leonard. *Crimes of Perception: An Encyclopedia of Heresies and Heretics*. New York: Paragon House, 1995.

Gerber, Jane S. *The Jews of Spain: A History of the Sephardic Experience*. New York: Free Press, 1992.

Gibbon, Edward. *Memoirs of My Life*. Edited and with an introduction by Betty Radice. London: Penguin Books, 1984.

Gibran, Jean, and Kahlil Gibran. *Kahlil Gibran: His Life and Work*. New York: Interlink Books, 1981.

Gibran, Kahlil. *Spirits Rebellious*. Translated by Anthony Rizcallah Ferris. New York: Philosophical Library, 1947.

Goethe, Johann Wolfgang von. *The Sorrows of Young Werther*. Translated and with an introduction by Michael Hulse. London: Penguin Books, 1989.

———. *The Sorrows of Young Werther and Selected Writings*. Translated by Catherine Hutter. Foreword by Hermann J. Weigand. New York: New American Library, 1962.

———. *The Sufferings of Young Werther*. Translated and with an introduction by Bayard Quincy Morgan. New York: Frederick Ungar Publishing, 1957.

Gould, Stephen Jay. *Ever Since Darwin: Reflections on Natural History*. New York: W. W. Norton, 1977.

Grane, Leif. *Peter Abelard: Philosophy and Christianity in the Middle Ages*. Translated by Frederick Crowley and Christine Crowley. New York: Harcourt, Brace and World, 1970.

Green, Jonathon, and Nicholas J. Karolides, reviser. *The Encyclopedia of Censorship, New Edition*. New York: Facts On File, 2005.

Greene, Graham. *A Sort of Life*. New York: Simon and Schuster, 1971.

———. *The Power and the Glory*. New York: Penguin Books, 1971.

———. *Ways of Escape*. New York: Simon and Schuster, 1980.

Haight, Anne Lyon. *Banned Books: 387 BC to 1978 AD.* Updated and enlarged by Chandler B. Grannis. New York: R. R. Bowker, 1978.

Hall, Constance Margaret. *The Sociology of Pierre Joseph Proudhon (1809–65).* New York: Philosophical Library, 1971.

Hampshire, Stuart, ed. *The Age of Reason: The 17th-Century Philosophers.* New York: New American Library, 1956.

———. *Spinoza: An Introduction to His Philosophical Thought.* London: Penguin Books, 1988.

Harrison, James. *Salman Rushdie.* New York: Twayne Publishers, 1992.

Harris, William H., and Judith S. Levy, eds. *The New Columbia Encyclopedia.* 4th ed. New York: Columbia University Press, 1975.

Harth, Erica. *Cyrano de Bergerac and the Polemics of Modernity.* New York: Columbia University Press, 1970.

Harvey, Sir Paul, ed. *The Oxford Companion to English Literature.* 3d ed. Oxford: Oxford University Press, 1955.

Haskins, Jim. *Voodoo & Hoodoo: Their Traditional Crafts as Revealed by Actual Practitioners.* New York: Original Publications, 1988.

Hassler, Donald M. *Erasmus Darwin.* New York: Twayne Publishers, 1973.

Hays, Denys. *Polydore Vergil: Renaissance Historian and Man of Letters.* Oxford, U.K.: Clarendon Press, 1952.

Hazard, Paul. *European Thought in the Eighteenth Century: From Montesquieu to Lessing.* Cleveland: World Publishing, 1973.

Hedayat, Sadegh. *The Blind Owl.* Translated by D. P. Costello. New York: Grove Weidenfeld, 1989.

Heilbroner, Robert. *The Worldly Philosophers: The Lives, Times and Ideas of the Great Economic Thinkers.* New York: Simon and Schuster, 1986.

Heins, Marjorie. *Sex, Sin and Blasphemy: A Guide to America's Culture Wars.* New York: New Press, 1993.

Hentoff, Nat. *Free Speech for Me, but Not for Thee.* New York: HarperCollins, 1992.

Hoffman, Eleanor. *Realm of the Evening Star: A History of Morocco and the Lands of the Moors.* Philadelphia: Chilton Books, 1965.

Hoffman, Robert L. *The Social and Political Theory of P.-J. Proudhon.* Urbana: University of Illinois Press, 1972.

Hollier, Denis. *A New History of French Literature.* Cambridge, Mass.: Harvard University Press, 1989.

Hornstein, Lillian Herlands., ed. *The Readers' Companion to World Literature.* New York: New American Library, 1956.

Hume, David. *An Inquiry Concerning Human Understanding.* Edited and with an introduction by Charles W. Hendel. Indianapolis, Ind.: Bobbs-Merrill, 1979.

———. *On Human Nature and the Understanding.* Edited and with an introduction by Anthony Flew. New York: Macmillan Publishing, 1975.

Hyams, Edward. *Pierre-Joseph Proudhon: His Revolutionary Life, Mind and Works.* New York: Taplinger Publishing, 1979.

Jaspers, Karl. *The Great Philosophers.* Vol. 3. New York: Harcourt Brace, 1993.

Jefferson, Carter. *Anatole France: The Politics of Skepticism.* New Brunswick, N.J.: Rutgers University Press, 1965.

Jenkinson, Edward B. "The Bible: A Source of Great Literature and Controversy." In *Censored Books: Critical Viewpoints,* edited by Nicholas J. Karolides, Lee Burress, and John M. Kean, 98–102. Metuchen, N.J.: Scarecrow Press, 1993.

Jolley, Nicholas. "The Reception of Descartes' Philosophy." In *The Cambridge Companion to Descartes*, edited by John Cottingham, 393–423. Cambridge: Cambridge University Press, 1992.

Jones, Sherry. *The Jewel of Medina*. New York: Beaufort Books, 2008.

Jordan, W. K. *The Development of Religious Toleration in England*. Vols. 3 and 4. Gloucester, Mass.: Peter Smith, 1965.

Kant, Immanuel. *The Critique of Pure Reason*. Translated by N. Kemp Smith. New York: St. Martin's Press, 1965.

———. *The Philosophy of Kant: Immanuel Kant's Moral and Political Writings*. Edited and with an introduction by Carl J. Friedrich. New York: Modern Library, 1993.

Kaplan, Fred, ed. *Oliver Twist: A Norton Critical Edition*. New York: W. W. Norton, 1993.

Kazantzakis, Helen. *Kazantzakis: A Biography Based on His Letters*. Translated by Amy Mims. New York: Simon and Schuster, 1968.

Kazantzakis, Nikos. *The Last Temptation of Christ*. Translated and with an afterword by P. A. Bien. New York: Simon and Schuster, 1960.

Kilcullen, John. *Sincerity and Truth: Essays on Arnauld, Bayle and Toleration*. Oxford, U.K.: Clarendon Press, 1988.

King-Hele, Desmond. *Erasmus Darwin and the Romantic Poets*. New York: St. Martin's Press, 1986.

Klausen, Jytte. *The Cartoons That Shook the World*. New Haven, Conn.: Yale University Press, 2009.

Kolakowski, Leszek. *Bergson*. Oxford: Oxford University Press, 1985.

The Koran. Translated and with an introduction by N. J. Dawood. Baltimore: Penguin Books, 1968.

Kundera, Milan. *Testaments Betrayed*. Trans. Linda Asher. New York: HarperCollins, 1995.

Küng, Hans. *Infallible? An Unresolved Inquiry*. Preface by Herbert Haag. New York: Continuum, 1994.

Laine, James W. *Shivaji: Hindu King in Islamic India*. New York: Oxford University Press, 2003.

Landau, Rom. *Morocco*. New York: G. P. Putnam's Sons. 1967.

Larson, Edward J. *Trial and Error: The American Controversy over Creation and Evolution*. New York: Oxford University Press, 1985.

Lea, Henry Charles. *History of the Inquisition of the Middle Ages*. Vols. 1 and 2. New York: Russell and Russell, 1955.

Leaman, Oliver. *Moses Maimonides*. Cairo: American University in Cairo Press, 1993.

Levy, Leonard W. *Blasphemy: Verbal Offense Against the Sacred, from Moses to Salman Rushdie*. New York: Alfred A. Knopf, 1993.

Li Hongzhi. *Zhuan Falun: The Complete Teachings of Falun Gong*. Gloucester, Mass.: Fair Winds Press, 2001.

Lin, Yutang, ed. *The Wisdom of Confucius*. New York: Modern Library, Random House, 1966.

Lippman, Thomas W. *Understanding Islam: An Introduction to the Muslim World*. New York: Penguin Books USA, 1990.

Lofmark, Carl. *What Is the Bible?* Buffalo, N.Y.: Prometheus Books, 1992.

Lutzer, Erwin W. *The Da Vinci Conspiracy*. Carol Stream, Ill.: Tyndale House, 2004.

Mahfouz, Naguib. *Children of Gebelawi*. Trans. Philip Stewart. Washington, D.C.: Three Continents Press, 1988.

———. *Children of the Alley*. Translated by Paul Theroux. New York: Doubleday, 1996.

Malti-Douglas, Fedwa, and Allen Douglas. "Reflections of a Feminist." In *Opening the Gates: A Century of Arab Feminist Writing*, edited by Margot Badran and Miriam Cooke, 394–404. Bloomington: Indiana University Press, 1990.

Mandeville, Bernard. *The Fable of the Bees*. Introduction by Philip Harth. London: Penguin Books, 1970.

Manguel, Alberto. *A History of Reading*. New York: Viking, 1996.

———, ed. *God's Spies: Stories in Defiance of Oppression*. Toronto: Macfarlane Walter and Ross, 1999.

Markman, Roberta, and Peter Markman. *The Flayed God: The Mythology of Mesoamerica*. New York: HarperCollins, 1992.

Mason, John Hope. *The Indispensable Rousseau*. London: Quartet Books, 1979.

McIntyre, Ruth A. *William Pynchon: Merchant and Colonizer*. Springfield, Mass.: Connecticut Valley Historical Museum, 1961.

Mernissi, Fatima. *Islam and Democracy: Fear of the Modern World*. Translated by Mary Jo Lakeland. Reading, Mass.: Addison-Wesley, 1992.

———. *The Veil and the Male Elite: A Feminist Interpretation of Women's Rights in Islam*. Trans. Mary Jo Lakeland. Reading, Mass.: Addison-Wesley, 1991.

Mill, John Stuart. *Essential Works of John Stuart Mill*. Edited and with an introduction by Max Lerner. New York: Bantam Books, 1971.

Montaigne, Michel de. *Essays*. Edited and with an introduction by J. M. Cohen. Middlesex, England: Penguin Books, 1958.

Montesquieu. *The Persian Letters*. Translated and with an introduction by George R. Healy. Indianapolis, Ind.: Bobbs-Merrill, 1964.

Moore, John Robert. *Defoe in the Pillory and Other Studies*. New York: Octagon Books, 1973.

Morgan, Edmund S. *Roger Williams: The Church and the State*. New York: Harcourt, Brace and World, 1967.

Nasrin, Taslima. *Lajja (Shame)*. New Delhi, Penguin Books, 1994.

———. *Meyebela: My Bengali Girlhood*. Royalton, Vt.: Steerforth Press, 2002.

Nauert, Charles G., Jr. *Agrippa and the Crisis of Renaissance Thought*. Urbana: University of Illinois Press, 1965.

New York Public Library. *Censorship: 500 Years of Conflict*. New York: Oxford University Press, 1984.

Noyes, Alfred. *Two Worlds for Memory*. Philadelphia: J. B. Lippincott, 1953.

Numbers, Ronald L., ed. *Creation-Evolution Debates*. New York: Garland Publishing, 1955.

O'Connor, James. *Kepler's Witch: An Astronomer's Discovery of Cosmic Order Amid Religious War, Political Intrigue and the Heresy Trial of His Mother*. San Francisco: HarperSanFrancisco, 2004.

Olsen, Tillie. *Silences*. New York: Dell Publishing, 1978.

O'Neil, Robert M. "The Bible and the Constitution." In *Censored Books: Critical Viewpoints*, edited by Nicholas J. Karolides, Lee Burress, and John M. Kean, 103–108. Metuchen, N.J.: Scarecrow Press, 1993.

O'Prey, Paul. *A Reader's Guide to Graham Greene*. New York: Thames and Hudson, 1988.

Osborne, Richard. *Philosophy for Beginners*. New York: Writers and Readers Publishing, 1991.

Paine, Thomas. *The Age of Reason*. Introduction by Philip S. Foner. Secaucus, N.J.: Citadel Press, 1974.

Parker, T. H. L. *John Calvin*. Batavia, Ill.: Lion Publishing Corporation, 1975.

Parsipur, Shahrnush. *Touba and the Meaning of Night.* New York: The Feminist Press of the City University of New York, 2006.

———. *Women Without Men: A Novel of Modern Iran.* Afterword by Persis M. Karim. Translator's note by Kamran Talattof. New York: Feminist Press at the City University of New York, 2004.

Pascal, Blaise. *The Provincial Letters.* Edited and with an introduction by J. Krailsheimer. Harmondsworth, England: Penguin Books, 1967.

Penelhum, Terence. *David Hume: An Introduction to His Philosophical System.* West Lafayette, Ind.: Purdue University Press, 1992.

Perrin, Noel. *Dr. Bowdler's Legacy: A History of Expurgated Books in England and America.* New York: Anchor Books, 1971.

Peters, Edward. *Inquisition.* New York: Free Press, 1988.

Pipes, Daniel. *The Rushdie Affair.* New York: Carol Publishing, 1990.

Polishook, Irwin H. *Roger Williams, John Cotton, and Religious Freedom: A Controversy in New and Old England.* Englewood Cliffs, N.J.: Prentice Hall, 1967.

Popkin, Richard, and Avrum Stroll. *Philosophy Made Simple.* New York: Doubleday, 1993.

Price, John V. *David Hume.* New York: Twayne Publishers, 1968.

Pullman, Philip. *The Golden Compass.* New York: Alfred A. Knopf, 1995.

———. *The Subtle Knife.* New York: Alfred A. Knopf, 1997.

———. *The Amber Spyglass.* New York: Alfred A. Knopf, 2000.

Putnam, George Haven. *The Censorship of the Church of Rome.* 2 vols. New York: G. P. Putnam's Sons, 1906–07.

Ravitch, Diane. *The Language Police: How Pressure Groups Restrict What Children Learn.* New York: Alfred A. Knopf, 2003.

Redman, Ben Ray, ed. and intro. *The Portable Voltaire.* New York: Penguin Books, 1977.

Reill, Peter Hanns, and Ellen Judy Wilson. *Encyclopedia of the Enlightenment.* New York: Facts On File, 1996.

Renan, Ernest. *The Life of Jesus.* Introduction by John Haynes Holmes. New York: Modern Library, 1955.

Rex, Walter. *Pascal's Provincial Letters: An Introduction.* New York: Holmes and Meier Publishers, 1977.

Richetti, John J. *Daniel Defoe.* Boston: Twayne Publishers, 1987.

Ridley, Jasper. *Thomas Cranmer.* Oxford: Clarendon Press, 1962.

Ritvo, Lucille B. *Darwin's Influence on Freud: A Tale of Two Sciences.* New Haven, Conn.: Yale University Press, 1990.

Rogers, Donald J. *Banned! Book Censorship in the Schools.* New York: Julian Messner, 1988.

Roth, Cecil. *The Spanish Inquisition.* New York: W. W. Norton, 1964.

Rowling, J. K. *Harry Potter and the Chamber of Secrets.* New York: Scholastic Press, 1999.

———. *Harry Potter and the Deathly Hallows.* New York: Scholastic Press, 2007.

———. *Harry Potter and the Goblet of Fire.* New York: Scholastic Press, 2000.

———. *Harry Potter and the Half-Blood Prince.* New York: Scholastic Press, 2005.

———. *Harry Potter and the Order of the Phoenix.* New York: Scholastic Press, 2003.

———. *Harry Potter and the Prisoner of Azkaban.* New York: Scholastic Press, 1999.

———. *Harry Potter and the Sorcerer's Stone.* New York: Scholastic Press, 1998.

Rummel, Erika, ed. *The Erasmus Reader.* Toronto: University of Toronto Press, 1990.

Rushdie, Salman. *Imaginary Homelands: Essays and Criticism 1981–1991.* New York: Penguin Books, 1991.

———. *The Satanic Verses.* New York: Viking Penguin, 1989.

Ruthven, Malise. *A Satanic Affair: Salman Rushdie and the Wrath of Islam.* London: Hogarth Press, 1991.

El Saadawi, Nawal. *The Fall of the Imam.* London: Minerva, 1989.

———. *The Hidden Face of Eve: Women in the Arab World.* Foreword by Irene L. Gendzier. Boston: Beacon Press, 1982.

———. *The Hidden Face of Eve: Women in the Arab World.* Preface by Nawal El Saadawi. Translated by Sherif Hetata. London: Zed Books, 1980.

Scammel, Michael. "Censorship and Its History: A Personal View." In *Article 19: World Report 1988*, edited by Kevin Boyle, 1–18. New York: Times Books, 1988.

Schechter, Danny. *Falun Gong's Challenge to China.* New York: Akashic Books, 2001.

Scott-Kakures, Dion, Susan Castegnetto, Hugh Benson, William Taschek, and Paul Hurley. *History of Philosophy.* New York: HarperCollins, 1993.

al-Shaykh, Hanan. *The Story of Zahra.* New York: Anchor Books, 1994.

Sherry, Norman. *The Life of Graham Greene.* Vol. 2: *1939–1955.* New York: Viking Penguin, 1994.

Shklar, Judith N. *Montesquieu.* Oxford: Oxford University Press, 1987.

Sigmund, Paul E. *Liberation Theology at the Crossroads: Democracy or Revolution?* New York: Oxford University Press, 1990.

Simon, Edith. *The Reformation.* New York: Time-Life Books, 1966.

Smith, D. W. *Helvétius, A Study in Persecution.* Oxford: Clarendon Press, 1965.

Smith, George H. *Atheism, Ayn Rand, and Other Heresies.* Buffalo, N.Y.: Prometheus Books, 1991.

Smith, Joseph H., ed. *Colonial Justice in Western Massachusetts (1639–1702): The Pynchon Court Record.* Cambridge, Mass.: Harvard University Press, 1961.

Spence, Jonathan D., *The Search for Modern China.* New York: W. W. Norton, 1990.

Spitz, Lewis W., ed. *The Protestant Reformation.* Englewood Cliffs, N.J.: Prentice Hall, 1966.

Standley, Arline Reilein. *Auguste Comte.* Twayne Publishers, 1981.

Steinsaltz, Adin. *The Essential Talmud.* New York: Basic Books, 1976.

Stendhal. *Red and Black: A Norton Critical Edition.* Translated and edited by Robert M. Adams. New York: W. W. Norton, 1969.

Stuart, Gene S., and George E. Stuart. *Lost Kingdoms of the Maya.* Washington, D.C.: National Geographic Society, 1993.

Sullivan, Robert E. *John Toland and the Deist Controversy: A Study in Adaptations.* Cambridge, Mass.: Harvard University Press, 1982.

Sutherland, James. *Daniel Defoe: A Critical Study.* Cambridge, Mass.: Harvard University Press, 1971.

Swift, Jonathan. *The Portable Swift.* Edited and with an introduction by Carl Van Doren. New York: Penguin Books, 1978.

———. *A Tale of a Tub and Other Satires.* Intro. by Lewis Melville. New York: E. P. Dutton, 1955.

———. *A Tale of a Tub: Written for the Universal Improvement of Mankind.* Foreword by Edward Hodnett. New York: Columbia University Press, 1930.

Synnestvedt, Sig. *The Essential Swedenborg.* New York: Twayne Publishers, 1970.

Talbot, Emile J. *Stendhal Revisited.* New York: Twayne Publishers, 1993.

Tedlock, Dennis, trans. *Popol Vuh: The Definitive Edition of the Mayan Book of the Dawn of Life and the Glories of Gods and Kings.* New York: Simon and Schuster, 1985.

Tetel, Marcel. *Montaigne: Updated Edition.* Boston: Twayne Publishers, 1990.

Thilly, Frank. *The History of Philosophy*. Revised by Ledger Wood. New York: Holt, Rinehart and Winston, 1957.

Thompson, David, and Ian Christie, eds. *Scorsese on Scorsese*. London: Faber and Faber, 1989.

Toksvig, Signe. *Emanuel Swedenborg: Scientist and Mystic*. Freeport, N.Y.: Books for Libraries Press, 1972.

Toulmin, Stephen. *Cosmopolis: The Hidden Agenda of Modernity*. Chicago: University of Chicago Press, 1990.

Trowbridge, George. *Swedenborg, Life and Teaching*. New York: Swedenborg Foundation, 1938.

Urvoy, Dominique. *Ibn Rushd (Averroës)*. Translated by Olivia Steward. Cairo: American University in Cairo Press, 1993.

Van Hollthoon, F. L. *The Road to Utopia: A Study of John Stuart Mill's Social Thought*. Assem, Netherlands: Van Gorcum, 1971.

Veidmanis, Gladys, "Reflections on 'the Shylock Problem,' " In *Censored Books: Critical Viewpoints*, edited by Nicholas J. Karolides, Lee Burress, and John M. Kean, 370–378. Metuchen, N.J.: Scarecrow Press, 1993.

Voltaire. *Philosophical Dictionary*. Edited, translated and with an introduction by Theodore Besterman. New York: Penguin Books, 1972.

Weatherby, W. J. *Salman Rushdie: Sentenced to Death*. New York: Carroll and Graf Publishers, 1990.

Weinstein, Donald. *Savonarola and Florence: Prophecy and Patriotism in the Renaissance*. Princeton, N.J.: Princeton University Press, 1970.

Weiss, Bernard J., ed. *People Need People*. Holt Basic Reading Series. New York: Holt, Rinehart and Winston, 1983.

———. *Riders on the Earth*. Holt Basic Reading Series. New York: Holt, Rinehart and Winston, 1983.

Welsby, Paul A. *A History of the Church of England, 1945–1980*. Oxford: Oxford University Press, 1984.

Wilcox, Donald J. *In Search of God and Self: Renaissance and Reformation Thought*. Boston: Houghton Mifflin, 1975.

Wildes, Harry Emerson. *William Penn*. New York: Macmillan Publishing, 1974.

Winslow, Ola Elizabeth. *John Eliot, "Apostle to the Indians."* Boston: Houghton Mifflin, 1968.

Wippel, John F., and Allan B. Wolter, eds. *Medieval Philosophy: From St. Augustine to Nicholas of Cusa*. New York: Free Press, 1969.

Wolff, Robert Paul, ed. *Ten Great Works of Philosophy*. New York: New American Library, 1969.

Yep, Laurence. Afterword to *Dragonwings*. New York: Scholastic, 1990.

Zagorin, Perez. *How the Idea of Religious Toleration Came to the West*. Princeton, N.J.: Princeton University Press, 2003.

PERIODICALS

Abou El-Magd, Nadia. "Book That Nearly Cost Naguib Mahfouz His Life Resurfaces in Egypt." Associated Press (January 12, 2007). Available online. URL: http://thedailynewsegypt.com/article.aspx?ArticleID=4933. Accessed June 6, 2010.

———. "The Prophet Is Back." *Al-Ahram Weekly* (August 5–11, 1999). Available online. URL: http://weekly.ahram.org.eg/1999/441/eg8.htm. Accessed June 6, 2010.

Adams, Lorraine. "Thinly Veiled." *New York Times Sunday Book Review* (December 12, 2008). Available online. URL: http://www.nytimes.com/2008/12/14/books/review/Adams-t.html?_r=1&scp=1&sq=publisher%20of%20O.J.%20book%20to%20handle%20Muhammad%20novel&st=cse. Accessed November 16, 2009.

Ahmed, Kamel. "Bangladesh Bans New Taslima Book." BBC News (August 13, 1999). Available online. URL: http://news.bbc.co.uk/2/hi/south_asia/419428.stm. Accessed December 16, 2004.

Akkara, Anto. "'Don't Hijack the Pope.'" *The Southern Cross* (March 8, 1998). Available online. URL: http://www.thesoutherncross.co.za./ Accessed December 16, 2004.

Allen, Nick, and Aislinn Simpson. "Mohammed Novel: Academic Faces Calls to Apologise over 'Pornographic' Remarks." *Daily Telegraph* (September 29, 2008). Available online. URL: http://www.telegraph.co.uk/news/3102416/Mohammed-novel-Academic-faces-calls-to-apologise-over-pornographic-remarks.html. Accessed October 12, 2009.

Alrawi, Karim. "Fiction's Freedom: The Government and Its Islamic Opponents Join Forces to Cripple Egyptian Publishing." *Index on Censorship* 25, no. 2 (March/April 1996): 172–175.

Alter, Alexandra. "Decades after the 'Monkey Trial,' Creationists Turn to Science." *Miami Herald* (August 15, 2005). Available online. URL: http://centredaily.com/mid/centredaily/news/12424164.htm. Accessed December 16, 2004.

American Library Association. *Newsletter on Intellectual Freedom* 33, no. 1 (January 1984): 11; 36, no. 1 (January 1987): 36–39; 39, no. 3 (March 1990): 46; 39, no. 6 (November 1990): 201; 40, no. 1 (January 1991): 16; 40, no. 2 (March 1991): 47; 41, no. 3 (May 1992): 78; 41, no. 5 (September 1992); 137; 41, no. 6 (November 1992): 196; 42, no. 1 (January 1993): 11; 42, no. 4 (July 1993): 127; 42, no. 5 (September 1993): 157; 43, no. 3 (May 1994): 200; 44, no. 1 (January 1995): 19–20; 45, no. 4 (July 1996): 134; 47, no. 5 (September 1998): 156; 54, no. 1 (January 2005); 54, no. 3 (May 2005).

Amnesty International. *The Crackdown on Falun Gong and Other So-Called Heretical Organizations.* London: Amnesty International, 2000.

Anis, Mona, and Amira Howeidy. "'I Dream of a Better Future.'" *Al-Ahram Weekly* (June 22–29, 1995) in *World Press Review* (October 1995): 19–21.

Applebaum, Anne. "Chipping Away at Free Speech." *Washington Post* (September 15, 2009). Available online. URL: http://www.washingtonpost.com.

Aronsfeld, C. C. "Book Burning in Jewish History." *Index on Censorship* 11, no. 1 (February 1982): 18.

Article 19. "Iran: Press Freedom Under the 'Moderates.'" *Censorship News*, no. 15 (August 17, 1992).

Associated Press. "Ban on 'The Witches' Sought." (October 19, 1989).

———. "Ontario Catholic School Board Pulls Fantasy Book following Complaint about Atheist Author." *International Herald Tribune* (November 22, 2007). Available online. URL: http://www.iht.com/bin/printfriendly.php?id=8443713. Accessed June 12, 2009.

Atwood, Margaret. Untitled. *Women's Review of Books* 12, nos. 10–11 (July 1995): 28.

Baldauf, Scott. "How a U.S. Historian Sparked Calls for His Arrest—in India." *Christian Science Monitor* (March 29, 2004). Available online. URL: http://www.csmonitor.com/2004/0329/p01s04-wosc.html. Accessed December 16, 2004.

Baldwin, Gordon B. "The Library Bill of Rights: A Critique." *Library Trends* 45, no. 1 (Summer 1996): 7–21.

Bardach, Ann Louise, "Tearing Off the Veil." *Vanity Fair*, August 1993, 123.

Barnes, Julian. "Staying Alive." *New Yorker*, February 21, 1994, 99–105.

Barnes, Michael. "Warrant for Professor's Arrest Issued in India." *MAC Weekly* (April 2, 2004). Available online. URL: http://www.macalester.edu/weekly. Accessed October 2, 2004.

Beaumont, Peter. "China's Falun Gong Crackdown: 'Persecution Is Almost Underground.'" *Guardian* (July 18, 2009). Available online. URL: http://www.guardian.co.uk/world/2009/jul/18/china-falun-gong-crackdown. Accessed June 6, 2010.

Benson, Ophelia. "Fear and Censorship." *Guardian* (January 5, 2010). Available online. URL: http://www.guardian.co.uk/commentisfree/belief/2010/jan/04/religion-islam. Accessed June 6, 2010.

Bhaumik, Subir. "India State in Total *Da Vinci* Ban." BBC News (May 23, 2006). Available online. URL: http://news.bbc.co.uk/go/pr/fr/2/hi/south___asia/5009778.stm. Accessed July 8, 2009.

Bhaumik, Subir. "Indian State Lifts Ban on Writer." BBC News (September 22, 2005). Available online. URL: http://news.bbc.co.uk/1/hi/world/south_asia/4272858.stm. Accessed January 20, 2006.

Bingham, John. "Radical Islamic Clerics Warn of Further Attacks after Publisher Is Firebombed." *Daily Telegraph* (September 28, 2008). Available online. URL: http://www.telegraph.co.uk/news/uknews/3097350/Radical-Islamic-clerics-warn-of-further-attacks-after-publisher-is-firebombed.html. Accessed November 14, 2009.

Birley, Robert. "Freedom of the Press." *Index on Censorship* 5, no. 1 (Spring 1976): 32.

Blakely, Rhys. "Pope Criticises Harry Potter." *Times* (London) (July 13, 2005). Available online. URL: http://www.timesonline.co.uk/article/0,,1=1692541,00.html. Accessed January 20, 2006.

Boff, Leonardo. Leonardo Boff's official Web site. Available online. URL: http://fly.to/boff.

Bohlen, Celestine. "Heresy Brings Hint of Martyrdom to Sri Lanka Priest." *New York Times* (January 15, 1997). Available online. URL: http://www.newyorktimes.com/. Accessed December 16, 2004.

———. "A Sri Lankan Priest Is Excommunicated for His Relativism." *New York Times* (January 7, 1997). Available online. URL: http://www.newyorktimes.com/. Accessed December 16, 2004.

———. "Vatican Sets Rules for Doctrinal Debates." *New York Times* (August 30, 1997). Available online. URL: http://www.newyorktimes.com/. Accessed December 16, 2004.

Bone, James. "Salman Rushdie Attacks 'Censorship by Fear' over 'The Jewel of Medina.'" *Times* (London) (August 16, 2008). Available online. URL: http://entertainment.timesonline.co.uk/tol/arts_and_entertainment/books/article4543243.ece. Accessed June 2, 2009.

———. "Yale University Press Accused of Cowardice over Muhammad Cartoons." *Times* (London) (August 18, 2009). Available online. URL: http://www.timesonline.co.uk/tol/news/world/us_and_americas/article679968. Accessed June 6, 2010.

Borst, John, et al. "Golden Compass 'Review' Causes Media Firestorm." Tomorrow's Trust, A Review of Catholic Education, blog archive (November 26, 2007). Available online. URL: http://tomorrowstrust.ca/?9=1129. Accessed June 12, 2009.

Broder, Henryk M. "After Attack on Danish Cartoonist, the West Is Choked by Fear." Spiegel Online International (January 4, 2010). Available online. URL: http://www.spiegel.de/international/Europe/0,1518,669888,00.html. Accessed June 10, 2010.

Brown, Ron. "Children's Book Challenges: The New Wave." *Canadian Children's Literature* 68 (1992): 27–32.

Bunting, Madeleine. "A Question of Faith." *Guardian* (October 6, 2007). Available online. URL: http://www.guardian.co.uk/books/2007/oct/06/society1.html. Accessed October 7, 2009.

Burkeman, Oliver. "'Heretic' Priest Defies Inquisitors in Rights Battle." Gemini News Service (October 10, 1997).

"Calgary Catholic School Board Dumps Golden Compass." *Globe and Mail* (December 5, 2007). Available online. URL: http://www.theglobeandmail.com/servlet/story/RTGAM.20071205.wgoldcompass1205/B. Accessed December 6, 2007.

Campbell, Duncan, and Julian Borger. "Rushdie Furor Stuns Honours Committee." *Guardian* (June 20, 2007). Available online. URL: http://www.guardian.co.uk/uk/2007/jun/20/books.pakistan. Accessed June 6, 2010.

Carroll, Diane. "Evolution Issues Again Gets Look from Board." *Kansas City Star* (August 9, 2005). Available online. URL: http://www.kansascity.com/mld/Kansascity/news/local/12336247.htm. Accessed January 20, 2006.

Carver, Peter. "Good Impressions—and Bad." *Canadian Children's Literature* 68 (1992). Available online. URL: http://libnt1.lib.uoguelph.ca/. Accessed September 29, 2004.

Chansanchai, Athima. "Darkness and Delight of Potter's Creator." *Baltimore Sun* (October 20, 2000). Available online. URL: http://www.baltimoresun.com/. Accessed November 2, 2000.

Christoffersen, John. "Yale Criticized for Nixing Muslim Cartoons in Book." Associated Press (September 8, 2009). Available online. URL: http://abcnews.go.com/US/wireStory?id=8512341. Accessed June 6, 2010.

Churnin, Nancy. "Bible Belt Beware: Harry Potter Isn't So Controversial Anymore." *Dallas Morning News* (July 13, 2005). Available online. URL: http://www.freerepublic.com/focus/f=news/1443583/posts. Accessed November 15, 2005.

Clark, Charles S. "Why Are Complaints about American Schoolbooks on the Rise?" *CQ Researcher* (February 19, 1993). Available online. URL: http://www.collegeofsanmateo.edu/library/cqresrre1993021900.htm.

Cohen, Patricia. "PEN Urges Yale to Publish Images of Muhammad." *New York Times* (September 11, 2009). Available online. URL: http://www.campus-watch.org/article/id/8289. Accessed June 6, 2010.

———. "Yale Press Bans Images of Muhammad in New Book." *New York Times* (August 13, 2009). Available online. URL: http://www.nytimes.com/2009/08/13/books/13book.html. Accesed June 6, 2010.

Collen, Lindsey. "The Rape of Fiction." *Index on Censorship* 12, nos. 4–5 (September/October 1994): 210–212.

"Court Laughs at Cartoonist's Trial." *Kathimerini* (April 4, 2005). Available online. URL: http://www.ckathimerini.com/4dcgi/_w_articles_politics_100014_14/04/2005_55187. Accessed January 20, 2006.

Courtright, Paul. "Studying Religion in an Age of Terror: Internet Death Threats and Scholarship as a Moral Practice." Academic Exchange, Emory University (April 15, 2004). Available online. URL: http://www.emory.edu/ACAD EXCHANGE/2004/aprmay/courtnight.html. Accessed November 15, 2004.

Crossette, Barbara. "A Cry for Tolerance Brings New Hatred Down on a Writer." *New York Times*, July 3, 1994, p. 7.

"Da Vinci Code Ban in India State." BBC News (June 1, 2006). Available online. URL: http://news.bbc.co.uk/go/pr/fr/-/2/hi/south___asia/5036094.stm. Accessed July 8, 2009.

"Da Vinci Code Book Banned in Iran." BBC News (July 26, 2006). Available online. URL: http://news.bbc.co.uk/go/pr/fr/-/2/hi/entertainment/5216490.stm. Accessed July 27, 2009.

Davis, Thulani. "Taslima Nasrin Speaks (Still)." *Village Voice* (November 13–19, 2002). Available online. URL: http://www.villagevoice.com/news/0246,davis,39832,1.html. Accessed November 16, 2004.

Dawoud, Khaled. "Did *Hisba* Ever Go Away?" *Al-Ahram Weekly On-line* 539, no. 9 (June 21–27, 2001). Available online. URL: http://weekly.ahram.org.eg/2001/539/eg7.htm.

Dehghan, Saeed Kamali. "The Gag Is Tightened." *Guardian* (January 6, 2008). Available online. URL: http://www.guardian.co.uk/books/2008/Jan/06/fiction.iran/print. Accessed July 8, 2009.

———. "Iranian Writers in a Literary Depression." PowellsBooks.Blog. Posted October 3, 2007. Available online. URL: http://www.powells.com/blog/?p=2492. Accessed June 16, 2009.

deLuzuriaga, Tania. "Man from Ministry Bans Potter." *Boston Globe* (Octber 25, 2007). Available online. URL: http://www.boston.com/news/local/articles/2007/10/25/man_from_ministry_bans_potter/. Accessed June 6, 2010.

Devi, Sharmilia. "Book on Danish Cartoons Sparks Ruckus." *National* (September 9, 2009). Available online. URL: http://www.campus-watch.org/article/id/8273. Accessed June 6, 2010.

Dhar, Sujoy. "Bangladeshi Author's New Book Upsets Prurient Fans." Inter Press Service (November 27, 2003).

Dhavan, Rajeev. "Ban, Burn, Destroy." *The Hindu* (January 23, 2004). Available online. URL: http://www.hindu.com/2004/01/27/stories/2004012701571004.html. Accessed December 16, 2004.

Dimbleby, Jonathan. *Index on Censorship* (December 18, 2009). Available online. URL: http://www.indexoncensorship.org/2009/12/jonathan-dimbleby/. Accessed June 6, 2010.

Diver, Krysia. "Cartoonist Faces Greek Jail for Blasphemy." *The Guardian* (March 23, 2005). Available online. URL: http://www.guardian.co.uk/arts/news/story/0,11711,1443908,00.html. Accessed January 20, 2006.

Drabble, Margaret. "Black Listings." *Autodafe: The Journal of the International Parliament of Writers* 1 (Spring 2001): 247. New York: Seven Stories Press, 2000.

Dworkin, Ronald. "The Right to Ridicule." *New York Review of Books 53*, no. 5 (March 23, 2006). Available online. URL: http://www.nybooks.com/articles/18111. Accessed June 6, 2010.

Ehab, John. "Publish and Be Damned." *Daily News Egypt* (April 11, 2008). Available online. URL: http://www.dailystaregypt.com/article.aspx?ArticleID=13056. Accessed June 6, 2010.

Eltahawy, Mona. "Yale's Misguided Retreat." *Washington Post* (August 29, 2009). Available online. URL: http://www.washingtonpost.com. Accessed June 6, 2010.

Engineer, Asghar Ali. "The Politics of Attack on Bhandarkar Institute." Centre for Study of Society and Secularism, Mumbai (February 1–5, 2004). Available online. URL: http://www.csss-isla.com/archive/archive.php?article=http://www.css-isla.com/archive/2004/feb 1_15.htm. Accessed January 20, 2006.

"Excommunication Is an Inordinate Threat." *National Catholic Reporter* (December 27, 1996). Available online. URL: http://findarticles.com/p/articles/mi_m1141/is_n9_v33/ai_19013597#continue. Accessed November 16, 2005.

Family Friendly Libraries. "Family Friendly School Policies" (2002). Available online. URL: http://www.fflibraries.org/Book_Reports/PSBookPolicies. htm.

Fan, Maureen. "Confucius Making a Comeback in Money-Driven Modern China." *Washington Post* (July 24, 2007). Available online. URL: http://www.washingtonpost. com/wp-dyn/content/article/2007/07/23/AR2007072301859.html.AccessedJune6, 2010.

Faroaq, Umer. "Pakistan Bans *Da Vinci Code*, Christians Happy." Islam Online (June 5, 2006). Available online. URL: http://www.islamonline.net/servlet/Satellite?c=Artic le__C&cid=1162385911282&pagename. Accessed July 8, 2009.

Fish, Stanley. "Crying Censorship." Think Again blog. *New York Times* (August 24, 2008). Available online. URL: http://fish.blogs.nytimes.com/2008/08/24/crying-censorship/index.html. Accessed August 27, 2008.

Fisk, Robert. " 'The Prophet' Falls Foul of Egyptian Thought Police." *Independent* (July 28, 1999). Available online. URL: http://www.independent.co.uk/news/world/ the-prophet-falls-foul-of-egyptian-thought-police-1109157.html?cmp=ilc-n. Accessed June 6, 2010.

Flood, Alison. "Publication of Controversial Muhammad Novel Delayed." *Guardian* (October 10, 2008). Available online. URL: http://www.guardian.co.uk/books/2008/ oct/10/jewel-of-medina-sherry-jones-aisha/print. Accessed July 9, 2009.

Freitas, Donna. "God in the Dust." *Boston Globe* (November 25, 2007). Available online. URL: http://www.boston.com/bostonglobe/ideas/articles/2007/11/25/god_ in_the_dust. Accessed June 12, 2009.

Fresno, Adam. "Radical Muslims Guilty of Firebomb Plot on Publisher of Prophet Mohammed Book." *Times* (London) (May 15, 2009). Available online. URL: http:// www.timesonline.co.uk/tol/news/uk/crime/article/article6295795.ece. Accessed November 14, 2009.

Goldenberg, Suzanne. "Novel on Prophet's Wife Pulled for Fear of Backlash." *Guardian* (August 9, 2008). Available online. URL: http://www.guardian.co.uk/ books/2008/aug/09/fiction.terrorism/print. Accessed July 9, 2009.

Goldstein, Evan R. "The Book That Shook Yale." *Chronicle of Higher Education* (September 29, 2009). Available online. URL: http://chronicle.com/article/The-Book-Shook-Yale/48634. Accessed June 6, 2010.

Goodstein, Laurie. "Defenders of Christianity Rebut *The Da Vinci Code*." *New York Times*, April 27, 2004, p. A22.

———. "Judge Rejects Teaching Intelligent Design." *New York Times* (December 21, 2005). Available online. URL: http://www.nytimes.com/. Accessed December 27, 2005.

"Groups United to Ban Textbooks." *IFAS Freedom Writer* (March/April 1991). Available online. URL: http://www.publiceye.org/ifas/fw/9103/textbooks.html. Accessed January 20, 2006.

Gunter, Lorne. "Faith Strengthened by a Good Test." *Edmonton Journal* (November 25, 2007). Available online. URL: http://lgunter@shaw.ca. Accessed June 12, 2009.

Gupta, Tilak D. "Autobiography of a Controversial Writer." *Tribune* (September 5, 1999). Available online. URL: http://www.tribuneindia.com/1999/99sep05/ sunday/head10.htm. Accessed October 2, 2004.

Hart, Ariel. "Judge in Georgia Orders Anti-Evolution Stickers Removed from Textbooks." *New York Times* (January 14, 2005). Available online. URL: http://www. nytimes.com. Accessed January 14, 2005.

El-Hennawy, Noha. "Publish and Perish." *Egypt Today* (February 2006). Available online. URL: http//www.egyptoday.com/article.aspx?ArticleID=6361. Accessed June 6, 2010.

Hertzberg, Arthur. "Swimming without Drowning: New Approaches to the Ocean of the Talmud." *New York Times Book Review*, March 27, 1994, pp. 12–14.

Hiel, Betsy. "'Da Vinci' Unlikely to Pass Egypt Censors." *Pittsburgh Tribune-Review* (May 14, 2006). Available online. URL: http://www.pittsburghlive.com/x/pittsburghtrib/mostread/s_453828.html. Accessed August 25, 2009.

Hitchens, Christopher. "Yale Surrenders." *Slate* (August 17, 2009). Available online. URL: http://www.slate.com/toolbar/aspx?action=print&id=2225504. Accessed June 6, 2010.

Hogan, Ron. "Judge for Yourself: *Jewel of Medina* in U.S. Bookstores." *GalleyCat* (October 6, 2008). Available online. URL: http://www.mediabistro.com/galleycat/authors/judge_for_yourself_jewel_of_medina_in_us_bookstores_96577.asp. Accessed October 12, 2009.

Howard, Jennifer. "Academic and Free-Speech Groups Join Criticism of Yale U. Press over Cartoons in Book." *Chronicle of Higher Education* (September 16, 2009). Available online. URL: http://chronicle.com/article/AcademicFree-Speech/48441/. Accessed June 6, 2010.

Howeidy, Amira. "The Persecution of Abu Zeid." *Al-Ahram Weekly* (June 22–28, 1995) in *World Press Review* (October 1995): 18–19.

Hoyle, Ben. "Salman Rushdie Unrepentant about Satanic Verses." *Times* (London) (October 1, 2008). Available online. URL: http://entertainment.timesonline.co.uk/tol/arts_and_entertainment/books/clive_james/article4856150.ece. Accessed June 6, 2010.

Human Rights Watch. *Dangerous Meditations: China's Campaign Against Falungong.* New York: Human Rights Watch, 2002.

Hume, Mick. "A Festival of Grovelling to Terrorists." *Times Online* (August 12, 2008). Available online. URL: http://www.timesonline.co.uk/tol/comment/columnists/article4509698.ece?print=yes&rand. Accessed July 23, 2009.

"Iran Adamant over Rushdie Fatwa." BBC News (February 17, 2005). Available online. URL: http://news.bbc.co.uk/2/hi/middle_east/4260599.stm. Accessed January 20, 2006.

"Iran Bans *Da Vinci Code* Book after 8 Editions." Christians of Iraq (July 26, 2006). Available online. URL: http://www.christiansofiraq.com/irandavinci.html. Accessed July 8, 2009

Irvine, Lindesay. "Taslima Nasrin to Leave India." *Guardian* (March 17, 2008). Available online. URL: http://www.guardian.co.uk. Accessed June 6, 2010.

Jacobs, Andrew. "China Still Presses Crusade Against Falun Gong." *New York Times* (April 28, 2009). Available online. URL: http://www.nytimes.com/2009/04/28/world/asia/28china.html. Accessed June 6, 2010.

"Jail Term Surprises Bangladeshi Author." BBC News (October 14, 2002). Available online. URL: http://news.bbc.co.uk/1/hi/world/south_asia/2327329.stm. Accessed October 2, 2004.

"James Laine's *Shavaji: Hindu King in Islamic India* and the Attack on the Bhandarkar Oriental Research Institute." *The Complete Review* (February 2004). Available online. URL: http://www.complete-review.com/quarterly/vol5/issue1/laine0.htm. Accessed January 20, 2006.

Jaschik, Scott. "Darwin, From the Creationists." *Inside Higher Ed* (October 7, 2009). Available online. URL: http://www.insidehighered.com/news/2009/10/07/darwin. Accessed June 6, 2010.

Jones, Derek, ed. *Censorship: A World Encyclopedia.* Chicago and London: Fitzroy, Dearborn, 2001. Available online. URL: http://www.thefileroom.org/documents/dyn/DisplayCase.cfm/id/1212. Accessed June 16, 2009.

Jones, Sherry. "Censoring 'The Jewel of Medina.'" *PostGlobal: Islam's Advance.* Posted by Jack Fairweather (August 11, 2008). Available online. URL: http://newsweek. washingtonpost.com/postglobal/islamadvance/2008/08/censoring_islam.htm. Accessed October 12, 2009.

———. "Our Own Worst Enemy." *New Humanist* 124, no. 6 (November/December 2009). Available online. URL: http://newhumanist.org.uk/2163/our-own-worst-enemy. Accessed June 6, 2010.

Jong, Erica. "The Boy Who Became a Mouse." *New York Times Book Review* (November 13, 1983). Available online. URL: http://roalddahlfans.com/books/witcrev1.php. Accessed January 20, 2006.

Joshi, Vijay. "Three Malaysian Churches Attacked in 'Allah' Dispute." *Yahoo News.* Available online. URL: http://news.yahoo.com/s/ap/20100108/ap_on_re_as/as_malaysia_allah_ban/print.html. Accessed January 8, 2010.

Junas, Dan. *Report on the Religious Right in Washington State.* Seattle: American Civil Liberties Union of Washington, 1995. Available online. URL: http://www.aclu-wa. org/Issues/religious/3.html. Accessed April 27, 2004.

"Karen Armstrong: It's OK to Listen to Her but Don't Read Her Works." Centre for Independent Journalism, Malaysia (June 11, 2007). Available online. URL: http://www.cijmalaysia.org/content/view/214/6/.html. Accessed October 7, 2009.

Katakam, Anupama. "The Politics of Vandalism." *Frontline* (January 17–30, 2004). Available online. URL: http://www.flonet.com/fl2102/stories/20040130003802 802800.htm.

Katakam, Anupama, and Nandagopal R. Menon. "Politics of a Ban." *Frontline* (February 11–24, 2006). Available online. URL: http://www.hinduonnet.com/fline/fl2303/stories/20060224002609300.htm. Accessed June 6, 2010.

El-Katatney, Ethar. "Flawed Jewel." *Egypt Today* (October 2008). Available online. URL: http://www.egypttoday.com/article.aspx?ArticleID=8171. Accessed October 12, 2009.

Kern, Edmund. "Pope Should Spell Out Views on Potter." *The Scotsman* (July 29, 2005). Available online. URL: http://www.scotsman.com/opinion.ctm?sid=1700982005. Accessed January 20, 2006.

Klausen, Jytte. "Not Everything Can Be Explained by Words Alone." *Yale Alumni Magazine* (September 9, 2009). Available online. URL: http://www.yalealumnimagazine. com/extras/yup/klausen149.html. Accessed June 6, 2010.

Laine, James W. "In India, 'the Unthinkable' Is Printed at One's Peril." *Los Angeles Times*, January 12, 2004, p. B-13.

"Laine to Be Summoned to India, Says Police Chief." Express News Service, Mumbai, India (March 23, 2004). Available online. URL: http://cities.expressindia.com/fullstory.php?newsid=79728. Accessed January 20, 2006.

"Leonardo Boff." Inter Press Service (December 30, 1999).

Llosa, Álvaro Vargas. "The Freedom to Publish." *New Republic* (September 10, 2008). Available online. URL: http://www.tnr.com/story_print.html?id=6c96c81a-63d0-4bcd-8d06-fcfb9b84fccd. Accessed June 6, 2010.

Lloyd, Anthony. "Tomb of the Unknown Assassin Reveals Mission to Kill Rushdie." *Times* (London) (June 8, 2005). Available online. URL: http://www.timesonline. co.uk/article/0,,3-1645223,00.html.

"Lost Words: The Stories They Wouldn't Let *You* Read." *Index on Censorship* 25, no. 6 (November/December 1996).

"Malaysia: 18 Books Banned for Disrupting Peace and Harmony." Article 19 (July 10, 2006). Available online. URL: http://www.article 19. org. html. Accessed October 7, 2009.

"Malaysian Government Bans Eighteen Books on Islam and Religion." International Freedom of Expression Exchange (July 4, 2006). Available online. URL: http:// www.ifex.org/en/content/view/full/75464/.html. Accessed June 15, 2009.

Malik, Kenan. "Why We Should Not Censor Ourselves." *Index on Censorship* (December 18, 2009). Available online. URL: http://www.kenanmalik.com/debates/index_ cartoons.html. Accessed June 6, 2010.

Mead, Louise S., and Anton Mates. "Why Science Standards Are Important to a Strong Science Curriculum and How States Measure Up." National Center for Science Education (August 7, 2009). Available online. URL: http://springerlink. com/content/9u0610162rn51432/fulltext.html. Accessed June 6, 2010.

Meenan, Jim. "Mom: Parental Rights Central to Book Issue." *South Bend Tribune* (April 16, 2004). Available online. URL: http://www.southbendtribune.com/. Accessed April 27, 2004.

Mernissi, Fatema. Fatema Mernissi's official Web site. Available online. URL: http:// www.mernissi.net. Accessed April 27, 2004.

Middle East Studies Association of North America, Committee for Academic Freedom in the Middle East and North Africa. "Letter to Ayatollah Ali Khamenei, Supreme Leader of the Islamic Republic of Iran" (December 23, 2003). Available online. URL: http://fp.arizona.edu/mesassoc/CAFMENAletters.htm.

Mooney, Paul. "Confucius Comes Back." *Chronicle of Higher Education* (April 20, 2007). Available online. URL: http://chronicle.com/article/Confucius-Comes-Back/ 34363. Accessed June 6, 2010.

Moore, Celia. "Banned in Mauritius." *Ms.*, November/December 1995, 89.

Nandgaonkar, Satish. "Author Explains Oedipus Parallel—Not Derogatory, Says Laine." *Telegraph* (January 12, 2006). Available online. URL: http://www.telegraph-india.com/1060112/asp/nation/story_5711098.asp. Accessed June 6, 2010.

Nasreen, Taslima. "Homeless Everywhere: Writing in Exile." *SaraiReader04* (February 2004). Available online. URL: http://www.sarai.net/journal/04_pdf/59taslima.pdf. Accessed January 20, 2006.

Nasrin, Taslima. Taslima Nasrin's official Web site. Available online. URL: http:// taslimanasrin.com. Accessed January 20, 2006.

Nee, Ooi Ying. "The Bane of Book Banning." *Nut Graph* (August 8, 2008). Available online. URL: http://www.thenutgraph.com/the-bane-of-book-banning.html. Accessed October 7, 2009.

Newport, Frank. "On Darwin's Birthday, Only 4 in 10 Believe in Evolution." *Gallup Daily News* (February 11, 2009). Available online. URL: http://www.gallup.com/ poll/114544/darwin-birthday-believe-evolution.aspx. Accessed June 6, 2010.

Nomani, Asra Q. "You Still Can't Write about Muhammad." Op-Ed. *Wall Street Journal* (August 6, 2008). Available online. URL: http://online.wsj.com/public/ article_print/SB121797979790078815073.html. Accessed October 12, 2009.

Nugent, Philippa. "Of Such Is Reputation Made." *Index on Censorship* 25, no. 2 (March/April 1996): 160.

O'Neill, Brendan. "Censorship Is Being Justified by Imaginary Muslim Outrage." *Independent* (October 22, 2009). Available online. URL: http://license.icopyright.net/user/viewFreeUse.act?fuid=NTQ3MTY3NA%3D%3D. Accessed June 6, 2010.

"Pakistan Bans *Da Vinci Code* Film." BBC News (June 4, 2006). Available online. URL: http://news.bbc.co.uk/go/pr/fr/-/2/hi/south___asia/5045672.stm. Accessed July 8, 2009.

"Parents' Pressure Leads Trustees to Vote to Scrap Reading Series." *Vancouver Sun*, May 10, 1993, p. A3.

Parsipur, Shahrnush. "A Prelude to Touba and the Meaning of Night." Seattle Art Museum (October 7, 2006). Available online. URL: http://www.shahrnushparsipur.com/article9.htm. Accessed June 6, 2010.

Pasha, Kamran. "Yale and the Danish Cartoons." *Huffington Post* (September 8, 2009). Available online. URL: http://www.huffingtonpost.com/kamran-pasha/yale-and-the-danish-carto_b_279463.html. Accessed June 6, 2010.

Piggott, Jill. "Rage Deferred." *Women's Review of Books* 12, nos. 10–11 (July 1995): 28.

Pipes, Daniel. "John Esposito and Karen Armstrong Banned in Malaysia." Daniel Pipes Blog (June 15, 2006, updated January 31, 2008). Available online. URL: http://www.danielpipes.org/blog/2006/06/john-esposito-and-karen-armstrong-banned-in.html. Accessed June 3, 2009.

Poser, Bill. "Rushdie 1, Fish 0." *Language Log* (August 25, 2008). Available online. URL: http://languagelog.ldc.upenn/edu/nll/?p=525. Accessed August 27, 2008.

Price, Massoume. "Symbolism of Women in Hedayat's 'Blind Owl.'" *Persian Language and Literature*. Iran Chamber Society, 2001. Available online. URL: http://www.iranchamber.com/literature/articles/women_hedayat_blind_owl.php. Accessed July 9, 2009.

Pullella, Philip. "Vatican Blasts 'Golden Compass' as Godless and Hopeless." Reuters (December 19, 2007). Available online. URL: www.reuters.com/article/entertainmentNews/idUSL1958884920071219. Accessed November 18, 2009.

Pullman, Philip. "The Censor's Dark Materials." *Guardian* (September 28, 2008). Available online. URL: http://www.guardian.co.uk/books/2008/sep/29/philip.pullman.amber.spyglass.golden.compass. Accessed June 12, 2009.

"Pune's Institute's Desecration Shocks Author." *Mid Day* (January 6, 2004). Available online. URL: http://ww1.mid-day.com/news/nation/2004/january/73060.htm. Accessed January 20, 2006.

"Punjab Ban for *Da Vinci Code* Film." BBC News (May 25, 2006). Available online. URL: http://news.bbc.co.uk/go/pr/fr/-/2/hi/south___asia/5017498.stm. Accessed July 8, 2009.

Raffaele, Martha. "Controversial Step Taken in Rural Pennsylvania District." Associated Press (November 12, 2004).

"Random Error." *Washington Post*, Editorial (August 22, 2008). Available online. URL: http://www.washingtonpost.com/wp-dyn/content/article/2008/08/21/AR2008082103104.html. Accessed October 12, 2009.

Riaz, Ali. "Taslima Nasrin: Breaking the Structured Silence." *Bulletin of Concerned Asian Scholars* 27, no. 1 (January–March 1995): 21–27.

Ritter, Karl. "Muhammad Cartoonist Defiant After Attack." *Associated Press* (May 13, 2010). Available online. URL: http://www.google.com/hostednews/ap/article/ALeqM5gfyTngzJoXl5VLnRYFKryLwR. Accessed June 6, 2010.

Rowling, J. K. J. K. Rowling's official Web site. Available online. URL: http://www.jkrowling.com.

El Saadawi, Nawal. "Defying Submission." *Index on Censorship* 19, no. 9 (October 1980): 16.

———. Nawal El Saadawi's official Web site. Available online. URL: http://www.nawalsaadawi.net.

Salmon, Christian. "The Parliament of a 'Missing People.' " *Autodafe: Journal of the International Parliament of Writers* 1 (Spring 2001): 9. New York: Seven Stories Press, 2000.

Sarkouhi, Faraj. "Iran: Book Censorship the Rule, Not the Exception." Radio Free Europe/Radio Liberty (November 26, 2007). Available online. URL: http://www.rferl.org/articleprintview/1079193. Accessed July 8, 2009.

Schaeffer, Pamela. "Condemned Priest Is Restored to Church." *National Catholic Reporter* (January 30, 1998). Available online. URL: http://natcath.org/NCR_Online/archives013098/bala1.html. Accessed January 20, 2006.

Scholastic Press. Information on Harry Potter books. Available online. URL: http://www.scholastic.com/harrypotter.

"Self-Muzzled at Yale." *Washington Post.* Editorial (August 23, 2009). Available online. URL: http://www.washingtonpost.com. Accessed June 6, 2010.

Simon, Stephanie. "Texas Opens Door for Evolution Doubts." *Wall Street Journal* (March 28, 2009). Available online. URL: http://www.wsj.com/article/SB123819751472561761.html. Accessed June 6, 2010.

Singh, Vijay. "Bringing Laine Back: Easier Said Than Done." Rediff.com (March 27, 2004). Available online. URL: http://us.rediff.com/news/2004/mar/27laine.htm. Accessed January 20, 2006.

Sjolie, Marie Louise. "The Danish Cartoonist Who Survived an Axe Attack." *Guardian* (January 4, 2010). Available online. URL: http://www.guardian.co.uk/world/2010/jan/04/danish-cartoonist-axe-attack. Accessed June 6, 2010.

"Somali Charged Over Attack on Cartoonist." BBC News (January 2, 2010). Available online. URL: http://news.bbc.co.uk/2/hi/Europe/8437652.stm. Accessed June 6, 2010.

Southeast Asian Press Alliance/International Freedom of Expression eXchange. "Authorities Ban Films, Books, Television Talk Show; Film Director Appeals Ban" (March 1, 2007). URL: Available online: http://www.ifex.org/malaysia/2007/03/01/authorities_ban_films_books_television/. Accessed June 6, 2010.

Spellberg, Denise. "I Didn't Kill 'The Jewel of Medina.'" Letters. *The Wall Street Journal* (August 9, 2008). Available online. URL: http://online.wsj.com/article/SB121824366910026293.html#printMode. Accessed October 12, 2009.

Stanley, Alessandra. "Freud in Russia: Return of the Repressed." *New York Times,* December 11, 1996, pp. 1, 10.

Al-Tahhawi, Amira. "Egypt's 'Woman Rebel' Back in the Line of Fire." *Menassat* (July 2, 2008). Available online. URL: http://www.menassat.com/?q=en/news-articles/4034-egypts-woman-rebel-back-line-fire. Accessed June 6, 2010.

Tait, Robert. "Bestsellers Banned in New Iranian Censorship Purge." *Guardian* (November 17, 2006). Available online. URL: http://www.guardian.co.uk/world/2006/nov/17/books.iran.print. Accessed July 8, 2009.

Tax, Meredith. "Taslima Nasrin: A Background Paper." *Bulletin of Concerned Asian Scholars* 25, no. 4 (October–December 1993): 72–74.

———. "Taslima's Pilgrimage." *Nation* (November 18, 2002). Available online. URL: http://www.thenation.com/doc/20021118/tax. Accessed October 15, 2004.

"Textbook Panel Goes Witch-Hunting." *Atlanta Journal and Constitution* (September 29, 1990). Available online. URL: http://holysmoke.org/wicca/textbook.html. Accessed November 15, 2005.

Tinguet, Margaret. "Ethiopia: Destroy the Muslims." *Index on Censorship* 16, no. 4 (April 1987): 33–35.

Trachtenberg, Jeffrey A. "Bride of the Prophet." *Wall Street Journal* (October 4, 2008). Available online. URL: http://online.wsj.com/article/SB122306918228703347.html#. Accessed October 12, 2009.

U.S. Department of State. *Country Reports on Human Rights Practices—2003.* Washington, D.C.: U.S. Government Printing Office, 2004.

Vedantam, Shankar. "U.S. Scholars' Writings Inspire Hatred in India." *Washington Post*, April 10, 2004, p. A-1.

Viren, Sarah. "Does Film 'Compass' Steer Kids in Wrong Direction?" *Houston Chronicle*, December 7, 2007, p. A1.

Walker, Peter. "Three Jailed for Arson Attack over Muhammad Bride Novel." *Guardian* (July 7, 2009). Available online. URL: http://www.guardian.co.uk/2009/jul/07/muslims-jailed-arson-book-protest. Accessed July 9, 2009.

Weaver, Mary Anne. "A Fugitive from Justice." *New Yorker*, September 12, 1994, 47–60.

———. "The Novelist and the Sheikh." *New Yorker*, January 30, 1995, 52–59.

Whyatt, Sara. "Taslima Nasrin." *Index on Censorship* 23, nos. 4–5 (September/October 1994): 202–207.

Willis, Simon. "The Jewel of Medina." *Granta* (September 20, 2008). Available online. URL: http://www.granta.com/Online-Only/The-Jewel-of-Medina. Accessed November 14, 2009.

Wilson, G. Willow. "Sherry Jones Has the Right to Offend Me." *Red Room* (August 13, 2008). Available online. URL: http://www.redroom.com/blog/g-willow-wilson/sherry-jones-has-the-right-to-offend-me. Accessed November 14, 2009.

Wilson, Scott. "Fearing Repeat of the Past, Lebanon Bans a Book." *Washington Post* (October 17, 2004). Available online. URL: http://www.washingtonpost.com/wp-dyn/articles/A38753-2004Oct16.html. Accessed June 4, 2009.

Wing-on, James Wong. "M'sia Bans Oxford University Book on Islam." Clare Street: James Wong Wing-on Online (June 20, 2006). Available online. URL: http://jameswongwingon-online.blogspot.com.html. Accessed October 7, 2009.

"Writers Issue Cartoon Row Warning." BBC News (March 1, 2006). Available online. URL: http://news.bbc.co.uk/2/hi/Europe/4663520.stm. Accessed June 6, 2010.

Yusop, Husna, and Jacqueline Ann Surin. "Abim: Lift Ban on Armstrong Books" *Sun*, June 18, 2007, p. 2.

Works Discussed in Other Volumes of This Series

BANNED BOOKS ON POLITICAL GROUNDS

THE AFFLUENT SOCIETY
John Kenneth Galbraith

AFTER SUCH KNOWLEDGE, WHAT FORGIVENESS?—
  MY ENCOUNTERS WITH KURDISTAN
Jonathan C. Randal

THE AGE OF KEYNES
Robert Lekachman

ALL QUIET ON THE WESTERN FRONT
Erich Maria Remarque

AMERICA IN LEGEND
Richard M. Dorson

AMERICAN CIVICS
William H. Hartley and William S. Vincent

THE AMERICAN PAGEANT: A HISTORY OF THE REPUBLIC
Thomas A. Bailey

ANDERSONVILLE
MacKinlay Kantor

ANIMAL FARM
George Orwell

THE APPOINTMENT
Herta Müller

AREOPAGITICA
John Milton

THE BASTARD OF ISTANBUL
Elif Shafak

BLACK BOY
Richard Wright

*BLOODS: AN ORAL HISTORY OF THE VIETNAM WAR BY
    BLACK VETERANS*
Wallace Terry

BORN ON THE FOURTH OF JULY
Ron Kovic

BOSS: RICHARD J. DALEY OF CHICAGO
Mike Royko

BURGER'S DAUGHTER
Nadine Gordimer

BURY MY HEART AT WOUNDED KNEE
Dee Brown

BUS STOP (CHEZHAN)
Gao Xingjian

*BY WAY OF DECEPTION: THE MAKING AND UNMAKING
    OF A MOSSAD OFFICER*
Victor Ostrovsky and Claire Hoy

CANCER WARD
Aleksandr Solzhenitsyn

CAT'S CRADLE
Kurt Vonnegut, Jr.

THE CHINA LOBBY IN AMERICAN POLITICS
Ross Y. Koen

THE CIA AND THE CULT OF INTELLIGENCE
Victor Marchetti and John D. Marks

CITIES OF SALT
Abdul Rahman Munif

CITIZEN TOM PAINE
Howard Fast

THE FRAGILE FLAG
Jane Langton

THE FUGITIVE (PERBURUAN)
Pramoedya Ananta Toer

FUGITIVES (TAOWANG)
Gao Xingjian

GIRLS OF RIYADH
Rajaa Alsanea

THE GRAPES OF WRATH
John Steinbeck

THE GULAG ARCHIPELAGO 1918–1956
Aleksandr Solzhenitsyn

GULLIVER'S TRAVELS
Jonathan Swift

HANDBOOK FOR CONSCIENTIOUS OBJECTORS
Robert A. Seeley, editor

THE HOAX OF THE TWENTIETH CENTURY
Arthur R. Butz

I AM THE CHEESE
Robert Cormier

INSIDE RUSSIA TODAY
John Gunther

INSIDE THE COMPANY: CIA DIARY
Philip Agee

IN THE SPIRIT OF CRAZY HORSE
Peter Matthiessen

AN INTRODUCTION TO PROBLEMS OF AMERICAN CULTURE
Harold O. Rugg

THE INVISIBLE GOVERNMENT
David Wise and Thomas B. Ross

IT CAN'T HAPPEN HERE
Sinclair Lewis

JOHNNY GOT HIS GUN
Dalton Trumbo

THE JOKE (ŽERT)
Milan Kundera

A JOURNEY FROM ST. PETERSBURG TO MOSCOW
Aleksandr Nikolaevich Radishchev

JULIE OF THE WOLVES
Jean Craighead George

THE JUNGLE
Upton Sinclair

KEEPING FAITH: MEMOIRS OF A PRESIDENT
Jimmy Carter

KISS OF THE SPIDER WOMAN
Manuel Puig

THE LAND AND PEOPLE OF CUBA
Victoria Ortiz

LAND OF THE FREE: A HISTORY OF THE UNITED STATES
John W. Caughey, John Hope Franklin, and Ernest R. May

LAUGHING BOY
Oliver La Farge

EL LIBRO NEGRO DE LA JUSTICIA CHILENA
  (THE BLACK BOOK OF CHILEAN JUSTICE)
Alejandra Matus

THE MAN DIED: PRISON NOTES OF WOLE SOYINKA
Wole Soyinka

THE MANIFESTO OF THE COMMUNIST PARTY
Karl Marx and Friedrich Engels

MARXISM VERSUS SOCIALISM
Vladimir G. Simkhovitch

MEIN KAMPF
Adolf Hitler

LES MISÉRABLES
Victor Hugo

A MONTH AND A DAY: A DETENTION DIARY
Ken Saro-Wiwa

MY BROTHER SAM IS DEAD
James Lincoln Collier and Christopher Collier

MY NAME IS ASHER LEV
Chaim Potok

MY PEOPLE: THE STORY OF THE JEWS
Abba Eban

NELSON AND WINNIE MANDELA
Dorothy Hoobler and Thomas Hoobler

1984
George Orwell

NOVEL WITHOUT A NAME
Duong Thu Huong

OIL!
Upton Sinclair

ONE DAY IN THE LIFE OF IVAN DENISOVICH
Aleksandr Solzhenitsyn

*ONE PEOPLE, ONE DESTINY: THE CARIBBEAN AND
CENTRAL AMERICA TODAY*
Don Rojas

*THE OPEN SORE OF A CONTINENT: A PERSONAL NARRATIVE
OF THE NIGERIAN CRISIS*
Wole Soyinka

OUR LAND, OUR TIME: A HISTORY OF THE UNITED STATES
Joseph Robert Conlin

PARADISE OF THE BLIND
Duong Thu Huong

THE PATRIOT (HA PATRIOT)
THE QUEEN OF THE BATHTUB (MALKAT AMBATYA)
Hanoch Levin

THE POLITICS OF DISPOSSESSION
Edward W. Said

THE PRINCE
Niccolò Machiavelli

PRINCIPLES OF NATURE
Elihu Palmer

PROMISE OF AMERICA
Larry Cuban and Philip Roden

REPORT OF THE SIBERIAN DELEGATION
Leon Trotsky

THE RIGHTS OF MAN
Thomas Paine

RUSSIA
Vernon Ives

SECRECY AND DEMOCRACY: THE CIA IN TRANSITION
Stansfield Turner

EL SEÑOR PRESIDENTE (THE PRESIDENT)
Miguel Angel Asturias

SLAUGHTERHOUSE-FIVE, OR THE CHILDREN'S CRUSADE
Kurt Vonnegut, Jr.

SNOW
Orhan Pamuk

SPYCATCHER
Peter Wright

THE STATE AND REVOLUTION
Vladimir I. Lenin

STRONG WIND (VIENTO FUERTE)
THE GREEN POPE (EL PAPA VERDE)
Miguel Angel Asturias

THE STRUGGLE IS MY LIFE
Nelson Mandela

A SUMMARY VIEW OF THE RIGHTS OF BRITISH AMERICA
Thomas Jefferson

SYLVESTER AND THE MAGIC PEBBLE
William Steig

TEN DAYS THAT SHOOK THE WORLD
John Reed

THE THINGS THEY CARRIED
Tim O'Brien

THIS EARTH OF MANKIND
CHILD OF ALL NATIONS
Pramoedya Ananta Toer

365 DAYS
Ronald J. Glasser

TODAY'S ISMS: COMMUNISM, FASCISM, CAPITALISM, SOCIALISM
William Ebenstein

THE UGLY AMERICAN
William J. Lederer and Eugene Burdick

UNCLE TOM'S CABIN
Harriet Beecher Stowe

UNITED STATES–VIETNAM RELATIONS, 1945–1967
(THE PENTAGON PAPERS)
U.S. Department of Defense

THE VANĚK PLAYS
Václav Havel

WAITING
Ha Jin

WHY ARE WE IN VIETNAM?
Norman Mailer

*A WOMAN IN BERLIN: EIGHT WEEKS IN
   THE CONQUERED CITY*
Anonymous

*WORDS OF CONSCIENCE: RELIGIOUS STATEMENTS
   ON CONSCIENTIOUS OBJECTION*
A. Stauffer Curry, editor (first edition)
Shawn Perry, editor (ninth edition)

YANGTZE! YANGTZE!
Dai Qing

BANNED BOOKS ON SEXUAL GROUNDS
ALICE SERIES
Phyllis Reynolds Naylor

ALWAYS RUNNING—LA VIDA LOCA: GANG DAYS IN L.A.
Luis T. Rodriguez

*AMERICA (THE BOOK): A CITIZEN'S GUIDE TO DEMOCRACY
   INACTION*
Jon Stewart, Ben Karlin, David Javerbaum

AN AMERICAN TRAGEDY
Theodore Dreiser

*THE ARABIAN NIGHTS, OR THE THOUSAND AND
   ONE NIGHTS*
Sir Richard Burton, trans.

THE ART OF LOVE (ARS AMATORIA)
Ovid (Publius Ovidius Naso)

THE AWAKENING
Kate Chopin

BESSIE COTTER
Wallace Smith

BLESS ME, ULTIMA
Rudolfo Anaya

THE BLUEST EYE
Toni Morrison

BOY
James Hanley

THE BUFFALO TREE
Adam Rapp

CANDIDE
Voltaire (François Marie Arouet Voltaire)

CANDY
Maxwell Kenton

THE CARPETBAGGERS
Harold Robbins

CASANOVA'S HOMECOMING (CASANOVA'S HEIMFAHRT)
Arthur Schnitzler

THE CHINESE ROOM
Vivian Connell

CHRISTINE
Stephen King

THE CLAN OF THE CAVE BEAR
Jean Auel

CONFESSIONS
Jean-Jacques Rousseau

THE DECAMERON
Giovanni Boccaccio

THE DEER PARK
Norman Mailer

THE DEVIL RIDES OUTSIDE
John Howard Griffin

THE DIARY OF SAMUEL PEPYS
Samuel Pepys

DROLL STORIES
Honoré de Balzac

DUBLINERS
James Joyce

EAT ME
Linda Jaivin

THE EPIC OF GILGAMESH
Unknown

FANNY HILL, OR MEMOIRS OF A WOMAN OF PLEASURE
John Cleland

THE FIFTEEN PLAGUES OF A MAIDENHEAD
Anonymous

FLOWERS FOR ALGERNON
Daniel Keyes

THE FLOWERS OF EVIL (LES FLEURS DU MAL)
Charles Baudelaire

FOREVER
Judy Blume

FOREVER AMBER
Kathleen Winsor

FROM HERE TO ETERNITY
James Jones

THE GENIUS
Theodore Dreiser

THE GILDED HEARSE
Charles O. Gorham

THE GINGER MAN
J. P. Donleavy

THE GOATS
Brock Cole

GOD'S LITTLE ACRE
Erskine Caldwell

GOSSIP GIRL SERIES
Cecily von Ziegesar

THE GROUP
Mary McCarthy

HAGAR REVELLY
Daniel Carson Goodman

THE HANDMAID'S TALE
Margaret Atwood

*THE HEPTAMERON (L'HEPTAMERON OU HISTOIRES
   DES AMANS FORTUNEZ)*
Marguerite d'Angoulême, Queen of Navarre

THE HISTORY OF TOM JONES, A FOUNDLING
Henry Fielding

HOMO SAPIENS
Stanley Przybyskzewski

HOW THE GARCÍA GIRLS LOST THEIR ACCENTS
Julia Alvarez

HOW TO MAKE LOVE LIKE A PORN STAR
Jenna Jameson

IF IT DIE
André Gide

ISLE OF PINES
Henry Neville

*IT'S PERFECTLY NORMAL: CHANGING BODIES,
   GROWING UP, SEX, AND SEXUAL HEALTH*
Robie H. Harris

JANET MARCH
Floyd Dell

JUDE THE OBSCURE
Thomas Hardy

JURGEN: A COMEDY OF JUSTICE
James Branch Cabell

JUSTINE, OR THE MISFORTUNES OF VIRTUE;
JULIETTE, HER SISTER, OR THE PROSPERITIES OF VICE
Marquis de Sade

THE KAMA SUTRA OF VATSAYANA
Sir Richard Burton, F. F. Arbuthnot, translators

THE KREUTZER SONATA
Leo Tolstoy

LADIES IN THE PARLOR
Jim Tully

LADY CHATTERLEY'S LOVER
D. H. Lawrence

LA TERRE (THE EARTH)
Émile Zola

LOLITA
Vladimir Nabokov

THE LUSTFUL TURK
Anonymous

MADAME BOVARY
Gustave Flaubert

MADELEINE
Anonymous

MADEMOISELLE DE MAUPIN
Théophile Gautier

THE MAID OF ORLEANS (LA PUCELLE)
François-Marie Arouet Voltaire

MEMOIRES
Giovanni Casanova de Seingalt

MEMOIRS OF A YOUNG RAKEHELL
Guillaume Apollinaire

MEMOIRS OF HECATE COUNTY
Edmund Wilson

THE MERRY MUSES OF CALEDONIA
Robert Burns

MOLL FLANDERS
Daniel Defoe

MY LIFE AND LOVES
Frank Harris

NATIVE SON
Richard Wright

A NIGHT IN A MOORISH HAREM
Anonymous

NOVEMBER (NOVEMBRE)
Gustave Flaubert

THE 120 DAYS OF SODOM (LES 120 JOURNÉES DE SODOME)
Marquis de Sade

OUR LADY OF THE FLOWERS (NOTRE-DAME-DES-FLEURS)
Jean Genet

OUTLAW REPRESENTATION
Richard Meyer

PAMELA, OR VIRTUE REWARDED
Samuel Richardson

PANSIES
D. H. Lawrence

THE PERFUMED GARDEN
Sir Richard Burton, trans.

THE PERKS OF BEING A WALLFLOWER
Stephen Chbosky

PEYTON PLACE
Grace Metalious

THE PHILANDERER
Stanley Kauffmann

POEMS AND BALLADS
Algernon Charles Swinburne

POINT COUNTER POINT
Aldous Huxley

RABBIT, RUN
John Updike

THE RAINBOW
D. H. Lawrence

REPLENISHING JESSICA
Max Bodenheim

SANCTUARY
William Faulkner

SARI SAYS
Sari Locker

THE SATYRICON
Gaius Petronius Arbiter

SEPTEMBER IN QUINZE
Vivian Connell

SERENADE
James M. Cain

SEX
Madonna

SEXUS
Henry Miller

SHANGHAI BABY
Wei Hui (Zhou Weihui)

SIMON CALLED PETER
Robert Keable

*1601—A FIRESIDE CONVERSATION IN YE TIME
  OF QUEEN ELIZABETH*
Mark Twain

SLEEVELESS ERRAND
Norah C. James

SNOW FALLING ON CEDARS
David Guterson

SONG OF SOLOMON
Toni Morrison

SOPHIE'S CHOICE
William Styron

A STORY TELLER'S HOLIDAY
George Moore

STUDS LONIGAN
James T. Farrell

SUSAN LENOX: HER FALL AND RISE
David Graham Phillips

SWEETER THAN LIFE
Mark Tryon

TEN NORTH FREDERICK
John O'Hara

TESS OF THE D'URBERVILLES
Thomas Hardy

THEIR EYES WERE WATCHING GOD
Zora Neale Hurston

THEN AGAIN, MAYBE I WON'T
Judy Blume

THE THIEF'S JOURNAL
Jean Genet

THIS BOY'S LIFE
Tobias Wolff

THREE WEEKS
Elinor Glyn

TOBACCO ROAD
Erskine Caldwell

TRAGIC GROUND
Erskine Caldwell

TRILBY
George du Maurier

THE TRIUMPH OF DEATH
Gabriele D'Annunzio

TROPIC OF CANCER
Henry Miller

TROPIC OF CAPRICORN
Henry Miller

TWILIGHT SERIES
Stephenie Meyer

ULYSSES
James Joyce

VENUS AND TANNHAUSER (UNDER THE HILL)
Aubrey Beardsley

THE WILD PALMS
William Faulkner

WOMEN IN LOVE
D. H. Lawrence

*WOMEN ON TOP: HOW REAL LIFE CHANGED WOMEN'S SEXUAL
    FANTASIES*
Nancy Friday

A YOUNG GIRL'S DIARY
Anonymous

BANNED BOOKS ON SOCIAL GROUNDS
THE ABSOLUTELY TRUE DIARY OF A PART-TIME INDIAN
Sherman Alexie

ADVENTURES OF HUCKLEBERRY FINN
Mark Twain

THE ADVENTURES OF SHERLOCK HOLMES
Sir Arthur Conan Doyle

THE ADVENTURES OF TOM SAWYER
Mark Twain

ALICE'S ADVENTURES IN WONDERLAND
Lewis Carroll

THE AMBOY DUKES
Irving Shulman

*THE AMERICAN HERITAGE DICTIONARY OF THE
    ENGLISH LANGUAGE*

AM I BLUE?
Marion Dane Bauer

AND STILL I RISE
Maya Angelou

AND TANGO MAKES THREE
Justin Richardson and Peter Parnell

ANNE FRANK: THE DIARY OF A YOUNG GIRL
Anne Frank

ANNIE ON MY MIND
Nancy Garden

ANOTHER COUNTRY
James Baldwin

APHRODITE
Pierre Louÿs

APPOINTMENT IN SAMARRA
John O'Hara

AS I LAY DYING
William Faulkner

THE AUTOBIOGRAPHY OF BENJAMIN FRANKLIN
Benjamin Franklin

THE AUTOBIOGRAPHY OF MALCOLM X
Malcolm X, with Alex Haley

THE AUTOBIOGRAPHY OF MISS JANE PITTMAN
Ernest J. Gaines

BABY BE-BOP
Francesca Lia Block

THE BASKETBALL DIARIES
Jim Carroll

BEING THERE
Jerzy Kosinski

THE BELL JAR
Sylvia Plath

BELOVED
Toni Morrison

THE BEST SHORT STORIES BY NEGRO WRITERS
Langston Hughes, ed.

BLACK LIKE ME
John Howard Griffin

BLESS THE BEASTS AND CHILDREN
Glendon Swarthout

BLUBBER
Judy Blume

BRAVE NEW WORLD
Aldous Huxley

BRIDGE TO TERABITHIA
Katherine Paterson

CAIN'S BOOK
Alexander Trocchi

CAMILLE
Alexandre Dumas, Jr.

THE CANTERBURY TALES
Geoffrey Chaucer

CAPTAIN UNDERPANTS (SERIES)
Dav Pilkey

CATCH-22
Joseph Heller

THE CATCHER IN THE RYE
J. D. Salinger

THE CHOCOLATE WAR
Robert Cormier

A CLOCKWORK ORANGE
Anthony Burgess

THE COLOR PURPLE
Alice Walker

CUJO
Stephen King

DADDY'S ROOMMATE
Michael Willhoite

A DAY NO PIGS WOULD DIE
Robert Newton Peck

DELIVERANCE
James Dickey

A DICTIONARY OF AMERICAN SLANG
Harold Wentworth

DICTIONARY OF SLANG AND UNCONVENTIONAL ENGLISH
Eric Partridge

DOCTOR DOLITTLE (SERIES)
Hugh John Lofting

DOG DAY AFTERNOON
Patrick Mann

DOWN THESE MEAN STREETS
Piri Thomas

DRACULA
Bram Stoker

THE DROWNING OF STEPHAN JONES
Bette Greene

EAST OF EDEN
John Steinbeck

ELMER GANTRY
Sinclair Lewis

END AS A MAN
Calder Willingham

ESTHER WATERS
George Moore

FAHRENHEIT 451
Ray Bradbury

FALLEN ANGELS
Walter Dean Myers

A FAREWELL TO ARMS
Ernest Hemingway

FINAL EXIT
Derek Humphry

THE FIXER
Bernard Malamud

FREAKONOMICS
Steven D. Levitt and Stephen J. Dubner

*FRUITS OF PHILOSOPHY: OR THE PRIVATE COMPANION
OF YOUNG MARRIED PEOPLE*
Charles Knowlton

GARGANTUA AND PANTAGRUEL
François Rabelais

GENTLEMAN'S AGREEMENT
Laura Z. Hobson

THE GIVER
Lois Lowry

GO ASK ALICE
Anonymous

GONE WITH THE WIND
Margaret Mitchell

GORILLAS IN THE MIST
Dian Fossey

GO TELL IT ON THE MOUNTAIN
James Baldwin

THE GREAT GATSBY
F. Scott Fitzgerald

GRENDEL
John Gardner

HEATHER HAS TWO MOMMIES
Leslea Newman

A HERO AIN'T NOTHIN' BUT A SANDWICH
Alice Childress

HOWL AND OTHER POEMS
Allen Ginsberg

I KNOW WHY THE CAGED BIRD SINGS
Maya Angelou

IN THE NIGHT KITCHEN
Maurice Sendak

INVISIBLE MAN
Ralph Ellison

JAKE AND HONEYBUNCH GO TO HEAVEN
Margot Zemach

JAMES AND THE GIANT PEACH
Roald Dahl

JAWS
Peter Benchley

JUNKY
William S. Burroughs

KING & KING
Linda de Haan and Stern Nijland

KINGSBLOOD ROYAL
Sinclair Lewis

THE KITE RUNNER
Khaled Hosseini

LAST EXIT TO BROOKLYN
Hubert Selby, Jr.

LEAVES OF GRASS
Walt Whitman

A LIGHT IN THE ATTIC
Shel Silverstein

LITTLE BLACK SAMBO
Helen Bannerman

LITTLE HOUSE ON THE PRAIRIE
Laura Ingalls Wilder

LITTLE RED RIDING HOOD
Charles Perrault

LORD OF THE FLIES
William Golding

MANCHILD IN THE PROMISED LAND
Claude Brown

MARRIED LOVE
Marie Stopes

MOTHER GOOSE'S NURSERY RHYMES AND FAIRY TALES
Unknown

MY HOUSE
Nikki Giovanni

THE NAKED APE
Desmond Morris

NAKED LUNCH
William S. Burroughs

NANA
Émile Zola

NEVER LOVE A STRANGER
Harold Robbins

NEW DICTIONARY OF AMERICAN SLANG
Robert L. Chapman
(discussed with *A DICTIONARY OF AMERICAN SLANG*)

OF MICE AND MEN
John Steinbeck

OF TIME AND THE RIVER
Thomas Wolfe

THE OLD MAN AND THE SEA
Ernest Hemingway

ONE FLEW OVER THE CUCKOO'S NEST
Ken Kesey

ORDINARY PEOPLE
Judith Guest

THE OX-BOW INCIDENT
Walter Van Tilburg Clark

THE RED PONY
John Steinbeck

THE SCARLET LETTER
Nathaniel Hawthorne

A SEPARATE PEACE
John Knowles

SISTER CARRIE
Theodore Dreiser

SOUL ON ICE
Eldridge Cleaver

STEPPENWOLF
Hermann Hesse

STRANGE FRUIT
Lillian Smith

STRANGER IN A STRANGE LAND
Robert A. Heinlein

THE SUN ALSO RISES
Ernest Hemingway

TO HAVE AND HAVE NOT
Ernest Hemingway

TO KILL A MOCKINGBIRD
Harper Lee

UNCLE REMUS
Joel Chandler Harris

UNLIVED AFFECTIONS
George Shannon

WE ALL FALL DOWN
Robert Cormier

WELCOME TO THE MONKEY HOUSE
Kurt Vonnegut, Jr.

THE WELL OF LONELINESS
Radclyffe Hall

WHALE TALK
Chris Crutcher

WOMAN IN THE MISTS
Farley Mowat
(discussed with *GORILLAS IN THE MIST*)

WORKING: PEOPLE TALK ABOUT WHAT THEY DO ALL DAY
  AND HOW THEY FEEL ABOUT WHAT THEY DO
Studs Terkel

A WORLD I NEVER MADE
James T. Farrell

INDEX

Note: **Boldface** page numbers indicate major treatment of a topic; *b* denotes entries located in the biographical section.